Racism, Colonialism, and Indigeneity in Canada

A READER

Edited by
Martin J. Cannon
& Lina Sunseri

OXFORD
UNIVERSITY PRESS

OXFORD
UNIVERSITY PRESS

8 Sampson Mews, Suite 204, Don Mills, Ontario M3C 0H5
www.oupcanada.com

Oxford University Press is a department of the University of Oxford.
It furthers the University's objective of excellence in research, scholarship,
and education by publishing worldwide in

Oxford   New York
Auckland   Cape Town   Dar es Salaam   Hong Kong   Karachi
Kuala Lumpur   Madrid   Melbourne   Mexico City   Nairobi
New Delhi   Shanghai   Taipei   Toronto

With offices in:
Argentina   Austria   Brazil   Chile   Czech Republic   France   Greece
Guatemala   Hungary   Italy   Japan   Poland   Portugal   Singapore
South Korea   Switzerland   Thailand   Turkey   Ukraine   Vietnam

Oxford is a trade mark of Oxford University Press
in the UK and in certain other countries

Published in Canada
by Oxford University Press

Library and Archives Canada Cataloguing in Publication

Racism, colonialism, and indigeneity in Canada : a reader / editors, Martin J. Cannon & Lina Sunseri.
Includes bibliographical references.

ISBN 978-0-19-543231-2

1. Native peoples—Canada—Social conditions.   2. Native peoples—Canada—Government relations.
3. Canada—Race relations.   I. Cannon, Martin John, 1969–   II. Sunseri, Lina

E78.C2N68 2011   305.897'071   C2010-906645-6

Cover image: Brenden S. Jemison

Oxford University Press is committed to our environment. This book is printed on
Forest Stewardship Council certified paper, harvested from a responsibly managed forest.

Mixed Sources
Product group from well-managed
forests and other controlled sources
www.fsc.org Cert no. SW-COC-000952
© 1996 Forest Stewardship Council

FSC

Printed and bound in Canada

1 2 3 4 — 14 13 12 11

Contents

Part Four: Racialization, Sexism, and Indigenous Identities   87

Part Five: Family, Belonging, and Displacement   111

Part Six: Indigenous Rights, Citizenship, and Nationalism   137

Part Seven: Decolonizing Indigenous Education   163

Part Eight: Poverty, Economic Marginality, and Community Development   189

Part Nine: Violence and the Construction of Criminality   231

Foreword

I have fond memories of the many times Martin Cannon and I had lunch together when he was teaching at the University of Saskatchewan. We would talk about our common scholarly engagement with Indigenous identity politics and confirm our mutual passion to develop and promote a race analysis of the experiences of Indigenous peoples in Canada. Now I see a culmination of this passion as Martin has joined with Lina Sunseri to collaborate on an important and probing collection of scholarly writings that explores the effects of racism on all facets of Indigenous life in Canada. I look at *Racism, Colonialism, and Indigeneity* in Canada and I see an insightful and commanding presentation of Indigenous voices.

In this volume, Canon and Sunseri, both of them eminent scholars of Indigenous history and contemporary culture, have combined their academic interests and community commitments. Given their university teaching experiences, they are all too familiar with the need for a book that provides a multidisciplinary Indigenous perspective on the impact of colonialism and racism on the socio-economic and political conditions and aspirations of Indigenous peoples. Now Cannon and Sunseri have provided the academy a most valuable and essential text.

Indigenous scholars and community activists are the authors of all chapters in *Racism, Colonialism, and Indigeneity in Canada*. Although the selected writers hail from homelands located across Canada and the United States, they are drawn together in this book by their common interest in analyzing and challenging the colonization and racialization of Indigenous peoples. As scholars and activists, these authors exemplify the pursuit of engaged scholarship in its purest, most honest sense. Their chapters insist that scholarship and research, while maintaining the highest standards of excellence, make a difference in the everyday lives of people. History, for example, is seen as a process of construction, vulnerable to human biases, and therefore a body of scholarship that must be examined rather than taken at face value. As Cannon and Sunseri explain in their introduction, history has provided a neutral account of processes of genocide, and in doing so normalizes racism against Indigenous peoples. This quality of critical engaged scholarship places the book solidly on what I believe is the foundation of Indigenous studies.

An important aspect of the book is that it focuses primarily on Indigenous peoples in Canadian contexts, inviting the reader to learn about Canadian racialized policies and practices and their profound effects on Indigenous peoples. This focus on Canadian examples fills a noticeable gap in the literature while demonstrating commonalities with racial analyses from other parts of the world.

But the book is not just about Indigenous peoples and their struggles. John Milloy, in the introduction to his book *A National Crime: The Canadian Government and the Residential School System, 1879–1986*, recounts the story of a young residential school graduate who, when asked to write his memories of his schooling experiences, insightfully responded, 'when I was asked to do this paper I had some misgivings, for if I were to be honest, I must tell of things as they were and really this is not my story but yours' (1999: xviii). The comments of this young Indigenous boy express a principal theme of *Racism, Colonialism, and Indigeneity in Canada*: that the colonization and marginalization of Indigenous peoples is not just an Indigenous story, but also the story of Canada. This story is still largely untold and, if told, largely unheard. Cannon and Sunseri's volume takes up the important challenge of exposing this overlooked dimension of Canadian history. Therefore, the book represents a unique pedagogical opportunity for Canadians while remaining an excellent resource for international scholars and community organizers concerned with promoting the rights of Indigenous peoples.

Racism, Colonialism, and Indigeneity in Canada joins a growing body of scholarship, including my own, dealing with the particular challenges of advancing a race analysis in Canada. Many Canadians still feel deeply invested in a national identity that would suggest the country has been nothing but fair, generous, socially just, and innocent of racism. In her book *Colour-Coded: A Legal History of Racism in Canada, 1900–1950*, legal scholar Constance Backhouse explores Canada's insistence, despite evidence to contrary, that it is a country devoid of racism. Canada's commitment to promoting itself as raceless and innocent has made it all the more difficult to engage in anti-racist education; so many, including scholars within our educational institutions, simply do not see the need for it. Racism in Canada is not only denied, or designated as taboo, but also often understood as something that took place in the distant past or in other places, as I have written about in *Troubling National Discourses in Anti-Racist Curricular Planning*. The complex challenges of exploring racism in Canada make Cannon and Sunseri's book all the more important.

One of the special features of *Racism, Colonialism, and Indigeneity in Canada* is that it addresses the need for newly arriving immigrants to become aware of Canada's inequitable treatment of Indigenous peoples. Unless the multiple ways in which Indigenous peoples in Canada have been racially oppressed are made more widely known, the simplistic picture of Canada as a paragon of fairness and equity will not be challenged. By exposing Canadian racism as well as Canada's promise, this book provides a realistic platform for all Canadians.

By adopting a multidisciplinary approach, *Racism, Colonialism, and Indigeneity in Canada* touches on a number of fields with current and potentially important connections to Indigenous studies. The book reaches out, often through the selected writers' own disciplinary ties, to many fields, including political science, education, anthropology, history, gender studies, literature, governmental studies, law, sociology, native studies, and community development, and to many professionals, such as lawyers, judges, teachers, social workers, police officers, physicians, psychologists, nurses, and politicians. With its wide and searching relevance, the book demonstrates how the condition of Indigenous peoples can be at the centre of theory and analysis, regardless of disciplinary affiliation or profession. At the same time, it skillfully expands our understanding of how colonization and racism have had an impact on Indigenous peoples. For example, the book examines how Canadian laws and policies tore apart families and communities by determining who could or could not belong to Indigenous communities, how Indigenous families were constituted, and how families could or could not raise their own children. It also explores how racism in Canada has ensured a mostly negative schooling experience for Indigenous children, not only through stereotyped and racist teachings about Indigenous peoples, but also through what was offered as schooling through residential schools and what is offered in integrated public schooling today. The text acknowledges that racism designates far too many Indigenous bodies as disposable, whether through the all-too-common occurrence of violence against Indigenous women or the number of deaths that occur while Indigenous peoples are in police custody. And finally, it investigates how racialized colonial violence is sanctioned through the law by making invisible the common denial of basic human and Indigenous rights and ensuring the economic and political marginalization of Indigenous peoples.

With such a wide and provocative variety of authors, approaches, and disciplines, it is reasonable to ask how a reader is to navigate the book. Here Cannon and Sunseri have stepped forward to provide firm and sensitive guidance. With their skillful use of powerful and provoking section headings, they have woven individual chapters into a comprehensive and integrated picture of the impact of racism and colonialization on Aboriginal peoples. The reader can almost hear the many dialogues developing between selected writers, producing a unified picture of the challenges and promises of Indigenous studies. As well, after each section, the editors provide a number of additional teaching resources, including recommended readings and audio-visual materials, and discussion questions. These features make the book into an active learning and teaching tool for university courses.

As an Indigenous professor and scholar of anti-racist education in Canada, I have often felt the enormity of the task of analyzing and exposing the dimensions and implications of racism towards Indigenous peoples. It is not an easy road to travel. In fact, I titled a recent keynote address 'Does talking about race make matters worse?', Of course, I answered the question with a resounding *No*. The problem is precisely that we don't talk enough about racism, and not enough of that talk actually leads to action.

In my work I constantly seek to move forward with a racial analysis, realizing that the difficulty of the task only makes my committed approach that much more necessary. In my efforts to move forward, I will look to this book by Cannon and Sunseri as not only a valuable resource but also a foundation upon which to build. *Racism, Colonialism, and Indigeneity in Canada* follows a path blazed by Maria Campbell, whose autobiography, *Halfbreed*, marked a significant moment in contemporary writings about the impact of racism on the lives of Indigenous peoples in Canada.

I recently completed *A Study of Canadian Aboriginal Teachers' Professional Knowledge and Experience*. Among many concerns raised by these Aboriginal teachers was the sheer number of ways in which they had experienced racism in education. They spoke about how their qualifications and capabilities were discounted, and how they were frequently excluded and marginalized. And they stated that expectations were often lowered for Aboriginal students; that Aboriginal content and perspectives were trivialized or ignored; and that the effects of colonization and oppression of Aboriginal peoples were discounted. One Aboriginal teacher in that study pointed out that although racism against Aboriginal peoples remains acceptable, 'we have to say that it is NOT' (2010: 45, original capitalization).

Racism, Colonialism, and Indigeneity in Canada adds its scholarly and powerful voice to stand beside that Aboriginal teacher, and many others, to instruct us about the nature and functions of racism against Indigenous peoples, and how we can mount an effective and informed resistance. As Cannon and Sunseri state in the introduction to part seven of their book, 'racism exists each time an Indigenous child is taught a history that neither describes nor reflects her experience as an Indigenous person; or conversely, is denied a vocabulary with which to describe and challenge histories of colonization that continue to shape his everyday life.' As editors, they are making sure a vocabulary is made available, offering praxis for action and change.

—Verna St Denis
November 2010

References

Backhouse, Constance. 1999. *Colour-Coded: A Legal History of Racism in Canada, 1900–1950*. Toronto: University of Toronto Press.

Campbell, Maria. 1973. *Halfbreed: A Proud and Bitter Canadian Legacy*. Toronto: McClelland and Stewart.

Milloy, John. 1999. *A National Crime: The Canadian Government and the Residential School System, 1879–1986*. Winnipeg: University of Manitoba Press.

Schick, C., and Verna St Denis. 2005. 'Troubling National Discourses in Anti-Racist Curricular Planning', *Canadian Journal of Education* 28 (3): 295–317.

St Denis, Verna. 2010. *A Study of Aboriginal Teachers' Professional Knowledge and Experience in Canadian Schools*. Ottawa: Canadian Teachers' Federation and the Canadian Council on Learning.

All Our Relations: Acknowledgements

This anthology of writings stems from conversations we have had about them as scholarly works, and in general, since meeting each other as graduate students at York University in the mid-1990s. Faced with the formidable responsibility of teaching courses concerning social inequality, Indigenous peoples, and racism, we have incorporated these writings in our classes and discussions, and we have spoken about them with friends, family, colleagues, students, and sometimes, the authors themselves. In each case, we feel they contain instructive insights, indispensable to those wishing to explore and combat racism and colonialism in Canada.

As colleagues and friends, we share much in common as Indigenous peoples. We are both Haudenosaunee—our fathers English and Italian respectively. We also share in our experience of postsecondary education wherein, as students of the Sociology of Race and Ethnic Relations, it seemed at times that racism and colonialism—and its impact on Indigenous peoples—did not fare centrally enough. The inspiration for this book thus emerged, at least in part, out of our undergraduate frustrations. We hope this anthology—and pedagogical components—will work toward fostering change within the academy, and for younger generations of Indigenous and non-Indigenous peoples.

There are many people to be acknowledged for the realization of this book. We especially wish to extend our gratitude to Oxford University Press for their diligence and enthusiasm at every stage of the publication process. Nancy Reilly helped us to realize *Racism, Colonialism, and Indigeneity in Canada*. Jennifer Mueller provided editorial suggestions in the early stages of the book's production. Jodi Lewchuk and Jennifer Wallace were very helpful in the technical aspects of this book, including the selection of maps and the illustration of Guswentah, or Two Row Wampum. Jessie Coffey provided meticulous editorial feedback and a careful and close reading of the entire anthology.

A number of colleagues and friends have supported and challenged us over the years and also need to be acknowledged. We are grateful to Trish Monture (Mohawk), Celia Haig-Brown, Bonita Lawrence (Miqmaw), Taiaike Alfred (Mohawk), and Beverley Jacobs (Mohawk). Martin wishes to acknowledge colleagues, including Verna St Denis (University of Saskatchewan), Sherene Razack, George Dei, and Roger Simon (OISE/University of Toronto). Lina wishes to acknowledge her colleagues at Brescia, University of Western Ontario, in particular Lisa Jakubowski, Pat Burman, and Ed Bell. While we are both responsible for the articles, openers, and pedagogical material, we have included in this book, these individuals have in some way supported us and shaped our ideas and thinking.

We wish to acknowledge students who have assisted us in realizing this book, including Kate Milley and Becky Boock, both of whom provided research assistance. Martin also wishes to thank Tara Leigh McHugh, Lynn Caldwell, Patricia McGuire, and Tyler McCreary.

We also thank friends and family for loving and supporting us over the many years. Martin wishes to thank Melissa Reddekopp, his parents, Alva and Gordon Cannon, Susan Ward, immediate and extended family, and his nieces, Sarah, Melissa, Emma, Deanna—and 'Lily' Marrai. Lina wishes to thank her parents, immediate and extended family, and her partner Chris and his children.

But most importantly, we want to give our thanks to the Creator, Sky Woman and All Our Relations for nurturing us, and providing us with daily gifts.

Credits

Grateful acknowledgement is made for permission to reprint the following:

Alfred, Taiaiake, 'Colonial Stains on Our Existence', from Wasáse, *Indigenous Pathways of Action and Freedom*. Copyright © University of Toronto Press Inc., 2005 (originally published by Broadview Press), pp. 101–78. Reprinted with permission of the publisher.

Alfred, Taiaiake and Jeff Corntassel, 'Being Indigenous: Resurgences against Contemporary Colonialism', *Government and Opposition*, vol. 40, no. 4, 2005: 587–614.

Andersen, Chris and Claude Denis, 'Urban Native Communities and the Nation: Before and After the Royal Commission on Aboriginal Peoples', *Canadian Review of Sociology and Anthropology*, vol. 40, no. 4, 2003: 373–90.

Anderson, Kim, 'Marriage, Divorce and Family Life'. In Kim Anderson, *A Recognition of Being: Reconstructing Native Womanhood* (Sumach Press, 2000), pp. 79–98. Reprinted by permission of Canadian Scholars' Press Inc.

Baskin, Cyndy, 'Aboriginal Youth Talk about Structural Determinants as the Cause of their Homelessness', *First Peoples Child & Family Review*, vol. 3, no. 3, 2007: 31–42.

Battiste, Marie, 'Micmac Literacy and Cognitive Assimilation'. In Jean Barman, Yvonne Hébert, and Don McCaskill, eds., *Indian Education in Canada: Volume 1: The Legacy*, pp. 23–44. Copyright © 1986 by University of British Columbia Press. Reprinted with permission of the Publisher. All rights reserved by the Publisher.

Battiste, Marie and Sakej Henderson, 'Eurocentrism and the European Ethnographic Tradition'. In *Protecting Indigenous Knowledge and Heritage: A Global Challenge* (Saskatoon: Purich Publishing, 2000), pp. 21–34.

Cannon, Martin J. 'Revisiting Histories of Legal Assimilation, Racialized Injustice, and the Future of Indian Status in Canada'. In Jerry P. White, Erik Anderson, Wendy Cornet, and Dan Beavon, eds., *Aboriginal Policy Research: Moving Forward, Making a Difference, Volume V* (Toronto: Thompson Educational Publishing, 2007), pp. 35–48.

Doxtator, Deborah, 'The Idea of Indianness and Once Upon a Time: The Role of Indians in History'. In Deborah Doxtator, *Fluffs and Feathers: An Exhibit on the Symbols of Indianness: A Resource Guide* (Brantford: Woodland Cultural Centre), p. 199.

Fournier, Suzanne and Ernie Crey, ' "Killing the Indian in the Child": Four Centuries of Church-Run Schools'. In Roger C.A. Maaka and Chris Anderson, eds., *The Indigenous Experience: Global Perspectives* (Toronto: Canadian Scholars' Press Inc./Women's Press, 2007), pp. 141–9. Reprinted by permission of Canadian Scholars' Press Inc.

Green, Joyce, 'From Stonechild to Social Cohesion', *Canadian Journal of Political Science*, vol. 39, no. 1, 2006.

Ing, Rosalind, 'Canada's Indian Residential Schools and Their Impacts on Mothering'. In Lavell-Harvard, Dawn Memee, and Jeanette Coribiere Lavell, eds., *'Until Our Hearts Are on the Ground': Aboriginal Mothering, Oppression, Resistance, and Rebirth* (Demeter Press, 2006), pp. 157–72.

King, Thomas, 'You're Not the Indian I Had in Mind'. In Thomas King, *The Truth about Stories: A Native Narrative* (Toronto: Anansi Press, 2003), pp. 31–60.

Lawrence, Bonita, 'Rewriting Histories of the Land: Colonization and Indigenous Resistance in Eastern Canada'. In Sherene Razack, ed., *Race, Space and the Law: Unmapping a White Settler Society* (Toronto: Between the Lines Press, 2002), pp. 21–46.

Lawrence, Bonita, 'Mixed Blood Urban Native People and the Rebuilding of Indigenous Nations'. In Bonita Lawrence, *'Real' Indians and Others: Mixed Blood Urban Native Peoples and Indigenous Nationhood*. (University of British Columbia Press, 2004), pp. 227–46. Reprinted with permission of the Publisher. All rights reserved by the Publisher.

Lawrence, Bonita and Enakshi Dua, 'Decolonizing Anti-Racism', *Social Justice*, vol. 32, no. 5, 2005: 120–43.

Little Thunder, Beverly, 'I Am a Lakota Womyn'. In Sue-Ellen Jacobs, Wesley Thomas, Sabine Lang, eds., *Two-Spirit People: Native American Gender Identity, Sexuality, and Spirituality* (Copyright 1997 by the Board of Trustees of the University of Illinois Press), pp. 203–10. Used with permission of the University of Illinois Press.

Montour, Martha, 'Iroquois Women's Rights with Respect to Matrimonial Property on Indian Reserves', *Canadian Native Law Reporter*, vol. 4, 1987: 1–10. Martha Montour is a member of the Mohawks of Kahnawake. In 1990 she was admitted to the Bar of the Province of Quebec and Bar of the State of New York. She is also a registered nurse. She is a part-time administrative judge for ethics complaints against native police officers in Quebec. Contact information: reception939@bellnet.ca.

Monture-Okanee, Patricia and Mary Ellen Turpel, 'Aboriginal Peoples and Canadian Criminal Law: Rethinking Justice', *University of British Columbia Law Review* (Special edition), vol. 26, 1992: 239–77.

Silver, Jim, Parvin Ghorayshi, Joan Hay, and Darlene Klyne, 'Sharing, Community, and Decolonization: Urban Aboriginal Community Development'. In Jim Silver et al., *In Their Own Voices: Building Urban Aboriginal Communities* (Fernwood Publishing. 2006).

Simpson, Audra, 'On Ethnographic Refusal: Indigeneity, "Voice" and Colonial Citizenship', *Junctures: The Journal for Thematic Dialogue*, vol. 9, 2007: 67–80. Published by Otago Polytechnic, Dunedin, New Zealand.

Smith, Andrea, 'Sexual Violence as a Tool of Genocide'. In Andrea Smith, *Conquest: Sexual Violence and American Indian Genocide* (South End Press, 2005), pp. 7–33.

Spears, Shandra, 'Strong Spirit, Fractured Identity: An Ojibway Adoptee's Journey to Wholeness'. In Kim Anderson and Bonita Lawrence, eds., *Strong Women Stories: Native Vision and Community Survival* (Sumach Press, 2003), 81–94.

St Denis, Verna, 'Rethinking Culture Theory in Aboriginal Education'. In Cynthia Levine-Rasky, ed., *Canadian Perspectives on the Sociology of Education* (Don Mills, Oxford University Press, 2009), pp. 163–82. Reprinted by permission of the publisher.

Stevenson, Winona, 'Colonialism and First Nations Women in Canada'. In Enakshi Dua and Angela Robertson, eds., *Scratching the Surface: Canadian Anti-Racist Feminist Thought* (Toronto: Canadian Scholars' Press Inc./Women's Press, 1999), pp. 49–80. Reprinted by permission of Canadian Scholars' Press Inc./Women's Press.

Sunseri, Lina, 'Moving Beyond the Feminism versus the Nationalism Dichotomy: An Anti-Colonial Feminist Perspective on Aboriginal Liberation Struggles', *Canadian Woman Studies*, vol. 20, no. 2: 143–8.

Voyageur, Cora and Brian Calliou, 'Aboriginal Economic Development and the Struggle for Self-Government'. In Les Samuelson and Wayne Anthony, eds., *Power and Resistance: Critical Thinking about Canadian Social Issues, 3rd Edition* (Fernwood Publishing, 2003), pp. 121–44.

Not Disappearing: An Introduction to the Text

Over the past several decades, the history of institutional racism aimed at Indigenous nations has attracted the attention of scholars, activists, and those concerned with social change. The nature and breadth of this work extends over many generations and defies any simple categorization. Our aim in this book is to present an overview of this work as written by Indigenous peoples in what is now North America. The scholarship we consider belongs to a diverse and heterogeneous generation of individuals residing on Turtle Island. We share with them in the desire to describe and explore the series of profound links between racism, sexism, and colonialism. We wish to explore the way colonial injustices have worked together to shape our experiences as Indigenous peoples and in the making of settler colonial relations.

The range of theoretical perspectives written by and about Indigenous North Americans on racism and race-relations is vast in scope. This book could not possibly capture all of these voices. Instead, we seek to provide an initial overview of perspectives, as well as some of the issues, themes, and concerns that have been raised when it comes to addressing matters of racism and Indigeneity. Some of these perspectives draw attention to the structural and interpersonal impacts of racism on the lives of our peoples and nations. Others draw attention to the obligations of Indigenous peoples and settler colonialists where understanding, acknowledging, and taking responsibility for racism is concerned. We would like to suggest that early nation-to-nation agreements represent an important set of organizing principles where realizing the shared responsibility to both understand and end racism is concerned.

Turtle Island is a word that is commonly used by Indigenous peoples to refer to North America. For Haudenosaunee[1] (sometimes called the Six Nations or Iroquois) our story of creation describes how this land came to be. Our elders tell us that before this earth was created, there was only water and water beings. There also existed the sky world and sky beings. One day, Sky Woman fell from this world and brought with her the medicines: the corn, squash, beans, tobacco, and strawberries that sustain us. The water beings laid Sky Woman and her medicines upon a turtle's back and Mother Earth was created. This version of the creation story, albeit shortened for our purposes here, has been told in slightly different ways. Our elders have kept these teachings alive, even when forbidden by racist legislation, and we give Yawa:ko (thanks) for their ongoing resistance.

We take the maintenance of our traditional stories seriously. We are also both concerned with the memory of historic treaties made on a nation-to-nation basis between our ancestors, the Haudenosaunee, and the newcomers to Turtle Island.

We believe these agreements hold original instructions and are key to showing how Indigenous and non-Indigenous peoples alike might address colonial injustice and racism. The Two Row Wampum or Guswentah in particular is an historic wampum—a beaded belt embroidered from fresh water shells—which serves to formalize or 'certify' original nation-to-nation agreements. Wampum are of great significance to our ancestors because they function to formalize agreements and, as Patricia Monture-Angus (1999: 36–7) has explained, were neither easily forgotten nor destroyed.

The Two Row Wampum dates to 1613 and is represented on a beaded belt which contains two purple beaded lines against a white backdrop (see Illustration A). As Williams and Nelson (1995: 3) have described, 'The two row wampum . . . symbolizes the river of life on which the Crown's sailing ship and the Haudenosaunee canoe both travel.' The three white rows are recognized as symbolizing an everlasting 'peace, friendship, and respect between the two nations' (quoted in Johnston, 1986: 32, also see Monture-Angus, 1999: 37). The metaphor of the European vessel and Confederacy canoe functions to characterize two distinct jurisdictions which were ordained in 1664 to co-exist independently (Borrows, 1997: 164–5). Originally exchanged with Dutch traders, and subsequently the British Crown, the Two Row Wampum belt speaks of separate jurisdictions. As Johnston (1986: 11) writes:

> The two were to co-exist as independent entities, each respecting the autonomy of the other. The two rows of purple wampum, representing the two governments, run parallel, never crossing. The two vessels travel together, as allies, but neither nation tries to steer the other's vessel. In the relationship envisioned by the Two Row Wampum, neither government has the authority to legislate for the other.

In the twenty-first century, the Two Row Wampum continues to be of tremendous significance. For the Six Nations Confederacy, the Guswentah establishes an historic relationship with the British Crown as an independent nation and also as allies. Moreover, the Two Row Wampum embodies the principle of separate jurisdictions. From this perspective, racism—in seeking as it does to disrupt and restrict the lives of Six Nations peoples ranging from issues of land administration to the ability for us to determine our own peoples—constitutes a British 'foot' in the Haudenosaunee canoe.

Although we use racism here to mean a violation of original principles set out in original nation-to-nation agreements, racism has been and can be defined academically in several different ways. Henry and Tator (2006: 5) define racism as a set of 'assumptions, attitudes, beliefs, and behaviours of individuals as well as to the institutional policies, process, and practices that flow from those understandings'. Combined, racism refers to societal disadvantages experienced by a people or group. Racism can be further divided into the forms it takes in society, including: individual, systemic, and structural racism (ibid., 350–2).

Individual racism stems from an individual's conscious and/or personal prejudice (ibid., 350). It refers to outward and overt attitudes of intolerance or bigotry. Systemic racism refers to policies and practices that result in the exclusion of individuals, or that work to effect considerable disadvantages on a specific group.

Systemic racism can be both institutional and structural; the former referring to 'racial discrimination that derives from individuals carrying out the dictates of others who are prejudiced or of a prejudiced society' (ibid., 352). Lastly, structural racism refers to inequalities that are 'rooted in the system-wide operation of a society' (ibid., 352). They refer to practices that 'exclude substantial numbers . . . of particular groups from significant participation in major social institutions' (ibid., 352).

Racism is not always obvious, overt, or even impolite. Indeed, Henry and Tator have focused on racism as it is effected in liberal and democratic societies like Canada. They define racism as essentially 'democratic', describing it as 'any set of justificatory arguments and mechanisms that permit individuals to maintain racist beliefs while championing democratic values' (ibid., 19). It is through 12 popular discourses that racism is structured and effected, including the discourse of denial, political correctness, colour-blindness, equal opportunity, blaming the victim, white victimization, reverse racism, binary polarization, moral panic, multiculturalism, liberal tolerance, and the discourse of national identity (for a detailed discussion, see Henry and Tator, 2006).

We take these academic definitions of racism seriously, but as discussed, we define racism as something that violates ancient principles set out in Two Row Wampum. This treaty has not been fully respected but the spirit of this relation-ship—however wounded it has become—cannot be so easily broken. Indeed, it is our objective to first revisit the original principles and to remind all future generations, Indigenous or otherwise, of its terms.

Each author in this collection is re-telling the story of 'settlement' (read col-onization) through Indigenous eyes, hearts, minds, and souls and in the process has never forgotten, metaphorically speaking, that the Two Row Wampum's prin-ciples were originally meant to guide us in our relationship with one another. The one party has never forgotten the original intention of the wampum, and through-out the centuries has kept reminding the colonizer to keep its foot out of its canoe; in short to respect the autonomy of Indigenous peoples as we have respected set-tler colonialists. The voices in this collection will vary somewhat because of the multiplicity of our experiences, but we feel that we share in common a commit-ment to restore the original balance upon which the two entities ought to be travelling. We believe that in order to restore balance, each side needs to remem-ber the principles of the treaty and to know of the historical forces that upset them and brought about much disruption on Turtle Island. Once that happens, then healing can begin and a new peaceful and just journey re-taken.

The word Haudenosaunee, or People of the Longhouse, is one that we use to describe our individual sense of identity and well-being. And while we might be just as comfortable with using words like Ukwehuwé (the Original People), Onyota'a:ka (People of the Standing Stone) , or even 'Six Nations', we resist the concept of 'Indian' to describe our collective identity. Naming is a powerful act of self-determination; in naming ourselves Haudenosaunee we are explicitly con-necting ourselves to the League of the Six Nations, (re)claiming our connections with the past, present, and future peoples who make up that League wherever they or their spirits might reside in Turtle Island.

We are bound together as Haudenosaunee through kinship and clan affiliation and have an interdependent responsibility that therefore guides our every thought and act. As Monture (2008: 156) writes:

[O]ne must understand something of the person's tribal tradition as this grounds who they are, as well as the symbols and styles they will use. . . . my name grounds me in the gift of words Creator gave me. It is both identity and direction. It is strength and responsibility. It is this location, as Mohawk citizen and woman, which guides the way I see the patterns that in turn ground my understanding of who I am and what I know.

Both of us are positioned as Ukwehuwé, Onyota'aka, and Turtle Clan. Not all Haudenosaunee are Longhouse or possess traditional names. Yeliwi:saks is the spiritual name belonging to Lina assigned to her by her clan mother which translates as 'She Is Gathering Stories/Knowledge'. Through the naming, she carries the responsibility of gathering stories and sharing the power of these words with others. Naming ourselves Onyota'aka is a powerful act of decolonization as it (re)juvenates our national identity, and tells the rest of the world that we were and are nations and are calling on others to see and treat us as such. The history of governing ourselves dates back many centuries before the arrival of non-Ukwehuwé.

This book stems, in part from our individual and collective sense of resistance to the term Indian, as it is one that embodies the historic and contemporary violation of Guswentah, and the autonomous right of Haudenosaunee and other Indigenous nations to determine their own citizenry. Indian embodies the very first act of colonial injustice and, we believe, that neither decolonization nor self-determination can be realized unless we challenge this history that institutionalized Indianness. We agree with other Ukwehuwé scholars in seeing the act of self-determination to begin first with the Self (Monture, 1999). We must resist foreign impositions that require the terms Aboriginal, First Nations, and Indian to be used when describing Indigenous people (Alfred, 2005). We must begin to (re)identify ourselves as Ukwehuwé and claiming our clans, our nations, and our broader affiliation with other Haudenosaunee (ibid.).

Indigenous peoples became Indians under a legal classification that did not distinguish between their linguistic and cultural differences, or the multiplicity of Indigenous nations at the time. People became Indians so that the state could delimit the occupation of lands to Indians alone. It was through these sorting out of lands that the concretization of race as a social construct took place in Canada. Prior to colonization, Indigenous peoples defined themselves as distinct nations with their own socio-economic and political systems. Under settler colonialism, the Canadian state treated all Indigenous nations as one 'Indian race'; their oneness constructed by virtue of otherness. This process coincided with the conceptualization of Turtle Island as 'terra nullius', a land imagined as empty and unoccupied. Property was therefore equated with whiteness (Harris, 1993); a process that allowed the colonizer to dispossess Indigenous nations of their lands.

Another motive for instituting the Indian Act was to protect Indians from outside land encroachments (Tobias, 1983). Early Indian policies sought to encourage the gradual civilization of the Indians through enfranchisement (ibid., 42). Enfranchisement aimed to assimilate the Indians of Canada. The premise of the legislation was simple: upon meeting certain criteria, men who were literate, free of debt, and of good moral character could (along with their 'dependents') give up legal Indian Act status and become ordinary Canadians with all the according rights and privileges (ibid., 42) The title and premise of enfranchisement law reveals its racist underpinnings: one could not be a 'civilized person' without giving up their Indian status. This is how racial categories were institutionalized. The first group to be racialized in Canada were the Indigenous peoples.

The Indian Act held the potential to reorganize Haudenosaunee kinship structures, in particular because they were both matrilocal and matrilineal prior to contact. Kinship structures were based on the clan system, where descent was passed through the women's line. This stood in opposition to the patrilineal registration criteria of the Indian Act. If one considers that in Canada, and in most of Europe, women were not considered persons but merely the property of men, the Indian Act clearly devalued females and the powers they enjoyed in some Indigenous nations. The process of establishing the category Indian was therefore also informed by patriarchal understandings. What this history suggests to us is that the colonial enterprise of racism is inseparable from (hetero)sexism and patriarchy as this has been argued by many Indigenous scholars (see Anderson, 2000; Cannon, 1995; Green, 2007; Lawrence, 2004; Monture, 1995; Smith, 2005, 2006; Sunseri, 2000).

Patriarchy has been defined as:

> [H]ierarchical relations between men and women, manifested in familial and social structures alike, in a descending order from an authoritarian—if oftentimes benevolent—male head, to male dominance in personal, political, cultural and social life, and to patriarchal families where the law of the father prevails (Code, 2000: 378).

Patriarchy invaded our nations, transforming what was largely egalitarianism into an imbalanced set of gender relations. In this book, we wish to investigate these and other ideological transformations of race and gender, as well as the interlocking ways in which patriarchal notions were reaffirmed through Indian policy and other broader sets of social relations.

The Indian Act entrenches a set of legalized parameters involving lands. As political economists have pointed out (Satzewich and Wotherspoon, 1993), the Indian Act provided for the appropriation of Indigenous territories and the accumulation of capital. 'The land was acquired [through] the forcible and relentless dispossession of Indigenous peoples, the theft of their territories, and the implementation of legislation and policies designed to effect their total disappearance as peoples' (Lawrence, 2002: 23). As such, 'any theorizing of race must go beyond simple cultural politics [and] acknowledge the centrality of broader political and economic developments' (Anderson quoted in Wallis and Fleras, 2009: xv). The history of capitalist relations is therefore inseparable from the emergence of race as a social construct in North America. Having said that, Canada has tried to erase its historical record. It is through storytelling that we might hope to reveal and redress the hidden dimensions of political economy. As Monture (2008: 156) notes, storytelling traditions are very common in our Indigenous nations, and 'through our stories we learn who we are. These stories teach about identity and responsibility.' Through the stories we gather by writers in this book, we openly name the Indian Act and all other socio-political structures imposed by the Canadian State as imperialist projects.

The Indian Act imposed an 'elected' band council system of governance upon Indigenous nations. These councils were empowered to make by-laws and, upon approval of the Superintendent of Indian Affairs, to deal with all other concerns. An elective system of governance remained a choice for Indigenous nations in Canada until an amendment in 1895. After this time, the government delegated itself the authority to depose both chiefs and councillors of bands not following an elected system (Tobias, 1983: 46–7; Indian Act [S.C. 1895, c.35, s.3] reprinted in Venne, 1981: 141). It is important to acknowledge that the Indian Act represented an imposition to already established, hereditary forms of government. We see this as a blatant act of colonialism. In seeking to replace traditional governance with an elective model, the belief in European political superiority and higher civilization became institutionalized. These ways of thinking are not confined to the past: an example of ongoing beliefs about European superiority takes place whenever the contributions of Indigenous peoples are said to have offered nothing to the building of North American civilization (*The Globe & Mail*, 24 October 2008).

We want to suggest that the Indian Act and other policies represent the very first instance of racialized thinking and institutionalized racism in Canada. We also want to examine how an Indian/white colour line is established and constructed under settler-colonialism. The processes that continue today to uphold, maintain, and reproduce a set of racialized ways of thinking were put into place over 150 years ago. By settler colonialism, we are referring to the process whereby Indigenous peoples were dispossessed of their lands through a series of genocidal acts, including the imposition of racial hierarchy through Indian status distinctions. Whiteness itself became constructed as the superior racial category and consequently white supremacy has become legitimatized and normalized (Razack, 2002).

The category of Indian is by no means a neutral one. It is an arbitrary category established by Europeans to refer to Indigenous difference. These arbitrary distinctions are inherent to processes of racialization. As Wendy Cornet (2003: 124–5) writes, racialization is

a term used by critical race theorists to describe the process by which the socially constructed concept of race assumes meaning within and between societies. Arbitrary elements of physical appearance or arbitrary descent criteria typically form the basis of race classification schemes. These classifications are social constructions and can be further entrenched by the law. The arbitrariness of race classification in an Indigenous context is twofold: first, in the selection of arbitrary physiognomic features as the basis of classification (by society) or of rigid descent criteria (by law—the Indian Act); while ignoring cultural distinctions and the nation(al) identities of the peoples concerned.

The construction of Indigenous difference takes place through processes of racialization and additional sets of discursive practices. Edward Said (1978) referred to an 'Orientalist' discourse, a Western construction of the Orient seen as essentially 'different' and inferior to the 'West'. When Indians are represented as the Other in their own lands, they are seen in contrast to the colonizer. Within the binary framework of Self and Other, the outcomes provide for injustice. Indigenous peoples are pathologized as genetically inferior and deviant, while the Western Self becomes the progressive, modern, and civilized subject (Sunseri, 2007). It also provides the ideological justification for the ongoing dispossession of lands, the accompanying attack on sovereignty, and the maintenance of cultural imperialism required for the furthering of capitalist exploitation.

Issues of race are not easily introduced into conversations about the self-determination of Indigenous peoples. Indeed, as Bob Porter (1999: 158) suggests, transforming conceptions of separate political status into matters of race works ultimately to erode the status of Indigenous peoples as citizens of separate sovereigns. He writes:

> Even though Indigenous society is rooted in a sovereignty separate and apart from American sovereignty, Indians today appear to be suggesting that they should be treated in the same way as such racial minority groups as African Americans and Asian Americans . . . While it certainly is the case that Indians have long been thought to be of a different 'race', protestations solely along racial lines can only serve to undermine the perception that Indian nations have a political existence separate and apart from that of the United States (ibid., 154).

It is incumbent upon us as Ukwehuwé to think seriously about the issues raised by Porter. In contemplating our own Haudenosaunee existence, we acknowledge that original nation-to-nation agreements were made at the time of contact with settler-colonists, including Guswentah or Two Row Wampum. These wampum do not make reference to Ukwehuwé as races of people, but rather sovereign nations whose inherent rights were granted by the Creator, or as Augie Fleras has put it, nations who 'share the sovereignty of Canada through multiple and overlapping jurisdictions' (2009: 78). We also feel that before a timeless and unbroken assertion of sovereignty can be fully realized, it will be necessary to acknowledge that colonial injustice, racism, and sexism are inextricably linked, historically, and even still today.

To begin to think about the interconnections we are describing, it is important to revisit Canada's Indian Act, and more specifically, Indian status distinctions. The Indian Act exemplifies the institutionalized racism and patriarchy that has characterized colonial dominance. Indian status is the process whereby Indigenous nations became Indians for state administrative purposes. It refers to a set of practices, beliefs, and ways of thinking that made—and continue to make—Indianness compulsory. In order to restore our status as Indigenous nations; indeed as separate political entities, it will be important to think about these historic processes, and as the Cree leader Phil Fontaine has put it, 'to move citizenship to the jurisdiction where it properly belongs and that is with First Nations governments'. In this book, we want to suggest that asserting our political status as Indigenous nations is impossible without challenging histories of racialization.

We are not suggesting that the Indian Act is everything when it comes to determining Indigenous identities. Indeed, many Ukwehuwé prefer to talk of identity and citizenship—as we have in this Introduction—in nation-specific terms. But even as we assert our nation-based identities—indeed even as we know who it is that we are—the Indian Act continues to make possible the ongoing *involuntary enfranchisement* of our people. Involuntary enfranchisement takes place in Canada whenever a status Indian (registered under S. 6(2) of the Indian Act) marries and has children with a non-Indian person (Cannon, 2008: 15). This act of exogamous, 'out-marriage' is by no means a neutral one because under current provisions it works to disenfranchise the grandchildren of women who married non-Indians before 1985. These individuals are a new class of 'involuntarily enfranchised' Indians—their loss of legal entitlements is brought on by their parent's choice to marry non-Indians (ibid.).

Under amendments to the Indian Act in 1985, those who register as status Indians now do so under one of seven different sections of the Indian Act. The major difference lies between sections 6(1) and 6(2). S. 6(1) Indians pass on Indian status to offspring; s. 6(2) Indians pass on status to offspring only if married to an Indian (Magnet, 2003: 55). This matter of discrimination has been raised at both the Superior Court and Court of Appeal levels in British Columbia in what is known as the McIvor case. It has been found that S. 6, in the conferring of Indian status, discriminates between the descendants of Indian men and women who married non-Indians because it is women's children who are registered under S. 6(2). The justices have all agreed unanimously: the treatment for Indian women and their children who claim Indian descent through them is unequal to that afforded to Indian men and their descendants (*McIvor v. Canada, Registrar, Indian and Northern Affairs*, 2007 BCSC 827 at 236). They have concluded that it is now *the grandchildren of Indian women* who are being treated differently than the *grandchildren of Indian men* based on their grandparents sex and/or marriage to non-Indians. We will return to a fuller discussion of this case and its consequences in our concluding chapter.

Section 6(2) of the Indian Act shows how pervasive the impact of sexism has been on the lives of Indigenous peoples. Of course sexism is not the only issue involved. Race and racism can also be used to describe historic injustices imposed by the Indian Act. The process whereby Indigenous nations became status Indians for state administrative purposes involves deeply racialized thinking. The issue itself is one that even our courts have been unable to address and acknowledge, even in progressive BC Court of Appeal judgments like the McIvor case. The case itself shows how intractable the institutionalized racism that characterizes the colonial present has become. The category Indian literally disappears below the surface of progressive politics and the law. Furthermore, in order to resist the category, we must appropriate and affirm its use. Bonita Lawrence describes the paradox we are highlighting. As she writes: 'Legal categories . . . shape peoples' lives. They set the terms that individuals and communities must utilize even in resisting these categories' (2004: 230).

We concur with Bob Porter that being awarded racial minority status cannot be understood as the central issue facing Indigenous peoples today. Having said that, we feel it is important to raise as a matter of political scrutiny and critical reflection, the process through which we became racialized as Indians in Canada. This thinking does not start with adopting racial minority status but in revisiting

Indianness itself. If the very first act of historical and colonial injustice involved the re-naming of our diverse nations, then the urgency of dismantling racialized regimes cannot be underestimated or denied. If it is true that histories of racialization have made racism so intractable, so institutionalized, then we cannot be truly free of colonial domination if the racism directed at our nations remains intact.

In saying that we are nations and citizens of Indigenous nations, we are not only opposing the Indian Act and other racialized processes, we are also opposing an identity-making process that was—and is still today—key to the building of Canada as a nation (Thobani, 2007). In that sense, this book is as much about whiteness as it is about racism and Indigeneity. By refusing the category Indian, we are asking Canadians to think about how identity legislation plays a part in creating colonial settlements, and indeed lands for the taking. We are intent on illustrating the many ways in which 'white men name and mark others, thereby naming and marking themselves' (Weis, Proweller, and Centrie, 1997: 214). We are saying that our territories extend far beyond the identity classification schemes used to define them as 'reserve-based lands'. We are asserting our political status as separate political entities, but we are simultaneously challenging the racialization and sexism that comprises colonialism.

In contemplating the future of self-determination, including the struggle for sovereignty that characterizes contemporary politics, it will be necessary to revisit and acknowledge histories of racialization and to provide a context for understanding sexism, colonial injustice, and the formulation of settler identities. In order to challenge settler colonialism and the primary claim to the land and to the nation, we must make visible the historic processes whereby we became Indians for state administrative purposes. The regulation of identities in this regard is by no means a relic of the past. As Bonita Lawrence has put it, 'it is part of the way in which Canada and the United States continue to actively maintain physical control of the land base they claim' (2004: 38).

Both in general and in light of these considerations, a series of questions come to mind concerning racism, Indigeneity, and citizenship: Who do Canadian citizens know themselves to be and how much of this depends on keeping racialized Others—status Indians in particular—firmly in place? How do we explain the white need for certainty about Indian difference? What are modern practices of difference-making, where are they located, and how do they operate in the contemporary world? What sorts of work go into the dispossession of lands, including the urban spaces we occupy and have always occupied? In addition to providing an overview of the writings of Indigenous peoples on and about racism, it is our hope that this book will shed critical insight into these types of questions.

Organization of the Book

As surely as racism is not disappearing in North America, neither are Indigenous peoples. We offer only a glimpse of the work that is being done to understand the interconnections between race, racialization, racism, sexism, and colonialism over the past centuries. In outlining the resistance to these systems of inequality, the book draws from multiple theoretical frameworks and crosses disciplinary boundaries. This is inevitable, if not desirable: many standpoints, views, identities, and backgrounds make up Indigenous knowledge and scholarship, and our experience is shaped by where we are located within communities, the academy, and mainstream society. These differences are sources of strength because the authors in this collection offer their own gifts, their own ways of knowing and being Indigenous on Turtle Island. Each is focused on specific themes, issues, and questions that offer a unique set of perspectives about race, racism, colonialism, and decolonization.

We open up the book with a review of some central theoretical foundations. How are we to explain what has occurred, and continues to occur, to Indigenous people across this land? In Chapter 1, Taiaiake Alfred tackles this question by suggesting that 'we need to understand clearly who and what constitutes our enemy', and the 'imperial arrogance, the institutional and attitudinal expressions of the prejudicial biases inherent in European and Euro-American cultures'. His chapter provides readers with a look at who/what this enemy is and how, through its own arrogance, it has actively participated in the imperialist and colonialist processes that have sought to dispossess Onkwehonwe from territorial, political, and cultural autonomy.

In Chapter 2, Marie Battiste and Sakej Henderson focus on Eurocentrism and how this serves as the ideological basis upon which the superiority of Europeans over non-Europeans was first conceptualized; and consequently, materialized in the encounter between the two groups. They examine the 'diffusionism' that has resulted in viewing Europe as the centre of progress and civilization and the non-European world as an 'emptiness of basic cultural institutions and peoples'. As Battiste and Henderson illustrate, this idea of diffusionism is deeply embedded in settler colonialism and it provided Europeans with the ideological justification for their beliefs and actions towards Indigenous peoples. The authors urge that these beliefs be re-evaluated and challenged.

Bonita Lawrence and Enakshi Dua, in their article 'Decolonizing Antiracism', provide a critique of antiracist scholarship. Theoretically, this scholarship has excluded Indigenous peoples and perspectives, and as a result, Indigenous peoples are disconnected from antiracist theories and activism. The authors make a call for a change in antiracism and postcolonial theories that takes seriously the theft of Indigenous lands, Indigenous movements, and decolonization. Their chapter seeks to integrate the specificity of Indigenous experiences, identities, and struggles, and is aimed at having a practical significance for Indigenous communities.

Part Two of this book consists of three chapters outlining the history of nation-building in Canada and the construction of a racialized Indian Other. In Chapter 4, Deborah Doxtator shows how the idea of Indian was created using labels such as ferocious, drunkards, and primitive, and through stereotypical symbols like tepees, totem poles, and face paint. These symbols persist in the colonial imagination and have little to do with the actual people of the past or present. Doxtator shows how 'Indians' have been portrayed in history textbooks: either as tools, as threats, as allies; nevertheless always secondary to the official heroes and builders of the nation. Colonialism is hardly ever taken up seriously in history textbooks; instead it is conceptualized as 'settlement', as something that 'just happened'. In this way, we concur with Doxtator: the mythology of the 'two founding nations' and the disappearing Indian endures within the minds of most Canadians. It is no wonder Indigenous youth feel alienated by the educational system. How are they able to see themselves reflected in textbooks if the history of their ancestors is not honestly represented?

Thomas King picks up on this review by Doxtator in Chapter 5. He is concerned with the Indian that exists in our collective imaginations. He looks closely at representation of 'Indianness' in popular culture, photography, and postcards, suggesting that many of these media have relegated us to past domains. Much has been ignored in this representation, including the dispossession of lands, struggles against the State, and other everyday events. King offers a counter-response by revisiting his own experience and, with great humour, setting the record straight about who is a 'real' Indian.

In the final chapter of Part Two, Winona Stevenson provides an overview of the various phases of colonialism with a focus on how it affected Indigenous women and gender relations. She looks at early representations of Indigenous women held by first Europeans, and how these have negatively impacted Indigenous women as patriarchy and sexism infiltrated their way into our communities. These histories of sexism and patriarchy are inseparable from the building of Canada as a nation.

Part Three of the book looks at how Indigenous spaces and territories have been shaped by racism and colonial formations. Chris Andersen and Claude Denis examine the relationship between state formation and the construction of Aboriginal identities in Chapter 7. They focus on the way public inquiries and commissions tend to legitimize and normalize land-based identities, which perpetuates, in turn, divisions and exclusions between Indigenous peoples. In Chapter 8, Bonita Lawrence challenges the dominant historical narratives of Canada and rewrites them from an Indigenous perspective. She examines the impact of racism and colonialism on Indigenous lands and communities in what is now called Eastern Canada. Although we cannot homogenize Indigenous experiences with colonialism, there are similar patterns that link them. In the final chapter of Part Three, Martha Montour shows how Iroquois women's rights with respect to matrimonial property were diminished by colonialism, in particular the Indian Act, and she proposes some remedies so that women's rights can be restored in Indigenous territories.

Racism and colonialism have had a profound influence on Indigenous identities. How we see ourselves, how others perceive us, how we treat each other, and how we treat those outside of our groups is all shaped by colonial discourses of Indigeneity. These discourses have very little to do with traditional ways of being and governing. In Chapter 10, Martin Cannon looks at matters of citizenship and how governments have inadequately dealt with these, in turn preventing the reconciliation of Indian status injustices. His work is informed by 10 interviews conducted with Indigenous peoples on this subject. There is a diversity of views on matters of belonging and citizenship, and a variety of experiences based on age, gender, spirituality, and political orientation. Despite these differences, there are a set of shared experiences based on racism and colonial history, as well as assimilation and resistance.

Chapters 11 and 12 address how different individuals are impacted by essentialist, racist and (hetero)sexist modes of thinking as these are embedded in colonial relations. In Chapter 11, Bonita Lawrence focuses on the identities of mixed-blooded individuals: people who have struggled to belong and be accepted as Indigenous in their own communities and in urban environments. Due to essentialist notions of identity constructed through colonialist government regulation, these individuals are most often not seen or treated as 'real' Indians. A similar set of exclusionary practices function to preclude the alternative realization of erotic and gendered diversity. As Beverly Little Thunder discusses in Chapter 12, colonialism has lumped the many possible ways of being and loving into fixed labels, wherein a womyn struggles to locate herself within a comfortable and suitable place. Her own spirituality is compromised by external definitions of self; a process failing two spirit individuals, leaving them feeling displaced, silenced, and forced to choose between fixed identity constructions.

Part Five addresses issues of belonging, displacement, and the dismantling of traditional family life. In Chapter 13, Kim Anderson examines traditional concepts and practices of marriage, divorce, and family life and how these have been transformed by colonialism. Through the influence of Christianity and other Western ideals, Indigenous societies have moved away from egalitarian, women-centred relations and have come to resemble the patriarchal families of Euro-Christian society. Many communities are trying to recover concepts of traditional family life. Rosalyn Ing looks at the impact of residential schooling on communities, families, and mothering. In Chapter 14, she asks: how are the women who attended these schools able to mother their children given the traumatic experiences they had to endure? What are the impacts on the grandchildren of these individuals? How have colonialist practices of assimilation marked current family relations, and how does this effect communities?

The Sixties Scoop and transracial adoption have also impacted on traditional family relations. Many children were taken away from their biological families because they were deemed unfit to parent. In Chapter 16, Shandra Spears explores her own personal narrative, looking at the impact these policies had on children who later grew up disconnected from their birth families and communities. These are traumatic experiences that were part of a genocidal attempt by the state to get rid of the 'Indian problem'. By appropriating these children and placing them into white families and communities, it was thought that Indians would just disappear.

Part Six of the book explores Indigenous nationhood and citizenship through Indigenous perspectives. In Chapter 16, Taiaiake Alfred and Jeff Corntassel analyze Indigenous identity in the context of contemporary colonialism. They argue that being Indigenous means having a place-based existence, a unique heritage to the land and its original peoples, and a consciousness of being in struggle against a colonial state. A person who identifies as Indigenous seeks to restore a nation to nation relationship with Canadian society, something we initially argued in this introduction.

In Chapter 17, Audra Simpson shows how Indigeneity has been historically tied to colonialism and anthropology. Anthropology has been an authoritative voice of the West in describing and 'knowing' Indigenous peoples. But these techniques of knowing were part of a larger colonial project, in turn constructing an essentialist, exotic, and dying culture stuck in a timeless past preoccupied with rituals. In contrast, and as Simpson shows, Indigenous notions of identity are not merely preoccupied with rituals and representations of an exotic, nostalgic past, but also with issues of nationhood, citizenship, rights, justice, territory, autonomy, and ways of relating with each other and others.

In Chapter 18, Lina Sunseri provides an anticolonial feminist perspective on nationalism by incorporating women's issues in nationalist discourses and practices challenging in turn colonial concepts of nation and belonging. Such a perspective tries to recover Indigenous ways of governing that could restore balance and gender relations as well as accommodating various contemporary identities.

Part Seven of the book deals with the educational experiences of Indigenous peoples. How have racism and colonialism shaped these experiences? Marie Battiste examines the ambivalence surrounding literacy education. This ambivalence is due to the assimilationist agenda of education imposed upon Indigenous peoples: a form of cognitive imperialism that devalues Indigenous traditions and attempts to replace them with Western educational methods. She provides some examples of Indigenous communities like the Micmaq who have developed Indigenous literacy models based on their own culture and traditions.

Suzanne Fournier and Ernie Crey revisit the history of residential schools in Chapter 20. They provide some context for understanding these schools by outlining the colonial dominance and racism that informed their emergence. Their article provides some insight into the institutional administration of these schools, as well as the kinds of abuse that characterized them. They outline histories of genocide to which much of the early education of Indigenous peoples has been so intimately connected.

Verna St. Denis, in Chapter 21, revisits the usage of culture theory in Indigenous education and questions the extent to which studying culture can disrupt unequal power relations that exist between Indigenous and non-Indigenous peoples. She argues that the current focus on cultural difference and incommensurability does little to displace the unequal power relations that have arisen in a racist society. This prevents all students from thinking critically about colonial realities and the strategies that might be used to repair them.

In Part Eight we link poverty with colonial histories of dispossession that left many nations and communities in the economic margins of one of the wealthiest countries in the world. In Chapter 22, Cyndy Baskin shows how the current homelessness of Indigenous youth in cities is linked to colonialism, in particular child welfare policies. She concludes by making some proposals for positive change for Indigenous youth and the general Indigenous population. Cora Voyageur and Brian Calliou, in Chapter 23, provide a review of the barriers that have historically existed for Indigenous communities. Much of this history has prevented communities from prospering economically. They examine cultural and systemic barriers that have contributed to the current economic marginalization of

Indigenous communities. The later part of this article is focused on the potential to revitalize economies and to explore external opportunities, internal assets, and alternative development strategies.

In the last chapter of Part Eight, Jim Silver et al. examine concrete examples of the revitalization introduced by Voyageur and Calliou. Based on examples from the city of Winnipeg, the authors outline the kinds of community development that are holistic, based upon Indigenous values of community, sharing, healing, and revitalization of Indigenous culture. Such a model of development differs from a Western model centred upon capitalistic values of individualism, profit, and devaluation of the environment. This chapter demonstrates that Indigenous peoples have the vision and ability to heal from oppressive socio-economic conditions, and to develop their own strategies of community and capacity-building that are decolonizing and rooted in Indigenous ways of being and knowing.

The last Part of the book covers issues of violence and criminality as experienced by Indigenous peoples. Joyce Green starts with a critical overview of the freezing death of Neil Stonechild and the public and legal responses to it. Green links systemic and institutional racism and demands that Canadian society take racism in all its existing forms before social cohesion can take place. Only then, can justice be delivered to the family of Neil Stonechild and others who froze to death—as well as those facing similar abuses and violence at the hands of the police.

In Chapter 26, Patricia Monture-Okanee and Mary Ellen Turpel offer an Indigenous perspective on criminal justice. They do so by deconstructing concepts embedded in the Canadian criminal justice system: justice, equal access to justice, equitable treatment, and respect. They also examine concepts such as alternative justice, parallel justice system, and a separate justice system. They suggest that criminal justice be looked at in a holistic manner: its institutions, norms, and how these have treated Indigenous people. For justice to be truly served, it is necessary to acknowledge and respect Indigenous difference as well as their separate political status.

The last chapter is written by Andrea Smith who examines sexual violence as a tool of genocide. Her article is a poignant and vivid reminder of the violence perpetuated against Indigenous bodies serving to violate their sexuality, womanhood, and Indigeneity. Such violence was used as a tool of patriarchal control, a means of treating individuals as subhuman. Hence, in the context of colonialism, racism and sexism interconnect and Indigenous women are violated as both Indigenous peoples and as women.

The intent of this book is to examine the interplay of racism and colonial forces and how these have shaped the lives of Indigenous peoples and their relations with settler colonialists. Our aim is to provide insight into what can be done to address historic wrongdoings and envision a different path, one where the founding principles of the Two-Row Wampum are re-established.

Notes

1. The word Haudenosaunee, meaning 'People of the Longhouse' (a reference to the distinctive houses in which our ancestors once resided), may differ depending on the Six Nations person or community to whom one is speaking. For example, Taiaiake Alfred refers to his people (the people of Kahnawake Mohawk Nation) as Rotinohshonni (1995: 38; 1999: xi). Doxtator (1996) chose the word Rotinonhsyonni. We use the word Haudenosaunee as it is one that is familiar to us, and also one that has been used by the Six Nations people in political dealings with the Canadian state (see Haudenosaunee Confederacy, 1983). Several words used henceforth in this book, including the words Ukwehuwé (the Original People) and Onyota'a:ka (People of the Standing Stone), are in Oneida (the language of both of our Indigenous ancestors), and we are grateful for the advice that has been provided to us in this regard by several Oneida speakers.

PART ONE

Theoretical Foundations

This book begins with a selection of theoretical perspectives offered by Indigenous scholars on matters of colonial dominance and racism. The literature we have selected provides a way of thinking about racism as a continually evolving process that is informed by—and indeed inseparable from—early colonial precedents. The readings provide a glimpse of the kinds of assumptions and understandings that continue to structure and inform academic scholarship, contemporary knowledge production, and the politics of recognition, as well as redress and reconciliation.

According to Alfred, racism cannot be reduced to individuals alone. Indeed, the enemy is not even the 'white man' in racial terms. Instead, racism is a way of thinking with an imperialist's mindset. Combating racism must therefore employ institutional analyses centred on its ideological basis and underpinnings. It is 'the belief in the superiority and universality of Euro-American culture' that requires our unwavering attention and scrutiny. We must revisit and ask critical questions about taken-for-granted practices, such as capitalism, democracy, and individual rights. These practices embody apparatuses of power now firmly entrenched into settler–colonial consciousness.

Imperialist ways of thinking are not easily dismantled. This is because they are continually enabled through social and political processes that fashion the Indian as Other within the racialized colonial imaginary. Indigenous nations are consumed under the category 'Aboriginal' or even 'Indian'—a process that is exemplary of the material and ideological violence that erases colonial histories of dispossession, nation-to-nation agreements, and the diversity that exists among us as Ukwehuwé. 'Aboriginalism', writes Alfred, expunges histories of dominance aimed at Indigenous peoples. Furthermore, it structures social and political outcomes.

The reparation of colonial and racialized injustices will remain complicated so long as they are shaped by Eurocentric principles. Before Indigenous peoples can take their rightful place as partners in the founding of Canada—and before any real change can be realized in the areas of law, politics, and economics—the meaning of justice itself must be entirely reconceptualized. Reparation must also be seen as a duty—not a gift—of white settler society. It will be necessary to decolonize our own ways of thinking as Indigenous peoples; that is, to think outside of the racialized categories and taken for granted processes that have been made available to use by the colonizer.

Meaningful change also requires that we think about knowledge production. Whose knowledge is valued and with what set of consequences? How have Indigenous knowledges been defined, addressed, incorporated or assumed out of existence in courts, curricula, and other sites of power? What knowledges inform and structure legal and political outcomes? For Battiste and Henderson, we need to look at the history of white settler knowledge; and more importantly, at the histories of European colonial thought.

Whiteness is by no means incidental in the writings of Indigenous scholars. In the first instance, white settler identities were premised on the idea of Indian—a category later established in law so that lands could be designated as either 'reserved' for them as Other or available to white settlers for securing the accumulation of capital. The construction of white settler identities also required that some knowledge be deemed deficient, backward, or lacking. As Battiste and Henderson show, Indigenous knowledge has always served as a convenient and 'self-congratulatory reference point against which Eurocentric society could measure its own progressive evolution'.

The idea of knowledge as a yardstick—as static and unchanging—has played a part in maintaining colonial dominance. While knowledge systems are themselves dynamic, adaptable, and transformative, they are often treated as timeless, or even disappearing. The confusion results from what Battiste and Henderson call the 'myth of primitive culture'—the idea that Indigenous knowledge is authentic and legitimate only when it has been untouched by European influence. The colonizer exerts dominance over Indigenous peoples through this practice and ways of thinking.

Theoretically, the readings we have selected for this chapter suggest that the injustices facing Indigenous peoples cannot be reduced to racism alone. Lawrence and Dua in particular suggest that matters of colonialism, the dispossession of lands, and sovereignty all require the attention of antiracism activists and scholars. Antiracism scholarship must change the questions it asks of inequality and injustice and do a better job at considering the issues stemming from colonization before it can hope to prioritize histories of Indigenous peoples and for antiracist movements to build coalition with them.

Until now, as Lawrence and Dua suggest, antiracism and postcolonial scholarship has not taken colonialism, decolonization, and Indigenous nationhood seriously. This has 'meant that Aboriginal peoples' histories, resistance, and current realities have been segregated from antiracism'. At best, Indigeneity receives only token recognition. At worst, it is thought to have little to do with histories of immigration or peoples of colour. In order for antiracism to be truly decolonizing, the link between peoples of colour to Indigeneity must be treated as a complex, dynamic interaction embodying in turn its own set of power relations.

Lawrence and Dua remind us that while differences do exist among peoples of colour, they too are settlers living on contested lands. Tensions can and therefore do exist between these groups. In general, many questions about non-white history have gone unanswered. For example, in what historical relation do new Canadians stand in relation to Indigenous struggles at reclaiming land and sovereignty (Sharma and Wright, 2008)? Questions such as these and others must be examined in order for postcolonial scholarship and antiracism to confront its colonial framework and for coalition building to occur.

Chapter 1

Colonial Stains on Our Existence

Taiaiake Alfred

Imperial Arrogances

If Onkwehonwe movements are to force Settler societies to transcend colonialism, we need to understand clearly who and what constitutes our enemy. The 'problem' or 'challenge' we face has been explained in many ways, but to move our discussion forward I will state it in a blunt and forcefully true way: the problem we face is Euroamerican arrogance, the institutional and attitudinal expressions of the prejudicial biases inherent in European and Euroamerican cultures. This is not the abstract concept it may appear to be on first reading; it is the fundamental source of stress, discord, and injustice and capitalizes on the ubiquitous nature of imperialism and the threat it presents. The challenge we face is made up of specific patterns of behaviour among Settlers and our own people: choices made to support mentalities that developed in serving the colonization of our lands as well as the unrestrained greed and selfishness of mainstream society. We must add to this the superficial monotheistic justifications for

the unnatural and misunderstood place and purpose of human beings in the world, an emphatic refusal to look inward, and an aggressive denial of the value of nature. . . .

So, in the framework of this struggle, what kinds of people make up Settler societies today? From the position of a movement for change, it is very important to distinguish between the various elements of the Settler population and to develop appropriate strategies of contention for each of the adversaries and enemies. There are those whom Albert Memmi called the 'colonizers who refuse' to accept their position and role in the unjust state, usually left-wing intellectuals (Memmi, 1991: 43).[1] These are people whose indignation at the theoretical injustices of imperialism as an historical process (usually thought of as happening in foreign countries rather than their own beloved backyards) is not accompanied by action. They may be progressive politically, but they usually hold a strong attachment to the colonial state and to their own privileges within Settler society. They are effectively silenced by being caught in the squeeze between their intellectual deconstructions of power and their moral cowardice when it comes to doing something about injustice in a real sense. The colonizers who refuse to acknowledge their privilege and inheritance of wrongs are practising another form of selfishness and hypocrisy—they claim the right and privilege of indignation and the power to judge those cruder colonizers among them and attempt to use this rhetorical posture to release themselves of their own responsibility for the colonial enterprise, both historically and in the way it has affected their own lives, their families' privileges, and their communities' formation. These people are paralyzed by fear. Their guilt renders them useless to our struggle and paradoxically makes them one of the strongest blocs of hard-core conservatism in Settler society. Put so eloquently by the African-American writer Audre Lorde, 'guilt is just another name for impotence, for defensiveness destructive of communication, it becomes a device to protect ignorance . . . the ultimate protection for changelessness' (Lorde, 1984).

Another arm of the colonial body is the colonizer who accepts his or her role, who has internalized colonial myths, mainly racist histories, notions of white superiority, and the lie of progress (or the immigrants' hope that material accumulation and expansion of wealth is indeed the formula for happiness, acceptability by the white man, and legitimacy as citizens). This posture is simple enough to understand and hardly needs further elaboration, except to acknowledge that the majority of the Settler population is in this category, an indication of the vastness of the challenge ahead of us. . . .

Onkwehonwe rights and freedoms are always falsely identified in the mass media and public commentary (which are tacitly supported by the government) as the instruments by which Settlers are victimized. Recognizing and respecting Onkwehonwe rights is played off against white people's property values and their personal and emotional security, which are all at base an assertion of convenience and entitlement to continue in the benefit of crimes by earlier generations without recompense to the actual people who suffered in the relationship. The convenience of this assertion

as justification for the unwillingness of the white population to take serious stands against injustice should not be lost on anyone; the pronouncement that Onkwehonwe rights harm white people is simply not true and cannot be supported with evidence. It is nothing but a Rhodesian projection of white power onto a framework of potential Onkwehonwe achievement and re-empowerment.

These false decolonization processes also demand clear demarcations of the territorial bounds of the concept of Onkwehonwe nationhood. This may not sound like such a problem at first glance, but it is, in fact, a conscious tactic designed to ensure the failure of meaningful negotiations. The demand for territorial clarity and non-overlapping negotiations on land issues is predicated on an acceptance of the Euroamerican way of viewing land, demarking and dividing the land and environment and relationships between peoples on the basis of European-derived notions of property, ownership, and jurisdiction (Seed, 1995).

These are the fundamentals of Euroamerican arrogance projected onto the politics of decolonization. This is what Memmi's disease of the European looks like to us today. Is there a cure? Is there a way to break the grip of this powerful sickness in the hearts and minds of Settler society?

These questions are of enormous significance. How do we make their history and their country mean something different to people who feel entitled to the symbolic and real monopoly they enjoy on the social dynamics of our relationship and on the cultural landscape?[2] It seems that if we are to move beyond the charitable racism of current policies or paternalist progressivism of liberal reconciliation models, justice must become a *duty* of, not a *gift* from, the Settler.[3] And for this to happen, Settler society must be forced into a reckoning with its past, its present, its future, and itself. White people who are not yet decolonized must come to admit they were and are wrong. They must admit that Onkwehonwe have rights that are collective and inherent to their indigeneity and that are autonomous from the Settler society—rights to land, to culture, and to community. The

Settlers' inability to comprehend justice for Onkwehonwe from within their own cultural frame is simple. Why are the Settlers' supposed gifts and concessions, stingy and reluctant though they are, toward Onkwehonwe not seen as duties? Because that would mean the Settlers must admit that they were and are wrong and would imply a set of rights for Onkwehonwe.

The Other Side of Fear

The colonial relationship is a dynamic one of arrogance, complacency, and complicity. Aboriginalist complicity with the injustice and Onkwehonwe complacency toward our rights and freedoms enable this arrogance. Euroamerican pretensions are empowered and emboldened by the unwillingness of Onkwehonwe to defend the truth and by people's participation in the white man's lies. As Onkwehonwe who are committed to the Original Teachings, there is not supposed to be any space between the principles we hold and the practice of our lives. This is the very meaning of integrity: having the mental toughness and emotional strength to stand up for what we believe is right. The challenge is to master, not conquer, fear and to engage in the constant fight to resist both the corrupting effects of the financial, sensual, and psychological weapons used by the colonial authorities to undermine Onkwehonwe people and the corrosive effect on the Onkwehonwe mind and soul of Euroamerican culture and society. The question here is a real and immediate one for Onkwehonwe who enter the struggle actively: How do we deal with the psychological and physical battle fatigue which, in most cases, leads to eventual despair and defeatism? . . .

Five hundred years of physical and psychological warfare have created a colonial culture of fear among both subdued and dominant peoples. We have emerged out of a shameful past, a history of racial and religious hatreds, of extreme violence, and of profound injustice. It is impossible to even acknowledge it truthfully. Colonial culture, for both the victims and the perpetrators, is fundamentally a denial of the past and of its moral implications. It is an aversion to the truth about who we really are and where it is that we come from. More than the moneyed privilege of the newcomers, more than the chaotic disadvantage of the original peoples, this is what we have inherited from our colonial past: relationships founded on hatred and violence and a culture founded on lies to assuage the guilt or shame of it all. We are afraid of our memories, afraid of what we have become, afraid of each other, and afraid for the future. Fear is the foundation of the way we are in the world and the way we think about the future. It is normal, and we have grown used to it.

All of what we know as government and law is founded on these fears. The powerful in our society manage the words we hear and the images we see to ensure that we remain afraid. Although the past and its implications are self-evident, we are complicit in their denial because it is too painful or arduous or costly to imagine an existence unbound from the lies. Emotionally and psychologically, we are attached to this mythology of colonialism because it explains the Euroamerican conquest and normalizes it in our lives. The perpetrators know that it is wrong to steal a country and so deny it is a crime; the victims know that it is shameful to accept defeat lying down. Yet, complacency rules over both because the thought of what might come out of transcending the lies is too . . . fearsome.

Lying complacent in a narrow conception of the past and nearly paralyzed by fear in a constrained vision of the future, both the colonized and colonizers have been forced to accept and live with a state of unfreedom. This is the most profound meaning of colonialism's modern turn. Of course, this is made possible because the vast lie has been embedded in every aspect of our lives for so long as memory, as identity, and as political and economic relations of domination and exploitation.

What kind of culture has been produced by this denial of truth and wearing down of authenticity—of rooted, healthy, and meaningful ways of life—in the service of political and economic power? This question must be asked not only of the subdued but of the dominant as well. Colonialism is a total relationship of power, and it has shaped the existence, not only of those who have lost, but also those who have profited. . . .

Spaces We Occupy

In many countries, the term 'aboriginal' is seen as an inoffensive and innocuous substitute for more caustic words like 'Indian', or 'Native'. Unpacked as a social, political, and intellectual construction, however, it is a highly offensive word. It reflects the prevailing colonial mentality in its redefinition of Onkwehonwe away from our original languages,[4] because it fashions 'the people' as a symbol and concept constructed on, and totally amenable to, colonialism. Being aboriginal, once the implications are fully understood, is repugnant to anyone who desires to preserve Onkwehonwe ways of life. The ideas that Onkwehonwe will be inevitably integrated wholly into the Settler society (meaning that their autonomous existences will be terminated actively or voluntarily) and that their governments and lands will be subsumed within the colonial state have become the accepted ideological frame of Settler society, state governments, and many Onkwehonwe themselves. It is the lens through which they view the problem of colonial injustice. Aboriginalism is the new paradigm. But what is it, exactly?

Aboriginalism is assimilation's end-game, the terminological and psychic displacement of authentic indigenous identities, beliefs, and behaviours with one designed by Indian Department bureaucrats, government lawyers, and judges to complete the imperial objective of exterminating Onkwehonwe presences from the social and political landscape. It is the final stage of the annihilation of an independent existence for the original peoples, a cultural and political-economic process of state-sponsored identity invention to dispossess and assimilate the remnants of the Onkwehonwe who are still tied to this land and to indigenous ways of life.

Aboriginalism is the ideology of the Onkwehonwe surrender to the social and mental pathologies that have come to define colonized indigenous exist-

ences and the inauthentic, disconnected lives too many of our people find themselves leading. It is the latest version of the many ideologies of conquest that have been used to justify assaults on our peoples' rights and freedoms. The Settlers have been very successful, through education and religion, in turning Onkwehonwe against one another and creating a segment of people in our communities who will collaborate with government to do the work formerly assigned to colonial agents. But beyond this obvious complicity, there is also the widespread descent into defeatism among many of our people. In fact, the real effect of this widespread defeatism—social suffering by Onkwehonwe—is the most visible feature of our communities to the outside world. Aboriginalism obscures everything that is historically true and meaningful about Onkwehonwe—our origins, languages, and names; our land, our heritage, and our rights—and puts in their place views of history and of ourselves and our futures that are nothing more than the self-justifying myths and fantasies of the Settler. Onkwehonwe, Anishnaabe, and Dene are denied their full and rooted meaning, and our people are made to become aboriginal; in the process real and meaningful connections to our pasts, our rights, and our strength are severed. This is the genocidal function of aboriginalism, the prettied-up face of neo-colonialism that is dispassionately integrated into the media, government, and academic discourses as integration, development, and, sometimes more honestly, as assimilation. It is the attempt to destroy authentic existences and replace them with ways of life and self-definitions that best serve Euroamerican wants, needs, and beliefs. . . .

Aboriginalism is a sickness, an aspiration to assimilation, expanded into a wholesale cultural project and political agenda. It is a false consciousness, a thorough and perpetual embedding of colonial identities. Within this inauthentic consciousness are non-contentious cooperative identities, institutions, and strategies for interacting with the colonizer. The lost people who accept the aboriginal status created for them by the colonizer can assume various postures; lacking an identity rooted in an Onkwehonwe culture, they find it necessary to select identities and cultural choices from the menu presented to them by the Settler society and the machinery of the state. The most pronounced and obvious of these are the 'victims of history', who seek only to *recover* from the past and live in peace with the Settlers, and the 'aboriginal litigants', who pray with their white brothers and sisters to a Christian god and strive before white judges for *reconciliation* between Settler and Onkwehonwe. Both the victim and litigant reflect the essential colonial process of civilizing the Onkwehonwe, making us into citizens of the conquering states, so that instead of fighting for ourselves and what is right, we seek a *resolution* that is acceptable to and non-disruptive for the state and society we have come to embrace and identify with.

This is the basic vocabulary of aboriginalism as a political ideology: recovery, reconciliation, and resolution. To this I may also add *resistance*, because, even though it is outwardly hostile to the 'enemy', constructing one's identity and life strictly in opposition to the colonizer is another form of white-man worship. All of these are false representations of the Onkwehonwe heritage of struggle. All of them, from the soft and passive legalist to the hard-core guerrilla fighter, demand on the part of Onkwehonwe an abandonment of our rooted identities and the adoption of one that is consistent with a submissive culture or a foreign culture. To fight against genocide, we are told to arm ourselves and take vengeance upon the white man. To fight against economic oppression, we are told to become capitalists and to live for money. To fight against unfair laws, we are told to become lawyers and change the system from within. None of these paths is our own! And none of them are capable of liberating us from colonialism with our Onkwehonwe spirits and identities intact. They demand that we surrender our true selves to become what it is we are fighting against, so that we may better it or defeat it. . . .

Meaningful change, the transcendence of colonialism, and the restoration of Onkwehonwe strength and freedom can only be achieved through the resurgence of an Onkwehonwe *spirit* and *consciousness* directed into *contention* with the very foundations of colonialism. Onkwehonwe do need to challenge the continuing hateful conquest of our peoples, but not with a misguided rage channelled through the futile delusions of money, institutional power, or vengeful violence. Seriously, what is the best hope these can offer us? Social order and cultural stasis enshrined in law; mass conversion to the white man's religion of consumerism; or killing a few whites. None of these reflect the ideals of peace, respect, harmony, and coexistence that are the heart of Onkwehonwe philosophies. We are taught to confront hate with the force of love and to struggle to live in the face of ever-present death and the bringers of it. But we must do it *our* way, or risk being transformed by the fight into that (and those) which we are struggling against. . . .

In contrast to this internalist approach—which we could summarize as an acceptance of assimilation with demands for mediation of its effects *within* the state—a more rooted indigenous peoples' movement has been emerging globally over the last 30 years as a movement *against* the state and *for* the re-emergence of Onkwehonwe existences as cultural and political entities unto themselves. Onkwehonwe are in relationships with Settlers, but are not subsumed within the state and are not drawn into its modern liberal ideology of selfish individualism and unrestrained consumption. Central to this, and in stark opposition to the reformist internalist aboriginal approaches, has been indigenous peoples' direct contention with capitalism. Especially in Ecuador and Bolivia, and with the Zapatista movement in Mexico (Selverston-Scher, 2001; Brysk, 2000; Holloway and Peláez, 1998), Onkwehonwe have acted on their realization that capitalist economics and liberal delusions of progress are not opportunities for indigenous peoples' gain, but the very engines of colonial aggression and injustice towards their peoples. The goals of this globalized indigenous movement have been developed to reflect the people's sensitive understanding of the political economy of neo-colonialism: the recognition of Onkwehonwe national existences along with collective rights of self-determination; respect for Onkwehonwe connections to their lands and the rights that flow from those connections; and the preservation and revitalization of indigenous cultures, especially languages, religions, and forms of governance.[5]

These indigenous movements are truly movements against what the dominant societies see as modernity. They share the notion of a balanced existence tied in meaningful ways to their heritage and the belief in the necessity of actively defending their existence. For Onkwehonwe, their politics is the carrying-out of the right and responsibility to be different from mainstream society. This is indeed the fight of all Onkwehonwe who remain true to the spirit of their ancestors: it is a fight for independence and for connection to one's heritage. . . .

In my mind, *regeneration* is the direct application of the principle of acting against our ingrained and oppressive fears. Imagine if regeneration of ourselves and our nations took the place of the goal of 'recovery' (so individualizing and terminal and so much a part of the industry built up around residential school and substance abuse healing among our peoples). Think of the freedom inherent in embracing the struggle to transcend what has been done to us rather than the effort to gain compensation for the crimes or to placate feelings and sensibilities.

Restitution, which is the application of the principles of clarity and honesty to politics, would take the place of the goal of 'reconciliation', which is promoted so vehemently by liberal thinkers and church groups, but which is fatally flawed because it depends on the false notion of a moral equivalency between Onkwehonwe and Settlers and on a basic acceptance of colonial institutions and relationships. Reconciliation gives Onkwehonwe a place inside of Settler society with no requirement for Settlers to forego any of their ill-gotten gains personally or collectively. Restitution, as the alternative antidote and perspective, is based on the proven notion that real peace-making requires making amends for harm done before any of the

other steps to restore the fabric of a relationship can be taken. Restitution is, in fact, the precondition for any form of true reconciliation to take place (Redekop, 2003).

Resurgence, which applies the principle of courageous action against injustice, could replace the notion of seeking 'resolution' to the colonial problem. Certainty and finality of land settlements are the objective in the Settler society's courts and are promoted through state-sponsored negotiation processes to achieve order in the relationship, order which ratifies colonial institutions and facilitates the perpetuation of the original injustice, from which comes their very existence. Resurgence is acting beyond resistance. It is what resistance always hopes to become: from a rooted position of strength, resistance defeats the temptation to stand down, to take what is offered by the state in exchange for being pacified. In rejecting the temptation to join the Settlers and their state, seeking instead to confront Settler society in a struggle to force an end to the imperial reality and to lay down the preconditions for a peaceful coexistence, we would choose to use contention as a means of widespread enlightenment and societal change. . . .

Reconciliation itself needs to be intellectually and politically deconstructed as the orienting goal of the Onkwehonwe struggle. How do we break the hold of this emasculating concept? The logic of reconciliation as justice is clear: without massive restitution, including land, financial transfers, and other forms of assistance to compensate for past harms and continuing injustices committed against our peoples, reconciliation would permanently enshrine colonial injustices and is itself a further injustice. This much is clear in our Onkwehonwe frame of understanding. But what about other people's understandings of the nature of the problem we are facing? The nearly complete ignorance of the Settler society about the true facts of their people's relationship with Onkwehonwe and their wilful denial of historical reality detract from any possibility of meaningful discussion on true reconciliation. Limited to a discussion of history that includes only the last five or ten years, the corporate media and general public focus on the billions of dollars handed out to the Onkwehonwe per year from federal treasuries and spent inefficiently. The complex story of what went on in the past and the tangled complexities of the past's impact on the present and future of our relationships are reduced to questions of 'entitlements', 'rights', and 'good governance' within the already established structures of the state. Consider the effect of lengthening our view and extending society's view. Considering 100 or 300 years of interactions, it would become clear, even to the Settlers, that the real problem facing their country is that two nations are fighting over questions of conquest and survival, of empire or genocide, and moral claims to be just societies. Considering the long view and true facts, the Indian Problem becomes a question of the struggle for right and wrong, for justice in its most basic form. Something was stolen, lies were told, and they've never been made right. That, I believe, is the crux of the problem. We must shift away from the pacifying discourse and reframe people's perception of the problem so that it is not a question of how to reconcile with colonialism that faces us. Instead, we must think of restitution as the first step towards creating justice and a moral society out of the immoral racism that is the foundation and core of all colonial countries. What was stolen must be given back, amends must be made for the crimes that were committed, from which all Settlers, old families and recent immigrants alike, have gained their existences as citizens of these colonial countries. . . .

Even the act of proposing a shift to this kind of discussion is a radical challenge to the reconciling negotiations that try to fit Onkwehonwe into the colonial legacy rather than to confront and defeat it. When I speak of restitution, I am speaking of restoring ourselves as peoples, our spiritual power, dignity, and the economic bases for our autonomy. . . .

Recasting the Onkwehonwe struggle as one of seeking restitution as the precondition to reconciliation is not extremist or irrational. Restitution, as a broad goal, involves demanding the return of what was stolen, accepting reparations (either land, material, or monetary recompense) for what cannot be returned, and forging a new socio-political relationship based on the Settler state's admission of wrongdoing and acceptance of the responsibility and obligation to engage Onkwehonwe peoples in a restitution-reconciliation peace-building process. . . .

Unprejudiced logics of decolonization point . . . to the need to create coexistence among autonomous political communities. Eventual peaceful coexistence demands a decolonization process in which Onkwehonwe will be extricated from, not further entrenched within, the values, cultures, and practices of liberal democracy. If the goals of decolonization are justice and peace, then the process to achieve these goals must reflect a basic covenant on the part of both Onkwehonwe and Settlers to honour each others' existences. This honouring cannot happen when one partner in the relationship is asked to sacrifice their heritage and identity in exchange for peace. This is why the only possibility of a just relationship between Onkwehonwe and the Settler society is the conception of a nation-to-nation partnership between peoples, the kind of relationship reflected in the original treaties of peace and friendship consecrated between indigenous peoples and the newcomers when white people first started arriving in our territories. And the only way to remove ourselves from the injustice of the present relationship is to begin to implement a process of resurgence-apology-restitution and seek to restore the pre-colonial relationship of sharing and cooperation among diverse peoples. . . .

Just as Onkwehonwe have commonality in our basic demands, responses to those demands have been the same across borders among the (so-called) progressive Settler states, those with significant indigenous populations and that seek an accord with those peoples. These state governments have refused territorial concessions to halt or redress patterns of colonial occupation; they insist that all resource development be jointly administered; they defend the legal and constitutional supremacy of the colonial state and insist on a subordinate governmental status for Onkwehonwe nations; and they insist on rights equivalency among Settler populations and Onkwehonwe, even in those territories recognized as Onkwehonwe homelands and in settlement lands within the indigenous nations' recognized spheres of governmental authority. From Nunavut in the Arctic to Tierra del Fuego and across the Pacific Ocean to Aotearoa, there is consistency in this pattern of demand and response.

The intransigence of Settler states has resulted in further degradations of Onkwehonwe lives and sparked serious violent conflicts in all countries with significant Onkwehonwe presence, ranging from the overt violent racism in Australian society, to the intractable and costly legal disputes over land title in Canada, to the armed insurgencies and violent repression common in Latin American countries. Unfortunately for Onkwehonwe, the intransigence of the Settler has been a profitable strategy, as Onkwehonwe groups have found it extremely difficult to continue to push for their demands in the face of the multiple strategies of delay, distraction, and containment employed by state governments. . . .

In the face of this intransigence, this generation of Onkwehonwe have some serious choices to make. Depending on whether we confront the challenge before us or not, there are a number of possible scenarios that may play out for our people. Our societies may collapse, and our next generations will die of self-destruction because of our decision to allow things to continue the way they are going. We may choose to retreat from the challenge in front of us, to become stagnant and passive, and to rely upon bureaucracy and technology for solutions to our problems, giving the Settlers even more control over our lives. Or, we can choose to fight for our existence as Onkwehonwe and our inherent rights and freedoms; we can embrace our challenges and engage our predicament.[6] . . .

Cycles of oppression are being repeated through generations in Onkwehonwe communities. Colonial economic relations are reflected in the political and legal structures of contemporary Onkwehonwe societies, and they result in Onkwehonwe having to adapt culturally to this reality and to individuals

reacting in particularly destructive and unhealthy (but completely comprehensible) ways. These social and health problems seem to be so vexing to governments; large amounts of money have been allocated to implement government-run organizations and policies geared towards alleviating these problems in both the United States and Canada, for example, but they have had only limited positive effect on the health status of our communities. But these problems are not really mysterious nor are they unsolvable. The social and health problems besetting Onkwehonwe are the logical result of a situation wherein people respond or adapt to unresolved colonial injustices. People in indigenous communities develop complexes of behaviour and mental attitudes that reflect their colonial situation and out flow unhealthy and destructive behaviours. It is a very simple problem to understand when we consider the whole context of the situation and all of the factors involved (Chandler and Lalonde, 1998). . . .

Notes

1. A notable and honourable exception from Memmi's own time is Jean-Paul Sartre.
2. For more on the urgency of redefining the colonial reality, see Memmi, *The Colonizer and the Colonized*, 103.
3. For more on this point see Richard Day, 'Who is This "We" That Gives the Gift? Native American Political Theory and "the Western Tradition" ', *Critical Horizons* 2, 2 (2001): 173–201,
4. I will remind the reader here that I am using the word 'Onkwehonwe' because I am Kanien'kehaka, and that in rejecting the white man's word, in this act of linguistic resurgence. I am not meaning to obscure or discourage the use of *Asishnaabe, Dene, Dakelh*, or any of the other authentic words for the people in indigenous languages.
5. For further discussion of the globalized indigenous movements' structure and goals, see Brysk, *From Tribal Village to Global Village*, 59.
6. These scenarios for the future draw on Duane Elgin, *Voluntary Simplicity*, rev. ed. (New York, NY: William Morrow, 1993) 179–91.

References

Brysk, Allison. 2000. *From Tribal Village to Global Village: Indian Rights and International Relations in Latin America*. Stanford, CA: Stanford University Press.

Chandler, Michael J., and Christopher Lalonde. 1998. 'Cultural Continuity as a Hedge against Suicide in Canada's First Nations', *Transcultural Psychiatry* 35: 191–219.

Holloway, John, and Eloina Peláez. 2000. *Zapatista!* London, UK: Pluto Press.

Kaplan, Robert D. 2001. 'Looking the World in the Eye', *The Atlantic* December: 68–82.

Lorde, Audre. 1984. 'The Uses of Anger', *Sister Outsider*. Freedom, CA: Crossing Press.

Memmi, Albert. 1991. *The Colonizer and the Colonized*. Boston, MA: Beacon Press.

Redekop, Vern. 2003. *From Violence to Blessing: How an Understanding of Deep-Rooted Conflicts Can Open Paths to Reconciliation*. Montréal, QC: Novalis.

Seed, Patricia. 1995. *Ceremonies of Possession in Europe's Conquest of the New World*. Cambridge, UK: Cambridge University Press.

Selverston-Scher, Melina. 2001. *Ethnopolitics in Ecuador: Indigenous Rights and the Strengthening of Democracy*. Miami, FL: North-South Center Press.

Chapter 2

Eurocentrism and the European Ethnographic Tradition

Marie Battiste and Sakej Henderson

Eurocentrism is the imaginative and institutional context that informs contemporary scholarship, opinion, and law. As a theory, it postulates the superiority of Europeans over non-Europeans. It is built on a set of assumptions and beliefs that educated and usually unprejudiced Europeans and North Americans habitually accept as true, as supported by 'the facts', or as 'reality'.

A central concept behind Eurocentrism is the idea of diffusionism. Diffusionism is based on two assumptions: (1) most human communities are uninventive, and (2) a few human communities (or places, or cultures) are inventive and are thus the permanent centers of cultural change or 'progress'. On a global scale, this results in a world with a single center—Europe—and a surrounding periphery. Europe, at the center (Inside), is historical, invents, and progresses, and non-Europe, at the periphery (Outside), is ahistorical, stagnant, and unchanging. From this framework, diffusionism asserts that European peoples are superior to Indigenous peoples. This superiority is based on some inherent characteristic of the European mind or spirit and because non-European peoples lack this characteristic, they are empty, or partly so, of ideas and proper spiritual values. The theory argues that because Europeans are superior, Indigenous peoples need the diffusion of creativity, imagination, invention, innovation, rationality, and sense of honor or ethics from Europe in order to progress.

Classical Eurocentric diffusionism exists as many variations of this proposition. First, for much of the non-European world, diffusionist literature asserts an emptiness of basic cultural institutions and people and equates an absence of established settlements with a lack of law. This idea has a particular connection to settler colonialism and to the physical movement of Europeans into non-European regions, such as North America, Africa, Australia, and New Zealand, displacing or eliminating the Indigenous inhabitants (Blaut, 1993). This proposition of emptiness supports a series of claims about an Indigenous emptiness of intellectual creativity and spiritual values, sometimes described by Europeans (as, for instance, by sociologist Max Weber) as an absence of 'rationality'. . . .

Diffusion explains any progress made by non-Europeans as resulting from the spread of European ideas, which flow into the non-European world like air flows into a vacuum. This diffusion may also be achieved by the spread of products through which European values are distributed. . . . Since Europe was believed to be advanced and non-Europe backward, any ideas that diffused into Europe from elsewhere were perceived to be inevitably uncivilized (Blaut, 1993).

The core of Eurocentric thought is its claim to be universal. There were two inspirations that forbade Europeans to rest content with developing their own part of the world. The first inspiration was curiosity. . . . The second inspiration was the messianic prophecy contained in monotheistic religions Eurocentric thought has a belief in, and commitment to, a messianic dream of a millennium: a new heaven, a new earth, and a transformed people. This belief was expressed in the Judaic vision of linear time moving toward a predetermined end and in the Christian vision of the spiritual transformation of the old into the new. . . .

At the beginning of a new millennium, this idea of a universal mission has created a global crisis. Although Eurocentrism has created unheard-of material wealth for the European minority, it has also created a techno-scientific realm that is threatening the foundations of human life, especially among the Indigenous majority. It is a dismaying legacy. Violence, war, and oppression have taken a heavy toll on Indigenous peoples' ecologies, lives, and knowledge. . . .

Eurocentrism and its belief in its superiority, in its explanation of the developmental patterns of progress, and in its synthesis of individualism, rationalism, and scientism has made modern

scholarship unable to grasp the crisis or to resolve it. . . . The global state of affairs casts doubt on the once-dominant and persuasive Eurocentric model and its beliefs about the natural world and human nature. These beliefs have to be re-evaluated.

Assumptions About the Natural World

In Eurocentric thought, the natural world is usually thought of as a single, wholly determinable realm. The world is a background against which the mind operates, and knowledge is regarded as information that originates outside humanity. Eurocentric thought can be justified only if several assumptions about the nature of the world and anyone's knowledge of it are accepted. These assumptions can be reduced to four fundamental statements: (1) the natural world exists independent of any beliefs about it; (2) perceptions may provide an accurate impression of the natural world; (3) linguistic concepts may describe the natural world; and (4) certain rules of inference are reliable means for arriving at new truths about the natural world. Upon these four delicate assumptions rest most Eurocentric beliefs about reality. To reject any one of them requires the rejection of a large number of other beliefs that depend upon it and introduces a massive dislocation in the Eurocentric system of beliefs about the world.

These four assumptions about the relation of Eurocentric thought to the natural world are empiricist in character—that is to say they rely on practical experience. The problem is that these assumptions are impossible to prove. . . .

(1) The Natural World Exists Independent of Any Beliefs About It

Most Eurocentric and Indigenous thinkers agree that an animate natural world exists, and that we are born into it. The difference between Eurocentric and Indigenous thought lies in the perceived relationship between people and the natural world. Eurocentric thought wants humanity to be at one with the natural order, but believes people are denied this unity because of their terrifying exclusion from the Garden of Eden. . . . As Eurocentric consciousness artificially constructs a place for its existence, it treats the natural world as a practical source of the means to achieve its own objectives. In contrast to the Eurocentric view, Indigenous peoples do not view humanity as separate from the natural world; thus they do not have to face the Eurocentric terror of separation from nature, nor do they have to construct artificial organizations—or human 'culture'—to overcome this separation.

(2) Perceptions May Provide an Accurate Impression of the Natural World

. . . The Eurocentric consciousness perceives events in the natural world as sensations, and these sensations are the basis for Eurocentric knowledge. In an indefinite number of ways, the Eurocentric mind can combine and recombine sensations, but these mental processes do not change the events themselves, since the natural world is oblivious to the working of the Eurocentric consciousness.

In the Eurocentric view, perceptions always act as a filter between human consciousness and the natural world so people can never experience reality directly. For example, humans describe objects as having a certain smell and some events as noisy, implying that these are properties of the objects and events themselves. . . .

Indigenous thought is closer to the ancient Greek idea of 'intelligible essences'. This theory argues that everything in the world contains within itself characteristics that can be known directly to the human mind; hence categories exist independently of the mind, and the mind can understand what the world is really like.

(3) Linguistic Concepts May Describe the Natural World

Eurocentric philosophers have consistently attempted to demonstrate that human beings are significantly different from all other forms of life, and they have stressed that this uniqueness lies in

language. To the ancient Greeks, language depended on the comprehension of intelligible essences in the natural world. Since the European Renaissance, modern thinkers have rejected the idea of intelligible essences and have asserted instead that creating categories is an arbitrary procedure. Because of the modern denial of intelligible essences, most sensory qualities are rejected as forming the categories of language. Instead it is thought that every person has the power to create rules of inference and to apply these rules to conceptualize and describe the natural world. The modern view of linguistics considers any language to be an arbitrary but conventionally agreed upon code. Language is a way of representing the perceived natural world, without any objective connection to the world. . . .

In the Indigenous worldview, humans perceive the sensuous order of the natural world through their eyes, noses, ears, mouths, and skins (Abram, 1996). Perceptions of the sensory world unfold as affective sounds and rhythm. As these sounds become words, humans participate in 'singing the world' (Merleau-Ponty, 1962). Since people enter into language through their sensory relationships with the natural world, languages cannot be understood in isolation from the ecologies that give rise to them.

(4) Certain Rules of Inference Are Reliable Means for Arriving at New Truths About the Natural World

In Eurocentric thought, the idea that languages are conventional codes is reflected in the rules of inference used for arriving at truths about the natural world. The Eurocentric mind is understood to be a machine that analyzes sensations and combines them into categories. This process of analysis and combination produces ideas, but it does not affect the natural world, which is oblivious to the workings of the human intellect. As categories are not fixed in anything that exists independently of the human mind, these ideas can be broken down again into their elementary sensations and recombined into new categories. . . .

The problem with Eurocentric theoretical analysis is that it is a way of looking at the world; it is not knowledge of how the world is, and Eurocentric theories of how the world operates change over time. Historian and philosopher of science Thomas Kuhn studied the process of intellectual transformations in the Eurocentric sciences. In his book *The Structure of Scientific Revolutions* (1970), Kuhn argued that there are long periods of 'normal science' in which fundamental assumptions and concepts are accepted and not seriously questioned. The unreflective era then gives way to a 'scientific revolution', in which new assumptions, theories, and ideas change the conceptual foundations of science. Kuhn called these competing conceptual foundations 'paradigms'. Paradigms include not only fundamental assumptions but also theories, principles, and doctrines. A paradigm shift occurs when scientists cannot explain certain data or natural phenomena by reference to established scientific theories. . . .

Modern thinkers have shown that the standards of inference, logical entailment, and causality, once thought reliable for arriving at truths about the natural world, are no longer judged to be reliable. Modern Eurocentric theorists have asserted that they need to find an alternative to logical and causal explanation. . . . Yet modern thought has not been able to develop a precise and detailed definition of a non-logical, non-causal method of inference that is both generalized in its method and rich in its historical references. . . . In the Indigenous worldview, the world operates according to a dynamic, circular flux in which human beings participate directly. Life is to be lived not according to universal, abstract theories about the way things work but as an interactive relationship in a particular time and place.

Assumptions About Human Nature

The rules of inference used to arrive at truths about the natural world are reflected in the Eurocentric view of human nature. Given certain assumptions about the natural world, the human mind uses reason to discover that some things are 'by nature' right for human beings and that others are created by artificial convention. As the categories imposed by reason are arbitrary, the question is, 'What impels the mind to analyze the world in one way rather than in another?' The generally accepted answer is desire. . . . This relationship of desire to reason establishes the modern context of Eurocentric philosophy, liberal psychology, humanities, and social sciences. It creates the categories of a human will that desires, and a mind that understands and knows. These ideas create the Eurocentric notions of self, morality, society, and law. People are subject to arbitrary desires and accept certain assumptions about the natural world. Based on their desires and assumptions, they use reason to explain and structure the world around them.

Scientific paradigms, therefore, have their counterparts in the rules of inference used in the social sciences and in law. In Eurocentric disciplines, such explanatory paradigms are called 'contexts'. Just as a paradigm reflects current scientific thought about the natural world, so a context reflects current social, political, and legal thought about the human social order. Brazilian legal scholar Roberto Unger has asserted that if a context allows people to move within it to discover everything about the natural world they can discover, it is a 'natural' context. If the context does not allow such natural movement, it is an 'artificial' context derived from selected assumptions (1984: 5–15; 1987: 18–25).

Unger asserts that three theses define artificial contexts. The first thesis is the principle of contextuality. It is the belief that assumptions or desires that humans take as given shape their mental and social lives. These assumptions form a picture of what the world is really like, and even a set of premises about how thoughts and languages are or can be structured. They also provide a framework for explaining and verifying worldviews. These worldviews are artificial because they are dependent on assumptions made about human nature or society and not on what the world is really like, independent of people's beliefs about it (1984: 18–19).

The second thesis is that these artificial world-views are conditional and can be changed, but such changes are exceptional and transitory. Any context can be supplemented or revised by other empowering ideas about features that make one explanatory or society-making practice better than another (1984: 9). Thus, small-scale, routine adjustments in a context can turn into a more unconfined transformation. If the conditionality of any context is overcome, people do not simply remain outside all context, but rather they create new assumptions and contexts (1987; 19).

The third thesis is that, just as in Kuhn's 'normal science', the conditionality of any artificial context is rarely recognized. Changes to artificial contexts are exceptional and transitory because the contexts are relatively immune to theories or activities. The distinction between routine and transformation maintains the immunity of the artificial context and prevents its conditionality from being questioned or opened up to revision (1984: 10). Against the background of change, the context is viewed as 'normal' or 'natural'. As Unger explains, however, the more people become aware of the conditionality of a context, the more likely they are to be able to effect meaningful change to that context (1984: 10–11).

Assumptive Quandaries

Because of the artificial nature of Eurocentric thought, all that has been said so far is unavoidably abstract. Whether or not these assumptions about the natural world and human nature are well founded, they have profoundly influenced Eurocentric thought, and colonization has carried them around the earth. Although these assumptions have been challenged by both Eurocentric and Indigenous thinkers, they remain the foundations of orthodox educational and political thought. . . .

If modern Eurocentric thought, in seeking to understand the natural world and human nature, employs linguistic concepts that do not correspond to an independent natural order and that are justified by questionable standards of infer-

ence, is it unreasonable to think that even those ideas that are well supported do not accurately describe the natural world and human nature? If this is the case, what are the implications of imposing Eurocentric models on Indigenous peoples? Why should we be forced to assimilate to an artificial reality?

What options remain in this disturbing predicament? The easy way out, the traditional solution of some Eurocentric thinkers, is to deny the primary assumption: that the natural world exists independent of any beliefs about it. Instead, they assert their beliefs and concepts constitute reality. The only authoritative reality, in this contradictory worldview, is the one of Eurocentric paradigms, theories, and contexts. . . .

Another option is to retain faith in the four basic assumptions despite clear evidence of the falsity of all but the first. Faith or practical grounds usually justify this approach. This option asserts that as a framework of belief, those assumptions have enabled Eurocentric thinkers to relate successfully to the physical environment and there is no better framework of beliefs that modern thinkers could adopt. Both apologies assert a bold mystical metamorphosis: if it works then it must be *true*; and if it is *true*, then it alone must be *true*. This position is based on Eurocentric artificial ways of thinking represented by logic and causality. But this practical option is a partial view—a censored view. It ignores the tragic consequences of this thinking, consequences that have brought the world to the brink of ecological disaster. A key issue today is whether these Eurocentric assumptions contain the latencies of ecological ruin. To our mind there is also the critical question of whether it matters that biological creatures are attempting to inhabit a non-biological, ideological environment. As Indigenous peoples, we find the Eurocentric assumptions could more accurately be described as *imaginality* than *reality*. The fundamental issue to us is this: does reality matter or is desire enough?

In our view, a fundamental adjustment of the Eurocentric assumptions about the natural world and human nature is necessary. The adjustment should accommodate unlimited human desires and needs to a limited planetary ecosystem. A sustainable relationship between humans and the natural world must enable us to manage our livelihoods by controlling humans while sustaining and nourishing the complexity and stability of diverse ecologies. This relationship requires a revision of the Eurocentric view of humans being separate from the natural world. It also requires a revision of ideas about language and about causal-positivistic modes of inference. The new context must view Europeans and colonialists as one species among others embedded in the intricate web of natural processes that contain and sustain all forms of life. . . .

The Ethnographic Tradition

For Eurocentric thought to adjust its assessments of non-European peoples and their attributes requires an interrogation of the Eurocentric ethnographic tradition. The study of Indigenous peoples has been a staple of the Eurocentric discipline of anthropology. To avoid the perils of subjective analysis, anthropology and the related discipline of ethnography seek to describe human societies as manifest through their cultures in scientific terms. The idea of 'culture' is derived from the idea of tillage—the cultivation of the soil in English, *cultura* in Latin. In Eurocentric thought, culture represents the totality of human achievement and awareness: the transmitted behaviors, arts, beliefs, institutions, and styles of human works and thoughts characteristic of a people, community, society, or class. The disciplines of anthropology and ethnography impose rational patterns on human behavior in the same way that science imposes general paradigms on observed events.

Eurocentric anthropologists have traditionally organized the descriptive details of the Indigenous cultures they studied into ethnographies. In these ethnographies they recorded the languages, child-rearing practices, totems, taboos, signifying codes, work and leisure interests, standards of behavior

and deviance, social classification systems, and jural procedures shared by members of the studied people. From these descriptive data, they inferred patterns that knit the societies they were studying into integrated wholes with all-embracing and largely taken-for-granted ways of life. They then inferred the pattern or patterns that differentiated these societies from other societies that had been studied.

By defining culture as a set of shared meanings, the classic norms of anthropological analysis made it difficult to study zones of difference within and between cultures. Indigenous cultures became homogenous rather than diverse. Yet, Indigenous consciousness has always required particular responses to particular ecologies built on flux. European ethnographers understood these cultural borderlands as annoying exceptions rather than as central areas for inquiry. Actual Indigenous knowledge, heritage, and consciousness came to be seen as too messy, even too downright chaotic, to be studied. The Eurocentric emphasis on coherent wholes at the expense of unique processes of change and internal inconsistencies, conflicts, and contradictions was and remains a serious limitation to Eurocentric understanding of Indigenous knowledge and heritage. In this sense, Eurocentric thinkers have taken culture as their abstract possession and Indigenous knowledge as merely symbolic and ideational. This search for stable, systematic régimes has reduced the knowledge that Eurocentric scholars claim to value 'on its own terms'.

Eurocentric anthropologists and ethnographers were inescapably complicit with the imperial domination of their epochs. For example, anthropology has always focused on the powerless, yet few anthropologists have attempted any evaluation of the effects of colonialism on these cultures. Behind their analyses of Indigenous people lay an assumptive realm continually betrayed in their writings. . . . . The contents of their writings represent the human objects of the civilizing mission's global enterprise as if Indigenous people were the ideal recipients of the White man's burden. Most often, they depicted Indigenous people as members of harmonious, internally homogeneous, unchanging cultures. From such a perspective, Indigenous knowledge and heritage appeared to 'need' progress, and economic and moral uplifting.

Moreover, the Eurocentric concept of static traditional Indigenous knowledge and heritage served as a self-congratulatory reference point against which Eurocentric society could measure its own progressive evolution. Europeans conceived the civilizing journey as more of a rise than a fall, as a process more of perfection than of degradation—a long and arduous journey upward, culminating in being 'them'. Often they called this process 'assimilation'. Eurocentric values not only had to be accepted, they also had to be absorbed. As a result, some colonized peoples immersed themselves in the imported Eurocentric culture; many even denied their origins in an attempt to become 'more English than the English'.

The contexts of colonial rule shaped the works of the classic ethnographers. By assuming the answers to questions that they should have asked, Eurocentric scholars confidently asserted that Indigenous knowledge and heritage do not change, only European society progresses. The monumentalism of timeless accounts of homogeneous Indigenous cultures and the objectivism of strict divisions of labor between the detached ethnographers and their Indigenous subjects are symptoms of imperial value contagion. . . . The ethnographers were literate, the Indigenous peoples were not. The ethnographers recorded the 'utterances' their Indigenous peoples spoke and then returned to their university communities to write 'definitive works' on culture based on raw data provided by Indigenous people in the field. . . .

Because the classic descriptions do not present fair interpretations of Indigenous worldviews, Indigenous people have had to suggest a total revision of anthropological analyses. Around the globe, Indigenous thinkers have had to prove that European scholars were mistaken in their notion of Indigenous culture as unchanging and homogeneous. We have had to prove that Indigenous societies are not timeless events in nature, that the so-called classic works confuse local cultures with universal human nature. We have had to demonstrate how ideology often makes cultural facts appear natural. We have had to use social analysis to attempt to reverse the process: to dismantle the ideological to reveal the cultural (a peculiar blend of objective arbitrariness and subjective taken-for-grantedness). The interplay between making the familiar strange and the strange familiar is part of the ongoing transformation of knowledge.

Still, the classic notion that the stability, orderliness, and equilibrium that the Eurocentric scholars described actually characterizes Indigenous society prevails in modern thought. The rhetoric of ethnography derives part of its resiliency from the Eurocentric concept of time and the illusion of a timeless Indigenous culture that it created. The classical understanding of Indigenous life, of how Indigenous people should look and act, and even what lies ahead of them, are now seen as being a part of Eurocentric time and thought. So strong are these written views that one can often predict from them what modern society demands of Indigenous people. Much too often these classic notions organize Indigenous lives and limit Indigenous futures.

The alleged timelessness of Indigenous culture creates another demon: the total demise of this culture, wherein any change in material reality is equated with the demise of Indigenous consciousness. The pioneering ethnographers achieved some insights into Indigenous consciousness, but more often they made interpretative mistakes. Central to their cultural confusion is the myth of a 'primitive culture', untouched by Eurocentric influences. Following in the footsteps of their predecessors, later ethnographers made their own mistakes, as well as duplicating or replicating those of others: the cumulative snarl is difficult to untangle. What is more important is that this timelessness is a Eurocentric attempt at limiting the future—another way of forcing Indigenous culture to accept the inevitability of imitating Eurocentric modes of thought and dress.

It is important to note that many scholars, both Indigenous and non-Indigenous, have been examining similar phenomena from various perspectives. In attempting to understand Indigenous knowledge and its processes of knowing, we recognize that the existing knowledge system used in educational systems must be interrogated. This means challenging Eurocentric researchers, their methodologies, and their investigators' skill. Often this interrogation causes discomfort. Grasping the holistic structure and processes of Indigenous knowledge requires an investigator's assumptions and perspective to stretch and develop. The researcher will have to explore uncharted territory without a conventional map.

A strong critique of Eurocentrism is under way in all fields of social thought. These critiques, such as postcolonial, poststructural, and postmodern thought, reveal that the assumptions that constructed Eurocentrism are not universal: they are derived from local and artificial knowledge. Under such thought, many assumptions of Eurocentrism are being exposed as false (e.g., Rosaldo,1989; Coombe, 1991; Said, 1992; Blaut, 1993; Noël, 1994; RCAP, 1996). Moreover, critical scholars have exposed the empirical beliefs of Eurocentric history, geography, and social science, which have often gained acceptance not because they relate to existing structures but rather because Eurocentric thought only recognizes confirming evidence as valid. . . . Thus, as long as Eurocentrism retains its persuasive intellectual power in academic and political realms, it will be resistant to change.

The limited awareness of Indigenous knowledge and heritage in academia indicates the biases and weakness of Eurocentric thought. Contemporary anthropologists have focused on developing a critique of ethnocentrism in both academic theory and popular culture. They have sought to develop participatory and collaborative research methodologies based on the assumption that anthropological texts are the product of dialogues between researchers and research subjects, rather than the authoritative, objective accounts of individual experts (Clifford, 1983; Clifford and Marcus, 1986; Marcus and Fisher, 1986). Others have created a critical anthropological perspective concerned with the situated, constructed, and political processes of knowledge production, distribution, and consumption. They attempt to contribute to the development of a critical anthropology of colonial and postcolonial relations (Coombe, 1991; Rosaldo, 1989; Said, 1992). What has emerged is an anthropology of anthropology and a recognition of the historicity of the discipline (Fox, 1991; Rosaldo, 1989). Critical theorists argue that the traditional liberal critique of ethnocentrism does not address the relationship of colonialism or racism (Coombe, 1991; Morre, 1988; Ulin, 1991). They argue that the anthropologist's 'canon' is not a realist's description of Indigenous peoples or their knowledge, but a history of European colonial thought (Said, 1992). . . .

References

Abram, David. 1996. *The Spell of the Sensuous: Perception and Language in a More-Than-Human World*. New York: Pantheon Books.

Blaut, J.M. 1993. *The Colonizer's Model of the World: Geographical Diffusionism and Eurocentric History*. New York: Guilford Press.

Clifford, James. 1983. 'On Ethnographic Authority', *Representations* 2: 118-46.

Clifford, James and George Marcus, eds. 1986. *Writing Culture: The Poetics and Politics of Ethnography*. Berkeley, CA: University of California Press.

Coombe, Rosemary J. 1991. 'Objects of Property and Subjects of Politics: Intellectual Property Laws and Democratic Dialogue', *Texas Law Review* 69: 1853–80.

Fox, Richard, ed. 1991. *Recapturing Anthropology: Working in the Present*. Santa Fe, NM: School of American Research Press.

Marcus, George, and M. Fisher. 1986. *Anthropology as Cultural Critique: An Experimental Moment in Human Sciences*. Chicago: University of Chicago Press.

Merleau-Ponty, Maurice. 1962. *Phenomenology of Perception*. Trans. Colin Smith. London: Routledge and Kegan Paul.

Morre, Henrietta. 1988. *Feminism and Anthropology*. Cambridge: Cambridge University Press.

Noël, Lise. 1994. *Intolerance, A General Survey*. Trans. A. Bennet. Montreal and Kingston: McGill-Queen's University Press.

RCAP. 1996. Bridging the Cultural Divide. A Report on Aboriginal Peoples and Criminal Justice in Canada. Ottawa: Canada Communication Group.

Rosaldo, Renato. 1989. *Culture and Truth: The Remaking of Social Analysis*. Boston: Beacon Press.

Said, Edward. 1992. *Culture and Imperialism*. Cambridge, MA: Harvard University Press.

Ulin, Robert. 1991. 'Critical Anthropology Twenty Years Later: Modernism and Postmodernism', *Anthropology: Critique of Anthropology* 11 (1): 81–132.

Unger, Roberto Mangabeira. 1984. *Passion: An Essay on Personality*. New York: Free Press.

Chapter 3

Decolonizing Antiracism

Bonita Lawrence and Enakshi Dua[1]

Introduction

In continuous conversations over the years, we have discussed our discomfort with the manner in which Aboriginal people and perspectives are excluded within antiracism. We have been surprised and disturbed by how rarely this exclusion has been taken up, or even noticed. Due to this exclusion, Aboriginal people cannot see themselves in antiracism contexts, and Aboriginal activism against settler domination takes place without people of colour as allies. Though antiracist theorists may ignore the contemporary Indigenous presence, Canada certainly does not. Police surveillance is a reality that all racialized people face, and yet Native communities are at risk of direct military intervention in ways that no other racialized community in Canada faces.[2] This article represents a call to postcolonial and antiracism theorists to begin to take Indigenous decolonization seriously. . . .

Despite our different positioning, experiences, and concerns, we have reached a common conclusion: that antiracism is premised on an ongoing colonial project. As a result, we fear that rather than challenging the ongoing colonization of Aboriginal peoples, Canadian antiracism is furthering contemporary colonial agendas. We will argue that antiracism theory participates in colonial agendas in two ways. First, it ignores the ongoing colonization of Aboriginal peoples in the Americas. Second, it fails to integrate an understanding of Canada as a colonialist state into antiracist frameworks. In this article, we seek ways to decolonize antiracism theory. Our goal in writing this is to begin to lay the groundwork that might make dialogue possible among antiracist and Aboriginal activists.

What Does It Mean to Look at Canada as Colonized Space? What Does It Mean to Ignore Indigenous Sovereignty?

Antiracist and postcolonial theorists have not integrated an understanding of Canada as a colonialist state into their frameworks. It is therefore important to begin by elaborating on the means through which colonization in Canada as a settler society has been implemented and is being maintained. We also need to reference how Indigenous peoples resist this ongoing colonization.

Settler states in the Americas are founded on, and maintained through, policies of direct extermination, displacement, or assimilation. The premise of each is to ensure that Indigenous peoples ultimately disappear *as* peoples, so that settler nations can seamlessly take their place. Because of the intensity of genocidal[3] policies that Indigenous people have faced and continue to face, a common error on the part of antiracist and postcolonial theorists is to assume that genocide has been virtually complete, that Indigenous peoples, however unfortunately, have been 'consigned to the dustbin of history' (Spivak, 1994) and no longer need to be taken into account. Yet such assumptions are scarcely different from settler nation-building myths, whereby 'Indians' become unreal figures, rooted in the nation's prehistory, who died out and no longer need to be taken seriously. . . .

To speak of Indigenous nationhood is to speak of land as Indigenous, in ways that are neither rhetorical nor metaphorical. Neither Canada nor the United States—or the settler states of 'Latin' America for that matter—which claim sovereignty over the territory they occupy, have a legitimate basis to anchor their absorption of huge portions of that territory (Churchill, 1992: 411). Indeed, nationhood for Indigenous peoples is acknowledged in current international law as the right of inherent sovereignty. The notion that peoples known to have occupied specific territories, who have a common language, a means of subsistence, forms of governance, legal systems, and means of deciding citizenship, are nations—particularly if they have entered into treaties. As Churchill notes (ibid., 19–20), only nations enter into treaty relationships.

In contrast, the legal system in Canada, a settler state, is premised on the need to preempt Indigenous sovereignty. The legal system does this through the assertion of a 'rule of law' that is daily deployed to deny possibilities of sovereignty

and to criminalize Indigenous dissent. Because this rule of law violates the premises on which treaties were signed with Aboriginal people, the Supreme Court occasionally is forced to acknowledge the larger framework of treaty agreements that predate assertions of Canadian sovereignty.[4] Historically, however, court decisions have been a chief instrument of the disenfranchisement of Aboriginal peoples. Recently, they have alternated between enlarging the scope of the potential for a renewed relationship between the Crown and Aboriginal peoples and drastically curtailing those possibilities. . . .

The immediate problem facing Aboriginal peoples in Canada is that the status quo of a colonial order continues to target them for legal and cultural extinction, while undermining the viability of communities through theft of their remaining lands and resources.[5] Aboriginal people need to re-establish control over their own communities. They must have their land returned to them, making communities viable and rebuilding nationhood, with a legal framework that brings Aboriginal peoples' existing and returned lands under their own authority. This requires a total rethinking of Canada. Sovereignty and self-determination must be genuinely on the table as fundamental to Indigenous survival, not as lip service. If they are truly progressive, antiracist theorists must begin to think about their personal stake in this struggle, and about where they are going to situate themselves.

We also need a better understanding of the ways in which Aboriginal peoples resist ongoing colonization. At the core of Indigenous survival and resistance is reclaiming a relationship to land. Yet, within antiracism theory and practice, the question of land as contested space is seldom taken up. From Indigenous perspectives, it speaks to a reluctance on the part of non-Natives of any background to acknowledge that there is more to this land than being settlers on it, that there are deeper, older stories and knowledge connected to the landscapes around us. To acknowledge that we all share the same land base and yet to question the differential terms on which it is occupied is to become aware of the colonial project that is taking place around us. . . .

How Has Antiracism/Postcolonial Theory Been Constructed on a Colonizing Framework?

. . . International critical race and postcolonial theory has failed to make Indigenous presence and colonization foundational in five areas. First, Native existence is erased through theories of race and racism that exclude them. Second, theories of Atlantic diasporic identities fail to take into account that these identities are situated in multiple projects of colonization and settlement on Indigenous lands. Third, histories of colonization are erased through writings on the history of slavery. Fourth, decolonization politics are equated with antiracist politics. Finally, theories of nationalism contribute to the ongoing delegitimization of Indigenous nationhood. Though often theorizing the British context, these writings have been important for shaping antiracist/postcolonial thinking throughout the West. . . .

Most of these works on the Americas fail to raise, let alone explore, the ways in which such identities have been articulated through the colonization of Aboriginal peoples, or the ways in which the project of appropriating land shaped the emergence of black/Asian/Hispanic settler formations. Paul Gilroy's (1993: 17) influential text, *The Black Atlantic*, illustrates this. In it, Gilroy explicates two interrelated projects. The first is to rethink modernity via the history of the black Atlantic and the African diaspora, and the second is to examine the ways in which diasporic discourses have shaped the political and cultural history of black Americans and black people in Europe. However, Gilroy's history of the black transatlantic does not make any significant reference to Indigenous peoples of the Americas or Indigenous nationhood. Similar to Hall, when Gilroy mentions Indigenous peoples or colonization, it is to locate them in the past. In one of the few references to Indigenous peoples, Gilroy states, 'striving to be both European and black

requires some specific forms of double consciousness. . . . If this appears to be little more than a roundabout way of saying that the reflexive cultures and consciousness of the European settlers and those of the Africans they enslaved, the "Indians" they slaughtered, and the Asians that they indentured were not, even in situations of the most extreme brutality, sealed hermeneutically from each other, then so be it' (ibid., 2–3). Reducing Indigenous peoples to those slaughtered suggests that Indigenous people in the Americas no longer exist, renders invisible their contemporary situation and struggles, and perpetuates myths of the Americas as an empty land. . . .

There is also a curious ambiguity in terms of integrating issues of Indigenous sovereignty. 'The claims made by peoples who have inhabited the territory since before recorded history and those who arrived by steamboat or airplane,' Clifford notes, 'will be founded on very different principles' (1997: 253). Rather than elaborate on such principles, Clifford focuses more on assertions that Aboriginal peoples are also diasporic, which leads him to raise what he sees as ambiguities in Indigenous nationhood. For example, in contrasting Indigenous and 'diasporic' claims to identity, Clifford suggests that Indigenous claims are primordial. For him, Indigenous claims 'stress continuity of habitation, Indigeneity, and often a "natural" connection to the land,' while 'diaspora cultures, constituted by displacement, may resist such appeals on political principle' (ibid., 252). Such a characterization of Indigenous claims ignores the contemporary political, social, and economic realities of Indigenous peoples, and fails to address the ways in which diasporic claims are premised on a colonizing social formation. Thus, despite exploring how diasporic identities articulate with or resist colonization projects, Clifford fails to take into account that these identities are situated in multiple projects of colonization and settlement on Indigenous lands.

We can see a similar erasure of colonialism and Indigenous peoples in writings on slavery. Writers such as Gilroy, Clifford, and others have emphasized the ways in which the enslavement of

Africans has shaped European discourses of modernity, European identity, and contemporary articulations of racism. As Toni Morrison powerfully states, 'modern life begins with slavery' (cited in Gilroy, 1993b: 308). We do not contest the importance of slavery, but we wonder about the claim that modernity began with slavery, given the significance of colonialism and Orientalism in constructing Europe's sense of itself as modern. Equally important, the claim that modernity began with slavery, rather than with the genocide and colonization of Indigenous peoples in the Americas that preceded it, erases Indigenous presence. The vision evoked is one in which the history of racism begins with the bringing of African peoples as slaves to what became the United States and Canada.

How does such theorizing about slavery fail to address the ways in which modes of slavery, and the anti-slavery movement in the United States, were premised on earlier and continuing modes of colonization of Indigenous peoples? For example, out of whose land would the '40 acres' be carved? How do we account for the fact that the same week President Lincoln signed the Emancipation Proclamation, he approved the order for the largest mass hanging in US history, of 38 Dakota men accused of participating in an uprising in Minnesota (Cook-Lynn, 1996: 63)? Such events suggest connections between the anti-slavery movement, the ongoing theft of Indigenous land, and the forced relocation or extermination of its original inhabitants. There was also a resounding silence among anti-slavery activists, women's suffragists, labour leaders, and ex-slaves such as Frederick Douglas concerning land theft and Indigenous genocide. Such silences reveal an apparent consensus among these diverse activists that the insertion of workers, white women, and blacks into US (and Canadian) nation-building was to continue to take place on Indigenous land, regardless of the cost to Indigenous peoples. In short, the relationship between slavery, anti-slavery, and colonialism is obscured when slavery is presented as the defining moment in North American racism.

Thus, critical race and postcolonial scholars have systematically excluded ongoing colonization from the ways in which racism is articulated. This has erased the presence of Aboriginal peoples and their ongoing struggles for decolonization, precluding a more sophisticated analysis of migration, diasporic identities, and diasporic countercultures. Equally disturbing, when we look at the few scholars who include Aboriginal peoples and decolonization in their theoretical frameworks, decolonization politics are equated with antiracist politics. Such an ontological approach places decolonization and antiracism within a liberal-pluralist framework, which decenters decolonization. . . .

Theories of nationalism render Indigenous nationhood unviable, which has serious ramifications in a colonial context. The postcolonial emphasis on deconstructing nationhood furthers Indigenous denationalization for those targeted for centuries for physical and cultural extermination, and facing added fragmentation through identity legislation (Grewal and Kaplan, 1994; Jackson and Penrose, 1993; Anderson, 1991; Hall, 1994). Such deconstructions can ignore settler state colonization (Anderson, 1991). Or they theorize, from the outside, about how communities 'become' Indigenous solely because of interactions with colonialist nationalist projects (Anderson, 2003; Warren, 1992). If the epistemologies and ontologies of Indigenous nations do not count, Indigeneity is evaluated through social construction theory. More problematic still are works that denigrate nationalism as representing only technologies of violence (McClintock, 1997), or a reification of categories that can degenerate into fundamentalism and 'ethnic cleansing' (Penrose, 1993; Nixon, 1997). There is also the simple dismissal of 'ethnic absolutism' as an increasingly untenable cultural strategy (Hall, 1996b: 250, quoted in Weaver, 1998: 14), which calls into question the very notion of national identity. None of these perspectives enable Indigenous peoples in the Americas to envision a future separate from continuous engulfment by the most powerful colonial order in the world, or their continuous erasure, starting with Columbus, from global international political relations (Venne, 1998). In this respect, postcolonial deconstructions of nationalism appear to be premised on what Cree scholar Lorraine Le Camp calls 'terranullism', the erasure of an ongoing post-contact Indigenous presence (Le Camp, 1995). Perhaps it is not surprising that from these perspectives, decolonization, nationhood, and sovereignty begin to appear ridiculous and irrelevant, impossible, and futile (Cook-Lynn, 1996: 88).

For Aboriginal peoples, postcolonial deconstructions of nationalism simply do not manifest any understanding of how Aboriginal peoples actualize nationhood and sovereignty given the colonial framework enveloping them. According to Oneida scholar Lina Sunseri (2005), Indigenous nationhood existed before Columbus; when contemporary Indigenous theorists on nationalism explicate traditional Indigenous concepts of nationhood, they redefine the concept of a nation by moving beyond a linkage of a nation to the state and/or modernity and other European-based ideas and values. . . .

Beyond Innocence: The Failure of Canadian Antiracism to Make Colonialism Foundational

The refusal of international scholarship to address settler state colonization and Indigenous decolonization is problematic, especially since the same epistemological and ontological frameworks are reproduced in Canadian antiracism theory, which is written on land that is still colonized. The failure of Canadian antiracism to make colonization foundational has meant that Aboriginal peoples' histories, resistance, and current realities have been segregated from antiracism. In this section, we will explore how this segregation is reflected in theory, as well as its implications for how we understand Canada and Canadian history. Second, we shall complicate our understandings of how people of colour are located in the settler society.

Antiracism's segregation from the knowledge and histories of resistance of Aboriginal peoples is

manifested in various ways. Aboriginal organizations are not invited to participate in organizing and shaping the focus of most antiracism conferences. Indigeneity thus receives only token recognition. Their ceremonies feature as performances to open the conference (regardless of the meaning of these ceremonies for the elders involved). Usually, one Aboriginal person is invited as a plenary speaker. A few scattered sessions, attended primarily by the families and friends of Aboriginal presenters, may address Indigeneity, but they are not seen as intrinsic to understanding race and racism. At these sessions, Aboriginal presenters may be challenged to reshape their presentations to fit into a 'critical race' framework. Failure to do so means that the work is seen as 'simplistic'. In our classes on antiracism, token attention—normally one week—is given to Aboriginal peoples, and rarely is the exploration of racism placed in a context of ongoing colonization. In antiracist political groups, Aboriginal issues are placed within a liberal pluralist framework, where they are marginalized and juxtaposed to other, often-contradictory struggles, such as that of Quebec sovereignty.

These practices reflect the theoretical segregation that underpins them. Within antiracism scholarship, the widespread practice of ignoring Indigenous presence at every stage of Canadian history fundamentally flaws our understandings of Canada and Canadian history. In this view, Canadian history is replete with white settler racism against immigrants of colour. If Aboriginal peoples are mentioned at all, it is at the point of contact, and then only as generic 'First Nations', a term bearing exactly the degree of specificity and historical meaning as 'people of colour'. The 'vanishing Indian' is as alive in antiracism scholarship as it is in mainstream Canada. . . .

These practices of exclusion and segregation reflect the contradictory ways in which peoples of colour are situated within the nation-state. Marginalized by a white settler nationalist project, as citizens they are nonetheless invited to take part in ongoing colonialism. The relationship of people of colour to Indigeneity is thus complex. We turn now to the dynamic interaction between people of colour, Indigeneity, and colonialism.

People of colour are settlers. Broad differences exist between those brought as slaves, currently work as migrant labourers, are refugees without legal documentation, or émigrés who have obtained citizenship. Yet people of colour live on land that is appropriated and contested, where Aboriginal peoples are denied nationhood and access to their own lands. This section will examine how people of colour, as settlers, participate in, or are complicit in, the ongoing colonization of Aboriginal peoples. Histories of the settlement of people of colour have been framed by racist exclusion and fail to account for the ways in which their settlement has taken place on Indigenous land. As citizens, they have been implicated in colonial actions. Moreover, there are current, ongoing tensions between Aboriginal peoples and people of colour, notably in terms of multiculturalism policy and immigration.

Let us turn to the history of settler formation in Canada and the role of people of colour in the colonial project. The Canadian nation-state project was one of white settlement. It displaced Aboriginal peoples and targeted them for physical and cultural extermination to open land for settlers, while marginalizing and restricting the entry into Canada of people of colour. Much of Canadian antiracist scholarship has attempted to document the exclusion and marginalization of people of colour from the emerging nation. However, this work does not examine the ways in which the entry of people of colour into Canada put them in colonial relationships with Aboriginal peoples.

Take, for example, the discussion of black loyalists in Nova Scotia who were denied lands promised to them, or awarded poor lands that whites did not want (Hill, 1981: 10, 63–64; Walcott, 1997: 35–36; Mensah, 2002: 46). Failure to reference who was being forced off the territories being settled erases the bloodiest interval of genocide in Canadian history.[6] The black settler population in Nova Scotia, ex-slaves with few options, was largely denied the opportunity to appropriate Native land, so that many eventually left for Sierra Leone (Mensah, 2002: 47). However, to speak of the loss of black land rights without referencing those being exterminated to 'free up' the land for settlement is to be complicit in erasing genocide. . . .

Perhaps the most difficult and contentious area in which Aboriginal realities conflict with the interests of people of colour regards immigration and multiculturalism. Aboriginal theorists and activists, particularly in Canada, have largely been silent on these issues. This reflects the discomfort and ambivalence of many Aboriginal people when official policies and discourses of multiculturalism and immigration obscure Native presence and divert attention from their realities, and when communities of colour resist their marginalization in ways that render Aboriginal communities invisible. Canadian language policy is a classic example. Multiculturalism policy overrides the redressing of assaults on Indigenous languages, with funding provided first for 'official' languages and then for 'heritage' languages. Only then are the dregs divided up among the 50-odd Indigenous languages in Canada currently at risk of extinction given ongoing cultural genocide.

Ongoing settlement of Indigenous lands, whether by white people or people of colour, remains part of Canada's nation-building project and is premised on displacing Indigenous peoples. Regarding immigration, Aboriginal peoples are caught between a rock and a hard place. Either they are implicated in the anti-immigrant racism of white Canadians, or they support struggles of people of colour that fail to take seriously the reality of ongoing colonization. Often overlooked by antiracist activists is that the *Delgamuuk'w* decision clearly sets out instances in which Aboriginal title could be infringed (i.e., limited or invalidated) by continuing immigration (Persky, 1998: 20). Canada's immigration goals, then, can be used to restrict Aboriginal rights. Antiracist activists need to think through how their campaigns can preempt the ability of Aboriginal communities to establish title to their traditional lands. Recent tendencies to advocate for open borders make this particularly important. Borders in the Americas are European fictions, restricting Native peoples' passage and that of peoples of colour. However, to speak of opening borders without addressing Indigenous land loss and ongoing struggles to reclaim territories is to divide communities that are already marginalized from one another. The question that must be asked is how opening borders would affect Indigenous struggles aimed at reclaiming land and nationhood.

Scholarship is needed on ending segregation practices and on the complex histories of inter-actions between peoples of colour and Aboriginal peoples. How did passage of the Multiculturalism Act in 1969 connect with Canada's attempt, in the same year, to pass the White Paper to eliminate 'Indian' status and Canada's fiduciary responsibil-ity to status Indians? To what extent did black-Mi'kmaq intermarriage in Nova Scotia represent resistance to extermination policies against Mi'kmaw people and the marginalization of black loyalists? How did Chinese men and Native com-munities interact during the building of the Canadian railroad? Is there a connection at the policy level between the denial of West Coast Native fishing rights and the confiscation of Japanese fishing boats during the internment? In what ways did people of colour support or chal-lenge policies used to colonize Aboriginal peoples? What were the moments of conflict and of collaboration?

With these questions, we are asking antiracism theory to examine how people of colour have con-tributed to the settler formation. We are not ask-ing every antiracism writer to become an 'Indian expert'. This is not desirable. Nor should histories of blacks, South Asians, or East Asians in Canada focus extensively on Aboriginal peoples. Yet, when speaking of histories of settlement, an explicit awareness and articulation of the intersection of specific settlement policies with policies control-ling 'Indians' is needed. This requires recognition of ongoing colonization as foundational. Such a clear rendition of the bigger picture naturally sac-rifices any notion of the innocence of people of colour in projects of settlement and colonial relations.

Summary: Taking on Decolonization

This article has addressed the multiple ways in which postcolonial and antiracist theory has maintained a colonial framework. We would like to suggest the following areas as topics to be taken up.

1. Aboriginal sovereignty is a reality that is on the table. Antiracist theorists must begin to talk about how they are going to place antiracist agendas within the context of sovereignty and restoration of land.
2. Taking colonization seriously changes anti-racism in powerful ways. Within academia, antiracist theorists need to begin to make ongoing colonization central to the construc-tion of knowledge about race and racism. They must learn how to write, research, and teach in ways that account for Indigenous realities as foundational.
3. This article has focused on antiracism theory, but the failure of antiracist activists to make the ongoing colonization of Indigenous peoples foundational to their agendas is also import-ant. Most antiracist groups have not included Indigenous concerns; when they do, they employ a pluralist framework. There is a strong need to begin discussions between antiracist and Aboriginal activists on how to frame claims for antiracism in ways that do not disempower Aboriginal peoples.

. . . A final word must be said about antiracism *within* Native communities. Aboriginal peoples have long and bitterly resisted the racism shaping Canada's colonial project, yet colonial legislation on Native identity has profound implications in terms of racialization, and the forms that racism can take, within Native communities. This article has focused on the need to decolonize antiracism as we now know it. Aboriginal peoples may also wish to ask how their communities would shape an antiracism project to address the violence col-onization has inflicted on Indigenous identity. The legacy of cultural genocide and legal classification by 'blood' and descent means that Aboriginal peoples must find their way through a morass of 'racial thinking' about basic issues relating to Native identity and nationhood. Their ways of doing this may move between re-traditionalization and deconstruction, between Indigenous and Western ways of addressing how Indigenous identity has been reduced to biology. Most of all, it means finding ways of working 'with a good heart'.

Wel'alieq!—Thank you.

Notes

1. This project represents an equal collaboration by both authors. The choice to put Bonita Lawrence's name first was explicitly political. Because antiracism is named here as part of a colonial project, and the positioning of peoples of colour as innocent of colonizing relationships is challenged, both authors struggled with a sense that Bonita Lawrence would face greater criticism and marginalization from antiracism circles if her name came first, than Enakshi Dua would, as a woman of colour with a long history of antiracism theory and activism. We decided to challenge these practices by situating the Aboriginal person first in the byline.

2. The specter of 'Native unrest' appears to have haunted the Canadian government since the 1885 uprising, so that the military is usually on the alert whenever Native activism appears to be spreading. As Sherene Razack has noted, the Canadian government, in sending the Airborne Regiment to Somalia in 1993, was highly aware that they might not have enough military power left at home in the event that the country was faced with another Oka (Razack, 2004: 147).

3. The meaning of the term 'genocide', as coined by Raphael Lemkin in 1944 during the discussions leading to the United Nations Genocide Convention, was given as follows: 'Generally speaking, genocide does not necessarily mean the immediate destruction of a nation, *except when* accomplished by mass killing of all the members of a nation. It is intended rather to signify a coordinated plan of different actions aimed at destruction of the essential foundations of the life of national groups, with the aim of annihilating the groups themselves. The objective of such a plan would be disintegration of the political and social institutions, of culture, language, national feelings, religion, and the economic existence of national groups, and the destruction of personal security, liberty, health, dignity, and the lives of individuals belonging to such groups. . . . Genocide has two phases: one, destruction of the national pattern of the oppressed group; the other, the

imposition of the national pattern of the oppressor' (Lemkin, 1944, quoted in Churchill, 1994: 12–13).

4. In the 1999 *Marshall* decision, for example, concerning the rights of Mi'kmaw people in the Maritimes to fish, the courts upheld the integrity of 18th-century treaties between Britain and the Mi'kmaw nation (Coates, 2000: 7) as superseding the authority that Canada had vested in institutions such as the Department of Fisheries and Oceans.

5. The combined acreage of all existing Indian reserves in Canada is less than one-half the amount in the Navajo reservation in Arizona (St. Germain, 2001).

6. Mi'kmaw people fought the English for over a century, up and down the Eastern Seaboard, in conjunction with other allied nations of the Wabanaki confederacy. With the 18th-century peace treaties, the British Crown unleashed a concentrated campaign of extermination efforts, including the posting of a bounty for the scalps of Mi'kmaq men, women, and children in 1744, 1749, and 1756, 'scorched earth' policies to starve out survivors (Paul, 2000: 182–84), the absolute denial of land for reserves for most of a century after asserting military control in 1763, and the accompanying spread of epidemics that brought the Mi'kmaq people to near extinction. Daniel Paul notes that by 1843, only 1,300 were left of a people whose numbers had been estimated at 30,000 to 200,000. Extermination efforts were most concentrated in periods immediately preceding the settling of loyalists, white and black, in Nova Scotia.

References

Alfred, Gerald (Taiaiake). 1999. *Peace Power and Righteousness: An Indigenous Manifesto.* London: Oxford University Press.

Anderson, Benedict. 2003. 'Nationalism and Cultural Survival in Our Time: A Sketch', pp. 165–90 in Bartholomew Dean and Jerome M. Levi, eds, *At the Risk of Being Heard: Identity, Indigenous Rights, and Postcolonial States.* Ann Arbor, MI: University of Michigan Press.

———. 1991. *Imagined Communities: Reflections on the Origin and Spread of Nationalism.* London and New York: Verso.

Churchill, Ward. 1994. *Indians Are Us? Culture and Genocide in Native North America.* Toronto: Between the Lines Press.

———. 1992. *Struggle for the Land: Indigenous Resistance to Genocide, Ecocide, and Expropriation in Contemporary North America.* Toronto: Between the Lines Press.

Clifford, James. 1997. *Routes: Travel and Translation in the Late Twentieth Century.* Cambridge, MA: Harvard University Press.

Cook-Lynn, Elizabeth. 1996. *Why I Can't Read Wallace Stegner and Other Essays: A Tribal Voice.* Madison, WI: University of Wisconsin Press.

Dua, Enakshi. 2003. ' "Race" and Governmentality: The Racialization of Canadian Citizenship Practices', in

Deborah Brock, ed., *Making Normal: Social Regulation in Canada*. Toronto: Nelson.

Gilroy, Paul. 1993. *The Black Atlantic: Modernity and Double Consciousness*. Cambridge, MA: Harvard University Press.

Grewal, Inderpal, and Caren Kaplan. 1994. *Scattered Hegemonies: Postmodernity and Transnational Feminist Practices*. Minneapolis: University of Minnesota Press.

Hall, Stuart. 1996a. 'The West and the Rest: Discourse and Power', pp. 184–224 in Stuart Hall, David Held, Don Hubert, and Kenneth Thompson, eds, *Modernity: An Introduction to Modern Societies*. London: Open University.

———. 1996b. 'When Was "The Post-Colonial?" Thinking at the Limit', pp. 242–60 in Iain Chambers and Lidia Curti, eds, *The Post-Colonial Question: Common Skies, Divided Horizons*. London: Routledge.

———. 1994. 'Cultural Identity and Diaspora', pp. 392–403 in P. Williams and L. Chrisman, eds, *Colonial Discourse and Postcolonial Theory*. New York: Columbia University Press.

Hill, Daniel G. 1981. *The Freedom Seekers: Blacks in Early Canada*. Toronto: Stoddart Publishing.

Le Camp, Lorraine. 1998. 'Terra Nullius/Theoria Nullius— Empty Lands/Empty Theory: A Literature Review of Critical Theory from an Aboriginal Perspective'. Unpublished manuscript. Toronto, Canada: Department of Sociology and Equity Studies, Ontario Institute for Studies in Education.

McClintock, Anne. 1997. ' "No Longer in a Future Heaven": Gender, Race, and Nationalism', pp. 89-112 in Anne McClintock, Aamir Mufti, and Ella Shohat, eds, *Dangerous Liaisons: Gender, Nation, and Postcolonial Perspectives*. Minneapolis: University of Minnesota.

Mensah, Joseph. 2002. *Black Canadians: History, Experiences, Social Conditions*. Halifax, NS: Fernwood Press.

Penrose, Jan. 1993. 'Reification in the Name of Change: The Impact of Nationalism on Social Constructions of Nation, People and Place in Scotland and the United Kingdom', pp. 27–49 in Peter Jackson and Jan Penrose, eds, *Constructions of Race, Place and Nation*. London: UCL Press.

Persky, Stan. 1998. *Delgamuukʼw: The Supreme Court of Canada Decision on Aboriginal Title* (Commentary.) Vancouver/Toronto: Greystone Books.

Razack, Sherene. 2004. *Dark Threats and White Knights: The Somalia Affair, Peacekeeping, and the New Imperialism*. Toronto: University of Toronto Press.

Spivak, Gayatri. 1994. Presentation at University of Toronto. (May).

Sunseri, Madelina. 2005. 'Theorizing Nationalisms: Intersections of Gender, Nation, Culture, and Colonization in the Case of Oneida's Decolonizing Nationalist Movement', Unpublished PhD Thesis (June). Toronto: Department of Sociology, York University.

Venne, Sharon. 1998. *Our Elders Understand Our Rights: Evolving International Law Regarding Indigenous Rights*. Penticton, BC: Theytus Books.

Walcott, Rinaldo. 1997. *Black Like Who? Writing/Black/Canada*. Toronto: Insomniac Press.

Warren, Kay. 1992. 'Transforming Memories and Histories: The Meanings of Ethnic Resurgence for Mayan Indians', pp. 189–219 in Alfred Stepan, ed., *Americas: New Interpretive Essays*. New York: Oxford University Press.

Weaver, Jace. 1998. 'From I-Hermeneutics to We-Hermeneutics: Native Americans and the Postcolonial', pp. 1–25 in Jace Weaver, ed., *Native American Religious Identity: Unforgotten Gods*. Maryknoll, NY: Orbis Books.

Part One

Additional Readings

Alfred, Taiaiake (Gerald). *Peace, Power, Righteousness: An Indigenous Manifesto*. Toronto: Oxford University Press, 1999.

———. *Heeding the Voices of our Ancestors: Kahnawake Mohawk Politics and the Rise of Native Nationalism*. Toronto: Oxford University Press, 1995.

Deloria, Vine. *Custer Died For Your Sins: An Indian Manifesto*. New York: Macmillan, 1969.

Monture, Patricia. *Thunder in My Soul: A Mohawk Woman Speaks*. Halifax: Fernwood Publishing, 1995.

———. *Journeying Forward: Dreaming First Nations Independence*. Halifax: Fernwood Publishing, 1999.

Relevant Websites

Royal Commission on Aboriginal Peoples (All Volumes)
http://www.collectionscnada.gc.ca/
webarchives/200711150553257/
http://www.ainc-inac.gc.ca/ch/rcap/sg/sgmm_e.html

The RCAP was released in 1996 and consists of five volumes. While not an exhaustive source, it offers a great deal of information and history of the Indigenous peoples of Canada and their relationships with the Canadian State.

Films

The Disappearing Indian. Dir. Grant McLean. National Film Board of Canada, 1995.
The Other Side of the Ledger: An Indian View of the Hudson's Bay Company. Dir. Willie Dunn and Martin De Falco. National Film Board of Canada, 1972.

Edward Said on Orientalism. Dir. Sut Jhally and Sanjay Talreja. Media Education Foundation, 1998.

Key Terms

Aboriginalism
Eurocentrism
Indigenous knowledge
Colonization
Decolonization

Antiracism
Imperialism
White settler society
Resurgence
Racism

Discussion Questions

1. What is meant by 'Aboriginalism'? How does it structure and disregard the aspirations of Indigenous nations? How does it embody the history of colonialism?
2. What are the implications for Indigenous populations in referring to the Canadian nation in postcolonial terms?
3. What are the similarities and differences between the following terms: anticolonialism, postcolonialism, and neocolonialism?
4. What is 'Eurocentric diffusionism'? What has this meant for Indigenous peoples?

Activities

Take 10–20 minutes to reflect on what you have been taught about Indigenous and Canadian histories. Discuss your individual reflections as a class. What kinds of patterns and differences emerge? How do these lessons make you feel? How have they impacted on the way you think of yourself and the land on which you live?

Watch the 1955 National Film Board production *The Disappearing Indian* (written and directed by Grant McLean). What colonial tropes, Eurocentric knowledge, and assumptions are present in this film?

Imagine that you were to take part in forming an antiracist group in your city or town. How could you ensure that Indigenous peoples interest and needs were included? Do you foresee any tensions or conflicts arising between Indigenous people and non-Indigenous people? If so, what would they be and why? How might you work to overcome and resolve them?

Nation-Building and the Deeply Racialized Other

In his book *Everything You Know About Indians is Wrong*, Comanche curator Paul Chaat Smith asks Americans to think *seriously* about the representation of Indigenous peoples in the historic colonial imaginary. His concern is with romanticism, or the depiction of Indigenous peoples based on myths, stereotypes, and oversimplification. Romanticism has long constituted a distinct form of racism aimed at Indigenous peoples. As Chaat Smith writes, it is 'a specialized vocabulary created by Euros for Indians' ensuring in turn 'a status as strange, primitive and exotic' (2009: 17). In this chapter, we provide a selection of articles written by Indigenous scholars on this matter.

Mohawk scholar Deborah Doxtator raises the idea of Indianness. In her view, the concept cannot be considered without addressing historic acts of racism and settler colonial injustice. Indianness is required in order to construct Indigenous peoples as different and Other. In the minds of white settler colonists, Indians are everything that civilization is not. They live in a world of long ago. They refuse to adopt modern conveniences. Their deficits also inform and enable histories of dispossession. Defined as just so many teepees, headdresses, and totem poles, Indianness makes possible what Cherokee scholar Andrea Smith (2006: 68) refers to as a pillar in the logic of genocide: the idea that Indigenous peoples must always be disappearing.

Histories of genocide are made possible through rigid assertions of difference between 'real Indians' and Others. Without the difference produced through myths and stereotypes about 'authentic' or 'real Indians', there can be nothing gained or lost by Indigenous peoples. They cannot move past the primitivism that defines their culture, or become civilized, for that matter. Resistance is paradoxical. The refusal to perform Indianness only reaffirms the idea that they have all but disappeared. Romanticism makes possible the ongoing dispossession of Indigenous peoples. So long as Indians are incapable of being themselves, rendered invisible, or no longer living, the act of land appropriation ensues.

Romanticism makes possible a caricature of Indigenous identities. It forecloses the breadth of Indigenous identities that exist and are possible in modern contexts. As Chaat Smith writes, 'silence about our own complicated histories supports the colonizer's idea that the only real Indians are full blooded, from a reservation, speak their language, and practice the religion of their ancestors' (2009: 26). How do we explain this need for authenticity? What are modern practices of difference making, where are they located, and how do they operate in the contemporary world? These are just some of questions being asked by Indigenous scholars about colonial representations of Indianness.

The politics of representation is just as much tied to whiteness as it is to Indianness. In saying this, we are not suggesting that Indigenous peoples abandon the work that is done in communities in order to focus on non-Indian issues. Rather, we want to take seriously the meaning of Indianness in the mind of the colonizer. If the privilege of whiteness is to pass as invisibly the norm, then the time has come to expose the difference that Indianness makes. As Carol Schick and Cree/Métis scholar Verna St Denis have put it 'addressing racism means more than examining the experience of those who experience racism' (2005: 299). Challenging racism also involves exposing the ways that 'white men name and mark Others, thereby naming and marking themselves' (ibid.)

Naming and marking Others as different does not only involve racist beliefs about the inherent superiority and inferiority of individuals. Historically, the process of difference making was gendered—often involving sexist and demeaning assumptions about Indigenous women. This was especially true of early colonialism in what is now Canada. As Cree scholar Winona Stevenson illustrates, stereotypes about Indigenous women were often used to create boundaries between Indigenous and white settler populations. Many of these understandings served to justify early colonial dominance and policies of exclusion.

Representations of Indianness are central to the construction of white settler identities. The colonizer imagines himself as civilized, but only insofar as he establishes himself in contrast with the mythical construction of savagism. The ideal woman construct discussed by Stevenson is inseparable from this process of upholding the binary between civility and savagism. As she suggests, missionary accounts are rife with examples of 'exploited, overworked drudges, abused, misused, [and] dirty'. Put simply, the pinnacle of European womanhood would likely never have been accomplished without colonial representations of Indigenous womanhood.

In order to justify the appropriation of Indian lands, the colonizer has always to prove the inferiority of Indigenous peoples. The rationale for these kinds of dispossession found their early ideological basis in colonial representations of Indianness and savagery. As Stevenson quotes the work of Sarah Carter in showing, 'expounding the righteous triumph of civilization over savagery' required 'proving the inferiority of the Indian'. These understandings enabled the transfer of Indian lands into the colonizers hands, gave way to the statutory subjugation of Indigenous women, and have stood the test of time into the twenty-first century.

The challenge we face as Indigenous peoples today is very much dependent on the ability to claim a more dynamic representation of our peoples. Thomas King focuses on the task of reinventing ourselves as 'Indians'—and in the face of popular and scholarly representations that have relegated us to past domains. There is another story to be told in his estimation. They tell the story of contemporary

Indians, including traditional symbols and meanings resituated in the present (Simpson, 1998: 52). They force us to 'reflect on what . . . things meant, and what they now mean' (ibid., 52–3). The task of reinvention will remain as much urgent as it is difficult. As Chaat Smith suggests, they 'require invention, not rewriting' (2009: 52). They may even require 'a final break with a form that was never about us in the first place' (ibid.).

Chapter 4

'The Idea of Indianness' and Once Upon a Time: The Role of Indians in History

Deborah Doxtator

Just a little more than a hundred years ago school texts were describing Indians as being 'ferocious and quarrelsome', 'great gluttons' and 'great drunkards' (Miles, 1870: xxii). How have attitudes towards Indian people changed? Do people still carry in their minds the idea, even if it goes unsaid, that Indian culture is 'primitive' and incapable of survival in a twentieth-century environment? Are some people still looking for the disappearing Indian? What does 'Indian' mean?

Teepees, headdresses, totem poles, birch bark canoes, face paint, fringes, buckskin, and tomahawks—when anyone sees images, drawings, or paintings of these things they immediately think of 'Indians'. They are symbols of 'Indianness' that have become immediately recognizable to the public. To take it one step further, they are the symbols that the public uses in its definition of what an Indian is. To the average person, Indians, *real* Indians, in their purest form of 'Indianness', live in a world of long ago where there are no high-rises, no snowmobiles, no colour television. They live in the woods or in places that are unknown called 'Indian Reserves'. The Indians that people know best are the ones they have read about in adventure stories as a child, cut out and pasted in school projects, read about in the newspaper. They may have 'played Indian' as a game, or dressed up as an Indian for Halloween. To many people 'Indians' are not real, anymore than Bugs Bunny, Marilyn Monroe, or Anne of Green Gables are real to them. So it is not surprising that when they do meet Indian people they have some very strange ideas about how 'Indians' behave, live, and speak.

In their excitement at meeting this celebrity, this 'Indian', people sometimes say foolish things, that if they thought about it, they would never ask anyone: 'Is that your own hair?', 'What is the significance of that design, is it sacred?', 'Say something in *Indian*.' Other Indian people have been asked whether or not their blood is red, or if feathers once grew out of their heads.

It is very difficult to discuss 'Indianness' with any measure of neutrality. The emotions and experience of both parties in the relationship between

'Indians' and 'Whites' has been such that there is no easy way to discuss the facts. It is impossible to discuss the concept of 'Indianness' without addressing racism and the injustices that have occurred. It is impossible to talk about 'Indianness' without facing the uncomfortable reality of the dispossession of one people by another. . . .

'Indian' has meant so many things, both good and bad: from an idealized all-spiritual, environmentalist, to a 'primitive' down-trodden welfare case. These popular images of 'Indians' have very little to do with actual people. Instead they reflect the ideas that one culture has manufactured about another people. These images influence the concept of 'Indianness' held by many people.

Definitions of 'Indianness' have changed a little over the past four hundred years. In the seventeenth century, there were debates concerning whether or not Indians were animals or human beings. In the twentieth century, the debate about Indians has shifted to whether or not 'Indians' are competent human beings, capable of running their own affairs. For decades, Indian children grew up being told that their culture was inferior, their religion was wrong, and their language useless.

The concept of 'The Indian' as primitive, undeveloped, and inferior has a long history, that extends back into the sixteenth century (Dickason, 1984: 35). Ever since the two races first met, non-Indians have been trying to teach, convert, 'improve' or otherwise change Indian peoples. The idea has persisted that, somehow, Indians are really just undeveloped human beings in desperate need of training in the proper way to live and make a living.

Academic disciplines still have great difficulty accepting Indian art, history, literature, music, and technology as art, history, literature, music, and technology without first placing it in an anthropological context. Museums continue to foster the view of Indians as 'pre-historic'. They have special galleries that focus on presenting something called 'Native Culture' in ways that are perceived inappropriate for 'Canadian culture'. It is not particularly unusual for museums such as the National Museum of Civilization to display human remains from a native culture which have included skeletal remains in their archaeological exhibits. It is seen as being comparable to scientific displays of the skeleton of 'Early Man'. But it is not likely that the bones of Laura Secord will be installed in any museum exhibit in the near future. Indians, like the 'Iron-Age' man, are seen as being separated from modern technological society by the fact that their technology, or rather perceived lack of it, makes them 'primitives' or 'wild-men', ancient ancestors that just don't exist anymore.

It has been difficult for industrial Canadian society to accept that non-industrial cultures are still viable. To Canadian society, Indian cultures are based firmly in the past, and Western culture has a tradition of repudiating the past as out-of-date and irrelevant to the present. Since the sixteenth century 'Indians' have been seen as representing an earlier, less civilized versions of Europeans. They have, in the minds of Europeans and Canadians, come to symbolize human beings at an earlier, less complex stage of development.

This has meant that images of 'Indians' created by Western society have emphasized their perception of Indian inferiority. In the nineteenth and early twentieth centuries 'Indian' culture was either denounced as immoral or seen as having degenerated from a higher form of culture. To those who were inclined to see the world as a struggle between good and bad, God and the Devil, Indians were 'pagans', devil worshippers. To those who accepted Darwin's theories of evolution, Indians were seen as halfway between men and beasts, simple people who needed to be eventually 'raised' to the level of Western civilization through education and training. To those who saw the world in terms of a 'golden past' against which everything in the present could never measure up, 'Indians were simply no longer what they used to be' (Barbeau, 1923). No matter what the approach, all of these views concluded that Indian societies were ultimately inferior to Western societies.

Every culture creates images of how it sees itself and the rest of the world. Incidental to these images of self-definition are definitions of the 'other'. Canadian society through control over such tools as advertising, literature, history, and the entertainment media has the power to create images of other peoples and these images often operate as a form of social control. For example, images in the media of women as incompetent, physically inferior, and scatter-brained have justified why women should not hold executive positions in Canadian business. Racial stereotypes in television situation-comedies have justified why it is all right to deny other racial groups access to power and financial rewards. Indians as part of a different racial group have been subject to this type of 'control' but also to a unique form of physiological warfare. Minority groups often endure discrimination but they never experience situations in which the discriminating group usurps their identity. The image of the 'romantic Indian princess' was created for the benefit and imagination of Euro-Canadian, not for the benefit of Indian people. It uses symbols derived from Indian cultures and changes them so that they better suit the needs of Canadian society. Through use of the romantic images of 'Indian princesses' and 'Indian chiefs' non-Indian people can become 'noble Indians' in their own minds. . . .

Once Upon a Time: The Role of Indians in History

In disposition the Savages were fierce, cruel and cunning. They seldom forgave an affront. They used to SCALP the enemies whom they had killed, and to torment those whom they had taken alive. . . . However, as the Indians were so cruel and bloodthirsty, we cannot but lament and condemn the practice of using their services in warfare. Those who used them were often unable to manage them. (Miles, 1870)

Eighteen days after setting out Davis handed over his charges to the personnel at Fort Battle ford—from outside the buildings. Realizing from personal experience the effect of such close contact with over a thousand Indians, the personnel there suggested that before presenting his dispatches it might be well for Davis to strip to the skin, burn his clothing and take a bath. (Robins, 1948)

Interpretations of history can best be understood as a series of stories or myths. My generation grew up with the story of how North America was 'discovered' by Christopher Columbus and of how civilization was 'started' by the French. There were lots of statements in the textbooks about 'virgin land', 'uninhabited territories'. Then suddenly into the picture came the Indians. Sometimes they were portrayed as tools, sometimes as threats, sometimes as allies. Indians were incidental because the story was not about them. They were just there—in the way.

I remember learning about Cartier, about Frontenac, about Brock and feeling disappointed that the Indians always lost. When we studied the fur trade, the Indians were always doing foolish things, giving up all their valuable fur resources worth thousands of dollars for a few pots and pans, selling huge tracts of land for a handful of shiny beads. I didn't want to accept it, but there it was in print, in the textbook that never lied.

It wasn't until I went to University that I understood that what I had read, studied, and reiterated in my test answers was a type of story. It was somebody else's story about how Canada was settled, and it functioned as a justification and explanation for 'the way things happened'. This fall I discovered that the story still functions in this way. One of my tutorial students remarked to me that he felt it was unfair to blame the Canadian government for the reserve system and broken treaties because it was unintentional that the treaty promises were not kept, that no one had planned that the Cree in Saskatchewan would starve, that it 'just happened'.

The Canadian history textbook was sprinkled with references to the clash between 'primitive and civilized societies'. It stated that 'despite their nomadic habits and their mixed blood the Métis were not savages', but 'unsophisticated peoples'. Métis people had 'primitive nationalism', Crees didn't advance to the battle, they 'prowled' around neighbourhoods frightening townspeople. Riel himself was said to be filled with 'primitive aggressiveness and hostility' (Francis et al., 1986). In the bulk of the reading, Indians still were in the periphery of the story, their part was still that of the obstacle, and source of conflict.

Historically, these stories about Indians being 'primitive', violent, and generally incompetent at self-government justified two elements of Canadian Indian policy: non-Indian land settlement and non-Indian control over Indians. For example, it was easy for nineteenth and often twentieth century analysts to justify why Indians no longer should control the land. They simply didn't know how to use it 'properly'. They built no roads, no fences, raised no cattle, they were not 'improving' the land with European technology. Regulations were passed in the Canadian Parliament to control Indians—where they could live, how they were governed, how they should make their living. In the years following the second Riel Rebellion, Indians in the west were not allowed to leave their reserves without the permission of the Indian agent. The government decided who was an Indian and who was not. During the nineteenth century, no other group in Canada was as closely regulated and controlled.

Why were Indian people so closely watched and regulated? Why has this regulation seemed understandable to the public? Why does the phrase 'wild Indians' make the public feel uneasy if not frightened? Conflict between Indians fighting for their land and settlers fighting to take the land happened in the relatively recent past, only a hundred years ago. Or it may be as some have argued, that Indians have always been viewed by historians and other scholars as being a submerged, frighteningly violent part of the Euro-North American psyche (Fielder, 1968).

Indians have always been viewed by Euro-North Americans in comparison with themselves. In the seventeenth century, Europeans believed that all of mankind was descended from Adam, the first man. Europeans also believed in a hierarchy of mankind. At the top of the hierarchy of societies, not surprisingly, were Europeans, and under them in development and 'civilization' were all of the other peoples who were not Europeans.

From the beginning, Europeans had tried to set Indians into this order of peoples. The earliest perceptions of Indians were that they were more like the ancient Romans or Biblical Israelites than they were like Europeans. Lafitau, an early French 'Indian' scholar went to great pains to demonstrate the similarity of North American customs and language to classical models. Early engravings of Indians often present them in poses and clothing that suggests a connection with ancient Greece or Rome. . . .

This tradition of presenting Indian individuals as classical figures has continued well into the twentieth century in the form of heraldry on coats of arms of Canadian cities, (City of Toronto, City of Brantford), provinces (Newfoundland, Nova Scotia), and historical cultural organizations (coat of arms of Ontario Historical Society).

In establishing the hierarchy of societies, the major criteria for classification was industrial technology and material wealth—two accomplishments of which Europeans were very proud. When this criteria was applied to Indians, most Europeans came to the conclusion that 'Indians' were also 'savages'. They lacked all the things that were necessary to be accepted as 'civilized' and as Europeans. They had no printing presses, no books, no wine, no factories, no European style government, no Christianity, no guns, and 'no polite conversations' (Dickason, 1984: 52). The associations of Indians with the European tradition of the 'primitive' half-animal 'wild man' were so strong that Indians were often depicted with long flowing beards and body hair even though explorers repeatedly remarked upon the fact that surprisingly, Indians were not very hairy and did not have beards.

To Cartier on the Gaspe coast in 1534, there was no doubt that the occupants of the new land were to be considered 'wild' men:

This people may well be called savage; for they are the sorriest folk there can be in the world and the whole lot of them had not anything above the value of five sous, their canoes and fishing nets excepted . . . They have no other dwelling but their canoes which they turn upside down and sleep on the ground underneath. They eat their meat almost raw, only warming it a little on the coals and the same with their fish. (Hoffman, 1961: 135)

Described as being without houses, possessions, and comforts, the Indian nonetheless attracted some interest from those Europeans who were interested in changing materialistic European society. Like unfallen man, Adam, the Indians appeared to be very generous with their possessions and as some saw them, completely, 'without evil and without guile' (Berkhofer, 1979: 11). This idyllic 'Adam' side to the 'savage' 'uncivilized' man was used to great effect by those who were dissatisfied with society and sought to reform it. They presented 'Indians' in ways that directly criticized European society.

Peter Martyr's sixteenth century history of the conquest of the 'New World' contrasted the 'crafty deceitful' Europeans with the 'Indians' who lived instead in a world of innocence, liberty, and ease uncorrupted by civilized ideas of property, greed, and luxury (Crane, 1952: 4). In Montaigne's 'On Cannibals', Brazilian people were used to criticize French poverty and social inequality. He contrasted the aboriginal practices of cannibalism with the common European practice of torture and concluded 'better to eat your dead enemy as do the Amerindians than to eat a man alive in the manner of the Europeans' (Dickason, 1984: 56). Similarly the women of France were chastened for their lack of affection for their children, scarcely waiting 'the birth of their children to put them out to nursemaids', unlike 'savage women' who breastfed their own children with no ill physical effects (Jaenan, 1976: 33).

By the seventeenth century, Europeans had certain fixed ideas about what an Indian was supposed to look like. The 'official costume' of Indians in European art was a feather skirt and upright headdress occasionally with some feathers at the wrists and ankles (Chiapelli, 1976: 504). The physical remoteness of Indians to Europeans made it possible to create representations of abstract 'Indians' that bore no resemblance to reality. In a sixteenth century illustration depicting Amerigo Vespucci awakening 'America' from the sleep in her hammock, America is represented as being a nude Indian woman. She is surrounded by European-looking animals in a forest scene; a spear

is propped against a tree. These abstract depictions of Indians created a visual symbolic language that was immediately recognizable as 'Indianness'; nudity, feathers, headdresses, bows and arrows. It was upon this system of symbols that nineteenth and twentieth century symbolic language about 'Indianness' was elaborated and developed.

Whenever Canadian and American society has found itself in competition with Indians over land and resources, the images generated about Indians by the non-Indian public are predictably negative. They are designed to create feelings of hate and anger. The newspaper engravings of the late nineteenth century provide ample examples of images of hate. 'The Sentinel's Evening Visitors', depicting Indian women waiting to get a drink of the guard's whiskey, possibly in exchange for certain services, and the sketch entitled 'Indian Loafers' both from Canadian newspapers, illustrate the feeling of disgust that the public was expected to share with the artist. Depictions of leering crazed Indians threatening women and children, riding demented through their camps crying for scalps, making off with stock animals and anything else that was portable, were common in newspapers of the 1870, and 1880s such as *The Graphic* and *The Illustrated War News*.

The pictorial story in these same newspapers of the Canadian and American participants in the wars with the Indians are strikingly heroic. Although an Indian may be depicted as scowling, demented, savage beyond all reason, the settler or the soldier is neat, calm, and in control. Although threatened, they appear as though they will never be defeated. This sense of the superiority, of 'British cheer and pluck' in the Battle of Batoche was reflected in the newspaper coverage of the victory for the Canadian forces:

The charge started at high noon by routing them out of the advanced pits. At 3:30 p.m. the enemy were totally routed, many having been killed and wounded, many more were prisoners in our hands and others had fled and were hiding in the surrounding bushes. Col. Williams said simply: 'Men will you follow me?' The answer was drowned in a roar of cheering such as I never heard before. Over the bluff we went, yelling like mad. The Indians fired one volley and ran. Neither the Indians nor halfbreeds stood their ground. (Winnipeg Free Press, 13 May 1910)

References

Barbeau, Marus. 1923. *Indian Days in the Canadian Rockies.* Toronto: MacMillan.

Berkhofer, Robert. 1979. *The White Man's Indian.* New York: Vintage Books.

Chiapelli, Fred. 1976. *First Images of America,* Vol. 1. Berkeley: University of California.

Crane, Fred. 1952. 'The Noble Savage in America 1815–1860'. Unpublished PhD Thesis, Yale University.

Dickason, Olive. 1984, *Myth of the Savage.* Calgary: University of Alberta Press.

Fielder, Leslie. 1968. *The Return of the Vanishing American.* Toronto: Stern and Day.

Francis, Douglas, et al., eds. 1986. *Readings in Canadian History: Post Confederation.* Toronto: Holt Rinehart and Winston of Canada, Ltd., pp. 63–127.

Hoffman, Bernard. 1961. *Cabot to Cartier.* Toronto: University of Toronto Press.

Jaenen, C.J. 1976. *Friend and Foe.* New York: Columbia University Press.

Miles, Henry. 1870. *The Child's History of Canada: For the Use of the Elementary Schools and of the Young Reader.* Montreal: Dawson Brothers.

Robins, John D., ed. 1948. 'West by North' in *A Pocketful of Canada,* written for the Canadian Council of Education for Citizenship. Toronto: Collins.

Winnipeg Free Press. 1910. Friday, 13 May. Souvenir Reprint, Glenbow Archives.

Chapter 5

You're Not the Indian I Had in Mind

Thomas King

In 1994, I came up with the bright idea of . . . travelling around North America and taking black-and-white portraits of Native artists for a book and a millennium project. I figured I'd spend a couple of months each year on the road travelling to cities and towns and reserves in Canada and the United States, and when 2000 rolled around, there I'd be with a terrific coffee-table book to welcome the next thousand years.

I should tell you that I had not come up with this idea on my own. As a matter of fact, Edward Sheriff Curtis had already done it, by photographing Indians, that is. Indeed, Curtis is probably the most famous of the Indian photographers. He started his project of photographing the Indians of North America around 1900, and for the next thirty years he roamed the continent, producing some forty thousand negatives, of which more than twenty-two hundred were published.

Curtis was fascinated by the idea of the North American Indian, obsessed with it. And he was determined to capture that idea, that image, before it vanished. This was a common concern among many intellectuals and artists and social scientists at the turn of the nineteenth century, who believed that, while Europeans in the New World were poised on the brink of a new adventure, the Indian was poised on the brink of extinction.

In literature of the United States, this particular span of time is known as the American Romantic Period, and the Indian was tailor-made for it. With its emphasis on feeling, its interest in nature, its fascination with exoticism, mysticism, and eroticism, and its preoccupation with the glorification of the past, American Romanticism found in the Indian a symbol in which all these concerns could be united. Prior to the nineteenth century, the prevalent image of the Indian had been that of an inferior being. The Romantics imagined their Indian as dying. But in that dying, in that passing away, in that disappearing from the stage of human progress, there was also a sense of nobility. . . .

Edgar Allan Poe believed that the most poetic topic in the world was the death of a beautiful woman. From the literature produced during the nineteenth century, second place would have to go to the death of the Indian.

Not that Indians were dying. To be sure, while many of the tribes who lived along the east coast of North America, in the interior of Lower Canada, and in the Connecticut, Ohio, and St Lawrence river valleys, had been injured and disoriented by the years of almost continuous warfare, by European diseases, and by the destructive push of settlers for cheap land. The vast majority of the tribes were a comfortable distance away from the grave.

This was the Indian of fact.

In 1830, when the American president, Andrew Jackson, fulfilling an election promise to his western and southern supporters, pushed the Removal Act through Congress, he did so in order to get rid of thousands of Indians—particularly the Cherokees, Choctaws, Chickasaws, Creeks, and Seminoles—who were not dying and not particularly interested in going anywhere.

These were not the Indians Curtis went west to find.

Curtis was looking for the literary Indian, the dying Indian, the imaginative construct. And to make sure that he would find what he wanted to find, he took along boxes of 'Indian' paraphernalia—wigs, blankets, painted backdrops, clothing—in case he ran into Indians who did not look as the Indian was supposed to look.

I collect postcards. . . . Postcards that depict Indians or Indian subjects. . . .Some of these postcards are old, but many of them are brand new, right off the rack. Two are contemporary pieces from the Postcard Factory in Markham, Ontario. The first shows an older Indian man in a full beaded and fringed leather outfit with an eagle feather war bonnet and a lance, sitting on a horse, set against a backdrop of trees and mountains. The second is a group of five Indians, one older man in a full headdress, sitting on a horse and four younger men on foot: two with bone breastplates, one with a leather vest, and one bare chested. The interesting thing about these two postcards is that the solitary man on his horse is identified only as a 'Cree Indian', while the group of five is designated as 'Native Indians' . . ., as if none of them had names or identities other than the cliché. Though to give them identities, to reveal them to be actual people, would be, I suppose, a violation of the physical laws governing matter and antimatter, that the Indian and Indians cannot exist in the same imagination. . . .

And the Indians do not.

It is my postcard Indian that Curtis was after. And in spite of the fact that Curtis met a great variety of Native people who would have given the lie to the construction, in spite of the fact that he fought vigorously for Native rights and published articles and books that railed against the government's treatment of Indians, this was the Indian that Curtis believed in.

I probably sound a little cranky. I don't mean to. I know Curtis paid Indians to shave away any facial hair. I know he talked them into wearing wigs. I know that he would provide one tribe of Indians with clothing from another tribe because the clothing looked more 'Indian'.

So his photographs would look authentic.

And while there is a part of me that would have preferred that Curtis had photographed his Indians as he found them, the men with crewcuts and moustaches, the women in cotton print dresses, I am grateful that we have his images at all, for the faces of the mothers and fathers, aunts and uncles, sisters and brothers who look at you from the depths of these photographs are not romantic illusions, they are real people.

Native culture, as with any culture, is a vibrant, changing thing, and when Curtis happened upon it, it was changing from what it had been to what it would become next. But the idea of 'the Indian' was already fixed in time and space. Even before Curtis built his first camera, that image had been set. His task, as he visited tribe after tribe, was to sort through what he saw in order to find what he needed.

But to accuse Curtis of romantic myopia is to be petty and to ignore the immensity of the project and the personal and economic ordeal that he undertook. He spent his life photographing and writing about Indians. He died harnessed to that endeavour, and, when I look at his photographs, I can imagine this solitary man moving across the prairies, through the forests, along the coast, dragging behind him an enormous camera and tripod and the cultural expectations of an emerging nation, and I am humbled. . . .

In Roseville, California, where I grew up, race was little more than a series of cultural tributaries that flowed through the town, coming together in confluences, swinging away into eddies. There were at least three main streams, Mexicans, the Mediterranean folk—Italians and Greeks—and the general mix of Anglo-Saxons that a Japanese friend of mine, years later, would refer to as the Crazy Caucasoids. But in Roseville, in the late 1950s and early 1960s, there were no Asian families that I can remember, and the picture I have of my 1961 graduating class does not contain a single black face.

If there was a racial divide in the town, it was the line between the Mexicans and everyone else. Some of the Mexican families had been in the area long before California fell to the Americans in 1848 as a spoil of war. . . .

I went to school with Hernandezes and Gomezes. But I didn't socialize with them, didn't even know where they lived. . . .

Racism is a funny thing, dead quiet on occasion, often dangerous. But sometimes it has a peculiar sense of humour. The guys I ran with looked at Mexicans with a certain disdain. I'd like to say that I didn't, but that wasn't true. No humour here. Except that while I was looking at Mexicans, other people, as it turned out, were looking at me.

In my last year of high school, I mustered enough courage to ask Karen Butler to go to the prom with me. That's not her real name, of course. I've changed it so I don't run the risk of embarrassing her for something that wasn't her fault. . . .

Karen was from the south side, one of the new subdivisions and what cultural theorists in the late twentieth century would call 'havens of homogeneity'.

Karen's mother was a schoolteacher. Her father was a doctor. My mother ran a small beauty shop out of a converted garage. Karen's family was upper middle class. We weren't. Still, there was a levelling of sorts, for Karen had a heart defect. It didn't affect her so far as I could tell, but I figured that being well off with a heart defect was pretty much the same as being poor with pimples. So I asked her if she wanted to go to the prom with me, and she said yes.

Then about a week before the big evening, Karen called me to say that she couldn't go to the dance after all. I'm sorry, she told me. It's my father. He doesn't want me dating Mexicans. . . .

It took my brother and me four days to drive to New Mexico. We could have made the trip in three days, but we kept getting sidetracked by interesting stops. My favourite was a McDonald's on the Will Rogers Turnpike near Claremore, Oklahoma. I generally avoid places like McDonald's but this one had a tiny Will Rogers museum on the first floor of the restaurant, as well as a statue of Rogers himself, twirling a rope, in the parking lot, standing next to a flag-pole. . . .

During the 1930s Rogers was probably the most famous man in North America. He performed in circuses and Wild West shows. He starred in the Zeigfeld Follies, and from 1933 to 1935 he was the top male motion-picture box-office attraction. Over forty million people read his newspaper columns on everything from gun control to Congress, and even more listened to his weekly radio show . . .

Rogers was born near Claremore Oklahoma, and his family was prominent in the Cherokee Nation. But he didn't look Indian, not in that constructed way. Certainly not in the way Curtis wanted Indians to look. And tourists pulling into the parking lot and seeing the statue for the first time would never know that this was an Indian as famous as Sitting Bull or Crazy Horse of Geronimo. Christopher must have read my mind. "The Indians we're going to photograph", he said, walking over to the statue. "What if they all look like Rogers? I know he's Indian", said my brother, "and you know he's Indian, but how is anyone else going to be able to tell?"

Curtis wasn't the only photographer in the early twentieth century who was taking pictures of Indians. So was Richard Throssel. Unless you're a photography buff, you won't know the name and will therefore have no way of knowing that Throssel was not only a contemporary of Curtis's, but that he was also Native. He is Cree to be exact, adopted by the Crow. Throssel even met Curtis, when Curtis came to the Crow reservation.

Throssel took many of the same sort of romantic photographs as Curtis. . . . But he also took other photographs, photographs that moved away from romance toward environmental and social comment. Photographs that did not imagine the Indian as dying or particularly noble, photographs that suggested that Indians were contemporary as well as historical figures. His photograph of Bull Over the Hill's home titled 'The Old and the New', shows a log house with a tipi in the background, and his 1910 photograph 'Interior of the Best Indian Kitchen on the Crow Reservation,' which shows an Indian family dressed in 'traditional' clothing sitting at an elegantly set table in their very contemporary house having tea, suggest that

Native people could negotiate the past and the present with relative ease. His untitled camp scene that juxtaposes traditional tipis with contemporary buggies and a family of pigs, rather than with unshod ponies and the prerequisite herd of buffalo, suggests, at least to my contemporary sensibilities, that Throssel had a penchant for satiric play.

But I'm probably imagining the humour. Throssel was, after all, a serious photographer trying to capture a moment, perhaps not realizing that tripping the shutter captures nothing, that everything on the ground glass changes before the light hits the film plane. What the camera allows you to do is to invent, to create. That's really what photographs are, not records of moments, but rather imaginative acts. . . .

In Curtis's magnum opus, *Portraits from North American Indian Life*, we don't see a collection of photographs of Indian people. We see race. Never mind that race is a construction and an illusion. Never mind that it does not exist in either biology or theology, though both have, from time to time, been enlisted in the cause of racism. Never mind that we can't hear it or smell it or taste it or feel it. The important thing is that we believe we can see it.

In fact, we hope we can see it. For one of the conundrums of the late twentieth century that we've hauled into the twenty-first is that many of our mothers and fathers, who were pursued by missionaries, educators, and government officials (armed with residential schools, European history, legislation such as the Indian Act, the Termination Act, and the Relocation Program of the 1950s), who were forcibly encouraged to give up their identities, now have children who are *determined* to be *seen* as Indians. . . .

When I was going to university, there was an almost irresistible pull to become what Gerald Vizenor calls a 'cultural ritualist', a kind of 'pretend' Indian, an Indian who has to dress up like an Indian and act like an Indian in order to be recognized as an Indian. And in the 1970s, being recognized as an Indian was critical. And here tribal affiliation was not a major consideration. We didn't dress up as nineteenth-century Cherokees or as the Apache, Choctaw, Lakota, Tlingit, Ojibway, Blackfoot, or Haida had dressed. We dressed up as the 'Indian' dressed. We dressed up in a manner to substantiate the cultural lie that had trapped us, and we did so with a passion. I have my own box of photographs. Pictures of me in my 'Indian' outfits, pictures of me being 'Indian', pictures of me in groups of other 'Indians'.

Not wanting to be mistaken for a Mexican or a White, I grew my hair long, bought a fringed leather pouch to hang off my belt, threw a four-strand bone choker around my neck, made a headband out of an old neckerchief, and strapped on a beaded belt buckle that I had bought at a trading post on a reservation in Wyoming. Trinkets of the trade.

I did resist feathers but that was my only concession to cultural sanity.

Not that university was my first experience with the narrow parameters of race. In 1964, I fell into a job as a junior executive at the Bank of America in San Francisco. Junior executive sounds grand, but as I discovered after the first few days, this was what the bank called men who worked as tellers, as opposed to the women who worked as tellers and who were just called tellers. . . .

The steamship company she worked for was called Columbus Lines, an irony that was not lost on me, and, occasionally, she told me, they would take on 'passengers' who could earn their one-way passage to Australia by working aboard the ship.

As it happened, I knew quite a bit about Australia. Just before I moved to San Francisco, I had worked at South Shore Lake Tahoe, a gambling, fun-in-the-sun mecca in the Sierra Nevada Mountains, where I had dated a woman from Australia. Her name was Sharon or Sherry and she told me all about the country, its beaches, the outback, the sharks. . . .

Amazing the way things come around.

The next week I asked the woman from the steamship company what the chances were of my getting a one-way job on one of the company's ships, and she told me she thought they were good. I must admit I could hardly contain my excitement.

Tom King, on a tramp steamer. Tom King, sailing off on a great adventure. Tom King, explorer of known worlds.

So I was disappointed when she came back the next week to tell me that the list of people who wanted to work their way to Australia was quite long and that nothing would come open for at least a year. However, there was a ship sailing for New Zealand in a week, and there was one spot left on the crew. If I wanted it, she said, it was mine.

And so I went. Packed everything I owned into two cheap metal trunks and hauled them to the docks. By the end of the week, I was at sea.

The ship was a German vessel out of Hamburg, the SS SS Cap Colorado. The captain was German. The crew was German. The cook was German. I wasn't German. As a matter of fact, none of the crew was sure what I was. When I told them I was Cherokee, or to keep matters simple, a North American Indian, they were intrigued.

And suspicious.

The cook, who could speak passable English, told me that he had read all of Karl May's novels and had a fair idea of what Indians were supposed to look like and that I wasn't what he had imagined.

'You're not the Indian I had in mind,' he told me.

Here was a small dilemma. Of all the crew members on that ship, the one person I didn't want to offend was the cook. I knew that Indians came in all shapes and sizes and colours, but I hadn't read Karl May, had no idea who he was. The cook had read May but had never actually seen an Indian. So we compromised. I confessed that I was a mixed-blood, and he allowed that this was possible, since May had described full-blood Apaches and not mixed-blood Cherokees.

I discovered some years later that May had never seen an Indian, either, but on board that ship it was probably just as well that I did not know this.

I spent almost a year in New Zealand. I worked as a deer culler, a beer bottle sorter, a freezer packer, and a photographer. I liked the country and might well have stayed had it not been for a phone call I got early one morning. It was a British-sounding man who introduced himself as an official with the immigration department.

If I'm not mistaken, he said, clipping the edges off each consonant, you entered the country eleven months ago on a thirty-day tourist visa and are therefore in violation of New Zealand immigration laws.

I agreed that he was probably correct.

"When might we expect you to leave?" he wanted to know.

As I said, I liked the place, had no plans to leave, so I asked him if there was any chance of applying for an immigration visa.

It turned out my immigration man had only newly arrived from England the month before to take up his duties and wasn't sure if this was possible. But he would check into it, he told me. In the meantime, would I give him some of my particulars.

It was the usual stuff. Name. Colour of hair. Colour of eyes. Height. Weight. Race.

Black, brown, six feet six inches, 230 pounds. Indian.

"Dear me," he said. "I don't believe we take applications from Indians."

I have to admit I was stunned. "Why not?" I wanted to know.

"Policy," said the immigration man.

"Do you get many?" I asked.

"Oh, yes," he said, "thousands."

I hadn't heard of any mass exodus of Native peoples from Canada or the States. These Indians, I asked him, where are they from? Alberta? Saskatchewan? Arizona? South Dakota? Oklahoma?

Dear me, no, said my British voice. They're from, you know, New Delhi, Bombay . . .

When Karen told me her father wouldn't let me take her to the prom because he didn't want her dating Mexicans, I told her I wasn't Mexican. I was Indian.

When the immigration officer told me I couldn't apply for a visa because I was Indian, I told him I wasn't East Indian, I was North American Indian.

As if that was going to settle anything.

Without missing a beat, and at the same time injecting a note of enthusiasm into his otherwise precise voice, the immigration man said, "What? Do you mean like cowboys and Indians?"

The next week, I was on a ship for Australia. . . .

But in all my travels, I never met an indigenous Australian. In New Zealand, I had met a great many Maoris, and while there had been friction between Maoris and Europeans, the two groups seemed to have organized themselves around an uneasy peace between equals. In Australia, there was no such peace. Just a damp, sweltering campaign of discrimination that you could feel on your skin and smell in your hair.

The Aboriginal people, I was told, were failing. They were dying off at such a rate that they wouldn't last another decade. It was sad to see them passing away, but their problem, according to the men who gathered in the bars after work, was that they did not have the same mental capacities as Whites. There was no point in educating them because they had no interest in improving their lot and were perfectly happy living in poverty and squalor.

The curious thing about these stories was I had heard them all before, knew them, in fact, by heart.

Eventually I wound up in Sydney and lied my way into a job as a journalist with a third-rate magazine called *Everybody's*—a disingenuous name if ever there was one. . . .

There was a photographer who worked for the magazine. Let's say that, after all these years, I've forgotten his name. So, we'll call him Lee. Lee was a decent enough guy, but, because there were no Aboriginal people in the immediate vicinity, Lee spent many of these smoky evenings sharpening his soggy wit on me.

Lee didn't know any more about Indians than had the cook on the tramp steamer or Karl May or the immigration man, but he reckoned that North Americans had taken care of the problem in a reasonably expedient fashion. I'm embarrassed to repeat his exact words but the gist of it was that North Americans had shot Native men and bred Native women until they were White.

In a perverse way, I've always liked people like Lee. They are, by and large, easy to deal with. Their racism is honest and straightforward. You don't have to go looking for it in a phrase or a gesture. And you don't have to wonder if you're being too sensitive. Best of all, they remind me how the past continues to inform the present.

One Monday, Lee stopped by my desk with a present for me. It was a cartoon that he had gotten one of the guys in the art department to work up. It showed a stereotypical Indian in feathers and leathers with a bull's eye on his crotch and flies buzzing around him. 'Office of Chief Screaching [sic] Eagle Goldstein', the caption read. 'Payola and bribes acceptable in the form of checks or money orders. No silver please.' Just above the Indian was 'Happy Barmizvah Keemosaby' and just below was 'only living Cherokee Jew.'

Lee stood at my desk, waiting for me to smile. I told him it was funny as hell, and he said, yeah, everyone he had showed it to thought it was a scream. I had the cartoon mounted on a board and stuck it on my desk.

I still have it. Just in case I forget.

So it was unanimous. Everyone knew who Indians were. Everyone knew what we looked like. Even Indians. But . . . I realized, for perhaps the first time, that I didn't know. Or more accurately, I didn't know how I wanted to represent Indians. My brother was right. Will Rogers did not look like an Indian. Worse, as I cast my mind across the list of Native artists I had come west to photograph, many of them friends . . . I realized that a good number of them didn't look Indian, either.

Yet how can something that has never existed—the Indian—have form and power while something that is alive and kicking—Indians—are invisible?

Edward Sheriff Curtis.

James Fenimore Cooper, George Catlin, Paul Kane, Charles Bird King, Karl May, the Atlanta Braves, the Washington Redskins, the Chicago Blackhawks, Pontiac (the car, not the Indian), Land O'Lakes butter, Calumet baking soda, Crazy Horse Malt Liquor, *A Man Called Horse*, Iron Eyes Cody, *Dances with Wolves*, *The Searchers*, the Indian Motorcycle Company, American Spirit tobacco, Native American Barbie, Chippewa Springs Golf Course, John Augustus Stone, the Cleveland Indians, Disney's Pocahontas, Geronimo shoes, the Calgary Stampede, Cherokee brand underwear, the Improved Order of Red Men, Ralph Hubbard and his Boy Scout troop, Mutual of Omaha, Buffalo Bill's Wild West Show, the Boston Tea Party, Frank Hamilton Cushing, William Wadsworth Longfellow, the Bank of Montreal, Chief's Trucking, Grey Owl, *The Sioux Spaceman*, Red Man chewing tobacco, Grateful Dead concerts, Dreamcatcher perfume.

In the end, there is no reason for the Indian to be real. The Indian simply has to exist in our imaginations.

But for those of us who are Indians, this disjunction between reality and imagination is akin to life and death. For to be seen as 'real', for people to 'imagine' us as Indians, we must be 'authentic'.

In the past, authenticity was simply in the eye of the beholder. Indians who looked Indian were authentic. Authenticity only became a problem for Native people in the twentieth century. While it is true that mixed-blood and full-blood rivalries pre-date this period, the question of who was an Indian and who was not was easier to settle. What made it easy was that most Indians lived on reserves of one sort or another (out of sight of Europeans) and had strong ties to a particular community, and the majority of those people who 'looked Indian' and those who did not at least had a culture and a language in common.

This is no longer as true as it once was, for many Native people now live in cities, with only tenuous ties to a reserve or a nation. Many no longer speak their Native language, a gift of colonialism, and the question of identity has become as much a personal matter as it is a matter of blood. N. Scott Momaday has suggested that being Native is an idea that an individual has of themselves. Momaday, who is Kiowa, is not suggesting that anyone who wants to can imagine themselves to be Indian. He is simply acknowledging that language and narrow definitions of culture are not the only ways identity can be constructed. Yet, in the absence of visual confirmation, these 'touch-stones'—race, culture, language, blood—still form a kind of authenticity test, a racial-reality game that contemporary Native people are forced to play. And here are some of the questions.

Were you born on a reserve? Small, rural towns with high Native populations will do. Cities will not.

Do you speak your Native language? Not a few phrases here and there. Fluency is the key. No fluency, no Indian.

Do you participate in your tribe's ceremonies? Being a singer or a dancer is a plus, but not absolutely required.

Are you a full-blood?

Are you a status Indian?

Are you enrolled?

You may suspect me of hyperbole, but many of these were questions that I was asked by a selection committee when I applied for a Ford Foundation Grant for American Indians in order to complete my PhD. I've told this story a number of times at various events, and each time I've told it, one or two non-Natives have come up to me afterwards and apologized for the stereotypical attitudes of a few misguided Whites. But the truth of the matter is that the selection committee was composed entirely of Native people. And the joke, if there is one, is that most of the committee couldn't pass this test, either, for these questions were not designed to measure academic potential or to ensure diversity, they were designed to exclude. For the real authenticity is in the rarity of a thing.

Of course, outside grant selection committees and possibly guards at the new and improved US border crossings, not many people ask these questions. They don't have to. They're content simply looking at you. If you don't look Indian, you aren't. If you don't look White, you're not. . . .

When I came up with my bright idea for a photographic expedition, I sat down with a number of granting agencies to see if there was any chance of getting some financial support for the project.

Several of them thought the idea had merit, but they weren't sure why I wanted to do it.

Which Indians did I have in mind, they wanted to know. How would I find these Indians? How would taking photographs of Native artists benefit Native people?

Had J.P. Morgan asked that question of Edward Curtis, Curtis probably would have told him that such photographs were necessary because the Indian was dying, and if he hesitated, the Noble Red Man would be gone and that part of America's antiquity would be lost forever. Curtis might have even thrown up John Audubon and Audubon's great endeavour to paint the birds of North America, many of whom were on the verge of extinction and might well have been helped on their way, since, in order to paint the birds, Audubon first had to kill them.

So they wouldn't move and spoil the sitting.

How will taking photographs of Native artists benefit Native people?

It wasn't a question I would have ever asked. It was a question—and I understood this part clearly—that came out of a Western Judeo-Christian sense of responsibility and that contained the unexamined implication that the lives of Native people needed improvement. I knew, without a doubt, that the pictures I was taking would not change the lives of the people I photographed any more than the arrivals and departures of, say, anthropologists on Native reserves had done anything to improve the lives of the people they came to study. . . .

Appearance.

I want to look Indian so that you will see me as Indian because I want to be Indian, even though being Indian and looking Indian is more a disadvantage than it is a luxury.

Just not for me.

Middle-class Indians, such as myself, can, after all, afford the burden of looking Indian. There's little danger that we'll be stuffed into the trunk of a police cruiser and dropped off on the outskirts of Saskatoon. Not much chance that we'll come before the courts and be incarcerated for a longer period of

our non-Indian brethren. Hardly any risk
hildren will be taken from us because we
e to cope with the potentials of poverty.

That sort of thing happens to those other Indians.
My relatives. My friends.

Just not me. . . .

What's important are the stories I've heard along
the way. And the stories I've told. Stories we make
up to try to set the world straight.

Take Will Rogers's story, for instance. It's yours.
Do with it what you will. Make it the topic of a
discussion group at a scholarly conference. Put it
on the Web. Forget it. But don't say in the years to
come that you would have lived your life differently if only you had heard this story.

You've heard it now.

Chapter 6

Colonialism and First Nations Women in Canada

Winona Stevenson

The intent of this chapter is to provide a brief
overview of the historic colonization of First
Nations women from contact to the end of the
early reserve era.[1] More specifically, it will describe
the goals and rationalizations of colonial agencies,
demonstrate how colonial agencies manipulated
public perceptions of First Nations women to
rationalize their subjugation, and describe the process by which the Victorian patriarchy was imposed
on First Nations women and societies through
federal legislation.[2] This chapter is intended as an
outline history; as such, it draws heavily from
existing studies on various aspects of Aboriginal
women's history. . . .

French–First Nations Relations

Early French colonial policy towards Aboriginal
Peoples was shaped by two influential ideologies—

mercantilism and Roman Catholicism (Frideres,
1998: 15). Initially, only a handful of merchants
emigrated to New France and they were totally
dependent on Aboriginal Peoples for subsistence,
survival, and fur gathering skills. In order to secure
Indian trade partners, fur traders entered into
already existing Aboriginal trade networks and alliance systems which were quite unlike any they
were used to. In most Aboriginal societies trade
was more than an economic venture—trade was
facilitated through diplomatic relationships which
included personal, social, political, and military
obligations (Dickason, 1992). These alliances were
cemented through marriage, adoption, and ceremony. Interracial marriages unsanctioned by
church ceremony followed Indigenous rites and
became known as *mariages à la façon du pays*, or
'marriage according to the custom of the country'.
Marriages between French fur traders and

Aboriginal women were initially common practice and, for a short time, became French policy (Dickason, 1985). . . .

The French Crown relied on the Roman Catholic missionaries to convert Aboriginal Peoples on the grounds that Christian conversion and French 'civilizing' influences would make them more loyal and stronger allies. One of the missionary priorities was to regularize interracial marriages according to Christian practices and to facilitate their work, they convinced the colonial authorities to offer official incentives. In 1680, Versaille allocated 50 livres, each as dowries to French and Aboriginal women marrying French men. Funds were also allocated for the education of Aboriginal girls to prepare them for marriage, which the Ursulines had been providing since they arrived in 1639 (Dickason, 1992; Ray, 1996). The overall objective of the program was the creation of a settled and farming mixed-blood population that was culturally French yet possessing the physical strength, knowledge, and skills of their mothers' people. . . .

'[P]acification and reconciliation' through Indigenous alliance systems were the foundations for French Indian policy throughout the seventeenth century (Jaenen, 1991: 27). The primary objectives were conversion to Catholicism and the eventual assimilation of Aboriginal Peoples into French civil and commercial life through incorporation, rather than by force or extinguishment of Aboriginal title. This policy required French authorities to restrict settlement to the lower St Lawrence Valley, allowing only small fur trade and military posts in First Nations territories beyond. Within New France a number of mission reserves were established, but beyond its boundaries First Nations self-determination and territorial rights were respected (Jaenen, 1991).

English–First Nations Relations

The English entered present-day Canada on two fronts: the eastern seaboard colonies of New England and Hudson's Bay in the far Northwest. Relations between Aboriginal Peoples and English colonists to the south of New France were negative,

almost from the start. Unlike the French, the English fur trade on the eastern seaboard was inconsequential in light of the rush for agricultural settlement.[3] Aboriginal survival skills in New England were only required when English colonists first arrived. Once established, the English colonists expanded by pushing into coveted Aboriginal lands by force. Driven by land lust and exonerated by manifest destiny ideology, English colonists waged war on Aboriginal communities. . . . The English followed a policy of expediency—when ignoring Aboriginal Peoples was no longer feasible in their rush for land, they annihilated them or pushed them onto small, isolated, and marginal tracts of land. English colonials on the eastern seaboard maintained that 'a "savage" could never validly exercise sovereignty' which only organized states, and some added Christian states, could assert (Dickason, 1992: 177). . . .

Initially the fur trade was characterized by mutual exchange and interdependency. As the fur trade became increasingly entrenched, however, the balance of power shifted. Ron Bourgeault (1991) describes how the patriarchy and the commodification of First Nation resources and labour introduced by the fur trade slowly destroyed egalitarian or communal relations between First Nations men and women. As the fur trade expanded in Western Canada, female labour power and sexuality were commodified and male private property introduced. In some instances, Aboriginal women benefited materially from their roles as intermediaries between their peoples and fur traders, but many more were exploited and abused (Bourgeault, 1991; Van Kirk, 1987). . . .

Colonial Representations of First Nations Women

Smandych and Lee stress that any attempt to explain aspects of 'the relationship linking law, colonialism and gender relations in post-contact societies' needs to address issues raised in recent feminist and Native ethnohistorical studies (1995: 29). In an effort to explain the rationales behind the subjugation of First Nations women, scholars have paid special attention to how stereotypical images of Aboriginal women were historically constructed. European colonialists arrived on our shores with predetermined ideas of appropriate female behaviour and status which served as their lens for 'understanding' the behaviour and status of Aboriginal women.

Recent studies demonstrate that the ideal condition of women in Western European society served as an index of 'civilization' (Shoemaker, 1995; Acoose, 1995; Smith, 1987; Weist, 1983; Smits, 1982; Fee, 1973). According to this index, how a society treated its women indicated its place on the social evolutionary scale. The status and condition of European women represented the pinnacle of civilization, the result of a 'long and painful evolutionary struggle away from nature' (Fee, 1973: 24) and a 'victory of self-discipline over instinct' (Cominos, 1963: 219).

The European ideal of womanhood, or the 'cult of true womanhood', revolved around female domesticity (Riley, 1986). The appropriate position of women was confinement to the household where they were enjoined to subordinate their wills to their fathers, husbands, or nearest appropriate male relative, and to direct their energies to the efficient management of the resources their men provided. The ideal woman was characterized by the virtues of piety, purity, submissiveness, and domesticity (Weist, 1983). She was defined as a nurturer, providing 'selfless, gentle, benign, and humane' support for her family. She was further burdened with the responsibility of socializing her children, of transmitting the cultural disciplines, morals, and values of her society to the next generation (M. Young, 1980: 98). By the nineteenth century, the ideal woman emerged as the prime symbol of civility and represented female emancipation at its peak (Riley, 1986).

The European ideal of womanhood was projected on Aboriginal societies throughout the colonized world where it functioned as 'the single most important criterion for contrasting savagism with civility' (Smits, 1982: 298). Victorian morality was the severe standard against which Aboriginal women were judged. They were ultimately found

wanting because almost everything about their being—their appearance, their social, economic, political, and spiritual positions, activities, and authority—was a violent affront to the European ideal. Compared to European women, Aboriginal women appeared 'antithetical to the presumed natural condition of women' (Weist, 1983: 39).

Confronted by women who were almost the exact counter-image of their own culture's ideal, initially caused much confusion in the minds of early European observers in present-day Canada. Where European women were fragile and weak, Aboriginal women were hard-working and strong; where European women were confined to affairs of the household, Aboriginal women were economically independent and actively involved in the public sphere; where European women were chaste and dependent on men, Aboriginal women had considerable personal autonomy and independence—they controlled their own sexuality, had the right to divorce, and owned the products of their labour (Leacock, 1980; Grumet, 1980; Devens, 1992; J. Brown, 1975).

In the early phases of the Western fur trade, many of the traits that set Aboriginal women apart from European women were valued by European men. A number of studies demonstrate that European men soon became dependent on the traditional hunting, gathering, and manufacturing skills of Aboriginal women, for their personal survival, and on their abilities as interpreters, cultural mediators, and guides to further the trade (Van Kirk, 1996, 1980; J.S.H. Brown, 1980). Many fur traders were intimately associated with Aboriginal women and learned much about traditional societies, but their documented perceptions strongly reflect their Western European sensitivities and biases. . . . Fur traders were shocked by the physical strength of Aboriginal women, by their clothing and beautifying styles, marriage and child-rearing practices, and by what they perceived as the drudgery of Aboriginal women's lives. In their ideal world, women were frail, dependent on men, and incapable of laborious tasks. In contrast, Aboriginal women made substantial contributions through small animal hunting, fishing, and gathering, and among some First Nations were full-time horticulturalists. When big game hunting failed, women were the sole providers for their families and communities. Furthermore, the economic contributions they made translated into considerable personal autonomy, since women were generally responsible for distributing the products of their labour and were owners of the household (Bourgeault, 1991; Etienne and Leacock, 1980; Van Kirk, 1980; Anderson, 1992).

The cumulative affect of all this was that Aboriginal women were understood and represented in ambiguous and contradictory terms—the 'noble savagess' (Princess) or the 'ignoble savagess' (Squaw Drudge).[4] The former is the archetypal Indian Princess, 'a Pocahontas type who was virginal', 'childlike, naturally innocent', beautiful, helper and mate to European men, and inclined to civilization and Christian conversion (Smith, 1987: 65). Her antithesis, the Squaw Drudge, is characterized as a 'squat, haggard, papoose-lugging drudge who toiled endlessly', who 'lived a most unfortunate, brutal life', and 'fought enemies with a vengeance and thirst for blood unmatched by any man' (Smith, 1987: 65). In contrast to her noble sister, the Squaw Drudge is also sexually licentious, ugly, beast of burden, and slave to men (Weist, 1983; Acoose, 1995).

This binary classification has its roots in the patriarchal Victorian virgin–whore dichotomy. However, colonialist imperatives, supported by racist ideology, intensified the binary imaging of Aboriginal women. In the minds of European men, the perceived condition of First Nations women was understood as an inevitable condition of their savagery. Unlike European women, Aboriginal women faced a 'peculiar kind of sexism . . . grounded in the pernicious and ever-present ideologies of racism' (Albers, 1983: 15). Also unlike European women, their burden was even more severe—to be 'good' they had to defy their own people, exile themselves from them, and transform into the European ideal (Green, 1990: 18). Their nobility as 'princesses' or their savagery as 'squaw drudges' were defined in terms of their relationship

to or with European men. Images of Aboriginal women, initially ambivalent and contradictory, became unambiguously negative and unidimensional when missionaries arrived on the scene. . . .

More than any other colonial agency, missionaries represented the condition of Aboriginal women in fatalistic and derogatory terms. Missionaries found no redeeming qualities; in their indigenous form Aboriginal women had no value (Carter, 1984). While many fur traders viewed Aboriginal women multidimensionally, missionaries could only see the debased 'savage'. Missionaries condemned almost everything about First Nations ways of life that appeared to challenge or violate 'civilized' Christian norms. However, they were especially damning of those aspects of Aboriginal women's lives and characters that appeared to blatantly transgress the European 'ideal woman' construct. Vivid descriptions of Aboriginal women as exploited, overworked drudges, abused, misused, dirty, haggard, resigned, and beaten abound in missionary literature (Devens, 1992; Carter, 1984; Leacock, 1980; E.R. Young, 1893; McLean, 1889; Jones, 1861; West, 1823). Missionaries generally believed that 'mutual love and sympathy' in Aboriginal family life 'was unknown in their pagan state' (E.R. Young, 1893: 63). Whereas civilized people 'pampered their women; savage people mistreated them' (Smith, 1987: 66). At best, Aboriginal women were pitied and their wretched state was blamed on the savagism of their men. Images of Aboriginal women created by men like the Reverend Egerton Ryerson Young, a Methodist missionary among Lake Winnipeg Cree and Saulteaux Peoples from 1868 to 1876, reflect their Eurocentric biases:

> This was one of the sad aspects of paganism which I often had to witness as I travelled among those bands that had not, up to that time, accepted the Gospel. When these poor women got old and feeble, very sad and deplorable is their condition. When able to toil and slave, *they are tolerated as necessary Evils.* When aged and weak, they are shamefully neglected, and, often, put out of existence. (E.R. Young 1893: 48, emphasis added)

Young was a popular and prolific writer of frontier adventure stories based on his experiences among First Nations Peoples. His representations of First Nations Peoples reached a huge audience. Speaking from personal experience, Janice Acoose reminds us that the negative images created in the past have an enduring quality that has dramatically impacted First Nation women's history and life:

> Such representations create very powerful images that perpetuate stereotypes, and perhaps more importantly, foster dangerous attitudes that affect human relations and inform institutional ideology. (1995: 39–40).

Missionaries directly attacked those aspects of Aboriginal women's lives and characters that exemplified their personal autonomy and independence. More specifically, they assailed the lack of patriarchal family structures, complementarity in gender relations, female authority in the household, polygamy, the rights of both sexes to divorce, sexual freedom outside of marriage, and female ownership of and control over lands, resources, and produce (Anderson, 1992; Carter, 1984; Weist, 1983; Smits, 1982; Leacock, 1981, 1980).

As early as the 1650s, Jesuit missionaries among the Montagnais and Naskapi of present-day Quebec attempted to restructure their society by introducing the European family organization complete with male authority, female fidelity, and the elimination of the right of divorce (Leacock, 1980). . . . Divorce, polygamy, and sexual freedom were a major 'source of horror' to missionaries (Nock, 1988, 55; Devens, 1992; Buffalohead, 1983; Leacock, 1980). . . .

While missionaries recognized that their cultural replacement programs would be difficult to impose, they did not anticipate vehement resistance from Aboriginal women, especially as they were accustomed to female submissiveness.

Female Resistance to Christian Conversion

Aboriginal women resisted Christian conversion and its concomitant social imperatives. This resistance was effective enough to compel missionaries, as agents of social change, to seek the coercive backing of the state. . . .

While European missionaries represented Aboriginal women's lot in life in super-negative terms, they also provide evidence that Aboriginal women had far more personal freedom, independence, and security than Western European women. As recent studies demonstrate, one of the many ironies of the Christian–Aboriginal encounter was that Aboriginal women had far more personal autonomy and self-determination than their 'emancipated' European counterparts (Devens, 1992; Smith, 1987; Lurie, 1972). As such, they had little or nothing to gain by converting to Christianity until external pressures became intolerable.

The work of the late Eleanor Leacock into seventeenth century Jesuit mission records provides fascinating insights into the female conversion process used on the Montagnais-Naskapi of Quebec and into female resistance. Missionaries first had to convince men of the righteousness of the patriarchy, especially male domination and the principle of punishment. Once converted, a handful of Montagnais men were encouraged to forcefully impose their newly acquired authority on women and children who suffered terrible psychological and physical pain at their hands. Some of the punishments LeJeune's neophytes subjected their women to included withholding food, public and private beatings, head-shearing, and incarcerations. Women resisted covertly by sabotaging neophyte men's work; and overtly by physically fighting back and running away (Leacock, 1981, 1980).

Aboriginal women resisted marital monogamy because polygamy was both practical and preferred (Leacock, 1980; Devens, 1992). Warfare and the dangers of male occupations reduced the number of marriageable men; polygamy ensured that all women desiring marriage could acquire it. . . .

Many Aboriginal women resisted Christian marriage to maintain control over access to resources and the right to distribute the products of family labour. Tlingit women in Northern British Columbia, for example, handled all family wealth and managed trade activities. When urged to 'legitimate' their marriages they resisted on the grounds that they refused to hand over their 'purse strings' to their husbands (Klein, 1976: 173). . . . Privately, mothers resisted the mission education of their daughters in an effort to protect and hide them from missionary influences, especially during their early formative years (Devens, 1992). Mission schools posed a threat to the socialization of their children and to the cultural integrity of the community. . . .

Indian agents reported that women resisted 'any progress towards modernization' and were 'a hindrance to the advancement of men' (Carter, 1996a: 162). The reality was that women preferred traditional airy and clean tents over dark, dirt-floored cabins, plus there was always a great shortage of household maintenance supplies. . . .

The historical evidence demonstrates that when Aboriginal women were faced with losing personal autonomy and power, they resisted. They resisted the patriarchy because it threatened to undermine their socio-economic autonomy and because it threatened the socio-cultural cohesion of their communities. . . . The strength and tenacity of female resistance to colonial intrusion is well known among Aboriginal Peoples—as the old Cheyenne proverb goes, 'A nation is not conquered until the hearts of its women are on the ground.'

Missionary and State Strategies and Collaboration

. . . To garner support for the mission enterprise, missionary literature employed what Gerald Berreman (1962) calls 'impressionistic management'. Missionaries wrote to please their readers and to elicit public and government support. In their attempts to persuade readers of the righteousness of their vocation missionaries capitalized on negative stereotypes—they had to convince their readers of the savage wretchedness of Aboriginal life. Since the condition of women 'was the single most important criterion for contrasting savagism with civility' (Smits, 1982: 298), missionaries represented Aboriginal women's lives and characters in the most negative light. If anything could

touch the hearts of philanthropists and good Christians, it was 'woman as victim'.

Missionary representations of the degraded condition of women served an even larger object— they provided the ideological rationale for colonial conquest, dispossession, and cultural genocide. As Sarah Carter points out in her study of missionary literature, by 'proving the inferiority of the Indian, the missionaries provided justification for the appropriation of their land' and convinced their readers 'that there was every justification and, indeed, a great need to transfer the future of the Indians and their lands into more capable hands' (1984: 41, 40). Expounding on the righteous triumph of civilization over savagery, missionaries also provided relief to those experiencing guilt or 'personal anxieties about the destruction of Indian societ[ies]' (Smits, 1982: 281).

Rayna Green demonstrates further that colonial representations of the ignoble Squaw Drudge, and all she stands for, reduce Aboriginal women to powerless and depersonalized objects of scorn. Like her male counterpart, the Bloodthirsty Savage, she can be easily destroyed without reference to her humanity and 'her physical removal can be understood as necessary to the progress of civilization' (Green, 1990: 20–1).

The fact that Aboriginal women resisted Christian conversion provided missionaries with even more justification to employ coercive conversion tactics and to solicit support from the state. Since missionary goals for Aboriginal peoples differed little from the goals established by the Canadian Indian Department, these two powerful colonial agencies combined their forces—missionaries provided the ideological rationale for government to develop and employ coercive cultural transformation strategies. . . .

The Statutory Subjugation of First Nations Women

From 1850 on, colonial legislatures, and later the Federal Government of Canada, imposed a series of regulations intended to enforce the patriarchy and coerce Aboriginal women to conform to the regiments and edicts demanded by local missionaries and Indian agents in present-day eastern Canada. . . .

The authority under which the Federal government based its coercive powers was the 1867 British North America Act. Section 91(24) of the BNA Act gave the Federal Government of Canada exclusive jurisdiction over the administration of Indians and lands reserved for Indians. . . .

Following the transfer of Rupert's Land from the HBC to Canada, the federal government extended its authority over Western Canada through a series of Treaties with First Nations from 1870 to 1921. These treaties, combined with the imposition of the 1876 Indian Act on Western First Nations, strongly demonstrate that the federal government's primary concern was to clear the land for newly arriving settler populations. . . .

Missionaries provided the state with (mis)information about the lives and conditions of Aboriginal people that justified the colonial enterprise and sanctioned, or authorized, the wholesale attack on Aboriginal cultures. Not only did missionaries provide the ideological rationale for the subjugation of Aboriginal Peoples, they also had direct input into the development of federal Indian policies and regulations (Deven, 1992; Cole, 1990; Nock, 1988; Fiske, 1987; Grant, 1984; Fisher, 1983). . . .

Perhaps the most oppressive and controversial legal manoeuvre of the colonial, and later federal, government was to usurp the right to determine who was, and who was not, an 'Indian'. The first definition was passed by the Lower Canada legislature in 1850 for the purpose of Indian administration, but it wasn't until 1869 that definition by patrilineage was imposed (Canada, SPC 1850, c.41; Canada, SC 1869, c.6).[5] . . . By the stroke of a pen First Nations women and their children could be denied their birth right as First Nation citizens, depending on whom they married—if born registered Indians, they could only remain 'Indian' if they married a registered Indian man or never married at all. . . .

First Nation responses to the membership provisions of the 1869 Indian Act were immediate. In 1872 the Grand Council of Ontario and Quebec Indians sent letters of protest on behalf of the Six Nations First Nation of Brantford, Ontario, demanding that the provision be amended,

so that Indian women may have the privilege of marrying when and whom they please; without subjecting themselves to exclusion or expulsion of their tribes and the consequent loss of property and rights. (cited in Jamieson, 1978: 31–2).

During the Treaty No. 1 negotiations at the Stone Fort in Manitoba, Saulteaux First Nation leaders strongly opposed the exclusionary definition of 'Indian'. . . .

The immediate and long-term effect of this provision was to reduce the number of status Indians the government was responsible for,[6] impose the European patrilineage system, and elevate the power and authority of men at the expense of women. . . .

In 1951 this regulation was amended, making it even more stringent by denying women who married-out, their First Nation/Band membership. Under law, she in fact ceased to be an 'Indian', denied protection and benefits under the Indian Act and her First Nations membership. The loss of First Nations membership meant, in tangible terms, that women lost the right to live on-reserve free from taxation or liens; be buried on-reserve; receive their fair share of First Nation annuities, revenues, and any on-reserve services like health and education (Canada, SC 1951, c.29). In more intangible terms, it meant they lost the right to live on traditional lands, participate in First Nations local activities (cultural, social, economic, spiritual), and raise their children in the traditional extended family system. They were legally stripped of their identity and forced to make their way, as best they could, in an alien society. This regulation remained in effect until the Indian Act was revised in 1985 by Bill C-31.[7]

The primary goal of the federal government's Indian policy was the destruction of tribal organization, cultural transformation, and the eventual assimilation of all First Nation Peoples into the Canadian mainstream body politic (Tobias, 1983). . . .

The impact of this provision on First Nations women was severe. First Nations men were given the unilateral authority to enfranchise their dependents—wives and children (Canada, SC 1876, c.18, s.86; Canada, SC 1918, c.26, s.6(2)). Women's legal status as First Nation citizens could be unilaterally and irrevocably stolen by federal legislation that allowed their fathers or husbands to make decisions on their behalf. This regulation was a major affront to women's autonomy— women had no recourse if their fathers or husbands 'sold' them out of status. It also seriously undermined the matrilineal descent rule of many tribes by giving men authority to decide whether or not their families would retain First Nation membership. The voluntary enfranchisement provisions remained in effect until 1985.

To facilitate assimilation, the Indian Act also provided for compulsory or involuntary enfranchisement. Any First Nations individual who lived in a foreign country for five simultaneous years could lose their First Nations membership and be denied the right to return home (Canada, SC 1876, c.18, s.3a). In addition, any . . . First Nations person who exhibited any of the qualities considered 'civilized' could no longer remain a First Nations person in the eyes of the government. The long-term objective of the federal government was succinctly stated by Superintendent General of Indian Affairs, Duncan Campbell Scott, in 1920:

> Our objective is to continue until there is not a single Indian in Canada that has not been absorbed into the body politic, and there is no Indian question and no Indian Department. (cited in Jamieson, 1978: 50).

Despite the hopes of Indian Department officials and missionaries, however, the involuntary enfranchisement provision was repealed after a few years, following considerable opposition from First Nations leadership. In 1933 involuntary enfranchisement was slipped into the Indian Act once more and while it remained in effect until 1951 it was made ineffectual and eventually abandoned because of First Nations protest (Canada, SC 1932–33, c.42, s.110(14)). . . .

Women who had children out of wedlock also came under attack. . . . The sexual autonomy of Indigenous women and their right to divorce were also violated in the 1876 Indian Act. . . . A final assault on women's rights to divorce occurred when the federal government imposed federal divorce laws on status Indians. In order to obtain a legal divorce, Indian women were bound by Canadian law which required more burdensome grounds of proof for women than for men (Montour, 1987). . . .

Provisions in the 1869 Gradual Enfranchisement of Indians Act were the first to officially exclude First Nations women from participating in local First Nation governance. . . . In its attempt to destroy traditional First Nations governments the state introduced an elected local government system based on the European municipal model. . . . Women were totally excluded from voting or running for office. The Act required that the Chief and council be elected 'by the male members of each Indian settlement of the full age of twenty-one years at such time and place, and in such manner, as the Superintendent General of Indian Affairs may direct' (Canada, SC 1869, c.6, s.10). . . .

Regardless of how resistant traditional leaders were to the elective system, women were not allowed to participate at any level of local government until 1951 revisions to the Indian Act (Canada, SC 1951, c.29).

The Indian Act also undermined female authority by denying them the right to participate in decisions concerning the disposition of reserve lands. The authority of Iroquois women as guardians and inheritors of the land, for example, was thwarted by the Indian Act which gave the authority to release and surrender reserve lands exclusively to men. The regulation stated that land surrenders were to be 'assented to by a majority of the male members of the band of the full age of twenty-one' (Canada, SC 1876, c.18, s.26(1)). . . .

Conclusion

From the first arrival of missionaries in our lands, the status and autonomy of First Nations women was attacked. When colonial authorities, later the Federal Government of Canada, assumed authority over First Nations Peoples, the attack on First Nations women was institutionalized. Through various Indian Acts and amendments, First Nations women's autonomy in the areas of membership, marriage, divorce, and sexuality were undermined, along with female relations to land and family property, and political decision-making. The overall intent of this legislation was to reduce First Nations women to a condition of dependency on their male relatives.

However, First Nations women did rot readily bow down to the foreign patriarchy. They resisted their oppression and retained much of their traditional knowledge and roles. Over time, many of the discriminatory sections of the Indian Act were repealed, but not in time to stay the internalization of many European patriarchal notions and practices. The irony in this story is that, in direct contrast to the experiences of Euro-Canadian women, Aboriginal women's 'emancipation', in fact, intended their subjugation.

While colonialist transformation programs wreaked terrible damage on First Nations communities, they were not entirely successful. Traditional knowledge and skills were hidden by those Aboriginal men and women who resisted total cultural transformation. The healing and spiritual revitalization efforts in our communities today attest to the tenacity of traditional Indigenous lifeways.

Notes

1. The cut-off date for this overview was selected because it somewhat marks the end of the classical colonial era and the beginning of the neo-colonial or internal colonial era we presently experience.

2. For the purposes at hand, this chapter is necessarily general in its approach and analyses. A broad (aka Canadian) overview of any subject in Native Studies requires considerable sensitivity and rigour to avoid falling prey to overgeneralization and misrepresentation. The reality is that no one general study can fairly represent the lives and experiences of all Aboriginal women in Canada because not all Aboriginal Peoples are alike. Within the geopolitical boundaries of Canada there are hundreds of distinct

and autonomous Aboriginal Nations and societies and all have unique traditions and histories. Readers are strongly urged to consult the growing numbers of more regionally and First Nations-specific studies.

3. The New England colonies were located south of the primary beaver habitats and while some fur trapping occurred it was inconsequential because of the poor quality of southern furs.

4. Historically and contemporarily the term 'squaw' is loaded with negative connotations. It originates from 'esqwew' or 'iskwew' which in most Algonquian languages signifies woman. However, it has been bastardized by non-Aboriginal peoples into a derogative term embodying a range of nasty stereotypes.

5. In 1850 legislation was passed in Lower Canada that determined who was entitled to live on Indian lands. It included the first definition of an 'Indian'—all persons of Indian ancestry, and all such persons married to such persons, belonging to or recognized as belonging to an Indian Band and living with that Band (*Statutes of the Province of Canada*, chap. 42). The following year the definition was amended to exclude non-Aboriginal spouses of both sexes but the children of mixed marriages were not excluded (Jamieson, 1986: 116). Patriarchal definition was imposed in 1869.

6. In 1869 the federal government's stated purpose in imposing this regulation was to prevent the relatively large numbers of non-Indian men who were married to First Nations women from living on reserves and dividing First Nation revenues into smaller per capita portions, which, the government claimed, impoverished Indians. However, First Nation revenues seldom accounted for much of their incomes. In reality, declining economic opportunities due to settler encroachments into hunting, trapping, and fishing territories were the primary sources of First Nations poverty (Canada, House of Commons, 1869: 83; Fenton, 1928: 161).

7. The sexual discrimination against Indian women through this section of the Indian Act remained in effect until 1985. That year the Indian Act was revised by Bill C-31 which repealed the discriminatory sections of the Act and allowed for the reinstatement of women and their children who lost status and Band membership by marrying-out. Bill C-31 also transferred the authority to determine Band membership over to First Nations governments. See Joyce Green, 'Sexual Equality and Indian Government: An Analysis of Bill C-31 Amendments to the Indian Act', *Native Studies Review* 1 (1985): 81–95.

References

Acoose, Janice. 1995. *Iskwewak Kah'ki yaw ni Wahkomakanak: Neither Indian Princess Nor Easy Squaws*. Toronto: Women's Press.

Albers, Patricia. 1983. 'Introduction: New Perspectives on Plains Indian Women', in Patricia Albers and Beatrice Medicine, eds, *The Hidden Half: Studies of Plains Indian Women*. Lanham: University Press of America.

Anderson, Karen. 1992. 'Commodity Exchange and Subordination: Montagnais-Naskapi and Huron Women, 1600–1650', in David Miller, Carl Beal, James Demspey, and R. Wes Heber, eds, *The First Ones: Readings in Indian/Native Studies*. Piapot: Saskatchewan Indian Federated College.

Berreman, Gerald D. 1962. *Behind Many Masks: Ethnography and Impression Management in a Himalayan Village*. New York: Society for Applied Anthropology.

Bourgeault, Ron. 1991. 'Race, Class, and Gender: Colonial Domination of Indian Women', in Ormond McKague, ed., *Racism in Canada*. Saskatoon. Fifth House Publishers.

Brown, Jennifer S.H. 1980. *Strangers in Blood: Fur Trade Company Families in Indian Country*. Vancouver: University of British Columbia Press.

Brown, Judith. 1975. 'Iroquois Women: An Ethnohistorical Note', in Payna Pelter, ed., *Towards an Anthropology of Women*. New York: Monthly Review Press.

Buffalohead, Priscilla K. 1983. 'Farmers, Warrior, Traders: A Fresh Look at Ojibway Women', *Minnesota History* 48 (6): 236–44.

Canada. *Statutes of the Province of Canada*. 1850, chap. 41; 1857, chap. 29.

———. House of Commons. 27 April 1869.

———. *Statutes of Canada*. 1868, 31 Victoria, chap. 42; 1869, 32–33 Victoria, chap. 6; 1876, 39 Victoria, chap. 18; 1884, 47 Victoria, chap. 27; 1951, 15 Victoria, chap. 29.

Carter, Sarah. 1984. 'The Missionaries' Indian: The Publications of John McDougall, John McLean and Egerton Ryerson Young', *Prairie Forum* 9 (1): 27–44.

———. 1996a. 'First Nations Women of Prairie Canada in the Early Reserves, the 1870s to the 1920s: A Preliminary Inquiry', in Christine Miller and Patricia Chuchryck, eds, *Women of the First Nations: Power, Wisdom, and Strength*. Winnipeg: University of Manitoba Press.

Cole, Douglas, and Ira Chaikin. 1990. *An Iron Hand upon the People: The Law Against the Potlatch on the Northwest Coast*. Toronto: University of Toronto Press.

Cominos, Peter T. 1963. 'Late-Victorian Sexual Respectability and the Social System', *International Review of Social History* 8: 18–48.

Devens, Carol. 1992. *Countering Colonization: Native American Women and Great Lakes Missions, 1630–1900*. Berkeley: University of California Press.

Dickason, Olive Patricia. 1985. 'From 'One Nation' in the Northeast to 'New Nation' in the Northwest: A Look at the Emergence of the Metis', in Jacqueline Peterson and Jennifer S.H. Brown, eds, *The New Peoples: Being and Becoming Metis in North America*. Winnipeg: University of Manitoba Press.

———. 1992. *Canada's First Nations: A History of Founding Peoples from Earliest Times*. Norman: University of Oklahoma Press.

Etienne, Mona, and Eleanor Leacock, eds. 1980. *Women and Colonization: Anthropological Perspectives*. New York: Praeger Publishers.

Fee, Elizabeth. 1973. 'The Sexual Politics of Victorian Social Anthropology', *Feminist Studies* (Winter–Spring): 23–39.

Fenton, William N. 1988. 'The Iroquois in History', Eleanor Burke Leacock and Nancy Oestreich Lurie, eds, *North American Indians in Historical Perspective*. Prospect Heights: Waveland Press, Inc.

Fisher, Robin. 1983. *Contact and Conflict: Indian-European Relations in British Columbia, 1774–1890*. Vancouver: University of British Columbia Press.

Fiske, Jo-Anne. 1987. 'Fishing is Women's Business: Changing Economic Roles of Carrier Women and Men', in Bruce Alden Cox, ed., *Native Peoples, Native Lands: Canada's Indians, Inuit and Metis*. Ottawa: Carleton University Press.

Frideres, James A. 1998. *Aboriginal Peoples in Canada: Contemporary Conflicts*, 5th ed. Scarborough: Prentice Hall, Allyn and Bacon Canada.

Grant, John Webster. 1984. *Moon of the Wintertime: Missionaries and the Indians of Canada in Encounter Since 1534*. Toronto: University of Toronto Press.

Green, Joyce. 1985. 'Sexual Equality and the Indian Government: An Analysis of Bill C-31 Amendments to the Indian Act', *Native Studies Review* 1 (2): 81–95.

Green, Rayna. 1990. 'The Pocahontas Perplex: The Image of Indian Women in American Culture', in Ellen Carol Dubois and V.L. Ruiz, eds, *Unequal Sisters: A Multicultural Reader in U.S. Women's History*. New York: Routledge.

Grumet, Robert Steven. 1980. 'Sunksquaws, Shamans, and Tradeswomen: Middle Atlantic Algonkian Women During the 17th and 18th Centuries', in Mona Etienne and Eleanor Leacock, eds, *Women and Colonization*. New York: Praeger Publishers.

Jamieson, Kathleen. 1978. *Indian Women and the Law in Canada: Citizens Minus*. Ottawa: Minister of Supply and Services, Canada.

———. 1986. 'Sex Discrimination and the Indian Act', in J. Rick Ponting, ed., *Arduous Journey: Canadian Indians and Decolonization*. Toronto: McClelland and Stewart.

Jaenen, Cornelius. 1991. 'French Sovereignty and Native Nationhood During the French Regime', in J.R. Miller, ed., *Sweet Promises: A Reader on Indian–White Relations in Canada*. Toronto: University of Toronto Press.

Jones, Peter. 1970. *History of the Ojebway Indians: With Especial Reference to Their Conversion to Christianity*. 1861. Reprint, Freeport: Books for Libraries.

Klein, Laura F. 1976. ' "She's One of Us, You Know": The Public Life of Tlingit Women: Traditional, Historical, and Contemporary Perspectives', *The Western Canadian Journal of Anthropology* 6 (3): 164–83.

Leacock, Eleanor. 1980. 'Montagnais Women and the Jesuit Program for Colonization', in Mona Etienne and Eleanor Leacock, eds, *Women and Colonization: Anthropological Perspectives*. New York: Praeger.

————, ed. 1981. *Myths of Male Dominance: Collected Articles on Women Cross-Culturally*. New York: Monthly Review Press.

Lurie, Nancy O. 1972. 'Indian Women: A Legacy of Freedom', in B.L. Fontana, ed., *Look to the Mountaintop*. San Jose: Gousha Publishers.

McLean, John. 1889. *The Indians of Canada: Their Manners and Customs*. Toronto: William Briggs.

Montour, Martha. 1987. 'Iroquois Women's Rights with Respect to Matrimonial Property on Indian Reserves', *Canadian Native Law Reporter* 4: 1–10.

Nock, David C. 1988. *A Victorian Missionary and Canadian Indian Policy: Cultural Synthesis vs. Cultural Replacement*. Waterloo: Wilfrid Laurier Press.

Ray, Arthur. 1996. *'I Have Lived Here Since the World Began': An Illustrated History of Canada's Native People*. Toronto: Lester Publishing.

Riley, Glenda. 1986. *Inventing the American Women: A Perspective on Women's History*. Arlington Heights: Harlan Davidson, Inc.

Shoemaker, Nancy. 1995. 'Introduction', in Nancy Shoemaker, ed., *Negotiators of Change: Historical Perspectives on Native American Women*. New York: Routledge.

Smandych, Russell, and Gloria Lee. 1995. 'Women, Colonization and Resistance: Elements of an Amerindian Autohistorical Approach to the Study of Law and Colonialism', *Native Studies Review* 10 (1): 21–46.

Smith, Sherry L. 1987. 'Beyond the Princess and Squaw: Army Officers' Perceptions of Indian Women', in Susan Armitage and Elizabeth Jameson, eds, *The Women's West*. Norman: University of Oklahoma Press.

Smits, David D. 1982. 'The "Squaw Drudge": A Prime Index of Savagism', *Ethnohistory* 29 (4): 281–306.

Tobias, John. 1991. 'Protection, Civilization, Assimilation: An Outline History of Canada's Indian Policy', in J.R. Miller, ed., *Sweet Promises: A Reader on Indian-White Relations in Canada*. Toronto: University of Toronto Press.

Van Kirk. Sylvia. 1980. *'Many Tender Ties': Women in Fur Trade Society, 1670–1870*. Winnipeg: Watson & Dwyer.

————. 1987a. 'The Role of Native Women in the Creation of Fur Trade Society in Western Canada, 1670–1830', in Susan Armitage and Elizabeth Jameson, eds, *The Women's West*. Norman: University of Oklahoma Press.

Weist, Katherine M. 1983. 'Beast of Burden and Menial Staves: Nineteenth Century Observations of Northern Plains Indian Women', in Patricia Albers and Beatrice Medicine, eds, *The Hidden Half: Studies of Plains Indian Women*. Lanham: University Press of America.

West, John. 1823. *The Substance of a Journal During a Residence at the Red Colony, British North American in the Years 1820–1823*. Reprinted ed. Vancouver: 1967, Alcuin Society.

Young, Egerton R. 1893. *By Canoe and Dog Team Among the Cree and Saulteaux Indians*. London: Charles H. Kelly.

Young, Mary E. 1980. 'Women, Civilization, and the Indian Question', in Mabel E. Deutrich and Virginia C. Purdy, eds, *Clio was a Woman: Studies in the History of American Women*. Washington: Howard University Press.

Part Two

Additional Readings

Acoose, Janice (Misko-Kìsikàwihkwè). *Iskwewak Kah'Ki Yaw Ni Wahkomakanak: Neither Indian Princesses Nor Easy Squaws*. Toronto: Women's Press, 1995.

Chaat Smith, Paul. *Everything You Know About Indians Is Wrong*. Minneapolis, MN: University of Minnesota Press, 2009.

Lawrence, Bonita. *'Real' Indians and Others: Mixed-Blood Urban Native Peoples and Indigenous Nationhood*. Vancouver: University of British Columbia Press, 2004.

LaRocque, Emma. *When the Other Is Me: Native Resistance Discourse, 1850–1990*. Winnipeg: University of Manitoba Press, 2010.

Mackey, Eva. *The House of Difference: Cultural Politics and National Identity in Canada*. Toronto: University of Toronto Press, 1999.

Rollins, Peter C., and John E. O'Connor, eds. *Hollywood's Indian: The Portrayal of the Native American in Film*. Lexington, KY: University Press of Kentucky, 1998.

Schick, Carol, and Verna St Denis. 'Troubling National Discourses in Anti-Racist Curricular Planning', *Canadian Journal of Education* 28, 3 (2005): 295–317.

Relevant Websites

The National Museum of the American Indian
http://www.nmai.si.edu/
According to The National Museum of the American Indian website, the 'NMAIs the sixteenth museum of the Smithsonian Institution. It is the first national museum dedicated to the preservation, study, and exhibition of the life, languages, literature, history, and arts of Native Americans. Established by an act of Congress in 1989 (amendment in 1996), the museum works in collaboration with the Native peoples of the Western Hemisphere to protect and foster their cultures by reaffirming traditions and beliefs, encouraging contemporary artistic expression, and empowering the Indian voice.'

MNet ('Common Portrayals of Aboriginal People')
http://www.media-awareness.ca/english/issues/
stereotyping/aboriginal_people/aboriginal_portrayals.cfm
MNet 'is a Canadian non-profit organization that has been pioneering the development of media and digital literacy programs since its incorporation in 1996'. This link is to a page called 'Common Portrayals of Aboriginal People' which overviews stereotypes and constructions of Indigenous people in the media.

Films

Aboriginality. Dir. Dominique Keller and Tom Jackson. National Film Board of Canada, 2008.
Couple In The Cage: A Guatinaui Odyssey. Dir. Coco Fusco and Paula Heredia. Third World Newsreel, 1993.
Reel Injun. Dir. Neil Diamond. National Film Board of Canada, 2009.

Shooting Indians: A Journey with Jeffrey Thomas, A Film by Ali Kazimi. Dir. Ali Kazimi. Peripheral Visions Film and Video Inc., 1997.

Key Terms

Colonial imaginary
Romanticism
Authenticity
Stereotype

Representation
The Other
Squaw Drudge/Indian Princess binary
Dehumanization

Discussion Questions

1. Identify and discuss strategies of dehumanization. How have they been deployed and used in the colonial enterprise?
2. How do images of 'Indians', created by Western society, work to perpetuate racist stereotypes? How do they work to uphold and benefit settler colonialism? What are the implications of the 'Noble Savage' or renderings of Indigenous peoples as a 'disappearing race'?
3. Discuss the relationship between the virgin/whore dichotomy and the Squaw Drudge/Indian Princess dichotomy. What similarities and differences exist between these archetypes? Whose interests are served? What is the relationship between patriarchy and colonialism, and how can these systems be understood as interlocking?
4. How do we explain the need for certainty about Indian difference? Where are these practices located and how do they operate in the contemporary world? What kinds of material consequences does keeping the racialized Other firmly intact have in legitimating and perpetuating Canadian colonialism?

Activities

Identify different representations of 'Indians' in popular culture (e.g., Disney films, children's literature, 'Cowboy and Indian' figurines, Halloween costumes, etc.). For whom and what do these representations serve?

Locate some local, provincial, state, or national sports teams that have 'Indian' names or mascots. How are these altogether common and racist practices allowable? What does their persistence suggest?

How have representations of 'Indians' been handled by regional media in your area over the last five years? How are the individuals and stories being portrayed? If you were to rework these representations differently, how would you do it and why?

PART THREE

Race, Space, and Territoriality

The idea of North America as a once vast open wilderness, historically unoccupied and empty prior to the arrival of first white settlers is a powerful myth informing much of Canadian and US history. The early and sometimes forcible displacement of Indigenous peoples and territories rests on this fiction, furthered by an assumption that racism does not define the colonial past. 'In order for Canada to have a viable national identity', writes Miqmaw scholar Bonita Lawrence, 'the historical record of how the land was acquired must be erased.' In this chapter, we provide a selection of writings contesting this erasure, the institutionalized sexism that defines early settlement, and the future of self-determination shaped by territorial displacement.

The displacement of Indigenous peoples has a long history. The history varies regionally, but in many cases it involved the movement of people from traditional territories to lands created for them by the colonizer. From the mid-1800s, it was effected through colonial policy aimed at putting our people on Indian reserves—originally meant to protect us and thought to provide us with the Eurocentric education and instruction necessary for our assimilation into an emerging capitalist economy. The idea was that reserves and other rural, remote, and economically marginalized lands were the only appropriate place for us as Indians. These and other kinds of symbolic violence persist even today.

Today, many Indigenous peoples live in cities. In 2001, only slightly more than half of the registered Indian population lived on reserves in Canada. The statistic is revealing of a choice by Indigenous peoples to reject the economic marginalization of reserve life and move into urban contexts. Social scientists have spent countless hours documenting the experience of 'aboriginal peoples in cities'. Much of this literature has focused on the cultural incommensurability of Indians and urban ways of life, including the social problems plaguing Indigenous populations when they arrive in cities. These analyses offer little, if any, insight into difference-making practices that have long characterized settler colonialism.

In order to mark spaces as urban, Indigenous bodies are regulated. Historically, this took place through policy, including the pass system. Indians belonged on reserves and required the approval of Indian agents to leave them. Today, the policing of Indigenous bodies is as symbolic as it is material. It is accomplished through the invisibility of countless urban Indigenous peoples thought assimilated, or who, as the Cree politician Ovide Mercredi once put it, 'blend effortlessly into the multicultural framework of Canadian society'. It is also accomplished through over-policing, racial profiling, and police brutality, as evidenced in Cree scholar Tasha Hubbard's 2004 film *Two Worlds Colliding* about the freezing deaths of Indigenous men in Saskatoon.

The challenge we face as urban Indigenous peoples is as much a problem of poverty, inadequate housing, and ineffectual services delivery as it is a problem of exclusion and recognition. Indigeneity and urbanity are by no means incompatible to one another, nor do they stand in a dichotomous, either/or relation. The assumption is that we do not belong in cities. This prevents us from seeing that many of us as Indigenous peoples—the authors included—have lived in urban locations for generations. It negates the reality that many Canadian cities are situated on or near traditional Indigenous territories. It prevents us from acknowledging exclusionary practices and from understanding the work that goes into providing the ongoing ideological justification for the displacement of our peoples.

The racism effected through difference-making and other spatial practices has not been experienced uniformly among all Indigenous peoples. For Indigenous women, racism and sexism intersected to separate them from communities and to erode their rights and influence within communities. In Canada, the requirement that all women lose status as Indians—and therefore all birthrights and entitlements upon marriage to non-Indian men—contributed to their relocation to cities until the 1985 Indian Act amendments. Others came to cities because of federal and provincial/territorial laws that fell short of addressing the distribution of matrimonial real property upon dissolution of marriage. This matter was not addressed by Canada until 2009. The Government of Canada is presently trying to resolve Indian status injustices, as they currently remain unresolved.

The issue of matrimonial real property is by no means a new one. In 1987, Martha Montour wrote about the lack of protections for Indigenous women upon divorce on reserves. The article, which is included in Chapter 9 of this anthology, provides insight into women's once esteemed status in Indigenous communities, particularly the Haudenosaunee. More importantly, she outlines how both colonialism and patriarchy placed property and land ownership into the hands of men, thereby reorganizing gender relations. The process through which women's status was transformed in communities as a result of these changes has not been thoroughly documented. Nor has the accommodation of colonialism by Indigenous communities been thoroughly understood.

Bonita Lawrence is also interested in histories of colonialism, particularly as this relates to both land theft and dispossession. In Chapter 8, she rewrites histories of the land, challenging the normative and Eurocentric frameworks that have defined some as academic scholarship. As she suggests, some historians have written of dispossession in ways that prevent us from understanding the perspectives of Indigenous peoples experiencing it. Her chapter aims to 'decolonize the history of Eastern Canada', dismantling in turn a number of myths that are crucial to Canadian nation-building, including the idea that colonization was a benign process, innocent of both racism and genocide.

Andersen and Denis examine histories of dispossession and land theft from an altogether different perspective. They examine the 1996 Royal Commission on Aboriginal Peoples and how this report affirmed a model of nationhood and self-government that privileged 'Aboriginals with a land base'. The model proposed, excludes those who do not live in defined reserve-based or treaty territories and, furthermore, erases the colonial histories that lead many of us to relocate to cities. The politics of recognition is at once oblivious to histories of dislocation and to the sorting out of lands. Moreover, they are structured in ways that do not address geographies of exclusion, our presence in cities, and they effect the further dispossession of Indigenous peoples.

Chapter 7

Urban Native Communities and the Nation: Before and After the Royal Commission on Aboriginal Peoples

Chris Andersen and Claude Denis

This chapter examines the relationship between Canadian state formation and the construction of Aboriginal identities via the legitimating function of the public inquiry.

There are two major parts. The first part is fairly theoretical, focusing on a discussion of the concept of the state and situating our analysis in the context of discourse analysis/theory. Specifically, it highlights the modern liberal distinction between 'political' and 'civil' society, and focuses on two important abstractions necessary to sustain this demarcation, citizenship and the 'individual'. The second component of Part 1 sharpens the focus on the modern liberal conception of the state by discussing the importance of public

inquiries in legitimating specific instances of this concept of the state—what is it about the relationship between public inquiries and the state that gives both such legitimacy?

Part 2 of the paper takes up the theoretical threads delineated in the first, in order to inform our empirical evidence. Thus, we discuss, in broad strokes, the incorporation of the *nation model* in government–Aboriginal relations. In the context of Aboriginal politics, actors view the nation model as the primary vehicle through which self-determination of Aboriginal peoples is to be achieved. In practice, the nation is often understood to be somewhere 'above' individual Aboriginal communities (despite these calling themselves

'First Nations'), and generally[1] somewhere 'beneath' the sovereignty of the Canadian state. It includes such aspects as lands and territory, notions of citizenship, jurisdiction, internal organization, and inter-Aboriginal government organization.[2] So, for example, the 'Cree Nation' can be comprised of geographically proximate Cree communities (for example, Bigstone Cree Nation of Alberta, as well as the numerous Tribal Councils that are composed of proximate First Nations) identifying with this larger 'nation', whereas the borders of a large number of other self-described First Nations match those of an individual band—and it is important, in all cases, to maintain the conceptual and political distinction between band and nation.

We are particularly interested in the rise to prominence of the nation model into government-Aboriginal relations *prior to* the Royal Commission on Aboriginal Peoples (RCAP), primarily with regard to *urban* Aboriginals. What we want to know is to what extent the nation form is addressing the claims of *all* Aboriginals in Canada, and what effects the dominance of the nation model has on their forms of political representation. The final section of Part 2 takes up these issues as they have been affirmed, stabilized, normalized, and transformed in the RCAP Report, which functions as a legitimating tool of the state. We conclude by arguing that the RCAP Report serves to reinforce the nation as the cultural model of the state. It does so in a way that perpetuates, rather than rethinks, a long-established but conceptually contingent relationship between nation and territory. As a result, it naturalizes relations of power that marginalize urban Aboriginal communities.

The Nation and Foucauldian Discourse Analysis

The preceding lines probably make it clear that we are critical of the nation model. This should not be taken to mean that the nation is an inherently bad (or good) social form, or that a better alternative should be readily at hand. . . .

Discourse analysis is more interested in asking *how* these concepts function socially than *why* certain concepts are adopted and others are not. There are epistemological reasons for this interest, often encapsulated under the heading of anti-foundationalism. This is to say, first, that once we adopt a discursive view of the social world, it becomes impossible to answer 'why' questions without opening the door to the infinite regression of looking for the 'thing' lying behind the word/concept. Second, there is no easy (or even difficult) correspondence between word and thing, because every 'thing' is in fact a naturalized concept. Consequently, the social use—the meaning—of a concept cannot be assumed to be self-evident, and therefore the question of how the concept functions becomes central to social analysis. Hence, in this paper, the importance of discerning how the concept of nation functions among and around Indigenous peoples.

Among the key components of the social functioning of concepts, we focus on two dimensions. On the one hand, that of the discursive environment from which the concept is drawn, in this case, the way in which the concept of nation has been operating in Western societies for two hundred years, including, especially, in Canada; and its intimate relationship with the concept of state. On the other hand, the dimension of its internal differentiation: given that, structurally, concepts are built relationally, as systems of difference, of inclusion/exclusion. These are the sorts of questions that make sense in discourse analysis, in that they arise from its logic of investigation. In this case, we are interested in how Indigenous peoples are differently positioned with respect to 'nation', whether they are (considered) Status Indians or non-Status Indians, band members or not, Métis, Inuit, men or women, urban or reserve dwellers.

The State and the Public Inquiry

Modern State Formation

Since the early 1970s in Canada, Aboriginal political resurgence has meant that certain kinds of Aboriginal political claims have been legitimized. At the same time, other such claims—or potential claims—have not gained the same visibility. Specifically, the needs and aspirations of urban Aboriginals have remained marginal, while many government negotiations with Aboriginals on (or linked to) a recognized land base have moved ahead. It is in this latter context that the term 'First Nation' is, in general, applied to the political identity/organization of bands or groups of bands, rather than Aboriginal peoples at large. Recognizing this reality, certain segments of the Aboriginal population in Canada have attempted to avoid marginalization by shaping their political projects in ways consistent with the dominant narrative of nation; but this has been achieved at the expense of much of their conceivable constituency.

These developments are all bound up in the facts that: (a) Canada's Indigenous peoples function in the context of a relationship with the Canadian *state*; (b) the Canadian state's legitimating discourse has been and remains that of nationhood; and (c) political projects gain legitimacy (or not) based, in part, on the type of discourses prominent in the society and institutions in which they arise. This raises the theoretical question, what is the state? For our present purposes however, questioning what the state is may not be helpful. Here, it is more appropriate not to ask what the state *is*, but rather what it *does* (Denis, 1989, 1993).

Corrigan and Sayer (1985: 5), in their lucid and extensively documented study of English state formation, argue that 'states . . . state. . . . They define in great detail, acceptable forms and images of social activity and individual and collective identity; they regulate, in empirically specifiable ways, much—very much, by the twentieth century—of social life' (1985: 3). This is where 'citizens', conceived as the equal protagonists of the modern polity, occupy centre stage. However, the 'equality' infusing these modern regulatory processes is built on a number of otherwise, unacknowledged hierarchies. Among the most fundamental of these are racialized and gendered oppression, both of which are simultaneously concealed and perpetuated in the abstractions of 'citizenship' and the 'individual' (Sayer, 1987). In other words,

notions of citizenship and the citizen could only be understood in relation to excluded categories of people—in Canada, Aboriginals and, until recently, women.

It is not an accident, in this perspective, that the leading European states—the ones that most contributed to defining what the modern state was to become—developed not only as national states, but also as *colonial* states. . . .

Racial oppression, then, is a legacy of most modern (read Western) nation-states; that is to say, before they were nation-states most countries were imperially/colonially constituted—whether they were metropolis or colony. State formation in colonial territories, and concomitantly in the metropolis, was monumentally concerned with 'containing' the purity of the 'white race', and great effort was extended to ensure that this would be done. Notions of the citizen were strongly rooted in these racializing discourses. For example, Stoler (1995) notes that '[l]ate nineteenth-century and early twentieth century discourses on miscegenation combined notions of tainted, flawed, and pure blood with those of degeneration and racial purity in countless ways' (1995: 50). Similarly, Young (1995) suggests that colonial hierarchy was constructed to prevent the 'nightmare' of 'the unlimited and ungovernable fertility of *unnatural* unions' (1995: 98, emphasis added). . . .

To a large extent nowadays, the rhetoric of race, including, in particular, claims to racial (im)purity, has been replaced by a language of culture. However, Young (1995) shows that deconstructing the concept of culture historically discloses its intimate connection with race: race has always been culturally constructed, and vice versa (1995: 54). In general, these understandings of race and culture are bound together in the notion of *difference*. Said (1979; 1993) argues that this hierarchy of difference is constitutive of Western (*modern*) culture, which is and has always been predicated on an understanding of difference in which the 'other' (for him 'the Oriental', for us 'the Aboriginal') is not just *different*: s/he is also *lesser* (see also RCAP, 1996, Vol. 4: 45).[3] Western culture thus presupposes that 'the colonised either deserves to be overwhelmed, or is benefiting from the arrangement in obtaining the fruits of social, religious, and other measures of modernity and enlightenment' (Green, 1997: 6).

A second hallmark of the (Western) state is its conception of the individual as freed from the oppressiveness of previous forms of social organization (Anderson, 1991; Gellner, 1997; Giddens, 1985). This freedom is formally enshrined in the basic ideological separation of the state and civil society and, more importantly, in the *autonomy* of civil society from the state. . . .

Now, the Canadian state, like all states, is historically constituted. Its formation and imposition on Indigenous communities took place in the broader context of a conflict between a mercantile fur trade economy and an approaching industrial/agricultural-based economy. For First Nations, treaties, residential schools, disease and starvation ushered in an era of political and cultural marginalization (Carter, 1990; Milloy, 1999)—for the Métis, the inequities of the Scrip system (Tough, 1996), the maladministration of the *Manitoba Act, 1870* and the death of Louis Riel following the Northwest Rebellion, did the same. More recently, the last thirty years have borne witness to the seemingly inexorable decay of once-vibrant Métis communities and the overcrowding of First Nations reserve communities, both of which have conspired to force the migration of Native people off contiguous land bases and into Canada's cities.

The Public Inquiry as State Legitimation

The Royal Commission on Aboriginal Peoples was the largest and most ex(t/p)ensive public inquiry undertaken in Canadian history—as critics and pundits alike have enjoyed pointing out. The commission interviewed Aboriginals from across the country and came with a price tag of nearly $60 million. And, as with most inquiries, the RCAP Report, as it was finally published, condensed hundreds upon hundreds of interviews and scholarly submissions into five concentrated volumes—a winnowing process that was surely fraught with

all the same give-and-take negotiations that characterize the Canadian government's relationship with Aboriginal peoples. And, as has happened in other contexts,[4] the more radical Aboriginal views (such as, for example, Indigenous sovereignty discourses) were marginalized in favour of the more moderate ones. . . .

While public inquiries are often extremely expensive to conduct and usually received with much fanfare, most often very little is done about the recommendations contained in the final report. The RCAP Report is hardly an exception on this count: since its release in 1996 very few (if any) of its recommendations have been implemented.[5] . . . What has also occurred, however, is that the federal government has used the Report as an example of its willingness to engage in fair and respectful dialogue with Aboriginal peoples. In affirming formally the legitimacy of the nation model, even as it applies to Aboriginal peoples, the Canadian state reaffirms, at the same time, the nation as the cultural (and moral) form of the modern state.

On Some Aspects of Aboriginal Politics since 1982

The Nation Model Before RCAP

The nation model has in recent years become a very powerful and widely accepted legitimating discursive tool for Indigenous peoples attempting to throw off the yoke of colonialism that has bound them (in some cases) for the last few centuries. Canadian politics, particularly in the last few decades, is emblematic of the rise of this new narrative of Aboriginal nationhood. Thus, in 1975,

> The Dene Nation, the association representing Indian people of the Northwest Territories, became the first aboriginal group to assert nationhood within Canada, with the Inuit Tapirisat of Canada following quickly behind them (Zlotkin, 1983: 21).

This has happened in part as a result of Aboriginal reaction to the Canadian government's *White Paper* of 1969, which called for the assimilation of Indians into the 'whitestream' Canadian tapestry (Boldt, 1993), and, in part, following court decisions concerning the nature of Aboriginal rights (Zlotkin, 1983).

A peculiar outcome of the rise of the nationhood narrative has been its privileging of certain forms of Aboriginal collectivity over others. Specifically, the political claims of Aboriginal communities and organizations situated on defined territories (i.e., reserves and treaty territories) are legitimated at the expense of individuals and communities living off a recognized Aboriginal land base. And although government deals largely with 'bands', there are significant examples of First Nations operating collectively 'above' the band level (one can look at the Prince Albert and Meadow Lake Tribal Councils in Saskatchewan, the Athabasca and Yellowhead Tribal Councils in Alberta, and the recent Treaty 8 *Benoit* tax case as examples of this, not to mention existing Assembly of First Nations and Saskatchewan Indian Federated Nations efforts). In any case, urban (or non-reserve) Aboriginals without a formal, collective land base (and who in some cases do not even identify with a particular land base) are particularly affected by this hierarchy.[6] Indeed, Wherrett and Brown (1992) characterize the 1980s pre-RCAP Report era of self-government talks as one 'focus[ing] on reserve-based or Northern communities result[ing] in the virtual exclusion of a large segment of the Aboriginal population from discussion of self-government . . .' (1992: 84). And if Bill C-31 has potentially opened the door for some First Nations people to return to a reserve, this potential is mitigated by the lack of life opportunities in contemporary reserve communities—part of the reason why many leave reserves to begin with (see RCAP, 1996).

This marginalization of urban Natives is puzzling for several reasons, of which we will highlight four. First, while self-government negotiations between the various levels of government and the different Aboriginal communities are overwhelmingly based on the presumption of a land base, demographic trends suggest that at least half of the total self-identifying Aboriginal population do not live in these circumstances (Hanselmann, 2001; Peters, 1995; Statistics Canada, 2003). . . . More recently, the 2001 Census figures on Aboriginal residence continue to bear out these trends: more than a half million self-identifying Aboriginal (and more than two thirds of all self-identifying Métis) people live in urban areas (Statistics Canada, 2003).

To date, there appears to be tacit agreement between several segments of the Aboriginal population in Canada and the various levels of government involved, that serious discussion of 'self-government' for Aboriginal people *must* assume a land base of one kind or another (see Schwartz [1986] for an in-depth discussion of the flavour of the First Ministers' Conferences in this regard). However, as Weinstein (1986: 4) points out:

> [T]his is not a particularly helpful or productive approach as it fails to address the aspirations of a large part of Canada's aboriginal population, who are recognized in the Constitution and are as much entitled to participate in the identification and definition of the rights of the Aboriginal peoples to be included in the Constitution as those living on a land base.[7]

Second, it is likely that self-government agreements will include, like the Nisga'a Treaty, some measure of jurisdiction over urban Aboriginals who, while linked to a particular reserve community, still live in an urban area. Yet, the current tendency to deal specifically with the band councils may result in little opportunity for urban Aboriginals to participate meaningfully in this process (Falconer, 1985 in Peters, 1992), despite recent court decisions that directly address this issue (see *Corbiere v. Canada*, 1999). And since urban Aboriginals may, in many cases, comprise only a small proportion of the community they believe themselves connected to, their concerns risk being given the lowest of priority. Aboriginal women in particular have emphasized this problem[8] (see for example Green, 1997).

Third, as self-government agreements are reached in this current context, there is little discussion of the ways in which access to various government agencies (health and welfare, taxation, etc.) would work for Aboriginals caught in the 'urban netherland' (Brown, 1992).[9] Finally, there has been limited discussion of the mobility of any Aboriginal rights negotiated in the context of a specific piece of land.[10]

What all of this suggests is that prior to the RCAP Report, the processes of marginalizing urban Native concerns had begun. By privileging a nation model as inherently land-based—a 'conceptually convenient' policy orientation (see Peters, 1992: 52)—the provincial and federal governments were brushing under the rug the cultural and political realities faced by large groups of Aboriginals in Canada. In other words, although during the 1980s and 1990s governments in Canada claimed a grudging acquiescence to the wishes of Aboriginals to govern themselves in limited ways, the range of models deemed feasible was exceedingly narrow, because they began with the *a priori* assumption of a land base.

The important question here is whether assuming that a land base is necessary to the nation model as it applies to Indigenous peoples was/is unavoidable. If it is, the political marginalization of urban Aboriginals is also likely to have been unavoidable. But it seems hard to see why this would be the case. Three factors need to be considered. First, while nations are necessarily bounded, and therefore always exclude as much as they include, there is no automatic formula for drawing the (social) boundaries. In this sense, Aboriginal nations will always exclude non-Aboriginals—this very act of exclusion constitutes them as Aboriginal and as nations. But the definition(s) of who counts as an Aboriginal person, a member of the nation, is(are) plastic and it is entirely imaginable, in the abstract, for urban Aboriginals to be fully included. . . .

The second factor to keep in mind with regard to the relationship between a land base and the nation model is rather more basic, and it also leaves open the possibility of re-imagining the nation: as human life (among others) is fundamentally grounded in time and space, it makes no sense to say that urban Aboriginals have *no* relationship to territory. Their relationship may be to a different territory, or to the same territory as reserve-based Aboriginals, but in a different way. Indeed, this is what defines, to a significant extent, the relationship of urban Aboriginal people to each other, to reserve-based Aboriginals and to non-Aboriginals. In this perspective, what is called for is *thinking* this territory, *imagining* this relationship so as to include urban Aboriginals in the nation(s).

Third, we need to start thinking about urban communities as legitimate communities, rather than as depositories of poverty and pathology. Urban Native communities are real, they endure, they are growing, and it is long past the time when we can make the mistake of perceiving them as vestiges or missives of some more legitimate land-based community. Moreover, these Native communities both include and transgress existing bureaucratic categories, and they are the source of new forms of culture, association and self-perception—both individual and collective—about what it means to be Aboriginal. That is to say, urban Native communities produce chains of meaning—cultural forms—that adhere specifically to the mental and physical geography of the city and as such may, from time to time, produce political projects that conflict with those issued by land-based Aboriginal communities.

The existence of such a re-imagining possibility is important because it remains difficult today to think politically outside the nation model—witness talk of the emergence of 'cybernation' in the context of the politics of Internet. Indeed, as we witnessed an Aboriginal political awakening since the 1970s, it is hard to imagine what *other* political language it might have adopted: not only was it just about 'the only game in town', but it was also a language that other political actors would recognize instantly and would likely find compelling. Denying this discursive resource to destitute Aboriginal communities would make no political sense, and would be morally indefensible.

The Royal Commission on Aboriginal Peoples as a Normalizing Process

If we conceive of the normalization process as one in which 'some norms and qualities (appropriate to the life situation of some social groups) [are] elevated to become value, normality, and the quality of life itself' (Corrigan and Sayer, 1985: 123), we gain a better understanding of the discourse of Aboriginal culture as it appears in the RCAP Report. We argued in the previous section that the various levels of Canadian government(s) have dealt with Aboriginal political claims in very specific, 'national', ways, resulting in marginalizing the aspirations of urban Aboriginal populations in the contemporary Aboriginal political rebirth.

The RCAP Report quite explicitly upholds (and solidifies) these previous marginalizations, by affirming the 'nation-to-nation' model as the basis of the renewed relationship between Aboriginals and the Canadian state.

> [A] crucial component of the renewed relationship will be the nation rebuilding and nation recognition. All our recommendations for governance, treaty processes, and lands and resources are based on the nation as the basic political unit of Aboriginal peoples (RCAP, 1996, Vol. 5: 5).

The difficulty is that, as with virtually all nation-building processes, the nation-to-nation approach advocated in the Report is intimately connected to a geographical land base. This is especially the case for Aboriginals in the RCAP Report, which picks up the dominant narrative of Aboriginal people possessing a fundamental connection to the land and its resources:

> [L]and touches every aspect of life: conceptual and spiritual views; securing food, shelter and clothing; cycles of economic activities including the division of labour; forms of social organization such as recreational and ceremonial events; and systems of governance and management (RCAP, 1996, Vol. 2, Part 2: 448).

In other words, to Aboriginal people, 'land is not simply the basis for livelihood but of life and must be treated as such' (448).

We do not mean to suggest that this narrative should be abandoned as somehow false. Clearly, many Aboriginal people recognize themselves in this picture. But not all do, and it is not a matter of individual dissidence, but of social positioning: a half million, or so, urban Natives are in great danger of being left out. In their comparatively brief treatment of them, the writers of the RCAP Report suggest that urban Aboriginals will, in most cases, be forced to eschew a cultural revitalization project based on a land-based nation model in favour of attempting either to assure more Aboriginal representation on municipal service boards and committees, or to construct a 'community of interest' including Aboriginal peoples of diverse origins, by creating voluntary associations (RCAP, 1996, Vol. 4: 584; also see Dunn, 1986). For example, with regard to urban Métis specifically, writers of the RCAP Report suggest that, off a land base of some kind, governance would take the form of 'locals' and would affect only those who chose to participate in them (Vol. 2, Part 1: 161).

It would be unfair, however, to leave the reader with the impression that the RCAP Report authors simply dismissed urban issues as an afterthought—the issue is more complex. In their chapter on urban issues, the authors make a sincere attempt to place urban people into a nation-based governance context. And yet, it is clear that the RCAP Report suggestions are firmly planted in the idea that Aboriginal nations are located in 'traditional' home communities, such that urban communities themselves are not presented as legitimate alternatives.

> [M]aintaining cultural identity requires creating an Aboriginal community in the city. Following three decades of urbanization, *development of a strong community still remains largely incomplete*. Many urban Aboriginal people are impoverished and unorganized. No coherent or co-ordinated policies to meet their needs are in place, despite the fact that they make up almost half of Canada's Aboriginal population. They have been largely excluded

from discussions about self-government and institutional development. Aboriginal people in urban areas have little collective visibility or power (RCAP, 1996, Vol. 4: 531, emphasis added).

Moreover, their approaches to urban governance take, as their origin, urban Aboriginal peoples' nations of origin (1996, Vol. 4: 588). In fact, the writers of the urban chapter largely avoid referring to urban Aboriginal 'communities' at all—rather, they use 'Aboriginal people in urban areas' (1996, Vol. 4: 520).

Conclusion

The aim of this paper has been to explore the way that pre-existing marginalizing trends in Aboriginal politics were addressed, reconstructed, and officialized in the RCAP Report. Our argument was that the Report (re)affirmed several of these marginalizing trends, particularly those in relation to urban Aboriginals. We went on to argue that the solidification of these trends is particularly important because of the legitimating function that the Report possesses. . . . As the information from the RCAP Report is slowly disseminated into popular consciousness, and as it becomes a/the basis for policy negotiations between Aboriginals and the Canadian state, the construction of future political projects is likely to have to conform increasingly to the (land-anchored) nation model. Those who are unable to do so are likely to remain orphans of history—not as some unchanging, doomed, primitive people, but out of their displacement, within modernity, towards the margins of what generally counts as nationhood.

In a sense, there is nothing surprising about the outcome presented here; structurally, it makes sense for dominant Canadian society to marginalize the social power of Aboriginal communities (although it should be kept in mind that the Canadian government was partly responsible for the rise of Native political organizations in the 1970s in the first place—see Sawchuk, 1998). Moreover, and without lapsing into tired 'divide-and-conquer' arguments, it is strikingly apparent

that there is nothing 'post' about Canada's colonialism—indeed, it is alive and well. These days, however, Canada maintains its power not simply through the crude assimilation attempts that characterized its historical dealings with Aboriginal communities, but with far more indirect and subtle structural arrangements that encourage and ensconce the effective political marginalization of large segments of the Aboriginal community in Canada.

Notes

1. But not always: a number of Indigenous peoples, from the Mohawk to some Treaty peoples on the Prairies, are claiming sovereignty on the same level as the Canadian state, or indeed in the stead of the Canadian state.

2. This largely commonsensical description is officialized in the Report of the Royal Commission on Aboriginal Peoples (RCAP, 1996, Vol. 2: 250), in a process that is one of the primary objects of this paper's analysis.

3. In the same spirit as Said's work on orientalism (1979), Young (1995: 35) argues that '[h]owever much [indigenous peoples] may have been denigrated by being placed lower on the [civilization] scale, these other societies were . . . essential to the European sense of self and conception of civilization.'

4. See the Canadian government's treatment of Aboriginal women's concerns during the 1982 Constitution talks (Green, 1993; Weaver, 1993). In addition, see Sawchuk (1998) for a discussion of the ways in which the federal and provincial governing bodies discipline Aboriginal political organizations.

5. In its 1999 Budget, the federal government earmarked sufficient additional funding to the Department of Indian Affairs and Northern Development to allow for the bulk of the Report's recommendations to be carried out. Concretely, little has yet changed, including in the aftermath of subsequent Budgets.

6. To a certain extent, some bands (in Saskatchewan, for example), have attempted to create 'urban reserves' in cities (Saskatoon, Prince Albert and Regina)—these, however, have been used primarily for commercial, rather than residential purposes (see Barron and Garcea, 1999). And although it is conceivable that a minority of urban Native people might one day reside in an 'urban reserve', there are tens of thousands of non-Status Indians and Métis without this option. Moreover, the rate of outmarriage means that, in coming generations, increasing numbers of (currently) Status Indians will lose their status, thus further reducing their chances of living on a land base such as a reserve, urban or otherwise.

7. On this issue, see also Dunn (1986).

8. The extent to which the recent Supreme Court of Canada *Corbiere* decision will mitigate this marginalization remains to be seen. The *Corbiere* decisions found that band election rules that prohibited off-reserve Status Indian band members from voting violated section 15 of the Charter of Rights and Freedoms.

9. Partially, this is because funding agencies that would normally assume responsibility for Aboriginal issues (for First Nations, the Department of Indian Affairs and Northern Development, for example), argue that they lack a mandate to deal with First Nations living off reserve, given that they chose to interpret section 91(24) of the BNA Act of 1867 to deal exclusively with Indians residing on reserves.

10. Although these problems are not discussed in anything like the depth of a host of land-based issues, they nevertheless, have been addressed. Dunn (1986), in particular, discusses in great detail the potential problems relating to mobility and citizenship problems. In addition, Weinstein (1986) explores the pitfalls of Aboriginal self-government off a land base.

References

Anderson, B. 1991. *Imagined Communities: Reflections on the Origin and Spread of Nationalism*. London and New York: Verso.

Barron, F.L., and J. Garcea. 1999. *Urban Indian Reserves: Forging New Relationships in Saskatchewan*. Saskatoon: Purich Publishing Ltd.

Boldt, M. 1993. *Surviving as Indians: The Challenge of Self-Government*. Toronto: University of Toronto Press.

Brown, D. 1992. *Aboriginal Governments and Power Sharing in Canada*. Kingston: Queen's University, Institute of Intergovernmental Relations.

Carter, S. 1990. *Lost Harvests: Prairie Indian Reserve Farmers and Government Policy*. Montreal and Kingston: McGill-Queen's University Press.

Coon Come, M. 2003. 'Emperor Nault: Building His Own Kingdom', *The Hill Times*, 7 April: 10.

Corrigan, P., and D. Sayer. 1991. *The Great Arch: English State Formation as Cultural Revolution*. Oxford and New York: Basil Blackwell.

Denis, C. 1989. 'The Genesis of American Capitalism: An Historical Inquiry into State Theory', *Journal of Historical Sociology* 2 (4): 328–56.

Denis, C. 1993. 'Distinct Society as Conventional Wisdom: The Constitutional Silence of Anglo-Canadian Sociology', *Canadian Journal of Sociology* 18 (3): 251–69.

Dobbin, M. 1981. *The One-and-a-Half Men*. Vancouver: New Star Books.

Dunn, M. 1986. *Access to Survival: A Perspective on Aboriginal Self-government for the Constituency of the Native Council of Canada*. Kingston: NCC Constitutional Secretariat, Institute of Intergovernmental Relations, Queen's University.

Gellner, E. 1997. *Nationalism*. New York: New York University Press.

Giddens, A. 1985. *The Nation-State and Violence: A Critique of Historical Materialism*. Berkeley: University of California Press.

Green, J. 1993. 'Constitutionalizing the Patriarchy', *Constitutional Forum* 4 (4): 1–21.

Green, J. 1997. 'Exploring Identity and Citizenship: Aboriginal Women, Bill C-31 and the Sawridge Case'. PhD thesis, University of Alberta.

Hanselmann, C. 2001. *Urban Aboriginal People in Western Canada: Realities and Policies*. Calgary: Canada West Foundation.

Milloy, J.S. 1999. 'The Founding Vision of Residential School Education, 1879 to 1920', Pp. 23–47 in *A National Crime: The Canadian Government and the Residential School System, 1879–1986*. Winnipeg: University of Manitoba Press.

Peters, E. 1992. 'Self-government for Aboriginal People in Urban Areas: A Literature Review and Suggestions for Research', *Canadian Journal of Native Studies* 12 (1): 51–74.

Peters, E. 1995. *Aboriginal Self-Government in Urban Areas: Proceedings of a Workshop May 25 and 26, 1994*. Kingston: Institute of Intergovernmental Relations, Queen's University.

Royal Commission on Aboriginal Peoples (RCAP). 1996. *Report of the Royal Commission on Aboriginal Peoples*. Ottawa: Minister of Supply and Services.

Said, E.W. 1979. *Orientalism*. New York: Vintage Books.

Said, E.W. 1993. *Culture and Imperialism*. New York: Knopf.

Sanders, D. 1983. 'The Indian Lobby', pp. 301–32 in K. Banting and R. Simeon, eds, *And No One Cheered: Federalism, Democracy & The Constitution Act*. Toronto: Methuen.

Sawchuk, J. 1998. *Métis Politics in Western Canada: The Dynamics of Native Pressure Groups*. Saskatoon: Purich Publishing Ltd.

Sawchuk, J. 2001. 'Negotiating an Identity: Métis Political Organizations, the Canadian Government, and Competing Concepts of Aboriginality', *American Indian Quarterly* 25 (1): 73–92.

Sayer, D. 1987. *The Violence of Abstraction: The Analytic Foundations of Historical Materialism*. Oxford: Basil Blackwell.

Sayer, D., ed. 1989. *Readings from Karl Marx*. London and New York: Routledge.

Schwartz, B. 1986. *First Principles, Second Thoughts: Aboriginal Peoples, Constitutional Reform and Canadian Statecraft*. Montreal: Institute for Research on Public Policy.

Statistics Canada. 2003. *Aboriginal Peoples of Canada: A Demographic Profile*. Catalogue No. 96F0030XIE2001007.

Stoler, A.L. 1995. *Race and the Education of Desire: Foucault's History of Sexuality and the Colonial Order of Things*. Durham, NC: Duke University Press.

Tough, F. 1996. *'As Their Natural Resources Fail': Native Peoples and the Economic History of Northern Manitoba, 1870–1930.* Vancouver: UBC Press.

Weaver, S. 1993. 'First Nations Women and Government Policy, 1970–92: Discrimination and Conflict', in S. Burt, L. Code, and L. Dorney, eds, *Changing Patterns: Women in Canada.* Toronto: McClelland & Stewart.

Weinstein, J. 1986. *Aboriginal Self-Determination Off a Land Base. Aboriginal Peoples and Constitutional Reform.* Background Paper No. 8. Kingston: Institute of Intergovernmental Relations, Queen's University.

Wherrett, J., and D. Brown. 1992. *Self-Government for Aboriginal Peoples Living in Urban Areas.* Prepared for the Native Council of Canada. Kingston: Institute of Intergovernmental Relations, Queen's University.

Young, R. 1995. *Colonial Desire: Hybridity in Theory, Culture and Race.* London and New York: Routledge.

Zlotkin, N. 1983. *Unfinished Business: Aboriginal Peoples and the 1983 Constitution Conference.* Kingston: Institute of Intergovernmental Relations, Queen's University.

Court Cases

Corbiere v. Canada (Minister of Indian and Northern Affairs). 1999. File No. 25708. Supreme Court of Canada.

R. v. Powley. 2000. 2 C.N.L.R. 233. Ont. S.C.

R. v. Powley. 2001. 2 C.N.L.R. 291. Ont. C.A.

Chapter 8

Rewriting Histories of the Land: Colonization and Indigenous Resistance in Eastern Canada

Bonita Lawrence

The claim to a national culture in the past does not only rehabilitate that nation and serve as a justification for the hope of a future national culture. In the sphere of socioaffective equilibrium, it is responsible for an important change in the native. Perhaps we have not sufficiently demonstrated that colonialism is not simply content to impose its rule upon the present and future of a dominated country. Colonialism is not merely satisfied with holding a people in its grip and emptying the native's brain of all form and content. By a kind of perverse logic, it turns to the past of an oppressed people, and distorts, disfigures, and destroys it.

—Frantz Fanon, *The Wretched of the Earth*

Canadian national identity is deeply rooted in the notion of Canada as a vast northern wilderness, the possession of which, makes Canadians unique and 'pure' of character. Because of this, and in order for Canada to have a viable national identity, the histories of Indigenous nations,[1] in all their diversity and longevity, must be erased. Furthermore, in order to maintain

Canadians' self-image as a fundamentally 'decent' people innocent of any wrongdoing, the historical record of how the land was acquired—the forcible and relentless dispossession of Indigenous peoples, the theft of their territories, and the implementation of legislation and policies designed to effect their total disappearance as peoples—must also be erased. It has therefore been crucial that the survivors of this process be silenced—that Native people be deliberately denied a voice within national discourses (LaRocque, 1993).

A crucial part of the silencing of Indigenous voices is the demand that Indigenous scholars attempting to write about their histories conform to academic discourses that have already staked a claim to expertise about our pasts—notably anthropology and history. For many Aboriginal scholars from Eastern Canada who seek information about the past, exploring the 'seminal' works of contemporary non-Native 'experts' is an exercise in alienation. It is impossible for Native people to see themselves in the unknown and unknowable shadowy figures portrayed on the peripheries of the white settlements of colonial Nova Scotia, New France, and Upper Canada, whose lives are deduced solely through archaeological evidence or the journals of those who sought to conquer, convert, defraud, or in any other way prosper off them. This results in the depiction of ancestors who resemble 'stick figures'; noble savages, proud or wily, inevitably primitive. For the most part, Indigenous scholars engaged in academic writing about the past certainly have little interest in making the premises of such works central to their own writing—and yet the academic canon demands that they build their work on the back of these 'authoritative' sources. We should be clear that contemporary white historians have often argued in defence of Aboriginal peoples, seeking to challenge the minor roles that Native people have traditionally been consigned in the (discursively created) 'historical record.' What is never envisioned, however, is that Indigenous communities should be seen as final arbiters of their own histories.

What is the cost for Native peoples, when these academic disciplines 'own' our pasts? First of all,

colonization is normalized. 'Native history' becomes accounts of specific intervals of 'contact', accounts which neutralize processes of genocide, which never mention racism, and which do not take as part of their purview the devastating and ongoing implications of the policies and processes that are so neutrally described. A second problem, which primarily affects Aboriginal peoples in Eastern Canada, is the longevity of colonization and the fact that some Indigenous peoples are considered by non-Native academics to be virtually extinct, to exist only in the pages of historical texts. In such a context, the living descendants of the Aboriginal peoples of Eastern Canada are all too seldom viewed as those who should play central roles in any writing about the histories of their ancestors.

Most important, however, is the power that is lost when non-Native 'experts' define Indigenous peoples' pasts—the power that inheres when oppressed peoples choose the tools that they need to help them understand themselves and their histories:

> The development of theories by Indigenous scholars which attempt to explain our existence in contemporary society (as opposed to the 'traditional' society constructed under modernism) has only just begun. Not all these theories claim to be derived from some 'pure' sense of what it means to be Indigenous, nor do they claim to be theories which have been developed in a vacuum separated from any association with civil and human rights movements, other nationalist struggles, or other theoretical approaches. What is claimed, however, is that new ways of theorizing by Indigenous scholars are grounded in a real sense of, and sensitivity towards, what it means to be an Indigenous person. . . . Contained within this imperative is a sense of being able to determine priorities, to bring to the centre those issues of our own choosing, and to discuss them amongst ourselves. (Smith, 1999: 38)

For Indigenous peoples, telling our histories involves recovering our own stories of the past and asserting the epistemological foundations that inform our stories of the past. It also involves documenting processes of colonization from the perspectives of those who experienced it. As a result, this chapter, as an attempt to decolonize the history of Eastern Canada, focuses on Indigenous communities' stories of land theft and dispossession, as well as the resistance that these communities manifested towards colonization. It relies primarily on the endeavours of Indigenous elders and scholars who are researching community histories to shape its parameters. Knowledge-carriers such as Donald Marshall Senior and Indigenous scholars who carry out research on behalf of Indigenous communities such as Daniel Paul, Sakej Henderson, and Georges Sioui are my primary sources. For broader overviews of the colonization process, I draw on the works of Aboriginal historians such as Olivia Dickason and Winona Stevenson. In some instances, I rely on non-Native scholars who have consulted Native elders, such as Peter Schmalz, or who have conducted research specifically *for* Indigenous communities involved in resisting colonization (where those communities retain control over ownership of the knowledge and how it is to be used), such as James Morrison. In instances where no other information is available, the detailed work of non-Native scholars such as Bruce Trigger and J.R. Miller is used to make connections between different events and to document regional processes. The issues at hand are whether the scholar in question is Indigenous and the extent to which the scholar documents the perspectives of Indigenous communities about their own pasts.

As history is currently written, from outside Indigenous perspectives, we cannot see colonization *as* colonization. We cannot grasp the overall picture of a focused, concerted process of invasion and land theft. Winona Stevenson has summarized how the 'big picture' looks to Aboriginal peoples: 'Mercantilists wanted our furs, missionaries wanted our souls, colonial governments, and later, Canada, wanted our lands' (Stevenson, 1999: 49). And yet, this complex rendition of a global geopolitical process can obscure how these histories come together in the experiences of different Indigenous nations 'on the ground'. It also obscures the *processes* that enabled colonizers to acquire the land, and the *policies* that were put into place to control the peoples displaced from the land. As a decolonization history, the perspectives informing this work highlight Aboriginal communities' experiences of these colonial processes, while challenging a number of the myths that are crucial to Canadian nation-building, such as the notion that the colonization process was benign and through which Canada maintains its posture of being 'innocent' of racism and genocide. Other myths about Native savagery and the benefits of European technologies are challenged by Native communities' accounts of their own histories and are explored below.

Mercantile Colonialism: Trade and Warfare

The French and early British trade regimes in Canada did not feature the relentless slaughter and enslavement of Indigenous peoples that marked the Spanish conquest of much of 'Latin' America. Nor did they possess the implacable determination to obtain Indigenous land for settlement, by any means necessary, that marked much of the British colonial period in New England. Thus the interval of mercantile colonialism in Canada has been portrayed as relatively innocuous. And yet, northeastern North America was invaded by hundreds of trade ships of different European nations engaged in a massive competition for markets; an invasion instrumental in destabilizing existing intertribal political alliances in eastern North America. It is impossible, for example, to discount the central role that competition for markets played in the large-scale intertribal warfare that appears to have developed, relatively anomalously, throughout the sixteenth, seventeenth, and eighteenth centuries in much of eastern Canada and northeastern United States. Oral history and archeological evidence demonstrate that these wars were unique in the history of these Indigenous nations.

It is important to take into consideration the extent to which the new commodities offered by the Europeans gave obvious material advantages to those nations who successfully controlled different trade routes. Inevitably, however, as communities became reliant on trade to obtain many of the necessities of life, access to trade routes became not only desirable but actually necessary for survival (particular as diseases began to decimate populations, as the animal life was affected, and as missionaries began to make inroads on traditional practices).[2] These pressures resulted in such extreme levels of competition between Indigenous nations that an escalation into continuous warfare was almost inevitable. . . .

Warfare and trade among Indigenous nations profoundly changed the ecology of the land and way of life for nations of many regions. Yet these should not be seen as evidence of Indigenous savagery or of a breakdown of Indigenous values;[3] rather, these profound changes, in part, resulted from the severe pressures caused by the intense competition of European powers during mercantile colonialism to depopulate entire regions of all fur-bearing animals.

Disease and Christianization in the Huron-Wendat Nation

Although French colonial policies focused primarily on the fur trade, under the terms of the Doctrine of Discovery, the monopolies they granted to different individuals in different regions included the mandatory presence of Christian missionaries.[4] The missionaries relied on trade wars (and the epidemics frequently preceding or accompanying them) to harvest converts from Indigenous populations physically devastated by mass death. Nowhere is this more obvious than among the Huron-Wendat people.

The Wendat, whom the Jesuits labelled 'Huron', were the five confederated nations of the territory known as Wendake (now the Penetanguishene Peninsula jutting into Georgian Bay). It was made up of twenty-five towns, with a population that peaked at thirty thousand in the fifteenth century (Sioui, 1999: 84–5). The Wendat relied both on agriculture and fishing, and until extensive contact

with French traders began in 1609, they enjoyed remarkable health and an abundance of food.

Georges Sioui suggests that Wendat communities first came into contact with disease through the French, who were dealing with large groupings of Wendat living together as agricultural people. It was not until 1634, however, when the Jesuits, who had visited in 1626, returned to set up a mission that the Wendat encountered a continuous wave of epidemics, which culminated in the virulent smallpox epidemic of 1640 that cut their population in half (Trigger, 1994: 51). So many elders and youths died in the epidemics that the Wendat began to experience serious problems in maintaining their traditional livelihoods and grew extremely dependent on French trade for survival. The epidemics also had a catastrophic effect on the Wendat worldview. The psychological shock of such an extreme loss of life was experienced as sorcery, as the introduction of a malevolent power into the Wendat universe (Sioui, 1999: 86).

It was into this weakened population that the Jesuits managed to insinuate themselves, using their influence in France to have French traders withdrawn and replaced by Jesuit lay employees. The Jesuits sought to impress the Huron with their technological superiority and allowed their traders to sell certain goods, particularly guns, only to Christian converts (Trigger, 1994: 54). As the number of Christian converts grew in response to such virtual blackmail, the Jesuits gradually obtained enough power in the communities to forbid the practising of Wendat spiritual rituals. . . .

Many lost their tribal status in Kansas, but a small group of Wyandot acquired a reserve in northeastern Oklahoma where they continue to live today. A small number of Wendat remained in Ontario and maintained two reserves in the Windsor region. In the early nineteenth century, both reserves were ceded and sold by the Crown. A small acreage remained and was occupied by a group known as the Anderdon band. This band, consisting of the remaining forty-one Wendat families in Ontario, were enfranchised under the *Indian Act* in 1881, at which point they officially ceased to exist as 'Indians'. Their land base was divided up into individual allotments. Despite the loss of a collective land base and 'Indian' status, the descendants of the forty-one families in Windsor still consider themselves Wendat (Trigger, 1994: 55–61). . . .

The catastrophic changes that the Huron-Wendat have undergone are perhaps less important than the fact that they have survived as a people, and that their worldview has changed but remains fundamentally Wendat. These myths of savagery and of a 'loss of culture' form an essential part of contemporary settler ideology—a justification for the denial of restitution for colonization, the backlash against Aboriginal harvesting rights, and policies of repression against Native communities. Through exploring Huron-Wendat history informed by their own realities, a culture regarded as 'dead' by the mainstream speaks to us about its contemporary world.

The Mi'kmaq: Diplomacy and Armed Resistance

Not all nations faced the Wendat experience of Christianization. The Mi'kmaq nation was perhaps unique in the way it used Christianity as a source of resistance to colonization in the earliest years of contact with Europeans.

Mi'kmaki, 'the land of friendship', covers present-day Newfoundland, St-Pierre and Miquelon, Nova Scotia, New Brunswick, the Magdalen Islands, and the Gaspé Peninsula. It is the territory of the Mi'kmaq, which means 'the allied people'. The Mi'kmaq nation became centralized during a fourteenth-century war with the Iroquois Confederacy. Since then it has been led by the Sante Mawiomi, the Grand Council, and has been divided into seven regions, each with its Sakamaws or chiefs. It is part of the Wabanaki Confederacy, which includes the Mi'kmaq, the Abenakis in Quebec, the Maliseets in western New Brunswick, and the Passamaquoddies and Penobscots in New England (Richardson, 1989: 78). . . .

The Mi'kmaq people were the first Native people in North America to encounter Europeans, and

were aware of the political implications of contact. The French entered their territory in earnest in the sixteenth century and had set up small maritime colonies by the early seventeenth century. Knowledge of the genocide of Indigenous peoples in the Caribbean and Mexico by the Spanish . . . reached the Mi'kmaq by the mid-sixteenth century. In response to this information, and to the spread of disease that increased with greater contact, the Mi'kmaq avoided the French coastal settlements and consolidated their relationships with other Eastern nations of the Wabanaki Confederacy (Henderson, 1997: 80–1). However, Messamouet, a Mi'kmaw[5] scholar and prophet who had travelled to France and learned of how the Europeans conceptualized law and sovereignty, developed another option known as the 'Beautiful Trail', which would involve the Mi'kmaq nation negotiating an alliance with the Holy See in Rome. . . .

By building an alliance with the Holy See, the Mi'kmaq nation sought recognition as a sovereign body among the European nations. In this way, Mi'kmaki could resist the authority of the French Crown. In 1610, Grand Chief Membertou initiated an alliance with the Holy See by negotiating a Concordat that recognized Mi'kmaki as an independent Catholic Republic. As a public treaty with the Holy See, the Concordat had the force of international law, canon law, and civil law. Its primary effect was to protect the Mi'kmaq from French authority 'on the ground'. . . . Under the Concordat and alliance, the Mawiomi maintained a theocracy which synthesized Catholic and Mi'kmaq spirituality and maintained Mi'kmaq independence from the French Crown.[6]

In 1648, the Treaty of Westphalia ended the Holy See's rule over European monarchies. The treaty's settlement of territorial claims placed some lands under the control of nation-states and others under the control of the Holy See: Mi'kmaki 'reverted' to Mi'kmaq control and all protections ceased to exist.

Unfortunately for the Mi'kmaq, the French were not the only colonial power to invade their world. What the British sought was not furs and missions but land where they could build colonies for their surplus populations. . . . Nineteen out of twenty Indigenous people who came into contact with the British succumbed to disease. The British initiated a number of attacks against Indigenous villages, attacks which often escalated into full-scale wars. British slavers scoured the Atlantic coast for Indigenous people who were sold in slave markets all over the world. Indeed, they began raiding Mi'kmaq territory for slaves in the mid-1600s (Stannard, 1992: 238; Churchill, 1994: 34–5; Forbes, 1988: 54–8; Dickason, 1992: 108).

As the British encroached north from New England to Nova Scotia, the Mi'kmaq responded with open resistance. From the mid-1650s until the peace treaty of 1752 (which was reaffirmed in the treaty of 1761), they waged continuous warfare against the British, fighting land battles and capturing almost one hundred British ships. As the long war proceeded, and the Mi'kmaq were gradually weakened, the ascendant British developed policies to exterminate the Mi'kmaq. They used a variety of methods, including distributing poisoned food, trading blankets infected with diseases, and waging ongoing military assaults on civilian populations (Dickason, 1992: 159; Paul, 2000: 181–2). . . . The British introduced scalping policy as another method of extermination. For two decades, the British paid bounty for Mi'kmaq scalps and even imported a group of bounty hunters known as Goreham's Rangers from Massachusetts to depopulate the surviving Mi'kmaq nation (Paul, 2000: 207).

Those who survived this genocide were destitute, left with no food and without the necessary clothing to keep warm in a cold climate. Many were reduced to begging. Thousands died of starvation and exposure until limited poor relief was implemented on a local basis. Others eked out a bare existence selling handicrafts, cutting wood for whites, or working as prostitutes (which resulted in outbreaks of venereal disease). Those who struggled to acquire individual land plots were denied title; as a result, it was not uncommon for Mi'kmaw families to engage in the backbreaking labour of clearing and planting a patch of land, only to find that when they returned from fishing, hunting, or gathering excursions, white squatters had taken the land (Redmond, 1998): 116–17. When the British opened up the region for white settlement, they refused to set aside land for the Native peoples. . . .

By the early 1800s, the Mi'kmaq population had fallen from an estimated two hundred thousand to less than fifteen hundred people. Most whites were predicting that the Mi'kmaq would soon become extinct. During this period, Mi'kmaw leaders continuously petitioned London, finally managing to obtain a handful of small reserves. . . . The Mi'kmaq endured policies that tried to centralize and liquidate the few reserves that had been created, divide their bands, and dissolve their traditional governance. These policies aimed in every way to erase their existence.

Since the signing of the 1752 treaty, which brought an end to warfare, the Mi'kmaq have sought to resolve the ongoing land and resource theft, with little success. In 1973, the *Calder* case decision forced the Canadian government to recognize that it had some obligation to deal with land claims. . . .

In exploring Mi'kmaq resistance efforts—negotiating a Concordat with the Holy See, waging the longest anti-colonial war in North America, surviving policies designed to exterminate them—we see a picture of Native peoples as resourceful and capable of engaging a powerful enemy in armed conflict for a significant period of time. Perhaps even more important, we see Mi'kmaq people as actors on an international stage, engaging the European powers not only through warfare but through diplomacy, signing international treaties as a nation among nations. . . .

It is impossible to understand contemporary struggles for self-determination without this view of Native peoples as nations among other nations. Today, the spirit that enabled the Mi'kmaq to resist genocide is being manifested in the continuous struggles over the right to fish. . . . It is believed that Canada usurped lands accorded to the Mi'kmaq under the Concordat's international law. By reestablishing communication with the Holy See, the Mawiomi wish to recreate its partnership in ways that enhance the autonomy and spiritual uniqueness of the Mi'kmaq (Henderson, 1997: 104).

Geopolitical Struggles between the Colonizers and Indigenous Resistance in the Great Lakes Region

The British entered the territory now known as Canada from two fronts: the East Coast region (primarily for settlement purposes) and Hudson's Bay (under the charter of the Hudson's Bay Company for the purpose of the fur trade). . . .

The struggle between Britain and France over the Great Lakes region had profound effects on the Iroquois and Ojibway peoples who lived there. The trade struggle between Europeans forced, first, one party, and then the other, to lower the prices of trade goods relative to the furs that were traded for them. Ultimately, when warfare broke out, the effect was devastating, as colonial battles fought in Native homelands destroyed these regions and drew Native peoples into battles, primarily to ensure that a 'balance of power' resulted (which would ensure that both European powers remained deadlocked and that one power would not emerge victorious over another).[7]

In 1763, the warfare between France and Britain ended when France surrendered its territorial claims in North America. . . . Because it was important for Britain to reassert its formal adherence to the Doctrine of Discovery and to ensure that its claims to eastern North America would be respected by other European regimes, the British government consolidated its imperial position by structuring formal, constitutional relations with the Native nations in these territories. The Royal Proclamation of 1763 recognized Aboriginal title to all unceded lands and acknowledged a nation-to-nation relationship with Indigenous peoples which the Indian Department was in charge of conducting. Department agents could not command; they could only use the diplomatic tools of cajolery, coercion (where possible), and bribery (Milloy, 1983). The nation-to-nation relationship was maintained until the end of the War of 1812 when the post-war

relationships between Britain and the American government became more amicable and made military alliances with Native nations unnecessary.

In the meantime, Britain's ascendancy in the Great Lakes region marked a disastrous turn for Native peoples. . . . It was also obvious to Indigenous people that one unchallenged European power was far more dangerous to deal with than a group of competing Europeans. During this desperate state of affairs, a number of Indigenous nations attempted to form broad-ranging alliances across many nations in an effort to eliminate the British presence from their territories, culminating in the Pontiac uprising of 1763.

Pontiac, an Odawa war chief, was inspired by the Delaware prophet Neolin. He wanted to build a broad-based multinational movement whose principles involved a return to the ways of the ancestors and a complete avoidance of Europeans and their trade goods. At least nineteen of the Indigenous nations most affected by the Europeans shared this vision. Their combined forces laid siege to Fort Detroit for five months, captured nine other British forts, and killed or captured two thousand British. Within a few months, they had taken back most of the territory in the Great Lakes region from European control.

Between 1764 and 1766, peace negotiations took place between the British and the alliance. The British had no choice in the matter; the Pontiac uprising was the most serious Native resistance they had faced in the eighteenth century (Dickason, 1992: 182–4). As a consequence, the British were forced to adopt a far more respectful approach to Native peoples within the fur trade and to maintain far more beneficial trade terms. However, the dependency of many of the Indigenous nations on British trade goods and their different strategies in dealing with this dependency weakened the alliance and it could not be maintained over the long term.[8] This, unfortunately, coincided with the British plan to devise ways of removing the military threat that Native peoples clearly represented, without the cost of open warfare. The primary means they chose were disease and alcohol.

There is now evidence to suggest that the small-pox pandemic—which ravaged the Ojibway and a number of the Eastern nations including the Mingo, Delaware, Shawnee, and other Ohio River nations, and which killed at least one hundred thousand people—was deliberately started by the British (Churchill, 1994: 35). The earliest evidence of this deliberate policy is the written request of Sir Jeffrey Amherst to Colonel Henry Bouqet at Fort Pitt. In June 1763, Amherst instructed Bouqet to distribute blankets infected with smallpox as gifts to the Indians. On June 24, Captain Ecuyer of the Royal Americans noted in his journal, 'We gave them two blankets and a handkerchief out of the smallpox hospital. I hope it will have the desired effect' (Wagner and Stearn, 1945: 44–5). . . .

The 'chemical warfare' of alcohol was waged against the Ojibway in a highly deliberate manner. Major Gladwin articulated this policy clearly: 'The free sale of rum will destroy them more effectively than fire and sword.' The effects of widespread alcohol distribution were immediate.

In the Great Lakes region, chemical and germ warfare were used by the British as the primary means to acquire land and impose control. . . . The Pontiac uprising demonstrated the power of Indigenous nations organized in armed resistance to colonization. . . . These changes to Indigenous ways of life had long-term and highly significant effects on the possibilities of maintaining sover-eignty and resistance to European expansion. The centuries-long fur trade changed the course of Indigenous history in Eastern Canada, as the con-siderable military power of the Indigenous nations was subverted by their need for trade goods to support their changing way of life.

Ojibway Experiences of Colonization

Immigration, Deception, and Loss of Land

As the fur trade spread further west, the British government consolidated its hold over the Great Lakes area by implementing settlement policies. At the end of the American Revolution, Loyalists poured into the territory that had become known as Upper Canada, bringing new epidemics of smallpox that decimated the Ojibway around Lake Ontario. . . .

Between 1781 and 1830, the Ojibway gradually ceded to the British most of the land north of what is now southern Ontario. The British knew that the Ojibway were aware of the warfare being com-mitted against Native peoples in the United States, where uncontrolled, violent settlement and poli-cies of removal were being implemented. Using this knowledge to their advantage, the British pre-sented land treaties as statements of loyalty to the Crown and as guarantees that the lands would be protected from white settlement. Through the use of gifts and outright lies, to say nothing of improperly negotiated and conflicting boundaries, most of the land of southern Ontario was surren-dered over a fifty-year period. The British used the following procedures to negotiate land treaties:

1. By the Proclamation of 1763, the rights of Indigenous peoples to the land were acknowledged.
2. The Indigenous peoples of each area were called to consider a surrender of lands, nego-tiated by traders or administrators that they already knew and trusted.
3. Only the chiefs or male representatives were asked to sign.[9]
4. The surrender was considered a test of loyalty.
5. The area ceded was deliberately kept vague.
6. Some compensation, in the form of gifts, was given.
7. In many cases, the land was left unsettled for a few years, until disease and alcohol had weakened potential resistance. When the set-tlers began to come in and the Native people complained, they were shown the documents they had signed and told there was no recourse (Schmalz, 1991: 123). . . .

Settler Violence and Loss of Land

When the first two waves of land cessions were over in what is now southern Ontario, two million acres remained in the hands of Native peoples.

Over the next fifty years, the British exerted continuous pressure on the Saugeen Ojibway, whose territories of the Bruce Peninsula and its watershed were still unceded. Eager to acquire their land, the British developed a new way of obeying the letter of the law while violating its spirit—they began to use the threat of settler violence to force land surrenders. The constant encroachment of armed, land-hungry settlers forced the Saugeen Ojibway to continuously retreat, negotiating small land surrenders, a piece at a time. Often the treaties were negotiated with individuals who had no authority within their communities to negotiate treaties; these treaties, therefore, were illegal. . . .

A large influx of settlers, primarily refugees from the Irish potato famine and from English industrial slums, put pressure on the colony for even greater tracts of land. Once again, armed squatters were allowed to invade and seize lands. . . .

The above discussion demonstrates how the British fur trade interests in Upper Canada were gradually supplanted by settlement policies, which allowed the Crown to use whatever means were at hand to consolidate its hold over former 'Indian' territories. These policies resulted in the endless misery of relocation and land loss for the Ojibway people, of what is now southern and central Ontario, and left many unresolved claims for restitution of stolen lands. These claims include the efforts of the Caldwell Ojibway to obtain a reserve[10] after being forced off their land near Lake Erie during the first wave of land grabs in the early 1800s, and the monumental struggles around fishing rights waged by contemporary Saugeen Ojibway communities.[11]

Moving North: Resource Plunder of Ojibway and Cree Territories

The consolidation of the land and resource base of what is now northern Ontario . . . took place within the twentieth century.

Once the land base in southern Ontario was secure, business interests in the colony looked to the rich resources in the north. Within a few years,

the vast timber forests were being cut, and the growing presence of mineral prospectors and mining operations in northern Ontario caused a number of Ojibway leaders to travel to Toronto to register complaints and demand payment from the revenues of mining leases. When there was no response to these or other entreaties, the Ojibway took matters into their own hands and forcibly closed two mining operations in the Michipicoten area. Soon troops, which were not called in to protect the Saugeen Ojibway from violent white settlers, were on the scene to quell the 'rebellion', and government investigators began to respond to the issues that leaders were bringing to them (Dickason, 1992: 253). The Ojibway wanted treaties, but they demanded a new concession—that reserve territories be specified before the treaties were signed. After considerable discussion and many demands from the Ojibway leaders, the Robinson-Huron and Robinson-Superior Treaties were signed in 1850. These treaties ceded a land area twice the size of that which had already been given up in southern Ontario, set aside reserves (although much smaller than the Ojibway had hoped for), and provided the bands with a lump-sum payment plus annual annuities of $4 per year per person. Most important, hunting and fishing rights to the entire treaty area were to be maintained.

With these treaties, the colony gained access to all the land around Lake Huron and Lake Superior, south of the northern watershed. All land north of this was considered Rupert's Land, the 'property' of the Hudson's Bay Company. . . . Inherent in the concept of 'Canada', then, was the notion of continuous expansion, a Canadian version of 'manifest destiny', no less genocidal than the United States in its ultimate goals of supplanting Indigenous peoples and claiming their territory.

Under section 91(4) of the Constitution Act, 1867, the Canadian federal government was given constitutional responsibility for 'Indians and Lands reserved for the Indians', while section 109 gave the provinces control over lands and resources within provincial boundaries, subject to an interest 'other than that of the Province in the same' (Morrison, 1992: 4). . . .

In the late 1890s, the Liberal regime of Oliver Mowat, dominated by timber 'barons' whose immense profits had been made through logging central Ontario and the Temagami region, was succeeded by the Conservative regime of James Whitney. Proponents of modern liberal capitalism, the Conservatives pushed aggressively ahead with northern development, focusing on railways, mining, and the pulp and paper industry (Hodgins and Benidickson, 1989: 88–9). Three northern railways were constructed to access timber, develop mineral resources, and access potential hydroelectric sites to power the resource industries. The railways opened up the territory to predators at an unprecedented rate. As a rule, if the presence of Cree or Ojibway people hindered development, the newly created Department of Indian Affairs relocated them away from the area.

It is important to understand the scale of the mineral wealth taken from the lands of the Ojibway and Cree in the past century, at great disruption to their lives and without any compensation. Since the early 1900s, the Cobalt silver mines brought in more than $184 million; Kirkland Lake gold mines produced $463 million; and Larder Lake produced $390 million (Longo, 1973: 66–107). Meanwhile, the Porcupine region, one of the greatest gold camps in the world, produced over $1 billion worth of gold and had the largest silver, lead, and zinc mines in the world (Guilbert and Park, Jr, 1986: 863).

Across northeastern Ontario, hydroelectric development was sought primarily for the new mining industry. In 1911, however, timber concessions for the pulp and paper industry were granted, mainly to friends of government ministers, on condition that hydroelectric dams be built to power them out of the industry's money. In many cases, pulp cutting and dam construction proceeded well before permits were granted to do so.[12]

Reasserting a Silenced History

This chapter has introduced only a few examples of Indigenous writers, or non-Native historians working with Elders, who have recorded Indigenous nations' stories of their past. These stories introduce new perspectives to what is considered 'Canadian' history. . . .

Writing from the perspectives of the Indigenous nations enables specific communities to give a full and honest account of their struggles with colonizers intent on their removal and elimination as peoples, and to name the racism, land theft, and policies of genocide that characterize so much of Canada's relationships with the Indigenous nations. Even more important, Indigenous peoples are not cast as faceless, unreal 'stick figures' lost in a ferment of European interests, but as the living subjects of their own histories. . . .

It perhaps goes without saying that the histories of Indigenous nations will decentre the histories of New France and Upper Canada as organizing themes to the histories of this land. Canadian historians who are currently considered the experts could work in conjunction with Indigenous peoples wanting to tell their stories of the land. But the works of the experts alone, which provide powerful and detailed histories of the Canadian settler state, do not represent the full picture. It is the voices of Indigenous peoples, long silenced, but now creating a new discourse, which will tell a fuller history.

Notes

1. I have used a number of terms interchangeably to describe the subjects of this article. Generally, I use the term 'Indigenous peoples', as it is the international term most commonly selected by Indigenous peoples to describe themselves. However, Indigenous peoples in Canada often use the term 'Aboriginal' or 'Native' to describe themselves; as a result, I have included these terms as well, particularly when focusing on the local context. Occasionally, the term 'Indian' is included when popularly used by Native people (such as the term 'American Indians').

2. Losing access to the European trade appears to have been devastating for many communities. In *The Ojibwa of Southern Ontario* (Toronto: University of Toronto Press, 1991), Peter S. Schmalz recounts how Captain St. Pierre arrived at Madeline Island in 1718 to find an isolated community of Ojibway who had, over the past twenty-two years, lost access to the fur trade as a result of geographic isolation, war with the Iroquois, and the deadly trading competition between the French and the English, which

involved continuously cutting off each others' markets. After a century of growing dependence on European technology, the community no longer had the endurance to hunt without guns or the skills to make stone, bone, and wood tools and utensils to replace the metal ones they had become dependent on using. The women had lost many of the skills of treating skins (when they were able to obtain them) for clothing. St. Pierre found a ragged and starving community, desperate to enter into trade relationships again. It is not a matter, after all, simply of individuals 'roughing it' and re-adapting to Indigenous forms of technology. Indigenous communities had to be able to live off the land on a scale that would keep whole communities viable.

3. Contemporary attacks on Aboriginal harvesting, as well as the distrust that many environmentalists apparently hold for Native communities' abilities to maintain ecological relationships with the environment, have only been accelerated by the interest on the part of some historians in 'debunking' notions of the viability of Aboriginal ecological relationships in the past. Calvin Martin, for example, has advanced theories that suggest Aboriginal peoples lost their respect for animals during the fur trade because of the breakdown of their spiritual framework, which was caused by illness contracted from Europeans.

4. The Doctrine of Discovery was the formal code of juridical standards in international law that had been created by papal edict to control the different interests of European powers in the different lands they were acquiring. For its primary tenets, see Ward Churchill, *Struggle for the Land: Indigenous Resistance to Genocide, Ecocide and Expropriation in Contemporary North America* (Toronto: Between the Lines, 1992), p. 36.

5. Mi'kmaq people generally wish to be referred to in the terms of their own language, rather than through the generic term 'Micmac,' which had been applied to them. My limited understanding of the Mi'kmaq language suggests to me that individuals and family groups are referred to as 'Mi'kmaw,' while the nation and its language is referred to as 'Mi'kmaq.' My apologies to those who are better language speakers, for whom my use of terminology may not be accurate enough.

6. The independence enjoyed by the Mi'kmaq under the Concordat did not sit well with the Jesuits who came to Acadia to minister to both Acadian colonists and Mi'kmaqs. The Mi'kmaq rejected the Jesuits' authoritarian ways, after which the Jesuits attended only to the Catholics of New France. Mi'kmaki continued a relatively anomalous independence from French missionaries and colonists for most of the period of French ascendancy in North America and indeed, for the most part considered themselves, and were considered as, allies with the French Crown in its escalating war with the British in North America.

7. Many of the Indigenous nations affected by this warfare appeared to have fought strategically to ensure that

a balance of power between competing Europeans was maintained. It is significant that as the French and British became locked in a death struggle, the Ojibway appear to have signed a pact of non-aggression with the Iroquois. In general, as the extent of European interference in their affairs became crucial, many of the Great Lakes nations appear to have resisted fighting each other by the mid-eighteenth century. See Schmalz, *The Ojibwa of Southern Ontario*, p. 58.

8. Schmalz, *The Ojibwa of Southern Ontario*, has suggested that during the Pontiac uprising, the Ojibway and other nations were too divided by their dependence on European trade goods and by the inroads that alcohol was making in the communities to successfully rout the British from the Great Lakes region, as they might have been capable of doing in earlier years. Although driving the British out of the region was undoubtedly the wish of some of the Ojibway communities, there were other communities situated far away from encroaching British settlement, but equally dependent on European technology, that were less certain of the threat the British ultimately posed.

9. Excluding Native women from the process was central to its success. In eastern Canada, Native women's voices were in many cases considered extremely authoritative in matters of land use. Excluding them from the signing process made land theft that much easier, by allowing those who did not control the land to sign it over. See Kim Anderson, *A Recognition of Being: Reconstructing Native Womanhood* (Toronto: Sumach Press, 2001).

10. The traditional territory of the Caldwell band is Point Pelee, which is now a national park. The Caldwell band were involved in the War of 1812 as allies to the British Crown, where they were known as the Caldwell Rangers. After the war in 1815, the British Crown acknowledged their efforts and their loyal service and awarded them their traditional territory 'for ever more'. But it wasn't classified as a reserve, and meanwhile, British soldiers who retired after the war were awarded most of the land. By the 1860s the few remaining members of the Caldwell band that were still living on their traditional territories were beaten out of the new park by the RCMP with bullwhips. By the 1970s, the Caldwell band members dispersed throughout southern Ontario began to take part in ritual occupation of the park to protest their land claim. A settlement process is currently in effect (Anonymous Caldwell band member, interview with author, 1999).

11. After a series of struggles towards resolving historic land claims, the Chippewas of Nawash, one of two remaining Saugeen Ojibway bands, were recognized in 1992 as having a historic right to fish in their traditional waters. This decision led to three years of racist assaults by local whites and organized fishing interests, including the sinking of their fishing boats, the destruction of thousands of dollars of nets and other equipment, assaults on local Native people selling fish, the stabbing of two Native men in

Owen Sound and the beating of two others. No charges were laid by the Owen Sound Police or the OPP for any of this violence until the band called for a federal inquiry into the attacks ('Nawash Calls for Fed Inquiry into Attacks', *Anishinabek News*, June 1996, p. 14).

Meanwhile, the Ontario Ministry of Natural Resources, in open defiance of the ruling recognizing the band's rights, declared a fishing free-for-all for two consecutive years, allowing anglers licence-free access to the waters around the Bruce Peninsula for specific weekends throughout the summer ('Fishing Free-for-all Condemned by Natives', *Anishinabek News*, July 1995, p. 1).

In 1996, despite considerable opposition, the band took over the fishery using an *Indian Act* regulation that severed their community from the jurisdiction of the provincial government (Roberta Avery, 'Chippewas Take Over Management of Fishery', *Windspeaker*, July 1996, p. 3). The other Saugeen Ojibway band on the peninsula, the Saugeen First Nation, announced the formation of the Saugeen Fishing Authority and claimed formal juris-diction of the waters of their traditional territory. They demanded that sports fishermen and boaters would have to buy a licence from them to use their waters. The prov-incial government recognized the claims of neither bands, instead demanding they limit their catch and pur-chase licences from the provincial government in order to be able to fish at all (Roberta Avery, 'Fishery in Jeopardy, Says University Researcher', *Windspeaker*, Aug. 1996, p. 16).

By 1997, a government study into fish stocks in Lake Huron revealed that certain fish stocks were severely impaired. While the report was supposed to be for the whole Lake Huron area, it in fact zeroed in on the Bruce Peninsula area a number of times, feeding the attitudes of non-Natives about Native mismanagement of the fishery (Rob McKinley, 'Fight Over Fish Continues for Nawash', *Windspeaker*, Sept. 1997, p. 14). To add to the difficulties, in 1997, Atomic Energy of Canada announced their desire to bury 20,000 tonnes of nuclear waste in the Canadian shield. This brought to the band's attention the extent to which the fishery was already affected by nuclear contam-ination from the Bruce Nuclear Power Development on Lake Huron, 30 km south of the reserve (Roberta Avery, 'No Nuclear Waste on Indian Land', *Windspeaker*, April 1997, p. 4).

12. Howard Ferguson, then minister of Lands and Forests, had so consistently awarded timber and pulpwood con-cessions without advertisement, public tenders, or even formal agreements on price to individuals like Frank Anson who founded the powerful Abitibi Power and Paper Company, that he was found guilty in 1922 of vio-lating the *Crown Timber Act*—one of the few whites to ever be prosecuted for disobeying federal legislation con-cerning Indigenous land. See Morrison, 'Colonization Resource Extraction and Hydroelectric Development'.

References

Churchill, Ward. 1994. *Indians Are Us? Culture and Genocide in Native North America*. Toronto: Between the Lines.

Dickason, Olive. 1992. *Canada's First Nations*. Toronto: Oxford University Press.

Forbes, Jack D. 1988. *Black Africans and Native Americans: Color, Race and Caste in the Evolution of Red-Black Peoples*. Oxford: Basil Blackwell.

Guilbert, John M., and Charles F. Park, Jr. 1986. 'Porcupine-Timmins Gold Deposits', in *The Geology of Ore Deposits*. New York: W.H. Freeman and Company.

Henderson, J.S.Y. 1997. *The Mi'kmaw Concordat*. Halifax, NS: Fernwood Publishing.

Hodgins, Bruce W., and Jamie Benidickson. 1989. *The Temagami Experience: Recreation, Resources and Aboriginal Rights in the Northern Ontario Wilderness*. Toronto: University of Toronto Press.

LaRocque, Emma. 1993. 'Preface—or "Here Are Our Voices—Who Will Hear?"', in Jeanne Perrault and Sylvia Vance, eds, *Writing the Circle: Native Women of Western Canada*. Edmonton: NeWest Publishers.

Longo, Roy M. 1973. *Historical Highlights in Canadian Mining*. Toronto: Pitt Publishing Co.

Milloy, John S. 1983. 'The Early Indian Acts: Developmental Strategy and Constitutional Change', pp. 56–63 in I.A. Getty and A.S. Lussier, eds, *As Long as the Sun Shines and the Water Flows: A Reader in Canadian Native History*. Vancouver: University of British Columbia Press, 1983.

Morrison, James. 1992. 'Colonization, Resource Extraction and Hydroelectric Development in the Moose River Basin: A Preliminary History of the Implications for Aboriginal People.' Report prepared for the Moose River/James Bay Coalition, for presentation to the Environmental Assessment Board Hearings, Ontario Hydra Demand/Supply Plan, November.

Paul, Daniel N. 2000. *We Were Not the Savages: A Mi'kmaq Perspective on the Collision between European and Native American Civilizations*. Halifax: Fernwood Books.

Redmond, Theresa. 1998. ' "We Cannot Work Without Food": Nova Scotia Indian Policy and Mi'kmaq Agriculture, 1783–1867', in David T. McNab, ed., *Earth, Water, Air and Fire: Studies in Canadian Ethnohistory*. Waterloo, ON: Wilfrid Laurier University Press.

Richardson, Boyce, ed. 1989. *Drumbeat: Anger and Renewal in Indian Country*. Toronto: Summerhill Press and the Assembly of First Nations.

Schmalz, Peter S. 1991. *The Ojibwa of Southern Ontario*. Toronto: University of Toronto Press.

Sioui, Georges E. 1999. *Huron Wendat: The Heritage of the Circle*. Vancouver: University of British Columbia Press.

Smith, Linda Tuhiwai. 1999. *Decolonizing Methodologies: Research and Indigenous Peoples*. London: Zed Books.

Stannard, David E. 1992. *American Holocaust: The Conquest of the New World*. Toronto: Oxford University Press.

Stevenson, Winona. 1999. 'Colonialism and First Nations Women in Canada', in Enakshi Dua and Angela Robertson, eds, *Scratching the Surface: Canadian Anti-Racist Feminist Thought*. Toronto: The Women's Press.

Trigger, Bruce G. 1994. 'The Original Iroquoians: Huron, Petun, and Neutral', in E.S. Rogers and D.B. Smith, eds,

Aboriginal Ontario: Historical Perspectives on the First Nations. Toronto: Dundurn Press.

Wagner, E., and E. Stearn. 1945. *The Effects of Smallpox on the Destiny of the Amerindian*. Boston: Bruce Humphries.

Chapter 9

Iroquois Women's Rights with Respect to Matrimonial Property on Indian Reserves

Martha Montour

Introduction

My objective is to present a comparison between the traditional superior rights of the Iroquois women and their present day inferior rights, with respect to matrimonial property upon dissolution of marriage on Indian reserves under the Indian Act, R.S.C. 1970, c.I-6. It will be traced from pre-contact with the Europeans to the present time. I have restricted the scope of my paper to the matrimonial property rights of the Iroquois Confederacy in Canada. My conclusion will briefly present some political solutions and two possible legal arguments to resolve this unsatisfactory state of affairs. . . .

The Woman in Traditional Iroquois Family Life

The women enjoyed more privileges and possessed greater freedom than the women of other tribes, this was due . . . to the important place that agriculture held in their economic life and the distribution

of labor . . . [which left] the entire cultivation of the fields and the acquisition of the greater part of the food supply to the women. (Brown, 1978: 151)

The Iroquois women enjoyed an equal, if not superior position with respect to family property because of their control over the basic economic unit called the family and their economic contribution.

An Iroquois matron controlled the Longhouse where the extended family lived. There were several Longhouses in a village. The Longhouse was a large structure with many compartments and each family occupied one compartment. Stored food was the main wealth and it was under the control of the matron who supervised the cooking and dispensed it. The matron ruled supreme and all domestic arrangements were through this matron. Her power was socially recognized and institutionalized because the matron had the power to nominate and impeach the male chiefs who were the political representatives of the Confederacy. All inheritance and succession went through the female to the exclusion of the male. They also arranged all marriages. It was a matrilineal society.

Upon marriage, the husband moved into the Longhouse of his wife. Since all the women in the home were related, it was ruled by the women. If the husband failed to provide enough meat by hunting because he was lazy, he could be ousted by the women. Even if the couple set up their own household, the husband was obliged to supply food to his mother-in-law. It was to the husband's honour that his family was well-kept.

The women planted and harvested the fields. The men cleared the fields but not much importance was given to this task. This was reflected in the traditional ceremonies based on food harvest themes which was the sole responsibility of the women.

Lands of the Iroquois were communally owned by the tribes. The belief was that the land belonged not only to the present generation, but to the future generations (Snyderman, 1951). Any land transactions have born the signatures of the matrons, the chiefs and the leading warriors (Carr, 1883: 214).

Upon dissolution of the marriage, by either party, the separate household or compartment of the Longhouse belonged to the woman. The husband had to leave with only his clothes and weapons. Since the woman controlled the household and the fields, she kept the home and the farming tools. The husband either returned to his mother's Longhouse or set up another matrimonial home (Carr, 1883: 222). This was the traditional property division between spouses.

The Iroquois woman's rights to the family property was based on political influence via the control over the economic wealth of the family. As one can see, she had real property rights even superior to those of her husband.

Changes in the Iroquois Woman's Status

As the Iroquois became more and more exposed to European values and technology, the woman's status with respect to matrimonial property greatly changed and diminished. At European common and civil law, the husband had either sole ownership, or management of any family assets and the wife ceased to be a legal person. Also, all succession and inheritance was patrilineal. This was completely opposite to the equal, if not, superior status of the Iroquois woman.

The Iroquois husband's occupation changed from hunter to either farmer (which formerly was the woman's domain) or skilled tradesman. This resulted in an increase in production by the male and a diminution in the contribution by the female. Stored food was no longer an important wealth. Since most food was purchased rather than grown, the woman became dependent on the husband. Upon marriage, a couple usually set up their own household where the matron no longer ruled supreme. The husband became the sole provider of the food supply because he was the income-earner.

The loss of the Iroquois woman's status was hastened by non-Iroquois religion, politics, and legislation where the male status and role was defined according to the European values. All family property was registered under the husband's name in accordance with European law and custom. The Iroquois woman no longer had an equal right to a divorce except on more burdensome grounds than her husband. . . . The woman had no right to vote or to be involved in politics. Her only right was to support payments, which was a personal right against her husband. This was not a real property right. The Iroquois gradually adopted these values due to the economic dependency of the Iroquois woman and the influence of European contact.

Another important factor was the change in the concept of communal land ownership. Land became a commodity which could be exchanged for liquor, annuities, etc. Legislation gave individual Indians private land ownership. The power of the woman was considerably diminished if the man was the sole legal owner of family assets. This changed the social, political and economic custom of preserving land for the future generations.

Another important factor was that an elected system for chiefs, instead of the matrons selecting chiefs, was imposed by legislation such as the Indian Act. Since women were not allowed to vote, they lost any influence over lawmaking.

The traditional position of the Iroquois woman was changed to the inferior status of the European woman. The Iroquois woman had no economic contribution nor any political influence. She no longer owned the family property. All income was controlled by her husband. She was a dependent homemaker in the marriage.

Present Day Status of the Iroquois Woman

The present matrimonial rights of all spouses upon dissolution of marriage are governed by provincial legislation under section 92(13) of the Constitution Act, 1867. Each province has legislation for division of family property, depending on the residence of the spouses and the location of their property. A problem arises when Iroquois spouses apply to the courts for a division of property or any possessory or occupational rights to the matrimonial home under provincial legislation. They will be denied their request. This problem is the result of the federal exclusive jurisdiction over "Indians, and Lands reserved for the Indians" under section 91(24) of the Constitution Act, 1867. Since section 20 of the Indian Act is valid federal legislation, which regulates possession and occupation of reserve land by the elected chiefs and the Minister of Indian Affairs, any provincial matrimonial property legislation which deals with the same property rights is inoperative due to direct conflict between the legislation and operation of the paramountcy doctrine.

Case law from the Supreme Court of Canada has pronounced definitively on the issues of the right of possession and occupation of a matrimonial home on reserve land by an Indian spouse.

In *Derrickson v. Derrickson*, [1986] 2 C.N.L.R. 45, a wife applied for a half interest in her husband's interest in reserve land for which he held a certificate of possession under the Indian Act, or

for an order for compensation in lieu of division pursuant to the British Columbia Family Relations Act. The Supreme Court of Canada unanimously held that the right to possession of lands on an Indian reserve is manifestly the very essence of federal exclusive legislative power under section 91(24) of the Constitution Act, 1867. Provincial legislation dealing with the right of possession and ownership of immoveable property, while valid with respect to other immoveable property, cannot apply to reserve lands. Where division is not possible because reserve lands cannot be divided, a spouse, however, may be entitled to an order for compensation for the purposes of adjusting the division of family assets. No conflict exists between section 91(24) and a compensation order.

Another Supreme Court decision is *Paul v. Paul*, [1986] 2 C.N.L.R. 74. The Supreme Court upheld the decision of the British Columbia Court of Appeal that an order, pursuant to provincial legislation, granting exclusive interim occupation of the matrimonial home on an Indian reserve was in conflict with the Indian Act. It was held that, since occupation is part of possession under the Indian Act, provincial legislation granting occupation to the applicant wife was in conflict with the federal legislation which granted possession. Such an order could not be operative on an Indian reserve. One of the aims of provincial matrimonial legislation was to remedy the inequity of the 'separate as to property regime' with respect to matrimonial property rights at common law. It was to give each spouse an interest in the family assets, whether or not the property was in one spouse's name. The doctrine of constructive or resulting trust was unsatisfactory as the spouse was required to prove intention to share or actual contribution to claim ownership or a share.

It seems that the Iroquois spouses on Canadian reserve lands are suffering the same inequities as they cannot apply for relief under the provincial matrimonial legislation due to the conflict with federal jurisdiction. It would seem to be the same situation in Quebec civil law, where a matrimonial regime is imposed in absence of a marriage contract. In *Quebec No. 233*, [1985] C.A. 512, the

Quebec Court of Appeal held that community property regime applied to Indian spouses on reserves by virtue of section 88 of the Indian Act. Section 88 makes general provincial legislation applicable to Indians *but not to lands reserved for Indians*. The judgment does not pronounce on whether community property provisions can apply to Indian reserve lands.

It seems that the only recourse for spouses is under the trusts doctrine or a compensation order for the purpose of adjusting the division. Although either spouse may possess property under the Indian Act, the reality is that the introduction of European values has resulted in the allotment of reserve land to the male spouses, who are the income-earners. Since the Iroquois woman has lost her superior economic status, she will generally be the loser in a marriage dissolution. Although she can apply under provincial compensatory schemes, she will have difficulty enforcing such an order as it is not a real property right. The provincial legislation cannot disrupt a valid certificate of possession on reserve land.

The property situation of the modern day Iroquois woman is vastly different from her historical sister prior to European contact. There has been a complete demotion. If she is not the legal owner of the family asset situated on an Indian reserve, then upon marriage dissolution, she has no possibility of real property rights. She has no recourse under provincial matrimonial legislation as it conflicts with the land use scheme essential to the federal jurisdiction over reserve lands under section 91(24) of the Constitution Act, 1867. Her situation is equivalent to that under the 'separate as to property regime' which was remedied by provincial matrimonial legislation in the common law provinces. She has recourse only under common law trust doctrines and provincial compensation schemes. She no longer has her traditional real property rights over family assets.

Conclusion

Some of the solutions are political and some are legal. These are only a few of them in brief. . . .

One could try to challenge the landholding scheme under the Indian Act as discriminatory under section 15 of the Canadian Charter of Rights and Freedoms. As a result of this federal scheme, Indian spouses have no equality before and under provincial matrimonial property law because of their ethnic origin. It could also be argued that the land scheme's most negative effect is on dependent spouses who are most likely to be women. Therefore, it discriminates on the basis of sex. If one could convince the courts of a contravention of section 15, then maybe one could apply for a remedy under section 24. This remedy could be to order the federal government to rectify the lack of matrimonial property legislation for Indian reserves. But this would be a remedy that the courts would be most reluctant to order.

The most realistic solution is for the tribes to enact matrimonial property regimes as part of their right of self-government. If the federal government were to legislate on the matter under section 91(24) of the Constitution Act, 1867, it could possibly be challenged as a colourable attempt to legislate in the provincial jurisdiction over property and civil rights between spouses. But the regime could be upheld as being valid because it is essential to the use of reserve lands by Indian spouses whether enacted under Indian self-government or under the exclusive federal power of section 91(24).

Another remedy is based on international law. In the *International Covenant on Civil and Political Rights*, Article 23 states, in part:

> 4. States Parties to the present Covenant shall take appropriate steps to ensure equality of rights and responsibilities of spouses as to marriage, during marriage and at its dissolution. In the case of dissolution, provision shall be made for the necessary protection of any children.

If neither the courts nor the government bodies rectify the inequity, Iroquois women could appeal to the international arena. Spouses, upon marriage dissolution, have equal rights according to the Covenant. This should include an equal right to family property. Although this is not binding on Canadian courts, it can be politically embarrassing for Canada as a signatory to the Covenant. They are obliged to take the necessary steps to remedy any inequality of rights upon marriage dissolution. This may result in appropriate legislative action by the federal government or Indian governments. This was the result when Sandra Lovelace appealed to the international court because she had lost her rights as an Indian woman, upon marriage to a non-Indian spouse. Her appeal was received and the federal government passed legislative amendments to the Indian Act ending sexual discrimination.

If the legislative avenue is chosen it will be an opportunity to achieve an ideal matrimonial property regime. One could aim at restoring the influential position of the Iroquois women in the social and economic life of their tribes by vesting real matrimonial property rights in them. However,

this will only happen if women become politically and economically strong as they were in the past when they selected the political representatives and produced the necessities of life. Otherwise, they may have limited access to real property rights depending on the classification of divisible family property under any future regime for matrimonial reserve lands.

References

Brown, J.K. 1978. *Economics of the Iroquois*, Reprint of the 1905 edition. New York: AMS Press.

Snyderman, G.S. 1951. 'Concepts of Land Ownership among the Iroquois and their Neighbors', *Bureau of American Ethnology Bulletin* 149: 13–34.

Carr, L. 1883. *The Social and Political Position of Women among Iroquois Tribes*, 16th Report of the Peabody Museum of American Archaeology and Ethnology.

Part Three

Additional Readings

Bastien, Elizabeth. 'Matrimonial Real Property Solutions', *Canadian Woman Studies* 26, 3–4 (2008): 90–3.

Goldenberg, André. '"Salmon for Peanut Butter": Equality, Reconciliation and the Rejection of Commercial Aboriginal Rights', *Indigenous Law Journal* 3 (2004): 61–110.

Goulding, Warren. *Just Another Indian: A Serial Killer and Canada's Indifference*. Calgary, AB: Fifth House Ltd., 2001.

Jackson, Deborah Davis. *Our Elders Lived It: American Indian Identity in the City*. DeKalb, IL: Northern Illinois University Press.

Razack, Sherene. 'Gendered Racial Violence and Spatialized Justice: The Murder of Pamela George', pp. 121–56 in Sherene H. Razack, ed., *Race, Space and the Law: Unmapping a White Settler Society*. Toronto: Between the Lines Press, 2002.

Shorten, Linda. *Without Reserve: Stories from Urban Natives*. Edmonton, AB: NeWest Press, 1991.

Relevant Websites

Library and Archives Canada Canadian Confederation website
http://www.collectionscanada.gc.ca/confederation/index-e.html
This website 'tells the story of how Canada came to be'. Consider carefully where the Indigenous People are found in this archive and what story the archive tells. Think about how Lawrence's piece might be useful in analyzing this website.

Native Women's Association of Canada
http://nwac-hq.org/research/matrimonial-real-property
The Native Women's Association of Women provides information about Matrimonial Real Property, which includes resources and reports on Indigenous women and property rights.

Films

Finding Dawn. Dir. Christine Welsh. National Film Board of Canada, 2006.
First Stories—Apples and Indians. Dir. Lorne Olson. National Film Board of Canada, 2006.
Kanehsatake: 270 Years of Resistance. Dir. Alanis Obomsawin. National Film Board of Canada, 1993.

Is The Crown At War With Us? Dir. Alanis Obomsawin. National Film Board of Canada, 2002.
Two Worlds Colliding. Dir. Tasha Hubbard. National Film Board of Canada, 2004.
You Are On Indian Land. Dir. Mort Ransen. National Film Board of Canada, 1969.

Key Terms

Dispossession
Nation-building
Royal Commission on Aboriginal Peoples (RCAP)
Urbanity/Indigeneity binarism
Self-government

Matrimonial real property
Institutionalized patriarchy
Silenced history
Settler violence

Discussion Questions

1. What is the relationship between race, space, and the law?
2. What role do spatial understandings play in ongoing settler colonialism, dispossession, and the disavowal of Indigenous identities?
3. Bonita Lawrence writes that '. . . in order for Canada to have a viable national identity, the histories of Indigenous nations, in all their diversity and longevity, must be erased.' What does she mean by this and what are the implications of this reality for *both* Indigenous and non-Indigenous peoples?
4. Identify some of the issues facing Indigenous peoples in cities with respect to nationhood, belonging, and recognition. How are these issues overlooked by Canada and with what effects and consequences?

Activities

Research the land on which your school, home, or community is built. To which Indigenous nation does it belong? What is the history of colonial settlement or resistance against settlement on this land? Are there any historical 'disputes' over this land? What are they? What are the central differences in these 'disputes'?

Watch the 2002 National Film Board production *Is The Crown At War With Us?* (written and directed by Alanis Obomsawin). How might you analyze the actions of non-Indigenous fishermen with respect to race, space, and the law? Discuss the role of violence in upholding the boundaries of race and space under settler colonialism. Where does this film and its history fit in relation to Lawrence's article on the history of Indigenous resistance in Eastern Canada?

Watch the 2006 television drama *One Dead Indian* (written by Hugh Graham and Andrew Wreggit, directed by Tim Southam). How might you analyze the actions of the provincial government and police with respect to racism, resistance, and the law? Where do their actions stand in relation to the findings and recommendations of the Ipperwash Inquiry? How did the inquiry process bring us closer to decolonizing relations between Indigenous peoples and majority Canadians? What needs to be done in both the short term and long term for these to be fully implemented?

PART FOUR

Racialization, Sexism, and Indigenous Identities

Since 1850, the point at which the category Indian was established in law, Indian
status has received increasing attention by courts of law, policy makers, and
politicians in Canada. The controversy surrounds amendments to the Indian Act,
specifically, the constitutionality of S. 12 of the 1951 Act and S. 6 of the 1985
legislation. These sections establish the entitlement of persons to be registered as
Indians and make invidious distinctions between male and female Indians. Today,
these sections treat the children of men and women who married non-Indians differently and unequally under the law. Indian status embodies a long history of
discrimination aimed at Indigenous communities, especially Indigenous women.

Not every Indigenous person is a status Indian. As a matter of historical fact,
Indigenous peoples became Indians under a legal classification that did not distinguish between them, or for that matter, their multiplicity at early colonialism.
People became Indians so that the state could delimit the occupation of certain
lands to Indians alone. It was through the sorting out of lands that the idea of
whiteness, and indeed race, became concretized in what is now called Canada. The
category 'Indian' is no more than a legal construction rooted in histories of colonial
domination. Prior to colonization, Indigenous peoples were not 'Indians'. They
defined themselves as distinct nations with diverse kin-based, socio-economic, and
political systems.

The very first act of colonial injustice is racialized injustice—literally, the process whereby Indigenous nations became status Indians for state administrative
purposes. Broadly speaking, racialization refers to a set of practices, beliefs, and
ways of thinking that have made Indianness compulsory. Governments have not
addressed this matter in Canada. The injustice is one that even courts have been
unable to reconcile despite progressive legal judgments like Canada's recent
'McIvor case'. This case found the Indian Act to perpetuate sex discrimination,
because it gives fewer rights to the descendants of female Indians based on sex

and/or marriage to non-Indians. The court, however, said nothing about histories of racialization (Cannon, forthcoming)

The entitlement of persons to be acknowledged legally as Indians in North America is pertinent to any discussion of racism, racialization, and colonial dominance. The criteria used to determine who is—and who is not—an Indian find their roots in early racist thinking about blood quantum and in colonial histories that did not recognize the linguistic and cultural differences between Indigenous groups. Today, many people—including Métis—fall short of the legal criteria established so long ago for registration and enrolment. The removal of Indigenous people's ability to determine who belongs, as well as their own membership, must be addressed before histories of racism can ever be reconciled. In this section, we provide a selection of articles written by Indigenous scholars on matters of racialization and identity.

Martin Cannon documents the nature of historic injustice as this relates to the 1985 Indian Act amendments. The legal assimilation of status Indians and reserve lands is furthered by an inability of governments (deliberate or inadvertent) to transfer knowledge about Indian status injustices to Indian communities. But even knowledge itself cannot prevent the involuntary legal enfranchisement of status Indians today. In general, it will be necessary to revisit the sexism and institutionalized racism out of which Indian status injustices emerged historically. The time has come to scrutinize the political and legal contexts that foreclose discussions about identification approaches to Indigenous identity, original treaties, and citizenship.

Indian policy not only worked to institutionalize a set of racialized understandings into law, it also made fundamental assumptions about gendered and erotic diversity, as well as the kinship organization of communities. As Beverly Little Thunder reminds us, the colonizer's imperative to divide the world into strict male/female binaries would have precluded the existence of two-spirited wimmin. While one must be careful not to describe the erotic and gendered diversity that existed prior to contact as homosexual (Cannon, 1998), in the words of the feminist poet and theorist Adrienne Rich, colonial policy did work to make European forms of heterosexuality compulsory. As Little Thunder illustrates, it also worked to institutionalize homophobia within many nations and communities.

Sexuality may seem altogether unrelated to the racism and sexism. But the writing we include by Indigenous scholars in this section suggests something in common that configurations of sexism and racialization worked together simultaneously with heterosexism and heteronormativity to structure distinct kinds of discrimination for Indigenous women, nations, and two-spirited people. Even today, the law in Canada assumes that Indian status will be passed to children through opposite-sex marriage, throwing the constitutionality of the Indian Act into question where discrimination on the basis of sexual orientation is concerned. Racism, sexism, and heterosexism need to be challenged, but how can this be accomplished if discrimination is considered separate, unrelated historically, or only to involve one history of domination?

Indian status injustices invite the people who want to challenge them to become even more deeply entrenched into the colonial frameworks that have been used to define and sometimes divide them. As Bonita Lawrence illustrates, seeing women and men in state-constructed terms, obscures the history of racialized distinctions that were imposed on Indigenous peoples, and furthermore, prevents us from having important conversations about issues such as land, urbanity, identity, intermarriage, and citizenship. Combined, the readings we include here give readers an entry into issues involving racialization, sexism, and Indigenous identities.

Chapter 10

Revisiting Histories of Legal Assimilation, Racialized Injustice, and the Future of Indian Status in Canada

Martin J. Cannon

Introduction

This paper is concerned with the history of injustice surrounding the 1985 *Indian Act* amendments. . . .

I wish to reflect on matters of citizenship and Aboriginal identity in this paper as well as the history of 'involuntary enfranchisement' as this relates to Status Indians and Canadian Indian policy. I hope to invigorate the thinking toward histories of policy-based enfranchisement, racialized injustice, and gender-based exclusion. My discussion also draws from my qualitative research concerning issues of Indian status, the accommodation of Indian policy, and the accessibility of legal knowledge in Status Indian communities (Cannon, 2005).

The 1985 *Indian Act* Amendments: Wherein Lies the (In)justice?

On 28 June 1985, Bill C-31: *An Act to Amend the Indian Act* was given royal assent in Canadian Parliament. It promised to end years of blatant sex discrimination directed toward Aboriginal women under section 12(1)(b) of the 1951 amendments. I have sought to develop a critical understanding of Bill C-31 (Cannon, 2006a, 2006b), and I have shared in that criticism with other academics, Aboriginal people, and non-Aboriginal individuals (Lawrence, 2004; Holmes, 1987; Indian and Northern Affairs Canada, 1990).

The 1985 amendments are now over twenty years old, but they have not received widespread attention from federal policy makers. Discrimination is still made possible under Bill C-31, but it is not always clear or obvious. Under the new legislation, three new types of discrimination were made possible. These include inequalities of Indian status (Holmes, 1987), discrimination toward unmarried or unwed women (Clatworthy, 2003b; Mann, 2005), and the development of Canadian case law concerning Aboriginal citizenship rights (Issac, 1995; Moss, 1990).

Those who register as Status Indians now do so under one of seven different sections of the *Indian*

Act (1985). The major difference lies between sections 6(1) and 6(2). These sections reproduce legal inequalities because the children of women who married non-Indians before 1985 cannot pass along Indian status under section 6(2) (Holmes, 1987). The children of men do not face this same restriction as they are registered under section 6(1). The inequality I am describing has been referred to as the second-generation cut-off rule (Huntley et al., 1999: 74).

The 'second generation cut-off' clause is something that affects people who are related as cousins. This . . . current generation of Status Indians . . . is being treated differently in law because of their grandmother's choice to marry a non-Indian. For example, my mother's grandchildren are not eligible for Indian status even though my uncle's grandchildren (their second cousins) are registered under section 6(2). His children maintained Indian status under section 6(1)(a) of the amendments, and his grandchildren therefore inherited section 6(2) status by birthright. My siblings and I reacquired Indian status under section 6(2) of the 1985 amendments and cannot therefore pass status on to our children unless we marry Status Indians.[1] This is an example of the inequality created by Bill C-31 between the second and subsequent generations of men and women marrying non-Indians.[2]

With the exception of Lawrence (2004), the community-based impact of *An Act to Amend the Indian Act* (1985) has been under-studied from a qualitative perspective in academic literature (but see Huntley et al., 1999; Public History Inc, 2004; Fiske and George, 2006). This is unusual, especially since the *Act* has created a series of complexities for many communities—and for individuals—in terms of identity (Cannon, 2005). I have employed in-depth interviews as a method of addressing the question of policy-based exclusion and its accommodation by individuals (Cannon, 2005). I will highlight some of this research as a way of illustrating histories of assimilation and the current injustices surrounding 'out-marriage' and the loss of legal entitlements. . . .

Revisiting Histories of Enfranchisement in Indian Policy

[Bill C-31] . . . aimed to shrink the number of 'Indians' in Canadian society in order to reduce the government's obligations and liabilities to the status community. (Miller, 2004: 45)

. . . Assimilation has always had a cultural and legal component in Canadian Indian policy. Cultural assimilation refers to 'the loss, by an individual, of the markers that served to distinguish him or her as a member of one social group' (Jackson, 2002: 74). The schooling of Aboriginal children in residential schools until 1969 is an example of the kinds of policy aimed at cultural assimilation. These were policies aimed at cultivating Euro-Christian behaviours, appearances, and values. They were intended to re-socialize Aboriginal peoples into productive members of an emerging capitalist economy.

Legal assimilation is the word that is used to describe the act of losing Indian status in Canada. This started in 1850 when Canada introduced *An Act for the Protection of the Indians in Upper Canada from Imposition, and the Property Occupied or Enjoyed by them From Trespass and Injury*. It was also a part of policy in 1857 to encourage the 'gradual civilization' of the Indian tribes (Miller, 2004: 17). These two statutes introduced two new racialized categories of Aboriginal peoples: Indian and non-Indian. It was assumed (and expected) that band council governments would administer these new categories of people.

Sociologists refer to this process, whereby a heterogenous, linguistically diverse population is singled out for different (and often unequal) treatment in Canada, as racialization (Li, 1990: 7). But racialization, as it is often defined, does not refer to the act of taking up or realizing racial categories, however conscious a person might be of that process. Aboriginal peoples did not play a part in creating the 'racial' category Indian, but policy has had the effect of institutionalizing the category as a system of relations among Status

Indians in Canada. This is what is meant by racialization.

The history I am describing is etched in the memory of some, but not all, Status Indians. I include myself as one of these individuals, because I am a Status Indian and I have personally witnessed what the *Indian Act* is capable of doing legally, especially section 6(2). The *Indian Act* has been just as concerned with constructing the legal category 'Indian' as it has been on getting rid of Status Indians. Legal assimilation must therefore refer to the process of becoming a Non-Status Indian—whether an Aboriginal person is made aware of it or not.

Legal assimilation was one of the motivations behind enfranchisement policy. Enfranchisement emerged in 1857 with the explicit and avowed purpose of assimilating Status Indians. The premise behind this policy was simple: upon meeting certain criteria, Indian men who were literate, free of debt, and of good moral character, could (along with their 'dependents') give up legal status and become non-Indians. Enfranchisement was re-established in three subsequent pieces of legislation, but it was not always voluntary in the way I have described.

In 1918, Indian men (along with their wives and children) could become voluntarily enfranchised if they lived away from their communities (*Indian Act* [S.C. 1918, c.26, s.6(122A)(1)] reprinted in Venne, 1981: 220; Indian and Northern Affairs Canada, 1991: 10–11). The policy of enfranchisement was not only racialized, it was therefore simultaneously patriarchal (Cannon, 1995; Stevenson, 1999: 57). Enfranchisement policy assumed that, like other women, Indian women were to be legally subject to their husbands (Jamieson, 1978). This was a foreign notion to my own nation of peoples, the Six Nations of Grand River Territory (Cannon, 2004).[3]

Enfranchisement continued well into the twentieth century. In 1951, enfranchisement was made possible for individuals meeting the variety of criteria established in sections 12, 15, and 108 (*Indian Act* [S.C., 1951, c.29] reprinted in Venne, 1981:

319, 348–349; Indian and Northern Affairs Canada, 1991: 15–17). These sections included (a) the involuntary enfranchisement of women marrying non-Indians and (b) the voluntary enfranchisement of entire bands of people who so desired upon approval of the Minister of Indian Affairs (ibid.). The children of women born prior to a woman's marriage to a non-Indian also became involuntarily enfranchised under an amendment to the *Indian Act* in 1956 (*Indian Act* [S.C., 1956, c.40, s.26] reprinted in Venne, 1981: 398, Indian and Northern Affairs Canada, 1991: 19).

The very concept of voluntary enfranchisement (or voluntarily becoming a Non-Status Indian) did not end in Canada until 28 June 1985 with the passing of section 6(1)(d) of *An Act to Amend the Indian Act* (*Indian Act*, R.S.C. 1985 (1st Supp.), c.32, s.6(1)(d)). In a manual on registration and entitlements legislation, Indian and Northern Affairs Canada proclaimed that section 6(1)(d) had 'abolished' the practice of enfranchisement under the *Indian Act* (1991: 21). However, there is reason to believe that involuntary enfranchisement survives the 1985 amendments to the *Indian Act*.

Involuntary Enfranchisement in Demographic Perspective

Enfranchisement, voluntary and involuntary, was not achieved, and by 1985 Canada had to abandon the policy after close to 130 years of frustration. (Miller, 2004: 271)

Involuntary enfranchisement takes place in Canada whenever a Status Indian (registered under section 6(2) of the *Indian Act*), marries and has children with a non-Indian person. This act of exogamy or 'out-marriage' may seem a relatively neutral one, but section 6(2) works to disenfranchise the grandchildren of women who married non-Indians before 1985. These individuals represent a new class of 'involuntarily enfranchised' Indians: the children of section 6(2) intermarriages.[4] These children lose their parents' birthright to be registered as Status Indians in Canada.

The loss of legal entitlements is brought on by their parent's choice to marry non-Indians.

Individuals often marry non-Indians in the process of migrating to cities. Their choices are sometimes influenced by the depletion of resources and the lack of economic opportunities on reserves in Canada (Frideres, 2005: 164–170). These decisions lead to a loss of inheritance for the children born of section 6(2) intermarriages. As I will demonstrate, it is superficial to assume that all Status Indians are aware of this process, or that it leads to their children's losing status. However conscious Status Indians may be of it, the children of section 6(2) intermarriages are not legally entitled to *Indian Act* status like the children of section 6(1) intermarriages.[5]

Section 6(2) of the *Indian Act* (R.S.C. 1985 (1st Supp.), c. 32, s. 6(2)) is little different in effect than section 12(1)(b) of the *Indian Act* (S.C. 1951, c. 29, s. 12(1)(b)). Both sections furthered the loss of Indian status by those who marry non-Indians. The only difference is that now men also involuntarily enfranchise their children and grandchildren when marrying non-Indians. The choices facing these *male and female* Indians of the Status Indian population registered under section 6(2) of the *Indian Act* are therefore not any different than those facing women from 1850–1985.

Despite the passage of Bill C-31, intermarriage is still not a neutral act for Status Indians in Canada. It is the children of those who are registered under section 6(2) and who marry non-Indians that are now being disinherited. These are the grandchildren of women who married non-Indians prior to 1985, as well as the grandchildren of men and women who married non-Indians after 1985. They are, collectively, a class of Indians that stand to alter and change the composition of Status Indian populations in Canada. Clatworthy (2003a, 2005) has placed these trends into demographic perspective by providing a series of population forecasts.

Clatworthy (2005: 32) predicts that the Registered Indian population will witness a dramatic decline because of section 6(2) and other changes stemming from the 1985 *Indian Act* amendments. He projects that on- and off-reserve populations entitled to membership and Indian registration will witness a population of 914,300 by the year 2077, a dramatic drop from the projected 987,600 in 2052 (ibid.).

As Clatworthy (2003a: 86–87) explains:

> Within two generations, most of the children born to First Nations populations are not expected to qualify for registration under the new rules. Within four generations, only one of every six children born to First Nations populations is expected to qualify for registration. Unlike the rules of the old *Act*, which guaranteed registration to nearly all of the descendants of Registered Indian males, Bill C-31's rules have the potential to result in the extinction of the Registered Indian population.

These forecasts raise a series of concerns about the future of Indian status in Canada. They suggest that policies of legal enfranchisement, including the long term effects of section 6(2), will result in the eventual legal assimilation of Status Indians and their lands in Canada. Several factors will influence the rate at which this takes place, including the frequency of exogamous marriage. But legal assimilation also depends on a people's familiarity with, and knowledge about, section 6(2) of the *Indian Act*. In general, what do Status Indians think about the *Indian Act*, and about the prospect of legal assimilation? Are people aware of the potential effects of section 6(2)? These questions require ongoing qualitative inquiry (Lawrence, 2004; Cannon, 2005).

Revisiting Histories of Legal Assimilation in Indian Policy

. . . It is important to ask how legal inequalities created by sections 6(1) and 6(2) are playing themselves out among status populations today. In fact, some of these inequalities have yet to be fully articulated in political, judicial, and social forums. This occurred to me in ongoing research where I asked a group of Status Indians, aged 19–35, what it meant to be registered under section 6(2) of the *Indian Act*.

In one interview, I asked one of my study participants if she knew of the consequences of being registered under section 6(2) of the *Indian Act*. She responded:

> I'm just categorized under section 6(2), what can I do? It's like, I just fall under that status under what their requirements are, you know? And so, I'm just another person basically categorized into a spot. That's about it. (Interview Transcript #7: 4)

In other interviews, people were very aware of the inequality produced by section 6(2) of the *Indian Act*, but these individuals expressed cynicism where finding a resolution to them is concerned. As one person explained:

> I can't see the government telling me 'Well, if you go and do this, your children won't have status.' I think they'd rather me just go and do it without my knowing and then my children would be screwed over. That is an issue for me, I'd like my children to be Status Indians, not for any reason in particular, it's just cause I feel like that's a right that every Native person in Canada should have . . . Having to worry about who you marry shouldn't be an issue, but it is, you know? . . . (Interview Transcript #3: 4)

Another person I interviewed for the purposes of this paper expressed confusion where understanding Indian registration is concerned. As she explained:

> [W]hen they gave me my status, they basically sent me a letter saying I was approved with my status number but it had nothing on there stating what I was considered to be like, you know, Bill C-31 or whatever. My parents are Bill C-31s, but I have no idea what that makes me, and I have no idea what that is gonna make my children. Like, I think that's a big problem. I haven't actually gone out and tried to figure it out on my own, but I've asked a lot of people, you know teachers, profs, and everything, to see if they can explain it to me. . . . (Interview Transcript #4: 3)

There exists both apathy and criticism about Indian status and citizenship injustices. Issues of knowledge, accessibility, and sharing create some of this apathy. Injustices must be therefore placed into terms that 'the general Native public' understands, particularly before individuals can take action (Huntley et al., 1999: 74). But issues of knowledge, accessibility, and dissemination will not alone eliminate the apathy that is expressed toward the 1985 amendments.

Apathy is also expressed because of some people's preference to talk of identity in terms of nations, territories, or a community of people to which they belong. . . .

According to one of the individuals I interviewed for this paper:

> Having a status card doesn't make you any more Indian. I definitely think it has a lot to do with your culture and how much of it you actually connect with, you know? . . . I've always enjoyed anything that has to do with my culture, like powwows, round dances, and feasts. My family has always been involved in a lot of that stuff. So I think being Native has to do with how much you connect with your culture. . . . (Interview Transcript #8: 2)

Another Status Indian identified herself as belonging to a community of people. This is what mattered in defining herself as an Aboriginal person. As she explained:

> I guess I've never even concerned myself with things like status. I see my children as Indians because I've raised them as such, and for me, what makes them Indians is the values, which is why the traditions and the ceremonies are important to me. Being part of a larger Indian community is really important to me, it's not about blood or what the government says. (Interview Transcript #5: 1)

Despite the imposition of status boundaries, identities are being realized outside of racialized status provisions, and in nation-specific terms (also see Lawrence, 2004). These identities are tied to communities, nation-to-nation agreements, and to historic treaties (Henderson, 2002). The capacity of liberal pluralism to acknowledge and grasp these identities is an outstanding matter of colonial injustice in Canada (Kymlicka, 2000; Green, 2001; Schouls, 2003).

Rethinking Indian Status and Engaging with Citizenship

The interviews I conducted . . . concerning the 1985 *Indian Act* amendments permit three major conclusions. First and foremost, that legal assimilation is furthered by the inability of governments (deliberate or inadvertent) to transfer knowledge concerning legal inequality to Status Indian communities. Second, that many people prefer to talk of identity and citizenship in nation-specific terms. Third and finally, that it is necessary to scrutinize the political and legal contexts that prevent 'identification approaches' to identity and citizenship from happening (Schouls, 2003: 35, 166).

According to my research, there is variable knowledge possessed by a new and emerging generation of individuals registered under section 6(2) of the *Indian Act*. Some of these individuals know what it means to be a Non-Status Indian while identifying as an Aboriginal person. Some of them endeavour to establish, or maintain, a connection with their own and other communities. But others know very little about status injustices. This is something that actually works in the interest of legally assimilating the Registered Indian populations of Canada.

If section 6(2) contributes to the loss of Indian status as demographers predict, then this knowledge must somehow be transmitted to each and every Status Indian. Aboriginal peoples are entitled to know about status inequalities, especially within the broader context of history aimed at their racialization, legal assimilation, and enfranchisement. The sharing of this knowledge ensures the right of Aboriginal peoples to revisit and decide on a more equitable system of defining Indian status—or of resisting this system altogether.

People have been made unequal to each other because of the *Indian Act*. To pretend that Indian status is inconsequential is to therefore undermine the importance of legal distinctions, and how these affect the relationship between Status Indians, both male and female. But the people I interviewed also suggested a way of thinking about identity outside of Indian status provisions. These issues of citizenship and belonging are of immediate importance to Aboriginal populations. The question is, how do we get around to debating them and where ought they to be debated?

Section 6(2) injustices invite the people who want to challenge them to become even more deeply drawn into the colonial frameworks that have been used to define and sometimes divide them (Lawrence, 2004: 42). Seeing women and men in state-constructed terms often conceals historic events which imposed racialized distinctions on all Aboriginal nations, and that later required people to be legislated outside of them. It also detracts from the kinds of conversations that governments could be having where Aboriginal identity and citizenship is concerned.

Correcting Historic Wrongs or Racialized Injustice?

Freedom from colonization is the sense of an unbounded self and the ability to live fully in a wide and open world. It is to feel and live large! Being 'Indian' and being 'Aboriginal' is accepting a small self, imprisonment in the small space created for us by the white man: reserves, Aboriginal rights, *Indian Act* entitlements, etc. (Alfred, 2005: 165)

A major change in thinking is required before issues of Indian status can be fully understood or rejuvenated in Canada. I believe the future is now being realized—and can be realized—by refusing to acknowledge the *Indian Act* as the source of determining Aboriginal citizenship. Legal assimilation is less threatening to individuals who are mindful of Aboriginal identity and community in all of its infinite capacities. But I have intended to show, in this paper, how even these individuals are unable to prevent the legal assimilation of Status Indians and their reserve lands in Canada.[6]

Indian status or status inequalities will require the ongoing attention of federal and band-based governments. Several issues will emerge out of these discussions involving citizenship and Indian status. Before meaningful discussion can take place around any one of them, it will be necessary to move beyond the *Indian Act*. This will require legally acknowledging a sense of belonging based on real or assumed bonds between people, their shared knowledge of traditional stories or history, original nation-to-nation agreements, common beliefs, and a tie to some specific territory— including urban areas (see Green, 2001; Lawrence, 2004; Schouls, 2003: 177).

It is also necessary to begin the process of *affirming* the nations of Aboriginal peoples in law and politics, including who it is that we define as our citizens (Denis, 2002: 115–117). Only after these issues are addressed are Aboriginal peoples able to become truly self-determining. Phil Fontaine, Grand Chief of the Assembly of First Nations, recently noted:

> It is morally, politically and legally wrong for one government to tell another government who its citizens are, and we are calling for a process to move citizenship to the jurisdiction where it properly belongs, and that is with First Nations governments. (*Prince Albert Grand Council Tribune*, 2005)

By focusing on 'intercultural identification' or 'intercultural belonging' (Henderson, 2002: 432), the *Indian Act* remains ineffective as a tool for regulating identity (Lawrence, 2004: 230). But this does not mean that Canada is prepared to acknowledge the people who no longer 'qualify' for Indian status and registration. It does not even require that nation-to-nation agreements, urban-based individuals, territories, or nation-specific understandings of citizenship be acknowledged (Anderson and Denis, 2003: 332–388). Nor does it justify the kinds of ongoing legal inequalities created under section 6(2) of the *Indian Act*. These things require the attention of governments, policy makers, and those most affected by citizenship injustices.

A change in the way of thinking about Indian status is required in Canada. Citizenship injustices have their origins in the racialized and sexist understandings that were introduced historically and that remain a part of colonial policy. It follows that historical analysis (or 'liberating strategies') be committed to realizing—and addressing—both types of discrimination (Cannon, 1995). The loss of Indian status—and Indian status in general—is not something that belongs to women or 'individuals'. The loss of Indian status is something that belongs to the Aboriginal collective because of the potential of section 6(2) to disinherit them, and because of complex injustices that exist at the intersection of racialization and patriarchy (ibid.). Indeed, many men are now included among individuals experiencing discrimination at the 'intersection' of race and gender.

A new politics of identity is forming in Canada, and it includes a generation of men and women who are disqualified from Indian status, even though they are Aboriginal peoples. Some of these individuals were registered under section 6(2) of the *Indian Act* and face the same choices available to their mothers as 'Indians'. For the generations affected by it, section 6(2) brings about a different way of thinking about 'Indianness'. It could even bring forward a new way of thinking about historical discrimination, preferably leading many of us to realize that citizenship injustices were never really about women. They were about state-inspired definitions, and the act of becoming (or not) a member of the racialized collective.

Notes

1. The details I am describing here about Indian status and the way it defines people differently within my own immediate family is, but one example, of how the *Indian Act* has complicated the lives of Status Indians in Canada. Many people share entirely different experiences where Indian status is concerned. In current research, I am seeking to better document these histories through the use of qualitative research methodology.

2. Section 6(1)(a) of *An Act to Amend the Indian Act* (1985) read: '6(1) a person is entitled to be registered if (a) that person was registered or entitled to be registered immediately prior to April 17, 1985.'

3. For an analysis of the matrilineal and matrilocal kinship organization of the Haudenosaunee or 'Iroquois', see Randle (1951), Richards (1967), Druke (1986), Brown (1975), and Eastlack-Shafer (1990). For an analysis of social change and cultural continuity with respect to matrilineal and matrilocal kinship structure, see Shoemaker (1991) and Doxtator (1996). Also see Fiske & George (2006) and Native Women's Association of Canada (1992).

4. This new generation of individuals also includes the children of women registered under section 6(2) who do not state paternity at the time of registration.

5. For a description of the process see Clatworthy (2007). For graphical representation of the process see S. Clatworthy, 'Impacts of the 1985 Amendments to the *Indian Act* on First Nations Populations' in Jerry White et al., *Aboriginal Conditions: Research as a Foundation for Public Policy* (Vancouver: UBC Press, 2003).

6. These individuals also face what Denis (2002: 115) calls the 'heavy burden of historical proof'. This refers to a set of expectations that have been placed upon Aboriginal peoples in legal arenas to demonstrate an unbroken and timeless connection with the past or face charges of being inauthentic or no longer entitled to rights-based claims (also see Garroutte, 2003).

References

Alfred, Taiaiake. 2005. *Wasase: Indigenous Pathways of Action and Freedom*. Peterborough: Broadview Press.

Anderson, Chris, and Claude Denis. 2003. 'Urban Natives and the Nation: Before and After the Royal Commission on Aboriginal Peoples', *Canadian Review of Sociology and Anthropology* 40 (4): 373–390.

Brown, Judith K. 1975. 'Iroquois Women An Ethnographic Note', pp. 235–51 in Rayna Reiter, ed., *Towards an Anthropology of Women*. New York: Monthly Review Press.

Cannon, Martin J. 2006a. 'First Nations Citizenship: An Act to Amend the *Indian Act* (1985) and the Accommodation of Sex Discriminatory Policy', *Canadian Review of Social Policy* 56: 40–71.

Cannon, Martin J. 2006b. Revisiting Histories of Gender-Based Exclusion and the New Politics of Indian Identity. Unpublished Paper Written for the National Centre for First Nations Governance.

Cannon, Martin J. 2005. 'Bill C-31—*An Act to Amend the Indian Act*: Notes Toward a Qualitative Analysis of Legislated Injustice', *The Canadian Journal of Native Studies* 25 (1): 153–67.

Cannon, Martin J. 2004. A History of Politics and Women's Status at Six Nations of the Grand River Territory: A Study of Continuity and Social Change Among the Iroquois. Unpublished Doctoral Dissertation. York University, Toronto.

Cannon, Martin J. 1995. Demarginalizing the Intersection of 'Race' and Gender in First Nations Politics and the Law. Unpublished Master of Arts Thesis. Queen's University, Kingston.

Clatworthy, Stewart. 2007. 'Impacts of the 1985 Indian Act Amendments: A Case Study of Brokenhead Ojibway Nation', pp. 75–91 in Jerry P. White, Erik Anderson, Wendy Cornet and Dan Beavon, eds, *Aboriginal Policy Research: Moving Forward, Making a Difference*. Toronto: Thompson Educational Publishing, Inc.

Clatworthy, Stewart. 2005. *Indian Registration, Membership and Population Change in First Nations Communities*. Ottawa: DIAND Strategic Research and Analysis Directorate.

Clatworthy, Stewart. 2003a. 'Impacts of the 1985 Amendments to the *Indian Act* on First Nations Populations', pp. 63–90 in Jerry P. White, Paul S. Maxim, and Dan Beavon, eds, *Aboriginal Conditions: Research as a Foundation for Public Policy*. Vancouver: UBC Press.

Clatworthy, Stewart. 2003b. *Factors Contributing to Unstated Paternity*. Ottawa: DIAND Strategic Research and Analysis Directorate.

Denis, Claude. 2002. 'Indigenous Citizenship and History in Canada: Between Denial and Imposition', pp. 113–26 in R. Adamoski, D.E. Chunn, and R. Menzies, eds, *Contesting Canadian Citizenship: Historical Readings*. Peterborough: Broadview Press.

Doxtator, Deborah. 1996. What Happened to the Iroquois Clans?: A Study of Clans in Three Nineteenth Century Rotinonhsyonni Communities. Unpublished PhD Dissertation. University of Western Ontario, London.

Druke, Mary. 1986. 'Iroquois and Iroquoian in Canada', pp. 302–24 in R. Bruce Morrison and Roderick Wilson, eds, *Native Peoples: The Canadian Experience*. Toronto: McClelland and Stewart.

Eastlack-Shafer, Ann. 1990. 'The Status of Iroquois Women' [1941], pp. 71–135 in W.G. Spittal, ed., *Iroquois Women: An Anthology*. Ohsweken, Ontario: Iroquois Publishing and Craft Supplies.

Fiske, Jo-Anne, and Evelyn George. 2006. *Seeking Alternatives to Bill C-31: From Cultural Trauma to Cultural Revitalization through Customary Law*. Ottawa: Status of Women Canada.

Frideres, James, and René Gadacz. 2005. *Aboriginal Peoples in Canada*, 7th edn. Toronto: Pearson Education Canada.

Garroutte, Eva Marie. 2003. *Real Indians: Identity and the Survival of Native America*. Berkeley: University of California Press.

Green, Joyce. 2001. 'Canaries in the Mines of Citizenship', *Canadian Journal of Political Science* 34 (4): 715–39.

Henderson, James (Sákéj) Youngblood. 2002. 'Sui Generis and Treaty Citizenship', *Citizenship Studies* 6 (4): 415–40.

Holmes, Joan. 1987. *Bill C-31: Equality or Disparity?* Ottawa: Canadian Advisory Council on the Status of Women.

Huntley, Audrey, et al. 1999. *Bill C-31: Its Impact, Implications and Recommendations for Change in British Columbia—Final Report*. Vancouver: Aboriginal Women's Action Network (AWAN).

Indian and Northern Affairs Canada. 1991. *The* Indian Act *Past and Present: A Manual on Registration and Entitlement Legislation*. Ottawa: Indian Registration and Band Lists Directorate.

Indian and Northern Affairs Canada. 1990. *Correcting Historic Wrongs? Report of the Aboriginal Inquiry on the Impacts of Bill C-31*. [Impacts of the 1985 Amendments to the Indian Act (Bill C-31)] vol. 1. Ottawa: Indian and Northern Affairs Canada.

Interview Transcript #3. Conducted by Martin J. Cannon. 1 March 2006. Saskatoon, SK.

Interview Transcript #4. Conducted by Martin J. Cannon. 3 March 2006. Saskatoon, SK.

Interview Transcript #5. Conducted by Martin J. Cannon. 4 March 2006. Saskatoon, SK.

Interview Transcript #7. Conducted by Martin J. Cannon. 6 March 2006. Saskatoon, SK.

Interview Transcript #8. Conducted by Martin J. Cannon. 10 March 2006. Saskatoon, SK.

Issac, Thomas. 1995. 'Case Commentary, Self-Government, Indian Women and their Rights of Reinstatement under the *Indian Act: A Comment on Sawridge Band v. Canada'*, *Canadian Native Law Reporter* 4: 1–13.

Jackson, Deborah Davis. 2002. *Our Elders Lived It: American Indian Identity in the City*. DeKalb, IL: Northern Illinois University Press.

Jamieson, Kathleen. 1978. *Indian Women and the Law in Canada: Citizens Minus*. Ottawa: Status of Women Canada.

Kymlicka, Will, and Wayne Norman, eds. 2000. *Citizenship in Culturally Diverse Societies: Issues, Contests, Concepts*. Oxford: Oxford University Press.

Lawrence, Bonita. 2004. *'Real' Indians and Others: Mixed Blood Urban Native Peoples and Indigenous Nationhood*. Vancouver: UBC Press.

Li, P.S., ed. 1990. *Race and Ethnic Relations in Canada*. Toronto: Oxford University Press.

Mann, Michelle. 2005. *Indian Registration: Unrecognized and Unstated Paternity*. Ottawa: Status of Women Canada.

Miller, J.R. *Lethal Legacy: Current Native Controversies in Canada*. Toronto: McClelland & Stewart.

Moss, Wendy. 1990. 'Indigenous Self-Government and Sexual Equality under the *Indian Act*: Resolving Conflicts between Collective and Individual Rights', *Queen's Law Review* 15: 279–305.

Native Women's Association of Canada. 1992. *Matriarchy and the Canadian Charter: A Discussion Paper*. Ottawa: Native Women's Association of Canada.

Prince Albert Grand Council Tribune. 2005. 'AFN Calls for Control of First Nations Citizenship 20 Years After Bill C-31: Population of Status Indians Will Decline Because of Bill C-31', *Prince Albert Grand Council Tribune*. August 2005; available at www.page.sk.ca/tribune/page14.php.

Randle, Martha Champion. 1951. 'No. 8: Iroquois Women, Then and Now', pp. 169–80 in William N. Fenton, ed., *Bulletin no. 149: Symposium on local diversity in Iroquois culture*. Washington, DC: Smithsonian Institution Bureau of American Ethnology.

Richards, Cara E. 1967. 'Huron and Iroquois Residence Patterns, 1600–1650', in Elizabeth Tooker, ed., *Iroquois Culture. History and Prehistory: Proceedings of the 1965 Conference on Iroquois Research*. Albany: University of the State of New York, State Education Dept., New York State Museum and Science Service.

Schouls, Tim. 2003. *Shifting Boundaries: Aboriginal Identity, Pluralist Theory and the Politics of Self-Government*. Vancouver: UBC Press.

Venne, Sharon H. 1981. *Indian Acts and Amendments, 1868–1975: An Indexed Collection*. Saskatoon: Native Law Centre, University of Saskatchewan.

White, Jerry, Paul Maxim, and Nicholas Spence. 2004. *Permission to Develop: Aboriginal Treaties, Case Law and Regulations*. Toronto: Thompson Educational Publishing, Inc.

Winona Stevenson. 1999. 'Colonialism and First Nations Women in Canada', pp. 55–57 in Enakshi Dua and Angela Robertson, eds, *Scratching the Surface: Canadian Anti-Racist Feminist Thought*. Toronto: Women's Press.

Chapter 11

Mixed-Blood Urban Native People and the Rebuilding of Indigenous Nations

Bonita Lawrence

. . . Government regulation of Native identity has created a complex array of categories of Nativeness that have been reflected in the very distinct sets of experiences recounted to me by participants who are status Indians (with full or partial status), Bill C-31 Indians (with or without band membership), nonstatus Indians, or Métis. On another level, however, are the differences in perspectives between those who grew up on-reserve, and came to the city as adults, and those who grew up urban—differences created by the genocidal policies of residential schooling, the sixties scoop, and a century of gender and racial discrimination in the Indian Act.

Genocide, Hegemony, and Native Identity

. . . The impact of hegemonic images and definitions of Indianness on urban mixed-blood Native peoples' sense of their own identities has been considerable. At the same time, it is obvious that the urban Native community, in general, is continually engaging in ways of subverting or actively resisting these ways of thinking about Indianness, with greater or lesser degrees of success. One of the greatest difficulties individuals face in attempting to work their way through these hegemonic ways of thinking is the fact that these constructs have power precisely because of their

ability to reflect reality in common-sense ways. Appearance *does* make a difference to Indianness. Having status *has* shaped the realities of status Indians in ways that are highly distinctive. Being reserve-based *has* provided for a stronger collective identity for band members than is typically the case for urban Indians. And yet, as the participants' family and individual experiences have demonstrated, none of these descriptors—appearance, status, or a reserve background—are ultimate signifiers of a Native identity.

For Native people, appearance has been one of the obvious ways in which boundaries have been maintained between members of Indigenous societies and a hostile colonizing society. And yet a crucial way in which the cultural distinctiveness—and the nationhood—of Indigenous societies has been denied within the colonizing society has been to reduce cultural identity to race, therefore reducing Nativeness to appearance, with its implicit connection to 'purity' of blood. . . .

Indian status, above all, is a system that enabled Canada to deny and bypass Indigenous sovereignty, by replacing 'the Nation' with 'the Indian'. . . . Canada has been able to use Indian status to define who can be considered Indian in ways that have alienated whole communities from any access to a land base and permanently fragmented Native identity through an extremely patriarchal and racist system that has torn large holes in the fabric of Native societies. Indian status has also been an extremely effective way to control access to Native territory, through legislation that for years has stipulated that only those recognized by Canada as status Indians can live on the reserves supposedly set aside for all Native people.

The fact that the participants were able in a relatively straightforward manner to reject hegemonic concepts of Indianness as determined by appearance or being reserve-based, but continued to wrestle with the implications of Indian status, indicates the profound power of the state to regulate identity. In many respects, the participants' opinions about status were entirely reflective of whether or not they actually possessed Indian status. While the status Indian participants all saw status as crucial to protecting Native people from extinction, virtually all of the nonstatus people saw Indian status as so ultimately divisive that it represented a significant weakness to Native empowerment. What both groups held in common was an avowed belief that status was irrelevant to Nativeness, combined with a generally deeply held, almost instinctive reaction that the only *real* Indians are those who have Indian status. This is the problem when legislation is introduced that controls a group's identity—once created and established, it cannot simply be undone. You cannot put the genie back in the bottle again—you have to deal with it. It is one thing to recognize that Indian Act categories are artificial—or even that they have been internalized—as if these divisions can be overcome simply by denying their importance. Legal categories, however, shape peoples' lives. They set the terms that individuals and communities must utilize, even in resisting these categories. . . .

For the participants, what complicated their opinions about Indian status was the fact that it is tied so closely to access to Native land. Meanwhile, because of conflicting ways in which the Indian Act externalized some mixed-blood Native people and allowed others to stay (on the basis of gender) for over a century, means that Indian status has also become inextricably connected both to issues of appearance and to gender.

Regardless of the opinions of the participants, however, in some respects the cities represent a space where status has *already* been uncoupled from the position it occupies in reserve settings as a crucial signifier of Indianness. In urban settings, where a significant proportion of the Native population is the product of loss of status (or never had it in the first place), status Indians and nonstatus Native people work side by side at different agencies and are involved in the same cultural activities in ways that simply cannot happen in reserve settings, where funding for any sort of activity or process is linked to status and where nonstatus people cannot live on reserve land (except through leasing it in the same way as non-Natives do); in any case, regardless of where they live, they cannot participate in the life of the community.

Urban centers, in fact, increasingly represent spaces where boundaries between Native people and the dominant society are maintained neither by appearance nor Indian status but primarily by cultural orientation. In this respect they represent a unique place to observe what happens to Native people who lack legal protection of their rights as Indians and who are flexible about the racial boundaries of Indianness. It is worth considering, however, that urban Native people are able to maintain this flexibility precisely because they have no collective land base, which, in addition to loss of language, is the most problematic aspect of urban Native identity.

The participants were extremely clear-headed about how being urban affected their identities as Native people. While some individuals wrestled with the hegemonic logic that links Native people to images of 'living on the land like an Indian', most of the participants were relatively clear that reserve-based individuals did have a stronger sense of their identities as Native people simply because they had grown up in places where Native people were the majority. These individuals, however, were also aware that the boundaries between urban and reserve culture are neither as distinctive nor as fixed as individuals believe—that considerable cross-fertilization continues to happen between urban centers and adjacent reserves. . . .

This suggests that urban Native people and the First Nations need ways of conceptualizing alliances—or nationhood—strategically, in ways that do not involve individual bands having to endlessly open their membership rolls to those who grew up alienated from community life, or urban Indians having to continuously engage in fruitless attempts to recreate themselves in identities that their families left behind. . . .

In many ways, it appears crucial that urban and on-reserve Native people begin to address common problems.

On a deeper level, another important issue is how urban Native people, particularly those who are mixed-race, might be involved in struggles for self-determination. How can the sovereignty goals of contemporary First Nations, and their desires and the kind aspirations of urban individuals who consider themselves to be members of Indigenous nations 'in the abstract', be brought together? In this chapter, I will be presenting the participants' thoughts on what roles urban mixed-race Native people might play in the rebuilding of their Indigenous nations. The close of this chapter will focus, in a preliminary manner, on the forms of nation-building that might subvert the history of divisions imposed on Native people by government regulation of Indianness and that could make urban and on-reserve alliances possible.

Mixed-Blood Urban Native People and the First Nations

A number of individuals spoke about what urban mixed-bloods are currently doing to strengthen Aboriginal presence within the cities. They referred to the daily grind of urban life that newcomers to the cities face and saw their roles as working with such individuals toward strengthening them, so they could return to their communities as empowered individuals. . . .

There was a general consensus that in some respects, urban Native people have roles to play for which we are uniquely positioned. Several people referred to the greater awareness of power dynamics in the larger society that urban people have.

One individual, for example, spoke of the manner in which reserve communities tend to ignore the presence of people of colour and act as if Canada still consisted only of Native people and white people. She noted that one role of urban Native people must be to ensure that newer immigrant agendas did not marginalize those of Native people. Another individual, however, suggested that urban Native people are also positioned to address forms of alliances between peoples of colour and Aboriginal peoples, which might be useful in challenging racism within the dominant society.

One individual felt that urban mixed-bloods, as individuals who have, had to viscerally wrestle with dominant culture images of Indianness, might have a handle on challenging stereotypes about what Indianness is that do not often get challenged on reserves. . . . Another participant pointed out the importance of having urban Aboriginal people creating Native spaces in the city that reserve people can utilize when they come there, and that, as a result of this considerable interaction, it is already happening between urban centers and nearby reserves. . . .

Several individuals spoke to the increasing importance that strong urban Aboriginal communities will be playing in the future. . . .

One individual cautioned that the urban Native community, while it has taken strong first steps in creating a viable urban culture and is beginning to create urban self-government organizations, will not ultimately be sustainable unless a considerable investment in language teaching and acquiring some sort of urban land base becomes a priority. . . . This individual pointed out that this is not only an urban problem—that reserves are also plagued by the fact that those who are trained to acquire power, and therefore exercise the leadership, are often those who are the most removed from rural traditional Native culture. . . .

Coming to the heart of the problem, one individual pointed out that reserve-based people need to stop thinking of their tiny 'postage stamp' bits of land as their entire nation—and that until Indigenous sovereignty is conceived in larger and more inclusive terms, the divisions between Native people cannot help but multiply. . . . Another individual pointed out that Native people as a whole have to reconceptualize what is meant by nationhood, to provide a broad diversity of approaches to rebuilding our nations. . . .

Reconceptualizing Indigenous Nationhood

While the participants have contributed a considerable level of clarification toward the subject of urban mixed-blood Native people and nation-rebuilding, most were stymied by the fundamental impasse that the federal government has created—the presence, across Canada, of over six hundred tiny, almost landless individual entities known as the First Nations, the only Native communities recognized as legally existing according to the Indian Act. These scattered communities, occupying only fragments of their original land base, exist alongside an ever-growing body of urban, dispossessed individuals with no land base at all, whose ties to their communities of origin have been weakened and in some cases obscured. This growing body of urban Native people, instead of having some mode of working from their own strengths toward common goals with the First Nations, are shut out of formal sovereignty processes and instead placed in the role of being in direct competition with reserve communities for federal dollars in the interests of their own separate survival. In such a context, it is important to consider the ancient political systems that Native communities are attempting to revive and how urban mixed-bloods might be able to find a place in such nation-building efforts. . . .

The difference between the ancient confederacies and current nationhood assertions through provincial territorial organizations such as the Nishnawbe-Aski Nation, or the Anishinabek Nation, is that those organizations are groupings primarily organized around specific territorial treaties, which in most instances follow the logic of the colonizer with respect to who was included or excluded in the process. The ancient confederacies reference older realities, where individuals

who are currently classified as nonstatus Indians or Métis, could potentially be entitled to citizenship outside of Indian Act categories. In a similar manner there is little inherent potential for discrimination between those who grew up in the cities, and those who grew up on reserves, as far as citizenship in the confederacies would be concerned, in that the confederacies are premised on the notion that the entire traditional land base, not just the reserve, is Native land.

The possibility exists, however, that the individuals who are currently reviving these confederacies could 'imprint' these revived frameworks with the same divisions as the Indian Act has created, whereby status Indians, and communities designated as reserves, are privileged over all other groups. An interesting development, in this respect, is the effort to create a Cree Confederacy with member communities from Quebec to British Columbia, as well as the United States (McKinley, 1998: 1). . . .

The confederacies represent a way out of the deadlock of fragmentation and divisions that Native people have been sealed into by the Indian Act for two reasons—they not only present the possibility of renegotiating the boundaries that have currently been erected around different categories of Indigeneity, but they envision a potentially sufficient land base to do so. While Bill C-31 Indians may struggle for the right to be members in their mothers' communities, the fact remains that the generations of individuals excluded from Indianness by gender and racial discrimination within the Indian Act will not all be able to rediscover 'home' within the approximately six hundred existing postage-stamp-sized communities that are currently called 'First Nations'. The only really viable way in which urban Native people would be able to have access to Native land is through the prospect of being citizens of the original Indigenous territories—the lands that correspond to those that were held by the different Indigenous nations at the time of contact. We must be clear, though, that if First Nations genuinely want an end to the divisiveness of the current system, they cannot create new national entities that simply replicate its logic. First Nations have to be genuinely willing to work with groups that at present they ignore or disdain—the Métis, non-status Indians, and urban Native people in general—based on the needs of all of these groups, in ways that are premised on providing all future citizens of Indigenous nations with the kind of privileges and rights that at present only status Indians enjoy. This does not mean denying the differences between the different groups that the Indian Act has created—but it means finding the connections that a history of colonial regulation has sought to obscure or destroy.

For mixed-blood urban Native people, the confederacies could be sites where urban Native communities affiliate *as* urban communities—where urban mixed-bloods do not have to fruitlessly struggle to remake themselves as 'full-blood traditionalists' in order to be considered members of Indigenous nations, and where struggles over entitlement framed as who is a 'real' Indian and who is not become meaningless.

We should be clear that Aboriginal peoples in Canada continue to face ongoing and recently accelerating actions by Canada, not only to erode or openly attack the hard-won Aboriginal rights framed in the Constitution and acknowledged in court decisions, but to entirely undermine the ability of First Nations governments to individually or collectively resist ongoing loss of lard or to acquire a resource base and economic viability.[1] These attacks are, in most cases, spearheaded by ongoing attempts to change the Indian Act in ways that weaken any protections it provides to First Nations land. An important example is the First Nations Governance Act (FNGA), a suite of nine pieces of legislation currently being pushed through the various levels of parliament despite massive and ongoing protest by Native organizations and Native people across Canada. . . .

The bill, in pushing the notion of imposing First Nations accountability, ignores the fact that governments can scarcely be held accountable for programs they do not design. Furthermore, while chiefs of First Nations must be answerable, first of all, to Indian Affairs (who provides them with the

funding), they are expected to be accountable as well to their own people, when in fact they lack any form of control over their own revenues that would give them the necessary authority (Barnsley, 2003a: 1, 2). . . .

First Nations fear, among other things, that the legislation will infringe on existing treaty rights and force upon them the status of municipalities. The minister of Indian Affairs has entirely refused any discussion with members of the Assembly of First Nations, has withdrawn funds from treaty organizations that oppose the FNGA, has openly stated that he will not listen to Native protestors, and has devoted $10 million (of money designated for Aboriginal peoples) into selling the bill to the Canadian public. He also states that he has no authority to address treaty issues and that the FNGA has nothing to do with treaty rights.[2] . . .

What these attacks represent is a response to the massive number of direct challenges by different Native communities to the colonial status quo in Canada today. Putting aside the huge volume of residential school cases and the two hundred ongoing court cases addressing the defects and mismanagement of the Indian Act, there are upward of one thousand court cases dealing with Aboriginal and treaty rights currently moving through the justice system.[3]

For these reasons, it is clear that existing organizations of Aboriginal people must continue to struggle to defend existing political and legal rights and to fight for restitution because of colonial policies that have robbed them of land and resources. At the same time, since Native resistance to these ongoing attacks is seriously weakened by the various ways in which we are divided *by* the Indian Act and other legislation, it is apparent that unless there is some attempt to reintroduce traditional forms of governance, it will be more and more difficult to stand up to ongoing colonial assault. Part of this embracing of traditional governments *has* to involve rethinking who is Indian and who is Métis; it involves questioning the meanings of divisions among those with status, those without status, and Bill C-31 Indians. It also has to involve significantly challenging the restrictions to our former land bases, to render meaningless the current divisions between those who live on-reserve and those who are urban.

The day when significant areas of what was formerly Canada have been renegotiated along the lines of sovereign Native confederacies will not be reached during our lifetimes. However, transforming how we think about Native identity does not have to wait until the designation as 'citizen of an Indigenous Nation' becomes a reality for most of us. Numerous interim processes could be tried that would provide individuals who lack Indian status or band membership with legal rights and entitlement to at least some of the existing benefits of Indian status. All of these attempts would rupture or bypass some aspect of the Indian Act, . . . determined to maintain existing divisions between Native peoples as central to our subordination.

With respect to a movement that is already at hand, in terms of renegotiating the numbered treaties, a move that would tremendously challenge colonialism is for communities to demand that the descendants of individuals who received half-breed scrip should be admitted into treaty. These individuals could then be considered 'treaty Métis' and could thus begin to negotiate sovereignty issues in conjunction with treaty Indian groups—in particular, the acquisition of a land base. This approach has the strength of undermining the central role of the Indian Act—of empowering (in a relative way) some Native people in order to disempower the rest. While there would still be numbers of nonstatus Indians (particularly in eastern Canada and in the cities) who were not eligible for Indian status, by challenging the historic exclusion of half-breeds, an estimated six hundred thousand individuals would be brought into fiduciary relationship with the federal government in ways that significantly challenge colonial divisions.

Another approach would be for status Indian organizations to formally challenge, in a concerted way, the limitations to Indian status in Section 6.2 of Bill C-31, so that the second-generation cut-off, and the continued bleeding off of individuals from Indian status if their parents of either gender inter-marry with non-Natives, would be stopped. At least a hundred thousand more individuals would therefore be eligible for reinstatement as Indians.

A third direction is to work toward promoting Canada's fiduciary obligation toward whole communities of nonstatus people in eastern Canada who were excluded from the treaty-making process (such as the Algonquin in Ontario and Quebec, and the Mi'kmaq and Innu of Newfoundland) and are asserting themselves as First Nations without recognition by the federal government.

A diversity of forms of affiliation—and of nation-rebuilding—could be taken up, which fit the diverse circumstances that Aboriginal peoples face across the continent. The important point is that these forms of affiliation are concrete ways of addressing the divisions that have been created by the Indian Act, divisions that are not going to go away simply by our labelling them as 'colonial divisions' or attempting to disregard them. They are ways of bringing together the very different strengths that urban and reserve-based Native people have developed out of their different circumstances, in the interests of our mutual empowerment.

Notes

1. Section 35 of the Canadian Constitution, developed from the British North America Act of 1867 and repatriated from Britain in 1982, recognized and affirmed existing Aboriginal and treaty rights. This means that these rights are recognized as already existing at the time of colonization—they are not delegated, and do not flow from the Crown, and therefore are acknowledged as inherent rights.

   With respect to court decisions, Patricia Monture-Angus, in her 1999 work *Journeying Forward: Dreaming First Nations Independence*, has extensively examined the history of Supreme Court cases and their effects on Aboriginal rights. She has concluded that between the 1990 *Sparrow* decision, which first ruled on the terms by which Aboriginal rights could be said to be extinguished, and the *Delgamuukw* decision of the late 1990s, which ruled on the extent to which section 35 could protect Aboriginal title to land, the Supreme Court of Canada has used its opportunities to define section 35 as a means to water down the protections it is intended to afford and to therefore limit the content and exercise of Aboriginal Rights protected by the Constitution.

2. Taiaiake Alfred, in *Peace, Power, and Righteousness*
    describes how Canada administers 'self-government' by
    divesting of any responsibility toward rectifying centuries
    of colonialism, while holding tight to the land base and
    resources, and by further entrenching in law and practice
    the real basis of its power while maintaining basic policies
    of assimilation and destruction unchanged. The First
    Nations Governance Act should be seen in such a light.
3. The implications for crown liability are enormous
    (Barnsley, 2003b: 14–25). Most notably, the case *Victor
    Buffalo v the Queen* involves a lawsuit by the Samson Cree
    Band against the federal government for mismanagement
    of $1.5 billion in oil and gas trust monies. The lawyer for
    the Samson Cree Band, veteran James O'Reilly, is sub-
    poenaing Prime Minister Jean Chretien and Minister of
    Indian Affairs Robert Nault to testify (Barnsley, 2003c, 9).

References

Barnsley, Paul. 2003a. 'Harvard Study Group Finds Fault with
    FNGA', *Windspeaker* (February): 1, 2.
Barnsley, Paul. 2003b. 'White Paper Revisited?', *Windspeaker*
    (March): 14, 25.
Barnsley, Paul. 2003c. 'Compelled and Compelling',
    Windspeaker (April): 9.
McKinley, Rob. 1998. 'Gathering Looks at Cree Confederacy',
    Alberta Sweetgrass (May): 1.

Chapter 12

I Am a Lakota Womyn

Beverly Little Thunder (Standing Rock Lakota)

The very mention of 'Washington, DC' is enough to trigger insecurities that I hold inside over my lack of formal academic educa-tion.[1] As I put my thoughts into writing for this work I can only pray that the words that come from my heart will be heard and understood.

I am glad that I was able to hear the words of all those who spoke during our meeting in 1993 in Washington, DC. It was good to hear where those who have written about my people are taking their studies these days. As I heard the word 'berdache' [*sic*] used, I found myself wondering, 'Where am I as a womyn in this word?' Its mean-ing had no place in the description of my life. The word is meant to describe males, not me. I am a Lakota womyn, and I know that my own people have a name for me.

Most tribes that I have had the honor of know-ing have specific names for men who love men and for wimmin who love wimmin. I have per-sonally spent much of my life being placed in the 'other' category in the Western world. The sug-gested label of 'designated other' (when referring to me in my relationship with a womyn partner) did not appeal to me. Because I had no role model to look toward for guidance, I found myself learn-ing and adopting the terms used by the main-stream feminist community I became involved in. Although I did not totally fit in with the beliefs of some of these wimmin, I was able to learn from them and empower myself to follow the path that I needed to.

I can understand that there may be a need for some to find a pan-Native term that can be used as a marker for the general population of Native lesbians and gays. We are all so different in so many ways, however. Culturally and physically, we are all different. Each tribe has its own name, its own structure. How can we all even be called 'Natives'?

Whether we are talking about the past or the present, in terms of tribal identity or sexuality, the tendency to lump us all under one label is still there. We may all be men who love men or wimmin who love wimmin, but we have all come to this place in a different manner.

I had read accounts of one or two people who lived in the past. The studies seem to focus on one or two individuals who lived their lives in a different time, under different social circumstances, and with varied influences. Frequently, these accounts were obtained from someone who knew someone who knew someone (in other words, gossip). The stories were often written as if those in the past were the only true two-spirit people to have lived.

The words I would like to see written about me and read fifty years from now should be words that reflect who I am as an individual. I am a female, and I have no desire to be a male. I am able to perform many tasks that are considered male jobs. Yet, I am also able to do and enjoy doing many things that are considered female. I am also able to bear children and have done so.

Being a womyn who loves another womyn does not mean that I reject being a mother. I am, in fact, a mother to five children: two daughters and three sons. Having children helped me to look closer at the world into which I had brought them. It was important for me to, at least, get them to the doorway of their ancestors and teach them the basic values of the Lakota people and culture.

Many two-spirit wimmin I meet are very involved with children. Sometimes the children are their own, other times the children in their lives are nieces or nephews. Like myself, these wimmin share an interest in providing guidance to young people that will enable them to live their lives in a good way. There is a concern that the young ones need to have encouragement to feel good about who they are and the decisions they make.

My experience has been that one of my daughters has many aunts and uncles in the two-spirit community. They are there for her. She is a beautiful and well-centered young womyn today as a result of the help and guidance she received growing up in the two-spirit community. In the recent past, our people raised their children with the collective support of all the tribal members. What we are doing in the two-spirit community is no different from that old way.

It can be hard for those who have unsupportive families. Once I heard a young two-spirit man cry because his sister would not allow him to hold his newborn nephew. She had told him that she did not want her son to be gay. Another two-spirit couple were parenting the natural son of one of the wimmin. The natural mother became ill and died. Her brother then used the tribal courts to have the child taken from the remaining parent and have her forbidden from seeing the child again. No one seemed to be concerned with how the child may have felt being taken from both of the only parents he had known.

Two-spirit womyn and men are concerned for the future of their people. Children are a respected part of that circle of human life. All adults are role models and teachers for the next generation. This gives adults the responsibility of showing the young ones how to honor themselves and respect their choices as well as their place on this earth.

My experience began in Los Angeles, California, where I was born to a mother who was not expecting me to arrive so soon. I was born in the county hospital. Mother told me that this was because she was not able to get home to North Dakota. She also told me that we did go home when I was older and spent some time there in a small town called Kenel, in North Dakota.

My mother and father were alcoholics. There were many quite remarkable things about my mother, however her alcoholism drove her to send me to live with my relatives for much of my early life. Sometimes people tell me that I was lucky. My relatives assume that somehow these experiences formed my spiritual nature. They want to believe that I was taught all there is to know about Lakota spirituality when I was a child. They are incorrect. I am spiritual because it is what I have chosen to be. It is a part of who I am as a person.

I grew up in foster homes, boarding schools, and detention centers. I even spent some time in two convents. During this period I even thought it would be fun to be a nun.

I was not overly fond of boys. I was molested frequently as a child and as a result was fearful of males. I did not want to get married and have children. Out of fear and to prove to myself that I was not 'queer', I did get married, and I did have children. I do not regret this. I do, however, feel just a little bit sorry for those men whom I must have made unhappy.

I felt torn between Christianity, which was part of my life, and the traditions in which I was raised. I did not seem to fit into the Christian world, yet I was also aware of the homophobia in the world of my people. I could not find peace in being who I was.

In my early twenties I became active in the American Indian Movement. It was very frightening. I attended the Sweat Lodge Ceremonies and in doing so became aware of my responsibility to teach my children and guide them in the ways of their ancestors. I felt that if this were a path that they chose to follow when they were adults, at least they would know how to access it. Of course, this meant that I had to learn it in order to teach them. It was certainly a crash course in spirituality. There I was, a young mother in her twenties trying to learn and teach my children Lakota in a small town where no one else spoke the language. The sweat lodge I was able to take my children to was being led by men who were just learning themselves. It was not easy.

As I became more deeply involved in the ceremonies of my people and began to participate in the Sun Dance Ceremony, I became more and more terrified of being 'found out'. I feared that if anyone knew of my desire to be with another womyn I would be stricken from the ceremonies

that were now such an important part of my life. My fears turned out to be real, but I never expected that the same people who taught me so much about the Lakota ways would be some of those who would later reject me so completely.

This rejection came in 1985 when I attended the Sun Dance Ceremony in South Dakota. I went there and told the community that I could no longer pretend to be someone I was not. I could no longer sit quietly while cruel jokes were made about lesbians and gays. The word *lesbian* was, at the time, the only way I knew how to identify the feelings I felt. European influences had almost eradicated the recognition and role of people like myself among my own people.[2] The rejection hurt. It hurt a lot.

My involvement in the Lakota spiritual community was a large part my life and who I am. Being turned away by the Lakota wimmin and men with whom I had prayed and danced was devastating. Before I left the community, two older wimmin came to see me. I was told that there was no need for me to be there and be the subject of this anger. I was told that our people have trouble remembering the place of honor that my kind once held. I was told to go and have a ceremony for others like myself. I was told to listen to Spirit.

After a year, I was directed by Spirit to have a ceremony for my own kind—a Sun Dance ceremony that was different from those that I had learned. And so it began. The first three years were hard. I had to separate myself from the first group I had led in the ceremony. I left because of the direction I saw them going. It was not the way I had been taught to honor my people. No matter what, I was determined to do what I had to do in an honorable way for the sake of my ancestors. Now, as part of my continued determination to hold wimmin-only Sun Dances, we have our ceremony each full moon of July in the hills of California. There are few dancers. Each is a two-spirit womyn willing to prepare and honor the ceremony.

I am sure that there are some of my own people who feel that what I do is wrong. I have been forced to find in my own way a means of continuing with the expressions of my spiritual beliefs. I have done the best I can. Sometimes I have made mistakes, and at other times I may have appeared rebellious. I may have even appeared to be disrespectful of my own people. To maintain my center I have needed to do the things I have done in my life.

In the non-Native community of lesbians and gay people, I have been told that being two-spirited means that I am a special being. It seems that they felt that my spirituality was the mystical answer to my sexuality. I do not believe this to be so. My spirituality would have been with me, regardless of my sexuality. This attitude often creates a feeling of isolation. I live in a white society that finds me exotic. At the same time, I can be ignored by people I love, respect, and sometimes work with.

I have had to learn that sometimes I am on the cutting edge when I do what is best for myself. To protect myself, I have learned to keep a lot of 'band-aids' handy—especially those nurturing and caring friends I call on when things get rough. Doing so has been helpful for the times when not just strangers, but people I love and care about attack and judge my actions. There are so many of us who have been involved in a struggle for dignity for such a long time. Often we have struggled on our own without the support of our people. Every now and then we come across someone who will listen to us and offer moral and emotional support. When this happens, as it did during the second Wenner-Gren Foundation Conference meetings in Chicago in 1994, I feel the struggle is worth it.

I hear the stories that my brothers and sisters tell, and I find that I feel a deep love for these human beings who have endured so much pain in their lives. Yet they were willing to take the risk of sharing some of their most hurtful moments with a room full of anthropologists in Washington, DC, Chicago, and now with the world. . .

It is time that anthropologists write about those of us who are alive now. And they must *listen* to us, hear us, and use our own words, not just their special anthropological language. The combined words are the ones people will read fifty (and more) years from now. There are not just two or three of us . . . There are hundreds, even thou-

sands, of us, and we all struggle to live our lives with dignity and pride.

Just as my Lakota ancestors continue to struggle, I have come before you and tried to use your language to help you understand that 'berdache' is not who I am. I have tried to understand the scope and purpose of those who continue to work in the field of anthropology. I have read paper after paper written by anthropologists and historians, . . . , and I continue to see this same inappropriate word used for us. In spite of the fact that the Native people . . . that the term is not acceptable, it is still being used by some who insist that our request that they stop doing so impinges on their 'academic freedom' or their 'right to free speech'. When I read or hear such statements, I feel invisible. I hear and read about men who lived before us and again I feel invisible. There is so little written about the role of wimmin loving wimmin in the various tribes. I can not help but wonder how the young wimmin of future generations will feel. Will they feel invisible too?

During our discussions in Washington, DC, I heard someone make the comment that two-spirit people must be innovative. I have found this to be true. In order to survive the attacks and the fear of others, I have had to be innovative. I have needed to find ways to validate myself, ways to maintain my integrity and pride. There may be some people who chose to see me as a spiritual leader. I want to be clear that I do not see myself in this way. When others ask me why I have chosen the path that I follow, I tell them that it is the path I have been directed to follow. Only the Creator can know why and what my purpose is.

The world of the academy seeks to find and provide answers to questions, such as why are some people lesbian or gay and others are not. There are those who swear 'it must have been the water in a town' or 'the way a person was brought up'. We have all heard the various theories, yet none of us knows the answer.

The next seven generations are going to be affected by the work that has begun . . . If I, as a Native womyn, sound angry and arrogant, then it may be because our voices have never been heard before without a non-Native person first editing our thoughts into something that they deem more 'suitable' and 'appropriate'. The unique experience of each person who has been a part of this long process is important. Whether we are a manly womyn, a womynly man, transgendered, heterosexual, asexual, or otherwise, we are all one with creation.

No one person can speak for so many Native two-spirit people, no single term can apply to all of us at any time. Instead of focusing on one or two people who lived in the past it is now time to begin to write about those of us who live today. Anthropologists of today have the opportunity to record the contemporary life of our people, not just our history, for future generations.

These days I no longer ask for respect, and I do not ask for sensitivity. I will not bend over backward to be seen or heard. These days I demand respect and sensitivity, and I demand to be seen and to be heard. I demand all of these because they are my right as a human being.

I hope these words provide another step toward what is going to happen in the next few years to change how people write about us and record our lives. I pray Native people can reach understanding and clarity among themselves so that the voices of all my people can and will be heard. I pray that all humans can honor and respect the individuality of everyone who lives on Mother Earth.

Notes

1. As indicated in the 'Introduction,' the first Wenner-Gren Foundation Conference and the American Anthropological Association session on 'Revisiting the 'North American Berdache' Empirically and Theoretically' were held in Washington, DC, in November 1993. I had considerable anxiety about being in that city for several reasons, only one of which was speaking to a group of academics.
2. It is ironic that while my people so strongly rejected me and others like me, certain white male academics had 'rediscovered' Lakota *winkte* and were making references to the 'privileged' and 'honored' status of the ancient ones found in old anthropological and historical writings. Some even went so far as to argue that modern *winkte* still had status in our communities (Williams, 1986), when my experience showed otherwise.

Reference

Williams, Walter. 1986. *The Spirit and the Flesh: Sexual Diversity in American Indian Culture*. Boston: Beacon Press. Reprint 1991, with a new preface.

Part Four

Additional Readings

Anderson, Kim and Bonita Lawrence, eds. *Strong Women's Stories: Native Vision and Community Survival*. Toronto: Sumach Press, 2003.

Green, Joyce, ed. *Making Space for Indigenous Feminism*. Halifax: Fernwood Publishing, 2007.

Justice, Daniel Heath, Mark Rifkin, and Bethany Scheider, eds. *A Journal of Lesbian and Gay Studies* (Special Edition on Sexuality, Nationality, Indigeneity) 16, 1–2 (2010).

Kauanui, J. Kehaulani. *Hawaiian Blood: Colonialism and the Politics of Sovereignty and Indigeneity*. Durham, NC: Duke University Press, 2008.

McIvor, Donna Sharon. 'Self-Government and Aboriginal Women', pp. 167–86 in Enakshi Dua and Angela Robertson, eds, *Scratching the Surface: Canadian Anti-Racist Feminist Thought*. Toronto: Women's Press, 1999.

Smith, Andrea. *Conquest: Sexual Violence and American Indian Genocide*. Cambridge, MA: South End Press, 2005.

Relevant Websites

Native Women's Association of Canada
http://www.nwac-hq.org
The Native Women's Association of Canada (NWAC) is a great resource of information. The website has a Media Centre, where you can read recent media releases or search through the archives. The site also provides access to research and data on Indigenous women in Canada. Take time to research and explore current and past initiatives, issues, and reports. The website also has a link to the Sharon McIvor case.

INCITE! Women of Color Against Violence
http://www.incite.national.org/
As described on their website, INCITE! Women of Color Against Violence 'is a national activist organization of radical feminists of color advancing a movement to end violence against women of color and our communities through direct action, critical dialogue and grassroots organizing'. Cherokee scholar Andrea Smith is a co-founder of this organization. INCITE! identifies 'violence against women of color' as a combination of 'violence *directed at* communities', such as police violence, war, and colonialism, and 'violence *within* communities', such as rape and domestic violence.

Films

Yuxweluptun: Man of Masks. Dir. Dana Claxton. National Film Board of Canada, 1998.
First Stories—Two Spirited. Dir. Sharon A. Desjarlais. National Film Board of Canada, 2007.

Keepers of the Fire. Dir. Christine Welsh. National Film Board of Canada, 1994.
Onkwa-nistensera: Mothers of Our Nations. Dir. Dawn Martin-Hill. Indigenous Health Research Development Program, 2006.

Key Terms

Racialization
Indian
Indian Act
Gender discrimination
Legal assimilation

Involuntary enfranchisement
Two-spirited
Compulsory heterosexuality
Heteronormativity

Discussion Questions

1. How does the Indian Act, even following amendments in 1985, continue to regulate Indigenous identities and nationhood in Canada? How would you describe the nature of discrimination facing Indigenous communities in contemporary times?
2. How have Indigenous women, in speaking out against unequal treatment within the Indian Act, created awareness in settler colonial societies? What are some examples?
3. How have Indigenous peoples in cities challenged hegemonic definitions of 'Indianness'? How have they provided new ways of conceiving of Indigenous identity?

4. Discuss Little Thunder's exploration of colonialism, heterosexism, queerness, and two-spiritedness. What kinds of issues does she highlight with respect to pan-Native terminology, Western-academic terminology, and Queer terminology? What kinds of connections does she draw between racism, sexuality, and spirituality, and how is this shaped by colonialism?

Activities

Invite an Indigenous activist to discuss the impact of the Indian Act on his or her own identity.

Watch the 2008 National Film Board production *Club Native* (written and directed by Tracey Deer). How is the status Indian collective represented in the film? How are issues of racialization being addressed? How have definitions of Indianness become central to people's own self-images? What is the difference between the racism institutionalized through federal legislation and the racism employed to resist further colonial encroachment? How do we explain the absence of men's voices in the film? What needs to happen before these voices are heard?

Watch the 2007 film *Two Spirits* (written and directed by Ruth Fertig). What factors contribute to Joey Criddle's confusion in terms of gendered and erotic diversity? How would you describe his aspirations as a two-spirited man and activist?

PART FIVE

Family, Belonging, and Displacement

On 11 June 2008 Prime Minister Harper officially apologized on behalf of the Canadian State and ordinary Canadians to the survivors of the residential schooling system and Indigenous peoples, in general, for the many forms of abuse that happened in the schools and for other negative impacts inflicted on individuals, their families, and communities. This apology recognizes that the impacts of colonial policies, like residential schooling, are still ongoing in Indigenous communities. Contrary to what some might wish to believe, colonialism is not a thing of the past and a new path of reconciliation and healing must be taken. This section of the book examines the impact of racism, colonialism, and displacement on familial relations and nationhood, in particular, the impact of these legacies on traditional ways of knowing, loving, caring, and nurturing.

Following the prime minister's apology, Beverley Jacobs, then President of the Native Women's Association of Canada (NWAC) spoke to the House of Commons. As she explained: 'We have had so much impact from colonization and that is what we are dealing with today. Women have taken the brunt of it all. In the end it must be about more than what happened in the residential schools. For women, the truth telling must continue' (Jacobs, 2008). In this section, all three authors tell their truths, covering various *ways* in which colonial ideologies and practices have attacked healthy and balanced familial, communal, and gender relations. Kim Anderson analyzes the displacement of traditional gender and familiar relations, highlighting how before colonization women had a large amount of power, authority, and respect in their nations.

Traditionally, 'the family was not the property of the man', Anderson writes, and mothering gave women status and was deemed an affirmation of their status in their respective nations. Polygamy, divorce, and homosexuality were neither uncommon nor negatively regarded. Because of the interdependence and kinship-based nature of communities, violence was not condoned and when it did occur, members of the community treated it as a community issue and dealt with it according to protocol. However, as Anderson suggests, colonization changed all of this. Western patriarchal ideals and models of gender and familial relations eventually displaced women's traditional power, status, and authority and enabled men to acquire whatever limited amount of power over women and children. Matrilineal and matrilocal societies were ultimately transformed into patrilineal, patrilocal, and patriarchal ones, modelling European relations of the time. As Anderson concludes, 'colonization in and of itself is a violent process. It brought many untold forms of violence against the women, children and men of the Americas. Today, we are faced with epidemic, lateral violence in our communities.'

The residential school system is one method through which violent transformation occurred within Indigenous communities. Both Anderson and Ing examine the direct and intergenerational impacts of Canada's residential schools on individuals, families, and whole communities. Through the separation of children from their families and communities, the State had hoped that the traditional cultures of Indigenous peoples would be forgotten, and assimilation to mainstream society would take place. In 2008, the House of Commons reported that this policy was racist because it deemed Indigenous cultures to be inferior to that of Eurocanadians. It reported the many violent forms of abuse that happened inside the walls of the schools, as well as the long term impact on the bodies, minds, spirits, and hearts of the survivors and their families that is still being felt today.

Indigenous children were expected to suppress their sexuality, were punished for speaking their language and for maintaining bonds with their siblings, and suffered abuse from their teachers and schoolmates in residential schools. Children were left with feelings of shame about their Indigenous identity; they did not learn positive parenting skills, confusing love with violence and self-hate. When returning to their communities, they no longer possessed the love, confidence, self-esteem, cultural knowledge, and often times, the language, to form positive relationships with their families. Many turned to negative coping behaviours to escape the internal turmoil, sometimes involving alcoholism and other addictions, as well as violence. As Ing points out, residential schools affected entire communities. Many of them 'suffered a disintegration of political and social institutions of culture, language, religion and economic existence'. Ing rightly argues that we must make the links of the current social-economic conditions of Indigenous communities to residential schools and to re-educate society of the harm done by racist colonial policies that targeted Indigenous traditional ways of relating with each other.

Residential schools are not the only ways in which Indigenous peoples were forced to forgo their identities and to assimilate into mainstream society. By documenting her personal story, Shandra Spears shows how transracial adoptions, as frequently practiced in Canada over many generations, displaced children from their Indigenous families and, in so doing, disconnected them from entire communities. This process links with the major theme of 'disappearing' underscoring this anthology. As Spears writes: 'In Canada, young Native people disappear into the dominant society through love, lies, and ideology—transracial adopting—disconnects them from nations, families.' These 'disappearances' embody an act of genocide: just like residential schools, the State had hoped to make 'Indians' disappear through placing children into white families, impeding their ability to form strong Indigenous identities.

As Spears' narrative illustrates, the outcome was unjustly dramatic: many emerged angry, unable to formulate a positive sense of belonging in either white society or in the Indigenous community. The outcome of this history was a 'fractured' identity, one characterized by 'a collection of shutdowns and self-destructive behaviour'. Just like the experience of residential schools, children were robbed through transracial adoption of their inherent right to Indigeneity and have had to struggle to recover and reclaim their identification.

Despite the genocidal nature of both residential schooling and transracial adoption, all three authors speak of their own resilience and the courage of Indigenous people to survive the racist colonial attacks on Indigeneity. This is evident through efforts to recover both traditional gender and familiar relations, and to pass on these traditions to the younger generations, both by educating oneself of the history of residential schools, as well as our family members who have experienced this history so that we can make sense of the lingering effects existing in our families and nations, and to find again our inner strength to heal and move forward. As Spears concludes, 'the colonizer can try to hurt us, but can only succeed if we change who we are.' In short, the work that we are doing today to both reclaim and resist past histories of racism and injustice suggest that Indigenous peoples are quite clearly 'not disappearing'.

Chapter 13

Marriage, Divorce, and Family Life

Kim Anderson

To discuss the concept of marriage as it existed in pre-Christian Native societies is difficult, as there were so many different traditions regarding this type of union. Women made autonomous decisions about these partnerships in some cases, but many societies practised arranged marriages. Polygamy was acceptable in many societies prior to Christian influence. Some societies expected that the union of two people was a lifetime arrangement but in others 'divorce' or separation was common and in others still 'marriage' was

viewed as a primarily economic relationship that had nothing to do with sexual fidelity or loyalty. Native women's status and experiences with marriage were therefore not uniform. Like the people of western society today, partnerships were formed, but the expectations of those partnerships were very different from nation to nation.

Regardless of these differences, Native women typically had power, respect, and recognition within their families. As part of a family unit, a Native woman was interdependent, yet in many nations her autonomy as an individual in this unit was also respected. It may be that the principle of non-interference which was prevalent in many Indigenous nations was helpful to Native women in the arena of marriage. The principle of non-interference meant, among other things, that no one person had the right to tell another what to do. . . .

In the matrilocal societies of the Navajo, Seminoles, Cherokee, and Iroquois, a woman's autonomy in marriage was even more pronounced. The central position of the woman in the family was sustained by living with her own kin. There was no way for men in these societies to assume the position of 'head' of the family; rather, they became part of the interdependent family unit that ensured the central role of the mothers. The man joined the woman's family to assist with the survival of that family; he would work for the well-being of the family that had descended from the mother's line. As Jeannette Armstrong points out, this meant that the woman's property was handed down through a line of women, and that women were assisted by the men. . . .

A number of societies (such as the Inuit, Lakota, and Siksika) practised polygamy. Some Native women argue that polygamy can not be considered according to western/Christian standards of marriage. In fact, it may have provided a better life for women. Virginia Driving Hawk Sneve writes, 'Polygamy—a practice that most whites found reprehensible—lessened an individual wife's duties. The more wives a man had, the more skins could be tanned for the comfort of the lodge; however, the more women in the lodge, the more they controlled the man' (Sneve, 1995: 11). She reports that Sioux women who married white men found themselves in monogamous marriages that increased their workload. . . .

Polygamy may not have been the most ideal situation for women, but it may have offered some advantages. If marriage is understood as a primarily economic relationship, it is possible that polygamous relationships served some particular needs for Native women. However, we need more research to better understand women's positions in these marriages. For example, what were the sexual liberties of women? How did they relate to the other wives? Were these marriages simply thought of as work-teams or socioeconomic units, and how was this at odds with European notions of love?

There were many types of unions in traditional societies, and many of these relationships could be ended quite simply. Separation from one's partner was not complicated by the religious and legal ramifications of western society. In numerous Indigenous nations, 'divorce' was uncomplicated, commonplace, and could be initiated by either the man or the woman (Albers, 1983: 191; Buffalohead, 1983: 242; Guemple, 1995: 149; Sattler, 1995: 222; Sharp, 1995: 54). In Navajo culture, for example, either the woman or the man could decide to end the marriage. . . .

'Divorce' was easier in many Native societies largely because of the understandings of property. As with the understanding that one can't 'own' land, there was an understanding in most Indigenous cultures that one can't 'own' people.[1] This meant that a man could not own his wife, nor could parents own their children. The family was not the property of the man. In this way, a woman was more free to marry or divorce as she saw fit. With relation to the principle of non-interference, the wife had autonomy and respect. This enabled her to make decisions on her own behalf.

Whether single or in a partnership, motherhood accorded Native women tremendous status in the family, community, and nation. Motherhood was an affirmation of a woman's power and defined her central role in traditional Aboriginal societies. This stemmed from the reverence for women's innate power to bring forth life. Yet this power belonged to all women, regardless of whether or not they biologically produced children. Indigenous societies highly valued their children and both biological and non-biological mothers were honoured for their work. Pre-conquest women, Paula Gunn Allen writes, 'were mothers, and that word did not imply slaves, drudges, drones, who are required to love only for others rather than for themselves, as it so tragically does for many modern women' (Allen, 1986: 7).

With colonization, this powerful role of mother and the position of woman in the family came under attack. Social, economic, and political power was ripped away through the imposition of the western family structure. European 'family values' were a keystone in the conquest strategy. From the outset, missionaries were instructed to change Aboriginal family structure as part of their project to convert Native peoples. The Jesuits of New France, headed by Father Lejeune, introduced the patriarchal family structure, 'with male authority, female fidelity, and the elimination of the right to divorce' (Leacock, 1980: 28). Field matrons were sent out to Native communities to 'civilize' and 'educate' Native women so they could meet the patriarchal ideals of wife and mother (Emmerich, 1991). In order to be civilized, Native women needed to learn how to obey. Residential schools taught Native women to be compliant to their husbands and prepared them for the domestic role that was expected of white women at the time (Fiske, 1996; Wittstock, 1980: 214). The intent was to break down extended family and clan systems, considered by the missionaries to be a degraded state, 'the outcome of looseness of morals and absence of social restraint' (Fiske, 1996: 171). . . .

With the diminishing family structure, the respect for women and children vanished, and men's responsibilities shifted dramatically. In her essay on the criminalization of single, destitute mothers, Lakota scholar Elizabeth Cook-Lynn relates family and social breakdown to the destruction of traditional values. Before contact, men had natural and ethical responsibilities towards children. Men who dishonoured women were not accorded political, spiritual, or social status and were often physically attacked by women. Today, this is no longer true: 'men who are known to degrade women and abandon children now hold positions of power, even sometimes sitting at the tribal council tables. They are directors of tribal council programs, and they often participate unmolested in sacred ceremonies.' Women were also traditionally held accountable for their actions in the case of irresponsibility towards children,

but they were not singled out and placed 'at fault' alone, as they are in the increasingly popular 'single-mother' bashing of today's society (Cook-Lynn, 1996: 115–16). With the loss of their traditional responsibilities and the honour accorded to their position, Native women have, in many cases, become oppressed by a role that was once a great source of strength and power.

Sex and Sexuality

Attitudes towards sex and sexuality were complex, and varied extensively among the nations. One thing they held in common, however, was the acceptance that sex was something natural for both women and men. . . .

According to many Native peoples, women's bodies, by virtue of their capacity to bring forth life, were powerful and celebrated through all their cycles. Respect for their bodies was related to the respect and responsibility they commanded in their families, villages and nations. Because of this respect, women were not seen as 'sex objects', and, as well, they had a great deal of individual control over their own sexuality. . . .

Attitudes towards marriage, sex, and love were so different that it is hard to imagine traditional Native marriage relations from a contemporary western viewpoint. However, if one considers that people married young into arranged marriages that were based on economic development for the families, it is not hard to imagine that there was acceptance of this type of sexual freedom in marriage. Jeannette Armstrong (Okanagan) says the existence of post-marital sexual freedom among her people is a practice that still exists in some families today.

The fear of unwanted pregnancy was also absent among Native women. Children were always welcome, and because women were esteemed for having children, pregnancy was a natural part of the sexual cycle. Nor did children born out of wedlock have the stigma that later came with European ideas about 'illegitimacy'. Women were not punished for having children out of marriage. Leslie Marmon Silko asserts: 'New life was so precious that pregnancy was always appropriate, and pregnancy before marriage was celebrated as a good sign' (Silko, 1996: 67–8). There was no such thing as a 'single mother', because children were accepted into large kin-based or clan-based communities, with all the supports that accompanied this. . . .

The idea that all children are welcome, regardless of where they come from, is such a persistent value in Native societies that it still exists today, even in communities that have been heavily Christianized. Myra Laramee says that teenage pregnancy does not carry the same stigma in the Aboriginal community, 'because a child is a sacred being, and it doesn't matter how it gets here'.

Despite children always being welcomed as sacred beings, it appears that Native women did have access to birth control. Beverly Hungry Wolf has recorded Siksika elder Ah'-dunn (Margaret Hind-Man) talking about the traditional knowledge and practice of birth control. . . .

The sexual freedom and fluidity of sexuality included homosexuality in many Native societies. Anthropologist Sue Ellen Jacobs has identified eighty-eight societies with documented references to gayness. Eleven other societies have denied the existence of homosexuality, and these societies were 'in areas of heaviest, lengthiest, and most severely puritanical white encroachment' (Allen, 1986: 197).

The fluidity of gender was inherent in Native cultural views of the world. Some Native cultures understood that there were four genders rather than two: man; woman; the two spirit womanly males; and the two spirit manly females. A wide variety of Native American languages have words to describe people that are a combination of the masculine and feminine (Lang, 1997: 103). Current literature suggests that two-spirited people were not traditionally understood as they are now; for instance, it was not as socially sanctioned to have sex between people of the same gender (i.e., man/man), but people could have sex with an individual of another gender, regardless of whether they were the same sex (i.e., man/two spirit womanly male). The prevalence of this

across Native societies and the acceptance within societies was such that people could marry members of the third and fourth gender (Laframboise and Heyle, 1990: 459). . . .

Although these practices may not necessarily imply homosexuality, they do indicate a lack of homophobia in the societies that would allow such gender fluidity.

Homosexuality was highly regarded in some cultures. Odawa Elder Liza Mosher states that homosexual men were traditionally considered special because they could do 'women's work' such as taking care of children or cooking for feasts when the women were on their moon time (cited in Kulchyski, McCaskill, and Newhouse, 1999: 149). . . .

With European contact, homosexuality, the open sexuality of women, and the acceptance of children out of wedlock immediately came under attack. In short, sexuality that did not fit into the patriarchal model was unacceptable. . . .

Homosexuality was viewed as the ultimate sin. Algonquin educator Helen Thundercloud explains: 'We honoured two-spirited people because they brought gifts to our communities that were very important. And all of a sudden the Christians came along and said, "Oh you can't do that. That is a sin against God." Over the years we took those beliefs, and that has destroyed our people.' Where God was not enough to regulate homosexuality, the state stepped in. The *Indian Act* institutionalized heterosexual marriage (and heterosexuality) as it was the only way by which an individual would be able to pass on Indian status and rights (Cannon, 1998: 118). Whether by way of the church or the state, Euro-Christian attitudes about homosexuality have borne their bitter fruit, as homophobia has now found a place in every Native community. . . .

I believe that the most tragic and devastating impact on both Native women and Native men's sexuality came during the residential school era, when sexuality and sexual expression were suppressed, distorted, and perverted. Schools were either all male or all female, as the churches believed that Native students were likely to be more sexually active than non-Natives. Historian J.R. Miller speculates that this fear that led to the 'fanatical segregation' of the sexes 'might have been based on a misunderstanding of the greater autonomy and control of their own bodies that females in some Native communities enjoyed' (Miller, 1997: 234–35). It could be that the missionaries confused Native children's personal control of their bodies with open sexual license. Whatever the cause, Native children suffered the consequences by being chastised and even beaten for even attempting to communicate with members of the opposite sex, who were often their siblings and relations (Miller, 1997: 219). Shirley Williams recalls the policing of sexuality and the hysteria associated with it at St Joseph's Residential School. She remembers that girls were accused of improper behaviour when they tried to make contact with boys: 'We were called boy crazy.' These attempts at contact were usually not sexually driven, but the attempts of lonely little girls who wished to speak to their brothers or cousins. Their excitement at catching periodic glimpses of family members was often met with anger from the nuns, who accused them of sexual behaviour.

At residential school, girls were taught that the female body was a locus for shame. Miller describes the measures taken by the nuns at the Blue Quills Residential School in Alberta to conceal the female body: At Blue Quills, school girls had to wear 'this real tight binder' so that their growing breasts would be flattened, and at all ages they had to wear 'a bathing suit' that resembled 'a grey flannelette nightgown' when taking a bath. Other schools demanded that boys wear shorts in the shower, but 'females had a greater obligation than males to be modest in dress, chaste in behaviour, and free of pregnancy. Their heavier burden was part of the misfortune of being a woman' (Miller, 1997: 235).

Shirley Williams knows too well the sense of worthlessness and the denigration that came out of these policies. She remembers that girls in her school had to wear clothing that was loose, 'because you couldn't show your shape of your body.' . . . Residential school priests and nuns fan-

atically instilled the dogma that sex was the most punishable of offences, while at the same time sexually abusing the children in their care. The prevalence of rape, sexual assault, induced abortion, and sexual/psychological abuse is well documented (Chrisjohn, Young, and Maraun, 1997; Assembly of First Nations, 1994), as are the outright and horrific pillaging of Native sexuality. . . .

Residential school survivor Shirley Williams says that she left residential school 'starved for love'. Presumably, this was the case for many residential school survivors. When these feelings were coupled with abusive and degrading teachings about sexuality, they had the potential to wreck havoc on Native individuals, families, and communities.

Family Violence

. . . The traditional respect accorded to Native women made it unthinkable in Aboriginal cultures to practise violence against them. Although some writers contend that violence against women existed in early Native societies (Brodribb, 1984: 89; Malz and Archambault, 1995: 47–8), there is overwhelming evidence that such behaviour was offset by strong taboos and severe punishment. Sylvia Maracle writes, 'Our elders tell us that incidents of violence—be they sexual, mental, emotional or spiritual—were rare and swiftly dealt with in our communities prior to contact with the Europeans' (Maracle, 1993: 1). Patricia Monture-Angus asserts that 'violence and abuse (including political exclusions) against women were not tolerated in most Aboriginal societies.' . . .

When violence against women happened, there were systems to deal with it. Abusers could be met with violence in return, often at the hands of the women. Lee Maracle recalls her grandmother physically beating a cousin who had been violent with his sister. In the Plateau societies, the women meted out punishment to rapists. . . .

There were also ways of dealing with the sexual abuse of children, which was not unknown to Native societies. In a 1992 consultation, a number of different nations in British Columbia testified that there were traditional sanctions and laws against child sexual abuse, and that the clan system did much to eliminate or control these crimes (Fournier and Crey, 1997: 144). In my conversation with Maria Campbell, she told me that Métis and Cree culture had stories that warned about pedophiles, and precautions were taken to keep children away from unknown men. Men were expected to socialize in a house away from the children, and old women had the responsibility to watch over them. Among the Sto:lo, watchmen elders could send their spirits through the walls of an extended family's house to make sure the children were safe. They were called upon to work with visions about what was happening to a certain child. Guardians who were suspected of child abuse were publicly identified and punished with banishment, segregation from children, and even death (Fournier and Crey, 1997: 114). The protection provided by the extended family, clan, and community systems was lost with the introduction of nuclear family models. As the 'head of the family' male sexual predators were handed control over their wives and children, a role that shielded them from public scrutiny (Fournier and Crey, 1997: 144).

Colonization in and of itself is a violent process. It brought many untold forms of violence against the women, children, and men of the Americas. Today, we are faced with epidemic, lateral violence in our communities. State and church policies started this vicious cycle by instilling violence in children who were placed in residential schools and abusive foster homes, and by degrading women sexually, politically, and socially (Maracle, 1993: 1, 4; MacDonald, 1993: 5).

Abused Native boys and girls have grown into adults who abuse or who accept abuse as part of a relationship. If the cycle of violence is not broken, adults can pass violence on to their children. Instead of being positive role models, they risk teaching children violent behaviours. . . .

Western patriarchal family structures enabled Aboriginal men to turn their violence inward: 'Aboriginal men who had been deprived of natural authority through impoverishment and the theft of land were handed in exchange the weapon of absolute possession and control over their wives and children . . .' (Fournier and Crey, 1997: 145). Frustrated and powerless men have exerted their anger in the only arena of power they were given by the colonizer: the power to dominate Native women and children. The introduction of alcohol and drugs exacerbated the violence. Our people have used (and continue to use) alcohol and drugs to fill the ugly gap left by the theft of our ways. . . .

The violence that has become a 'way of life' for many Native women has crippled their well-being. It feeds into all the other mainstream messages about the worthlessness of Native women, and creates a vicious cycle of abuse that is passed onto the future generations. This culture of violence works in direct opposition to an understanding of woman as a sacred source. As Calvin Morrisseau suggests, 'striking out against a woman is like striking out against every thing we hold sacred . . .' (Morrisseau, 1998: 40).

Notes

1. Some nations (for example, the Sto:lo) had slavery.

References

Albers, Patricia. 1983. 'Sioux Women in Transition: A Study of Their Changing Status in Domestic and Capitalist Sectors of Production', in Patricia Albers and Beatrice Medicine, eds, *The Hidden Half: Studies of Plains Indian Women*. Washington: University Press of America.

Allen, Paula Gunn. 1986. *The Sacred Hoop: Recovering the Feminine in American Indian Tradition*. Boston: Beacon Press.

Assembly of First Nations. 1994. *Breaking the Silence: An Interpretive Study of Residential School Impact and Healing as Illustrated by the Stories of First Nations Individuals*. Ottawa: Assembly of First Nations.

Brodribb, Somer. 1984. 'The Traditional Roles of Native Women in Canada and the Impact of Colonization', *Canadian Journal of Native Studies* 4 (1).

Buffalohead, Priscilla K. 1983. 'Farmers, Warriors, Traders: A Fresh Look at Ojibway Women', *Minnesota History* 48 (6).

Cannon, Martin. 1998. 'The Regulation of First Nations Sexuality', *The Canadian Journal of Native Studies* 18 (1).

Chrisjohn, Roland, Sherri Young, and Michael Maraun. 1997. *The Circle Game: Shadows and Subsistence in the Indian Residential School Experience in Canada*. Penticton, BC: Theytus Books.

Cook-Lynn, Elizabeth. 1996. *Why I Can't Read Wallace Stegner and Other Essays*. Madison: University of Wisconsin Press.

Emmerich, Lisa E. 1991. 'Right In the Midst of My Own People: Native American Women and the Field Matron Program', *American Indian Quarterly* 15 (2): 201–16.

Fiske, Joanne. 1996. 'Gender and the Paradox of Residential Education in Carrier Society', in Christine Miller and Patricia Chuchryk, eds, *Women of the First Nations: Power, Wisdom and Strength*. Winnipeg: University of Manitoba Press.

Fournier, Suzanne, and Ernie Crey. 1997. *Stolen from Our Embrace: The Abduction of First Nations Children and the Restoration of Aboriginal Communities*. Vancouver: Douglas and McIntyre.

Guemple, Lee. 1995. "Gender in Inuit Society', in Laura F. Klein and Lillian Ackerman, eds, *Women and Power in Native North America*. Norman, OK: University of Oklahoma Press.

Knack, Martha C. 1995. 'The Dynamics of Southern Paiute Women's Roles', in Laura F. Klein and Lillian Ackerman, eds, *Women and Power in Native North America*. Norman, OK: University of Oklahoma Press.

Kulchyski, Peter, Don McCaskill, and David Newhouse. 1999. *In the Words of Elders*. Toronto: University of Toronto Press.

Laframboise, Teresa D., and Anneliese M. Heyle. 1990. 'Changing and Diverse Roles of Women in American Indian Cultures', *Sex Roles* 22 (7/8).

Lang, Sabine. 1997. 'Various Kinds of Two Spirit People: Gender Variance and Homosexuality in Native American Communities', in Sue Ellen Jacobs, Wesley Thomas, and Sabine Lang, eds, *Two-Spirit People: Native American Gender Identity, Sexuality and Spirituality*. Chicago: University of Illinois Press.

Leacock, Eleanor. 1980. 'Montagnais Women and the Jesuit Program for Colonization', in Eleanor Leacock, ed., *Women and Colonization: Anthropological Perspectives*. New York: Praeger Publishers.

MacDonald, Alison. 1993. 'Holistic Healing', *Vis à Vis: A National Newsletter on Family Violence* 10 (4).

Malz, Daniel, and Joallyn Archambault. 1995. 'Gender and Power in Native North America: Concluding Remarks', in Laura F. Klein and Lillian Ackerman, eds, *Women and Power in Native North America*. Norman, OK: University of Oklahoma Press.

Maracle, Sylvia Maracle. 1993. 'A Historical Viewpoint', *Vis à Vis: A National Newsletter on Family Violence* 10 (4).

Miller, J.R. 1997. *Shingwauk's Vision: A History of Native Residential Schools*. Toronto: University of Toronto Press.

Morrisseau, Calvin. 1998. *Into the Daylight: A Wholistic Approach to Healing*. Toronto: University of Toronto Press.

Sattler, Richard A. 1995. 'Women's Status Among the Muskogee and Cherokee', in Laura F. Klein and Lillian Ackerman, eds, *Women and Power in Native North America*. Norman, OK: University of Oklahoma Press.

Sharp, Henry S. 1995. 'Asymmetric Equals: Women and Men Among the Chippewayan', in Laura F. Klein and Lillian Ackerman, eds, *Women and Power in Native North America*. Norman, OK: University of Oklahoma Press.

Silko, Leslie Marmon. 1996. *Yellow Woman and a Beauty of Spirit*. New York: Touchstone.

Sneve, Virginia Driving Hawk. 1995. *Completing the Circle*. Lincoln: University of Nebraska Press.

Wittstock, Laura Waterman. 1980. 'Native American Women: Twilight of a Long Maidenhood', in Beverly Lindsay, ed., *Comparative Perspectives of Third World Women*. New York: Praeger.

Chapter 14

Canada's Indian Residential Schools and Their Impacts on Mothering

Rosalind Ing

Indian residential schools have been a part of Canada's history since the sixteenth century. Very young children, some as young as three years, were forcibly separated from their parents to attend these schools that were miles away from their communities (Ing, 1991). The purpose of this paper is to find out if there are intergenerational impacts on individuals, families, and communities for those whose parents/ancestors attended government-run Indian residential schools. The participants interviewed are all graduates or students who only learned about residential schools through their university education. Before this the children were puzzled and hurt by the lack of affection and communication of their parents' (mothers') lives. Through their university education, as the children learned about their parents' experiences, healing occurred. The children understood then that their parents did the best they could to mother under the difficult and traumatic circumstances of their own childhood in the residential school system. For those children whose ancestors or parents attended residential schools, the impacts are intergenerational. This paper explores what these impacts are and how they affect the fragile relationship between mothers and their children. . . .

The Literature Review

There are three generations of First Nations people alive who attended residential schools; many of them attended during the 1920s. They were children separated from their parents to satisfy a goal of assimilation in Canadian Indian Policy where institutionalized racism was practiced in many forms. After separation, and away from parents and communities, First Nations languages were forbidden, and most children were punished if caught (Ing, 1991). Some had needles stuck through their tongues (Chrisjohn and Young, 1997: 243) and they suffered many other atrocities and indignities. Few of the staff advocated on their behalf when 'students often experienced a variety of abuses inflicted in part from the racist values of society at the time and from the people who administered the schools' (AFN, 1998: 4). Church-going was routinely forced on them, and Barbara-Helen Hill refers to it as the trauma of 'churchianity' because, she wrote, 'it is not necessarily Christian teachings that are wrong, rather, the church's interpretation that has destroyed our people' (1995: 13). First Nations culture was branded inferior. Schools carried out a program of cultural replacement so severe that it forced some of those leaving the schools to deny their identity as First Nations people. 'It took me years . . . before I could admit I was an Indian even to myself. I suppose this was natural after being raised in an environment that held little or no respect for Indians' (Deiter, 1999: 67). This experimentation became complete as children were also raised away from the nurturing environment of their elders and culture. Linda Bull wrote, 'This naturally breaks the tie between the child and . . . parents at a critical time in . . . life and denies . . . the affection . . . so much . . . desired' (1991: 25) and rightfully needed and wanted by children. Family structure and social organization were nearly destroyed and parenting was affected (Ing, 1991; Davis, 2000). The *Indian Act* was amended several times to force compliance to the goal of assimilation. For what purpose did all this manipulation serve? In the end, most of the children returned from the schools alienated from their communities and unable to fit in to the Euro-Canadian society because of the overt racism. Many of them had few resources to help them deal with this society because that important spiritual element of self-esteem was severely compromised or nearly destroyed. Others who attended these schools wrote about self-esteem to describe their plight (Willis, 1973; Bull, 1991; Ing, 1991; Knockwood, 1992). But more than self-esteem was affected. Community-based studies by Roland Chrisjohn, Charlene Belleau and others, Debbie Foxcroft, and Elaine Herbert also reveal sexual, emotional, physical, and cultural abuse. Rod McCormick (1995) discusses healing through nature for some of these residential school survivors. . . .

Many children suffered indignities, either directly or indirectly. Running away was a common practice of rebellion and resistance. Most were rounded up and returned to face severe punishment in humiliating ways, such as being stripped naked and strapped, 'whipped or beaten' (Jaine, 1993: viii) before all the other students, to show the consequences of running away (Brass, 1987). For girls who were menstruating they were further humiliated (Bull, 1991: 45; Manuel and Loyie, 1998: 93). There were allegations of murders committed in which young children were forced to watch, and other deaths are mentioned (Knockwood, 1992: 107; Ennamorato, 1998: 134).

Through these painful punishments, terrors, and humiliations, many children were unable to express feelings in any way. 'Closely tied to this pain, was that experienced by not being allowed to comfort, care for and have regular contact' (AFN, 1994: 41) with siblings due to separation of children. Bull and Chrisjohn both made comparisons between residential schools and Goffman's description of 'total institutions'. Chrisjohn took the description further in terms of the type of discipline and punishment that occurred there using Goffman's phrase 'mortification of the self' (qtd. in Chrisjohn and Young, 1997: 74) to describe the ways children were forced to watch others' punishment and that 'such demonstrations serve as warnings' (qtd. in Chrisjohn and Young, 1997: 75). He added,

> Even if a given child was personally able to avoid severe treatment [s/he] was likely to witness it being applied to other children . . . there may be occasions when an individual witnesses a physical assault upon someone to whom one has ties and suffers the permanent mortification of having . . . taken no action. (qtd. in Chrisjohn and Young, 1997: 75)

. . . Another way that children were forced into silent submission was through punishment when speaking the only language they knew (Bull, 1991; Ing, 1991; Chrisjohn and Young, 1997; Deiter, 1999; Knockwood, 1992; Atkinson, 1988; Brass, 1987). There are descriptions of one particular teacher who cuffed children on the ears saying 'You silly little hussy' (Deiter, 1999: 53), causing more than ear damage. For those who wet their beds at night, humiliation followed in the morning as some were forced to walk around with their sheets over their heads or wear signs (Sterling, 1992). This mistreatment caused what Bull calls 'distance (social distance) placed between' the staff and the children, 'and the fear—initially of the unknown, but later the fear that developed and that was instilled in their . . . minds as little children' for the environment was 'so overwhelming . . . strict . . . militaristic' (1991: 41).

Children were always hungry (Johnson, 1988: 137). There are similar stories of how they managed to survive by sneaking out and killing rabbits and cooking them (Bull, 1991: 43; Deiter, 1999: 74) or some other 'creative means' (Chrisjohn and Young, 1997: 75; Bull, 1991: 41). Nearby, in the staff dining room, they could smell the roast beef, or as Shirley Sterling recalls:

> They get bacon or ham, eggs, toast and juice . . . We got gooey mush with powder milk . . . Once I found a worm in my soup. When I told Sister Theo, she told me not to be ungrateful. There were starving children in Africa. (1992: 24–5)

In some families, three generations went to residential school but most of the living generation is affected. George Littlechild wrote: 'My mother and all her brothers and sisters went to these boarding schools, and so did my grandparents. They grew up without their families and never learned how to raise children of their own' (1993: 18). He was raised in a foster home. The toll has been that

> Every First Nations group has suffered a disintegration of political and social institutions of culture, language, religion and economic existence. The destruction of the personal security, liberty, health, dignity . . . has been felt by successive generations. (AFN, 1998: 4–5)

Not only were students emotionally deprived. Another destructive outcome has been the individual attack on the culture, making children feel ashamed of who they are, persons of a proud and thriving culture before European settlement. Many children left these schools with an inferiority complex, feeling so ashamed of themselves and their families that they lived a life of denial, some never returning to their communities. Ruth Kirk, in *Wisdom of the Elders*, despairingly reflected as she was growing up,

> I felt sorry I was Indian. You keep hearing you're not much good . . . I was fourteen by the time they let me go home . . . it was too late. I never got close

with my mother. I wanted a better life. . . . When my daughter came, I didn't want her to know the pain I've had. . . . I shielded her from being Indian (1986: 244).

This has had detrimental effects on their children who feel they have been deprived of learning and knowing the positive and beautiful things about their culture. Following are the findings connecting intergenerational impacts to the literature.

The Intergenerational Impacts

. . . One of the reasons for conducting this research is to help those who have experienced the residential schools, but it is also written for their descendants. For the fourth generation, only six of the participants (who have children) were qualified to provide answers. These stories will help to focus on the meaning of the results of the findings. . . .

Olga shared when she began to learn and made connections as to why children were sent away. As a mother her reaction was one of anger, too.

> For our parents it was mandatory or else they would have ended up in jail for not sending us and they were left with no children at home. I was angry that whole year in school. I would wake up in the morning and I would be [furious] just mad for no reason.

Coming to terms with one's identity is a long process if denial was the norm. It affects individuals in different ways but it is still devastating until you can begin to replace the shame and guilt with facts, particularly around a family history of alcoholism. Sara realized, through her education, that:

> The situation of my family wasn't because of who we were. It was an eye-opening, emotional experience to one day awaken and realize that there are many factors and forces outside of yourself that have affected your life and the life of your family. Until that particular point I think that I have believed the myth and the lies about our people. I did inherit the shame that my mother carried. I felt

guilty and I left home at seventeen to get away because my family was plagued with alcoholism. I resented my mother because she never gave me a real father. . . . I never met my father. . . . I grew up surrounded by violence, fighting. I packed my bags, hitch-hiked across Canada. . . .

. . . Olga had important issues to overcome such as being moved so much, parenting, fear over language, and the cruelty associated with it. There was no stability. She said,

I went to three residential schools and was moved four times. I sent my son (15 years old) one year to residential school when he had behavioural problems but my daughter didn't go. I tried to give my children a good life. I never talked about my boarding school experiences, and I didn't teach them my language because I didn't want them to go through the same thing [but] I still speak my language. I had this one awful teacher who was not very kind to me. In Grade One I had ear problems, painful, both my ears were infected. I told the teacher. She didn't believe me. She hit me where I had the ache. . . . It really hurt—I was never able to forgive her. She would always punish me for using my language, striking me with a ruler. I had no other way of communicating, so in turn, I had a hard time communicating with my children. It was hard to explain to them why.

In her childhood, Nora had many traumas, interfering with healthy emotional development, and was further hampered by the inability to communicate in a family parented by silenced endurers of a system by saying she has 'not fully dealt with my childhood.' She said,

My grandfather also went [to residential school] and he [physically] abused my father; and my grandfather sexually abused me. I've been able to discuss this with my mother, and so I went to therapy at seventeen.

Nora adds that her father, an alcoholic, was ashamed of the way he grew up and lived a life of deception. 'He kept his Aboriginal background hidden from his previous wife [non-Aboriginal] and child; he was abusive—physically and verbally—to my mother; and when she left him, he quit.' Growing up with an alcoholic and abusive father is recognized in the patterns that remain, as well as with other family members. . . .

Wynn shares this about her family:

Dad was militant about me making my bed. White shirts or T-shirts had to be worn with a vest or sweater, never alone; and shoes, they bought me the best shoes they could afford . . . they never had properly fitted shoes.

Wynn is aware of her father's regimented or militaristic style of cleanliness and deportment. Despite these hardships on her children Wynn's mother demonstrated positive behaviours in a bad marriage, as she 'was loyal to my father despite his weekend binge drinking, and instilled a strong loyalty to people . . . I love . . . and care [about].' But this stress has consequences. Her father's alcoholism is intergenerational but has been addressed by Wynn as she honestly declared her 'alcoholism . . . but I have maintained sobriety since age 25.' However, other undesirable traits appeared in the family as 'my brother abused me physically, emotionally and sexually; he died at 19 (still molesting me) when I was 16.' A resolution is successful as 'my mother turned to spirituality for healing when he died; she and I saw an elder regularly bringing us closer as a family.'

Rose adds a different slant as she recognizes some benefits and family strengths.

My mother attended residential school yet she values education. What a contradiction! I have trouble understanding her, having had such a bad experience yet highly valuing education. It was a profound realization for me that it was not the education per se that was troublesome but the school experience she had. She was able to separate her bad experiences and supported education for my brother and I. I kept my two children out of the school system [and home-schooled] until this year;

they're six and eight. [As a child] I found school a struggle and had forms of identity crisis. I see the tragedy of residential schools. It should never have happened. Some families have floundered; I see darkness daily. Many did not go on to higher education, live tragic lives, and their children too. Many of my aunts and uncles [my mother's side] attended and survived. I see the strength of their spirit, the human spirit. They didn't lose sight of the value of education and have wonderful lives. We have a doctor, lawyers, social workers, a publisher, professional counselors and educators from just one family. I think our own family strength helped us through. The life shared before residential school gave us all the strength to overcome the negative aspects of the schools.

Perhaps there are more children in Earl's category that we don't hear about. Those with odds against them to survive childhood traumas can ensure their children never go through what they did by making conscious decisions such as reading and learning about positive parenting.

Well, I think I was very fortunate that both my parents made an effort to give me a solid upbringing even though they both had very difficult, emotional traumatic lives. They made a decision to stop the cycle at my generation, for me and my brother, and the following generation [his daughter]. They had to work very hard to learn good parenting skills. I remember seeing books [that my mother read] about parenting and bringing up babies on the bookshelves.

But most influential was the role by a respected elder who is also a grandfather. Earl is also able to see his elder's inspiration in his nuclear and extended family.

We were particularly lucky to have a very strong family even though all of my mother's sisters and brothers went to residential school. They had a strong early upbringing from my grandparents; my grandmother died early but my grandfather . . . a very strong figure gave direction to everyone in the

family. Most of . . . my generation turned out well-adjusted to live and work in Canadian society, but [also maintain] . . . an identity as a First Nations person. I know some cousins didn't do as well. . . .

He admits he wasn't left unscathed as 'I didn't learn my [mother's] language, and had to learn some First Nations traditions on my own' that his mother didn't practice to hand down.

Hope said 'I think religion played a major support role for my mother, but my father turned away from it.' She feels that the racism she experienced and 'the stereotyping of the drunken and uneducated Indian' is a direct result of residential school. She is willing to say that

My parents had self-esteem issues. They married young and had my brother and I at an early age, and weren't prepared to have a family or a marriage. They never experienced a family, didn't know how to deal with family issues, and our family fell apart. It created self esteem issues for me, too, thinking I came from a broken home. That's the most direct effect that it's had [on me].

Her father went to university to study after residential school, where he met her mother,

then he spent 25 years on land negotiations . . . doing valiant work helping the community grow and heal itself but it was an ultimate sacrifice at the expense of time not spent with his family. . . . He's very respected and I admire him. My mom quit university to stay home with my brother and me, and I'm grateful. Mom later went back to complete a Bachelor and Masters degrees. We couldn't depend on each other for emotional support. There was no communication between us. I could only compare my family to TV families, and how they acted; we had no deep communication, no working out of issues as we never spoke about them. I also slept over at my girlfriend's and saw how their parents acted, communicated much more with each other, speaking about their day, nice things like that; it was comfortable to wake up and find both parents there.

Some of these are common problems that most children of divorced/separated parents have and understandably so. But one has to question the common theme of 'lack of communication' that is occurring so often in the study that is associated with silence. The intergenerational effects are the self-esteem issues, and due to father being away so much, it heightened the unspoken 'silence'. . . .

Nora may have given some insight into the silence and lack of affection in her family. In this example of 'mortification of the self', she describes this incident her mother shared. She

> . . . told me of a time that she was with some kids at school and they [staff] let some dogs loose, who were chasing this little boy and they viciously attacked him. By the sounds of it, he tried to run away and this was his punishment, but she told me she never saw this boy again.

Nora expresses these feelings and offers some advice.

> When I hear those stories I'm affected on so many different levels, that pain, complete outrage. [We have] to start talking about it, but gradually because I see the pictures and it's difficult. I'm reliving it all. Mom says when she talks/hears about residential schools she is depressed for days, so I can't get her to share or ask questions. I hate it when she's sad.

Nora has been able to process some of her experiences in terms of its effects as she said, 'residential school made people unable to communicate . . . my mother found it hard even to hug us . . . she wasn't always there [emotionally] for us. I remember feeling lonely and unloved.' An important way to nurture children was missing; her mother was forced to watch this brutal murder as a lesson not to run away; any expression (of feelings) may have been suppressed; and carried into parenthood, making her unable to be affectionate.

Rose describes this incident of terror that her mother shared unexpectedly:

> Once we went out for dinner together and quite out of the blue she told me about a really hard time for her at residential school where she was quite a young child and somebody from the school beat her quite badly, to the point where she was hospitalized. She had been left for dead in a boiler room, beaten with a poker. Somebody found her and took her to the school infirmary. The man came back and attempted to smother her. That was really difficult for her to share with me. To this day I don't know what possessed her to share that with me but it was a really hard story to listen to.

. . . Lara worked on

> Reclaiming culture through the sweat lodge ceremonies with my parents. That was a good way to connect spiritually. It also helped me get through university, as it wasn't easy. I participate in sun dancing. It helps my health. Like mom's sisters, it helps them reclaim identity, and their self-esteem. I haven't had the direct experience of residential school, but it feels like I've been there in terms of the emotional expression; those who went there can't [express the emotions] because it was just so overwhelming. Internalized racism turns anger inwards, people can't articulate to know why. I've tried to recapture some of the language by taking it at university. Mom still speaks it. [Spirituality and] the different ceremonies [show] there are ways to express this that are not verbal or emotional. The value of some of the traditions developed over thousands of years is that there is an awareness of what the body needs as you are traumatized through the body, right?

Rose claims, 'I was a teenager and I rediscovered my own spirituality, I feel strong in it now. . . . Originally education has been a tool of destroying us, but it became a tool we could use to fight with, to regain our sense of identity.' In her B.Ed. studies she found her identity and gained confidence to home school her two sons; understood her roots as a child of a woman who went to residential school and what it meant for her. Nora attends 'ceremonies with my mother' where 'I feel safe, loved, cared for. Now I'm committed to understanding traditional knowledge as it's more spiritually valuable to me than my university [Law] degree[s].'

In conclusion, the participants resolve to move on, effecting reconciliation amongst themselves and their parents (mothers did the best they could). They interact in *a successful way* to fight the odds against them *to achieve a university degree*; deal with prejudice and discrimination in an attempt to better their own lives and their children's; and throughout, they maintain their dignity. These are essential qualities creating positive accomplishments that can be passed on to strengthen the next generation of mothers. There are many examples of harm to individuals and families (do not forget that these were very young children receiving no mothering and little guidance at the time they were at residential school). Sara (a participant who is a teacher and has three children) shared how three generations of her family were affected chaotically including drugs, child apprehensions, alcohol, and incarcerations because her mother (whom she still loves) denied being 'Indian' and did not resolve her trauma and shame associated with residential school. Other intergenerational impacts include stories of different incidents that caused trauma and shame; some of these incidents and stories are criminal as they included assault on victims, disappearance of a child, and possible homicide being witnessed by young children. As Chrisjohn wrote, '. . . there may be occasions when an individual witnesses a physical assault upon someone to whom one has ties and suffers the *permanent mortification* of having . . . taken no action' (Chrisjohn and Young, 1997: 75). Any expression of feelings was suppressed by the traumas. Due to these traumas mothering for those who attended residential school was severely affected—as children they grew up not knowing how to give or show affection, necessary in the nurturance of children. Therefore, mothering became difficult and their children did not understand why mothers were unemotional and unable to show affection. . . . Education changed this group of participants— healing was affected through knowledge gained at university on the research topic of residential schools—and this inspired these mothers to gain social awareness about the injustices in this form of education and its impacts on their mothers' ability to parent. Mothering should or could have been enhanced if their mothers' experiences had been shared or resolved. This study is significant because it has consequences for all of Canadian society. All My Relations. *Ekosi, Kakinaw ni Wakomakanak.*

References

Assembly of First Nations (AFN). 1994. *Breaking the Silence: An Interpretive Study of Residential School Impact and Healing as Illustrated by the Stories of First Nations Individuals*. Ottawa: First Nations Health Commission.

Assembly of First Nations (AFN). 1998. *Residential School Update*. Ottawa: Assembly of First Nations Health Secretariat, March.

Atkinson, Jim. 1988. *The Mission School Syndrome* (film). Whitehorse, YT: Northern Native Broadcasting.

Brass, Eleanor. 1987. *I Walk in Two Worlds*. Calgary: Glenbow Museum.

Bull, Linda. 1991. 'Indian Residential Schooling: The Native Perspective', *Canadian Journal of Native Education* Supplement, 18: 1–63.

Chrisjohn, Roland, and Sherri Young, with Michael Maraun. 1997. *The Circle Game: Shadows and Substance in the Indian Residential School Experience in Canada*. Penticton: Theytus Books Ltd.

Chrisjohn, Roland, Charlene Belleau, et al. 1991. 'Faith Misplaced: Lasting Effects of Abuse in a First Nations Community', *Canadian Journal of Native Education* 18: 196–97.

Davis, Sarah. 2000. 'The Experience of Self-Destructive Behavior in First Nations Adolescent Girls'. Unpublished Master's thesis, University of British Columbia.

Deiter, Constance. 1999. *From Our Mother's Arms: The Intergenerational Impact of Residential Schools in Saskatchewan*. Toronto: United Church Publishing House.

Ennamorato, Judith. 1998. *Sing the Brave Song*. Richmond Hill, ON: Raven Press.

Foxcroft, Debbie. 1996. *Indian Residential Schools: The Nuuchah-nulth Experience*. Port Alberni: Nuu-chah-nulth Tribal Council.

Herbert, Elaine. 1994. 'Talking Back: Six First Nations Women's Stories of Recovering From Childhood Sexual Abuse and Addiction'. Unpublished Master's thesis, University of British Columbia.

Hill, Barbara-Helen. 1995. *Shaking the Rattle: Healing the Trauma of Colonization*. Penticton: Theytus Books Ltd.

Ing, N. Rosalyn. 1991. 'The Effects of Residential Schools on Native Child-Rearing Practices,' *Canadian Journal of Native Education* Supplement, 18: 65–118.

Jaine, Linda. 1993. *Residential Schools: The Stolen Years*. Saskatoon: University Extension Press.

Johnson, Basil. 1988. *Indian School Days*. Toronto: Key Porter Books Ltd.

Kirk, Ruth. 1986. *Wisdom of the Elders*. Vancouver: Douglas and McIntyre, in association with the British Columbia Provincial Museum.

Knockwood, Isabelle. 1992. *Out of the Depths: The Experiences of Mi'Kmaw Children at the Indian Residential School at Shubenacadie, Nova Scotia*. Lockeport: Roseway Publishing.

Littlechild, George. 1993. *This Land is My Land*. Emeryville, California: Children's Book Press.

Manuel, Vera, and Larry Loyie. 1998. *Two Plays About Residential School*. Vancouver: Living Traditions Writers Group.

McCormick, Rod. 1995. 'The Facilitation of Healing for the First Nations People of British Columbia', *Canadian Journal of Native Education* 21: 251–322.

Sterling, Shirley. 1992. *My Name is Seepeetza*. Toronto: Groundwood Books.

Willis, Jane. 1973. *Genish: An Indian Girlhood*. Toronto: New Press.

Chapter 15

Strong Spirit, Fractured Identity: An Ojibway Adoptee's Journey to Wholeness

Shandra Spears

Transracial adoption of Native children is more complex than anyone who has not lived through the experience can imagine. I have lived through it. Apart from the obvious disconnection from Native community and birth relatives, transracially adopted First Nations children face specific challenges, which we continue to face throughout the course of our adult lives. Mainstream society, when it acknowledges this issue at all, suggests that our trauma is a result of the abuse that we have experienced and that this abuse was inflicted by a few aberrant individuals. As with residential school survivors, this discourse can be stretched to say that many Native children did not experience violence first-hand and, therefore, have not experienced trauma.

By evaluating us as individual cases and by focusing primarily on our physical experience, the dominant society disconnects us from the larger aspects of politics and history. However, the removal of entire generations of Native children from our communities and families is a genocidal blow to our Nations, and we feel that violence in our bones. The myth of Native people as 'conquered' implies that we were defeated in battle, but cultural warfare attacks the hearts and minds of vulnerable children. The myth of adopted Native children as 'abandoned by troubled birth parents' denies the bonds of love between Native children and their families and communities and constructs white parents as heroic rescuers. . . .

In the context of colonization, the adoption of Native children by white families is an attempt to assimilate us into Canadian society. If Native children grow up as Canadians, we will presumably cease to be part of an 'Indian problem'. White adoptive parents are co-opted into this assimilation process by their urgent need to parent.

It is convenient to imagine that a parent's love can erase history and political conflict—but children grow up and conflict remains. Children are not 'bridges between two worlds'. Children cannot be programmed to become anyone but who they are. The attempt to mould Native children into an alien identity, out of laziness or self-interest, endangers our lives. Those of us who survive the experience often emerge angry at our loss and fiercely committed to our Native identity, once we rediscover it. The only way to have earned our loyalty in any permanent way would have been to meet our real cultural, spiritual, emotional, and physical needs with fairness and honesty. The possibility of finding accurate information about Native culture, which could lead parents to find culture-based support for Native children, is beyond the reach of the average Canadian, because this information is suppressed within dominant communication systems. In some totalitarian regimes, people disappear because death squads take them away. In Canada, young Native people disappear into the dominant society through love, lies, and ideology.

Challenging the Mythology of Adoption

My life story can be read from a couple of different ideological positions. One ideology states that colonization is a myth, that it no longer exists, that it wasn't bad for Indigenous people, and that it has had no lasting impact on our lives. This ideological position goes on to suggest that the Native way of life is unrealistic, backward and has little value, and that any child would be grateful for the chance to be raised by loving, white, middle-class parents and have access to good health care, education, and employment opportunities. Life on

the reserve leads to life in prison or on the streets, so adoptive parents can give Native children a chance at a better life. If I understand my life according to this mythology, it was blessed and prosperous. This is one truth.

Another truth, from another ideological position, is that I was robbed of a political, historical, spiritual, linguistic, and cultural base which could have given me a great sense of self-esteem and strength. This position also acknowledges that a large proportion of Native people who ended up homeless, incarcerated, addicted, or psychologically scarred, were products of this 'better life'. Native people who remained connected to community and culture didn't come over to our house for dinner. I never heard my language spoken, and I was never given accurate information about my culture. I grew up within an ideology that said I did not exist, because Native people did not exist, except as mascots or objects of desire (Barthes, 1970). Through this process of symbolic annihilation (Tuchman, 1978), I ceased to exist as a Native person within my own mind.

I was already part white and lived surrounded by white colleagues and relatives. How much further could I step away from 'Nativeness'—by marrying a white person and investing in a white, middle-class, Canadian way of life? Wouldn't that be simpler and less painful? How could my children return from that even greater distance? Love truly can conquer all. If I followed this process, it would use my own love relationships to turn me into a 'death sentence' for my own descendants, at least in terms of being 'practising' Ojibways. In my life, and in the history of my family, residential schooling and transracial adoption took me so far away from my language and culture that only a violent upheaval was able to bring me back. This is my story.

The Story of My Survival

I was born in 1968 and was surrendered at birth for adoption. I lived in Toronto with two foster families before being adopted at five months of age. My older sister was very excited to have a new baby sister in the house. I had big brown eyes and auburn hair, and I'd already had the first of six surgeries to correct my club feet. My baby picture shows me sitting in my car seat on the sidewalk of my foster family's home with tiny casts on my legs on the day I was brought home from Toronto.

My first memory is of laughing. I was at the Hospital for Sick Children. I was eighteen months old, and I was about to have my ankle broken and reset with a pin. The surgeon was explaining that holes would have to be cut into the little boots attached to the brace I wore at night. I remember sitting on the counter in the blue light of the X-ray display, looking from the doctor to my parents, thinking that this was the funniest thing I'd ever heard. 'Holes in my ankles; holes in my boots!' I thought it was hilarious.

Our family was playful, outdoorsy, and emotionally intense. We participated in a music society, the church, and Girl Guides. My sister and I took dance lessons and sang in the church choir. We had a little Pomeranian dog named Rusty. We camped almost every weekend, every summer, for most of my childhood. I loved it. When I was four years old, I learned that I was adopted. After many discussions, I came to understand that my other parents had been unable to take care of me, and that my Mom and Dad[1] were very happy that I was their little girl. I was adopted, and I had problems with my feet. My Dad's father had died. My Mom had health problems. My sister had allergies. Everyone in our family had her or his challenges.

My adoption story was that I was one-eighth Indian and that my grandfather had been an Indian chief. That made me an Indian princess. I had brown hair and brown eyes, and tanned well in the summertime. That was the extent of my Native identity.

Our home was also violent, and I became the family scapegoat. I experienced violence, shaming, and screaming. There were no cigarette burns and no rapes, and it didn't happen all the time. It was a pattern of domestic violence that had affected our extended family for several generations, so it did not begin as an attack on me as a Native child. But it was real. It happened—and it happened more to me than to my white sister. Conversations were dangerous and all members of the family were sensitized to signs of a fight. I couldn't negotiate my way through dangerous discussions very well, and I was a very sensitive child. Some Native adoptees say that they refused to cry when they were battered. I cried every time. I was always terrified of those experiences. . . .

The violence and fear didn't mean that I never had any fun. On the contrary, our family had family games, jokes, and traditions that were playful and imaginative. We could turn the smallest events into celebrations. We were voracious readers, and my earliest spiritual teachings came from the alternative worlds of fantasy and science-fiction novels. I loved my family and home. I didn't like feeling trapped and afraid.

I developed my sense of identity by internalizing everything around me. Having no Native women in my life, I had no way of knowing that I was a beautiful Native girl. I didn't even know that I was Native. There was no Native 'mirror' that reflected my beauty; only a white mirror that reflected my difference. I compared myself to the girls around me, with their small waists and cute noses. I didn't look like them, but I had no reason to believe I was supposed to look any other way. Therefore, I 'knew' that I was a white girl—an ugly white girl. I was a typical 'ugly duckling'. Having no one to tell me that I was worth protecting, I 'knew' that I was worthless and bad.

At twelve years old, I started high school and discovered acting. I needed acceptance and affection, and I looked for those things outside the home, finding a place for myself with the artsy alternative crowd. I started to come out of my shell. By the end of high school, my days and nights were filled with arts activities, volunteering, part-time jobs, and going to night clubs. I came out of my shell at home as well. I stopped being silent and became openly hostile. The violence was escalating, and one parent was afraid of seriously injuring me. My parents called the Children's Aid Society to see if I could be placed in foster care. They were told that I would probably not find a foster home and could end up homeless. I stayed. I screamed and fought. I was sometimes kicked out, and sometimes I kicked myself out. I started keeping a running count-down on my bedroom door: '135 days until I can leave this house.'

The violence stopped when I became physically large enough to fight back. No one in my family has hit me since my seventeenth birthday. Emotionally, however, I remained a scapegoat, and I acted out my role as a troublemaker. I smoked, drove when I was drunk, and engaged in other risky, self-destructive behaviours. I longed for affection from the young men who were most cruel to me and rejected those who treated me with respect. . . .

From White to Native in Four 'Easy' Years

The reunion with my birth mother was a positive experience, and we were very close for two years. She told me about my birth father, and that he was Ojibway. In that moment, I went from being 'one-eighth Indian' to being Ojibway: the half-white daughter of an Ojibway man. This information had been falsified in my CAS file, where my birth father was listed as 'one-quarter Indian'. For the first time, I had a name for my Nation and names for my birth parents. I had the name of the reserve that he was from. These identifiers were very powerful for me. I also had images of people who looked like me. Almost overnight, like the ugly ducking, I decided I was quite good-looking! I started mentioning my Ojibway identity to ran-dom Native people; once, to a customer at K-Mart, and then to a student. This was a probing, hesitant process. I was checking to see whether they would laugh at me, because it was still obvious to me that I was the same white Shandra I had always been. But they encouraged me to continue searching for my Native relatives and even to apply for my Indian Status.

I felt like I had permission to continue. However, Ojibway identity was completely new to me. As a 'one-eighth Indian', I lived in Canada as a white person and occasionally brought up the fact that I

was 'part-Indian'. This meant that one of my ancestors had been Native but that I was not. If asked, I would say that I was proud to be part-Native, but it was a pride in something I had no direct experience with, like my artistic ability, or my post-punk music, or my family role as a rebel, it made me different, and I had learned to take pride in my uniqueness. I began to understand that I was an Ojibway person, but it still felt very unreal. I had no idea what to do with any of it. I wasn't really conscious of race, because I half-consciously believed that 'race' referred only to 'non-white' people. I started noticing the races of my friends and began talking to them about iden-tity and culture.

My birth mother took me to events where I could meet other Native people and ask questions, and she took me to the first Toronto rally in sup-port of the activists in Kahnesetake who had been attacked by provincial police. Before our relation-ship went sour, she gave me a lot of help in taking those first steps. By the end of the summer of 1990, I had had a crash course in activism. At first, I felt most comfortable with non-Native support-ers. But then, I began to understand that Native activists would be maimed and killed while non-Native activists often faced less lethal conse-quences. That was a crucial moment, and it changed my sense of identity permanently.

Some Native women and men challenged my ethnicity in aggressive or insulting ways. I became very defensive about my fair skin, but didn't have enough confidence to really stand up for myself. Inside, part of me still felt like my Nativeness was a hoax, and I was seeing how far I could push it, but another part recognized that I had a right to pursue it and resented the discrimination I faced.

My life was full of 'firsts'. I worked in a Native organization for the first time and went to my first powwow. I lived with my first Native boyfriend. I was homeless and accessed a Native women's shel-ter for the first time. I learned to do beadwork and went to cultural events. I made friends with Native people who were homeless or middle class; who were ex-cons, activists, healers, artists, executive directors, or entrepreneurs. My friends from high school and university were graduating, marrying, and moving on with their careers, while I was synthesizing a whole new sense of identity at every level of my body, mind, and spirit. I was angry about the loss of Native culture I had experienced as a child, and I was mourning the 'white' direction that I was rejecting as an adult. This choice connected me to my new community and identity, and separated me from everything I had ever known. . . .

It had been four years since I met my birth mother, and I had immersed myself in the Toronto Native community without the legitimizing presence of an extended Native family. I was biracial, fair-skinned, non-status, urban, and culturally confused, and I had been raised by a white family, yet I had managed to make the identity shift. My reunion with my father's side of the family was my first trip to the reserve, and the family arranged for me to be instated as a band member. I was finally a Status Indian with a Native family. I even looked 'more Native' when I returned, so that friends asked if I had dyed my hair. But my birth father, who had been homeless, was deceased. He had died in 1987, eighteen months before I began my search, and he had been left to die with no treatment in a hospital hallway. For the next six years, I wandered through the stages of a very confusing grief. Like so many other elements of my story, it felt unreal. How could I be grieving for someone I didn't know? Did I have a right to grieve? Eventually, it was through ceremony that I found some peace.

Dressing Up Like An Indian

Ceremonies were very helpful to me, and I learned from excellent healers and traditional teachers. I learned to take on some responsibilities at our lodge. I learned my name and my clan and began to drum and sing. I explored the role of helper. I was learning to be respectful, and it felt good. My hair was very long and I kept it braided. I tried wearing skirts, as I had been taught to do. I even managed to find a way back to my teaching/leadership role, by teaching voice technique to Native women drummers. But I still felt I was out of my element.

The wild, expressive rebel that I had always been was being pushed aside for a long-haired, skirt-wearing woman working in social services between acting jobs. I wanted to be the irreverent, sarcastic, dynamic artist I had always been. I wore the uniform of a strong, traditional woman, but I still went home at night and felt crazy and self-destructive. I was invited to sing, but I couldn't speak the way I wanted to speak. I carried a journal around for those times when I wanted to say something that white or Native people in my life didn't accept or understand. I tried to be wild, expressive, proper, respectable, and rebellious all at once, but it was next to impossible. People could only accept a portion of me at a time. Lots of white friends dropped me completely, unable to cope with the changes I was going through.

I eventually split myself into different Shandras for each of these situations. One went home for weekends with the family, while another went to the lodge and sang, and yet another was an actor and martial artist. Switching from one reality to another gave me headaches, and triggered intense feelings of rage. I usually turned these rages on myself. There were times when I could barely recognize people I worked with every day, or forgot elements of traditional protocol because I was switched into 'white' mode. Few people went from acting class, to martial arts class, to a traditional ceremony, to an all-night party; and then back to a nine-to-five office job all in one day. But I had done this all my life. I was a cultural chameleon, just as I had been growing up. I was feeling better and I had some of the answers I needed, but I was still pretending.

It can be very humiliating to be a Native adoptee within our community. Community members act as though our return to our community will solve all our problems. They think we should leave our childhood histories in the past and focus on behaving more like 'real' Native people. After being constructed all our lives as 'the problem', we return to our communities to face more of the same treatment. As recently as last year, a Native friend told me that she thinks I am brighter than most adoptees and that's why I can understand our culture. That bigotry suggests that adoption equals stupidity. It seems unthinkable, but it exists.

Adoptees are called 'lost birds'. I don't feel like a lost bird! I am a strong, surviving Anishinaabe kwe who found my way back, alone, through a series of challenges, without any concrete or ideological support for my determination. That doesn't make me 'lost'. I understand the concept, though. What I call the 'Adoptee Syndrome', a collection of shutdown and self-destructive behaviours, is very much like that of a bird who has fallen from the nest or a person who is so seriously ill that she or he can no longer eat.

Healing the Fractures with Anger and Authenticity

How do I experience the Syndrome? It begins when situations restimulate my post-traumatic grief and rage. At this point, I either get what I need to relax the trigger or I stay triggered. For a while, I may continue to function, but I begin to lose some of my healthy habits. I eat proper meals and show up for work or appointments, but I stop using the prayers, meditation, or medicines that can help me. I dissociate, then shut down and go numb or feel overwhelmed by rage or panic. I reach out for help, but if the help isn't exactly what I need, I don't ask again. I beat up on myself. I start missing deadlines or I drop relationships. Sometimes, I get so 'stuck' that I do nothing while my work, or my rent, is not taken care of. Thoughts of self-injury or suicide repeatedly enter my mind. I have to stay away from knives, subway ledges, and high balconies, because I feel the temptation to jump, or to cut.

Sometimes, I self-injure just enough to break out of the spin, although as a general rule I try not to. I become obsessed with negative, harmful people or situations. I become critical of others and of myself. Sometimes, I can't focus, or I run out of the room crying. Sometimes, my feelings boil over into physical gestures; I throw things.

One such 'release' cost me an expensive camera last year, because that was what was in my hand at the moment. This kind of trigger can last anywhere from a day to a year. I am using the present tense, because this is an ongoing obstacle. The fact that I can describe it, or even cope with it, does not mean that it goes away. . . .

The thing is that, even though I was an 'instant Indian', I had knowledge and spiritual gifts the whole time, even as a child. 'Real (Catholic/reserve) Indians' like to mock 'urban Indians' who take up traditional spirituality. I was a prime target. I could even see their point! All they could see were assimilated Native people coming back, full of earnest longing and gobbling up teachings. But that 'wannabe' image didn't matter to me. The more I learned, the more I discovered that I had had dreams and spiritual guidance helping me throughout my life. I discovered that my birth family had been spiritual and political leaders for generations before the boarding school/adoption disruption. I am not a pre-Colombian Ojibway woman. But neither are the 'real Indians'. We are all struggling through different aspects of the same genocidal program. . . .

The Strong Spirit Knows What Is True

Back in 1991, at the abused women's shelter, a housemate gave me a strong teaching. She said that if I want to find my direction in life, I should go inside and find myself as a little kid and ask myself what I want to be. A few months later in ceremony, I had a chance to do just that. The ceremony brought us into connection with parts of ourselves. I was reunited with myself at four years old. I was dancing and laughing inside one of those columns of light that I had seen as a young girl. I asked my four-year-old self, 'Aren't you in pain? Don't your legs hurt? Aren't you afraid?' Four-year-old-me replied, 'No, silly. I'm dancing!' A couple of years later, when I was named, Elder Waabishkamigizikwe named me 'Laughter Woman'. My first memory is of laughing. It is who I am.

Another grandmother taught me that people can try to hurt us, but they cannot change who we are. Or, as my Mother says, 'Shandra, shit doesn't stick to you.' I have an inner strength that bounces back from trouble, and I celebrate that. That ability to heal also exists within our families and communities and will lead us to solutions.

We can hold state and civic institutions responsible for their genocidal practices but that will not ultimately solve our distress. We are responsible for our own healing, and we are strong enough to achieve it. Native-child welfare organizations and open adoptions are creating better options for our children, and Native people are tackling problems in a variety of ways. Fortunately, we are not all one type of 'Indian'. Each of us has a different history, bringing different strengths to this cultural and political battlefield. In the polite Canadian culture war that seeks to break apart our strong families, we have an opportunity to discover our greatest strengths. The colonizer can try to hurt us, but can only succeed if we change who we are.

Notes

1. The post-reunion life of an adoptee can be complicated for many reasons, including having two sets of parents. To clarify—my parents, who raised me, are called 'Mom and Dad', while my birth parents are called 'my birth parents', or are referred to by their first names. 'Mom' and 'Dad' have been capitalized throughout the essay to emphasize this distinction. I have been calling my parents Mom and Dad since I learned how to talk, and I have done so throughout this essay instead of using more clinical terms like 'my adoptive parents'. I prefer to express the normalcy and chaos of my adoption and post-reunion experience by using authentic language.

References

Barthes, Roland. 1970. *Mythologies*. Paris: Seuil.

Tuchman, Gaye. 1978. 'Introduction: The Symbolic Annihilation of Women by the Mass Media', in Gaye Tuchman, Arlene Kaplan Daniels, and James Benét, eds, *Hearth and Home: Images of Women in the Mass Media*. New York: Oxford University Press.

Part Five

Additional Readings

Anderson, Kim. *A Recognition of Being: Reconstructing Native Womanhood*. Toronto: Second Story Press, 2000.

Castellano, Marlene Brant, Linda Archibald, and Mike DeGagné. *From Truth to Reconciliation: Transforming the Legacy of Residential Schools*. Ottawa: Aboriginal Healing Foundation, 2008.

Chrisjohn, Roland, and Sherri L. Young. *The Circle Game: Shadows and Substance in the Indian Residential School Experience in Canada*, rev. ed. Penticton, BC: Theytus Books, 2006.

Grant, Agnes. *Finding My Talk: How Fourteen Native Women Reclaimed their Lives after Residential Schools*. Calgary, AB: Fifth House, 2004.

Relevant Websites

Aboriginal Healing Foundation (Research Series)
http://www.ahf.ca/publications/research-series
As described on their website, the Aboriginal Healing Foundation (AHF) was initiated 'to encourage and support, through research and funding contributions, community-based Aboriginal directed healing initiatives which address the legacy of physical and sexual abuse suffered in Canada's Indian Residential School System, including inter-generational impacts.' Of interest is the AHF research series which examines the ongoing impact of residential schools.

Office of the Prime Minister (Stephen Harper Apology)
http://www.pm.gc.ca/eng/media.asp?id=2149
This website contains the official apology given by the Canadian federal government to the survivors of the residential schooling system.

Films

A Place Between: The Story of an Adoption. Dir. Curtis Kaltenbaugh. National Film Board of Canada, 2007.
Onkwa-nistenhsera: Mothers of our Nations. Dir. Dawn Martin-Hall. Indigenous Health Research Development Program, 2006.

Our Healing Journey. Prod. and Dir. Kem Murch Productions Inc. 2001.
Stolen Children. CBC Learning, 2008.

Key Terms

Matrilocal/Matrilineal societies
Residential schooling
Intergenerational impacts

Transracial adoption
Fractured identity

Discussion Questions

1. Discuss how Indigenous concepts and practices of marriage, divorce, family, and sexuality have been transformed in Indigenous societies as a result of the influence of EuroChristian values. What are the impacts of those transformations on women?
2. Discuss the links between Canada's civilizing missions and the regulation of Indigenous sexualities. How have legacies of residential schooling and notions of civility worked to impose colonial conceptions of relationships onto Indigenous bodies?
3. There is much evidence that residential schooling has had lasting intergenerational impacts on Indigenous communities. What are some of these impacts and how have communities enacted healing processes for survivors and their families?
4. Shandra Spears details her personal experience as an adoptee and the difficulties she encountered as a result from being removed from her Indigenous community. How do her experiences reflect the effects of Canadian colonialism? Does her narrative have a different effect than detailing the impacts of residential schooling through quantitative research and/or theoretical analysis?

Activities

Watch the documentary *Unrepentant: Kevin Annett and Canada's Genocide* (available online). Discuss the ongoing implications of residential schools on both Indigenous and non-Indigenous identities.

On 11 June 2008 the Government of Canada officially apologized for the residential school system. Watch the apology online and discuss your thoughts about it. Should Canada have apologized for residential schooling? Is saying 'sorry' enough? What other concrete actions are needed for reconciliation and healing to begin, and to move forward? To prepare for this activity, read one or both of the following: (a) Sara Ahmed, 'The Politics of Bad Feeling', *Australian Critical Race and Whiteness Studies Association Journal* 1 (2005): 72–85; (b) Megan Boler, 'The Risk of Empathy: Interrogating Multiculturalism's Gaze', *Cultural Studies* 11, 2 (1997): 251–71.

PART SIX

Indigenous Rights, Citizenship, and Nationalism

On 13 September 2007 the United Nations adopted the Declaration on the Rights of Indigenous Peoples. The Declaration itself provided an overview of Indigenous peoples, including a framework for realizing a future of more just relations. States were urged to implement a series of steps to safeguard the rights of Indigenous nations. Moreover, and with great significance to the themes raised in this section of the anthology, the document acknowledged that 'indigenous peoples have suffered from historic injustices as a result of, inter alia, their colonization and dispossession of their lands, territories and resources.' It recognized 'the urgent need to respect and promote the inherent rights of Indigenous peoples which derive from their political, economic, and social structures and from their cultures, spiritual traditions, histories and philosophies, especially their rights to their lands, territories, and resources'.

The Declaration was not legally binding on member States and does not signify a threat to their sovereignty. Nevertheless, Canada was one of the four member States that did not sign the covenant. In choosing to reject the Declaration, Canada failed to acknowledge the distinct nature of equity claims and the historicity of Indigenous rights. As each of the authors in this section point out, Indigenous rights are as unique as the peoples themselves. They are rooted in the inherent and never before extinguished rights of nations, as well as a colonial experience wherein people were dispossessed—and continue to be dispossessed—of lands. Indigenous peoples do not wish to integrate into mainstream structures, but rather wish to have their rights and nation-to-nation relationships affirmed. These demands derive from, and indeed shape, what it means to be Indigenous in the contemporary world. Indigeneity, as Alfred and Corntassel explain, refers to an identity that is 'constructed, shaped, and lived in the politicized context of contemporary colonialism'.

Alfred and Corntassel suggest that contemporary Indigenous struggles are an affirmation of identity. The demand to have Indigenous rights affirmed is inherently decolonizing in nature. Remembering our ceremonies, traditions, laws, and auto-nomous nations is a journey of what they refer to as 'self-conscious traditionalism'. This type of traditionalism is a 'reconstruction of traditional communities based on the original teachings and orienting values'. Before we can break from the current colonial conditions, under which we have lived for centuries, we must 'start from the individual self, re-awaken oneself, re-generate oneself and move outward'. Indigenous nations will each have their own unique ways of working through this re-awakening, but what is shared is a colonial past, the need for resurgence, and the need to 'become forces of Indigenous truth against the lie of colonialism'.

Indigenous peoples are in a unique position relative to the Canadian political make-up. As Henderson (2002) writes, Indigenous peoples have a unique constitu-tional heritage enabling sui generis rights. Canada is 'based on the foundation of shared sovereignty' (ibid., 419), since our ancestors agreed to a treaty relationship, he writes, 'a relationship between nations . . . a belief in autonomous zones of power, freedom, and liberties' (ibid., 422). Although Canada has not respected our treaty rights, they are nonetheless real and binding to the parties originally promis-ing to uphold them. Indigenous peoples do not necessarily wish to become Canadian citizens. Instead, they are 'imagining and constructing an alternative pluralism from their traditions and teachings. They are criticizing, displacing and redefining Eurocentric rights, and discourses . . .' (ibid., 433).

Audra Simpson's article in this part of the book reveals how Indigenous nations have always and continue to imagine and construct alternative discourses of citizenship. In it, she addresses the complexities embedded in matters of citizen-ship, in particular the current challenges present in her own community, the Kahnawake Mohawk nation. As with other nations, Canada imposed a definition of membership at Kahnawake through the Indian Act. Through the Indian Act, traditional ways of defining nationhood and national membership have been dis-rupted, especially patrilineal definitions of citizenship which robbed Mohawk women who 'married out' of a right to be defined as Mohawk (Indian for that matter) and granted such rights to white women who 'married in'. In 1985 the state, in its attempt to redress gendered injustice granted 'reserves' the right to define their own membership. Out of this history, Kahnawake passed a code of 50 per cent blood quantum as a criterion for membership.

Blood quantum criteria have divided the communities, including Kahnawake, resulting in a 'refusal' to talk about it. But, as Simpson discusses, the policy must be understood by looking at the history of fractured nation-to-nation relationships. Having to live under and indeed resist the Indian Act for hundreds of years has produced an anxiety over resources and their scarcity, and the wrongful acknow-ledgement of some whites as 'Indians', leading people to treat Bill C-31 as another colonial imposition to be resisted. What now exist are different forms of recogni-tion that are simultaneously lived by people, and a new search of re-defining the nation, but this time the community is in the process of self-determining member-ship criteria, rather than having those set by a foreign State.

In her article, Sunseri proposes the possibility of progressive Indigenous nation-alist liberation movements that could eliminate oppression and re-establish balanced relations within Indigenous nations. Indigenous women are at the forefront of such nationalist movements and view their participation necessary as both women and Indigenous people. Women had been particularly attacked by colonialism as the status and authority they traditionally held have been devalued through colonial policies. Women view their participation to be crucially important in order to ensure that, in the journey towards decolonization, those traditions that were based on gender balance are remembered and re-established in decolonized Indigenous nations. Similar to Alfred and Corntassel, she argues that only a nationalism which discloses the lies of colonialism and recalls Indigenous ways of governing can be decolonizing and empowering for all members. After centuries of colonial transformations, it is difficult to remember those traditions but, as the authors in this section show, true warriors have always resisted colonial impositions and have insisted on the inherent rights to follow our own traditional ways of governing and be equal participants in a nation-to-nation relationship.

Chapter 16

Being Indigenous: Resurgences Against Contemporary Colonialism[1]

Taiaiake Alfred and Jeff Corntassel

Indigenousness is an identity constructed, shaped and lived in the politicized context of contemporary colonialism. The communities, clans, nations and tribes we call Indigenous peoples are just that: Indigenous to the lands they inhabit, in contrast to and in contention with the colonial societies and states that have spread out from Europe and other centres of empire. It is this oppositional, place-based existence, along with the consciousness of being in struggle against the dispossessing and demeaning fact of colonization by foreign peoples, that fundamentally distinguishes Indigenous peoples from other peoples of the world.[2]

There are, of course, vast differences among the world's Indigenous peoples in their cultures, political-economic situations, and in their relationships with colonizing Settler societies. But the struggle to survive as distinct peoples on foundations constituted in their unique heritages, attachments to their homelands, and natural ways of life is what is shared by all Indigenous peoples, as well as the fact that their existence is, in large part, lived as determined acts of survival against colonizing states' efforts to eradicate them culturally, politically and physically. The challenge of 'being Indigenous', in a psychic and cultural sense, forms the crucial question facing Indigenous peoples today in the era of contemporary colonialism—a form of post-modern imperialism in which domination is still the Settler imperative but where colonizers have designed and practise more subtle means (in contrast to the earlier forms of missionary and militaristic colonial enterprises) of accomplishing their objectives. . . .

In Canada today, many Indigenous people have embraced the Canadian government's label of 'aboriginal', along with the concomitant and limited notion of postcolonial justice framed within the institutional construct of the state. In fact, this identity is purely a state construction that is instrumental to the state's attempt to gradually subsume Indigenous existences into its own constitutional system and body politic since Canadian independence from Great Britain—a process that started in the mid-twentieth century and culminated with the emergence of a Canadian constitution in 1982. Far from reflecting any true history or honest reconciliation with the past or present agreements and treaties that form an authentic basis for Indigenous–state relations in the Canadian context, 'aboriginalism' is a legal, political, and cultural discourse designed to serve an agenda of silent surrender to an inherently unjust relation at the root of the colonial state itself.

The acceptance of being 'aboriginal' (or its equivalent term in other countries, such as 'ethnic groups') is a powerful assault on Indigenous identities. It must be understood that the aboriginalist assault takes place in a politico-economic context of historic and ongoing dispossession and of contemporary deprivation and poverty; this is a context in which Indigenous peoples are forced by the compelling needs of physical survival to cooperate individually and collectively with the state authorities to ensure their physical survival. Consequently, there are many 'aboriginals' (in Canada) or 'Native Americans' (in the United States) who identify themselves solely by their political-legal relationship to the state rather than by any cultural or social ties to their Indigenous community or culture or homeland. This continuing colonial process pulls Indigenous peoples away from cultural practices and community aspects of 'being Indigenous' towards a political-legal construction as 'aboriginal' or 'Native American', both of which are representative of what we refer to as being 'incidentally Indigenous'. . . .

Colonial legacies and contemporary practices of disconnection, dependency, and dispossession have effectively confined Indigenous identities to state-sanctioned legal and political definitional approaches. This political-legal compartmentalization of community values often leads Indigenous nations to mimic the practices of dominant non-Indigenous legal-political institutions and adhere to state-sanctioned definitions of Indigenous identity. Such compartmentalization results in a 'politics of distraction' (Smith, 2000: 211).[3] that diverts energies away from decolonizing and regenerating communities and frames community relationships in state-centric terms, such as aforementioned 'aboriginality'. . . .

Colonial Powers as Shape Shifters

It is important to identify all of the old and new faces of colonialism that continue to distort and dehumanize Indigenous peoples—often pitting us against each other in battles over authentic histories. Colonization is the word most often used to describe the experience of Indigenous encounters with Settler societies, and it is the framework we are employing here. However, there is a danger in allowing colonization to be the only story of Indigenous lives. It must be recognized that colonialism is a narrative in which the Settler's power is the fundamental reference and assumption, inherently limiting Indigenous freedom and imposing a view of the world that is but an outcome or perspective on that power. As stated earlier, we live in an era of postmodern imperialism and manipulations by shape-shifting colonial powers; the instruments of domination are evolving and inventing new methods to erase Indigenous histories and senses of place. Therefore, 'globalization' in Indigenous eyes reflects a deepening, hastening and stretching of an already-existing empire. Living within such political and cultural contexts, it is remembering ceremony, returning to homelands and liberation from the myths of colonialism that are the decolonizing imperatives. In their seminal treatise, *The Fourth World*, Manuel and Posluns explained the effects of contemporary colonial processes:

The colonial system is always a way of gaining control over another people for the sake of what the colonial power has determined to be 'the common good'. People can only become convinced of the common good when their own capacity to imagine ways in which they can govern themselves has been destroyed. (Manuel and Posluns, 1974: 60)

From such a Fourth World viewpoint, the 'common good' becomes whatever it is defined as by shape-shifting colonial elites. Nietschmann documents a number of shape-shifting strategies imposed by Settler states that confront Indigenous peoples on a daily basis—such as creating a bogus 'we are you' agenda, calling for a vote to legitimize the occupation, referring to state camps as 'economic development' and 'new communities', and offering amnesty to resistant military leaders and their forces in order to co-opt their movements (Nietschmann, 1995: 236–7). While some of these shape-shifting tactics may, on the surface, appear to be subtle, they, like other brutal forms of oppression, threaten the very survival of Indigenous communities. . . .

Such new faces of colonialism encroach on Indigenous sacred histories, homelands, and cultural practices in somewhat familiar ways, but use diplomatic language and the veneer of free trade to mask ugly truths. The great North African anti-colonial writer Frantz Fanon described this process as an ongoing dialectic:

Colonialism is not satisfied merely with holding a people in its grip and emptying the native's brain of all form and content. By a kind of perverted logic, it turns to the past of the oppressed people, and distorts, disfigures, and destroys it. This work of devaluing pre-colonial history takes on a dialectical significance today. (Fanon, 1963: 210)

It is these perverted logics and lies that must be confronted now, just as troops were fought courageously with guns and bombs in previous eras of the struggle for Indigenous freedom. When lies become accepted and normal, the imperative of the warrior is to awaken and enliven the truth and

to get people to invest belief and energy into that truth. The battle is a spiritual and physical one fought against the political manipulation of the people's own innate fears and the embedding of complacency, that metastasizing weakness, into their psyches. Fanon pointed out that the most important strength of Indigenous resistance, unity, is also constantly under attack as colonial powers erase community histories and senses of place to replace them with doctrines of individualism and predatory capitalism: 'In the colonial context . . . the natives fight among themselves. They tend to use each other as a screen, and each hides from his neighbor the national enemy' (Fanon, 1963: 306–7). . . .

How can we refocus and restore the original objective of Indigenous autonomy and nation-to-nation relations between original and immigrant peoples to its orienting primacy? In advocating a break from the colonial path, Nez Percé/Chicana scholar Inés Hernández-Ávila speaks of the power of Indigenous languages in articulating a transformative agenda in Mexico that is 'dignifying, validating and ensuring the continuance of their peoples' languages and cultures' (Hernández-Ávila, 2003: 56). Hernández-Ávila's interview with Feliciano Sanchez Chan, a Maya/Yucateco, highlights the need for 'zones of refuge' that are immune to the reaches of imperialism and globalization. These zones of refuge are places where:

knowledge has been historically guarded, exercised and sustained. These zones of refuge represent safe (physical and psychological) spaces where Mesoamerican cultural matrices continue to find expression, even as the advocates of the imaginary Mexico persist in their obstinate project of erasure and substitution. (Hernández-Ávila, 2003: 38)

This is a powerful conceptualization of a strategic and cultural objective that remains consistent with traditional goals yet stands against the integrative goals of the contemporary colonial agenda. In addition to creating zones of refuge and other breaks from colonial rule that create spaces of freedom, we will begin to realize decolonization in a real way when we begin to achieve the re-strengthening of our people as individuals so that these spaces can be occupied by decolonized people living authentic lives. This is a recognition that our true power as Indigenous people ultimately lies in our relationships with our land, relatives, language, and ceremonial life. As the eminent Lakota scholar Vine Deloria, Jr asserts, 'What we need is a cultural leave-us-alone agreement, in spirit and in fact' (Deloria, Jr, 1988: 27).

Complacency, Corruption, and Compartmentalized Communities

. . . What does it mean to be Indigenous, given the colonial legacies of blood quantum measurements (Snipp, 1989; Hagan, 1985), state assimilation policies, self-identification as a challenge to community citizenship standards, acceptance of colonial labels of 'aboriginalism', and gendered identity constructions (Anderson, 2000; Mihesuah, 2003)? Postmodern imperialists attempt to partition Indigenous bodies and communities by imposing political/legal fictions on cultural peoples. How can we promote balance between political and cultural notions of being Indigenous? Cree/Métis writer Kim Anderson outlines several 'foundations of resistance' for being Indigenous, which include: strong families, grounding in community, connection to land, language, storytelling and spirituality (Anderson, 2000: 116–36). For Anderson, these form a basis for action. However, we believe that the interrelationships between these fundamental principles must be examined further in order to generate a foundation for effective resistance to contemporary colonialism.

Peoplehood models, which discuss the interconnected factors of community, language and cultural practices, appear to have some promise for discussing the adaptability and resurgence of Indigenous communities. Indigenous peoples themselves have long understood their existence as peoples or nations (expressed not in these terms but in their own languages, of course) as formed around axes of land, culture and community. Scholars have investigated these traditional under-standings and derived theories based on such Indigenous philosophies. The concept of 'peoplehood' has its roots in anthropologist Edward H. Spicer's work on 'enduring peoples' (Spicer, 1962). Spicer's discussion of an 'Indian sense of identity' (as distinct from 'ethnic groups') centred on three key factors: their relationship to the land, common spiritual bond, and language use (Spicer, 1962: 576–8). The peoplehood concept was further developed by Cherokee anthropologist Robert K. Thomas, who added 'sacred history' as a fourth factor in community relationships (Thomas, 1990). Thomas also described the four peoplehood components as being interwoven and dependent on one another. . . .

Building on this notion of a dynamic and interconnected concept of Indigenous identity constituted in history, ceremony, language, and land, we consider relationships (or kinship networks) to be at the core of an authentic Indigenous identity. Clearly, it is the need to maintain respectful relationships that guides all interactions and experiences with community, clans, families, individuals, homelands, plants, animals, etc. in the Indigenous cultural ideal. If any one of these elements of identity, such as sacred history, is in danger of being lost, unified action can be taken to revitalize and restore that part of the community by utilizing relationships, which are the spiritual and cultural foundations of Indigenous peoples. Tewa scholar Gregory Cajete contrasts this Indigenous sense of kinship and 'ensoulment of nature' with the (relatively) one-dimensional Newtonian-Cartesian perspectives characteristic of European and colonial worldviews: '[Indigenous] people understood that all entities of nature—plants, animals, stones, trees, mountains, rivers, lakes, and a host of other living entities—embodied relationships that must be honored' (Cajete, 2000: 178). . . .

There are obvious strengths of the peoplehood model as a foundation for developing Indigenous cultures of resistance. But where should strategies to generate a resurgence of Indigenous nationhood be focused? Manuel and Posluns's theory of the Fourth World is again instructive, revealing the unifying nature of Indigenous action in the struggle against colonialism throughout the world:

> My belief in the Fourth World is an act of faith. But it is no illusion. I have told you of the strength of my ancestors. My faith is simply that the strength of the present generation and those who are still coming toward us is no less than the strength of our forebears. The Fourth World is far more of a Long March than an Eternal Resting Place. My faith is that we, and our children's children, are willing and able to take up the burden of our history and set out on our journey. Were there no more to it than that I should ask no more of other men than to let us pass freely. (Manuel and Posluns, 1974: 261)

For Manuel and Posluns, the Fourth World is founded on active relationships with the spiritual and cultural heritage embedded in the words and patterns of thought and behaviour left to us by our ancestors. The legacies of their struggles to be Indigenous form the imperatives of our contemporary struggles to regenerate authentic Indigenous existences.

A Fourth World theory asserting Indigenous laws on Indigenous lands highlights the sites of ongoing state–nation conflicts while reaffirming the spiritual and cultural nature of the struggle. This is not simply another taxonomy relating Indigenous realities in a theoretical way to the so-called First, Second, and Third Worlds, but a recognition of a spiritual 'struggle to enter the Fourth World' and to decode state motivations as they invade under the 'mantle of liberation and development' (Nietschmann, 1995: 235–6). The Canadian historian Anthony Hall describes this as a battle against the 'empire of possessive individualism' and the 'militarization of space': 'the idea of the Fourth World provides a kind of broad ideological umbrella to cover the changing coalitions of pluralistic resistance aimed at preventing the monocultural transformation of the entire planet . . .' (Hall, 2003: 523, 530). . . .

The larger process of regeneration, as with the outwardly focused process of decolonization, also begins with the self. It is a self-conscious kind of traditionalism that is the central process in the 'reconstruction of traditional communities' based on the original teachings and orienting values of Indigenous peoples (Alfred, 1999: 81). Colonialism corrupted the relationship between original peoples and the Settlers, and it eventually led to the corruption of Indigenous cultures and communities too. But our discussion thus far has, we hope, illustrated the fact that decolonization and regeneration are not, at root, collective and institutional processes. They are shifts in thinking and action that emanate from recommitments and reorientations at the level of the self that, over time and through proper organization, manifest as broad social and political movements to challenge state agendas and authorities. To a large extent, institutional approaches to making meaningful change in the lives of Indigenous people have not led to what we understand as decolonization and regeneration; rather they have further embedded Indigenous people in the colonial institutions they set out to challenge. This paradoxical outcome of struggle is because of the logical inconsistencies at the core of the institutional approaches. . . .

Indigenous Pathways of Action and Freedom

Indigenous pathways of authentic action and freedom struggle start with people transcending colonialism on an individual basis—a strength that soon reverberates outward from the self to family, clan, community, and into all of the broader relationships that form an Indigenous existence. In this way, Indigenousness is reconstructed, reshaped, and actively lived as resurgence against the dispossessing and demeaning processes of annihilation that are inherent to colonialism.

There is no concise neat model of resurgence in this way of approaching decolonization and the regeneration of our peoples. Nor are there clear and definite steps that we can list for people to check off as milestones on their march to freedom. But there are identifiable directions of movement, patterns of thought and action that reflect a shift to an Indigenous reality from the colonized places we inhabit today in our minds and in our souls.

Derived from experience of Indigenous warriors, old and new, who have generated an authentic existence out of the mess left by colonial dispossession and disruption, these pathways can be thought of as the direction of freedom whether we have in mind the struggle of a single person or conceptualizing an eventual global Indigenous struggle founded on the regeneration of ourselves and our communities.

These are the mantras of a resurgent Indigenous movement:

- *Land is Life*—our people must reconnect with the terrain and geography of their Indigenous heritage if they are to comprehend the teachings and values of the ancestors, and if they are to draw strength and sustenance that is independent of colonial power, and which is regenerative of an authentic, autonomous, Indigenous existence.
- *Language is Power*—our people must recover ways of knowing and relating from outside the mental and ideational framework of colonialism by regenerating themselves in a conceptual universe formed through Indigenous languages.
- *Freedom is the Other Side of Fear*—our people must transcend the controlling power of the many and varied fears that colonial powers use to dominate and manipulate us into complacency and cooperation with its authorities. The way to do this is to confront our fears head-on through spiritually grounded action; contention and direct movement at the source of our fears is the only way to break the chains that bind us to our colonial existences.
- *Decolonize your Diet*—our people must regain the self-sufficient capacity to provide our own food, clothing, shelter and medicines. Ultimately important to the struggle for freedom is the reconstitution of our own sick and weakened physical bodies and community relationships accomplished through a return to the natural sources of food and the active, hard-working, physical lives lived by our ancestors.
- *Change Happens one Warrior at a Time*—our people must reconstitute the mentoring and learning–teaching relationships that foster real

and meaningful human development and community solidarity. The movement toward decolonization and regeneration will emanate from transformations achieved by direct-guided experience in small, personal, groups and one-on-one mentoring towards a new path.

These mantras and the pathways they represent will be put into practice by every person in their own way, in response to the particular context and set of challenges that form each person and community's colonial reality.

Bringing it all together, *being Indigenous* means thinking, speaking, and acting with the conscious intent of regenerating one's indigeneity. Each Indigenous nation has its own way of articulating and asserting self-determination and freedom. For example, in Kanien'keha, the word is *Onkwehonweneha*, which translates as the 'way of the original people'. Tsalagi (Cherokee) have the tradition of *Wigaduwaga*, which translates into 'I will always be up above in all things that influence me in life; in the uppermost; for us to follow or emulate.' The Lyackson people have the term *Snuw'uw'ul*, Hopis say *Hopit Pŏtskwani'at*, and Maori say *Tino rangatiratanga*.[4] As Indigenous peoples, the way to recovering freedom and power and happiness is clear: it is time for each one of us to make the commitment to transcend colonialism as people, and for us to work together as peoples to become forces of Indigenous truth against the lie of colonialism. We do not need to wait for the colonizer to provide us with money or to validate our vision of a free future; we only need to start to use our Indigenous languages to frame our thoughts, the ethical framework of our philosophies to make decisions and to use our laws and institutions to govern ourselves.

Notes

1. This article is part of 'The Politics of Identity', an on-going series edited by Richard Bellamy.
2. This article draws on analyses and concepts developed in Taiaiake Alfred, *Wasáse: Indigenous Pathways of Action and Freedom* (Peterborough, ON: Broadview Press, 2005).
3. For examples of classic colonial-liberal discourse with liberatory pretences, see Patrick Macklem, *Indigenous Difference and the Constitution of Canada* (Toronto,

University of Toronto Press, 2001); Charles Taylor, *Multiculturalism and 'The Politics of Recognition'* (Princeton, Princeton University Press, 1992); and Will Kimlycka, ed., *The Rights of Minority Cultures* (Oxford, Oxford University Press, 1995).

4. See, for example, Roger Maaka and Augie Fleras, 'Engaging with Indigeneity: Tino Rangatiratanga in Aotearoa', pp. 89–109 in Duncan Ivison, Paul Patton, and Will Sanders, eds, *Political Theory and the Rights of Indigenous Peoples* (Cambridge: Cambridge University Press, 2000).

References

Alfred, Taiaiake. 1999. *Peace, Power, Righteousness: An Indigenous Manifesto*. Oxford: Oxford University Press.

Anderson, Kim. 2000. *A Recognition of Being: Reconstructing Native Womanhood*. Toronto: Sumach Press.

Cajete, Gregory. 2000. *Native Science: Natural Laws of Interdependence*. Santa Fe, NM: Clear Light Publishers.

Deloria, Jr., Vine. 1988. *Custer Died for your Sins*. Norman, OK: University of Oklahoma Press.

Fanon, Frantz. 1963. *The Wretched of the Earth*. New York: Grove Press.

Hagan, William T. 1985. 'Full Blood, Mixed Blood, Generic and Ersatz: The Problem of Indian Identity', *Arizona and the West*. 27: 309–26.

Hall, Anthony J. 2003. *The American Empire and the Fourth World*. Montreal: McGill-Queen's University Press.

Hernández-Ávila, Inés. 2003. 'The Power of Native Languages and the Performance of Indigenous Autonomy: The Case of Mexico', in Richard Grounds, George E. Tinker, and David E. Wilkins, eds, *Native Voices: American Indian Identity and Resistance*. Lawrence: University Press of Kansas.

Manuel, George, and Michael Posluns. 1974. *The Fourth World: An Indian Reality*. New York: Collier Macmillan Canada.

Mihesuah, Devon, A. 2003. *Indigenous American Women: Decolonization, Empowerment, Activism*. Lincoln: University of Nebraska Press.

Nietschmann, Bernard. 1995. 'The Fourth World: Nation Versus States', in George J. Demko and William B. Wood, eds, *Reordering the World: Geopolitical Perspectives on the 21st Century*. Philadelphia, PA: Westview Press.

Smith, Graham Hingangaroa. 2000. 'Protecting and Respecting Indigenous Knowledge', in Marie Battiste, ed., *Reclaiming Indigenous Voice and Vision*. Vancouver, BC: UBC Press.

Snipp, C. Matthew. 1989. *American Indians: The First of This Land*. New York: Russell Save Foundation.

Spicer, Edward H. 1962. *Cycles of Conquest: The Impact of Spain, Mexico and the United States on the Indians of the Southwest, 1533–1960*. Phoenix: University of Arizona Press.

Thomas, Robert K. 1990. 'The Tap-Roots of Peoplehood', in Daphne J. Anderson, ed., *Getting to the Heart of the Matter: Collected Letters and Papers*. Vancouver: Native Ministries Consortium.

Chapter 17

On Ethnographic Refusal: Indigeneity, 'Voice', and Colonial Citizenship

Audra Simpson

Anthropological Need

To speak of Indigeneity is to speak of colonialism and anthropology, as these are means through which Indigenous people have been known and sometimes are still known. In different moments, anthropology has imagined itself to be a voice, and in some disciplinary iterations, the voice of the colonized (Paine, 1990; Said, 1989). This modern interlocutionary role was not self-ascribed by anthropologists, nor was it without a serious material and ideational context; it accorded with the imperatives of Empire and in this, specific technologies of rule that sought to obtain space and resources, to define and know the difference that it constructed in those spaces and to then govern those within (Asad, 1973; Said, 1994; Deloria, 1988). Knowing and representing the 'voices' within those places required more than military might, it required the methods and modalities of knowing, in particular: categorization, ethnological comparison, linguistic translation, and ethnography.

These techniques of knowing were predicated upon a profound need, as the distributions in power and possibility that made Empire also made for the heuristic and documentary requirements of a metropolitan and administrative readership, hence the required accounts of the difference that 'culture' stood in for in these 'new'

places (Cohn, 1987; Thomas, 1994; Wolfe, 1999; Pratt, 1992). These accounts were required for governance, but also so that those in the metropole might know themselves in a manner that accorded to the global processes underway. Like 'race' in other contexts, 'culture' was (and still is in some quarters) the conceptual and necessarily essentialized space that stood in for complicated bodily and exchange-based relationships that enabled and marked colonial situations in Empire: warfare, commerce, sex, trade, missionization. 'Culture' described the difference that was found in these places and marked the ontological endgame of each exchange: a difference that had been contained into neat, ethnically-defined territorial spaces that now needed to be made sense of, to be ordered, ranked, to be governed, to be possessed.[1] This is a form of politics that is more than representational, as this was a governmental and disciplinary possession of bodies and territories, and in this were included existent forms of philosophy, history and social life that Empire sought to speak of and speak for.

In this paper I will argue that the techniques of representation and analysis that avail themselves to us when the processes sketched out above have been accounted for make for a form of representation that may move away from 'difference' and attendant containment as a unit of analysis. I am interested in the way that cultural analysis may look when difference is not the unit of analysis, when culture is disaggregated into narratives rather than wholes, when proximity to the territory that one is engaging in is as immediate as the self, and what this then does to questions of 'voice'. I will argue that in such a context of anthropological accounting—an accounting I started to do above but will do more robustly below—'voice' is coupled with sovereignty that is evident at the level of interlocution, at the level of method and at the level of textualization. Within Indigenous contexts, contexts that are never properly 'post-colonial', the sovereignty of the people we speak of, when speaking for themselves, interrupt anthropological portraits of timelessness, procedure, and function that dominate representations of their past and, sometimes, their present.

As an anthropologist I always found such portraits of Indigenous peoples to be strange in light of the deeply resistant, self-governing, and relentlessly critical people that I belong to and work with. When I started to do my work on a topic that simply matters to the Mohawks of Kahnawake— the question of who we are, and who we shall be for the future—I found that anthropological histories on the Iroquois[2] and analytics used for cultural analysis were exceedingly ritualistic and procedural, and so much so that they privileged particular communities and peoples in ways that stressed harmony and timelessness even where there was utter opposition to and struggle against the state. Again, this is more than a representational problem, or a superficially representational problem. The people that I work with and belong to do care deeply about ceremony and tradition, but hinged those concerns to nationhood, citizenship, rights, justice, proper ways of being in the world, the best way to be in relation to one another, political recognition, invigorating the Mohawk language—they did not talk about the usual anthropological fare that dominated the prodigious amount of research upon them. They clearly had and have critiques of state power, hegemony, history, and even one another that made them appear anomalous against the literature written upon them.

And so it was that I asked questions about the questions that mattered to us and had to write in certain ways, as these matterings sometimes were more our business than others, but clearly had import for much larger questions, questions concerning *just* forms of dominion, or sovereignty or citizenship. I want to reflect upon the dissonance between the representations that were produced by writing away from and to dominant forms of knowing and commitment to what people say (imperfectly glossed here as 'voice'). I do so in order to ask what the form of knowledge might look like when such histories as the one sketched out above are accounted for in disciplinary form and analysis. And further to that, I consider what analysis will look like, or sound like, when the goals and aspirations of those we talk to inform the methods and the shape of our theorizing and analysis.

Particular Ways of Knowing

Unlike anthropologies of the past, accounting for Empire and colonialism and doing so in the context of 'settler societies' (code for proximal-to, or once 'Indigenous') is now becoming more acceptable. This is owing to political currents, critiques, and philosophical trends outside of and within anthropology that have embedded the discipline within the history of colonialism, have highlighted ethics and form, and pluralized the places and peoples that are now considered viable for ethnographic analysis. Although more acceptable than in the past, anthropological analyses of indigeneity may still occupy the 'salvage' and 'documentary' slot for analysis, an elaboration of object that results from the endurance of categories that emerged in moments of colonial contact, many of which still reign supreme. In those moments, people left their own spaces of self-definition and became 'Indigenous'. And 'Indigenous' is a category that did not explicitly state or theorize the shared experience of having their lands alienated from them or that they would be understood in particular ways. This shared condition might be an innocent tale of differential access to power, of differing translations of events, were there a level field of interpretation within which to assert those different translations, as well as an agreed-upon vocabulary for comparison. No situation such as the one we all inherit and live within is 'innocent' of a violence of form, if not content, in narrating a history or a present for ourselves. But like the law and its political formations that took things from them, there are disciplinary forms that must be contended with by Indigenous peoples. Anthropology and the 'law' (both, necessarily, reified in this iteration) mark two such spaces of knowing and contention with serious implications for Indigenous peoples in the present.[3] . . .

Histories of Being Refused: The Indian Act in Canada

I was stimulated to frame my project on Mohawk nationhood and citizenship by the complete disjuncture between what was written about my own people and the things that mattered the most to us. I was interested in the unambiguous, sometimes virulent and violent boundaries that were being drawn within the reservation community of Kahnawake over the question of 'membership'. At the time I started to think about my research, the elected government of the community had already devised, with some participation from the membership, a 1984 code which would require a 50 per cent blood quantum for membership in the community. This membership code itself was stimulated by several factors, most recently an international human rights decision that made Canada amend its Indian Act and reinstate onto a federal registry previously disenfranchised Indian women and children ('Bill C-31'). Aimed at redressing the patrilineal bias in the Indian Act, Bill C-31 was passed into effect in 1984. With this legislation, Indian women who lost their status upon marriage to non-Indian men (or non-status Indian men) were put back on the federal registration list of Indians in Canada (Cassidy and Bish, 1989). It was now up to each reserve to devise membership codes that were of their own making, and to then admit (or deny) membership

to these women and their children in their own local registries.

Bill C-31 followed on the heels of a decade-long battle that saw non-status Indian women go head to head with their reserve, or band council governments, the state, and finally, international authorities. The women had unsuccessfully petitioned their band council governments to let them return, to raise their children, and to exercise their rights as Indians. The band council governments upheld the Indian Act and challenged the women to bring their case to the courts. The women then organized into political action groups, Equal Rights for Indian Women and the Native Women's Association of Canada, which then brought the Canadian government to court for the inherent gender bias in the Indian Act. They lost their case. It was only when they brought the case to the United Nations that Canada was forced to amend the Indian Act and remove the bias of determining membership in Indian bands along the father's line. Perceived as a victory for Indian women (and perhaps for all women, as there was some coalition-building between women's organizations at the time), Bill C-31 was intended to mend the fabric of Indian societies torn apart by unjust legislation. In practice, however, matters were much different.

Kahnawake had already assimilated some tenets of the Indian Act into the social fabric of the community. The means for defining kinship and determining community belonging, the traditional means for determining descent—through the mother's clan—was supplanted by the Indian Act and its European model of patrilineal descent as detailed above. Kahnawake had formally accepted the Indian Act in the community in 1890; however, as a reserve on Crown land, the community had been subject to elements of the Act as early as 1850. In 1850, however, Indian status was transferable to both male and female non-Indian spouses of Indians. Therefore non-Indian men or women could hold land, operate businesses, and claim tax exemption on the reserve. Unwilling to accept the possibility of white men holding land in the community, Kahnawake contested this aspect of the Act and brought it to the courts so that the Act would be changed.

As detailed above, as a result of the Indian Act, matrilineal descent and property holding was transferred to the father's line. This was an unambiguously raced and gendered injustice that Indian women, disenfranchised from their Indian status across Canada, fought against. But the complex of factors—Canada's bestowal of a right to reserves to determine membership after 100 years of living under Indian Act rules for recognition; Canada's reinstatement of the women on a federal registry—led, in part, to the development of a blood quantum code in Kahnawake, a code that was in defiance of Canadian norms for political recognition, but appeared to be 'objective' and gender-neutral. The membership code was contested and defended by, it seemed, everyone within the community and sometimes all at once. Bill C-31 appeared as a most recent imposition (read by some as being told who was an Indian, *again*) and this iteration of the code reflected a century of colonial impositions, along with a desire for scientific rigour and objectivity. No one was completely happy with the code but everyone agreed that 'something had to be done', and that membership was the number one issue facing the community. In such a context, there were not only boundaries being constructed and deconstructed daily, there was a heightened awareness and deep and generalized concern over what would be the means for determining who we were—and who was not eligible to be recognized by us as being who we are.

In such a context, I knew that there were limits to what I could ask—and then what I could say—within the scope of my project on Mohawk nationhood, and those limits extended beyond any statement on ethical forms of research that either the American Anthropological Association or the Social Sciences and Humanities Research Council of Canada (two professional and research-regulating bodies for anthropologists in Canada and the United States) required. And so it was that I wrote an ethnography that pivoted upon refusal(s). I was interested in the larger picture, in

the discursive, material, and moral territory that was simultaneously historical and contemporary (this 'national' space) and the ways in which *Kahnawakero:non*, the 'people of Kahnawake', had refused the authority of the state at almost every turn. The ways in which their formation of the initial membership code (now replaced by a lineage code and board of elders to implement the code and determine cases) was refused; the ways in which their interactions with border guards at the international boundary line were predicated upon a refusal; how refusal worked in everyday encounters to enunciate repeatedly to ourselves and to outsiders that 'this is who we are, this is who you are, these are my rights.'

There was no place in the existing literature for these articulations, nor was there a neat placement for them within post-colonial studies or analysis—there was not a doubleness to their consciousness, a still-colonial but striving to be 'post-colonial consciousness' that denied the modern self that Fanon, Bhabha, and Giddens, speak of and from (Bhabha, 1994; Giddens, 1991; Fanon, 1967). There seemed, rather, to be a tripleness, a quadrupleness, to consciousness and an endless play, and it went something like this: 'I am me, I am what you think I am and I am who this person to the right of me thinks I am and you are all full of shit and then maybe I will tell you to your face.' There was a definite core that seemed to reveal itself at the point of refusal and that refusal was arrived at, of course, at the very limit of the discourse.

Anthropology, in such a context is, I think, sometimes really funny. Others would say uncomfortable. But contemporary fieldwork with Iroquois peoples involves being pushed and pushing back, a kind of discursive wrestling. There are *multiple* sovereignties at work, all of which have worked to protect, to limit, to entrench what was already in place, an exercise of political will that generated an exception, in Agamben's theorisation, to the liability of the subject (Agamben, 2005). To speak of limits in such a way makes some liberal thinkers uncomfortable, and may, to them, seem dangerous. When access to information, to knowledge, to the intellectual commons is controlled by the people who generate that information, it can be seen as a violation of shared standards of justice and truth. However, in the context that I have worked and still work within, history rears its head at every turn and did so through the bodily presence of white women (with Indian status), through the bodily presence of the children that they had with Indian men. These are the inheritors of colonial rules of recognition and were rendered, in some dark moments, as colonial residues and reminders. Their juridical identities spoke not of Eastern Woodlands Fever, an historical and contemporary transgression and erotic fantasy which a cultural analyst with the vim, vigour, and verve of Spike Lee should dwell upon, but rather of something less sexy: Iroquois citizenships (a clan system) strangulated and arrested by the Indian Act.

The Indian Act of 1868 recognized the union between an Indian man and a white woman as one that maintained his legal recognition as an Indian, and would transfer the same recognition to the woman in the eyes of the state. The union of an Indian woman and white man, on the other hand, would deny her legal recognition as an Indian, her status under the Indian Act, and that of her children in the eyes of the state and, sometimes, the community. These bizarre logics of recognition and residues of history structured and still structure (in part) the bodies and persons and personalities and cousins and friends and enemies that comprise my version of Kahnawake. The punctuating, juridical bestowals of settler colonialism were read, like a text, with the status designations inscribed upon each one of us—'C-31, status, non-status'—co-existing with traditional Iroquois modalities of recognition: 'clan, no-clan'. Thus, historical and juridical moments were carried by us, upon our very bodies—historical moments which settled upon the body, read as rights. I saw, unfolding before me in a fleshy, Hegelian *present*, the processes of settlement and its contracting and expanding forms of recognition—in the form of the people before me who spoke endlessly, it seemed, of how we shall determine who we are and who is *not* who we are. They did so while simultaneously refusing these logics.

'No One Seems to Know': Doing History and Ethnography in the Familiar

This question of recognition has surfaced repeatedly through time and, although completely originating in Canadian settlement and the Indian Act, its contemporary guises are most local. In the beginning of my own research on this subject, the Mohawk Council of Kahnawake placed a notice in the weekly newspaper, *The Eastern Door*. It read: 'The following members of the community are housing non-natives,' with the name of the community member, their band number (number on the local Indian registry) and the name of their non-Indian guest. The concern over non-Indians in Kahnawake, I would later learn through archival research, extended back to the earliest correspondence between the Indian Agent and Ottawa. Readable now in Record Group 10, letters from the Agent documented Kahnawake's 'sensitivity' to outsiders: 'To the half breed Canadians of the village. We wish to have a final decision to know if DeLormier, Giasson, Deblois, Meloche and others are masters in our Reserve. There are eight of us who write (Indians) and if you do not leave the village look out for your heads, your buildings, your cattle and take warning of what we now tell you' (Reid, 2004). This was a warning to 'half-breeds' and whites living within Kahnawake in 1878, a time of great scarcity (of firewood and land). This warning, publicly posted to the 'half breeds' and 'whites', all of whom owned disproportionate amounts of property on the reserve, enunciated a still earlier anxiety over distribution of resources and power and the wrongful recognition of certain Whites as Indians in the eyes of the state.

Thus the notice in The Eastern Door was not without a context, and the context is the material and semiotic history from which Mohawk speak and by which they are simultaneously informed: land loss; scarcity of firewood; the one year that white men could legally obtain Indian status and buy and sell land; more encroachment; the earlier 'settling' of New York State and loss of the

Mohawk Valley; the end of the Indian Wars; the Riel Rebellion in Canada; the ascendancy and decline of the British in North America. I do not wish to say that managing these historical vicissitudes ethnographically and in the present is unusual for those who wish to understand sovereignty as central to the lives, and the territorial integrity and the dignity of people that we work with. But in my brief discussion of the ways in which I came to understand my project, this concern over membership is part of the anthropological and *colonial* accounting that must happen for ethnography to make sense. Recall that the Indian Act, a specific body of law that recognizes Indians in a wardship status in Canada, created the categories of person and rights that served to sever Indian women from their communities upon marriage to white men. It did the reverse to Indian men—white women *gained* Indian status upon their marriage into an Indian community. This created the conditions for blood quantum and the contestation (and accordance) of it that I examined as part of my research. How does one write about this or analyze what is so clearly offensive to the anthropological sensibilities of access, of replicable results, in some ways of 'fairness,' and reconcile all this with the plight of those who are struggling every day to maintain what little they have left? And when they are struggling so clearly with the languages and analytics of a foreign culture that occupies their semantic and material space, and naturalizes this occupation through history-writing and the very analytics that are used to know them?

The work of understanding these issues of membership, political recognition, sovereignty and autonomy within communities requires an historical sensibility (and reckoning) that is deeply horizontal as well as vertical. While there was a hearty oral archive of the structuring logics of exclusion—of how people got to get 'here', how they married each other when they did—there was co-terminously, the logic of the present, that I saw and lived and suffered through and enjoyed (and still do), of tolerance and exceptions and affections—what I call in other places 'feeling citizen-

ships' that are structured in the present space of intra-community recognition, affection and care, outside of the logics of colonial and imperial rule (re: the Indian Act or blood quantum). And here I give such an example of these alternative logics from someone I interviewed, but also of a refusal, or a denial within the space of ethnography:

Q. Tell me what you think our ideal form of citizenship is . .. are citizenship and membership the same thing?

A. From my understanding, and whomever I ask, I get these grey, cloudy answers in return, so I am not quite sure. I am a citizen of Kahnawake but I am not a member of Kahnawake. I am not on this mysterious list that no-one seems to have any information about. So although I dearly love Kahnawake, there are many positions I will never be able to hold until this membership issue is cleared up, so I don't know much about it, other than, I don't think it to be fair—there are those who leave the community, as I said, we all come back to Kahnawake, but there are those who leave for twenty-five years and they come back and they're a member, and they will have all these opportunities that I won't, even though I've never left. I don't think that's fair.

But I think there's a distinction—one could be a citizen without being a member.

Q. Interesting, and that citizenship is based on . . . let me push you on that then, how is that different, explain it to me?

A. Citizenship is, as I said, you live there, you grew up there, that is the life that you know—that is who you are. Membership is more of a legislative enactment designed to keep people from obtaining the various benefits that Aboriginals can receive. So I am a citizen, I live there, that is who I am, yet I cannot be a member because of these laws, which I feel is unfair. If I had been there my whole life I should have the same opportunity to run for Council that anyone else can. Yet I cannot.

Q. Do you think that's because of public sentiment, the Indian Act, is that because o . . .

A. I don't know what you know, or what others know—this is an area that I can't get straight answers from, no-one seems to know. . . .

We discussed further:

Q. *What do you think the legacy of C-31 is in Kahnawake?*

A. *I think I really don't know much about this. There's this generation of people, myself included, who were young during that time, and we had no recollection of that time or even of these laws—as I said, I inquire, but nobody seems to know; I don't seem to get answers from anybody . . .*

Q. *But you ask people?*

A. *I ask people—the same thing with this traditional government movement that is happening in Kahnawake, people speak of traditional government, they speak of Bill C-31 and no one seems to know anything about it.*

Q. *In your personal experience, how did you come to understand C-31?*

A. *With what I do understand with it, I think from my mother. From what I understand, she tends to avoid speaking of this; I believe she was one of the C-31 people, but I don't know for sure.*

Q. *To get it [her status] back?*

A. *To get back on, she married my father who was a Canadian, she was taken off this list, she got back on with C-31—and all the details I do not know.*

Q. *'Cause it's unpleasant?*

A. *She doesn't speak of it and, as I say, I inquire, but I receive no answers, people seem to side-step it or give these very vague summaries—it's almost like it is a taboo subject.*

Q. *Would you like to see it discussed more openly, or to find stuff out or be able to . . .*

A. *I would like to, out of curiosity, know a bit more about it—but if I don't, I will live my life and for the most part I don't think it will really bother me other than not being able to be on this list, I guess.* (Simpson, 2003)

'No one seems to know' was laced through much of my informant's discussion of C-31, and of his own predicament—which I knew he spoke of indirectly, because I knew his predicament. And I also knew everyone knew, because everyone knows everyone's 'predicament'. This was the collective 'limit'—that of knowledge and thus who we could or would not claim. So it was very interesting to me that he would tell me that 'he did not know' and 'no one seems to know'—to me these utterances meant, 'I know you know, and you know that I know I know . . . so let's just not get into this.' Or, 'let's just not say.' So I did not say, and so I did not 'get into it' with him, and I won't get into it with my readers. What I am quiet about is his predicament and my predicament and the actual stuff (the math, the clans, the mess, the misrecognitions, the confusion, and the clarity)—the calculus of our predicaments. And although I pushed him, hoping that there might be something explicit said from the space of his exclusion—or more explicit than he gave me—it was enough that he said what he said. 'Enough' is certainly enough. 'Enough', I realized, was when I reached the limit of my own return and our collective arrival. Can I do this and still come home; what am I revealing here and why? Where will this get us? Who benefits from this and why? And 'enough' was when they shut down (or told me to turn off the recorder), or told me outright funny things like 'nobody seems to know'—when everybody *does* know and talks about it *all the time*. Dominion then, had to be exercised over these representations, and that was determined when enough was said. The ethnographic limit then, was reached not just when it would cause harm (or extreme discomfort)—the limit was arrived at when the representation would bite all of us and compromise the *representational* territory that we have gained for ourselves in the past 100 years, in small but deeply influential ways, with a cadre of scholars from Kahnawake whose work has reached beyond the boundaries of the community (Alfred, G.R., 1995; Alfred, T., 1999, 2005; Simpson, 2001). . . .

The people I interviewed do know the different forms of recognition that are at play, the simultaneities of consciousness that are in work in any colonial encounter (including those with me) in the exercising of rights—and that knowledge translates into the 'feeling side' of recognition, one that is not juridical, is home-grown, and dignified by local history and knowledge. What is theoretically generative about these refusals? They *account* for the history detailed above; they tell us something about the way we cradle or embed our representations and notions of sovereignty and nationhood; and they critique and move us away from statist forms of recognition. In listening and shutting off the tape recorder, in situating each subject within their own shifting historical context of the present, these refusals speak volumes, because they tell us when to stop. Whether or not we wish to share that is a matter of ethnography that can both *refuse* and also take up *refusal* in generative ways.

Notes

1. Pieter Pels and Oscar Salemink trace the anthropological 'culture' concept back to the eighteenth century, to Johann Gottfried Herder's notion of a nation that is necessarily differentiated from others, and possessing a history that was generated internally and shaped by language. They argue that '[b]y assimilating the quantitative aggregate of "population" to an identity of type, he laid the ground work for the scientific conception of race and culture.' See 'Introduction: Locating the Colonial Subjects of Anthropology', p. 19 in P. Pels and O. Salemink, eds, *Colonial Subjects: Essays on the Practical History of Anthropology* (Ann Arbor: University of Michigan Press, 1999).

2. 'Iroquois' is a French transliteration of *Haudenosaunee*, or 'People of the Longhouse'. The Iroquois form a confederacy of six Indigenous nations—Mohawk, Oneida, Onondaga, Cayuga, Seneca, and Tuscarora—that extended their dominion across what is now the Northeastern United States. They now reside on 15 reservations and unrecognized/traditional communities and cities across the borders of the United States and Canada. The Mohawks of Kahnawake are a single nation, a reservation community located in what is now Southern Quebec (Canada).

3. For an examination of the dialectic between anthropological theory and the formation of racial categories (focusing on African Americans) and the law in the United States, see Lee Baker, *From Savage to Negro: Anthropology and the Construction of Race, 1896–1954* (Berkeley: University of California Press, 1998).

References

Agamben, G. 2005. *State of Exception*. Chicago: University of Chicago Press.

Alfred, G.R. 1995. *Heeding the Voices of our Ancestors: Kahnawake Mohawk Politics and the Rise of Native Nationalism*. Toronto: Oxford University Press.

Alfred, T. 1999. *Peace, Power and Righteousness: An Indigenous Manifesto*. Toronto: Oxford University Press.

Alfred, T. 2005. *Wasáse: Indigenous Pathways of Action and Freedom*. Peterborough: Broadview Press.

Asad, T. 1973. *Anthropology & the Colonial Encounter*. London: Ithaca Press.

Bhabha, H.K. 1994. *The Location of Culture*. London: Routledge.

Cassidy, F., and R.L. Bish. 1989. *Indian Government: Its Meaning in Practice*. Lantzville, BC: Oolichan Books.

Cohn, B. 1987. *An Anthropologist among the Historians and Other Essays*. Delhi: Oxford University Press.

Deloria, V. 1988. *Custer Died for Your Sins: An Indian Manifesto*. Norman: University of Oklahoma Press.

Fanon, F. 1967. *Black Skin: White Masks*. New York: Grove Press.

Giddens, A. 1991. *Modernity and Self Identity: Self and Society in the Late Modern Age*. Stanford: Stanford University Press.

Paine, R. 1990. 'Our Authorial Authority,' *Culture* 9 (2): 35–47.

Pratt, M.L. 1992. *Imperial Eyes: Travel Writing and Transculturation*. London: Routledge.Reid, G.F. 2004. *Kahnawà:ke: Factionalism, Traditionalism, and Nationalism in a Mohawk Community*. Lincoln: University of Nebraska Press.

Said, E.W. 1989. 'Representing the Colonized: Anthropology's Interlocutors', *Critical Inquiry* 15 (Winter): 205–25.

Said, E.W. 1994. *Orientalism*. New York: Vintage Books.

Simpson, A. 2001. 'Paths Toward a Mohawk Nation: Narratives of Citizenship and Nationhood in Kahnawake', pp. 113–36 in Duncan Ivison, Paul Patton, and Will Sanders, eds, *Political Theory and the Rights of Indigenous Peoples*. Cambridge: Cambridge University Press.

Simpson, A. 2003. 'To the Reserve and Back Again: Kahnawake Mohawk Narratives of Self, Home and Nation'. PhD diss., McGill University.

Thomas, N. 1994. *Colonialism's Culture: Anthropology, Travel, and Government*. Princeton: Princeton University Press.

Wolfe, P. 1999. *Settler Colonialism and the Transformation of Anthropology: The Politics and Poetics of an Ethnographic Event*. London: Cassell.

Chapter 18

Moving Beyond the Feminism Versus Nationalism Dichotomy: An Anti-Colonial Feminist Perspective on Aboriginal Liberation Struggles

Lina Sunseri

In writing this paper, I feel that I must clearly identify my position in our 'Canadian' society: I am of mixed Aboriginal-Southern White European ancestry. This mixed cultural/ethno-racial identity provides me with distinct experiences which have brought me to a point in my life where I support the anti-colonial self-determination struggles of Aboriginal peoples on this Turtle Island known as Canada. Many times I am asked by friends, intellectuals, feminists, and non-feminists, how I could support any nationalist struggle, especially in light of what has taken place in many parts of the world in the name of ethno-nationalism. Indeed, I often wonder if an Aboriginal 'nationalist' struggle can avoid the destructive results that have occurred elsewhere. I also wonder where I would be placed, and place myself, in this struggle, given my mixed ancestry. My 'hybrid' identity leaves me in what Homi Bhabha would call an 'in-between' place, not quite the colonizer or the colonized. Located as I am in this ambivalent place, having the 'privilege' of a mixture of cultures, it is not surprising then, that I might feel both pulled and pushed towards an Aboriginal anti-colonial movement. This tension is further complicated by my feminist ideology and culture, an ideology that has expressed justifiable skepticism about 'nationalisms', especially in light of the latter's relationship with women's rights.

This paper, written in the midst of all these emotions and recent events of 'nationalist' movements (such as the Serbian, Croatian, Kurdish, and Tamil cases), is an attempt to come to terms with my support for an Aboriginal anti-colonial nationalist movement. Mine is obviously then a situated knowledge, informed by both feminist knowledge and Aboriginal experiences, either of my own or of other Aboriginal peoples. A situated knowledge stresses and validates the importance of lived experiences and it incorporates these experiences within theory (Collins, 2000). While recognizing the limitations of past nationalist movements to liberate women, I believe that it is possible to envision a progressive nationalist liberation movement, one which could eliminate oppressive and unequal power relations. Given that Aboriginal women have lived for many centuries in an oppressive racist and sexist colonial society, which has brought them infinite political, economic, social, and cultural destruction, it is not surprising that these women would ally themselves with a movement that wants to restore and reaffirm their inherent right to govern themselves. . . .

Defining Feminism, Nationalism, and the Nation

A core part of this paper consists of the debate between feminism and nationalism, and how the two seem incompatible. Some earlier second-wave feminists believe that women's oppression is unique and tied to a universal patriarchy (Firestone, 1979; Friedan, 1965; Millett, 1977). They sought to unite women through a sense of a shared oppression, and tended to believe that women's interests can be best achieved through a women's movement that places women's rights the first priority in its agenda.

Many Aboriginal women, along with other women of colour and 'third world' women, have felt alienated by what they view as a 'Western' feminist movement that has either marginalized them or not accurately represented their experiences and interests. As Charles and Hintjens point out:

> In the context of the Third World, this rejection of feminism often arises from its association with western, middle-class women and with the negative consequences of modernisation. . . . However, feminism has also developed a critique of modernism. . . . Thus western feminism recognizes that women neither automatically share a gender identity nor do they necessarily have political interests in common. Their material circumstances and experiences differ significantly and a unity of interests between women from different cultures (and within the same society) cannot be deduced from their shared gender. (1998: 20)

The marginalization of non-White European women within mainstream Western feminism is a reality, and women of colour have challenged the members of the movement to analyze its own racism and its essentialist portrayal of the 'Universal' woman. As Charles and Hintjens indicate above, Western feminism has more recently provided its own critique of modernity and taken into account the diversity of women's experience. Although Western feminism has responded to the challenges presented by women of colour and Third World women, and re-evaluated its earlier assumptions, I still believe that more work needs to be done, especially vis-à-vis the further incorporation of issues of colonialism and racism into the theory and praxis of the movement. Until the women's movement completely faces the reality that many of its members are part of the colonial power, and therefore share some of the advantages that their male counterparts enjoy, most Aboriginals and other colonized groups will continue to view it with some skepticism. If we could all come to understand feminism as a theory and movement that wants to fight all forms of oppression, including racism and colonialism, then we could see it as a struggle for unity among all oppressed women and men. It is this meaning of feminism that I accept, and therefore I can call myself a feminist without reservations.

For the purpose of this paper, nationalism and nation are associated with movements for independence, liberation, and revolution. A classic definition of nation is that of Benedict Anderson, who constructs it as 'an imagined community', a collectivity of individuals who feel that they belong to a shared linguistic community. Anthony Smith presents a primordial definition of nation. For him, nation refers to an ethnic collectivity with a shared past. In my analysis, nation means not only a community that may share a common culture and historical experiences, but it is also a collectivity that is 'oriented towards the future' (Yuval-Davis, 1997: 19). Nationalism is that ideology or discourse which promotes and shapes the formation of such communities. There are different kinds of nationalism; some rely on an exclusionary and homogenous vision, but others can be empowering and culturally diverse. Partha Chatterjee argues, in the context of an anticolonial project,

> the national question here is, of course, historically fused with a colonial question. The assertion of national identity was, therefore, a form of the struggle against colonial exploitation. (1986: 18)

It is precisely this anti-colonial, liberation struggle to which I refer when I speak of nationalism in this paper. Within this framework, and within an Aboriginal context, nationalism means a process to revitalize the different institutions and practices of our various Nations (Alfred, 1995). An Aboriginal perspective on nation and nationalism differs from a Western one because its basis for nationhood is not rooted in notions of territoriality, boundaries, and nation-state (Alfred, 1995). Moreover, other concepts (such as 'pure' Indian, status-Indian, national and regional boundaries) are all constructs of a colonial state and are foreign, if not antithetical, to most Aboriginal cultures and ways of governance (Monture-Angus, 1995).

Feminist Critique of Nationalism

Feminist studies on nationalist and other liberation movements have revealed that, after national liberation, women generally have been pushed to domestic roles (Abdo, 1994). During nationalist struggles, women are often seen as the producers and reproducers of the national culture, and can acquire prestige and status as the bearers of 'pure' culture. However, they can also become increasingly controlled, as their reproductive roles and their portrayal as bearers of culture can also be used to control their sexuality and confine them to domestic roles (Enloe, 1993).

Embedded implicitly and explicitly in this discourse of women as the bearers of culture and 'tradition', is another discourse not exclusively tied to women: that of ethno/racial identity as immutable and connected to blood. Yet, when identity is viewed as uni-dimensional and biological, it marginalizes those who do not fit the strict categories of belonging to one specific ethnic/racial group, and in the process excludes all those individuals who have 'mixed' descent, because their blood cannot be easily and exclusively connected with one group. When ethno-racial nationalist movements connect their concept of belonging to the nation to this notion of purity, we can also see that they need to regulate the sexual relationships of the members of their community. In practice, this

regulation is more strictly applied, and with more negative sanctions, against women, because their reproductive roles become extremely important in the discourses of common origin and purity of blood (Yuval-Davis, 1997).

While recognizing some of the negative results of some nationalist discourses for women, we cannot ignore that some anti-colonial movements have provided the opportunity to mobilize women in their common struggle against the oppressive colonial or quasi-colonial power, as in the case of Algeria, South Africa, Palestine, and some Latin American countries. The women involved have increased their political consciousness and, in some cases, made the male nationalists more aware of exploitative and oppressive gender relations. Often enough though, the male nationalists argue that colonialism and/or capitalism has been the cause of women's problems and they have completely ignored or dismissed the patriarchal nature of women's oppression. Moreover, neither a nationalist nor a socialist revolution has yet integrated a feminist discourse (McClintock, 1995). Constructing a radical alternative discourse that can smash both the sexist emperor and the sexist 'colonized' is not an easy task. This project becomes even more difficult when other forces, both internal and external, such as global capitalism, religious fundamentalism, and reactionary 'traditionalism' are at work, limiting the possibility of a full transformation of social relations in the postcolonial world.

Aboriginal Self-determination Struggles

Aboriginal peoples of North America have, in recent decades, successfully articulated a discourse of 'self-determination', advocating a commitment on the part of non-Aboriginals to recognize Aboriginal inherent rights to govern ourselves. This discourse of self-determination is similar to that of self-government; however, I see it as having a much broader meaning and intent. Some may use the two terms interchangeably and argue that self-government means an inherent right of

Aboriginal peoples to 'be governed by rules of social, moral, political and cultural behaviour upon which they agree' (McIvor, 1999: 167). However, I tend to agree more with Monture-Angus (1999) and with other Aboriginals who claim that self-government implies a perpetuation of a colonial superior government that still makes the ultimate decisions about the meaning of aboriginal rights and how these are to be implemented. Self-government, then, is viewed by us as a 'limited form of governance' (Monture-Angus, 1999: 29) that maintains unacceptable and unjust colonial relations. Self-determination, on the other hand, holds a better promise for Aboriginal peoples, because it is premised on the notion that our rights to be independent and to determine our own futures were never extinguished. (Monture-Angus, 1999). What we demand is not merely equal opportunity within the mainstream Canadian system, but rather an inherent right of First Nations people to live by our own unique set of values (Schouls, 1992). Some of these different sets of values comprise a distinct definition of government, of land, and of land rights. For native peoples, 'government' constitutes a decision-making system based on consensus and on individuals maintaining significant responsibilities for their behaviour and decisions (Barnaby, 1992). Similarly, Aboriginals have a unique relationship to the land; in fact, this distinctive relationship to creation is reflected in our languages, hence our insistence that our rights to lands be recognized. Ours is a world view that moves far beyond the material utility of natural resources because we view our relationship with animals, plants, water, and all other living things as a very spiritual one. Land rights are, then, very different than proprietary rights. While the latter translates into individual ownership of land and is usually based on a market economy, the former 'needs to be understood in a context of culture and territoriality. . . . Similarly, tribal sovereignty must be understood in its cultural context, one that reflects self-determination and self-sufficiency traditionally predicated on reciprocity' (Jaimes-Guerrero, 1997: 102).

Many Canadians feel threatened by the demands of Aboriginal peoples; some fear they might have to relinquish any privilege they have enjoyed at the expense of Aboriginals' oppression, others feel that Aboriginal self-government may weaken an already shaky Canadian national identity. It is important to note that recognition of Aboriginal sovereignty does not automatically become national independence. As Glenn Morris argues,

> Given the difficult practical political and economic difficulties facing smaller states in the world today, most indigenous peoples may very well not opt for complete independent state status. Many would probably choose some type of autonomy or federation with existing states, preserving rights to internal self-governance and control as members of larger states. (1992: 78–9)

What is crucial here is that it is the choice of Aboriginal peoples to determine which course to take, rather than having one imposed on them, as has been the case with the Canadian state.

As in some other anti-colonial liberation struggles, Aboriginal women have had an important role in the 'national' struggle and their roles have not been free of contradictions and obstacles. Colonization of the Americas ultimately transformed all structures, including Aboriginal gender relations. Prior to this, women in most Aboriginal societies enjoyed a large amount of status and power. The Haudenosaunee (Iroquois, or a more appropriate translation, People of the Longhouse) women, for example, occupied prominent positions in all aspects of indigenous life. Within the laws of the Haudenosaunee people, the Kaianerekowa, known as the Great Law of Peace, it is clearly stated that women choose the Oyaneh (Clan Mothers), who had a large amount of power in each clan, including the power to remove chiefs, to decide on matters of intertribal disputes, and determine distribution of resources (Goodleaf, 1995).

The contact with European societies and the eventual colonization of Aboriginal peoples altered the conditions of Aboriginal women of Canada. As Cora Voyageur argues:

one of the primary reasons for the situation of Indian women today is that Indians, in general, were subjugated by the immigrant European society. . . . The British North American Act of 1867 gave the power of legislative control over Indians and their lands to the federal government. The Indian Act of 1876 consolidate legislation already in place. The measure depriving an Indian woman of her status when she married a non-Indian was first legislated in the 1869 Indian Act. This Act was also the first legislation that officially discriminated against Indian women by assigning them fewer fundamental rights than Indian men. (1996: 100)

Most Aboriginal women point out that, for them, the Canadian law is at the centre of our problems and the patriarchal nature of the Canadian state has different meanings and consequences for Aboriginal women (Monture-Angus, 1995). In order to fully understand how patriarchy works in Canada, we must look at the oppressive role that the Canadian state has had, and continues to have, in the everyday lives of Aboriginal women. Decolonization, therefore, is a necessary step for the full liberation of Aboriginal women, and it is the one point where Aboriginal men and women can come together as united. By 'decolonization' I mean the process by which the longstanding colonial relations between Aboriginals and non-Aboriginals are abolished and new relations formed. These relations will be based on principles of mutual respect, sharing, and recognition of the inherent rights of Aboriginal peoples to follow their traditional ways of governance.

Resorting exclusively to an agenda of decolonization, while simultaneously not integrating women's issues into it, as I have warned earlier, can be 'dangerous' for women. We cannot be certain that the national liberation will automatically translate into a women's liberation. More often than not, failing to combine a gender analysis with an anti-colonial one can only increase the chances that colonized women's lives will not be improved, as the new male leaders will be reluctant to give up any power they have recently gained. As Aboriginal women, we have an awareness of inequalities and injustices we surfer as women as well as Aboriginal peoples. These inequalities may have been created as a result of the colonization of out peoples, but some may have existed in some communities externally to it, and we need to look closer at this possibility. As Emma Laroque states, it is important to remember that:

> Culture is not immutable, and tradition cannot be expected to be always of value or relevant in our times. As Native women, we are faced with the very difficult and painful choices, but nonetheless, we are challenged to change, create, and embrace 'traditions' consistent with contemporary and international human rights standards. (1996: 14)

Canadian Indigenous women have, at times, found themselves in opposition to the male-dominated and federally funded Aboriginal associations. The two important historical moments where we witnessed this dissension between male leaders and female leaders occurred during the amendment of the Indian Act which reinstated Indian status to Aboriginal women who had married non-Indian men, and then later during the Charlottetown Accord talks, when the Native Women's Association of Canada (NWAC) argued that the collective rights of Aboriginal women related to gender equality were not protected and integrated in the Accord. Throughout these moments, the Assembly of First Nations, the main Aboriginal organization recognized and funded by the Canadian state, did not fully support the positions of Aboriginal women as advanced by the Native Women's Association of Canada (NWAC), often arguing that the women's arguments were based upon an individual rights discourse that undermined the struggle of First Nations for self-determination.

This particular way of looking at the dissension between the male-dominated political associations and the Native Women's Association of Canada ignores a critical issue: 'the discursive formation of ethno political identity that emerges as male and female political leaders contest each other's expressed collective aspirations and envisioned future nationhood' (Fiske, 1996: 71). Many Aboriginal women's groups (which do receive support from many traditional men) use a political discourse that looks at the intersection of ethnicity, class and gender and they want to bring back symbols and images that have been part of most Aboriginal traditional cultures. Some of the symbols include that of 'Woman as the heart of the Nation', 'the centre of everything' (Fiske, 1996). What Aboriginal women envision, then, is a feminized nation, where both men and women equally give birth to it, and following a traditional Aboriginal cultural world view, kin ties are 'evoked as symbols of a community and nation: blood and culture, not law, define ethnic identity and citizenship within a nation that nurture and sustains her people' (Fiske, 1996: 76–7). As I expect the word 'blood' to raise many eyebrows, I feel it is important to remark that as my elders and other Aboriginal peoples have told me, many Aboriginal traditional societies were very open to 'adopting' members of other 'tribes' who acquired their culture. At least, that was the case for the Haudenosaunee people. Therefore, it can be clarified that the notion of blood is not as rigid and exclusionary as the one more commonly used by other ethno-nationalist movements. It stands to represent one's affiliation to a clan, and one's membership to it can be obtained either by birth or adoption by the female members of the clan.

For the most part, Aboriginal male-led organizations use a different discourse, one which is masculinist and derived from the same European hegemonic power that they oppose. In this discourse, men are the natural citizens and women, instead, have to be accepted by the men and the Canadian state (Fiske, 1996). This masculinist discourse came into evidence during the proposed amendments to the Indian Act to reinstate women who had lost Indian status into their communities. In a subsequent period, in name of protecting the constitutional 'collective' rights of self-government, Aboriginal male leaders were ignoring the gender relations of power that presently exist in Aboriginal communities. Throughout both these debates, Aboriginal women asked for either re-instatement

or insurance that gender equality for Aboriginal women be protected in the Constitution, Aboriginal women have always argued that, if we truly want to reaffirm our traditional way of life, women's rights are to be considered collective by nature and to be at the core of Aboriginal notions of 'nation.' Moreover, to argue that women's rights (as Aboriginal women) are only individual rights is a colonized way of thinking, because for Aboriginal peoples the individuals are always part of the collective, not outside of, or contrary to it. We must also remember that many of the dividing lines (either of status, reserve residency, blood, or membership to bands) now existing in our communities were not originally drawn by Aboriginals themselves, rather by the Canadian state (Monture-Angus, 1999: 144–5). During our decolonization process, we Aboriginal women must ask the men and the leaders of Aboriginal communities to respect the powerful roles Aboriginal women held and which are part of many traditional laws (e.g., the Kaianerekowa). In doing so, we can then equally walk together towards the same path and have a similar vision, one in which we are, in the words of Sharon McIvor, 'united with our own people, on our own lands, determining our forms of government, deciding rules for membership in our Nations, and deciding who will live on our lands' (1999: 180).

Conclusion

In this paper, I have attempted to illustrate the complexities of the ongoing debate between feminists and nationalists. Throughout, I argue that there is not a single version of either feminism or nationalism and demonstrate that they can be either progressive or reactionary. For the most part, 'Western' feminism has been guilty of excluding, or at least marginalizing, women of colour and Third world women and has only recently begun to integrate issues of race and colonialism in its theories. In the context of Aboriginal women's issues, feminist theories need to look more closely at the issues of land rights, sovereignty, and colonization and the impact this has had on the lives of Aboriginal women. In their critique of nationalism, feminists need to look much deeper at issues of land rights, at the colonial state's erasure of the cultural practices of indigenous peoples, and should not be quick to define Aboriginal women's participation in nationalist struggles as non-feminist and inherently dangerous for women (Jaimes-Guerrero, 1997). However, we Aboriginal women should be also very careful not to prematurely dismiss all of feminist theories. Undoubtedly they have enriched our analyses of power relations, especially of those most directly related to gender. It is also true that many 'mainstream' feminists have attempted to reevaluate their earlier assumptions and are beginning to question their own colonization of 'others'. More importantly, most of the feminist skepticism about nationalisms should be taken seriously. Historically, women's participation on anti-colonial liberation movements has been vital, but has not translated into enduring gains for women in the new nation. There are many nationalisms, and only one that offers women an emancipatory place in all phases of the liberation movement would be the one that I could join. Most importantly, identities which are defined by an ideology of purity of 'race' have the potential to be very oppressive and dangerous, especially for women, since they are seen as bearers of the imagined pure nation. We must also acknowledge that 'tradition' is not static, but is always transformed by people; therefore, postcolonial Aboriginal nations must accommodate differences of experience and let traditional practices meet the continuously changing needs of their members.

Notes

1. I would refer readers to the works of Jayawardena (1986), Charles and Hintjens (1998), Moghadam (1994), and Alexander and Mohanty (1997) for an overview of the mobilization of women in anti-colonial movements.

References

Abdo, Nahla. 1994. 'Nationalism and Feminism: Palestinian Women and the Intifada—No Going Back', in Valerie Moghadam, ed., *Gender and National Identity*. London and New Jersey: Zed Books, 1994.

Alexander, M. Jacqui, and Chandra Talpade Mohanty, eds. 1997. *Feminist Genealogies, Colonial Legacies, Democratic Futures*. London and New York: Routledge.

Alfred, Gerald R. 1995. *Heeding the Voices of our Ancestors: Kahnawake Mohawk Politics and the Rise of Native Nationalism*. Toronto: Oxford University Press.

Anderson, Benedict. 1983. *Imagined Communities: Reflections on the Origin and Spread of Nationalism*. London: Verso.

Barnaby, Joanne. 1992. 'Culture and Sovereignty', in Diane Engelstad and John Bird, eds, *Nation to Nation*. Concord: Anansi.

Bhabha, Homi K. 1994. *The Location of Culture*. London and New York: Routledge.

Charles, Nickie, and Helen Hintjens, eds. 1998. *Gender, Ethnicity and Political Ideologies*. London and New York: Routledge.

Chatterjee, Partha. 1986. *Nationalist Thought and the Colonial World: A Derivative Discourse*. London: Zed Books.

Collins, Patricia Hill. 2000. *Black Feminist Thought: Knowledge, Consciousness, and the Politics of Empowerment*, 2nd edn. London and New York: Routledge.

Enloe, Cynthia. 1993. *The Morning After: Sexual Politics at the End of the Cold War*. Berkeley: University of California Press.

Firestone, Shulamith. 1979. *The Dialectic of Sex*. London: The Women's Press.

Fiske, Jo-Anne. 1996. 'The Woman is to the Nation as the Heart is to the Body', *Studies in Political Economy* 51: 65–89.

Friedan, Betty. 1965. *The Feminine Mystique*. Harmondsworth: Penguin.

Goodleaf, Donna. 1995. *Entering the War Zone*. Penticton, BC: Theytus Books.

Jaimes-Guerrero, Marie Anna. 1997. 'Civil Rights versus Sovereignty: Native American Women in Life and Land Struggles', in M. Jacqui Alexander and Chandra Talpade Mohanty, eds, *Feminist Genealogies, Colonial Legacies, Democratic Futures*. London and New York: Routledge.

Jayawardena, Kumari. 1986. *Feminism and Nationalism in the Third World*. London: Zed Books.

Laroque, Emma. 1996. 'The Colonization of a Native Woman Scholar', in Christine Millet and Patricia Chuchryk, eds, *Women of the First Nations*. Winnipeg: University of Manitoba Press.

McClintock, Anne. 1995. *Imperial Leather*. London and New York: Routledge.

McIvor, Sharon D. 1999. 'Self-Government and Aboriginal Women', in Enakshi Dua and Angela Robertson, eds, *Scratching the Surface: Canadian Anti-Racist Feminist Thought*. Toronto: Women's Press.

Millett, Kate. 1977. *Sexual Politics*. London: Virago.

Moghadam, Valerie. 1994. *Gender and National Identity*. London and New Jersey: Zed Books.

Monture-Angus, Patricia. 1995. *Thunder in My Soul: A Mohawk Woman Speaks*. Halifax: Fernwood Publishing.

Monture-Angus, Patricia. 1999. *Journey Forward: Dreaming First Nations' Independence*. Halifax: Fernwood Publishing.

Morris, Glenn. 1992. 'International Law and Politics', in M. Annette Jaimes, ed., *The State of Native America*. Boston: South End Press.

Schouls, Tim, John Olthuis, and Diane Engelstad. 1992. 'The Basic Dilemma: Sovereignty of Assimilation', in Diane Engelstad and John Bird, eds, *Nation to Nation: Aboriginal Sovereignty and the Future of Canada*. Concord: Anansi Press.

Smith, Anthony. 1986. *The Ethnic Origins of Nations*. Oxford: Basil Blackwell.

Voyageur, Cora J. 1996. 'Contemporary Indian Women', in David Man Long and Olive Patricia Dickason, eds, *Visions of the Heart*. Toronto: Harcourt Brace and Company.

Yuval-Davis, Nira. 1997. *Gender and Nation*. London: Sage Publications.

Part Six

Additional Readings

Alfred, Taiaiake. *Wasáse: Indigenous Pathways of Action and Freedom*. Toronto: Broadview Press, 2005.

———. *Peace, Power, Righteousness: An Indigenous Manifesto*. Don Mills, ON: Oxford University Press, 1999.

———. *Heeding the Voices of Our Ancestors: Kahnawake Mohawk Politics and the Rise of Native Nationalism*. Don Mills, ON: Oxford University Press, 1995.

Barker, Joanne, ed. *Sovereignty Matters: Locations of Contestations and Possibility in Indigenous Struggles for Self-Determination*. Lincoln, NE: University of Nebraska Press, 2005.

Henderson, James (Sákéj) Youngblood. 'Sui Generis and Treaty Citizenship', *Citizenship Studies* 6, 4 (2002): 415–40.

Ivison, Duncan, Paul Patton, and Will Sanders, eds. *Political Theory and the Rights of Indigenous Peoples*. Cambridge: Cambridge University Press, 2000.

Relevant Websites

United Nations Permanent Forum on Indigenous Issues
http://www.un.org/esa/socdev/unpfii/en/about_us.html
This website provides information about the issues faced by Indigenous peoples across the globe.

Defenders of the Land
http://www.defendersoftheland.org/
The Defenders of the Land describe themselves as 'a network of Indigenous communities and activists in land struggle across Canada, including Elders and youth, women and men'. According to their website, the organization 'was founded at a historic meeting in Winnipeg from November 12–14, 2008. Defenders is the only organization of its kind in the territory known as Canada—Indigenous-led, free of government or corporate funding, and dedicated to building a fundamental movement for Indigenous rights.'

Films

Kanehsatake: 270 Years of Resistance. Dir. Alanis Obomsawin. National Film Board of Canada, 1993.
Jidwa:doh—Let's Become Again. Dir. Dawn Martin-Hill. Indigenous Health Research Development Program, 2005.

Our Nationhood. Dir. Alanis Obomsawin. National Film Board of Canada, 2003.

Key Terms

Fourth World
Cartesian dualism
Globalization
Imperialism
Colonial/anticolonial/decolonial nationhood

Nationalism
Nation-state
Sui generis citizenship
Treaty

Discussion Questions

1. In their article Corntassel and Alfred identify different versions of neocolonialism. Trace their discussion of these re-modified forms of colonialism. What do they say about the role of white settlers in the ongoing colonialism?

2. Discuss Sunseri's analysis of feminism and nationalism. How and why has nationalism been critiqued by many feminist scholars? What problems does Sunseri identify in this type of feminist analysis, particularly with respect to Indigenous nationalisms?

3. Simpson's article highlights 'refusal' in ethnography and anthropology. How does she use the concept of 'refusal' in her work, and why does she find it necessary? How is this 'refusal' linked to the 'techniques of knowing' that she discusses earlier in the article?

4. What are the differences between the concepts of 'nation', 'nationalism', and 'nation-state'? Why is it important for many Indigenous scholars and peoples to differentiate between notions of statehood and nationhood?

Activities

Make a list of directions in colonial and anticolonial/decolonial thought and movements as discussed specifically by Corntassel and Alfred, Simpson, and Sunseri. What are the similarities and differences in the various articles? How could these various directions of thought influence our differing experiences of the world, and how could they structure the forms of resistance to colonialism?

Watch the film *Sewatokwa'tsher'at: The Dish with One Spoon* (2008), directed by Dawn Martin-Hill. Discuss the notions of nation and nationalism as presented in the film: what do many white residents in Caledonia imagine Canadian nationalism to be? What kinds of Canadian national narratives inform these white residents' actions? How do you account for the discrepancy between representations of Six Nations' actions on the one hand as peaceful resistance against colonialism, and on the other hand, as terrorist? What role does race play in this discrepancy? How does the film show the connections between colonial concepts of race, entitlement and land?

PART SEVEN

Decolonizing Indigenous Education

On 11 June 2008, the Prime Minister of Canada and three other political leaders stood in the House of Commons and offered a public apology to former students of Indian residential schools. The nation watched and listened as the leaders spoke of religious orders that ran these institutions, the brutality that defined them, and, indeed, Canada itself who funded them. Surrounded by media and religious officials, Indigenous political leaders took turns responding to the apology, each of them recounting its impact on our families and nations. The event itself marked a turning point in Canadian history, one that cannot go unnoticed in the history of racism, education, and colonial reparations.

In Canada, the history of education is rooted in missionary schooling. Early schools were aimed at making all Canadians productive members of an emerging capitalist economy. For Indigenous peoples, this was a particularly violent and disruptive process, involving at times their forcible removal from homes and communities. Pedagogically, our ancestors were subjected to instruction premised on colonial superiority, in turn marking them inferior along with their cultures and knowledges. The history of racism and education is unmistakably linked and inseparable for Indigenous peoples. Ideologies of racism continue, furthermore, to shape modern educational contexts and structure a devastating series of outcomes.

Disparities in educational achievements between Indigenous and non-Indigenous peoples are startling. In 2001, 58 per cent of status Indians aged 20–24 and living on a reserve in Canada did not complete a high school education (Statistics Canada, 2004: 12). This stood in contrast to a mere 15 per cent of non-Indians in precisely the same age category who had less than a high school diploma (ibid.). In terms of postsecondary education, the numbers are equally disturbing. Only two per cent of status Indians aged 25–34 and living on a reserve in Canada held a University degree in 2001, compared to 28 per cent of non-Indians in the same age group (ibid.). It is incumbent upon us as educators and as Indigenous peoples to both reconcile and comprehend these disparities in educational attainment.

A public apology does not, in itself, remedy years of colonial displacement, nor can it undo a century of cognitive, pedagogical, and linguistic supremacy that continues to shape the experience of schooling for us as nations. The modern face of racism no longer rests at the hands of Euro-Christian orders charged with the responsibility of 'civilizing' Indian children. Instead, racism exists each time an Indigenous child is taught a history that neither describes or reflects her experience as an Indigenous person; or conversely, is denied a vocabulary with which to describe and challenge histories of colonization that continue to shape his every-day life. It is precisely these kinds of practices that contribute to educational disparities and to Indigenous peoples being pushed out of institutions of formal learning.

Despite ameliorative efforts, disparities in educational attainment proliferate and appear endemic to Canadian society. The failure to acknowledge and under-stand these matters, including the complexity of challenges facing Indigenous nations in schools needs to be taken seriously. Reparations must start by asking: What is teaching? What is learning? For whom are we teaching and about what? It involves exposing the violence engendered in privileged ways of knowing, includ-ing the assumptions that accrue to individuals and teachers by virtue of whiteness, colonization, gender, and social capital. It also starts by contemplating the past and present as this has impacted, and continues to impact, on our nations.

In this section, we provide a selection of articles written by Indigenous schol-ars about education from past to present. Marie Battiste provides an historical account and context for understanding the conceptual disjuncture between Eurocentric and Indigenous knowledge systems. She uses the phrase 'cognitive imperialism' to describe assimilative processes that sought to reconfigure literacy, individual consciousness, teaching, and learning, as well as the imparting of cul-tural, spiritual, and linguistic knowledge among her own people, the Miqmaw of what is now Eastern Canada. The process she describes redefined notions of lit-eracy, transforming in turn the kinds of knowledge that came to be recognized and valued in education.

The Eurocentricism and epistemological violence discussed by Battiste is one that both structured and informed the pedagogy of residential schools. As Suzanne Fornier and Ernie Crey point out, the purpose of residential schools was premised on saving Indigenous children from their supposed positions of savagery and primi-tiveness. Although the operation of these schools changed hands through the decades, their reliance on a conceptual framework, vision, and praxis aimed at the colonization of Indigenous peoples remained the same. Disparities in education cannot be addressed, nor can education hope to be transformative for Indigenous peoples until these histories are amended.

Decolonizing education requires an understanding of the aspirations, proto-cols, philosophical foundations, and systems of knowledge that reflect Indigenous worldviews. But even these efforts will be complicated by histories of racism and difference making. As Cree/Métis scholar Verna St Denis outlines, culturally rel-evant education is only a partial solution to educational disparities and drop out rates, inadequate on its own for explaining or redressing the status quo of racism and structural inequality. Indeed, it is colonialism and not cultural incommensurability that must be addressed. In order to fully decolonize education, an approach that is centered on Indigenous knowledge as well as anti-racist and anti-colonial pedagogy is required.

Chapter 19

Micmac Literacy and Cognitive Assimilation

Marie Battiste

Literacy is an ambivalent process of modern consciousness. When people refer to the processes of becoming literate in terms of the youth of their own culture, literacy is called cultural transmission. But when a certain literacy is forced upon youths outside that culture, it becomes cultural and cognitive assimilation. The functions of literacy, as a shield in cultural transmission and as a sword of cognitive imperialism, have been hidden by the interactions of the myths and modern conceptions of literacy.

Certain myths have disguised the functions and value of literacy in society (Graff, 1979). Viewed as the benign liberator of the mind, literacy is perceived to be the modernizing agent of society and an economic commodity necessary for national development (Oxenham, 1981). Thus, guided by mistaken assumptions about the desirability and economic effects of literacy, tribal states and underdeveloped nations have instituted policies which have imposed modern values on tribal, preindustrial societies without regard for their language and culture in the hopes of being able to overcome their social, economic, racial, and political impotence.

Modern conceptions of literacy have further disguised its processes because they are fragmented and limited: fragmented by the search among western scholars for normative standards which can be universally applied; and limited by the bias toward instrumental objectives of modern liberal social theory and Western school practices. Literacy, however, is not an all or nothing proposition; its elements cannot be universally applied (Dauzat and Dauzat, 1977: 341; Heath, 1982). Rather, literacy is a relative social concept more reflective of culture and context than of the levels of formal instruction by which it is usually measured. . . .

Recent studies have shown, however, that literacy has not been used in the same way in all cultures, nor have its results been the same (Cole and Scribner, 1978; Clammer, 1976). Yet modern studies have not inquired about how literacy functions outside of Western institutions of learning, and, more importantly, what factors govern its acceptance, rejection, and diffusion. In the last two decades, the consistent failure of the schools to achieve societal literacy suggests that much more is involved than the formal processes taught in schools (Copperman, 1978).

Recent historical comparative and ethnographic studies in different communities reveal that the acquisition and diffusion of literacy are related to a society's perception of literacy's value and function (Spolsky, Englebrecht, and Ortiz, 1982; Walker, 1969, 1981). . . .

The hidden bias of the myths and concepts of literacy became apparent to me in 1975 when my people, the Micmac communities of eastern Canada, had to choose an orthography for use in reserve schools. A practical and efficient writing system, purported to reflect the phonemic system of the Micmac language, was introduced, but it was met with initial resistance. Reasons for community resistance to the new script lay in the sociocultural and historical factors associated with earlier scripts.

The Micmac Indians are an Algonkian-speaking tribe of northeastern America who for over three hundred years have had several different kinds of literacies which have served the social, cultural, and spiritual needs of tribal society. Pictographs, petroglyphs, notched sticks, and wampum were the primary Native texts of Algonkian ideographic literacy. These provide the context for all other kinds of literacies for the Micmac, who have remained faithful to the deep structure of the Micmac literacy and consciousness in the Algonkian traditions. Europeans adapted aboriginal symbols and designs found on earlier Native texts and developed hieroglyphic characters which were used for teaching prayers. These modified Algonkian hieroglyphics remain the essence of Micmac literacy, even though four roman scripts have also been developed to serve different purposes of European missionaries, Canadian governments, and Native groups over the last 250 years. The forceful attempt to create English literacy in Micmac society has created transitional problems of cognitive incoherence and cultural ambiguity. These problems raise important questions concerning the doctrine and actual functions of modern literacy in tribal society.

The Context of Aboriginal Literacy

Through the use of pictographs, petroglyphs, notched sticks, and wampum, early North American Indians achieved a form of written communication and recording which served the social, political, cultural, and spiritual needs of the early period, fully describing the ideal and material world. Aboriginal literacy embodied tribal epistemology in Native texts, which interacted with and depended upon the oral tradition. . . .

The various Native texts in tribal North America represented the worldview of tribal people, particularly their ideas and beliefs about knowledge, power, and medicine. These Native texts represented another form of knowledge that has since been eradicated from western thought. A fundamental element in tribal epistemology lay in two traditional knowledge sources:

1. from the immediate world of personal and tribal experiences, that is, one's perceptions, thoughts, and memories which included one's shared experiences with others; and
2. from the spiritual world evidenced through dreams, visions, and signs which were often interpreted with the aid of medicine men or elders.

. . . Native texts appear to have served both a public and private function. Wampum was the public record, maintained by a wampum keeper or tribal historian. The wampum—strings and belts of tubular shells—was regularly brought forward at ceremonial gatherings. Political records of treaties and presents, represented through conventional symbols, were woven with shells into strings or belts. The arrangement of shells in relation to colour conveyed knowledge and an attitude: for example, white shells represented peace and friendship, and purple shells represented war and death. . . .

Pictographs, petroglyphs, and notched sticks served more diversified, principally personal, uses. The Algonkian Indians used them to communicate information and messages to friends and relatives about their whereabouts or of routes and directions taken, to relate stories, to enlist warriors into battle, or to tell of herbal cures (Brinton, [1884] 1969: 217). . . .

Algonkian Indians were known to have also used pictographs and petroglyphs for communicating with the spirit world or for conveying individual visions and experiences with the spirit world (Robertson, 1973). The petroglyphs incised on birchbark scrolls of the *Midewiwin* or Grand Medicine society are an example of the written spiritual literacy among the Algonkian nations (Eliade, 1964: 314ff).[1] . . .

Through the use of symbolic literacy, the Algonkian nations, including the Micmac, achieved a form of written communication and recording which served their social, political, cultural, and spiritual needs. . . .

In symbolic literacy, reason was the awareness of a highly concrete ideal implicit in the reality of nature. It knew no distinction between *is* and *ought* or between theory and practice. Individual consciousness tended, faithfully, to reflect the collective culture, and obedience to the spiritual soul was obedience to the tribal society.

Micmacs had no need for authoritative or recorded human opinion since each person determined what was wisdom. Likewise, Micmac society had no need for elite scholars or experts: the most principled and persuasive speakers became leaders of the tribe because they expressed and lived Micmac ideals of the Good.

The Myth of the Illiterate Savage

Most of the aboriginal literacies of America were destroyed or transformed or neglected by Euro-Christian travellers and missionaries. Some of the neglect stemmed from ethnocentrism and from the mistaken belief that Indians were not capable of writing. In 1580, Montaigne spoke of the Tupi-Guarani of Brazil as 'so new and infantile, that he is yet to learn his A.B.C.' (Montaigne, 1580: 141). But when Europeans did encounter undeniable evidence of writing, of literacy equivalent to their own, they did their best to eradicate it as if it posed

a threat to the Scripture or literacies they brought with them, as for example, in the situation of the Toltec and Mayan parchment or paper books.

The lack of Western knowledge of the continent and its people, the nature of American Indian literacies, and the lack of European understanding of symbolic literacy were also threats to Native culture. The interaction of these factors created the myth that the Natives were illiterate savages who possessed only an oral tradition. This myth justified the need to teach them European literacy and knowledge. . . . Micmac experience with the Christian immigrants slowly fragmented the unity of consciousness of their symbolic system.

The tradition of aboriginal epistemology and symbolic literacy of the Natives were barely noted in the written observations of the Europeans. In 1497, John Cabot's exploration uncovered 'fallen trees bearing marks' which caught his attention (*Collections*, 1897). In 1652, Father Gabriel Druilletes reported the Algonkian Indians using coal for pen, bark for paper, and writing with peculiar characters. He noted: 'They use certain marks, according to their ideas as a local memory to recollect the points, articles, and maxims which they heard' (Ganong, 1910: 22). In 1653, Father Bressani reported Indians of New France using 'little sticks instead of books, which they sometimes mark with certain signs. . . . By the aid of these they can repeat the names of a hundred or more presents, the decisions adopted in councils and a thousand other particulars' (Ganong, 1910: 23). Few of the early travellers understood the significance of the symbolic literacy or its legacy because of the myth of the illiterate savage. . . .

It has always been difficult for Micmacs to accept the romantic humanitarian image of the righteous immigrant who laboured selflessly for mankind to spread Christianity and culture to the nonliterate Natives. . . . Both religious and governmental authorities have manipulated the nature of Micmac society and literacy to the Natives' psychological and economic detriment. The development of the myth of the illiterate savage was instrumental in denying them human dignity, respect, or entitlement to their wealth.

However, neither the myth of the illiterate savage nor the image of the Christian as a moral hero deceived Micmac leaders. Europeans boasted about their homeland and culture and condemned those of the Micmac, but Micmacs rejected their pretence since the conflict between European pretences and conduct was apparent (Thwaites, 1897; Mealing, 1963: 29–30). Critical reflection on secular European thought followed the same wisdom. Micmac society was an affluent and literate society comparable to European society. Micmac life was not 'nasty, brutish or short' as it was stereotyped; instead it was comfortable and ecologically stable, with great diversity of food and a steadier balance between humans and the natural environment. Micmac education was a vital part of ecological life; it was not an imagined preparation for the utility of aristocratic society. . . .

As Micmacs witnessed the puzzling dichotomy between Christian theology and conduct, they attempted to reconcile why the actions of the Christians revealed that which its teaching sought to prevent. As a consequence, the force of theology diminished in tribal society. But the best of the teachings became synthesized into broader aboriginal ideals. At the same time, the myth of the illiterate savage predominated in European thought. It dramatized the world vision and historical sense of colonialization, while ignoring centuries of aboriginal civilization. It justified the transformation of wealth and power through violence and oppression. It became the mythogenesis of Canada.

Literacy as Cognitive Assimilation

In 1610, Chief Membertou and 140 Micmacs voluntarily entered into a spiritual and political alliance with France in a ceremony which included baptism and a gift of wampum.[2] From that time to the French and English uprising in 1744, French Catholic missionaries lived and worked among Micmacs of eastern Canada, converting them to Catholicism and to a faith which blended well with the Micmacs' tribal spiritual rituals. The missionaries' continued presence among Micmacs

also assured the King of France of the Micmacs continued political and economic alliance. Missionaries learned the Native language, preaching to them about the road to salvation and teaching them the prayers which were to pave that road. The first use of ideographic symbolization for literary purposes is attributed to Father Christian Le Clerq, who in 1677 incorporated the Biblical ideals into the existing symbolic literacy of the Micmac which he called a 'formulary'. . . .

By incorporating the Catholic rituals into the existing symbolic literacy and the oral traditions, the Micmac families rapidly diffused this system throughout the nation within the traditional social and cultural contexts. Father taught son, mother taught daughter, and children taught each other. . . .

In 1735, Father Pierre Antoine Maillard began a twenty-seven year mission among Micmacs of Cape Breton Island, during which he expanded hieroglyphic literacy and contributed to the transformation of ideographic literacy to roman script. . . .

Unlike Le Clerq, who frequently characterized Micmacs as savages and barbarians incapable of advancing to letter literacy, Maillard perceived them as curious and intelligent people, capable of learning anything they wanted to earn. He was frequently challenged by their enquiring minds. He astutely realized that if Micmacs learned to write French, they would have access to sensitive political and religious literature. Maillard, a political activist in the French and English war, feared that if Micmacs knew how to read and write letters, they would be better able to incite each other through their correspondence, to the detriment of French Catholic interests. Despite the fact that Maillard had developed a roman script for the Micmac language, which he used for his own language and grammar improvement, he chose to teach them only the hieroglyphics. . . .

The similarity of spiritual function between Catholic priests and medicine people ensured the success of collective dialogues among the families. Medicine people had specialized knowledge of reading and writing the sacred symbols on birchbark which for centuries catalogued the proper rituals and chants for various spiritual functions. The priest and his reliance on the Bible was analogous to the Micmac traditions. The apprenticing of young men to the medicine society was a long and rigorous training involving the learning of symbols, chants, and rituals, and the nature of the interaction with the spirit world. As spiritual intermediaries, the medicine people aided tribal members in achieving a personal and direct interaction and communion with the spirits. From these quests came wisdom, knowledge, guidance, and a special place in the world. . . .

European theology and languages, which were familiar to the tribal worlds of the Micmacs, gave no hint of their latent use as instruments of domination and empire in European thought. . . . The negative mythical depiction of Micmac society, knowledge, and values became the justification for civilizing the Micmac and confiscating their wealth. While operating in the same manner described in other colonial situations, it took several centuries for the English grammar and literacy to become instruments of domination of the Micmac mind (Memmi, 1965: 79–89).

Despite Maillard's and earlier missionaries' attempts to restrict Micmacs to hieroglyphic literacy, Micmac ingenuity prevailed, and soon the Indians acquainted themselves with yet another mode of communicating with one another: alphabetic scripts. . . . Aiding in the pacification of Micmacs after 1744, he transcribed the Treaty of 1752 into his Micmac roman script. Maillard sought their approval of the peace plan. As a trusted friend of the Micmac Santewi Mawio'mi, or Grand Council, Maillard presided at the ceremony and read the treaty to the assembled Indians. Through these exchanges, the Micmacs discovered the political significance of expanding their literacy repertoire. Furthermore, they were very impressed with the new mode of writing that enabled them to record the words and thoughts of the writer exactly (Maillard, 1963). Yet, Maillard refused to teach them alphabetic script and further forbade Micmacs from going to local English public schools (Koren, 1962).

The English government sought literacy and education for Micmacs as the sword of assimilation. A century later, in 1842, the Nova Scotian government passed an act which provided for free tuition for Micmacs attending their schools; however, Micmacs were interested neither in having their children educated by others nor in the functions of English literacy. Government reports beginning in 1843 indicated Micmacs' growing interest in learning to read, although they were strongly adamant to transmit only their own culture through literacy in Micmac. The Micmacs' migratory lifestyle further prevented them from spending much time in school; thus literacy was taught at home by parents (Department of Indian Affairs, 1843–73).

By the time Reverend Silas Tertius Rand arrived among the Micmacs in 1845, they had already learned the fundamentals of how to read and write Micmac in the French roman script. . . . He frequently criticized the French priests who, in seeking to prevent Micmacs from learning how to read and write letters, forbade them to go to school (Koren, 1962). . . .

Hoping to show Micmacs the contradictions in Catholic dogma, Rand translated several sections from the Bible into Micmac and developed a Micmac dictionary and reading book. However, despite the courtesy Micmacs extended to Rand, neither he nor the Canadian government were able to dissuade Micmacs from their traditional habits and Catholic beliefs. Repeated governmental attempts to introduce Protestantism, Bible reading, and formal schooling into Micmac tribal society failed. But despite their refusal to accept the Protestant literature, Micmac literacy skills continued to grow through Rand's influence. Rand reported being pleased with the number of Micmacs who had learned to read (Rand, 1873).

Micmacs became consumers of English- and colonial-made goods and vices, partly to convince the British that they were not different from them and they therefore need not be feared or oppressed. But the Micmac never cognitively assimilated English knowledge or values. They did not forget the tribal knowledge, history, or language, nor did they change their tribal rituals or lifestyle. Micmac society continually rejected the English language, the Protestant worldview, and its individualist society as demonic in nature. . . .

Experience had taught the Micmac that assimilation to colonial life did not advance their interest. The colonist in Canada would not permit them to acquire any of their confiscated wealth or enforce their legal rights. Despite numerous petitions to the Queen, the Governor General, and the Legislative Assemblies, the colonial system denied equal rights or opportunity for Micmacs. The Micmacs' civilized efforts to use roman script to petition the legal authorities to return their wealth were met with disdain and neglect.

English Language Education as Cognitive Imperialism

Micmac literacy was at its height in 1920 when Canadian governmental policy instituted English language in all Indian day schools and compulsory schooling for all Indian children from the ages of six to sixteen years. Both the Nova Scotia government and the federal government had found that their efforts from 1800 to 1920 to attract Micmacs to the White man's habits and to domesticated farming had been repeatedly rejected in favour of symbolic literacy and a traditional lifestyle. . . .

Through the *Indian Act* of 1920, the Canadian parliament expanded its control over Indian lands and people by legislating regulatory provisions for Indian affairs. The administration of all schools for Indians was assumed by the Department of Indian Affairs, although some schools continued to be staffed by religious orders. In some communities, religious orders introduced Micmac literacy in the reserve day schools, using Pacifique's system for teaching the fundamentals of Catholic doctrines (Bock, 1966). However, the Canadian government considered these schools ineffective (Department of Indian Affairs, 1927). 'Effectiveness' of Indian schools was determined by their ability to transform the Indian. The commissioner of Indian affairs stated that the goal of federal education for

Indians was 'to give the rising generation of Indians such training as will make them loyal citizens of Canada and enable them to compete with their white neighbors' (Department of Indian Affairs, 1918: 23).

In 1930, the opening of residential boarding schools and the increased age for compulsory schooling to eighteen years led to a gradual decline in Micmac literacy. . . .

The Shubenacadie residential school in Nova Scotia became a nightmare which continued into the middle of the 1950s. Perhaps the most traumatic effect of the residential school was not its language restriction but its destruction of the tribal family cohesion and its replacement with peer group allegiance. . . .

The implicit goal of federal education was the annihilation of Micmac history, knowledge, language, and collective habits, thereby making Micmac youths believe that Anglo-Canadian society was culturally and technically superior to Micmac society. Catholic residential day schools based their curriculum on teaching Micmacs to reject their traditional cultural ways in favour of the life of the individual in the dominant Canadian society. Inherent in this policy was the destruction of tribal identity and values along with the tribal soul. This educational process is called cognitive imperialism, the last stage of imperialism wherein the imperialist seeks to whitewash the tribal mind and soul and to create doubt.

The displacement of a tribal worldview was justified by governmental interests. The gift of modern knowledge has been labeled the 'banking' concept (Freire, 1971). It views the students' minds as 'containers' to be filled by teachers, thus allowing the imposition of one world view over another, sometimes with a velvet glove. Knowledge is considered as

a gift bestowed by those who consider themselves knowledgeable upon those who they consider to know nothing. Projecting an absolute ignorance onto others, a characteristic of the ideology of oppression, negates education and knowledge as processes of inquiry. The teacher presents himself to his students as their necessary opposite; by considering their ignorance absolute, he justifies his own existence. . . . Indeed, the interests of the oppressors lie in changing the consciousness of the oppressed, not the situation which oppresses them. (Freire, 1971: 58–62)

Into the late 1960s, federal policy continued its destruction of tribal language and culture. . . .No respect was accorded the Native languages or culture and the use of the Micmac language became a badge of servitude in Canadian society. Federal education, as the tool of cognitive imperialism, rejected Micmac knowledge, history, spirituality, culture, and language in their mission to create a Canadian individual. Justified by the myth of the illiterate savage, Canadian educators divided ideas, reordered events, and wrote fictitious accounts of past events.

The 1971 Subcommittee on Indian Education for the Standing Committee on Indian Affairs and Northern Development found that federal, provincial, and church schools alike had failed to educate Indian children (Department of Indian Affairs, 1971). Their report laid the foundation for Indian control of education, but while these efforts have ended some of the drastic unilateral measures of the DIA, no real Indian control exists in education (*Indian Self-Government*, 1983).

Revival of a Fragmented Micmac Language

The initiation of Cultural Education Centres was the federal government's antidote to their attempts at destroying the cultural base. Based on the French language model of Quebec, Native Cultural Centres were established to support Native communities' efforts at developing culturally responsive educational materials. . . .

In 1974, the Micmac Association of Cultural Studies, serving the Nova Scotia Micmac communities, developed their own script with the help of Native and non-Native linguists. . . .

By the beginning of the 1980s, four different roman scripts existed, each having its proponents. Because each programme had its script preference and had operated independently, duplication of efforts and lack of resource sharing has resulted in a general lack of sequential literacy materials among all groups and a lack of consensus over which script to use for educational purposes. Meanwhile, through 1979, high dropout rates and recidivism continued to characterize Indian education (*Survey*, 1979).

The Charter of Rights and Freedoms in the *Constitution Act, 1982*, affirmed the rights of minority children to be educated in their own language. The charter cannot be interpreted so as to limit any of the aboriginal or treaty rights of Canada's Native peoples (section 25) and must be interpreted in a manner consistent with the presentation and enhancement of the multicultural heritage of Canadians (section 27). Thus, guarantees were affirmed of 'customary right or privilege' acquired or enjoyed before the charter, especially for aboriginal people (section 22). While no new funding has been provided by Parliament for implementation, the guarantee of customary language rights of the aboriginal peoples is an important affirmation to help the Micmac people 'preserve their culture and identity, their customs, tradition and languages' (*The Constitution and You*, 1982: 28).

Conclusion

. . . Western sequential literacy has not erased Native symbolic literacy and consciousness, which has been developed over millennia. Symbolic literacy still affects the Micmac mind, soul, and conduct.

Just as symbolic literacy continues, so have coercive methods of cultural and cognitive assimilation continued in Western liberal education and literacy. Despite good intentions, the seemingly innocuous textbooks continue the mythical portrait of Micmacs and their society, when mentioned at all. Canadian history remains a fictitious history, a by-product of nineteenth-century European society, and the Micmacs and other tribal nations are merely bystanders in the flow and flux of European and Canadian history. . . . Micmac language is the least valued by educators despite the fact it sustains the feeling, emotions, and dreams of most Micmac youth and preserves the ancient ancestry. This psychological and cultural regime is substantially the same in provincial, federal, and most band-controlled schools. . . .

A contemporary assessment of Micmac education suggests the need for the continued development of traditional and contemporary functions of literacy and knowledge. Although the forms of literacy to which the Micmacs have been exposed have been intrinsically different, the symbolic literacy and its consciousness have persisted. Micmac literacy remains spiritual and family-based rather than public. It continues to favour collective dialogue and ritual. . . .

Coercive methods of cultural assimilation through education and literacy must now be replaced with a Micmac education of cultural transmission and development of cultural adaptive strategies founded upon a choice of systems and knowledge. Bilingual, bicultural education must be the foundation upon which different knowledge bases and cultural processes are met with respect and chosen according to family preference.

Notes

1. See also Norman Feder, *American Indian Art* (New York: Abrahams, 1965), item 218, for an illustration of a section of the *Midewiwin* birchbark text of an initiation into the society. The illustration describes a certain stage or house, the knowledge totem, and how to set up and perform the ritual.
2. For an exact replica of this wampum belt, see Plate 1 in David I. Bushnell, 'Native Cemeteries and Forms of Burial East of the Mississippi', *Bulletin 71* (Washington, DC: Bureau of Ethnology, 1920).

References

Bock, Philip. 1966. *The Micmac Indians of Restigouche*. Bulletin nno. 213, Anthropological Series 77. Ottawa: National Museum of Manitoba.

Brinton, D.G. [1884] 1969. *The Lenape and Their Legends with the Complete Text and Symbols of the Walam Olum*. New York: AMS Press.

Clammer, J.R. 1976. *Literacy and Social Change*. Leiden: E.J. Brill.

Cole, Michael, and Sylvia Scribner. 1978. 'Literacy without Schooling: Testing for Intellectual Effects', *Harvard Educational Review* 40 (4): 448–61.

Collections and Proceedings. 1897. Second Series, vol. 8. Portland: Maine Historical Society.

Copperman, Paul. 1978. *The Literacy Hoax*. New York: William Morrow and Company.

Dauzat, Sam, and Joann Dauzat. 1977. 'Literacy: In Quest of a Definition', *Convergence* 10 (1): 341.

Department of Indian Affairs [DIA]. 1843–73. *Annual Reports* [AR].

Department of Indian Affairs. 1918. *Annual Reports* [AR].

Department of Indian Affairs. 1927. *Annual Reports* [AR].

Department of Indian Affairs. 1971. *Subcommittee on Indian Education*. Ottawa: DIA.

Eliade, Mircea. 1964. Shamanism: *Archaic Techniques of Ecstasy*. Princeton: Princeton University Press.

Freire, Paulo. 1971. *Pedagogy of the Oppressed*. New York: Herder and Herder.

Ganong, William, ed. and trans. 1910. *New Relations of Gaspesia*. Toronto: The Champlain Society.

Graff, Harvey. 1979. 'The Literacy Myth: Literacy and Social Structure in the Nineteenth Century'. PhD diss., University of Toronto.

Heath, Shirley Brice. 1982. 'Protean Shapes in Literacy Events: Evershifting Oral and Literate Functions' pp. 91–117 in Deborah Tannen, ed., *Spoken and Written Language: Exploring Orality and Literacy*. Norwood, NJ: Ablex Publishing.

Indian Self-Government in Canada. 1983. Report of the Special Committee to the House of Commons, Ottawa.

Koren, Henry. 1962. *Knaves or Knights: A History of the Spiritan Missionaries in Acadia and North America 1732–1839*. Pittsburgh: Duquesne University Press.

Maillard, Antoine Pierre. 1963. 'Lettre de M. L'Abbé Maillard sur les Missions de l'Acadie et Particulièrement sur les Missions Micmaques', *Soirées Canadiennes* 3: 291–426.

Mealing, R.S. 1963. *The Jesuit Relations and Allied Documents*, Toronto: McClelland and Stewart.

Memmi, Albert. 1965. *The Colonizer and the Colonized*. Boston: Beacon Press.

Montaigne. 1580. *Essayes*, Florio's translation, vol. 3. Paris.

Oxenham, John. 1981. *Literacy: Writing, Reading and Social Organization*. London: Routledge and Kegan Paul.

Rand, Silas Tertius. 1873. *A Short Statement of the Lord's Work among the Micmac Indians*. Halifax: W. MacNab.

Robertson, Marion. 1973. *Rock Drawings of the Micmac Indians*. Halifax: Nova Scotia Museum.

Spolsky, Bernard, Guillermina Englebrecht, and Leroy Ortiz. 1982. *The Sociolinguistics of Literacy: An Historical and*

Comparative Study of Five Cases. Final Report on Grant #NIE-G-79-0179. Washington: National Institute of Education.

Survey of Indian Education 1971–1979. 1979. Union of Nova Scotia Indians. Dalhousie University: School of Public Affairs.

The Constitution and You. 1982. Ottawa.

Thwaites, Reuben Gold, ed. *The Jesuit Relations and Allied Documents*, vol. 3. Cleveland.

Walker, William. 1969. 'Notes on Native Writing Systems and the Design of Native Literacy Programs', *Anthropological Linguistics* 2 (5).

Walker, William. 1981. 'Native American Writing Systems', in Charles Ferguson and Shierly Brice Heath, eds, *Language in the U.S.A.* Cambridge: Cambridge University Press.

Chapter 20

'Killing the Indian in the Child': Four Centuries of Church-Run Schools

Suzanne Fournier and Ernie Crey

Emily Rice's introduction to residential school will be etched on her soul for the rest of her life. Raised on a lush British Columbia Gulf Island replete with wild deer, gardens, and orchards and surrounded by straits that ran silver with salmon and herring, Rice spoke little English at the age of eight when she was told the priest was coming to take her to boarding school. . . .

'Our Alcatraz', as survivors would later call the Kuper Island residential school, was just across the channel from the Vancouver Island town of Chemainus. The huge brick building, which towered over the island's only wharf, was operated from 1906 to 1978 by two Catholic orders, first the Montfort Fathers and then the Oblates of Mary Immaculate. . . .

By the time Emily Rice left Kuper Island in 1959, at the age of 11, she had been repeatedly assaulted and sexually abused by Father Jackson and three other priests, one of whom plied her

with alcohol before raping her. A nun, Sister Mary Margaret, known for peeping at the girls in the shower and grabbing their breasts, was infuriated when Emily resisted her advances. 'She took a big stick with bark on it, and rammed it right inside my vagina,' recalls Rice. 'She told me to say I'd fallen on the stick and that she was just trying to get it out.' The girl crawled into the infirmary the next day, too afraid to name the perpetrator. . . .

The stories of residential school survivors like Emily Rice began to slowly make their way into mainstream Canadian consciousness in the early 1980s. The schools' destruction of the lives of Indian children, in stark contrast to their supposed purpose of 'saving' pagan youth from their parents' uncivilized fate, was known before that time to many Canadians who could have stopped it. . . . The schools persisted as 'internment camps for Indian children' for well over a century, ultimately affecting virtually every Aboriginal community in

Canada. The death toll, excessive discipline, and overall educational failure of the schools—well-known to any Indian Affairs bureaucrat who possessed a critical mind or a conscience—also leaked out frequently into the public eye, through the news media of the day or in the House of Commons. Aboriginal parents sometimes contacted journalists or politicians when their pleas to have their children better treated or returned home fell on deaf ears. In 1907, both the *Montreal Star* and *Saturday Night* reported on a medical inspection of the schools that found Aboriginal children were dying in astonishing numbers. The magazine called the 24 per cent national death rate of Aboriginal children in the schools (42 per cent counting the children who died at home, where many were sent when they became critically ill), 'a situation disgraceful to the country', and concluded, 'Even war seldom shows as large a percentage of fatalities as does the educational system we have imposed upon our Indian wards.' . . . The cumulative onslaught of criticism did little to deter Canada's complicity with the churches in obscuring the schools' failures until well into the 1960s.

Residential schooling reached its peak in 1931 with over 80 schools across Canada. From the mid-1800s to the 1970s, up to a third of all Aboriginal children were confined to the schools, many for the majority of their childhoods. The explicit mandate of the residential schools, throughout the lengthy partnership between the Canadian government and the churches who were responsible for operating them, was described succinctly by one federal bureaucrat: 'To obtain entire possession of all Indian children after they attain to the age of seven or eight years and keep them at the schools.'

Nowhere in Canada was the instrument of the residential school used more brutally and thoroughly than in British Columbia, where despite relatively late settlement by Europeans, the schools endured longer than anywhere else. The Anglican and United Churches, along with several Roman Catholic orders, divided up the province, which contained the largest population of Aboriginal people in Canada, into small religious fiefdoms. . . .

The seeds of a national system of institutions for Indian children were sown at the earliest contact between white Europeans and Aboriginal people in North America. . . . The Recollets were replaced by the Jesuits, the intellectual elite of European religious orders, who were better educated, more numerous and eager to try their hand with the 'savages' of the New World.

After decades of unrewarding toil with the downtrodden European underclasses, the Jesuits were entranced by the prospect of converting robust young Aboriginal children into francized Christians who might, through intermarriage, improve the class of French settlers in the new country. . . .

When the practice of removing Aboriginal children to France proved to be an abject failure—those children who did not die became neither miniature Frenchmen nor Christian proselytizers—the Jesuits moved to establish boarding schools in the new colony. They attempted at first to separate the children from their parents, so as not to be 'annoyed and distracted by the fathers while instructing the children'. But as their boarding schools stood empty, the priests tried siting schools closer to Aboriginal villages. They soon found, however, as Father Lejeune reported, that the influence of the priests paled beside that of the children's families: 'We could not retain the little Savages, if they be not removed from their native country, or if they have not some companions who help them to remain of their own free will . . . when the savages were encamped near us, our [sic] children no longer belonged to us.' . . .

It was their powerful cultural and spiritual traditions, founded on seemingly immutable bonds between children and extended families, that enabled Aboriginal nations to hold their ground in these early encounters with Europeans. The initial period of contact represented a profound clash of cultures, and nowhere can that conflict be seen more starkly than in the radically opposed attitudes towards childhood. . . .

The European cultural inverted pyramid, in direct contrast to Aboriginal cultures, was based on 'the profound oppression of women in society at large', Conrad points out. As women were devalued, so were children; they were the chattels of a patriarch. . . .

Although European religious orders were concerned with converting the 'pagans' right from the time of their arrival, direct intervention by colonial governments in the lives of Aboriginal people did not begin in earnest until British hegemony was established in 1812. . . .

By the 1820s, the new government of early Canada found itself pressured by a flood of British homesteaders who demanded the Indians be somehow neutralized or removed from the land. This political and economic imperative was a direct motivation for the colonial government's support of religious-run boarding schools for Indian children. . . . In 1846, the government resolved at a meeting in Orillia, Ontario to fully commit itself to Indian residential schools. Thus the interests of church and state merged in a marriage of convenience that was to endure more than a century: the churches could harvest souls at government-funded schools while meeting the shared mandate to eradicate all that was Indian in the children. The 'Indian problem' would cease to exist.

The major denominations had already carved up the country among themselves, with Catholics, Anglicans, and Methodists launching schools for Indian children as far west as Manitoba and Alberta. . . .

The churches soon received even more official support. With Confederation in 1867, the new national government was charged under the British North America Act with constitutional responsibility for Indian education. . . . As the local hand controlling the government purse strings, the Indian agent could threaten to withhold money from increasingly destitute Aboriginal parents if they did not send their children away to school; he could even throw them in jail.

Aboriginal leaders were not uninterested in educating their children for the emerging white man's world. They could see their destiny as a subjugated people if they did not adjust. Chief Paulus Claus of the Bay of Quinte Mohawks had told the government in 1846 that he viewed the supposed

'great cause of Indian improvement' as 'our only hope to prevent our race from perishing and to enable us to stand on the same ground as the white man'. Other leaders, weary of being displaced and dispossessed of their land, also regarded the education of their young as inevitable, and even desirable. . . . Day schools near Aboriginal children's homes were eliminated once it was determined they were unsuited to the primary *raison d'être* of Indian education. Institutions far from the reserves could completely remove Indian children from their 'evil surroundings' in favour of having them 'kept constantly within the circle of civilized conditions', as Regina MP Nicholas Flood Davin urged in a report to the federal government in 1879.

For a model of institutional care for Indians, the fledgling Canadian government looked with interest to the south, where the United States was establishing a system of industrial boarding schools in the wake of a long and bloody conquest of American Indian tribes by the US Army. The prototype of an Indian school there actually had its origins in a prison for 'pacified' Indians commanded by Lt Richard Henry Pratt. The US government embraced Pratt's methods and endorsed the evolution of American Indian policy from its guiding principle, 'The only good Indian is a dead Indian,' to Pratt's watchword: 'Kill the Indian in him and save the man.' Pratt established the Carlisle Indian School in Pennsylvania in 1878 with backing from the federal Bureau of Indian Affairs, which swiftly set up more 'industrial' schools offering meagre academics, augmented by agriculture and trades instruction for the boys and domestic training for the girls, sufficient to equip a servant class.

The American system was heartily recommended to the government of John A. Macdonald by backbencher Nicholas Flood Davin in the 1879 report. It was accepted that the Christian obligation to Indians could be discharged 'only through the medium of children'. The well-being of First Nations left bereft of their children was not addressed. Adults could not be rescued from 'their present state of ignorance, superstition and helplessness', as they were 'physically, mentally and morally . . . unfitted to bear such a complete metamorphosis'. Pragmatically, Indian Affairs bureaucrats advised Macdonald, the schools were 'a good investment' to prevent Indian children from becoming 'an undesirable and often dangerous element in society'.

By 1896, the Canadian government was funding 45 church-run residential schools across Canada. Almost a quarter of these were located in British Columbia. In any given year, as many as 1,500 children from virtually every one of BC's First Nations were interned in these schools. In addition to St Mary's Mission, the Roman Catholic Church operated schools at Kuper Island, North Vancouver, Lower Post on the BC–Yukon border, Kamloops, Christie on northern Vancouver Island, Sechelt, Lejac in northern BC, Cranbrook and Williams Lake. The Church of England, later the Anglican Church, operated three schools, the first in the model Indian village at Metlakatla, then St George's at Lytton and one at Alert Bay, while the Methodist Church, later the United Church, ran schools in northwest BC at Port Simpson and Kitimat, Coqualeetza school in the Fraser Valley, and two schools in Nuu-chah-nulth territory on Vancouver Island: the Alberni Indian Residential School and another further north at Ahousaht.

In persuading Indian parents to send their children to these schools, authorities were assisted by a growing famine in Indian villages in western Canada. In this environment of hunger, amid recurring outbreaks of smallpox and influenza, the government withheld food rations from parents who resisted the removal of their children. Indian agents marched in lockstep with the religious orders, preparing lists of children to be taken from the reserves and then organizing the fall roundup. Strapping young farm boys, aided by RCMP officers, herded the children onto buckboard trucks or trains like cattle.

Official policy called for children to be isolated not only from their family and homelands but also, once at school, from their friends and siblings. Isolation made children more vulnerable to the massive brainwashing that was undertaken to replace their 'pagan superstitions' with Christianity,

and their 'free and easy mode of life' with relentless labour and routine. . . . As soon as children entered school, their traditional long hair was shorn or shaved off; they were assigned a number and an English name and warned not to let a word of their language pass their lips.

Aboriginal parents were not complacent once their children were installed in the schools, even though their letters were censored and their visits, even by the few who could afford to make them, were discouraged. . . . Resistance among Indian parents manifested itself all across Canada and took many forms, from the withholding of children despite threatened sanctions to petitions, visits, and outright threats of violence. But despite these and other early signs of trouble, the Department of Indian Affairs continued to defend the boarding schools, declaring they were succeeding in 'the emancipation of the Indian from his inherent superstition and gross ignorance'.

References

Adams, David Wallace. 1995. *Education for Extinction: American Indians and the Boarding School Experience 1873–1928.* Lawrence, KS: University Press of Kansas.

Anderson, Karen. 1991. *Chain Her by One Foot: The Subjugation of Native Women in Seventeenth-Century New France.* New York: Routledge.

Assembly of First Nations. 1994. *Breaking the Silence: An Interpretive Study of Residential School Impact and Healing as Illustrated by the Stories of First Nations Individuals.* Ottawa: Assembly of First Nations.

Barman, Jean. 1991. *The West Beyond the West: A History of British Columbia.* Toronto: University of Toronto Press.

Barman, Jean, Yvonne Hebert, and Don McCaskill, eds. 1986–87. *Indian Education in Canada:* Vol. 1, *The Legacy,* and Vol. 2, *The Challenge.* Vancouver: University of British Columbia Press.

Berger, Thomas R. 1991. *A Long and Terrible Shadow: White Values, Native Rights in the Americas 1492–1992.* Vancouver: Douglas & McIntyre.

Choquette, Robert. 1995. *The Oblate Assault on Canada's Northwest.* Ottawa: University of Ottawa Press.

Fisher, Robin. 1977. *Contact & Conflict: Indian-European Relations in British Columbia, 1774–1890.* Vancouver: University of British Columbia Press.

Furniss, Elizabeth. 1992. *Victims of Benevolence: The Dark Legacy of the Williams Lake Residential School.* Vancouver: Arsenal Pulp Press.

Grant, Agnes. 1996. *No End of Grief: Indian Residential Schools in Canada*. Winnipeg: Pemmican Publications Inc.

Hyman, Irwin A. 1990. *Reading, Writing and the Hickory Stick: The Appalling Story of Physical and Psychological Abuse in American Schools*. Lexington, MA: Lexington Books.

Jaine, Linda, ed. 1993. *Residential Schools: The Stolen Years*. Saskatoon: University Extension Press.

Knockwood, Isabelle. 1992. *Out of the Depths: The Experiences of Mi'kmaw Children at the Indian Residential School in Shubenacadie, Nova Scotia*. Lockport, NS: Roseway Publishing.

Kuper Island Industrial School: Conduct Books, Daily Diaries, Attendance Records. 1891–1907. Victoria, BC. Provincial Archives, Dept. of Indian Affairs and Northern Development.

Looking Forward, Looking Back, Vol. 1, Report of the Royal Commission on Aboriginal Peoples. 1996. Ottawa: Canada Communication Group.

Miller, J.R. 1996. *Shingwauk's Vision: A History of Native Residential Schools*. Toronto: University of Toronto Press.

Nuu-chah-nulth Tribal Council. 1996. *Indian Residential Schools: The Nuu-chah-nulth Experience*. Port Alberni, BC: Nuu-chah-nulth Tribal Council.

Titley, E. Brian. 1986. *A Narrow Vision: Duncan Campbell Scott and the Administration of Indian Affairs in Canada*. Vancouver: University of British Columbia Press.

Trigger, Bruce G. 1995. 'Champlain Judged by His Indian Policy: A Different View of Early Canadian History', in Olive P. Dickason, ed., *The Native Imprint: The Contribution of First Peoples to Canada's Character*. Athabasca: Athabasca University Educational Enterprises.

Chapter 21

Rethinking Culture Theory in Aboriginal Education

Verna St Denis

Will teaching Native culture remedy the many wounds of oppression? (Hermes, 2005: 23)

Introduction

. . . When racialized conflict between Aboriginal and white Canadians erupts in a way that makes it clear that collective action is required, more often than not, what is recommended is not anti-racism education but cross-cultural awareness or race-relations training for the primarily 'white' service providers, including police officers, social workers, and teachers. Usually the recommended cross-cultural awareness or race-relations training does not include a critical race theory analysis that might explore 'how a regime of white supremacy and its subordination of people of color have been created and maintained' (Ladson-Billings, 1999: 14). Rather than acknowledging the need for a critical examination of how and why race matters in our society, it is often suggested that it is Aboriginal people and their culture that must be explained to and understood by those in position of racial dominance. A recent example is the Stonechild Inquiry that recommends race-relations training that will include 'information about Aboriginal culture, history, societal and family structures' (Wright, 2004: 213).

This chapter explores how the culture concept and the discipline of anthropology came to occupy such an important role in the conceptualizing and theorizing in the lives of Aboriginal people and especially in Aboriginal education. This knowledge is important because of the effects that the culture concept and discipline has had on the capacity for defining and suggesting solutions to Aboriginal educational problems. For example, in both explaining and seeking solutions to low achievement and high dropout rates for Aboriginal students, the call is usually made for 'culturally relevant' education rather than the need for a critical race and class analysis. This chapter will suggest that a cultural framework of analysis is partial and inadequate on its own for explaining Aboriginal educational failures and that culturally based solutions can inadvertently contribute to further problems.

Current concepts of Aboriginal education and the sub-discipline of educational anthropology evolved during the same time period and are as related as are anthropologists and Indians in North America. As has been observed, the discipline of anthropology was 'invented across the "red/white" color line' (Michaelson, 1999: xvi). Both Aboriginal and American-Indian educators have acknowledged the predominance of the culture concept and anthropology in Aboriginal and American-Indian education. In a review of literature on American-Indian education, Deyhle and Swisher (1997: 117) observed that, 'over the past 30 years, we found that the largest body of research was grounded in educational anthropology and sociology'. Furthermore they state that this research 'used the concept of culture as a framework for the analysis of schooling and the behaviour of Indian students, parents and their communities' (ibid.).

In the 1960s much of the educational anthropology literature suggested that racialized minority children failed in school because their cultural beliefs and practices predisposed them to failure, and they were, therefore, described as being 'culturally deprived' or even 'deviant' (McDermott, 1997). In the 1970s some adjustments were made to the cultural framework for analyzing educational failure, suggesting that it was not so much that some children were culturally deprived or culturally disadvantaged but that their way of life was merely 'culturally different'—not better or worse than that valued by schools, but definitely different (McDermott, 1997). The subsequent educational interventions suggested that cultural differences needed to be celebrated rather than eradicated. This shift in emphasis was meant to advantage Aboriginal and American-Indian children whose culture would now be celebrated and observed through research that would focus on learning styles and acculturation processes.

This shift towards prescribing the celebration of cultural difference as a means to bring about educational equality provided a foundation for the growing focus on the importance and necessity of cultural and language revitalization for Aboriginal students. American-Indian educators and researchers Tippeconnic and Swisher note that, 'beginning in the 1960s and into the 70s a revival of "Indianness" in the classroom was now encouraged' (1992: 75). In a Canadian review of policy on Aboriginal education, Abele, Dittburner, and Graham also explain that between 1967 and 1982 Aboriginal education was increasingly regarded as a 'means for the revitalization of Indian cultures and economies' (2000: 8).

As part of this cultural revitalization, the provision of culturally relevant education assumed great importance for improving the educational success of Aboriginal students, and the health and well-being of Aboriginal communities in general. This shift to regarding education as the means to revitalize Aboriginal culture and language is often attributed to processes of decolonization and, in Canada, to the policy outlined in 'Indian Control of Indian Education' (National Indian Brotherhood, 1972). The idea that culture and language could be revitalized, and that Aboriginal people needed a 'positive' cultural identity as a prerequisite to success in education and in life more generally, can also be understood to be derivative of anthropological concepts and theorizing.

In writing this chapter, I have been informed by my own experiences and professional knowledge as an Aboriginal teacher and educator. By the time I arrived on campus as a university student in the late 1970s, the move towards decolonizing education by Aboriginal people in Canada was already moving forward with the adoption of the policy position outlined in 'Indian Control of Indian Education' (National Indian Brotherhood, 1972). With the recognition of this policy came the establishment of Indian cultural centres, Indian Teacher Education programs, cultural survival schools, and Indian and Native Studies departments across the country (Posluns, 2007). It was a very exciting time for us Aboriginal students since we could now pursue specialized studies in Aboriginal education and Native Studies.

In 1978 I enrolled in the Indian Teacher Education Program at the University of Saskatchewan. I was going to become an 'Indian' teacher. I was younger than most students in the program at that time, and, although both my parents had spoken Cree, I myself was not fluent in Cree. Indian Teacher Education programs were at the forefront in calling for the cultural and language revitalization of Indian cultures, and Indian teachers were to play a significant role in this revitalization. In this educational context I sensed I was in trouble— I was well aware that my lack of fluency in my indigenous language placed me at a disadvantage. The analysis offered here in this chapter is one attempt to make sense of this 'trouble'.

I didn't realize back then the role that anthropological concepts and theory had in the formulations of Aboriginal education through notions like 'cultural discontinuity', 'cultural relevance', 'cultural difference', and 'acculturation/enculturation'. As a student and teacher of Aboriginal education and Native Studies, I never imagined that studying anthropology and its concepts would be useful in

unravelling some of the ways in which we interpret the problems and solutions we have named and pursued in Aboriginal education.

Although I have now been involved in Aboriginal education for almost three decades, it is only in the past decade that I realized I needed to know more about anthropology. I had avoided learning about anthropology partly because anthropology and history were two mainstream disciplines that Native Studies and Aboriginal education had rallied against in the 1970s and 1980s. I regarded the discipline of anthropology, as some in the late 1960s referred to it, as the 'child of colonialism' (Cough, in Caulfield 1969: 182) and therefore not worthy of attention. It was Rosaldo's *Culture and Truth: The Remaking of Social Analysis* (1989) that introduced me to a critique of classic notions in anthropology. Reading this book marked the beginning of my efforts to develop an understanding of how anthropologically informed social analysis has impacted the development of Aboriginal education. This chapter offers an analysis of how those of us in Aboriginal education have been historically and discursively constituted within and by anthropological theory and research.

I began to understand that the social and cultural analysis prevalent when I first enrolled in the Indian Teacher Education Program was informed not only by 'Indian philosophy and worldview' but also by the social and cultural analysis practised by American anthropologists who combined psychology and anthropology through their focus on culture and personality and acculturation studies. The culture and personality movement and acculturation studies inspired psychologists and anthropologists who were interested in cross-cultural education, and who contributed to the development of educational anthropology. In turn, the social and cultural analysis offered by scholars of educational anthropology influenced the conceptualizing of Aboriginal/Indian education. As someone who has been involved in Aboriginal/Indian education for almost 30 years, I find there is still much to learn about this legacy of anthropological ideas, concepts, problems, and solutions that helped to shape Indian education.

European Philosophical and Intellectual Legacies

> Culture is . . . itself the illness to which it proposes a cure. (Eagleton, 2000: 31)

. . . Efforts to develop a history of the culture concept invariably requires attempts to make sense of the relationships between the varied usages of the concepts of 'culture' and 'civilization', and 'Romanticism' and 'Primitivism' within European thought and social practice. . . .

Both Romanticism and Primitivism have influenced our understanding of 'culture' and 'civilization' through articulations of self and Other. Scholarly writing about the history of the development of modern notions of culture is often situated within histories of Romanticism, if not Primitivism. Although Romanticism and Primitivism are two different social and intellectual developments, there is some overlap and similarities between these two schools of thought. And although neither Romanticism nor Primitivism has been consistently or constantly invoked in European imagination and fantasies of the Other, one of their recurring and enduring emphases is a valorization of the Other, as a way to critique and register dissatisfaction with European society (Stocking, 1986). . . .

Herder conceptualized 'culture' as the 'uniquely distinct' way of life, values, and beliefs of a people; culture was what distinguished one people from another (1774: 44f.). . . .

Herder's conceptualization of 'culture' has lent itself to a belief in 'cultural essentialism' and 'cultural determinism' that is elaborated upon in Boasian anthropology. . . . It suggests an essential culture that is able to exist in the realm of the spiritual.

Herder also signalled language as important to the delineation of a nation, because within language dwells a people's 'entire world of tradition, history, religion, principles of existence; its whole heart and soul' (Herder, in Malik, 1996: 78–9). This idea that the culture of a people is invoked through its language and stories is further developed in the efforts made in Aboriginal education to participate in cultural and language revitalization, as it was also an idea brewing within anthropological studies of culture and personality and acculturation.

Another of Herder's beliefs was in the 'incommensurability of the values of different cultures and societies' (Malik, 1996: 78). . . .

This idea of the incommensurability of different cultures would eventually propel and motivate anthropology's interest in what makes people different. The idea would lend itself not only to an exaggeration of human difference but also a negative evaluation of these differences, making possible notions like folks who suffer, not from colonial oppression but, from 'cultural incongruence', and 'cultural discontinuity', both of which were seen as tangible threats to cultural self-preservation despite whatever cultural exchanges and accommodations have been made by cultural Others (Biolsi, 1997).

The idea of the 'incommensurability' of cultures led anthropologists in search of 'an Indian culture incommensurably alien from [their own]' (Biolsi, 1997: 140)—in other words, the search for the 'real' Indian (Biolsi, 1997; Waldram, 2004). The belief in twentieth-century social analysis about the incommensurability of different cultures encourages a trivializing of the impact of colonial oppression by attributing the effects and the conditions of oppression to this very factor of incommensurability. In the example of Aboriginal people, effects of oppression are cast as 'value conflicts' between white and Indian cultures, suggesting that inequality is inevitable, and merely an effect of different orientations to work, education, and family. When the affects of oppression are attributed to a 'conflict of values' it is easy to see how the remedy then becomes cross-cultural awareness training or a 'race'-relations program that does not disrupt the status quo of structural inequality while seemingly responding.

Understanding American Anthropological Legacies

. . .Through concepts like 'enculturation', this idea of a culture as a conditioning process became a central concept in educational anthropology, and suggested research into the 'enculturation processes' of culturally different students, families, and communities. In addition, this idea that culture is a conditioning process implied that it is not people who create culture through the conditions of their everyday lives, but rather 'culture' that creates people. It is as if culture is an object with its own agency divorced from people. This objectification of culture also suggests that culture is something to be 'lost' and 'found'. It is as if people are no longer agents; culture happens to them. A notion like 'cultural determinism' then becomes possible. Cultural determinism has been used to justify racism; hence the notion of 'cultural racism' (Hall, 1982; Gilroy, 1990) that becomes another way to justify discrimination. . . .

This idea of culture as an entity outside of people provides a foundation for the belief in the potential for 'cultural revitalization' and the very idea that culture can be retrieved. While the idea that culture resides deep inside one's 'core' may be reassuring in the early stages of an engagement with cultural revitalization, when that 'traditional' culture fails to appear or reveal itself, it can be very troubling. This failure of culture to appear becomes a very different kind of problem. It is a problem long familiar to those anthropologists who have been keenly interested in 'authentic' and 'real' Indians or the 'primitive', and for whom evidence of 'cultural change' would suggest otherwise, namely that culture is mutable.

Many have critiqued anthropologists' interest and fetishization of the most exotic and primitive Other (e.g., Biolsi, 1997; Caulfield, 1969; Deloria, 1969; Rosaldo, 1989). The implications for regarding cultural change as a threat and as a negative process continue to have repercussions for 'Others' such as Aboriginal people. . . .

Not only was cultural change regarded as dangerous for the 'primitive' Other, but 'rapid' cultural change was regarded as even more detrimental. Culture was something primitive people 'had', and it was understood that 'primitive' people needed culture more than 'civilized' people did. . . .

Educational anthropology would embrace the above ideas and to a large degree so would Aboriginal education. This conceptualization has resulted in that claim that it is 'cultural discontinuity' between the school and the Aboriginal family and community and the inability of Aboriginal students to make adequate cultural adjustments that causes high levels of school failure for Aboriginal students despite evidence that racism and classism are equally, if not more compelling reasons for these levels of school failure (Ledlow, 1992). Culturally relevant education, rather than anti-oppressive education, has become a common-sense solution. As well, the idea that 'primitives' learn less by instruction than by imitation led to research focusing on understanding different 'learning styles' and with the effect of creating a new set of stereotypes about the nature of Aboriginal learning styles. . . .

This method of anthropological social analysis, exemplified by Benedict and Mead, compared and contrasted cultures as a whole and paved the way for cross-cultural comparisons that continue to remain popular in educational research. In particular, this method has been used as a way of explaining the low academic achievement of Aboriginal students. . . .

Acculturation studies . . . promoted ideas that the retention of 'indigenous belief systems' was essential for Indians to adequately adjust to rapid social change (Waldram, 2004). Anthropologists were often not interested in documenting the creative and successful ways in which Indians were making cultural adaptations to their continually changing environments (Deloria, 1969). This was especially the case if anthropologists were particularly interested in finding the most 'incommensurable' and exotic Indian (Biolsi, 1997). Further advancing the belief that culture was a 'cure', studies of acculturation, such as those conducted among the Hopi, claimed that 'Personality disorders and social breakdown characterize Hopi communities that have lost their values and their ceremonies' (Thompson, 1946: 210, in Waldram, 2004: 37). This idea that Indian culture is 'lost' and that Indians have lost their culture is a deceptively benign but very common way to refer to the effects of colonial and racial oppression on Aboriginal people. In acculturation studies, suggesting that 'maintaining essential, internal cultural integrity' (Thompson, 1950, in Waldram, 2004: 35) is necessary for exploited and colonized people, has become a popular and common way to blame the victim of oppression.

The problem of inequality is now attributed to the Indian who does not have 'cultural integrity' rather than the social, economic, and political context that does not recognize the human rights of Aboriginal people. Acculturation, and culture and Personality studies, contributed to reducing the effects of colonial and racial oppression to a problem of an identity crisis. Restoring the Indian has become the imperative rather than ensuring social and political justice. The anthropological interest in a timeless and unchanging cultural Indian demeans Aboriginal and American-Indian Peoples who have had to constantly adjust to and live with the context of ongoing and normalized racism. . . . The idea that cultural adaptation is regarded as 'broken' relegates Indians as interesting to the degree that they can serve as windows to the past, ignoring the effects of colonization by aiming to celebrate and recoup as much 'traditional' culture as possible.

As many have stated, Boas and his many students 'never showed any real interest in studying the situation of conquest and exploitation' (Caulfield, 1969: 184, italics in original). This failure by the anthropology of that time to explore the consequences and situation of exploitation continued to have repercussions for at least the early years in the development of Aboriginal education by and for Aboriginal people rather than examining the situation of conquest and exploitation, anthropologists like Benedict were more interested in bringing attention to 'the desperate urgency of doing anthropological field work before the last precious and irretrievable memories

of traditional American Indian cultures were carried to the grave' (Mead, 197: 3). . . . Here we have an anthropology that cared more about 'Indian culture' than the people of that culture, yet another example of the belief in a culture as something outside and existing independently of its people.

This background knowledge of anthropology provides a basis to better understand the published conference proceedings of the first conference of educational anthropology. That conference helped initiate the field of Educational Anthropology, which has had its own set of implications for Aboriginal education.

The Legacy of Educational Anthropology

. . . In 1954, the anthropologist George Spindler hosted a conference that brought together several educators and anthropologists; among them were anthropologists Margaret Mead, Alfred Kroeber, and Cora DuBois. Several papers were presented, along with remarks by formal discussants; conference proceedings were published in the book *Education and Anthropology* (Spindler, 1955a) and later republished in the edited collection, *Education and Culture: Anthropological Approaches* (Spindler, 1963). . . .

Some of the many concepts utilized in the papers and the discussions that followed included ones familiar to those who work in the area of Aboriginal education, including: cultural transmission; enculturation; acculturation; cultural awareness; bicultural, monocultural, and intercultural learners; cultural gap; and cultural discontinuity.

Conference participants acknowledged that the discipline of psychology made it possible to combine educational and anthropological interests (Frank, 1955). Participants agreed that exploring cultural processes of socialization was one way in which anthropology could contribute to education. Socialization processes were understood to vary from culture to culture, and it was those 'differences' that could form the basis of investigation in developing educational anthropology. Building on acculturation and personality studies in anthropology, educational anthropology would also explore processes of cultural change, cultural adaptation, and cultural continuity. Knowledge of socialization practices and processes could, in turn, help educators and schools assist culturally different students adjust to change. . . .

This idea that schools and education are the site for cultural continuity and cultural transmission has become accepted wisdom in Aboriginal education (see, e.g., Royal Commission on Aboriginal Peoples, 1996). Through the conceptual framework of educational anthropology, schools are increasingly instructed to become a place where 'culturally relevant' education should occur so as to ensure cultural continuity and cultural transmission for the Aboriginal child. But in light of massive cultural change in regards to how Aboriginal people live, the task of providing culturally relevant education can prove to be perplexing and challenging for the well-intentioned Aboriginal teacher who asks, 'what is it exactly that you want to be taught in the classroom, the parents say let's teach culture in a classroom, but they don't come out and say what they mean by culture' (Friesen and Orr, 1995: 22). In the context of ongoing cultural change, this line of questioning remains relevant, but it is also the legacy of an anthropology that was once intent on 'reconstructing traditional culture' (Asad, in Stocking, 1991: 318).

By combining psychology and anthropology, the field of educational anthropology would pursue investigations that would seek to explain the impact of differences between the cultural values and beliefs of the culturally different child and the teacher. . . . It was proposed that this cultural knowledge could help teachers understand how 'imitation, participation, communication, and informal methods' socialize members into one's culture, as well as how 'cultural motivation incentives, values and school learning' are related (Quillen, 1955: 3).

Four decades later, this theorizing about difference has, more often than not, resulted in the production of stereotypes and classist and racist constructions of the culturally different child (Laroque, 1991; Razack, 1998). This anthropo-logical orientation to understanding 'difference' is now used to endorse the current demand that human service providers be 'culturally competent' in their delivery of services. Without examining the impact of racism and classism, this requirement for cultural competency has the potential to repeat stereotypes of Aboriginal people rather than focusing on how racial dominance and poverty continue to detrimentally impact Aboriginal people (Razack, 1998; Schick and St. Denis, 2005). . . .

There is no single straightforward trajectory to understanding how, when, and why the concept of culture, as opposed to the need for social and political justice, has come to occupy such a large role in articulating Aboriginal education. . . .

The politics of this articulation of culture as a concept associated with the Other, and the nation as a concept associated with the civilized person, has a long history, not only in anthropology but, in Western and European thinking, in general. It is not common for those in a position of racial dominance to risk relativizing their own way of life by describing it as a 'culture': as Eagleton puts it, 'One's own way of life is simply human; it is other people who are ethnic, idiosyncratic, culturally peculiar' (2000: 27). . . .

A review of literature reveals that teachers often have low expectations of Aboriginal and American-Indian students (Ambler, 1997; Delpit, 1995; Flail, 1993; Strong, 1998; Tirado, 2001; Wilson, 1991). Low expectations justify the lack of instruction and attention to Aboriginal students. Tirado (2001) found that teachers have a tendency to size up American-Indian students as underachievers; they don't expect the kids to do anything, so they don't teach them. Wilson found that 'even before teachers knew the [Aboriginal] students, they prejudged them. They could not have imagined that these students would ever be successful. Students were classified as unable to cope with a heavy academic load' (1991: 379). As a result, Aboriginal students are often placed disproportionately in vocational or special needs classes (Wilson, 1991). Rather than encouraging an examination of the ways in which class and racial bias impact educational processes, the legacy of the 1954 conference of anthropologists and educators has resulted in a large body of educational research primarily interested in 'culture' as the explanatory concept for understanding how the culturally Other would or would not adjust to school. . . .

The idea that the cultural Other is not able to make cultural adjustments without a great deal of trauma is an idea that continues to have a negative effect on discussions of how to improve educational achievement for Aboriginal students. To a large extent these discussions tend to promote a stereotyped idea of the Aboriginal student as vulnerable and non-resilient and enables the avoidance of addressing the far more difficult questions of racism and classism in education. . . .

This idea of the Aboriginal cultural Other as unwilling and unable to adapt to changing social, economic, and political contexts is a long entrenched assumption that justifies oppression and inequality. For example, Sarah Carter (1986, 1996), a prairie Canadian historian, challenges the taken-for-granted assumption that Aboriginal people were unwilling and unable to adapt to a farming-based economy. Carter uncovers the extent to which white settlers and the Canadian government colluded to ensure that Aboriginal farmers failed at farming. The introduction of the pass and permit system prevented Aboriginal farmers from succeeding by limiting their ability to purchase farm machinery, limiting what produce they could grow, and limiting when and where they could sell their produce.

The All Hallows School in British Columbia, a boarding school attended by both Aboriginal and white girls between 1884 and 1920, described in the work of Barman (1986), provides another historical and educational example of unwarranted assumptions about Aboriginal people unwilling and unable to adapt to change. The establishment of the All Hallows School was a case in which Aboriginal parents welcomed change and the opportunity to adjust to a changing world by requesting that a school be established for their girls.

Because of inadequate financial resources, the All Hallows School could only function if white girls were allowed to attend alongside Indian girls. In the first years of the school, the Indian and white girls seemed content with their integrated schooling situation. Then a white parent protested about this integrated situation, so the effort was made to separate the white and Indian girls. But in his annual report, the bishop in charge of the school commented that the Indian girls were as intellectually capable as the white girls, claiming that at times the Indian girls had 'the answers all respects being equal, and sometimes superior, to anything that could be expected from white children of the same age' (Barman, 1986: 117). Not only did the Indian girls achieve academically, but they also could from time to time serve as junior teachers, and their ability to learn the practices of another culture was demonstrated in two Indian girls, who alongside eight white girls passed the Royal Academy of Music exam.

These Indian girls did not seem to suffer any crisis due to the culture difference between the school and their home and community. When the Indian girls returned home for holidays and summer vacation, they often freely maintained contact with the teachers through letters. At least for one Indian girl, the only source of cultural conflict involved the dilemma of attending a potlatch even though it was 'forbidden by law' (Barman, 1986: 118). In a letter to the sisters at the school, this student tried to persuade them that the potlatch is not something they should be afraid of because it is just 'our way of praying' (Barman, 1986: 119).

Eventually the Indian and white girls were physically separated, although still offered equally challenging academic programs. But then the curriculum for the Indian girls shifted from a full academic program to one that included teaching them how to weave baskets. Finally, a shift in government policy lead to closing the school, a policy change justified by a larger concern that it was unwise to offer Indians an education that would allow them 'to compete industrially with our people' (Minister of Indian Affairs, 1897, in Barman, 1986: 120). Throughout the proceeding decades, Aboriginal people continued to be denied the high-quality education for which First Nations treaty negotiators assumed they had signed on. The inability of an anthropology and, in turn, an educational anthropology to acknowledge the effects of 'conquest and exploitation' of the cultural Other continues to reverberate.

As Biolsi (1997) explains, anthropologists such as those present at the time of that 1954 conference were typically not interested in Indians who accepted that change was inevitable. As a result, these examples of Indian farmers and the All Hallows School would not have drawn their attention. Not only were anthropologists not interested in Indians wanting to figure out how to adapt to the changing world around them, but anthropologists also typically maligned these Indians for not being 'real' Indians (Biolsi, 1997; Waldram, 2004).

Conclusion

> More powerful than their knowledge of cultural difference is their knowledge of the big picture— the context of socio-economic and cultural oppression of Native Americans. (Hermes, 2005: 21)

We started out a few decades ago in Aboriginal education believing that we could address the effects of racialization and colonization by affirming and validating the cultural traditions and heritage of Aboriginal peoples. There is increasing evidence that those efforts have limitations. As I have argued elsewhere, cultural revitalization encourages misdiagnoses of the problem (St. Denis, 2004). It places far too much responsibility on the marginalized and oppressed to change yet again, and once again lets those in positions of dominance off the hook for being accountable for ongoing discrimination. It is to the advantage of the status quo to have Aboriginal people preoccupied with matters of authenticity. If cultural authenticity is the problem then we don't have to look at what is the immensely more difficult task of challenging the conscious and unconscious ways in which the ideology of white identity as superior is normalized and naturalized in our schools and nation, both in the past and in the present (Francis, 1997; Willinsky, 1998).

Instead of doing anti-racism education that explores why and how race matters, we can end up doing cross-cultural awareness training that often has the effect of encouraging the belief that the cultural difference of the Aboriginal 'Other' is the problem. Offering cultural awareness workshops can also provide another opportunity for non-Aboriginals to resent and resist Aboriginal people. Offering cultural awareness education has become the mainstream thinking about proper solutions to educational and social inequality. In her research exploring the qualities of effective teachers of American Indians, Hermes, an American-Indian educator, found that 'more powerful than [teachers'] knowledge of cultural difference is their knowledge of the big picture— the context of socioeconomic and cultural oppression of Native Americans' (2005: 21). We often hear that addressing racism or doing anti-racism education is too negative and that we need to focus on a more positive approach. However, that often means tinkering with the status quo. As Kaomea suggests, when schools offer benign lessons in Hawaiian arts, crafts, and values, this approach tends to erase Hawaiian suffering, hardship, and oppression. 'It is time to tell more uncomfortable stories' (Kaomea, 2003: 23).

References

Abele, F., C. Dittburner, and K.A. Graham. 2000. *Towards a Shared Understanding in the Policy Discussion about Aboriginal Education*, pp. 3–24 in M.B. Castellano, L. Davis, and L. Lahache, eds, *Aboriginal Education: Fulfilling the Promise*. Vancouver and Toronto: University of British Columbia Press.

Ambler, M. 1997. 'Without Racism: Indian Students Could Be Both Indian and Students', *Tribal College Journal* 8 (4): 8–11. Available at http://www.tribalcollegejournal.org/themag/backissues/spring97/spring97ee.html; accessed 8 October 2002.

Barman, J. 1986. 'Separate and Unequal: Indian and White Girls at All Hallows School, 1884–1920', in J. Barman, Y. Hebert, and D. McCaskill, eds, *Indian Education in Canada*, Volume 1: The Legacy. Vancouver: University of British Columbia Press.

Biolsi, T. 1997. 'The Anthropological Construction of "Indians": Haviland Scudder Mekeel and the Search for the Primitive in Lakota Country', pp. 133–59 in Thomas Biolsi and L.J. Zimmerman, eds, *Indians and Anthropologists: Vine Deloria Jr. and the Critique of Anthropology*. Tucson: University of Arizona Press.

Carter, S. 1986. ' "We Must Farm to Enable Us to Live": The Plains Cree and Agriculture to 1900', pp. 444–70 in R.B. Morrison and C.R. Wilson, eds, *Native Peoples: The Canadian Experience*. Toronto: McClelland and Stewart.

Carter, S. 1996. 'First Nations Women in Prairie Canada in the Early Reserve Years, the 1870s to the 1920s: A Preliminary Inquiry', pp. 51–75 in C. Miller and P. Chuchryk, eds, *Women of the First Nations: Power, Wisdom, and Strength*. Winnipeg: University of Manitoba Press.

Caulfield, M.D. 1969. 'Culture and Imperialism: Proposing a New Dialectic', pp. 182–212 in D. Hymes, ed., *Reinventing Anthropology*. New York: Pantheon Books.

Deloria, V., Jr. 1969/1988. *Custer Died for Your Sins: An Indian Manifesto*. Norman, OK: University of Oklahoma Press.

Delpit, L. 1995. *Educating Other People's Children: Cultural Conflict in the Classroom*. New York: New Press.

Deyhle, D. 1992. 'Constructing Failure and Maintaining Cultural Identity: Navajo and Ute School Leavers', *Journal of American Indian Education* 31: 24–47.

Deyhle, D., and K. Swisher. 1997. 'Research in American Indian and Alaska Native Education: From Assimilation to Self-determination', *Educational Review* 22: 113–94.

Eagleton, T. 2000. *The Idea of Culture*. Oxford: Blackwell Manifestos.

Francis, D. 1997. *National Dreams: Myth, Memory and Canadian History*. Vancouver: Arsenal Pulp Press.

Frank, L.K. 1955. 'Preface', in Spindler (1955a: vii–xi).

Friesen, D.W., and J. Orr. 1995. 'Northern Aboriginal Teachers' Voices'. Unpublished manuscript, University of Regina, Saskatchewan.

Hall, J.L. 1993. 'What Can We Expect from Minority Students?', *Contemporary Education* 64 (3): 180–2.

Herder, J.G. 1774/1967. *Another Philosophy of History Concerning the Development of Mankind. Translation of Auch eine Philosophie der Geschichte zur Bildung der Menschheit*. Frankfurt am Main: Suhrkamp.

Hermes, M. 2005. 'Complicating Discontinuity: What about Poverty?', *Curriculum Inquiry* 35 (1): 9–26.

Kaomea, J. 2003. 'Reading Erasures and Making the Familiar Strange: Defamiliarizing Methods for Research in Formerly Colonized and Historically Oppressed Communities', *Educational Researcher* 32 (2): 14–25.

Ladson-Billings, G. 1999. 'Just What Is Critical Race Theory, and What's It Doing in a Nice Field like Education?', pp. 7–30 in L. Parker, D. Deyhle, and S. Villenas, eds, *Race Is . . . Race Isn't: Critical Race Theory and Qualitative Studies in Education*. Boulder, CO: Westview Press.

Larocque, E. 1991. 'Racism Runs through Canadian Society', pp. 73–6 in O. McKague, ed., *Racism in Canada*. Saskatoon: Fifth House.

Ledlow, S. 1992. 'Is Cultural Discontinuity an Adequate Explanation for Dropping Out?', *Journal of American Indian Education* 31: 21–36.

McDermott, R.P. 1997. 'Achieving School Failure, 1972–1997', pp. 110–35 in G. Spindler, ed., *Education and Cultural Process: Anthropological Approaches*, 3rd edn. Prospect Heights, IL: Waveland Press.

Malik, K. 1996. *The Meaning of Race: Race, History and Culture in Western Society*. New York: New York University Press.

Mead, M. 1974. *Ruth Benedict: A Humanist in Anthropology*. New York: Columbia University Press.

Michaelson, S. 1999. *The Limits of Multiculturalism: Interrogating the Origins of American Anthropology*. Minneapolis: University of Minnesota Press.

National Indian Brotherhood. 1972. 'Indian Control of Indian Education'. Ottawa: National Indian Brotherhood.

Posluns, M. 2007. *Speaking with Authority: The Emergence of the Vocabulary of First Nations' Self-Government*. New York: Routledge.

Quillen, J.I. 1955. 'An Introduction to Anthropology and Education', in Spindler (1955a: 1–4).

Razack, S. 1998. *Looking White People in the Eye: Race, Class and Gender in the Courtrooms and the Classrooms*. Toronto: University of Toronto Press.

Rosaldo, R. 1989. *Culture and Truth: The Remaking of Social Analysis*. Boston: Beacon Press.

Royal Commission on Aboriginal Peoples. 1996. *Report on the Royal Commission on Aboriginal Peoples*. 5 vols. Ottawa: Canada Communications Group.

Schick, C., and V. St. Denis. 2005. 'Troubling National Discourses in Anti-racist Curricular Planning', *Canadian Journal of Education* 28 (3): 295–317.

Spindler, G. 1955a. *Education and Anthropology*. Stanford: Stanford University Press.

———. 1955b. 'Anthropology and Education: An Overview', in Spindler (1955a: 5–22).

———. 1963. *Education and Culture: Anthropological Approaches*. New York: Holt, Rinehart and Winston.

St. Denis, V. 2004. 'Real Indians: Cultural Revitalization and Fundamentalism in Aboriginal Education', pp. 35–47 in C. Schick, J. Jaffe, and A. Watkinson, eds. *Contesting Fundamentalisms*. Halifax, NS: Fernwood.

Stocking, G.W., Jr. 1986. 'Essays on Culture and Personality', pp. 3–12 in Stocking, ed., *History of Anthropology Vol. 4. Malinowski, Rivers, Benedict and Others: Essays on Culture and Personality*. Madison: University of Wisconsin Press.

Strong, W.C. 1998. 'Low Expectations by Teachers within an Academic Context' Paper presented at the Annual Meeting of the American Educational Research Association San Diego, CA. (ERIC Document Research Service No. ED 420 62)

Tippeconnic, J.W., III, and K. Swisher. 1992. 'American Indian Education', pp. 75–8 in M.C. Alkin, ed., *Encyclopedia of Education Research*. New York: MacMillan.

Tirado, M. 2001. 'Left Behind: Are Public Schools Failing Indian Kids?', *American Indian Report* 17: 12–15. Available at Wilson Web. Accessed 9 October 2002.

Troulliet, M.R. 1991. 'Anthropology and the Savage Slot: The Poetics and Politics of Otherness', pp. 17–44 in R.G. Fox, ed., *Recapturing anthropology: Working in the Present.* Santa Fe, NM: School of American Press.

Waldram, J. 2004. *Revenge of the Windigo: The Construction of the Mind and Mental Health of North American Aboriginal Peoples.* Toronto: University of Toronto Press.

Willinsky, John. 1998. *Learning to Divide the World: Education at Empire's End.* Minneapolis: University of Minnesota Press.

Wilson, P. 1991. 'Trauma of Sioux Indian High School Students', *Anthropology and Education* Quarterly 22: 367–83.

Wright, D.H. 2004. *Report of the Commission of Inquiry into Matters relating to the Death of Neil Stonechild.* Available at http://www.stonechildinquiry.ca/.

Zenter, H. 1973. *The Indian Identity Crisis: Inquires into the Problems and Prospects of Societal Development among Native Peoples.* Calgary: Strayer Publications.

Part Seven

Additional Readings

Battiste, Marie, and Jean Barman, eds. *First Nations Education in Canada: The Circle Unfolds.* Vancouver, BC: UBC Press, 1999.

Dion, Susan D. *Braiding Histories: Learning from Aboriginal Peoples' Experiences and Perspectives.* Vancouver, BC: UBC Press, 2009.

Haig Brown, Celia. *Resistance and Renewal: Surviving the Indian Residential School.* Vancouver, BC: Arsenal Pulp Press, 1988.

Jaine, Linda, ed. *Residential Schools: The Stolen Years.* Saskatoon, SK: University Extension Press, 1993.

Jacobs, Beverley. 'Response to Canada's Apology to Residential School Survivors', *Canadian Woman Studies* 26, 3–4 (2008): 223–5.

Relevant Websites

Truth and Reconciliation Commission of Canada
http://www.trc-cvr.ca/index_e.html
This website provides useful information about the history of residential schools, the recently formed Truth and Reconciliation Commission of Canada, and the programs available to individuals and communities affected by the legacies of residential schooling system.

Films

Cold Journey. Dir. Martin Defalco. National Film Board of Canada, 1975.

Day at Indian Residential Schools in Canada. Dir. Leslee White-Eye and Donna Young. Indigenous Education Coalition, 2005.

The Fallen Feather: Indian Industrial Residential Schools and Canadian Confederation. Dir. Randy Bezeau. Kinetic Video, 2007.

Niigaanibatowaad: FrontRunners. Dir. Lori Lewis. National Film Board of Canada, 2007.

Pelq'ilc (Coming Home). Dir. Helen Haig-Brown and Celia Haig-Brown. V Tape, 2009.

Key Terms

Assimilation
Cognitive assimilation
Banking concept
Sequential/symbolic literacy

Cultural revitalization
Cultural fundamentalism
Acculturation

Discussion Questions

1. Marie Battiste explores the ways in which Eurocentric notions of progress were deeply embedded in colonialism and colonial educational policies. What role did literacy play in notions of progress, and how was this secured through particular kinds of erasure?

2. What is cultural and cognitive assimilation? How has educational policy worked to further cultural assimilation or genocide? How have Indigenous peoples of the past and today resisted these policies?

3. How does the focus on cultural education erase the systemic violence of colonialism in Canada? What are the implications of turning dehumanization into a problem of 'culture', 'cultural incommensurability', or 'cultural' misunderstanding?

4. How did residential schools encourage the assimilation of Indigenous peoples and with what set of consequences? How do these manifest themselves in contemporary contexts?

Activities

In their book, *The Circle Game*, Chrisjohn, Young, and Maraun write: 'The conceptual world-view that gave rise to the genocide of Indigenous peoples remains in place, unchallenged; its lineaments invade all aspects of present majority thinking about Indian residential school. Unless this world-view is recognized, and the damage it has done and continues to do brought into focus, the long-term agenda of Indian residential schooling will succeed' (2006: 23). What do they mean by this and what are the implications of this reality for both Indigenous and non-Indigenous peoples?

Read Roger Simon's 'Toward a Hopeful Practice of Worrying' and Sara Ahmed's 'The Politics of Bad Feeling' and organize a class discussion about the mandate of the Truth and Reconciliation Commission of Canada. What are the goals of the Commission overall and with respect to public education about the history of residential schools? How might the Commission elicit empathy among Canadians that makes possible a restorative project, a claiming of responsibility for the colonial past, and a more just and equitable future? What recommendations would your class make to the Commission?

Poverty, Economic Marginality, and Community Development

From 22 December to 25 December 2009, at the Oneida of the Thames Longhouse, mid-winter ceremonies were held honouring Mother Earth and all her natural gifts. During the ceremonies, new members of the nation were welcomed and given traditional Oneida names. At the end of the first day of the ceremonies our spiritual elder gave us teachings about the ceremonies and also remarked that as the original peoples of the land we should resist assimilation and re-awaken our traditions and ways of governing. He reminded us of our responsibility to protect our lands and natural resources from some 'development' projects that in actuality are threatening the climate, the waters, the trees, and the well-being of our nations. By resisting, we are not against all modern technological developments, or stating that we do not wish to participate in the economy or share the wealth created from our rich resources. But we do want sustainable economies that do not destroy the environment and Mother Earth; we must ensure that our present economies safeguard 'all our relations' for the next seven generations. Our Haudenosaunee traditional teachings instruct us to keep the concept of 'seven generations' in mind when making any decision. In actuality this means that any decision taken in the present must bear in mind the wellbeing of at least the next seven future generations (Lyons, 1989).

Indigenous ways of relating to the natural environments and the commitment to sustainable economies have not been appreciated by mainstream society and often have become, as Voyageur and Calliou point out in their article, a structural barrier to Indigenous economic development. Links between Indigenous peoples, poverty, and development policy have, in recent years, received attention by social researchers and analysts who have reported that 'development itself has failed to provide answers to human suffering and disadvantage' (McNeish and Eversole, 2005: 1). Moreover, it has finally been internationally recognized that 'indigenous peoples are nearly always disadvantaged relative to their non-indigenous counterparts. Their material standard of living is lower; their risk of disease and early death higher . . . there is a "cost" to being Indigenous' (ibid., 2). Their socio-economic conditions have been described to belong to that of 'Fourth World' communities, minority populations in their own lands, who suffer from a lack of political power, economic subjugation, and social and cultural stigmatization (Dick, 1985).

Rather than treating these conditions as outcomes of individual faults or bad personal choices we must recognize that their poverty and economic marginaliza-tion are linked to past and ongoing colonial policies, racist attitudes, and forms of discrimination. As Voyageur and Calliou explain, the economic underdevelopment is not a 'Native problem'. It is, instead, 'the Canadian state's institutionalized and oppressive, economic and legal structures have played a key role in Aboriginal com-munity underdevelopment, which has resulted in the increasing dependency of some Indigenous peoples on the state'.

Indigenous peoples' current economic conditions have been created by a com-bination of cultural barriers and systemic discrimination. Cultural barriers consist, for example, of the conflict between Indigenous values and Euro-Canadian ones, wherein Indigenous belief in collectivism and spiritual connection to the land clashes with the belief in individualism and treatment of land as a commodity. Racist ideologies have treated Indigenous values as inferior, hence justifying the devaluation of Indigenous peoples, their economies, and colonization. Their eco-nomic marginalization has been treated as a consequence of their outmoded value system and their unwillingness to let go of their 'Indianness'. Such racist ideologies disallow to closely examine any systemic barriers that have created and maintained Indigenous underdevelopment.

Systemic barriers in the educational or legal institutions have had negative impacts on the ability of Indigenous peoples to prosper. Experiences in the residential schools, the lack of culturally relevant curriculum, and the inability to secure good employment still present barriers to the well-being of Indigenous individuals. Legal institutions have also played a detrimental role in Indigenous socioeconomic life. As Voyageur and Calliou argue, 'the Canadian state, through its federal and provincial jurisdictions, often legislates access to land and resources that benefits corporate interests and is detrimental to Aboriginal peoples.' Therefore, a blame-the-victim ideology is inadequate in analyzing current Indigenous economic conditions as it fails to recognize how racism and colonial attitudes and policies have significantly contributed to both the creation and the maintenance of those conditions.

Homelessness, itself a by-product of economic marginalization, needs to be connected to the history of colonization. In her study of Indigenous youth in Toronto, Baskin explores the structural factors behind homelessness and the need for culturally appropriate and relevant programs and policies. Factors that can be identified as contributors to Indigenous youth homelessness are lack of affordable housing, addictions, poverty, residential schooling, racism, discrimination, cultural and geographical displacement, and violence in their homes and communities. Homelessness is, in fact, a symptom of a deep structural problem: colonization. 'Colonization did not only create the relationship between Aboriginal peoples and mainstream society—it is also experienced personally. Thus, we emphasize that the history of colonization and its current impacts explains, in large part, why some Aboriginal peoples are homeless in their own lands.'

Most Indigenous homeless youth, Baskin discovered during her study, have been under the child protection system, where they experienced loneliness, isolation, abuse, and racism, and ended up in the streets to escape their situation. Their biological families had not been able to provide for them due to poverty, addiction problems, violence—all factors related to lingering structural barriers partly resulted by colonization. Current child and family policies and programs do not recognize the particularities of Indigenous family problems, most importantly their link with poverty. Ultimately there is a need for Indigenous communities to build and own specific child and family services and policies that value the collective nature of parenting that have always existed in Indigenous nations. Additionally, support must be provided to extended family members in caring for children, so that they not end up in foster and adoptive families where, as history has shown, the experiences have largely been negative and often lead to homelessness.

In their article, Silver, Ghorayshi, Hay, and Klyne examine holistic and empowering initiatives of 'Aboriginal community development.' As the authors point out, 'Aboriginal community development' differs from other models that are rooted in values of capitalism and modernization. 'Aboriginal community development' is rooted in Indigenous values of collectivism, holistic healing, and sharing. One of the main aims of such a model of development is to decolonize the individual and community from oppressive legacies of colonialism. These legacies have disempowered communities and placed them into marginalized positions in a first world country like Canada.

By closely examining examples of community development initiatives taken up by and for Indigenous peoples in urban settings like Winnipeg, Manitoba, and by including the voices of community members involved in community development initiatives, one cannot help but be impressed by the resilience of Indigenous peoples. After reading the article, we are confident that readers will be hopeful that urban 'Aboriginal community development' can be rooted in traditional Indigenous values that can help people to rebuild their own lives, revitalize their cultures, and overall, rebuild a healthy sense of community.

Through community development—as participants in the initiatives outlined by Silver et al. point out—people learn of the dominant oppressive structures that have affected them. By addressing the colonizing agenda and deconstructing colonialism, they can reclaim their voices and agency. At the core of such a project lies a need to rebuild a positive sense of Indigenous identity, and to build skills that empower Indigenous peoples. Community development strategies like these, the authors remind us, need to start from where the people are, meaning that one needs to identify and incorporate local knowledge and to support people to make their own choices and develop their own agendas. A legacy of colonialism has led to a pervasive sense of powerlessness. As such, assisting people to find their own way, to believe in their own capacity, and to heal and move forward, is a powerful form of decolonization.

Silver et al. outline examples of such initiatives, like the building of the Indian Métis Friendship Centre in Winnipeg, the establishment of the Ma Mawi Wi Chi Itata—an urban 'Aboriginal child welfare agency'—and other projects. These examples demonstrate that, although Indigenous nations have suffered in numerous ways through histories of colonialism that attacked their cultures, spirit, and dispossessed them of lands, they have always and nonetheless resisted and have been resilient. One can see from this article that a decolonized movement of revitalization is emerging, one that is rooted in traditional ways, and that has the potential to heal and rebuild communities.

As the articles in this part of the book show, current socioeconomic conditions are deeply rooted in the history of colonization and we must allow Indigenous peoples to regain control of their economies, to partake in an equal share on the wealth that is produced by the natural resources of their territories, and to develop social policies and programs that are cognizant of the structural barriers that have been faced by Indigenous peoples.

Chapter 22

Aboriginal Youth Talk About Structural Determinants as the Causes of Their Homelessness

Cyndy Baskin

Introduction

This article, which is based on a research project, explores the structural factors that may have led to the homelessness of Aboriginal youth in an urban centre. It begins with definitions of homelessness, then examines the prevalence of homelessness for Aboriginal youth, and next turns to a brief discussion of colonization and the role of child welfare in this process. The article then reports on the findings of the project that was conducted with homeless Aboriginal youth in Toronto using a culture-based research methodology.

This research project was conducted by myself as the principal investigator and a youth who is currently attending university as the research assistant. I am of Mi'kmaq and Irish descent and a professor in a school of social work. The research assistant is a young, Ojibway woman with a social work degree who is now in law school. We are both active participants in Toronto's Aboriginal community and have many relatives who have been/are homeless youth and who have had involvement with child welfare.

Toronto was chosen as the site for this research project as both the principal investigator and research assistant reside there and have connections to several Aboriginal agencies that service youth. In addition, Toronto has a large Aboriginal population and represents many diverse Nations (Statistics Canada, 2003). The medicine wheel was selected as the research methodology for the project after consulting with Aboriginal youth workers and youth themselves. They confirmed that the majority of youth were familiar with the medicine wheel and it is a teaching tool used by many Nations such as the Cree and Ojibway.

While there does appear to be some overlap between Eurocentric models of structural determinants and those presented by Aboriginal scholars

(DuHanmel, 2003; Thomas, 2003), such as education, income, and diet, this article proposes that to adequately address determinants faced by Aboriginal youth, a framework that is culturally appropriate and addresses colonization needs to be implemented. It further proposes that an arm of colonization, which is likely related to homelessness among youth, is their involvement in state institutional child welfare (Cauce and Morgan, 1994; Fall and Berg, 1996; Fitzgerald, 1995; Lindsey, et al., 2000; Maclean et al., 1999).

Current research on Aboriginal youth is minimal, especially in the area of homelessness. Available statistics do not illustrate the extent of the problem, although most advocates suggest that the rate of homelessness for this population is dramatically increasing (Abrahams, 2000; United Native Nations Society, 2001). The purpose of this research project, then, was to explore with homeless Aboriginal youth the conditions under which they became homeless, how they may be assisted today, and what can be done to prevent homelessness from continuing in the future. The significance of this project is connected to the fact that Aboriginal youth are the fastest growing group in Canada while the non-Aboriginal population is aging (Hick, 2007; Hoglund, 2004; Statistics Canada, 2003). It asserts that it will become increasingly important to Canada's future, especially in terms of our workforce, to ensure that Aboriginal youth be healthy and productive members of society. This article contributes suggestions for change to social policies and direct practice focusing on control of child welfare by and with Aboriginal peoples.

Definitions

Common definitions of homelessness include people that live on the street, stay in emergency shelters, spend more of their income on rent, or live in crowded conditions which keeps them at serious risk of becoming homeless (Golden, et al., 1999). The Toronto Disaster Relief Committee (1998) states that homelessness means simply not having secure housing. . . .

With particular attention to youth, homelessness is usually defined as those youth aged 15–24 who are not living with a family in a home, or not in the care of child protection agencies. Homeless youth are also described as those living 'in an unsafe or temporary living environment' (Fitzgerald, 1995: 7). The Canadian Mortgage and Housing Corporation (2001) and Golden et al. (1999) describe homeless youth as those youth with no permanent address.

Prevalence

Many sources state that there is no accurate data regarding homeless Aboriginal peoples, let alone Aboriginal youth (Golden et al., 1999; Layton, 2000; Native Counseling Service of Alberta, 2000; UNNS, 2001). In Layton's *Homelessness: The Making and Unmaking of a Crisis* (2000), what statistics exist show that Aboriginal peoples in general do have a high rate of homelessness as compared to the rest of Canadian society. The NCSA states that 'the Aboriginal homeless rate is at about 40 per cent Canada wide' (2000: 3). Golden et al. (1999), in their major report for the City of Toronto, reports that Aboriginal peoples make up 15 per cent of the homeless population in Toronto and that 'many Aboriginal Canadian youth from reserves and urban communities end up on the streets of Toronto' (1999: 75). If this 15 per cent figure is correct, it means that Aboriginal peoples are overrepresented in the homeless population by more than a factor of three considering they make up only 4.4 per cent of the Canadian population (Statistics Canada, 2001).

It is also important to note that the rate of homelessness is usually derived from the number of people who use shelters. However, the UNNS (2001) indicates that shelter users do not represent the entire Aboriginal homeless population as many do not utilize the shelter system. Furthermore, the Aboriginal community is estimated to have a high rate of concealed homelessness and these numbers are not included in the official data. This category includes those in transition homes, jails and detox centres, and those who live in overcrowded, unstable, or inadequate housing. It also includes 'couch surfing', which is when people stay at a friend or family members' dwelling for a short period of time, then move on to another person's home. Another category that often goes unnoticed is those who are at high risk of becoming homeless. This category includes many Aboriginal peoples who live in poor housing conditions and pay more than 25 per cent of their income for rental accommodations. Therefore, to completely capture the Aboriginal homeless population, all of these categories of homelessness must be included (UNNS, 2001). . . .

Factors Associated with Homelessness

Within the literature, the most frequently cited cause of homelessness for all peoples in Canada is lack of affordable housing (Golden et al., 1999; Hulchanski, 2004; Shapcott, 2001; TDRC, 1998). Some authors (UNNS, 2001; Weinreb et al., 1998) argue that personal factors, such as fetal alcohol spectrum disorder, addictions, poverty, poor health, and/or dysfunctional family relations are the cause of Aboriginal homelessness. Other literature states that socio-economic status and the lack of resources on reserves are also causes of homelessness (Beavis et al., 1997).

However, UNNS (2001) argues that even what appear to be personal factors are in fact the effects of structural barriers. UNNS (2001) states that the homelessness of Aboriginal peoples is rooted in 'structural factors such as unemployment, low wages or lack of income, loss of housing, colonization, racism, discrimination (systemic or otherwise), patriarchy, cultural and geographic displacement, and the reserve system' (2001: 2). Other authors contend that the historical introduction of foreign systems such as education, justice, health, and child protection have left Aboriginal peoples in a 'cycle of economic dependency, including high rates of poverty and unemployment' (Morrissette et al., 1993: 94).

Based on the literature outlined above, we assert that the factors associated with homelessness are connected to the omnipresent concept of colonization. Colonization did not only create the relationship between Aboriginal peoples and mainstream society—it is also experienced personally. Thus, we emphasize that the history of colonization and its current impacts explains, in large part, why some Aboriginal peoples are homeless in their own lands. We also believe that a framework which addresses the negative impacts of colonization on Aboriginal peoples and emphasizes our strengths needs to be developed. A Eurocentric lens fails to do this as it tends to frame Aboriginal peoples as social and economic disadvantages to the rest of Canadian society while negating our political power.

Institutional Child Protection

The distinctive factor between homeless adults and homeless youth is that the latter are forced to leave home at an early age, before they have a chance to fully develop into healthy adults (Cauce and Morgan, 1994; Fitzgerald, 1995; Golden et al., 1999; MacLean et al., 1999). In general, many youth that are homeless come from the care of the child protection system such as adoptive homes, foster homes, or group homes (Cauce and Morgan, 1994; Fall and Berg, 1996; Fitzgerald, 1995; Lindsey et al., 2000; Maclean et al., 1999). According to one study, between 25 per cent and 50 per cent of homeless youth were previously in the care of foster homes (Lindsey et al., 2000). This may be connected to the fact that these systems are designed to care for young children (under 15), so youth encounter barriers to service because they are too old for children's services and not old enough for adult services. Therefore, they are often left with no choice but to live on the street (Fitzgerald, 1995).

The child protection system, historically a tool of colonization, continues to the present day (Anderson, 1998; Du Hamel, 2003; Hudson, 1997; McKenzie and Seidl, 1995; Report of the Aboriginal Justice Inquiry of Manitoba, 1998). Although there have been some Aboriginal child welfare agencies developed throughout Canada

(Anderson, 1998; Hudson, 1997; McKenzie and Seidl, 1995), Aboriginal children are still over represented in the child protection system (Hudson, 1997; Mckenzie and Seidl, 1995; Thomas, 2003). This may be due to the restrictions placed on Aboriginal child welfare organizations. These organizations do have some control over the policies and procedures within their agencies; however, they are still usually required to comply with federal and provincial laws and policies. . . .

For anyone to take an institution such as child welfare, that has left a challenging legacy for many Aboriginal peoples, and turn it into something appropriate for Aboriginal communities is an enormous task. Yet it is obviously the goal of Aboriginal child protection services. As Hoglund (2004) advocates, both research and policies developed within an Aboriginal context by Aboriginal peoples is crucial because:

> Understanding how contextual mechanisms foster as well as challenge Native children's healthy social development is essential for generating informed, strengths-based research priorities and supporting Native sponsored policy and program development . . . Researchers, educators, service providers, and policymakers need to look beyond Western European models of successful development to adequately understand favoured socialization and developmental processes within the sociocultural, historical, political, legal and socioeconomic contexts of Native children's lives and the families and communities in which Native children live. (Hoglund, 2004: 165, 168)

We stress that insider views are necessary in order to develop social policies that reflect Aboriginal worldviews and values. Thus, this research project explored the following questions with insiders—Aboriginal youth affected by homelessness:

- What is appropriate parenting within Aboriginal perspectives?
- What supports do Aboriginal parents, families, and communities need to raise children?
- How does prevention become a priority?

- How do we frame 'neglect' within the realities of poverty?

Aboriginal Youth Research Circles

In this research project with Aboriginal youth, which we (and an Aboriginal student research assistant) designed and conducted, one research circle took place at two youth programs within Toronto that service youth who are homeless or at risk of becoming so. A total of 24 youth participated. Basic information was obtained from the participants through a standard form that all of the youth filled out. Next, within the research circles, youth were invited to discuss specific areas about their past and current situations. They were free to decide for themselves which areas they wanted to contribute to. The research methodology was based on Aboriginal cultural protocols and integrated a tool known as the 'Medicine Wheel' as shown on page 196. . . .

Sixteen youth had completed grades eight through eleven. This illustrates that many of the youth had a high incompletion rate for academic studies. This is especially significant considering that many of the participants were in their early twenties. One particular question on the information form was 'what grade are you currently completing?' Six youth answered they were not completing any grade at the time and they had not completed grade twelve (needed for a high school diploma). This shows that in this group of Aboriginal youth in their early twenties, many have not completed high school and were not in the process of doing so. Of twenty-four youth, only three were currently completing a college education and none were attending university. This information demonstrates a great need for more comprehensive educational resources and greater access to education that addresses the worldviews and needs of Aboriginal youth.

Eastern Direction: Looking Back

The first topic raised with the youth was 'who they grew up with'. It was suggested to them that they

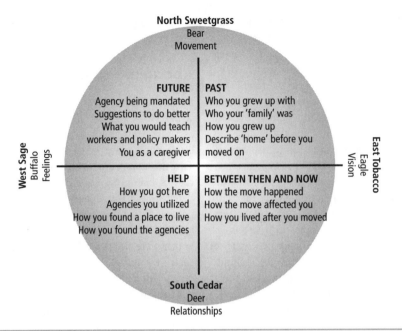

FIGURE 22.1   The Medicine Wheel

talk about who their family was/is, how they grew up, and what were their homes like before they moved on. Most of the youth stated that they grew up in the care of the Children's Aid Society (CAS), which included foster homes and group homes. More than half of all of the respondents mentioned having to relocate more than once. Those that stated they relocated said they moved to and from several different families and in some cases these homes or families were spread across the country. Four youth mentioned being in trouble with the law, were incarcerated, or always 'getting into trouble'. Seven youth mentioned living in a lone-parent female-headed family. Two of the youth lived with their mother, but later moved in with their father. One participant stated that he lived with his grandparents for awhile. Only two youth stated that they lived in two-parent families—one of whom was later placed in the care of CAS. Hence, only one of the twenty-four participants had lived with both parents for a significant amount of time. Many of the participants had also moved back and forth between their biological families and foster care while growing up.

The predominant theme in the youths' profiles is that the majority were not living with their biological parents. The responses of the youth illustrates that many of them did not have what mainstream society considers as the 'traditional' family. This in itself is not negative. What is negative is the fact that many of the youth were in the care of the state and placed in unstable homes meaning that they resided with families or in group homes where they experienced psychological, emotional, physical, sexual, and spiritual abuse, neglect, and acts of racism (e.g., one female youth was given the nickname of 'squaw' in her foster home). Those who lived in one-parent families also lived with an element of instability. Many moved from home to home, both biological and otherwise, without consistency in their lives.

Southern Direction: Between Then and Now

Youth were invited to talk about the move from their 'homes' into homelessness and how they lived after this move. The responses of the youth were varied. Each had a different story to tell. Some came to Toronto with their caregivers or relatives to look for work or obtain an education. One youth was passing through Toronto, but experienced a crisis and was forced to stay. One stated that her adoptive parents were abusive which forced her to move out on her own. She stated that the street life was easier because she could make her own rules. Although this life was preferable in comparison to her home life, it was tough living on the streets. Resources were difficult to access because of her young age. One participant stated that she was 'sick of group homes . . . too many rules' and that she was constantly moving from one group home to another. Two other participants explained how they lost their apartments due to lack of funds. Some of the youth that were in care, adopted, or in group homes stated that they lived in small towns and experienced a great deal of overt racism. They had believed that they could escape this by moving to a multicultural city like Toronto. A few youth explained how they were just released from jail, and how they were often in and out of jail. Three youth stated that they came to Toronto for opportunities; they wanted to change their lives around.

The major theme in these stories illustrates that growing up in the care of, or being involved long term with, CAS—whether that be adoptive homes, foster homes, group homes, or moving between biological and foster families—is often a profoundly negative experience. When asked about the reasons for moving back and forth between biological and foster homes, youth explained that when a biological parent complied with the demands of child welfare, such as staying in counselling for a long enough time period or attending a substance abuse treatment program, they were able to go back to these parents. However, when the parent stopped complying by starting to drink again or getting back with an abusive partner, the child would once again go to a foster home.

In a number of ways, this response on the part of child welfare authorities can be linked to looking at Aboriginal parents only through a Euro-centric lens. Often when Aboriginal parents are placed in a position of complying with demands to get their children back into their care, intentionally or not, it is a set up for failure. For example, they may not be voluntarily participating in programs, these programs may not be relevant in terms of examining structural reasons for their situations or they may not be culturally applicable, there may not be enough emphasis on support of and resources for the parent or the values and worldviews of Western society are being applied to Aboriginal parents which skews assessments.

Few of the youth who participated in this project experienced a positive home life. Many participants felt that they were forced to leave their homes. This was explained as, for example, not being wanted any longer by adoptive parents because they were rebelling, getting into trouble or questioning the rules. Even though some expressed how difficult street life was, none of them regretted their decisions for this was better than what they left behind. Among other things, this demonstrates that interventions need to be implemented before youth feel forced to leave their homes.

Western Direction: Help Along the Journey

The next area youth were asked to discuss was how they were able to receive help from social services agencies and how they were able to find a place to live once in Toronto. Some youth explained that they asked other Aboriginal peoples, they did not know, where they could stay for the night. Other youth stated that their friends or family members informed them of Aboriginal agencies in Toronto. One mentioned walking by a building that had an Aboriginal logo painted on the front, so he walked in. Four youth said that they were referred to an Aboriginal agency by mainstream organizations that service youth. Most of the participants agreed that they felt more comfortable at an Aboriginal agency. However, they also stated that it was good to get served by both Aboriginal and mainstream agencies. There were a few who expressed some dislike for certain Aboriginal organizations because of their experiences there regarding other peoples' behaviours such as intoxication and violence, but they still utilized them.

For the most part, the youth expressed a great sense of community amongst themselves, both within youth programs and on the streets. They spoke about helping each other out by sharing information about resources, agencies, and service providers within Toronto that were considered to be non-judgmental of them and some of their behaviours, such as substance using. Many youth talked about sticking together when on the streets for greater protection from both other people on the street and the police and letting others know about safe places to sleep. When they had something to share, whether that be money, alcohol, cigarettes, or food, they tended to share it with other youth. Some of them referred to each other as brothers and sisters even though they were not related by blood. They also shared secrets, stories, emotions, and laughter.

Northern Direction: Looking Towards the Future

The participants then explored what they would do to make the system better for future youth. They talked about what they would like to teach social workers and policy makers, especially with regards to the child protection system. To put this in context for themselves, the youth chose an Aboriginal child and family services agency becoming mandated as a child protection authority as an example to discuss what they would like social workers and policy makers to know. There were mixed feelings from the youth about the agency's change from offering voluntary services to taking on the responsibility of child protection. Many youth felt that bringing an Aboriginal perspective to child protection was vital. Others felt that it was a negative move because, in their opinions, the Aboriginal agency was too concerned with minor issues. One youth gave the example that '[a worker from the agency] stripped my kids because they had diaper rashes.' Another young mother stated that the agency

forced traditional ways on her, when she just wanted some emotional support. Another youth stated that other Aboriginal services were just as likely to involve child protection and related the example of an Aboriginal day care centre calling the Aboriginal child protection agency because her child had a 'running nose'. Some youth felt that the Aboriginal agency is 'too quick to jump on rumours'. Some of the participants who made these comments about the agency also expressed dislike for mainstream CAS, saying that they often felt like they were under 'a microscope' and that they did not believe that child protection—either mainstream or Aboriginal—would be so cautious with older adults. Thus, they felt like they were being discriminated against specifically because they were Aboriginal youth.

Although some youth disagreed with Aboriginal family services agencies becoming mandated, their suggestions for change did express some common themes. One raised a great difficulty with child protection stating that children have to be protected, but at the same time, Aboriginal families have different needs that are often neglected by these services. Next, they talked about the importance of incorporating Aboriginal culture into the lives of youth, no matter who their families are. The majority of the youth agreed that even though Aboriginal family services becoming mandated is an empowering concept, it does not work if these services have to use the same legislation as mainstream CAS. Although mandated Aboriginal child welfare agencies employ Aboriginal peoples as workers to varying degrees and incorporate some practices such as involving extended families as care givers of children, they must follow the same legislation—the Child and Family Services Act in Ontario—as all other mandated child welfare authorities. This Act is not inclusive of Aboriginal values, particularly around collective responsibilities for raising children, nor does it acknowledge the impacts of colonization or the inherent strengths of Aboriginal peoples and communities. It does not make clear distinctions between neglect and poverty nor does it include aspects of prevention which is crucial to the well being of the future of our children and youth. In keeping with these points, some youth spoke about how mainstream Canadian society decides what is acceptable child rearing for Aboriginal peoples and this is where the conflict lies. Other participants expressed that there is a need for more Aboriginal policy makers to change child welfare legislation or the cycle of oppression will continue. They explained that if this is not done, then it will simply mean 'putting a brown face on it' [Aboriginal control of child welfare]. They further explained that this may 'soften the blow' for some, but continue to oppress many.

The youths' suggestions about the need for more Aboriginal policy makers and changing child welfare legislation is brilliant. Since the current Child and Family Services Act does not address the sovereignty of Aboriginal peoples, what is necessary then is an Aboriginal Family and Child Services Act. Such an Act could address many of the concerns that the youth raised in this research project. For example, it would be developed by Aboriginal peoples according to our definitions of family, child care and parenting, This Act could clearly differentiate between poverty and neglect. It would reflect the values of Aboriginal peoples such as collective responsibility for children, communal sharing of resources and assisting families when they are struggling rather than taking their children away from them. Perhaps most importantly, an Aboriginal Family and Child Services Act would recognize the impacts of colonization upon all of us and focus our resources, both human and financial, on the well being of everyone in our communities and on the prevention of further internalized oppression which leads to the harm of all.

The next major issue that youth discussed was the policies governing who is allowed to be a customary care (foster) or adoptive parent and how these need to be transformed to better fit the circumstances of Aboriginal peoples. First, youth concurred that permanency planning should be key, ensuring that workers try to keep children with family members. Another point was to have more customary care homes and adoptive families in reserve communities. Overall, the youth expres-

sed their belief that there must be more Aboriginal families willing to adopt or care for children, and that the government needs to encourage and support this process through funding and legislation. Some of the examples they introduced were that some Aboriginal families may not have a lot of money, but that should not be a deciding factor in caring for children. They pointed out that many lower income families can do a good job of raising children. Furthermore, the youth took the stand that if being poor is such a concern, then the government should provide the necessary funds to foster families. They adamantly stated that, after all, the government is the reason why so many Aboriginal peoples are living in poverty in the first place. Moreover, these youth believe that preference should not be given to two parent families. Many Aboriginal families are headed by one parent who can raise children in a positive environment. Youth also stated that, if non-Aboriginal families are going to take in Aboriginal children, it needs to be mandatory that the children be connected to their cultures. They also believe that more effort needs to be put into keeping siblings together if families have to place their children into care. However, all of the youth were adamant that keeping families together must be of the greatest importance. One promising suggestion made to help keep families was that there could be a group of parents that can be used as an information resource for other parents who need it during times when they struggle with raising their children.

The participants also addressed the issue of child protection workers. They suggested that workers should be Aboriginal or, if not, have intensive training on issues affecting Aboriginal peoples. They stressed the need for greater consistency in training and education for helpers and how workers need to take into account what the client wants. They want workers to realize that everyone is different and what is 'normal' for an Aboriginal family may not be 'normal' for a mainstream one.

In conclusion, the theme for youth regarding the future was that for real positive change to occur, adding in a few cultural pieces is not enough, but rather legislation and social policies have to be completely changed to better suit the needs of Aboriginal families.

Coming Full Circle: Analysis

The depth of analysis these young people demonstrate, both in terms of their knowledge and understanding of the reasons for their homelessness, and the critical lens from which they view the world is amazing. They are insightful and articulate. They call it the way they see it and no one is fooling them.

These youth were easily able to comprehend their life experiences, which were, for the most part, contact with child protection and separation from their biological families and home communities, within the realities of colonization and oppression. A comment that stands out most perhaps is from a young man who said, 'mostly we're taken away by child welfare because of poverty and this translates into neglect by them.' For Aboriginal peoples, poverty is a direct result of colonization which destroyed the original economic basis of our communities. In contemporary society, breaking out of poverty is, in large part, dependent on acquiring formal education and employment. However, education has been historically genocidal and is currently alienating for many Aboriginal peoples so that 68.5 per cent of youth do not complete high school (Hick, 2007: RCAP, 1996). According to the RCAP report, both youth and parents are adamant that education does not prepare them for life in understanding themselves as Aboriginal peoples nor does it prepare them for life in the modern world. In fact, according to this report, youth stated they left school because they were made to feel ashamed of being Aboriginal, they experienced racism and there was no recognition of Aboriginal perspectives in history or respect for their cultures.

Certainly, low educational attainment affects peoples' future employment and income levels. However, according to the results of a study conducted by Kunz, Milan, and Schetagne (2000), Aboriginal peoples also have difficulty finding employment because of racism in the work place. They found that compared to white Canadians, Aboriginal peoples with university degrees are less likely to have managerial and professional jobs. In addition, they are over represented in the bottom 20 per cent and under represented in the top 20 per cent of income earners. Even with the same level of higher education, white Canadians are three times as likely as Aboriginal peoples to be in the top 20 per cent of income earners. These results are confirmed by Hick (2007) as well. Clearly, these studies reveal that even with university degrees, job opportunities are out of reach for many Aboriginal peoples.

Unlike the generation before them, this group of youth usually has a roof over their heads at night. But they do not have homes. Thanks to Aboriginal agencies that service youth, most of these young people are housed and have access to some health services. However, most struggle with poverty, have not completed high school, are transient, and, in the case of many female youth, are single mothers involved with child welfare who are often concerned that their children will be removed from them. This concern seems to come from a belief in the tendency for social service workers to 'blame the victim' (Anderson, 1998; Hudson, 1997; Thomas, 2003). Even within Aboriginal child welfare agencies, internalized oppression has caused some Aboriginal peoples to believe the negative stereotypes about some members of their community and thus they treat them just as the dominant society does.

From a structural perspective, for the most part, Aboriginal child protection agencies continue to be mandated to operate within the framework of legislation and social policies not based on Aboriginal values and perspectives. Since these policies do not incorporate the distinct needs of Aboriginal peoples, a major focus needs to be creating legislation and policies that are compatible with Aboriginal worldviews, in general, while taking into consideration the great diversity of our Nations. In addition to this, the legislation and policies must also take into account past injustices and the effects they have on the health and behaviours of Aboriginal peoples today. To simply add in 'culturally based practice' without any change to oppressive legislation is clearly detrimental for it changes little (Anderson, 1998; Hudson, 1997; RAJIM, 1998).

Furthermore, mainstream legal and political discourses regarding self-government, Aboriginal rights, and treaties are grounded in Western constructions of nationhood that originate from European history and cultures. Such discourses inevitably marginalize Aboriginal worldviews in the construction of nationhood in self-government and treaty negotiations. This approach, then, continues to entrench Eurocentric-Canadian structural power imbalances rather than creating positive economic, political, and social change for Aboriginal peoples. I emphasize that until constructs of nationhood can be examined from both an Aboriginal and a Eurocentric lens equally, self-government that creates inclusive and sustainable Aboriginal communities is impossible.

The preliminary work from this research project also has many encouraging messages. These youth are greatly concerned about the next generation. When they spoke about their experiences and recommendations, they did not do so in ways that will necessarily benefit them, but rather because they hope to make contributions to the future of both their children and all Aboriginal children in general. These youth also view positive change as centering on re-structuring child welfare legislation and social policy. They identified that change simply by creating Aboriginal child protection agencies with Aboriginal workers is not enough.

Aboriginal child and family services agencies are to be commended for picking up the responsibility of child welfare and attempting to incorporate traditional knowledges into their work. However, many colonial legacies have been passed on to their shoulders, such as internalized oppression, family violence, poverty, and suicide, which they are expected to heal. They also must face unrealistic expectations placed upon them by both the Aboriginal communities they serve and mainstream society and governments (Hudson and Taylor-Henley, 1995; Bennett, Blackstock, and De

La Ronde, 2005). Aboriginal peoples, including those who work in the area of child welfare, must re-claim the knowledge that prior to colonization, we lived as autonomous groups and our inherent right to self-determination—which included controlling the affairs affecting our families and children—was never abdicated despite the policies and actions forced upon us by Canadian governments (First Nations Child and Family Task Force, 1993; Association of Native Child and Family Services Agencies of Ontario, 2001; Bennett, Blackstock, and De La Ronde, 2005). Aboriginal responsibility and control must go beyond child welfare service delivery to the creation of legislation and policies that will restore traditional forms of government. This is crucial since present legislation and social policies related to child welfare are based on Eurocentric values and worldviews, thereby making them an ongoing tool of colonization. Hence, as the youth raised, Aboriginal peoples must become policy makers in this area. Without significant changes to social policies, the major request to keep families together and concentrate heavily on prevention, which one youth described as 'eliminating poverty', cannot possibly happen.

According to the voices of this group of youth, holistic good health rests largely on the value of supporting families through equitable access to resources to care for the well being of their children. Such resources include inclusive education that is representative of Aboriginal youth, job opportunities based on merit and anti-colonial, anti-racist policies and legislation all of which aim to eliminate poverty caused by colonization.

References

Abrahams, P. 2000. *The Toronto Report Card on Homelessness 2000*. Toronto: City of Toronto. Retrieved online 15 May 2004 from http://www.city.toronto.on.ca/homelessness/2000/index.htm.

Anderson, K. 1998. 'A Canadian Child Welfare Agency for Urban Natives: The Clients Speak', *Child Welfare* 77: 441–61.

Association of Native Child and Family Services Agencies of Ontario. July 2001. *Pre-Mandated Native Child and Family Service Agencies: Issues and Recommendations*. Thunder Bay, ON: The Association.

Beavis, M., Klos, N., Carter, T., and Douchant, C. 1997. *Literature Review: Aboriginal Peoples and Homelessness.* Winnipeg: Institute of Urban Studies. Retrieved online 15 May 2004 from http://www.ginsler.com/documents/ f_aborig.html.

Bennett, M., Blackstock, C., and De La Ronde, R. 2005. *A Literature Review and Annotated Bibliography on Aspects of Aboriginal Child Welfare in Canada.* Ottawa, ON: The First Nations Research Site of the Centre of Excellence for Child Welfare and the First Nations Child & Family Caring Society of Canada. Retrieved online 15 May 2004 from http://www.fncaringsociety.ca/docs/ AboriginalCWLitReview_2ndEd.pdf.

Canadian Mortgage and Housing Corporation. 2001. *Environmental Scan on Youth Homelessness.* Ottawa: CMHC.

Castellano, M. 2002. *Aboriginal Family Trends: Extended Families, Nuclear Families, Families of the Heart.* Ottawa: The Vanier Institute of the Family.

Cauce, A., and Morgan, C.J. 1994. 'Effectiveness of Intensive Case Management for Homeless Adolescents: Results of a Three Month Follow-up', *Journal of Emotional and Behavioural Disorders* 2: 219–27.

Du Hamel, P. 2003. 'Aboriginal Youth: Risk and Resilience', *Native Social Work Journal* 5: 213–24.

Fall, K.A., and Berg, R.C. 1996. 'Behavioural Characteristics and Treatment Strategies with Homeless Adolescents', *Individual Psychology* 52: 431–40.

First Nations Child and Family Task Force. November 1993. *Children First, Our Responsibility: Report of the First Nations Child and Family Task Force.* Winnipeg: Queen's Printer.

Fitzgerald, M.D. 1995. 'Homeless Youth and the Child Welfare System: Implications for Policy and Service', *Child Welfare* 74: 717–31.

Golden, A., Currie, W.H., Greaves, E., and Latimer, E.J. 1999. *Taking Responsibility for Homelessness: An Action Plan for Toronto.* Toronto: City of Toronto.

Hick, S. 2007. *Social Welfare in Canada: Understanding Income Security.* Toronto: Thompson Educational Publishing Inc.

Hoglund, W.L. 2004. 'Navigating Discrimination: The Interplay of Contexts on Native Children's Social Development', pp. 153–71 in C.A. Nelson and C.A. Nelson, eds, *Racism, eh? A Critical Inter-disciplinary Anthology of Race and Racism in Canada.* Concord, ON: Captus Press Inc.

Hudson, P. 1997. 'First Nations Child and Family Services: Breaking the Silence', *Canadian Ethnic Studies* 29 (3): 161–73.

Hudson, P., and Taylor-Henley, S. 1992. *Interactions Between Social and Political Development in First Nations Communities.* Winnipeg: University of Manitoba, Faculty of Social Work.

Hulchanski, D. 2004. *Question and Answer: Homelessness in Canada.* Retrieved online 15 May 2004 from http://www.tdrc.net.

Kunz J.L, Milan A., and Schetagne S. 2000. *Unequal Access: A Canadian Profile of Race Differences in Education, Employment and Income.* Toronto: Canadian Race Relations Foundation.

Layton, Jack. 2000. *Homelessness: The Making and Unmaking of a Crisis.* Toronto: Penguin.

Lindsey, E.W., Kurtz P.D., Jarvis, S., Williams, N.R., and Nackerud, L. 2000. 'How Runaway and Homeless Youth Navigate Troubled Waters: Personal Strengths and Resources', *Child and Adolescent Social Work Journal* 17: 115–40.

Maclean, M.G., Embry, L.E., and Cauce, A.M. 1999. 'Homeless Adolescents Paths to Separation from Family: Comparison of Family Characteristics, Psychological Adjustment, and Victimization', *Journal of Community Psychology* 27: 179–87.

Mckenzie, B., and Seidl, E. 1995. 'Child and Family Service Standards in First Nations: An Action Research Project', *Child Welfare* 74: 633–53.

Morrissette, V., McKenzie, B., and Morrissette, L. 1993. 'Towards an Aboriginal Model of Social Work Practice', *Canadian Social Work Review* 10 (1): 91–108.

Native Counseling Services of Alberta [NCSA]. 2000. 'Community Consultation on Homelessness Report'. Edmonton: NCSA. Retrieved online 15 May 2004 from http://www. edmonton-omelessness.ca/aboriginal/ consultation.doc.

Report of the Aboriginal Justice Inquiry of Manitoba. 1998. *The Justice System and Aboriginal People.* Winnipeg: Manitoba Government. Retrieved online 15 May 2004 from http://www.ajic.mb.ca/volumel/chapter14.html.

Royal Commission on Aboriginal Peoples. 1996. *Volume 1, Looking Forward, Looking Back.* Ottawa, ON: Canada Communication Group.

Shapcott, M. 2001. *Housing, Homelessness, Poverty and Free Trade in Canada.* Retrieved online 15 May 2004 from http://www.tdrc.net.

Statistics Canada. 2003. *2001 Census Analysis Series: Aboriginal Peoples of Canada, A Demographic Profile.* Retrieved online 15 May 2004 from http://www12.statcan.ca/english/ census01/Products/Analytic/companion/abor/pdf/ 96F0030XIE2001007.pdf.

Thomas, W. 2003. 'The Social Determinants of Aboriginal Health: A Literature Review', *Native Social Work Journal* 5: 270–86.

Toronto Disaster Relief Committee [TDRC]. 1998. *State of Emergency Declaration.* Retrieved online 14 May 2004 from http'//www.tdrc.net; 'Resources' section.

United Native Nations Society [UNNS]. 2001. *Aboriginal Homelessness in British Columbia.* Retrieved online 15 May 2004 from http://www.urbancenter.utoronto.ca/pdfs/ elibrary/UNNS_Aboriginal_Homelessn.pdf.

Chapter 23

Aboriginal Economic Development and the Struggle for Self-Government

Cora Voyageur and Brian Calliou

. . . It is no secret that in the past little, if any, of the vast economic wealth derived from the exploitation of the land and resources found its way to Canada's Aboriginal peoples.[1] One analyst argues that in all liberal democracies Aboriginal peoples are transformed into 'politically weak, economically marginal and culturally stigmatized members of national societies' (Dyck, 1985: 1). Another maintains that liberal lawyers who apply liberal laws to protect American 'Indian' rights have actually contributed to the loss of indigenous culture (Medcalf, 1978). By failing to examine the structural inequities inherent in Canadian Indian legislation and policies, some social scientists mistakenly characterize Native–white relations as 'the Aboriginal Problem' (Frideres, 1988). On the contrary, the Canadian state's institutionalized and oppressive economic and legal structures have played a key role in Aboriginal community underdevelopment, which has resulted in the increasing dependency of some Aboriginal peoples on the state. Institutional structures have had a profound impact on Aboriginal peoples. The constraints imposed by those structures have become the essence of the Aboriginal relationship with Canadian society.

Although First Nations people in Canada remain subject to state regulations and policies, they have never passively accepted the Canadian state's domination. They have long resisted both overtly and covertly, yet much has changed in recent years. First Nations peoples are gaining control over their lives and their communities. The current struggle for self-government plays a part in the First Nations peoples' resistance to the control exercised over them by the Canadian state and its institutions. They see the key to economic development in self-government—not in the sense of achieving a nation-state but in achieving official recognition of their inherent rights, treaty obligations, and land claims—and by gaining increased control over local and regional decision-making. But the struggle for self-government has produced a new form of resistance: now the Canadian state and various interest groups are resisting the attempts by First Nations peoples to control their own destinies.

If self-government can be achieved, a new social order for First Nations peoples and for all Canadians may truly be at hand. In the meantime, by examining Canada's institutional structures—as opposed to the standard focus on the shortcomings of First Nations peoples—we can come to a better understanding of the dispossession of Canada's First Nations peoples.

Barriers to Native Economic Development

Quite simply, the experiences of Aboriginal peoples are notably distinct from those of non-Aboriginals. Despite strides in educational attainment and the growing number of Aboriginal peoples in positions of power and prestige, Canada's First Nations are collectively at the lowest rung of the socioeconomic ladder; they are among the country's poorest and least educated. The average Aboriginal income in 1996 was $15,699, while the average non-Aboriginal income was $25,414 (Statistics Canada, 1999: 13). Some 9.3 per cent of Aboriginal people aged fifteen years and older reported no income at all during 1995, compared with 7.6 per cent of the total Canadian population (Statistics Canada, 2002: 1). Some 45.9 per cent of Aboriginal people complete high school, compared to 65.1 per cent of non-Aboriginals (Statistics Canada, 1999: 13). Fewer Aboriginals (25.4 per cent) complete some form of postsecondary education, compared to the non-Aboriginal community (41.0 per cent). This distinct Aboriginal experience is the result of cultural, legal–political, and economic barriers.

Cultural Barriers: 'Race' and Racism

Cultural differences can both directly and indirectly result in barriers to development. The different values and beliefs of non-Aboriginal people often conflict with Aboriginal worldviews. A non-Aboriginal worldview often includes a strong belief in the basic principles of liberalism: human control over nature, individualism, the notion of land as a commodity, and the private ownership of property. An Aboriginal worldview usually includes a strong belief in collectivism and stresses a spiritual connection to the land—of living with rather than controlling nature, and sharing rather than owning land. . . .

Problems arise particularly when racism and racist attitudes use cultural differences to treat Aboriginal peoples and their cultural practices as unworthy of respect. A belief in 'racial separateness' or 'racial difference' justified the undertaking by which settler populations took Aboriginal peoples' lands and resources. Race, as a sociopolitical concept, entails: 'an ideology of inherent White superiority [used] to justify White dominance and exploitation' (Frideres, 1988: 378). By characterizing others as inferior, Western

Europeans gave themselves leave to move in and take over the lands and lives of the indigenous peoples, avoiding or lessening their guilt. . . .

For the most part Canadians do not question the underlying racist notions or actions that played an integral role in establishing our country. The society appears to have little problem accepting the legal and political domination of Aboriginal peoples. The reality that Aboriginal people have been denied a fair share of Canada's wealth, resources, and land does not seem to disturb our collective conscience to any great degree. A covert or subtle form of racism occurs, for instance, when social scientists explain what is 'wrong' with Aboriginal people by focusing attention on the values and traditions of 'those' people.

The view that Aboriginal people must shed their 'Indianness' to make it in today's society barely masks the still-lingering racist ethos of Aboriginal inferiority. In this view, the Aboriginal notion of collective land ownership is not only outmoded but restricts First Nations peoples' access to, for example, bank loans for development projects. But as we shall see in the realm of legal barriers, restricted access to capital is more a function of the *Indian Act* than of differing cultural ideas about land tenure.

Systemic Discrimination

In theory, institutions in liberal societies promote equality of all citizens, but in reality certain groups continue to suffer from systemic discrimination—practices firmly set in place at all levels in society's structure. By examining societal structures we can better understand problems that have their roots in the institutional rather than the individual level. Systemic discrimination, for example, can have a negative impact on Aboriginal peoples' abilities to gain stable and worthwhile employment. . . .

Educational institutions play a role in systemic discrimination. Aboriginal people have long been, more often than not, unable to obtain extensive schooling. The last residential school closed only in the mid-1990s. Under that system Aboriginal children were forced to leave their homes and go to residential schools, where they were often punished simply for speaking their own languages. These conditions represent systemic discrimination: barriers to learning built into the institution of education. . . .

At one time Aboriginal people had low levels of education and job-related experience, but academic achievement and work experience levels have now increased significantly in the Aboriginal community. Yet Aboriginal persons are still often incorrectly labelled as unskilled labour. Helmar Drost (1995), in his study of Aboriginal unemployment, found that often the problem of high unemployment rates was linked to the lack of job opportunities and not to the Aboriginal people's lack of skills or job-related experience. He found that there were more qualified Aboriginal workers than there were available jobs.

Legal Barriers

Perhaps the most significant barrier to economic development for First Nations is a legal one: the lack of legal control over land and resources. The Canadian state, through its federal and provincial jurisdictions, often legislates access to land and resources that benefits corporate interests and is detrimental to Aboriginal peoples.

The *Constitution Act 1867* set out the legislative powers for federal and provincial governments, giving the federal government responsibility for 'Indians, and Land reserved for Indians' (McMillan, 1988: 287). The Canadian parliament exercised its authority by creating the *Indian Act* (1876). An Indian Affairs representative once stated, 'Probably there is no other legislation which deals with so many and varied subjects in a single act. It may be said indeed to deal with the whole life of a people' (MacInnes, 1946: 388). The *Indian Act*'s extensive regulation, in addition to fish and game laws and other legislation that restricts access to traditional resources, has damaged Aboriginal economies. The Canadian government has used the *Indian Act* to deny First Nations peoples their basic rights, such as freedom of association and the right to representation in the judicial system. A 1927 amendment made it illegal for anyone to raise money for an Indian band to bring claims against the government (Kellough, 1980). Over the years, amendments to the *Indian Act* have outlawed social, cultural, and religious gatherings such as the sun dance on the Plains and the potlatch on the West Coast. . . .

The political and legal structures that impose economic restrictions on Aboriginal peoples represent the state's attempts to control them. State laws and policies set out many legislative restrictions that act as barriers to Native economic development. Government policies again express the values of liberalism, which supports individual freedom, a free-market economy, private ownership, and the accumulation of wealth. Critics of liberalism argue that liberal law protects elite property interests and does not recognize Aboriginal peoples' rights to the land and resources (Loo, 1994).

A lack of financing for on-reserve ventures is a major problem in Aboriginal communities, stifling economic development. Financial institutions, situated in the metropolitan financial centres, generally do not lend to persons who do not have property as collateral. The *Indian Act* exempts land and property situated on a reserve from seizure. Banks cannot seize an Indian's property for defaulting on loan payments. Thus major banks tend to avoid giving loans to an Indian person because of the risk involved. Still, some changes are now making Indian ventures more viable. Governments give loan guarantees to some individuals, and Aboriginally owned and administered financing institutions are emerging. Federal funding has aided in the establishment of Aboriginal businesses. Today there are about 20,000 businesses owned and operated by Aboriginal people in Canada (Aboriginal Business Canada, 2000: K1). . . .

Explaining Barriers to Economic Development

Debate about the lack of Aboriginal participation in the Canadian economy involves, in general, assimilationist and anti-assimilationist. Assimila-tionists argue that the cultural differences of Aboriginal peoples and mainstream society place Aboriginals at a clear disadvantage. This stance does not account for the barriers derived from racism and systemic discrimination experienced by Aboriginal peoples in Canada. Meanwhile, human capital theory argues that Aboriginal peoples would be more 'successful' if they only accepted and attained education along Euro-Canadian lines. This approach does not account for those many Aboriginal people who have acquired education and skills and are still unemployed.

Modernization theory, a dominant theory within the assimilationist stream, views industrial-ization and technological change as both inevit-able and desirable. Modernists further state that traditional economies that fail to undergo indus-trialization will remain underdeveloped. Thus the lack of economic development within a region or amongst a particular population is linked to out-moded economic organization and ideas. The region or people are responsible for their own economic underdevelopment due to their inability or unwillingness to 'change with the times'. This approach does not consider factors such as geo-graphic isolation, lack of access to capital, or small economies of scale that might inhibit profitability as significant impediments to development. Modernization theory, in the final analysis, really 'blames the victim'.

Anti-assimilationist perspectives use an amalgam of theories to explain barriers to economic develop-ment. They include, among others, the metropolis-hinterland interaction, colonialism, and dependency theories that serve to underline the overt and systemic structures that explain the fre-quent economic marginalization of Aboriginal peoples.

The metropolis-hinterland and dependency theories examine the root of legal and political barriers. In the metropolis-hinterland paradigm, the political and economic elite of metropolitan centres are the decision-makers who exploit the hinterland's raw materials and sell the finished products back to the outlying areas. Hinterland communities have little or no say in choices made for them and their regions. Local interests have little priority in relation to large-scale capitalist interests. Thus, First Nations reserves, most of them located in rural areas, had no input in deci-sions made on their behalf in distant locales. Critics of the Canadian state's approach to eco-nomic development argue that development must proceed under local control to meet local needs and aspirations rather than serve only the goals of multinational corporations (Frideres, 1988).

Dependency theory emerges as a critique of modernization theory. According to dependency theorists, underdevelopment can only be under-stood through an analysis of the economic rela-tionships between developed and undeveloped economies. Hinterland populations become dependent upon the productive relationships established by the capitalist metropolis (McArthur, 1989). James Frideres (1991) argues that reserve Indians occupy a position of 'domestic depend-ency'. In other words, major decisions affecting their socioeconomic progress are made by individ-uals and institutions outside their communities. Aboriginal peoples, originally self-sufficient, became dependent over time. Although they enjoyed the convenience of European goods dur-ing the early days of the fur trade, historically those goods had not been essential to their sur-vival. They soon became more dependent upon trade goods such as guns and ammunition, and their dependence greatly increased when European immigrants settled their traditional lands and they found themselves limited to reserves. Because of the newly restricted land base, their traditional economies suffered and some of the peoples became more dependent on government transfer payments for support. . . .

Resistance and the Struggle for Independence

Aboriginal peoples resisted control by the Canadian state in many different ways. They made—and continue to make—persistent attempts to exercise independence through political, economic, and self-governing initiatives. They protested the *Indian Act* from the beginning. . . . They also long opposed the government's assimilation program. . . .

During the late nineteenth and early twentieth centuries, Aboriginal people 'were actors who pursued their interests and struggled to preserve their identity. They resisted, evaded, and defied efforts to control their decision making, limit their traditional rites, and deprive them of their children' (Miller, 1991: 340). More recently, Aboriginal people who entered treaties with the Crown vehemently expressed the sacredness of treaties and the importance of protecting their treaty rights. Any attempts by the state to infringe upon or reduce treaty rights were met with strong opposition, as evidenced by the reaction of chiefs across Canada to the 1969 *Statement of the Government of Canada on Indian Policy* (also known as the White Paper).

Courts

Aboriginal peoples have also used the courts to resist the dispossession of their land and resources. For example, Chief Frank Calder, on behalf of the Nishga people, launched a court challenge against the province of British Columbia over the development of traditional land (*Calder v. A.G. British Columbia* 1973). . . . This case had a dramatic impact on Aboriginal law and prompted the federal government to change its stance and move towards settling Aboriginal land claims. First Nations won a significant victory and wrestled power away from the federal government, which had previously refused to negotiate Aboriginal land claims. More importantly, the Calder case spawned a series of Aboriginal rights litigation in the Canadian courts.

In 1985 the Supreme Court of Canada made a significant ruling in the Guerin case, giving legal recognition to the Aboriginal peoples' view of their 'inherent rights' and thereby rejecting the state's notion that Aboriginal rights were 'derivative rights' (rights derived from the state's recognition of them). The case also stands as authority for the principle of fiduciary duty, which means that because First Nations people are in a trust-

like position vis-à-vis the federal government, the federal government must always act in their best interests. . . .

Politics

Aboriginal peoples have also expressed their resistance in the political arena. A growing number of Aboriginal lawyers, judges, doctors, and academic professors have become politically active in the last decade or so. An emerging group of Aboriginal professionals often takes leadership roles in the struggle for Aboriginal rights and Aboriginal peoples' share of Canada's wealth. . . .

The strong opposition to the 1969 *Statement of the Government of Canada on Indian Policy* led to amendments to the *Indian Act*, giving Aboriginal people more control over self-governing policies. In the 1960s the federal government introduced a policy of devolution of powers to band councils (Frideres ,1988). Perhaps partly in response to Aboriginal peoples' agitation, more control and responsibility were shifted onto the Aboriginal communities. . . . In the 1980s the Assembly of First Nations pressed for a seat at the first ministers' conferences on the Constitution and on the Quebec question. Aboriginal peoples have also used the existing political structures to achieve their goals. In 1990 Elijah Harper, a member of Manitoba's Legislative Assembly, used his power to withhold consent to halt the passage of the Meech Lake Accord constitutional amendments. Harper's objection was based on Canada's refusal to deal adequately with Aboriginal rights. . . .

Aboriginal resistance has also led to violent confrontations. In 1990 a highly publicized and violent crisis occurred when Mohawk warriors barricaded a road to protect land from being developed into a golf course near the town of Oka, Quebec. The Mohawks maintained that the land was the site of traditional burial grounds. Gunfire was exchanged and a police officer, Marcel Lemay, was killed in the mêlée. In 1996 another armed conflict, known as the Gustafson Lake incident, occurred in British Columbia when Native people claimed privately owned land as sacred ground and would not vacate. An armed standoff resulted and a heavy exchange of gunfire ensued. Subsequently the protesters were taken into custody, charged, and sentenced.

The summer of 1995 saw unarmed Aboriginal people using civil disobedience tactics to protest the provincial government's failure to settle an outstanding land claim at Ipperwash, Ontario. Provincial government leaders refused to negotiate and instead obtained a court injunction. When heavily armed police were sent in to deal with the Aboriginal protesters, an Indian man, Anthony 'Dudley' George, was killed by gunfire. A police officer was eventually convicted of the murder.

In general, then, Aboriginal peoples have struggled to gain more control over local matters and have reacted to the erosion of their treaty and Aboriginal rights. They have organized to gain greater control of their natural resources. They have pushed for the retention of their independent means of production, openly defying regulation by continuing to hunt and fish out of season (Gulig, 1994). . . .

Although Aboriginal people have won occasional victories, some commentators argue that such victories are exceptions rather than the rule and are meant only to pacify the dispossessed (Havemann, 1989). Whether these victories are truly significant or merely anomalous pacifiers, Aboriginal peoples have no choice but to compete for their share of economic development and self-sufficiency in what is clearly a continuing struggle (Wotherspoon and Satzewich, 1993: 261). . . .

In recent years, having become more assertive about their inherent rights to be self-governing on their own territories, Aboriginal peoples have devised, analyzed, and implemented initiatives in their communities. They have taken control of local issues, arguing that imposed Canadian government structures have continually failed them. The federal relationship with the First Nations began as a nation-to-nation partnership and many First Nations leaders continue to regard it in this way. This approach gives credence to the notion of self-government in international law. Sally Weaver (1990: 13) argues that the Department of Indian

Affairs' new way of thinking about its relationship with Aboriginal peoples must rest on the 'principles of the Aboriginal and democratic self-government, and the need for Aboriginally-designed and legitimated political institutions' if co-existence and self-determination are to prevail.

Self-Government

At the heart of the changes being pursued by First Nations people and their political organizations is the principle of self-government: the necessary step towards co-existence, self-determination, and actual economic development. The strategy of self-government is based on the 'special relationship' between Canada and First Nations, but the term cannot be rigidly defined. It is a necessarily fluid political concept: self-government will take different forms in different communities and at different times. Although the concept aims at a broad set of powers over local matters, under some circumstances the form adopted can resemble a provincial structure; under other circumstances the form could be that of a municipality. Self-governing forms could include 'self-administration' but ultimately must be more than that. Indeed, self-government could involve a devolution of powers from the Department of Indian Affairs, an approach attempted in Manitoba. The key is that the particular form must be defined by the community so that traditional practices and traditional forms of government can be accommodated and traditional values can underpin the more European-based forms of self-government. . . . In a self-governing system, parallel systems of governance could be established with bilateral agreements or tripartite agreements negotiated between the various governments; or co-management agreements could be established in which First Nations people become partners in the planning and management of lands and resources.

Over time First Nations' relationship with the federal government has changed. Before 1982 Aboriginal peoples dealt only with the Department of Indian Affairs. Since the repatriation of the Constitution that relationship has now expanded beyond a single federal ministry. First Nations leaders and political organizations now deal face-to-face with first ministers on constitutional issues. They now deal with various federal and provincial cabinet ministers and high-ranking bureaucrats and corporate managers on a range of issues. They wield more power and authority than they did in early Aboriginal–white relations. . . .

Generally, governments now consult Aboriginal people before passing legislation that would infringe upon their constitutionally protected inherent or treaty rights. As well, there is a growing trend for industry to consult First Nations about development projects planned in their traditional territories (British Columbia, 1997; RCAP, 1996b). Taking control of services such as health, education, and Policing on their own initiative represents a key step towards self-government (Delisle, 1984). . . .

Native Economic Development in the New Millennium

Now, in the early years of the twenty-first century, we seem to have the potential to revitalize Aboriginal communities, which in turn would benefit the country as a whole. But as the Royal Commission on Aboriginal Peoples argues, this potential hinges on a historic reversal: Aboriginal peoples must gain more control over their lives, territories, and resources; they must become self-governing. In their economic development, any strategies must be aware of three types of Aboriginal economies: Indian/Métis land economies, urban economies, and Northern economies (RCAP, 1996a). Furthermore, the RCAP (1996a) outlines three factors required for successful economic development on reserves. Based on case studies of reserves in the United States, the three factors are: (1) 'external opportunities', which refers to political control over reserve decision-making, access to capital financing, unique economic niches or markets based on the band's strengths and resources, and short distances to markets; (2) 'internal assets', which refers to the band's natural resources and lands, human capital, and institutions of govern-

ance and culture; and (3) 'development strategy', which refers to the choice of plans and approaches to development activity (Cornell and Kalt, 1990; RCAP, 1996a).

Progress has been made on the first set of factors. Financial institutions have recently begun to increase services to Aboriginal people. Banks have been set up on reserves. Native newspapers carry many advertisements from Canada's leading banks as they compete for First Nations business.

With regard to the second set of factors, various joint Aboriginal–government initiatives hold some promise. National Aboriginal organizations have entered into agreements with the federal government to give local control of training programs. Priorities might include short-term skills training or longer-term education within an individual's career plan. Criteria might be based on need or a proven track record. Nevertheless, planning and implementation are in the hands of local Aboriginal people. . . .

The third set of factors may be the most important to Native economic development. Within these choices lie the dangers of assimilation and co-optation. New Aboriginal economic organizations will, necessarily, operate within the context of a global capitalist structure. Entering this economic arena will require developing knowledge about and understanding of capitalist development. Such understanding does not mean accepting or reproducing the capitalist way of doing business. To avoid the political, social, and cultural assimilation that would follow such economic assimilation, Aboriginal organizations must be selective, adapting and modifying existing capitalist business practices to meet their cultural beliefs and needs. Indeed, some writers have argued that this is already the case (Newhouse, 1993). As Ian Chapman, Don McCaskill, and David Newhouse (1991) point out, the management of Aboriginal organizations differs from the capitalist norm in that those bodies are based on the values of consensus-making, elders, advisory boards, and holistic employee development.

Another development strategy could follow the more traditional path of licensing non-Aboriginal corporations to develop the resources on traditional lands. But, as the Royal Commission on Aboriginal Peoples (1996a) argues, these licences must include strict performance requirements that benefit Aboriginal communities. In the context of self-government, these requirements would include preferential training and employment at all levels of operations; preferential access to supply contracts; respect for traditional uses of the territories; acceptance of Aboriginal environmental standards; and union participation in these policies (RCAP, 1996a). Similarly, joint ventures and partnerships with non-Aboriginal people and corporations could be made to provide economic benefits to Aboriginal communities (Anderson, 1995).

Even with full control over their reserve lands and resources, some First Nations will not gain independence, at least in part because most reserves are very small. A land base must include reserve expansion and benefits from industrial development on traditional territories, even where title has been given up. . . . As the RCAP (1996a: 799) states, 'Aboriginal people must participate in federal, provincial and local economic planning mechanisms (such as economic development commissions, economic planning boards, and local economic task forces). The establishment of genuine partnerships with the non-Aboriginal private sector should also be encouraged.'

Joint ventures and partnerships with corporations and governments have been linked historically to the dispossession of Aboriginal peoples and thus may be a new path to cultural genocide. To avoid this new form of assimilation, government and industry must be pushed continually into the 'new paradigm' that fully accepts validation of Aboriginal rights, including the right to self-government. . . .

Conclusion

Aboriginal peoples were once distinct and sovereign nations on the land that is now recognized as Canada. They had their own system of laws, religion, and other institutions, all of which supported self-governance. Long after contact with Europeans they remained sovereign—so much so that they were not only partners in the fur trade economy but also participated in the wars between the European powers in North America. As European settlement in North America grew, the Europeans' desire for more lands and resources became insatiable. The newcomers justified taking First Nations' land by characterizing Aboriginal peoples—their former benefactors and allies—as being less than human. The Europeans created laws based on racist and religious intolerance to dispossess Aboriginal peoples of their land, resources, and cultures.

Over time, Aboriginal peoples' numbers were depleted by disease and epidemics. Non-Aboriginals saw them as a dying race. The First Nations increasingly came under the control of the state and its institutions and were subjugated by law. Many academics have explained this loss of control by applying the tenets of 'dependency theory', arguing that Aboriginal peoples were controlled by outside institutions and individuals and thus became dependent on the state, particularly the Department of Indian Affairs. The theory explains how Aboriginal peoples became dependent, but it does not adequately explain how Aboriginal people continually resisted the domination and control by outsiders. This resistance took many forms, from passive resistance to armed conflict; it was used to exercise their independence and, recently, to increase their control over their lives. The state and interest groups have met this increased control, however, with their own resistance, often based on the argument that no group should have special rights. Liberal ideology, with its dislike for collective rights, lends support, and the courts have given primacy to individual rights over collective rights. . . .

It makes sense for Canadian citizens to embrace the growing control of land and resources, and increasing powers of self-government for Aboriginal peoples. In this new millennium, Aboriginal peoples should be viewed more as partners in Canadian society and recognized for the important contributions they make, and have made, to Canadian society and its immense wealth. Their voices must be heard, respected, and accommodated in discussions and planning for resource development in their traditional territories. They still have important interests and rights to those lands, whether the territories have been ceded or not. . . .

Note

1. We use the terms Aboriginal and Native interchangeably throughout this chapter. The term Indian or First Nations speaks exclusively of those individuals or communities governed by the *Indian Act*.

References

Aboriginal Business Canada. 2002. *Aboriginal Entrepreneurs in Canada: Progress and Prospects*. Ottawa: Industry Canada.

Aboriginal Justice Inquiry of Manitoba. 1991. *The Justice System and Aboriginal People*, Volume I. Winnipeg: Queen's Printer.

Anderson, Robert B. 1995. 'The Business of the First Nations in Saskatchewan: A Contingency Perspective', *Canadian Journal of Native Studies* 15.

Anderson Robert B. 1999. *Economic Development Among the Aboriginal Peoples in Canada: The Hope for the Future*. Toronto: Captus Press.

Aubry, Jack. 1997. 'Tax Dollars Spent on Native Bands Not Controlled Enough, Many Say', *Edmonton Journal*, 20 June, A7.

Barron, F. Laurie. 1984. 'A Summary of Federal Indian Policy in the Canadian West, 1867–1984', *Native Studies Review* 1.

British Columbia. 1997. *Protection of Aboriginal Rights*. Victoria: Ministry of Forests.

Calder v. *A.G. British Columbia*. 1973. D.L.R. (3rd). 145. (Supreme Court of Canada).

Carter, Sarah. 1990. *Lost Harvests: Prairie Indian Reserve Farmers and Government Policy*. Montreal: McGill-Queens University Press.

Chapman, Ian, Don McCaskill, and David Newhouse. 1991. 'Management in Contemporary Aboriginal Organizations', *Canadian Journal of Native Studies* 11 (2).

Clairman, Cara L. 1993. 'First Nations and Environmental Groups in Ontario's Parks—Conflict or Cooperation?', *Canadian Native Law Reporter* 1.

Cleland, Charles E. 1990. 'Indian Treaties and American Myths: Roots of Social Conflicts over Treaty Rights', *Native Studies Review* 6.

Cornell, Stephen, and Joseph Kalt. 1990. 'Pathways from Poverty: Economic Development and Institution-Building on American Indian Reservations', *American Indian Culture and Research Journal* 14.

Delisle, Andrew. 1984. 'How We Regained Control over Our Lives and Territories: The Kahnewake Story', in Leroy Little Bear, Menno Boldt, and J. Anthony Long, eds, *Pathways to Self-Determination: Canadian Indians and the Canadian State*. Toronto: University of Toronto Press.

Drost, Helmar. 1995. 'The Aboriginal–White Unemployment Gap in Canada's Urban Labour Market', *Market Solutions for Native Poverty: Social Policy for the Third Solitude*. Toronto: C.D. Howe Institute.

Dyck, Noel. 1985. *Indigenous People and the Nation-State: Fourth World Politics in Canada, Australia and Norway*. St. John's, NF: Memorial University of Newfoundland.

First Nations Gazette. 1997. Volume 1, Number 1. Saskatoon: Native Law Centre, University of Saskatchewan.

Frideres, James. 1988. 'The Political Economy of Natives in Canadian Society', in James Frideres, ed., *Native Peoples in Canada: Contemporary Conflicts*. Scarborough, ON: Prentice.

_____. 1991. 'Indian Economic Development: Innovations and Obstructions', in John W. Friesen, ed., *The Cultural Maze: Complex Questions on Native Destiny in Western Canada*. Calgary: Detselig.

Friedman, Milton, and Walter W. Heller. 1969. *Monetary vs. Fiscal Policy*. New York: Norton.

Friesen, Gerald. 1987. *The Canadian Prairies: A History*. Toronto: University of Toronto Press.

Gulig, Anthony G. 1994. 'Rights and Resources: A Comparison of Native/Government Resource Relations in the Treaty Ten and Lake Superior Chippewa Ceded Territory'. Paper presented at the 1994 Canadian Historical Association Meeting, University of Calgary, May.

High, Steven. 1996. 'Native Wage Labour and Independent Production During the "Era of Irrelevance" ', *Labour/ La Travail* 37.

Hudson, D.R. 1990. 'Fraser River Fisheries: Anthropology, the State, and First Nations', *Native Studies Review* 6.

Indian Affairs and Northern Development (DIAND). 2001. *Basic Departmental Data, 2000*. Ottawa: Departmental Statistics Section, Information Quality and Research Directorate, Information Management Branch.

Johnston, Darlene. 1993. 'First Nations and Canadian Citizenship', in William Kaplan, ed., *Belonging: The Meaning and Future of Canadian Citizenship*. Montreal: McGill-Queen's University Press.

Kapashesit, Randy, and Murray Klippenstein. 1991. 'Aboriginal Group Rights and Environmental Protection', *McGill Law Journal* 36.

Kellough, Gail. 1980. 'From Colonialism to Economic Imperialism: The Experience of the Canadian Indian', in John Harp and John R. Hofley, eds, *Structured Inequality in Canada*. Scarborough, ON: Prentice-Hall.

Knight, Rolf. 1996. *Indians at Work: An Informal History of Native Indian Labour in British Columbia, 1858–1930*. Vancouver: New Star.

Krauter, Joseph, and Morris Davis. 1978. *Minority Canadians: Ethnic Groups*. Toronto: Methuen.

Kymlicka, Will. 1989. *Liberalism, Community and Culture*. New York: Oxford University Press.

Loo, Tina. 1994. *Making Law, Order and Authority in British Columbia, 1821–1871*. Toronto: University of Toronto Press.

MacInnes, T.R.L. 1946. 'History of Indian Administration in Canada', *Canadian Journal of Economics and Political Science* 12.

McArthur, Doug. 1989. 'The New Aboriginal Economic Development Institutions', in Paul Kariya, ed., *Native Socio-Economic Development in Canada: Change, Promise and Innovation*. Toronto: Institute for Urban Studies.

McMillan, Alan. 1988. *Native Peoples and Cultures of Canada: An Anthropological Overview*. Vancouver: Douglas and McIntyre.

Medcalf, Linda. 1978. *Law and Identity: Lawyers, Native Americans and Legal Practice*. Beverly Hills: Sage.

Miller, J.R. 1989. *Skyscrapers Hide the Heavens: A History of Indian–White Relations in Canada*. Toronto: University of Toronto Press.

Miller, J.R. 1991. 'Owen Glendower, Hotspur and Canadian Policy', in J.R. Miller, ed., *Sweet Promises: A Reader on Indian–White Relations in Canada*. Toronto: University of Toronto Press.

Milloy, John S. 1983. 'The Early Indian Acts: Development Strategy and Constitutional Change', in Ian Getty and Antoine Lussier, eds, *As Long as the Sun Shines and Water Flows*. Vancouver: University of British Columbia Press.

Newhouse, David R. 1993. 'Modern Aboriginal Economies: Capitalism with an Aboriginal Face', in *Royal Commission on Aboriginal Peoples, Sharing the Harvest: The Road to Self Reliance*. Ottawa: Supply and Services.

Parnell, Ted. 1976. 'The Process of Economic Underdevelopment', in Ted Parnell, ed., *Disposable Native*. Edmonton: Alberta Human Rights and Civil Liberties Association.

Penner, Keith. 1983. 'Minutes of Proceedings and Evidence'. Report of the Special Committee on Indian Self-Government in Canada 40 (12, 20 October). Ottawa: House of Common Standing Committee on Indian Affairs and Northern Development.

Powderface, Sykes. 1984. 'Self-Government Means Biting the Hand that Feeds Us', in Leroy Little Bear, Menno Boldt, and J. Anthony Long, eds, *Pathways to Self-Determination: Canadian Indians and the Canadian State*. Toronto: University of Toronto Press.

R. v. Sparrow. 1990. 4 *Western Weekly Reports* 410 (Supreme Court of Canada).

Ray, A.J. 1974. *Indians in the Fur Trade: Their Role as Trappers, Hunters, and Middlemen in the Lands Southwest of Hudson Bay, 1660–1870*. Toronto: University of Toronto Press.

Royal Commission on Aboriginal Peoples (RCAP). 1996a. 'Economic Development'. *Royal Commission on Aboriginal People*. Ottawa: Supply and Services.

Royal Commission on Aboriginal Peoples (RCAP). 1996b. 'Lands and Resources'. *Royal Commission on Aboriginal People*. Vol. II: Restructuring the Relationship. Ottawa: Supply and Services.

Satzewich, Vic. 1996. 'Where's the Beef?: Cattle Killing, Rations Policy and First Nations "Criminality" in Southern Alberta, 1892–1895', *Journal of Historical Sociology* 9.

Sloan, Pamela, and Roger Hill. 1995. *Corporate Aboriginal Relations: Best Practise Case Studies*. Toronto: Hill Sloan.

Smith, Mel. 1995. *Our Home or Native Land?* Victoria: Crown Western.

Statistics Canada. 1999a. *Labour Force Update*. Catalogue 71-005-XPB, Summer. Ottawa. Statistics Canada.

Statistics Canada. 1999b. 'General Social Survey: Time Use.' *The Daily*, November 9. Catalogue 12F0080XIE. Ottawa: Statistics Canada.

Statistics Canada. 2002a. *Canadian Economic Observer*. Catalogue 11-010-XPB, May. Ottawa. Statistics Canada.

Statistics Canada. 2002b. *Labour Force Information*. Catalogue 71-001-PPb, March. Ottawa. Statistics Canada.

Supreme Court of Canada. 1999. 'R. v. Marshall', *Canadian Native Law Reporter*. Saskatoon: University of Saskatchewan Native Law Centre.

Tough, Frank. 1985. 'Challenges to the Native Economy of Northern Manitoba in the Post-Treaty Period, 1870–1900', *Native Studies Review* 1.

Usher, Peter J. 1987. 'Indigenous Management Systems and the Conservation of Wildlife in the Canadian North', *Alternatives* 14(1).

Waldram, James B. 1994. 'Canada's 'Indian Problem' and the Indian's Canada Problem', in L. Samuelson, ed., *Power and Resistance: Critical Thinking about Canadian Social Issues*. Halifax: Fernwood.

Walter, Gerald R. 1994. 'Defining Sustainable Communities', *International Journal of Forestry* 10(2).

Watkins, Mel. 1977. *Dene Nation: The Colony Within*. Toronto: University of Toronto Press.

Weaver, Sally. 1985. 'Federal Difficulties with Aboriginal Rights', in Menno Boldt and J. Anthony Long, eds, *The Quest for Justice: Aboriginal Peoples and Aboriginal Rights*. Toronto: University of Toronto Press.

Weaver, Sally. 1990. 'A New Paradigm in Canadian Indian Policy for the 1990s', *Canadian Ethnic Studies* 22.

Wotherspoon, Terry, and Vic Satzewich. 1993. *First Nations: Race, Class, and Gender Relations*. Scarborough, ON: Nelson.

York, Geoffrey. 1990. *The Dispossessed: Life and Death in Native Canada*. Toronto: Little.

Chapter 24

Sharing, Community, and Decolonization: Urban Aboriginal Community Development

Jim Silver, Parvin Ghorayshi, Joan Hay, and Darlene Klyne

In this chapter, urban Aboriginal people, long-time activists in their community, outline an inspiring, holistic, Aboriginal approach to community development. Rooted in traditional Aboriginal values of sharing and community, this approach to community development starts with the individual and the individual's need to heal from the damage of colonization. The process of people's healing, of their rebuilding or recreating themselves, is rooted in a revived sense of community and a revitalization of Aboriginal cultures; this in turn requires the building of Aboriginal organizations. The process of reclaiming an Aboriginal identity takes place, therefore, at an individual, community, organizational and ultimately political level. This is a process now underway; it is a process of decolonization that, if it can continue to be rooted in traditional Aboriginal values of sharing and community, will be the foundation upon which healing and rebuilding are based,

This is a much different sense of 'development' from that often taken for granted in the West. It is more consistent with a set of ideas and practices that have been critical of Western notions of development.

The post-Second World War initiatives that led to the idea of development have been widely criticized as exclusionary. Critics argue that development models premised upon the Western notion of modernization and capitalism have predomin-antly benefitted those who already have economic power (Hart-Landsberg and Burkett, 2001; Sparr, 1994). By attempting to generate prosperity within the framework of the capitalist market economy, development strategies have ignored the well-being of many (Sen, 1999). Development has become a new colonialism, contributing to underdevelopment, which has turned the nations of the South into exploitable resources and dependent consumers (Zaoual, 1999), and created barriers to human development and freedom (Sen, 1999). Many people have begun to question this concept of development—with its emphasis on profit and the pursuit of growth, and its enrichment of some and impoverishment of many—both in the 'West' and in the 'rest' of the world.

Marginalized groups in northern countries, like their counterparts elsewhere, have been the target of development strategies. What came to be labelled as the key characteristics of underdevelopment in southern countries, such as poverty and lack of access to education, health care and employment, for example, also exist among various groups of people in the North (Veltmeyer and O'Malley, 2001; Labrecque, 1991). Aboriginal people are a good example of people in the North who have been living in what came to be known as 'underdeveloped conditions' and who have been the target of development policies (Loxley, 1981, 2000; Silver, 2003).

Community development has been advanced as an alternative. There are considerable differences between strategies, but in general, community development involves the continuous process of capacity building: building upon and strengthening local resources to generate well-being among community members (Dreier, 1996; Fals-Borda, 1992; Fisher and Shragge, 2002; Perry, n.d.: 1–21; Lewis, 1994; Fontan et al., 1999). Community development is based on the premise that community members need to gain control of resources to generate economic well-being. The general goal of community development is to benefit those who have been marginalized from the current economic system.

In this chapter, we focus on Aboriginal community development in an inner-city setting. We draw upon the experiences of twenty-six Aboriginal people, men and women, young and old, who have been and remain active in Winnipeg inner-city community development. We use this case study to enter into the debate on development in general, and community development for Aboriginal people in particular. We show how Aboriginal people have been constructed as the 'other' within Canadian society. Colonialism negatively affected, and continues to negatively affect, Aboriginal people: their economy, identity, culture, family, community, and well-being. Despite difficulties, urban Aboriginal people have continued their struggles to reclaim their history and reconstruct their lives. . . .

Construction of Aboriginal People as the 'Other': Colonization and Its Impact

The Canadian government's deliberate strategy from the late nineteenth and most of the twentieth century with respect to Aboriginal people was assimilation, which required the destruction of Aboriginal cultures. The justification for what can only be seen as a strategy of state-sanctioned violence against an entire people was that Aboriginal cultures were inferior to European-based cultures, and therefore the attempt to destroy

Aboriginal cultures was a 'civilizing' mission. Aboriginal people resisted this process and have clung tenaciously to their traditional ways of life, but the damage to individuals and to families from this campaign of cultural destruction has been massive.

Aboriginal people refer to the residential schools as their most painful encounter with colonialism. Those we interviewed expressed to us in a variety of ways that residential school was based on the idea that anything to do with Aboriginal people—knowledge, education, family, community, spirituality, language, their very way of being—had to be transformed. The residential schools did not prepare them for the outside world but put down their culture, broke their family ties and, worst of all, instilled a sense of shame. Former students rightly call themselves 'residential school survivors.' Residential school was a transformative experience for many Aboriginal people. Joseph[1] tells us:

> It produced individuals with new personalities. You never know who you are, there was a lost identity, and I speak really about myself, I didn't know who I was . . . consequently I was in no-man's land when I came out of residential school. . . .

Racism

Racism is an almost inevitable product of this process of colonization. All participants talk about racism and how it has affected, and continues to affect, their lives. Charles states: 'I remember as a child, there was a lot of racism, eh, and like more openly. . . . We grew up in a really heavily racist time, and it was like, openly, you know.' He describes the use of language:

> common phrases like . . . called us Indians, call us things like 'Chief' but like Indian was used like a swear word, it wasn't really used to describe a nation of people, it was used to describe, you know, people who were drunk, lazy, you know, all the sort of false images.

Racism continues to be a daily experience for Aboriginal people in Winnipeg. One of the things that most aggravates them is that non-Aboriginal people are so frequently oblivious to this. Maggie describes a recent high-level civic meeting, where an important city figure said, 'I have tried everything for Aboriginal students just to stay in the programs, I think they just need to be encouraged.'

> And I just looked at her . . . and I was just like, speechless, and that doesn't happen often, but I didn't even know what to say other than to look at her, like, 'are you for real? We just need to be encouraged?' How insulting. . . . It's all across the board, like, racism is very much alive in this city.

Destruction of Identity and Self-Esteem

The belief that Aboriginal cultures are inferior was constantly expressed by non-Aboriginal people. Some Aboriginal people have internalized those colonial beliefs, and they carry the pain of their supposed inferiority. It weighs them down because one needs a positive sense of oneself to cope with the world. (For a similar argument regarding African-Americans, see hooks, 2003.) . . .

For some, the burden of internalizing colonialism manifests itself in a lack self-esteem and self-confidence. Ethel remembers when she was young and carrying 'lots of shame'. Another woman, Ingrid, describes her teenage years as feeling 'very ashamed of who I was. I couldn't look anybody in the eye, you know, I walked half my life with my head down, very ashamed of who I was.'

These are typical examples of the difficulties that these exceptionally gifted inner-city community leaders have experienced at different stages of their lives. Despite these difficulties, they have made remarkable changes in their lives and in their communities. . . .

Community Development By and For Aboriginal People

We have already discussed the devastating impact of colonization on Aboriginal people and their way of life. The twenty-six participants in this study fought back, rebuilt their lives, and reclaimed their culture. All have become leaders in their communities. In particular, the older people in this group began doing 'community development' long before the term became popular in Canada. For these 'organic intellectuals', Aboriginal community development directly challenges Western models of development. It starts with decolonization; recognizes and builds on people's skills and empowers them; honours Aboriginal traditions, values and cultures; rebuilds a sense of community among Aboriginal people; goes beyond economic needs; and generates organizations and mechanisms for democratic participation. This approach to community development is holistic.

Decolonization

Through community development, people learn the true value of their work and how the dominant system excludes them (Freire, 1973; Morgan, 1996). Teaching the history of oppression to affected groups, so that community members can understand, articulate and recognize the forces that oppressed them, is essential (Okazawa-Rey and Wong, 1997). This raises political consciousness and is part of the process of decolonization (Shor and Freire, 1987; Freire, 1973). For the participants in this study, Aboriginal community development requires, as a starting point, an understanding that colonization has had a devastating impact on the lives of Aboriginal people. By addressing the colonizing agenda and deconstructing the colonial discourse, Aboriginal people can reclaim their voices and their collective post-colonial identity can emerge. Healing is an outcome of this program and requires both an understanding of the historical process of colonization and an immersion in Aboriginal culture. . . .

Josephine advocates that 'we have to get to know ourselves', because the process of colonization took away her sense of identity. As she puts it, you 'never knew who you are, there was a lost identity, and I speak really about myself, I didn't know who I was.' The same is stressed by Walter: 'Culture is a very big part of who we are as

Aboriginal people. . . . Once our culture is in place, people are learning it, they are practising it, and eventually you are going to know who you are . . . and we have to know who we are to be able to succeed anywhere.' Along the same line, Ethel believes that healing 'begins first with the person and then it just floods out, it's like a pebble dropping; once that pebble drops, it just has an effect—self, family, jobs, community. For our people I think the first thing they have to do is do their own piece. . . . The next level isn't there until that piece is done with yourself.' She adds that Aboriginal people won't become involved in community development 'unless they've done their own work first. Because why would they be concerned about community if they're just surviving?' This process of cultural retrieval is a crucial part of inner-city Aboriginal people becoming involved in community development. They cannot do it without first *healing* themselves, and the process of healing involves the promotion of Aboriginal cultures, so that they can regain a positive sense of identity. . . .

Again and again, in different ways, we were told that the first step in Aboriginal community development is rebuilding the sense of Aboriginal identity and the pride in being Aboriginal, and an understanding of the process and consequences of colonization. This is the foundation. As Jack states: 'if people don't feel good about themselves as a person, as a Cree or Ojibwa or whatever person . . . they tend to have low self-esteem and tend to be more involved in negative coping . . . alcohol, drugs.' Many problems that Aboriginal people face are rooted in their loss of identity. Ethel describes the sense of shame that she felt as a youngster, the product of both her institutionalization, first in residential school and then in the Manitoba Youth Centre, and the disconnection that she felt from her family and from mainstream institutions. She describes 'acting out', and nobody in the school appearing to understand that she was a little girl carrying a huge burden of pain.

Non-Aboriginal people are disconnected from that Aboriginal reality. This is a part of the disconnection from the dominant culture, most members

of which do not see the internalized consequences of colonization. They see the behaviour, the acting out, but they do not see that this is a product of the dominant culture, of the disruption caused by colonization. She says: 'it wasn't until that point of healing that I started truly understanding what colonization meant, first of all to myself, and then to our family and then to our community.' The process of healing, on a person-by-person basis, and the process of community-building are part of a holistic process of Aboriginal community development. . . .

Bringing Back the Sense of Community

Strong relationships and social ties are referred to as social capital. Community development, it is argued, entails building social relationships. . . . This empowers individuals, strengthens bonds and may also build a united political force. Aboriginal people need, Shirley believes, places and spaces to connect and to talk: 'a long time ago in our communities there were always . . . places in the community . . . where you could sit and talk and listen. So we need to somehow recreate that in a way that fits the urban environment.' Richard stresses the importance of establishing a sense of community:

> A lot of people who grew up in the North End do community development by virtue of the fact that they come from conditions that are not always ideal, that is, they're poor, they come oftentimes from visible minorities, so they experience racism and discrimination and all of those sorts of things, so growing up in that kind of environment, you naturally tend towards a sense of community, so when I grew up as a little boy and onwards there was a real powerful sense of community in the North End. I grew up all of my life there, so I'm what's called an urban Indian, I guess. I can recall very, very clearly the strong sense of community that existed.

. . . This sense of belonging generates Aboriginal involvement in the community, states Maggie:

> I think where people miss the mark on involving the Aboriginal community is really creating those

opportunities just to get together and talk. I've seen that on a local level, just with our community care centres, people coming to our centres, sitting around, having a coffee, getting to know each other and saying, 'hey, wouldn't it be nice if we put together a summer program for kids,' and [her organization] can do that, can support that.

Others doing Aboriginal community development share these values; they talk about building human relationships. For instance, Maggie states, 'building those relationships, going door-to-door, you know, knocking on people's doors, sitting around the kitchen table having a coffee and building that relationship'. Ethel adds: 'if you want community people involved, you've got to meet with your community . . . come right to your constituents, right to your neighbourhoods and get them involved.' . . . This idea is further stressed by Charles, who firmly believes that Aboriginal people need to build a sense of community in what others have called an 'asset-based' fashion (Kretzmann and McKnight, 1993):

> So when we look at community . . . look at the value of people, you know, what do they have to offer, what is good about them, eh? You know, you go into the North End or you go into any sort of poor community, you make tea, and people organize around a cup of tea, they bring cigarettes out, and they share, and you know, those are community development things that we overlook . . . people helping each other out.

Starting Where People Are, Empowering and Creating Opportunities

Community development starts where people are and values local knowledge and people's understanding and aspirations for their lives and their communities. There is a conscious attempt made to identify and incorporate local knowledge in community development programs. By adopting such an approach, community development has the potential to foster cultural preservation and to weaken exploitative outside forces (Voyageur and Calliou, 2003; O'Donnell and Karanja, 2000).

Many of the participants in this study stressed the importance of starting where people are and patiently building from there. The damage done by colonization is not undone overnight. They support people in finding their own ways and making their own choices, in their own time. This may be a lengthy process. Donna states that people

> come to the centre and they look like they are in crisis, and you just need to listen to them sometimes, and they just move, they are given options and they just fly on their own and some take years. But as long as there is that little movement on their part and stuff like that, we will support them if it takes twenty years. Because that is what it takes sometimes. You got to get them where they are at, where people are at. . . . You need to let them be at the point where they are ready, because why put them some place that they are not ready for it? Then they don't make it, and it is like, you know, because you get tired of failing, so you need to wait to see.

She adds:

> And so long as they are growing and that is where their comfort level is then you stay, there is never any push. . . . Let the creator do his work, stop trying to do his work for him. . . . Just give the opportunities and when people are ready they will get the strength they need to do what they need to do. It may not be the choice I make, but it might be the choice they need to make. . . .

Aboriginal Organizations, Aboriginal Leadership

Aboriginal organizations—those run by and for Aboriginal people in a way consistent with Aboriginal values—as we have seen earlier, have been a critical source of empowerment for all of the participants in this study. Therefore, for all of them, Aboriginal community development requires the building of Aboriginal organizations.

All participants reminded us that urban Aboriginal people have formed and run many Aboriginal organizations in Winnipeg. They also emphasized that much of this community development work, although not all, is being done by Aboriginal women. It is Aboriginal women who are, for the most part, the leaders in putting into practice an Aboriginal form of community development. . . .

Their organizing efforts reflect the movement toward enabling Aboriginal people to run their own affairs and creating an Aboriginal community development rooted in traditional Aboriginal values of sharing and community. This process has been going on for years in Winnipeg, at least since the 1960s, when Aboriginal people began coming to the city, but it is a story largely untold. Nonetheless, even the bare outline of the story reveals that building Aboriginal organizations has involved mobilizing Aboriginal people to challenge and to wrest power from those in control.

Indian Métis Friendship Centre

One of the first Aboriginal organizations in Winnipeg, indeed, perhaps the first, was the Indian Métis Friendship Centre (IMFC). John describes being part of the Company of Young Canadians in the early 1960s, charged with organizing Friendship Centres into the Manitoba Association of Friendship Centres. When the IMFC started, it was run by 'a white board, and a white director . . . the intent was good.' Within five years, the centre had elected an all-Aboriginal board and hired an Aboriginal director. This was not easy. There was considerable resistance to this change, because at that time it was believed that Aboriginal people could not run their own affairs. . . .

Now there are many Aboriginal organizations in Winnipeg: 'there are about seventy organizations in the city now that have been formed over the last thirty years and most of them owe their being to the Friendship Centres.'

Sometimes efforts to establish Aboriginal organizations did not succeed. John told us that the Main Street Project 'was originally a native organization, [it was a] native group of people who were concerned that their relations were dying in the back alleys of the hotels there and freezing in the cold.' One of our participants, Joseph, got involved with the Main Street Project and started

looking for funding, but the federal government backed off because it was off-reserve, and the provincial government dismissed it, saying it was not responsible for Treaty Indians. Someone with the provincial government said: 'Add some white people to the board, then we can consider funding, then it's not an Indian board.' They did as suggested and the province of Manitoba funded the Main Street Project, and the federal government followed suit, 'That's how it became funded, at the beginning, but then the Indian people got crowded out and it became a white board because the money started to flow. . . . People forget that it was a native initiative.'

Children of the Earth High School

Children of the Earth High School, the Aboriginal high school in Winnipeg's North End, has its origins in the early 1980s in a series of meetings of urban Aboriginal people who had been active in the community, especially around education issues. As Richard describes it: 'there was a strong sense that the schools were not providing the kind of education that our kids needed, that oftentimes they were very racist environments, that the content that was being taught in schools was very biased and very white mainstream Euro-Canadian information.' The inner-city Aboriginal community mobilized large numbers in support of educational changes. Several meetings were held that drew hundreds of Aboriginal students and youth, who said their first priority was educational change.

There was considerable outside opposition to an approach that involved mobilizing large numbers of Aboriginal people and challenging such a powerful institution of the dominant culture—the Winnipeg School Division. There was even opposition from within the Aboriginal community by people who did not want to offend the system. . . . Opposition from the School Division was intense:

because they had their own agenda, they didn't want to see the kinds of significant changes we were suggesting because it would mean changes to their curriculum and changes to their administration and really those changes being untested. And main-stream systems have a hard time dealing with unknowns and they have a hard time dealing with untested kinds of theories or ideas about how things ought to be done. So there's always a great deal of hesitancy when Aboriginal people or other minority groups approach mainstream systems for changes.

Nevertheless, as the result of a very significant mobilization of urban Aboriginal people over a period of years, urban Aboriginal people in Winnipeg were successful in establishing the inner-city Aboriginal high school, Children of the Earth.

Ma Mawi Wi Chi Itata

Like education, child welfare is an area in which Aboriginal people have had many negative experiences. These experiences led, by a similar process of large-scale mobilization and confrontation, to the establishment of the Ma Mawi Wi Chi Itata Centre, the urban Aboriginal child welfare agency. As Richard explains it, the Ma Mawi movement:

came from the Original Women's Network, and it came from the urban community, that whole initiative to make some changes in child welfare. . . . There was a whole coalition of Aboriginal organizations . . . to get some control over child welfare in Winnipeg and we were lobbying government to try and get some of the funding as well as some of the changes to the Child and Family Services Act so that it was more reflective of Aboriginal people and Aboriginal wants and needs. The people who were involved in this movement were people who were just from the community, you know. . . . There were some high-profile people, but high-profile people in terms of their involvement in community development already, people like Kathy Mallett, for example . . . and Linda Clarkson, who was also involved very strongly in community development in the late seventies, early eighties . . . and Wayne Helgason, when he was just beginning to, when he was actually working for Northwest Child and Family Services and he was beginning to get involved in community development and he

didn't like what he was seeing and what was happening so he was one of the . . . first 'system' people who was beginning to get involved. But this whole movement just, just escalated, just took off, it was a huge groundswell because obviously the issue that was at hand was one that affected the whole community, both urban and rural, because all of us had experiences that involved child welfare in one way or another, so people just jumped to the cause and put a lot, a lot, of pressure on government, which ended up in the changes to the Child and Family Service Act of 1984, and it also ended with the establishment of Ma Mawi Wi Chi Itata Centre. That was a community development initiative. That was a very purposeful agenda that was put together by grassroots people in the community to make some changes to a system.

The result is a completely Aboriginal organization, run according to Aboriginal values and deeply rooted in the inner-city Aboriginal community. But the creation of Ma Mawi, like the creation of Children of the Earth, required a form of community development that was mobilizing and challenging, and that was rooted in the community and the community's real needs, and in the Aboriginal values of community and sharing.

Without this kind of mobilizing and challenging political strategy, big gains like the establishment of Ma Mawi and Children of the Earth are not possible. This is because non-Aboriginal people, as Miles says, 'still have this view that they'll tell us what to do. With the growing confidence we have in the Aboriginal community, we want to do these things now ourselves, and there's a real kind of subtle undercurrent opposing that—giving the control to Aboriginal groups. . . . We want it now and I don't think they want to give it up.' He adds that this process is 'moving, oh, so slowly. . . . You can't even really see it's moving, but I think they know it's moving now.' This is the almost subterranean process—invisible to most outside the inner city—that is now occurring. It is a struggle. It is a process of throwing off the urban shackles of colonialism. It is a crucial part of the process of Aboriginal community development.

Aboriginal Organizations Run By and For Aboriginal People

There are, in Winnipeg's inner city, deeply held grievances about non-Aboriginal people delivering services to and for Aboriginal people, and thus earning good incomes from jobs built on Aboriginal people's grief. Central to the emergent Aboriginal form of community development is the belief that this is exploitative and ineffective, and must be replaced by Aboriginal organizations run by and for Aboriginal people in a fashion consistent with Aboriginal values. Alice says: 'but really, like social work . . . it's a system of employment, eh . . . where you're not making a product but you are still administering people's pain, managing people's pain.' . . .

Genuine community development involves Aboriginal people solving their own problems through their own organizations. Alice says: 'Having control over our own lives . . . it's the best community development you'll have.' She argues that:

> Aboriginal people need to do it ourselves, in our way. And underline our values. I mean the paradox is that everyone wants a good life for themselves and their families . . . but we have different ways of getting there. And our way of getting there is just as valid as a Western way of getting there. . . . If it is not 'ourselves doing it,' it becomes a form of 'development' that is tantamount to cultural imperialism.

. . . Today in the inner city there continues to be conflict between Aboriginal and non-Aboriginal organizations over the issue of Aboriginal control. A lot of inner-city money still goes to non-Aboriginal organizations working to meet the needs of Aboriginal people, and in many cases the staff employed are non-Aboriginal people. This creates a great deal of resentment. As Miles says: 'if you look at all those groups, the non-native groups, there's a lot of jobs there, there's a lot of resources go there,' but many Aboriginal people believe that soon they are going to have to 'transfer those organizations to the groups they work with.' . . .

But this process of Aboriginal people taking control is slow. There is resistance. And although 'the organizations that have helped us over the years have *not* led to change,' those who benefit from the system as it is now, according to Doug, 'have their teeth well-sunk into the status quo'. But, as he correctly observes, 'good community development challenges the status quo.'

Aboriginal Community Development Is Not Just About Economics

Aboriginal community development is holistic. It focuses on the individual, the family, the community, the cultures, the organizations. And it focuses on the spiritual and emotional aspects of people's lives, not just on economic development. Thus Walter states:

> So for me, for Aboriginal people to truly succeed, and for the communities to get better . . . you need sort of a holistic approach to community development. . . . Community economic development is just a small part of it. . . . When I talk about holistic we are not just talking about education, training, or employment, we are talking about supporting the individual.

. . . Economic issues need to be dealt with, but they have to be put in the context of the Aboriginal reality. As Doug puts it: 'I have a concern that all too often community development moves to community economic development too fast.' Richard adds:

> But those economic issues also need to be framed inside of our own understanding of who we are and about our values and our sense of community and our sense of sharing and our sense of co-operation. [Otherwise,] the values get removed from the initiative, right? And they simply then begin to act as corporations that make profit and they lose this notion of the sharing that needs to happen inside of any economic activity in the community.[2]

But doing this, developing and maintaining a specifically Aboriginal community development process grounded in the Aboriginal values of sharing and community is a difficult challenge, because when one tries to maintain those values in an organizational form there is a danger, Doug argues, that one will:

> get caught up or get sucked into that whole, larger sort of capitalist economic development notion . . . and it's going to continue to be a difficult challenge because as we more and more impact on those wider systems, we get pulled into them, we eventually become part of them, and when we become part of them, we sometimes simply adopt what's already in place rather than make changes to those systems ourselves. And when we do that we then begin to lose ourselves. . . .

Most of our interviewees expressed the belief that Aboriginal values, particularly those related to community and sharing, must be the basis of Aboriginal community development. This is a form of decolonization, in that, as Richard says 'we'd be strengthening who we are, we'd be reconstructing who we are.'

The use of traditional Aboriginal values as a fundamental part of Aboriginal community development has grown dramatically in recent decades and is the product of decades of work by urban Aboriginal people in Winnipeg's inner city. . . .

Even the language, the words, to enable Aboriginal people to talk about rebuilding their culture and their community along Aboriginal lines had to be retrieved and re-inserted into everyday discourse. This has been an important creative process and a central feature of Aboriginal community development. And Richard is saying that a part of this work is intellectual—building and articulating and making into 'common sense' the analysis of the decolonization process, for example. This suggests the importance to Aboriginal community development of 'organic intellectuals'—Aboriginal intellectuals rooted in traditional Aboriginal ways of thinking as well as the realities of the inner city. Richard continues: 'One of the things that we've learned, certainly that I've learned throughout all of that, is that

there's still a tremendous amount of work that we need to do around community development, and part of that work relates to strengthening that decolonization process and to continue to build the analysis inside of the community.' Organic intellectuals of the Aboriginal community have developed an analysis of the process of colonization and decolonization and of their relationship to Aboriginal people's often harsh inner-city lives. They interpret those lives through an Aboriginal lens, with an Aboriginal world view. It is the development of a 'counter-hegemony'—an interpretation of Aboriginal people's lives that is counter to, alternative to, the largely colonial views of the dominant culture.

Thus Aboriginal community development requires that Aboriginal people heal and go through the process of decolonization. But healing is not just an individual process; it requires a community that is strong and healthy. That in turn requires an understanding and appreciation of Aboriginal culture and knowledge, and to achieve this requires the development of Aboriginal organizations—organizations run by and for Aboriginal people and operated in ways consistent with and respectful of Aboriginal culture. And all of this requires adherence to an ideology rooted in an understanding of the historical effects of colonization and the necessity for decolonization. This in turn requires the development of 'intellectuals'— in at least some cases elders, but not only elders— capable of developing and articulating this ideology. So it is in this way that Aboriginal community development is holistic—it focuses on the individual, the family, the community, the cultures, and the organization. And it focuses on the spiritual and emotional aspects of people's lives, not just on economic development.

A Future Full of Hope

Those active in inner-city Aboriginal community development face a number of challenges, but they are hopeful about the future. Up to the early 1960s, very few Aboriginal people lived in Winnipeg. As their numbers have grown and their urban experience has deepened, they have built their own, distinctive Aboriginal forms of community development. The gains that they have made have been substantial and important, and theirs is a sophisticated and holistic form of urban community development. But the challenges that remain are daunting.

New and Old Challenges

The participants in this study are proud of their communities' achievements and believe there is no turning back. However, they are aware of the challenges that continue to face them. They are concerned about persistent poverty, racism, violence, lack of direction among youth, emerging class divisions among Aboriginal people, and the necessity for a collective voice.

Many talk about the difficulties that Aboriginal people are facing in Winnipeg. Alice believes that 'racism is . . . deep in this culture.' They remind us that many urban Aboriginal people are struggling with poverty, which affects their choices and life chances. James adds that the 'vast majority of our people are in the lower income strata; I believe that is probably one of the reasons why people sort of have a hard time trying to do things for ourselves.' He continues, 'I live down in the inner city and I see a lot of challenges that the inner city faces, you know there is poverty, there are young families that are just trying to make ends meet. . . . There are people on social assistance, there are Aboriginal youth there that have no direction as to what they want to do.' . . .

Violence in Aboriginal communities is a grave concern for the people we have talked to. Verna says: 'I wondered why is there still such a high suicide rate, why seven youth killed themselves in the past year in this community.' Walter says: 'what is happening out there, you know, youth violence seems to be increasing, you know every day you hear about a kid getting beaten or getting killed.' John warns us:

We've been very, very quiet and very, very silent, yet the problems in our communities continue to

escalate and ah, not so much in the cities but more in the reserves . . . and in the poverty stricken communities where a lot of our people are still languishing in poverty . . . drinking going on . . . gang problems and so on . . . absolute third world state.

The majority of Aboriginal people are struggling in their daily lives, but a small minority is succeeding, economically and otherwise. . . .

Indeed class divisions are already emerging in the Aboriginal community (Hull, 2001). And it is clear from our interviews that some Aboriginal leaders are ambitious in an individualistic sense, at odds with the Aboriginal values of community and sharing.

A gap is emerging between the 'haves' and 'have-nots' in Winnipeg's Aboriginal community because, John argues, Aboriginal organizations—community development and political organizations—are not rooted in Aboriginal values. He says: 'our Aboriginal values and traditions and customs and beliefs are all different from the larger society. . . . Until we establish our own identity as a distinct group of people it's not going to make any difference.' John believes that to undertake Aboriginal community development is to establish Aboriginal identity, and pride in it, as something different and then to build Aboriginal organizations rooted in that Aboriginal identity, in that differentness, in the traditional values of community and of sharing. . . .

Non-Aboriginal People: Walk Beside Us, Not in Front, Nor Behind

Aboriginal people regularly experience the divide between themselves and a non-Aboriginal community that does not want to listen. As Alice states:

To me that is all I call it, it's racism. There's a real divide between, I mean they don't hear us, we can say you know, jeez, we should have our own school and they don't hear us, they don't hear us. I mean . . . they got to fix themselves before they even begin to look at trying to help us. They really have to look at their own stuff.

People in this study genuinely believe, and have indicated in different ways, that they need non-Aboriginal people to be their allies in doing community development. They want non-Aboriginal people to be prepared to transfer some of their power and to operate on an equal footing with their Aboriginal allies. They want the non-Aboriginal community to listen to them and hear them, share their skills and experiences with them, without imposing their views and their ideas on Aboriginal people.

There is no doubt that non-Aboriginal people's involvement is needed. But only a particular kind of involvement is acceptable. Agatha puts it: 'There definitely should be a relationship, we cannot do this alone. Our non-Aboriginal brothers and sisters have to be walking beside us, not in front of us, not behind us but beside us in this work. But also they have to be very respectful as well and open to hearing a new way of doing things, and that hasn't always been the case, you know.' Similarly, Mary states: 'I think the idea of partnership is good, but I think it must be a true partnership and I think that, you know, we really cannot become effective partners until we have some power.'

Aboriginal people are asking for allies who respect their values and authority and will share with them their experience and skills and their power. . . .

To be an effective ally, non-Aboriginal people need to educate themselves. When they go into Aboriginal communities, they must be very sensitive and conscious of their position and their actions. This means being reflexive—being aware of white privilege and acting accordingly, acting supportively and co-operatively, with a full knowledge of one's position in the hierarchy. . . .

It is through learning and un-learning that non-Aboriginal people can reflect upon themselves and their relationship or non-relationship with the Aboriginal community, and can understand their place within this process. Through reflexivity, non-Aboriginal people can learn to become the kind of allies that Aboriginal people are asking for: those who will walk beside Aboriginal people, not in front, not behind them.

An Alternative Relationship with the State

Aboriginal people have always had a contradictory relationship with the state. On the one hand, the participants in this study are very critical of state institutions. Although they recognize both the power and limitations of the state, one after another has told us that the educational system has failed Aboriginal people; that Aboriginal people do not trust the system; that the justice system is biased against Aboriginal people; that government programs and policies—particularly those associated with Indian Affairs—are not in touch with the reality of Aboriginal people, and repeatedly betray a lack of understanding of Aboriginal issues; that government has created an 'Indian Industry'; that there are too many reports, too many programs, too many ineffective and costly big projects, as opposed to grassroots projects; that policies are short-sighted and do not have a long-term vision; and that government has created a culture of dependency among many Aboriginal people.

On the other hand, despite these and other criticisms, inner-city Aboriginal organizations depend on government and charitable organizations for their financial survival. They have to apply for funding, account for their spending and meet the expectations of the funders. This necessitates the creation and maintenance of good working relations with governments and others who control the flow of funds. These efforts deliver benefits, in the form of the maintenance and gradual growth of programs that assist inner-city Aboriginal people and the creation of jobs for inner-city Aboriginal people.

Politics of Access

The economic advantages of developing and maintaining these positive relationships with governments lead to what might be called a 'politics of access'. Community-based organizations need access to governments and other funders—those with money. In some cases this means a 'don't bite the hand that feeds you' form of politics. . . .

In other cases these economic realities lead inner-city Aboriginal activists to consider that they ought to join forces with those who allocate the resources. This strategy most often leads to developing close working relationships with, or even joining, the Liberal Party of Canada. The Liberal Party has usually governed at the federal level, where the largest resources are located and where First Nations people have historically negotiated with the state.

The 'politics of access' leads many of the best inner-city community development practitioners to refuse involvement at the broader political level. In some cases the lack of political involvement is attributable to a fear of offending potential funders. The majority of the Aboriginal people that we have interviewed see the importance of an *Aboriginal* community development rooted in the Aboriginal values of sharing and community, but do not for the moment see any way of expressing these values at the political level.

However necessary it may appear, given the financial dependency of community-based organizations, there are serious drawbacks to the 'politics of access'. Most importantly, it could be argued to lead, as Charles believes, not to 'solving' the problems of the inner city but to 'containing' them. By this he means that the dependency of community-based Aboriginal organizations on government funding may keep them silent and eliminate the political threat they might otherwise pose. . . .

It can be argued that governments and other funders do not really want to solve the problems of the inner city. Doing that would require public investment very far beyond what is now being committed to the inner city. Richard states: 'There is also a very conservative trend that sets in place today, even with the NDP government that we have, the NDP government is very much a careful government right now.' The current provincial government, for example, although more 'inner-city-friendly' than its predecessor, is committed to reducing taxes and running a balanced budget and 'inoculating' itself against criticism from its traditional foes (Flanagan, 2003). This approach increases the likelihood of re-election. This neces-

sitates responding positively to demands from the corporate community that taxes be cut and budgets balanced. It also necessitates responding positively to demands from the public and from powerful institutions that health and education be adequately funded. Once these demands have been met, there is little funding left for the inner city (Hudson, 2004). This is a political strategy designed not necessarily to *solve* problems, but rather to *manage* them so as to ensure re-election. If there is pressure on the provincial government to cut taxes and increase spending on health and education, they will do so. And if there is little public pressure on the provincial government to increase funding to the inner city—and there is not because the 'politics of access' practised by many inner-city community development organizations involves meeting the needs of funders to ensure continued funding—then they will not increase inner-city funding.

And to the extent that this is the case, the implicit strategy of governments—or at least the effect of government strategy—is simply to 'contain' the problems of the inner city. The result is a constant shortage of funding. As Walter says: 'Okay, government provides the resources but there is never enough, you know, to run a really effective program or programs . . . the resources are really spread thinly so there's never enough.'

An Alternative Approach: The Politics of Mobilization

To make real changes, significant and large changes that benefit the inner city, advocates require a different way of relating to the state, a different kind of politics, one built on mobilizing people and challenging systems. This alternative form of politics seeks power for Aboriginal people, but not power *over* others, rather power to enable all Aboriginal people to live in a healthy way in today's world and to do so as Aboriginal people.

This alternative way of relating to the state sees the virtues of and the necessity for the focus on healing and on community, but also sees its limitations. It argues the case for a politics that includes mobilization and confrontation, to speed the process of Aboriginal people governing themselves through their own organizations. This is a politics that has been used by urban Aboriginal people and has been successful in securing big victories—the creation of the Ma Mawi Wi Chi Itata Centre and Children of the Earth High School, for example. As William puts it:

> We have to get some power and . . . power is never given, you have to take it and you can only take it by building your knowledge, by organizing, and by doing things. . . . Then they begin to listen. . . . As long as you don't have power, you're going to be disadvantaged, so you have to organize.

. . . Existing institutions resist change and are unlikely to change voluntarily. In the case of Children of the Earth School, for example, the existing school division and some powerful Aboriginal leaders opposed the creation of an Aboriginal school. But Aboriginal people mobilized and demanded change. . . .

The politics of mobilization and confrontation, of collective and militant action, has a significant record of success in Winnipeg's inner city. In addition to Children of the Earth and Ma Mawi, the Aboriginal Centre might be seen as an example. Charles says:

> After the Oka crisis, for example, the budgets for Aboriginal organizations shot up dramatically. In the city, here, they developed the Aboriginal Centre. All kinds of resources went there and again, you know, you could see it as a process to cool down the masses, eh, you know, a process to put the fire out, because they knew there was a movement occurring.

There is another form of politics, another way of relating to the state that emerges logically out of the financial dependency of Aboriginal community-based organizations. This is the demand for a form of urban Aboriginal self-governance that would give Aboriginal people the legal authority to control the allocation of resources. . . .

A major part of the case for such a transfer of power and resources is that many, even most, of the bureaucrats who now make decisions about the allocation of resources do not really know Aboriginal people and their needs. William, who worked in Ottawa with the federal government for some years, says: 'One thing that amazed me when I went to Ottawa was the number of very bright young people . . . who would sit in offices and dream up solutions for people out there . . . sometimes with very little relationship to reality.' . . .

There Is No Turning Back: The Future Is Full of Hope

Although they expressed concerns about the future, our respondents are very optimistic and believe there is no turning back. Jack stresses the many positive things that are happening for the Aboriginal community and the momentum created. He states, 'Oh, yeah, I am optimistic' and adds, 'I see it already happening, a lot of training is going on, training and also employment initiatives are going on for our young people.' Agatha notes the changes that are taking place: 'I think things are changing because the mainstream organizations and government and funders have recognized that they need to include us, our voices at the table, and they need to hear our views of how things should be done. That wasn't always the case.' As Miles puts it: 'I was reading something about caterpillars, how they cocoon and then come out as butterflies. I think—maybe it is not a good analogy—but I think we are budding as a people; we are starting to bloom.'

When asked about the future, most of the people that we spoke to responded in collective terms about the future of Aboriginal people *as a people*. Most also spoke about the future in terms consistent with the values of Aboriginal community development. Their responses were not about personal accumulation or consumption, but rather about community and sharing. For example, when asked what she hopes the future would bring, Verna replies: 'Looking out for each other like they did years ago.' Others talked about Aboriginal people being more in charge of their own affairs and having more hope. When asked what she would like the Aboriginal community to look like twenty years from now, Ethel replies: 'my goal is . . . that our students are running their own organization. I want [her organization's] graduates running this program, people who've grown in this program.' Shirley says: 'We should be running the place! We should be running a lot of the mainstream organizations . . . [and] we need to be able to take our values with us, in there. . . . You really have to be able to come here and not check your belief system at the door in order to survive.' Linda adds to this: 'I'd like to see Aboriginal people taking the lead,' and expresses the importance of 'creating the opportunity for people to feel hopeful, to feel in control of their lives. . . . I mean community development to me is really human resource development, it's building people, providing opportunities for people, and standing by them when things fall, or being creative.' This reference to creativity acknowledges the fact that Aboriginal people are different and some may not want to fit into pre-existing slots in the system. So an Aboriginal community development approach, Linda says, needs to 'recognize who we are, and then build some economic opportunities around our situation and around who we are. You know, some of us are not going to be nine-to-fivers, and so you have to be creative about it.' . . .

Conclusion

We believe that by listening to the authentic voices of Aboriginal community leaders in Winnipeg's inner city, we have uncovered a story that is exciting and even inspiring. A process of decolonization is underway, and it is manifesting itself in a distinctive, Aboriginal form of urban community development.

This Aboriginal community development is rooted in the traditional Aboriginal values of community and sharing. Many of the people that we interviewed believe fervently in these values, and live and work in a way consistent with these values. They see Aboriginal community development starting with the individual, with the need for people to heal from the damage of colonization.

Part of this involves rebuilding Aboriginal people's identity and creating pride in being Aboriginal. The process of people rebuilding themselves, recreating themselves, although it happens person by person, requires a strong sense of community—one in which Aboriginal culture flourishes—and this in turn necessitates the creation of Aboriginal organizations. Just as Aboriginal people need to reclaim their identity as individuals, so do they need to reclaim their collective organizational identity via the creation of Aboriginal organizations. This is a process that has been going on for more than thirty years in Winnipeg: the Indian and Métis Friendship Centre, the Ma Mawi Wi Chi Itata Centre, the Urban Circle Training Centre, the Native Women's Transition Centre, the Aboriginal Centre, and the Children of the Earth High School are just a few examples. The process of reclaiming an Aboriginal identity has to take place at the individual, community, organizational and political levels. This process is well underway.

All of this—at the individual, the community, the organizational and the broader political levels—is a process of decolonization, a process of Aboriginal people seeking to take back control of their lives after many decades of colonial control. Their lives have been badly damaged. They have to rebuild. This has to start at the individual and local community level—healthy individuals require healthy communities, and vice versa. It has to mean Aboriginal-controlled organizations. And perhaps most significantly, it needs to be rooted in traditional Aboriginal values. Why? There are two reasons.

One is that large numbers of Aboriginal people do not want to assimilate. They want to live with and take advantage of the dominant culture but they want to do so as Aboriginal people, in a way consistent with Aboriginal values.

The second is that adherence to Aboriginal values is likely to reduce the chances of an Aboriginal elite emerging and leaving others behind. An Aboriginal community development process rooted in Aboriginal values places a premium on community and sharing, and this is most likely to keep leaders in close contact with the people.

Many of the individuals we interviewed adhere to these values, living and working in a way consistent with them. They grew up poor and lived rough. They have not forgotten their roots.

These organic urban Aboriginal intellectuals, as we described them earlier, are aware of the challenges they face. However, despite these challenges and difficulties, Aboriginal community development, with its strong emphasis on community and sharing, on respect for Aboriginal culture, is a reality in Winnipeg's inner city. Aboriginal people are building Aboriginal organizations in the inner city—run by and for Aboriginal people, and infused with Aboriginal values—to meet the needs of modern Aboriginal people. A process of healing and building is underway.

Notes

1. We have used pseudonyms for each of the twenty-six people interviewed for this chapter.
2. This is an important observation. If relatively sophisticated community economic development (CED) initiatives are put in place before people in the community are ready to participate, then these CED organizations are likely to become just another external agency—disconnected from the community. They may become an outside force, acting *upon* rather than *with* the community. At the same time, however, it is important to acknowledge that the various Aboriginal community-based organizations that we are talking about are themselves central elements of an economic strategy. They employ hundreds, perhaps thousands, of Aboriginal people. They have been called 'the invisible infrastructure', and Newhouse has recently calculated that there are approximately 3,000 such Aboriginal community-based organizations across Canada, most in urban centres (Newhouse, 2003: 245). Not only do they deliver needed services, but they also employ Aboriginal people to deliver the services, and this makes them a central part of a community economic development strategy. Also, Aboriginal people themselves have developed sophisticated approaches to CED, and these have been described in detail by Loxley (2000), and Loxley and Wien (2003). It is important, we believe, to accept that sometimes 'community development moves to community economic development too fast,' while holding to the view that economic development is important and that the urban Aboriginal community has made important contributions to devising and implementing appropriate and effective forms of community economic development.

References

Dreier, P. 1996. 'Community Empowerment Strategies: The Limits and Potential of Community Organizing in Urban Neighborhoods', *Cityscape: A Journal of Policy Development and Research* 2 (2).

Fals-Borda, O. 1992. 'Evolution and Convergence in Participatory Action Research', in J. Frideres, ed., *A World of Communities: Participatory Research Perspectives*. North York: Captus.

Fisher, R., and Shragge, E. 2002. 'Organizing Locally and Globally: Bridging the Divides', *Canadian Dimension* 36 (3).

Flanagan, Donne. 2003. 'Inoculating Traditional NDP Weaknesses Key to Doer's Success'. Unpublished paper, June.

Fontan, J.M., P. Hamel, R. Morin, and E. Shragge. 1999. 'Community Economic Development and Metropolitan Governance: A Comparison of Montreal and Toronto', *Canadian Journal of Regional Science* 22 (1–2).

Freire, Paulo. 1973. *Education for Critical Consciousness*. New York: Seabury Press.

Freire, Paulo. 1970. *Pedagogy of the Oppressed*. New York: Herder and Herder.

Hart-Landsberg, M., and P. Burkett. 2001. 'Economic Crisis and Restructuring in South Korea: Beyond the Free Market-Statist Debate', *Critical Asian Studies* 33 (3).

hooks, bell. 2003. *Rock My Soul: Black People and Self Esteem*. New York: Washington Square Press.

Hudson, Ian. 2004. 'The ndp's Dwindling Budget Options', *Fast Facts*. CCPA-Mb., 12 May 12.

Hull, Jeremy. 2001. *Aboriginal People and Social Classes in Manitoba*. Winnipeg: Canadian Centre for Policy Alternatives.

Hull, Jeremy. 1990. 'Socio-Economic Status and Native Education in Canada', *Canadian Journal of Native Education* 17 (1).

Hull, Jeremy. 1984. *Native Women and Work*. Report 2. Winnipeg: Institute of Urban Studies.

Hull, Jeremy. 1983. *Natives in a Class Society*. Saskatoon: One Sky.

Kretzmann, John P., and John L. McKnight. 1993. *Building Communities From the Inside Out: A Path Toward Finding and Mobilizing a Community's Assets*. Evanston, IL: Asset Based Community Development Institute, Institute for Policy Research.

Labrecque, M.F. 1991. 'Les femmes et le I: de qui parle-ton at juste?', *Recherches Féministes* 4 (2).

Lewis, M. 1994. *The Development Wheel: A Workbook to Guide Community Analysis & Development Planning*. The West Coast Series on ced, Second Edition. Vernon, BC: Westcoast Development Group.

Loxley, John. 2000. 'Aboriginal Economic Development in Winnipeg', in Jim Silver, ed., *Solutions That Work: Fighting Poverty in Winnipeg*. Winnipeg and Halifax: Canadian Centre for Policy Alternatives-Manitoba and Fernwood Publishing.

Loxley, John. 1981. 'The "Great Northern" Plan', *Studies in Political Economy* 6.

Loxley, John, and Fred Wien. 2003. 'Urban Aboriginal Economic Development,' in David Newhouse and Evelyn Peters, eds, *Not Strangers in These Parts: Urban Aboriginal Peoples*. Ottawa: Policy Research Initiative, Privy Council Office.

Morgan, M. 1996. 'Working for Social Change: Learning From and Building Upon Women's Knowledge to Develop Economic Literacy', in P. Ghorayshi and C. Belanger, eds, *Women, Work and Gender Relations in Developing Countries, A Global Perspective*. Westport, CT: Greenwood Press.

Newhouse, David. 2003. 'The Invisible Infrastructure: Urban Aboriginal Institutions and Organizations', in David Newhouse and Evelyn Peters, eds, *Not Strangers in These Parts: Urban Aboriginal Peoples*. Ottawa: Policy Research Initiative, Privy Council Office.

Newhouse, David, and Evelyn Peters, eds. *Not Strangers in These Parts: Urban Aboriginal Peoples*. Ottawa: Policy Research Initiative, Privy Council Office.

Newhouse, David. 2000. 'From the Tribal to the Modern: The Development of Modern Aboriginal Societies', in R.F. Lalberte, P. Settee, J.B. Waldrum, R. Innes, B. Macdougall, L. McBain, and F.L. Barron, eds, *Expressions in Canadian Native Studies*. Saskatoon: University of Saskatchewan Extension Press.

O'Donnell, S., and S. Karanja. 2000. 'Transformative Community Practice: Building a Model for Developing Extremely Low Income African-American Communities', *Journal of Community Practice* 7 (3).

Okazawa-Rey, M., and M. Wong. 1997. 'Organizing in Communities of Color: Addressing Interethnic Conflicts', *Social Justice* 24 (1).

Perry, S. n.d. 'Some Terminology and Definitions in the Field of Community Economic Development', *Making Waves* 10 (1).

Sen, A. 1999. *Development as Freedom*. New York: Anchor Books.

Shor, I., and P. Freire. 1987. *A Pedagogy for Liberation: Dialogues on Transforming Education*. South Hadley, MA: Bergin & Garvey Publishers, Inc. .

Silver, Jim. 2004a. 'To Help One Another: The Story of Ma Mawi', *Fast Facts*. Winnipeg: Canadian Centre for Policy Alternatives-Manitoba.

Silver, Jim. 2004b. 'Winnipeg's Urban Aboriginal Strategy', *Outlook: Canada's Progressive Jewish Magazine* 42 (2).

Silver, Jim. 2003. 'The Spence Neighbourhood', *Fast Facts*. Winnipeg: Canadian Centre for Policy Alternatives-Manitoba.

Silver, Jim. 2003. 'Persistent Poverty and the Push for Community Solutions', in L. Samuelson and W. Antony, eds, *Power and Resistance: Critical Thinking About Canadian Social Issues*. Halifax: Fernwood Publishing.

Silver, Jim, Kathy Mallett, Janice Greene, and Freeman Simard. 2002. *Aboriginal Education in Winnipeg Inner City High Schools*. Winnipeg: Canadian Centre for Policy Alternatives-Manitoba.

Sparr, P. 1994. *Mortgaging Women's Lives: Feminist Critique of Structural Adjustment*. London: Zed Press.

Veltmeyer, H., and A. O'Malley. 2001. *Transcending Neoliberalism: Community-based Development in Latin America*. Bloomfield, CT: Kumarian Press.

Voyageur, Cora J. 2000. 'Contemporary Aboriginal Women in Canada', in David Long and Olive Dickason, eds, *Visions of the Heart: Canadian Aboriginal Issues*, 2nd edn. Toronto: Harcourt Canada.

Voyageur, C., and B. Calliou. 2003. 'Aboriginal Economic Development and the Struggle for Self-Government', in L. Samuelson and W. Antony, eds, *Power and Resistance: Critical Thinking About Canadian Social Issues*, 3rd edn. Halifax: Fernwood Publishing.

Zaoual, H. 1999. 'The Maghreb Experience: A Challenge to the Rational Myths of Economics', *Review of African Political Economy* 82.

Part Eight

Additional Readings

Blaser, Mario, Harvey A. Feit, and Glenn McRae, eds. *In the Way of Development: Indigenous People, Life Projects, and Globalization*. London & New York: Zed Books, 2004.

Bodley, John H. *Victims of Progress*. Lanham: Altamira Press, 2008.

Manden, Jerry, and Victoria Tauli-Corpuz, eds. *Paradigm Wars: Indigenous Peoples' Resistance to Globalization*. San Francisco: Sierra Club Books, 2006.

Peters, Evelyn J., ed. *Not Strangers in These Parts: Urban Aboriginal Peoples*. Ottawa: Policy Research Initiative, 2003.

Westra, Laura. *Environmental Justice and the Rights of Indigenous Peoples: International and Domestic Legal Perspectives*. London: Earthscan, 2008.

Relevant Websites

Assembly of First Nations (Policy Areas)
http://www.afn.ca/article.asp?id=23
The Assembly of First Nations (AFN) website provides a number of Fact Sheets with respect to First Nations and has a section on policy, including a discussion of economic partnerships.

Films

Beating the Streets. Dir. Lorna Thomas. National Film Board of Canada, 1998.
Flooding Job's Garden. Dir. Boyce Richardson. Prod. Tamarack Productions, 1991.

No Address. Dir. Alanis Obomsawin. National Film Board of Canada, 1988.

Key Terms

Homelessness
Structural determinants
Poverty

Eurocentric models
'Aboriginal community development'

Discussion Questions

1. Discuss how Canadian colonial history has influenced the ways in which the youth involved in Baskin's research project have been marginalized by Eurocentric models of schooling and child welfare.

2. Assess the conclusion of the youth in Baskin's research project evidenced in the following quotation: 'an Aboriginal Family and Child Services Act would recognize the impacts of colonization upon all of us and focus our resources, both human and financial, on the well being of everyone in our communities and on the prevention of further internalized oppression which leads to the harm of all' (38). What is meant by this? Do you feel such an Act would be adequate remedy for the marginalization experienced by many Indigenous youth? How could internalized oppression be prevented?

3. How has liberal modernization theory viewed Indigenous traditional societies and affected their social and economic well being? How could self-government aid in alleviating Indigenous peoples' economic marginality?

4. What do Silver, Ghorayshi, Hay, and Klyne mean by Aboriginal community development? How does this type of development differ from other Western models of community development? How can an 'Aboriginal community development' revive a sense of community and revitalization of Indigenous cultures? Do you know of other examples of 'Aboriginal community development' aside from those discussed by the authors of the article?

Activities

Invite a local community worker in a social services sector to speak about issues of poverty, homelessness of Indigenous youth in the area, and how the community agency is working to address these.

Locate a recent news item that highlights the economic and social conditions of a reserve community. What are the main issues? Does the article link these conditions with a colonial context at all? What proposals, if any, are offered as possible solutions, and how do these reflect those offered by the authors of this part of the book?

Violence and the Construction of Criminality

In a democratic society like Canada, supposedly the law and the justice system are to treat all who live within its borders respectfully and equally. In fact, the image most people have of the law is that it is fair and objective. But, this presumes that the 'subject of law is a universal, abstract person. . . . Indeed, law's claim to impartiality is derived from its commitment to the view that it does not deal with different types of people' (Comack, 1999: 23). Yet, there are *different* groups with particular race, gender, class, sexuality, abilities, and ethnicities that make distinct subjects of law. Additionally, despite the myth that Canadian law and the justice system have been/are just, fair, and respectful, the reality is that racism is quite present within the legal institutions and practices. A number of studies have shown that racial minorities and Indigenous peoples have experienced racist treatment from the justice system in various ways: by the police, the courts, the enactment of discriminatory laws, and policies (Henry and Tator, 2006: 130).

One only needs to remember that it was the Indian Act—a law made by non-Indigenous peoples without the consent or participation of those to whom it was directed—that allowed the establishment of reserves, dispossession of lands, removal of children from their families and their placement in residential schools, and the termination of 'Indian status' to those women who married unregistered males. Evidently, Canadian law has not been an instrument of justice for Indigenous peoples; instead, it has been a tool of oppression and colonialism. In this section of the book, the three authors provide a critical examination of the role of the Canadian justice system and laws in constructing and perpetuating colonial injustices and violent oppression against Indigenous peoples.

Both the irrelevance and inequities within the justice system towards Indigenous peoples are discussed by Monture-Okanee and Turpel who argue that 'the criminal justice system is constructed with concepts that are not culturally relevant to an aboriginal person or to aboriginal communities. . . . [and this leads to question] whether, in the context of our experience to date, the criminal justice system can even be termed a 'justice' system for aboriginal peoples.' The irrelevance of the system can be traced to the differing conceptualizations of law, conflict, and punishment between Indigenous and non-Indigenous worldviews. As one example, impartiality, an essential criterion of law within the Canadian system, is not deemed as important, if even possible, within Indigenous systems. Given the close-knit kinship nature of Indigenous communities, the person with the authority to solve conflicts ought to be one who is well-connected with the community and well-respected because of wisdom acquired through life experiences. Non-Indigenous professionals who see and are seen as detached, impartial persons of authority are not necessarily better equipped to deal with the complex issues faced by the communities. In fact, Monture-Okanee and Turpel show how child welfare workers removed children from their Indigenous families due to different conceptualizations of family, neglect, and a 'best interest of the child' standard that did not serve Indigenous communities well.

Additionally, a major difference exists in how punishment is viewed and treated: while the Canadian system tends to punish those who have deviated from constructed social order by setting them into isolated institutions, from an Indigenous worldview such banishment is unusual. Indigenous societies emphasize restoration of balance and harmony between the 'offender' and the community. As Monture-Okanee and Turpel explain, 'this notion of restoring balance and harmony is the cultural equivalent of rehabilitation within aboriginal cultures.' However, Indigenous values and practices have not been part of the Canadian system and, overall, Indigenous peoples have not been treated equitably by an alien legal and judicial system.

Indigenous peoples are culturally and historically *different* from the rest of Canadians and this difference, Monture-Okanee and Turpel argue, ought not to be dismissed in the pursuit of *equality*. An assimilationist approach to justice would deny Indigenous histories, worldviews, and unique rights as the original peoples of the land. This would not serve justice, but rather further strip them of their Indigeneity. What is needed, indeed, is to allow Indigenous nations to 'design and control the criminal justice system inside their communities in accordance with the particular aboriginal history, language and social and cultural practices of that community . . . it will be our system and our law'.

That the current justice system has failed Indigenous people is a point reiterated by Green in her examination of the Stonechild case and other similar unjust treatments by the system. The case of Neil Stonechild and that of many other men who had been taken by the police and left to freeze to death in Saskatoon is a clear example of racism within the justice system that has literally killed our peoples. A public inquiry into these events was opened in 2003 and, in 2004, Justice David Wright released his report. In it, he clearly criticized the whole Saskatoon police for the way they treated Mr Stonechild and the way in which they investigated (or not) the matter. However, Green criticizes the report itself for not directly naming racism as the main perpetrator of the injustice served in the Stonechild case and other similar cases. As Green maintains, these are exemplars of the racism in the political culture, a racism that is ultimately linked to colonialism: 'The processes of colonialism provide the impulse for the racist ideology that is now encoded in social, political, economic, academic, and cultural institutions and practices, and which functions to maintain the status quo of the white dominance.'

The Stonechild case provides us with the opportunity to reveal the racism that exists within the structures and to call for fundamental change to the white privilege it maintains. Unfortunately, the report failed to recognize the structural and systemic element of racism and only treated it as a consequence of a 'chasm' between the different communities. As Green argues, this, though, would only see racism as caused by misunderstanding, rather than 'by the disproportionate power and malice held by those in the dominant community, who also benefit from the subordinate status of Aboriginal people'. Hence, what is required to ensure that such events do end, is to deconstruct racist ideologies and to dismantle the 'relations of dominance and, consequently, with the race-coded privileges that accrue to, especially, white Canadians'.

Similarly to their male counterparts, Indigenous women have been unjustly treated by Canadian white male-dominant society. That the bodies of Indigenous women have been the target of male (often white) violence and state violent oppression has insofar in this anthology been documented and this section reinforces the point. Amnesty International, together with the Native Women Association of Canada, has reported that over 500 Indigenous women have been missing and/or murdered in Canada and neither outcry by society nor serious investigation by the police has taken place. Would the same occur if these were the bodies of affluent white females? Aren't the lives of our Indigenous sisters as worthwhile? Why is the violence against them not treated with the same seriousness and punishment?

These questions preoccupy and are examined by the authors in this anthology who argue that racism and colonialism are the underlying and often unmentioned factors that can partly explain both the violent acts and the lack of action by the justice system. Racist ideologies have helped to construct Indigenous female bodies as dangerous, promiscuous, dirty objects of male desires. Racism also helps to explain why their violation does not receive harsh punishment: often it is their perceived promiscuity and 'risky' lifestyles that are the centre of media attentions, rather than the violent acts themselves.

Rape has always been a tool of patriarchal control and of genocide. Because Indian bodies are "dirty", they are considered sexually violable and rapable. Patriarchal gender violence is the process by which colonizers inscribe hierarchy and domination on the bodies of the colonized. Such violence had been frequently practiced in the early years of colonialism in the Americas and continues to impact the lives of Indigenous women and their whole communities. And the lack of interest by the police and all other social structures of our society lead us to have lots of reservations about the relevance, possibility, and application of justice towards Indigenous peoples by a current system that has been an alien and racist agent of colonialism.

Chapter 25

From *Stonechild* to Social Cohesion: Antiracist Challenges for Saskatchewan

Joyce Green

The frozen body of Neil Stonechild, a seventeen-year-old Cree university student, was found on the outskirts of Saskatoon, on 29 November 1990. While his body bore cuts and marks that suggested he had been assaulted, the cause of death was determined to be freezing. He was last seen in the back of a police car by a friend, Jason Roy, to whom Stonechild was appealing for help. Denying Roy's account and attacking his credibility, the police officers in question also denied having Stonechild in police custody that night.

Neil Stonechild was not the first, nor the last, Aboriginal man to freeze to death in apparently similar circumstances. Indeed, the police practice of taking Aboriginals out of town and leaving them even had its own moniker, 'Starlight Tours', used by both the police service and the Aboriginal community.

Ten years after Stonechild's body was found, Darrel Night was taken out of town and left to his fate. Night survived, and later filed a complaint. Two police officers were subsequently charged and convicted of unlawful confinement for their actions in his case. That same winter, in February 2000, the frozen bodies of Lloyd Dustyhorn, Lawrence Wegner, and Darcy Dean Ironchild were also found, on separate occasions, in the same area. Within a few weeks, the RCMP was called in to investigate the matter, and in 2001 it produced a report. No charges were laid. The public inquiry

looking into the circumstances surrounding Neil Stonechild's death, headed by Mr Justice David Wright, was not struck until September 2003. . . .

In October 2004, Mr Justice David Wright submitted the report of the Commission of Inquiry Into Matters Relating to the Death of Neil Stonechild (hereafter referred to as the Stonechild report), a provincial investigation. The report criticized the police investigation into Stonechild's death: 'The deficiencies in the investigation go beyond incompetence or neglect. They were inexcusable' (Harding, 2004; Wright, 2004: 199). Moreover, Wright condemned not just the individual behaviour of those involved, but the command structure of the Saskatoon Police Force, writing that these deficiencies 'would have been identified and remedied before the file was closed if the file had been properly supervised' (2004: 200). Wright concluded that the Saskatoon Police Service had conducted the investigation in a fashion that obfuscated the matter and, in particular, the role of officers on the force in the event. Wright found that Stonechild had been in the custody of the police on the night he was last seen alive, and that his frozen body bore injuries and marks likely caused by handcuffs. He found that the principal investigator on the case, Keith Jarvis, carried out a 'superficial and totally inadequate investigation' of the death, and 'dismissed important information' provided to him by members of the police. Wright wrote: 'The only reasonable inference that can be drawn is that Jarvis was not prepared to pursue the investigation because he was either aware of police involvement or suspected police involvement' (2004: 200).

Despite the Stonechild family's highly publicized concerns that racism was a factor in the quick closure of the file, the police chose not to investigate the officers implicated in the Stonechild death or to address racism in the Saskatchewan Police Service (Wright, 2004: 201–2). Wright found that in subsequent years, 'the chiefs and deputy chiefs of police who successively headed the Saskatoon Police Service, rejected or ignored reports . . . that cast serious doubts on the conduct of the Stonechild investigation.' Finally, he found that '[t]he self-protective and defensive attitudes exhibited by the senior levels of the police service continued . . . (and) were manifested by certain members of the Saskatoon Police Service during the Inquiry' (Wright, 2004: 212). Stonechild's family is now suing the Saskatoon Police Service for $30 million: for costs, exemplary, and punitive damages; for special damages, for behaviour characterized as trespass, assault and battery, deceit and conspiracy by police officers (CBC Radio One-Saskatchewan, 1 November 2005; Adam, 2005).

On 12 November 2004, Saskatoon Police Chief Russell fired Constables Larry Hartwig and Bradley Senger, announcing that they were 'unsuitable for police service by reason of their conduct' (Harding, 2004: A6). Despite Wright's finding that Stonechild had been in police custody on the night he died, no charges were laid in connection with this. And what was the impugned conduct that cost the men their jobs with the Saskatoon Police Service? Not racism, not criminal negligence, and not manslaughter; instead, their failure was characterized as administrative. Chief Sabo said they had failed to properly report information and evidence about Stonechild being in their custody on 24 November 1990. The fired officers appealed the Sabo decision.[1]

More recently, Saskatoon Deputy Police Chief Dan Wiks was disciplined with a one-day unpaid suspension for giving inaccurate information to a Saskatoon *Star Phoenix* journalist. Wiks, in 2003, had told the reporter that 'the police had no indication of officer involvement' in the Stonechild death, although he testified in 2004 to the Wright Inquiry that the Saskatoon police had, since 2000, known that the RCMP suspected constables Hartwig and Senger (Haight, 2005). The Saskatoon Police Force, under Chief Sabo's direction, appealed, seeking a more severe ruling. However, sources in the police force reported to the media that some officers disagreed with the decision to appeal, demonstrating that Chief Sabo faced some internal challenges to his approach and, possibly, to his policy direction on Aboriginal policing (CBC Radio One-Saskatchewan, 1 November 2005). Perhaps not co-incidentally, upon review in March 2006, Sabo's contract was not renewed and the chief, who had been recruited particularly to repair the police–Aboriginal relationship post-Stonechild, did not enjoy much support from the Saskatoon Police Force. However, obviously taking a different view, the Federation of Saskatchewan Indian Nations honoured Sabo at its winter legislative assembly, for 'healing the rifts between police and the First Nations community' (CBC Radio One-Saskatchewan, 14 March 2006; Warick, 2006: A7).

Aboriginal activists and organizations have called the police force racist. Spokespersons for the police have denied the accusation, and defended the force's reputation and the claims of the individuals involved in the Stonechild matter. And yet, a number of factors suggest something is amiss: the pattern of denial and obfuscation around the Stonechild case, which ultimately led to the Wright inquiry; the high degree of public awareness regarding the 'Starlight Tours'; and the anger toward and fear of cops in the sizeable Aboriginal community. In the white community[2] in Saskatoon, opinion was polarized between those supporting the police position and especially that of the officers involved, and those criticizing what appeared to be racism, apparent criminal behaviour on the part of some officers, and institutional practices violating human rights.

In this article, I look at the Stonechild and related incidents as exemplars of the racism in

Saskatchewan's (and Canada's) political culture, and consider what possibilities exist to erode this damaging and sometimes deadly phenomenon. I argue that the processes of colonialism provide the impulse for the racist ideology that is now encoded in social, political, economic, academic, and cultural institutions and practices, and which functions to maintain the status quo of white dominance. I suggest that decolonization, rather than 'revolt', 'assimilation' (Memmi, 1965) or 'cultural understanding', is the necessary political project to eradicate the kinds of systemic practices that arguably killed Neil Stonechild et al. I argue that decolonization is a political project capacious enough to include colonizer and colonized without erasing or subordinating either. . . .

Allegations of systemic racism are generally rejected by those who suggest that the way things are done, the status quo, is simply the product of social and intellectual consensus and is not laden with relations of dominance and subordination, nor the result of malicious intent. In order to challenge this, it is useful to employ the conceptual lens of Albert Memmi to Canadian colonial history. In Memmi's account, colonialism is tied to oppression, and is conditioned by 'the oppressor's hatred for the oppressed' (1965: xxvii). This hatred is manufactured and perpetuated by sets of racist assumptions that form the ideological foundation for the systematic, bureaucratic and individual implementation of racist practices, while also constructing 'self-absolution' of the racists (1965: xxvi). The consequence, racist ideology, both facilitates the maintenance of the economic potential and processes of colonialism, while simultaneously explaining its ineluctability and positive significance (1965: 82–83). . . .

Racism never happens in the absence of relations of privilege: 'privilege is at the heart of the colonial relationship—and . . . is undoubtedly economic' (Memmi, 1965: xii; see also Cesaire, 1972: 10–11; van Dijk, 1993: 21–22). And what is the nature of this economic privilege? It derives from the obliteration of the political, cultural and economic processes of the colonized, and their replacement by colonial models. This is done not to aid the 'development' of the colonized, but rather to appropriate their land and resources for economic and political gain by the colonizers (Memmi, 1965: 3–18). And that, after all, is the primary motivation of most Canadians' ancestors in immigrating: there were opportunities, especially economic opportunities, and access to cheap or free land here, that were not available at home. 'Colonization is, above all, economic and political exploitation' (Memmi, 1965: 149). . . .

Now, what might be termed 'second-generation colonialism' includes the expectations of the benefits that accrue to those with privilege, precisely because of the colonial conditions that created the privilege, and that deny it to the colonized; and because of those normalized assumptions that form the dominant political culture. Most of those with privilege are happily unaware of the particulars of Canada's colonial past and also of the contemporary consequences of colonialism, which include both Aboriginal trauma and white privilege. Yet, white privilege is a consequence of racism (as male privilege is a consequence of sexism) and so, too, is Aboriginal suffering. As Olson writes, 'Contemporary white privilege is like an "invisible weightless knapsack" of unearned advantages that whites draw on in their daily lives to improve or maintain their social position, even as they hold to the ideals of political equality and equal opportunity' (2002: 338). . . .

Confronting and eradicating racism requires unmasking the white-preferential, male-preferential processes that facilitate access to power, privilege, education, influences employment, political positions and so on. Because the effects of racism are unintended by individuals, and because most people in the dominant community are well intentioned and truly believe that their privilege is solely the result of their merit and diligence, the existence of intentional systemic patterns of discrimination and privilege is denied by most members of the settler population. This results in what Razack calls 'the dominant group's refusal to examine its own complicity in oppressing others' (1998: 40). Thus, systemic racism is embedded in Canadian political culture, in the service, first, of colonialism and subsequently, in the maintenance of settler and white privilege. . . .

The systemic racism embedded in our political culture is inherited from the colonial relationships that have now been transmuted into the Canadian social context, where descendants of settler populations carry with them a preferential entry into social, political, and economic institutions; and who see themselves reflected in those institutions and in the dominant culture, in ways that Aboriginal populations do not. Further, the very fact of normativeness is a social asset to those who enjoy it. Finally, this asset is especially strongly correlated with white skin privilege, rather than with those racialized Canadians that our society labels 'visible minorities'. Ultimately, this phenomenon both perpetuates racist assumptions and processes, even as it is so normalized as to be invisible and non-controversial (Green, 2005). Yet, it is inescapably visible to those whose 'race' constructs them as subordinate, and this realization is accompanied by anger at and resentment of those who benefit from race privilege while denying the existence and consequences of racism (for a good personal account of this see Fourhorns, 2005).

Systemic racism has material consequences, both for those who enjoy privilege, and for those who are subordinate. Statistics Canada data show that the likelihood of Aboriginal people completing school or acquiring post-secondary education is improving, but it is still significantly less than the national average (48 per cent of Aboriginal youth did not complete secondary school as of 2001; 37 per cent of non-reserve Aboriginal people had completed post-secondary studies, compared with 58 per cent for the total Canadian population). Health problems are distinctive and prevalent for Aboriginal populations: 'For every 10-year age group between the ages of 25 and 64, the proportion of Aboriginal people who reported their health as fair or poor was about double that of the total Canadian population.' Economic marginalization also shows up in the lack of adequate housing

and child-care facilities (Statistics Canada, 2003; Saskatchewan Labour, 2003). . . .

Colonialism and its accompanying racism are practiced through 'extreme discursive warfare' (Lawrence, 2004: 39). The trenches of this warfare lie in the media, in government bureaucracy and legislation, and in universities. The media write, speak, and produce for the 'average reader', the normative working-class or middle-class white model, with its set of social assumptions about the world. The advertisers that underwrite the media pitch to this category. For the most part, Aboriginal peoples do not exist for the media, except as practitioners of violence or political opposition, as marketing stereotypes, or as bearers of social pathologies. Virtually no real Aboriginal people write for or are portrayed in the media, especially the private media, for Aboriginal or settler consumption. (Doug Cuthand's occasional columns in the Regina and Saskatoon newspapers are so exceptional as to prove the rule.) The creators and enforcers of the laws and policies of the state are overwhelmingly non-Aboriginal, implementing regimes that are seldom directed at Aboriginal peoples and almost never with Aboriginal stakeholder or citizen participation. . . .

Stonechild provides us with a moment of opportunity, and is a call to arms for all who were appalled by this incident and who are committed to transformation of this damaging and sometimes deadly phenomenon. It is a moment when even those who have no race analysis, and no understanding of colonialism[3] are united with Aboriginal people in condemning the particular police actions that arguably led to the death of Neil Stonechild, and undeniably led to a set of institutionally sanctioned practices of police behaviour that frustrated the justice system. If we can trace the parameters of racism in political culture, it may be that the repugnance of those who reject police calumny and violence may also move them to reflect on our racist political culture, and how we are variously constructed within it. Then, we can move to strategies for building social solidarity, and for undermining race privilege as well as race discrimination.

Stonechild shows us that racism kills. The same lesson emerged from the Pamela George case, in which the young Saulteaux woman was assaulted and killed by two middle-class white men in Regina (Razack, 2002), and from the murders of Eva Taysup, Calinda Waterhen, Shelley Napope, and Mary Jane Serloin by a white man, John Crawford (Goulding, 2001). Racism maims, as demonstrated by the 2001 case of the 12-year-old Cree rape victim from the Melfort-Tisdale area, assaulted by three white adult males (Coolican, 2001; Prober, 2003; Buydens, 2005). Its pervasiveness limits opportunities and experience, depriving us all of human capital even as individuals' lives are marred. . . .

Razack argues that racism in Canada has a spatialized component. She suggests that the colonial society disciplines the colonized into particular and least valuable portions of communities. It is not only the bodies of people that are raced, but geographical space in communities, where whiteness constitutes a pass to all areas, but an exclusive pass to exclusively white areas; and where areas of predominantly Aboriginal occupation are coded as dangerous, degenerate spaces still available for white (and especially white male) tourism. It is in this white adventure into degenerate native space, Razack claims, that raced and gendered identities are enacted and confirmed—by the white agents, against the native ones. Thus, the Stroll in Regina, Saskatchewan, is worked predominantly by Aboriginal women, and white men can venture there for risky adventure, confirming the power relations between all as they act out their raced sexuality on Aboriginal bodies. However, the likelihood that the women would similarly enter the primarily white residential space of the murderers is slim. This spatialized relationship maintains the focus on the indigenous as needing to be controlled, for racism suggests they are ultimately not fit for civilized society (Razack, 2002). The Starlight Tours also fit with Razack's analysis, as they served to eject Aboriginal men from the primarily white urban society of Saskatoon.

Razack uses this analysis to illuminate the processes that played out in the murder of Pamela George. Her analytical framework can be applied to other situations to show similar or identical processes: the murdered women in Vancouver's notorious pig farm; the murdered sex workers in Edmonton and Saskatoon; the scores of missing Aboriginal women across the country. These cases show us the racial definition of space, into white space and Other space, and the racial conflation of Aboriginal with available and ultimately disposable women. In this way, the white public 'knows' there is no need to be concerned about these issues, for it believes (it is taught) that these women brought themselves into danger by 'choosing their lifestyles'. Consider the numbers of missing Aboriginal women whose cases are being documented and publicized by the Native Women's Association of Canada in its *Stolen Sisters* campaign. These women have been disregarded as objects for state concern and action because of the many factors in their lives that are a direct consequence of being Aboriginal: ultimately, they are ignored precisely because they are Aboriginal. . . .

In his book, *Just Another Indian*, Warren Goulding explores the context for the murders of four Aboriginal women by John Martin Crawford; the lack of media and state attention paid to the murders; Martin's eventual trial and conviction in Saskatoon, Saskatchewan; and the 'lurid details of a triple sex murder'. Goulding points out that, in contradistinction to the Paul Bernardo trial, the media didn't seem interested: the story had the ingredients of sex and violence, but it was about Aboriginal victims, not middle-class white girls. Racism played and plays a role; it was the in/significance of the Aboriginality of the victims to authorities, media and the white public that resulted in the lack of urgency around the case. Contrasting the response to the Crawford murders with those committed by Paul Bernardo and Karla Homolka, Goulding implies the middle-class whiteness of the latter rendered them subjects of empathy and interest. . . .The indifference of white media and the white public to the violence and misery that attend to many Aboriginal lives is a deeply racist position. . . .

While racism is most violently experienced by Aboriginal people, it also maims the humanity and civility of those who perpetuate it, deny it or ignore it. Racism injures the capacity of the body politic to work collaboratively toward common visions. It disables a common citizenship in a collective political project. In other words, the social cohesion that could sustain all of us is dependent on confronting and eliminating racism from Canada's social fabric.

This will be no easy task. Racism is the legitimating ideology of colonialism. Over decades, the racist assumptions that legitimate our politico-social order have been dignified by intellectuals, by policy, and by politics, until they have become part of what many understand as common sense. In families, in schools, and in popular culture, racism is reproduced intergenerationally and unconsciously by good people. This culture of white racism operates in ways that appear to be benign, unintentional, passive, or unknowing. It can only operate thusly because of its very normativeness, and because of the conventional consensus on the suspect nature of Aboriginal people. . . .

In his 'final comments' section in the Stonechild Inquiry, Mr Justice Wright wrote: 'As I reviewed the evidence in this Inquiry, I was reminded, again and again, of the chasm that separates Aboriginal and non-Aboriginal people in this city and province. *Our two communities do not know each other and do not seem to want to*' (2004: 208, emphasis added). He was troubled by the fact that 'the Saskatoon Police Service's submissions regarding the improvements to the Service did not contain any reference at all to attempts to improve the Service's interaction with Aboriginals and other racial groups' (2004: 210). Apparently, then, the police force did not think it had a race/ism problem that needed to be fixed. The Stonechild matter was interpreted as an incident, decontextualized from the political and institutional culture of racism and the specifics of colonialism in Saskatchewan. Particular individuals could be faulted, but the system remained uninterrogated. Wright, whose report was in so many ways illuminative of the depth and pervasiveness of racism in the Saskatoon Police Force, was unable to grapple with its systemic and structural nature, and he concluded with the erroneous implication that the 'chasm' is created by both communities, and is a matter of misunderstanding and of cultural differences, rather than systemic power relations with historical origins and contemporary practices. In concluding thusly, he invoked comforting myths of cultural difference to explain systemic racism—the myths of inalterable and incommensurate cultural essences that are mutually incomprehensible. While cultures assuredly have differences, some profound, these differences do not create the racism that leads to practices like Starlight Tours. . . .

Wright departed from the context for the institutional racism that led to the deaths of the frozen men by calling for greater 'understanding' between the two communities. This suggests that the problem of racism is caused by misunderstandings, rather than by the disproportionate power and malice held by those in the dominant community, who also benefit from the subordinated status of Aboriginal people. Stonechild et al. did not die due to a misunderstanding. Indeed, on the same page that Wright turned to culturalist explanations, he also cited evidence from witnesses demonstrating the awareness and fear of white racism with which Aboriginal people live (2004: 209). Yet he seemed unable to clearly analyze the discrete notions of culture and racism, nor could he distinguish between them. Cultural awareness activities, such as having police officers participate in a smudge ceremony, are a good start, but on their own they will not bring about a shift in racist practices or institutions.

Racism in Canada is the malaise of colonialism. The continued structural racism sustains the 'toxic gulf' between Aboriginal and settler communities that Wright identified but misunderstood, and its remedy will be found in positive strategies for decolonization. Wright misunderstood the toxic gulf because he saw it as personal and relational, and as being equally the responsibility of the dominant and Aboriginal communities. He did not conceptualize it as a logical consequence of the processes of colonialism. His even-handed condemnation of it, then, places an unfair portion of the blame on Aboriginal communities for the racism initiated by the dominant community's elites. This is not to suggest that there is no racism in Aboriginal communities—there is. But I argue that institutional racism on the order demonstrated by *Stonechild* is emblematic of relations of dominance and subordination, and the reactionary racism in Aboriginal communities is just that, not the legitimating ideology of dominance.[4] Destabilizing institutional and structural racism requires grappling with the relations of dominance and, consequently, with the race-coded privileges that accrue to especially white Canadians. White privilege is sustained by what Lawrence calls '[t]he intensely white supremacist nature of Canadian society, where power and privilege are organized along lines of skin colour' (2004: 175). The chasm is about unequal power relations, not moral equivalence. . . .

But a post-colonial Canada must have a place for the former holders of privilege. Unlike the British in India, the Belgians in Congo, and other instances of 'elsewhere' decolonization, Canada is a settler society. The solution of withdrawing from the colony is not available to the vast majority of non-Aboriginal Canadians. Time has done its work of erasing boundaries and options, and creating rootedness and community. We must, in all our diversity, and much hybridity (Said, 1994) find ways to live together, to 'bear with' each other in our stranger-hood (Hansen, 2004) and also in our commonalities. No collective public can be manufactured without some collective stake in a transformed future; no decolonization is probable in Canada without a beneficial future, both for the colonized, and those who are privileged by whiteness. And no profound transformation can occur without systemic, institutional, constitutional and, above all, cultural shifts.

Transforming any foundational inter-generational process is dicey. However, governments have on occasion taken the coercive apparatus and financing capacity of the state via government and initiated new directions in public policy, in acts of political will. This is what governments must do: provide a combination of ethical and pragmatic leadership in setting the conditions for and parameters of the Good Society for all of those to whom they are responsible. In the case of systemic, institutional and cultural racism, this is a challenge, as those who must take the lead on this are also those who, overwhelmingly, benefit from the relations of dominance and subordination that are the *raison d'être* of racism.

Notes

1. The hearing into the matter concluded on 31 October 2005, though a decision was not then made (CBC Radio One-Saskatchewan, 31 October 2005).
2. I use the term 'white' for two reasons. First, empirically, Saskatchewan's population is predominantly white, with the balance being almost entirely Aboriginal. Only a tiny percentage of Saskatchewan residents are 'visible minorities', something less than 4 per cent. Second, 'white' is intended to invoke the privileged component of a race-stratified society. Therefore, I also refer to 'white racism', and have not taken up the ways in which non-white members of settler society may also be racist, or affected by racism.
3. Colonialism is an always exploitative relationship, in which the political, cultural, and economic autonomy of one society or nation is appropriated by another via coercion. It is legitimated by myths of superiority, inevitability, and racism, and it is enforced by the socio-political institutions of the colonizer. These myths and the practices of colonialism are transmitted intergenerationally through political culture.
4. Teun van Dijk writes: 'Essential for racism is a relation of group power or dominance. (It is not) personal or individual, but social, cultural, political, or economic. . . . Given the definition of racism as a form of dominance, reverse racism or black racism in white-dominated societies is theoretically excluded in our framework' (1993: 21).

References

Adam, Betty Ann. 2005. 'Stonechild family sues for $30M', *Regina Leader-Post*, November 1.

Buydens, Norma. 2005. 'The Melfort Rape and Children's Rights: Why R v. Edmondson Matters to All Canadian Kids', Canadian Centre for Policy Alternatives-Saskatchewan. *Saskatchewan Notes* 4 (1) (January): 1–4.

Canadian Broadcasting Corporation (CBC). 2005a. 'Girls in gangs: disturbing reports from the inside', available at http://sask.cbc.ca/regional/servlet/View?filename=gangs-girls050321, 21 March.

CBC. 2005b. Morning Edition. 'They're young and often aboriginal—and they say they're waging a war', available at http://sask.cbc.ca/regional/servlet/view?filename=favel030522, 21 March.

CBC. 2005c. Radio One. 'Re Saskatoon Police Service appeal of Dan Wicks' one-day suspension', 31 October.

CBC. 2005d. Radio One. 'Re Hartwig and Senger appeals for their jobs with the Saskatoon Police Service', 1 November.

CBC. 2006. Radio One. 'Re Federation of Saskatchewan Indian Nations honouring outgoing Saskatoon Police Chief Russell Sabo', 14 March.

Cataldo, Sabrina. 2004. '$750,000 donation to fund chair in police studies', University Relations, University of Regina communication, 1 December.

Cesaire, Aime. 1972. *Discourse on Colonialism*. New York and London: Monthly Review Press.

Comeau, Lisa. 2004. 'The Purpose of Education in European Colonies: Mid-19th to Early 20th Century'. Unpublished paper presented to SIDRU (Saskatchewan Instructional Development & Research Unit), University of Regina, 25 February.

Coolican, Lori. 2001. 'Family wants look at accused', *Regina Leader-Post*, 16 October, A1, A2.

Dickerson, Mark, and Tom Flanagan. 1999. *An Introduction to Government and Politics: A Conceptual Approach*, 5th edn. Toronto: ITP Nelson.

Fourhorns, Charlene. 2005. 'Education for Indians: The Colonial Experiment on Piapot's Kids', *Canadian Dimension* 39 (3): 42–4.

Goodale, Ralph. 2003. Speaking Notes for The Honourable Ralph Goodale, P.C., M.P., 8 November; available at http://www.ralphgoodale.ca/Speeches/speech-ReginaAffordable Housing.html, retrieved 25 May 2004.

Green, Joyce. 2002. 'Transforming at the Margins of the Academy', pp. 85–91 in Elena Hannah, Linda Paul, and Swani Vethamany-Globus, eds, *Women in the Canadian Academic Tundra: Challenging the Chill*. Kingston and Montreal: McGill-Queen's University Press.

Green, Joyce. 2005. 'Self-determination, Citizenship, and Federalism: Indigenous and Canadian Palimpsest', pp. 329–52 in Michael Murphy, ed., *State of the Federation: Reconfiguring Aboriginal-State Relations*. Institute of Intergovernmental Relations, School of Policy Studies, Queen's University. Kingston and Montreal: McGill-Queen's University Press.

Goulding, Warren. 2001. *Just Another Indian: A Serial Killer and Canada's Indifference*. Calgary: Fifth House Limited.

Goulding, Warren. 2004. 'Reconnecting with Human Rights'. Notes for an address by Warren Goulding, Friday, 10 December, Regina, Saskatchewan. Unpublished, on file with the author.

Government of Saskatchewan. 2005. http://www.sask2005.ca/; http://www.cyr.gov.sk.ca/saskatchewans_centennial. html; http://www.gov.sk.ca/govinfo/news/premier speech. html?0085 (retrieved 22 May 2005).

Haight, Lana. 2005. 'Wiks going back to work', *Regina Leader-Post*, 8 October.

Hansen, Phillip. 2004. 'Hannah Arendt and Bearing with Strangers', *Contemporary Political Theory* 3 (1): 3–22.

Harding, Katherine. 2004. 'Two police officers fired in Stonechild case', *Toronto Globe and Mail*, 13 November, A6.

Irlbacher-Fox, Stephanie. 2005. 'Practical Implications of Philosophical Approaches Within Canada's Aboriginal Policy'. Unpublished paper presented to the Canadian Political Science Association, University of Western Ontario, London, Ontario, June.

Jaccoud, Mylene, and Renee Brassard. 2003. 'The Marginalization of Aboriginal Women in Montreal', pp. 131–45 in David Newhouse and Evelyn Peters, eds, *Not Strangers in These Parts: Urban Aboriginal Peoples*. Ottawa: Policy Research Initiative.

Kuokkanen, Rauna. 2005. 'The Responsibility of the Academy: A Call for Doing Homework'. Unpublished paper presented to the Canadian Political Science Association, University of Western Ontario, London, Ontario, June.

Lawrence, Bonita. 2004. *'Real' Indians and Others: Mixed-Blood Urban Native Peoples and Indigenous Nationhood*. Vancouver: UBC Press.

Memmi, Albert. 1965. *The Colonizer and the Colonized*. Boston: Beacon Press.

Olson, Joel. 2002. 'Whiteness and the Participation–Inclusion Dilemma', *Political Theory* 30 (3): 384–409.

Razack, Sherene. 1998. *Looking White People in the Eye: Gender, Race, and Culture in Courtrooms and Classrooms*. Toronto: University of Toronto Press.

Razack, Sherene. 2002. 'Gendered Racial Violence and Spatialized Justice: The Murder of Pamela George', pp. 121–56 in Sherene Razack, ed., *Race, Space, and the Law: Unmapping a White Settler Society*. Toronto: Between The Lines.

Prober, Rosalind. 2003. 'What no Child Should Endure: *R. v Edmonston, Kindrat and Brown*', *Beyond Borders Newsletter* 3 (Fall): 1–2.

Said, Edward. 1994. *Culture and Imperialism*. New York: Vintage Books.

Saskatchewan Labour, Status of Women Office. 2003. 'A Profile of Aboriginal Women in Saskatchewan'. Unpublished, on file with the author.

Smith, Linda Tuhiwai. 1999. *Decolonizing Methodologies: Research and Indigenous Peoples*. London and New York: Zed Books.

Statistics Canada. 2003. 'Aboriginal Peoples Survey: Well-being of the Non-reserve Aboriginal Population', *The Daily*, 24 September, available at http://www.statcan.ca/Daily/English/030924/d030924b.htm; retrieved 9 May.

van Dijk, Teun. 1993. *Elite Discourse and Racism*. Newbury Park: Sage.

Vipond, Mary. 2000. *The Mass Media in Canada*, 3rd ed. Toronto: James Lorimer and Company Ltd.

Warick, Jason. 2006. 'Saskatoon police chief to be honoured', *Regina Leader-Post*, A7.

Woloski, Rosalie. 2005. 'Re Donald Worme and systemic racism', *CBC Radio One*, Saskatoon, 21 June 2005. Script on file with the author.

Wright, David H., Mr Justice. 2004. *Report of the Commission of Inquiry Into Matters Relating to the Death of Neil Stonechild*. Regina: Government of Saskatchewan.

Chapter 26

Aboriginal Peoples and Canadian Criminal Law: Rethinking Justice

Patricia Monture-Okanee and Mary Ellen Turpel

Preface

This paper was prepared for the Law Reform Commission of Canada, in the context of a Reference placed before the Commission by the Minister of Justice, the Honourable Kim Campbell, on 8 June 1990, to consider '. . . the *Criminal Code* and related statutes, and the extent to which they ensure that: a) aboriginal persons; and b) persons in Canada who are members of cultural or religious minorities have equal access to justice, and are treated equitably and with respect.' . . .

I. Aboriginal Perspectives on Justice and the Criminal Code

A. Introduction: Scope of the Reference

It is difficult to locate a matter as large and complex as criminal justice within a cultural perspective without first critically examining the presuppositions and structures of the Canadian criminal justice system as it is currently imagined. The Reference letter from the Minister of Justice requesting the Law Reform Commission of Canada to study the *Criminal Code*[1] and related statutes with a view to considering the extent to which they ensure that aboriginal[2] persons have '*equal access to justice, and are treated equitably and with respect*' requires the Law Reform Commission of Canada to reflect upon aboriginal perceptions on the notions of justice, equal access to justice, equitable treatment and, most of all, respect.

These concepts need to be carefully deconstructed in order to give content to the mandate for the Commission's work.[3] Moreover, a series of related concepts which frequently come to the fore in political discussions of aboriginal people and the criminal justice system, such as 'alternative justice systems', 'parallel justice systems' or 'separate justice systems', should also be critically deconstructed and analyzed in light of the Commission's mandate. This analysis must first recognize that none of these expressions are found in aboriginal languages—they are English expressions more or less rooted in legal discourse.[4] . . .

First, to interpret the mandate of the Commission as focused narrowly on the text of the *Criminal Code* or related statutes, would be conceptually incomplete and overly constraining in terms of contributing to 'the development of new approaches'. . . . When considering the criminal justice system and aboriginal peoples, it is an indispensable prerequisite to move beyond the circumscribed confines of criminal statutes and consider the conceptual basis of Canadian criminal justice, the nature of the interaction between aboriginal people and the criminal justice system and aboriginal aspirations in this area. . . .

We would suggest to the Commission that the entire paradigm of the existing criminal justice system is one which needs to be looked at holistically in order to locate it in a context of Canadian cultural values and failings. By holistically we mean all aspects of the system, its institutions and its norms and also the broader jurisprudential goals of discipline, punishment and rehabilitation.[5]

The Canadian criminal justice system is completely alien to aboriginal peoples.[6] This is not a novel point and obviously the Minister's Reference is long overdue. Initial observations regarding the alien character of the criminal justice system can be made at this point to underscore the significance of holistic approaches to reform within the Canadian criminal justice system.

The criminal justice system is constructed with concepts that are not culturally relevant to an aboriginal person or to aboriginal communities. . . .

The notion of a written code or law is also foreign to aboriginal cultures.[7] This does not mean that aboriginal systems of law were not as 'advanced' or 'civilized' as European-based systems; these are racist stereotypes. It merely means that aboriginal law was conceptualized in different but equally valid ways. Laws were not written because law needs to be accessible to everyone. When an oral system is effective, the law is carried with each individual wherever he or she travels.

Thus, a system in which laws are accessible only through lawyers and professionals seems very remote, unapproachable, and not connected to the kinship structure of aboriginal communities.

The Canadian criminal justice system is operated by a professionally trained class of prosecutors and defenders who decide the fate of an offender on terms that reflect their privilege and perspective. . . . If representatives of a particular population do not secure access to the professional legal class, their participation at this level is non-existent and they are excluded from the processes used to select decision-makers in the legal system. This is an example of systemic discrimination impacting on aboriginal peoples. . . .

Another 'alien' norm of the Canadian criminal justice system, is the requirement that judges decide matters 'impartially.' This so-called 'impartiality' is the basis for the institutional authority of criminal justice officials acting on behalf of the Canadian system. In aboriginal cultures, impartiality is not the essential ingredient when we think of relations of justice. Aboriginal communities are closely-knit kinship communities. Even those individuals who reside in urban settings commonly retain intimate connections with their communities.[8] These individuals also take their own values and understandings of how justice will operate with them when they come to the cities. The person with authority to resolve conflicts among aboriginal peoples in their communities must be someone known to them who can look at all aspects of a problem, not an unknown person set apart from the community in an 'impartial' way. A 'judge' from a non-aboriginal context is simply an outsider without authority.

Within aboriginal communities, the equivalent actor to the judge is the Elder. This is not to say that the Elder is the same thing as a judge or assumes that role. Elders are the most respected members of aboriginal communities. Elders are respected because they have accumulated life experiences and hold the wisdom of the community in their hearts and minds. Although it is a qualitatively different value, this respect for a person's knowledge of their culture and language, and for their wisdom, is the equivalent to respect for impartiality in European-based systems. . . .

Wisdom, knowledge, and the respect of an aboriginal community are gained through experience; therefore professionals who come into contact with aboriginal people are not necessarily viewed with respect simply by virtue of their professional qualifications. Aboriginal people hold no respect for 'professionals,' simply because they hold a professional title. Respect is earned through life experience and by demonstrating that you are a good member of your community, a good speaker of your language and a committed helper of your people.

Aboriginal mistrust of professionals has been validated by our experience with professional authorities. To raise but one example, one should consider the many child welfare cases where children have been removed from their family home. The professional social worker was deemed to know what was best for the aboriginal child, more so than the aboriginal parents and/or the aboriginal community. We now understand that this standard, the 'best interest of the child,' was bound by race, culture and class.[9] Professional authority based on a tide, especially when the professional is white, is understandably suspect within aboriginal communities. Too often it means disrespect for cultural practices and the imposition of alien values. . . .

The problems we have identified in the application of Canadian criminal justice practices to aboriginal peoples go beyond this outline. It is not merely judgments which are biased by the colour of the accused person that are problematic. Beyond colour-related stereotypes and misunderstandings, the existing system involves a basic disrespect for aboriginal culture and different forms of social, political and spiritual life. The cultural barriers which separate aboriginal people from non-aboriginal people are at the heart of this problem, and these barriers must become clearly identified and understood. Aboriginal peoples do not have written laws. We do not have confidence in 'outsiders' to our cultures as our communities are closely-knit extended families. . . .

The existing criminal justice system must be considered in light of other values it projects and the corresponding claims to justice which it hopes to sustain. For instance, the Canadian system is grounded in a belief in 'correctional' punishment based on banishment to special institutions where the goals of retribution, deterrence and reform of the offender legitimize the punishment. Punishment is a concept which is not culturally relevant to aboriginal social experience.[10] Banishment is the most severe remedy available under aboriginal systems of justice. It means the end of social and cultural life with one's community. This is true for the individual who lives within his or her community as well as for the individual who lives in an urban area and is either directly connected to his or her community or understands what that connection is. Incarceration must be understood as banishment if the cultural perception of the aboriginal person facing a prison sentence (and their family as well as their community) is ever to be understood. If the goal of the social structure is to restore balance and harmony within the community, as it is for the aboriginal community, the act of pushing an 'offender' outside the circle of social life is not seen as a solution. It is seen as counter-productive, creating further obstacles to the restoration of balance and harmony after an anti-social act.

From an aboriginal perspective, balance and harmony can be restored only through strengthening connections with one's community. This notion of restoring balance and harmony is the cultural equivalent of rehabilitation within aboriginal cultures. Through the kinship system (and/or the clan system of government) and through the involvement of the Elders, balance and harmony is restored for the offender, the victim and the community. Within the Canadian penal structure, the supervision of the offender after banishment is by a person from a specialized corrections bureaucracy who does not know the offender, the offender's family, or the offender's community. This person may even be biased against the offender in subtle or obvious ways.[11] The Canadian criminal justice system's notion of rehabilitation or corrections is fundamentally alien to aboriginal communities. . . .

We raise these preliminary cultural concerns because we have serious reservations about the extent to which aboriginal peoples have equal access to, or receive equitable treatment within, the existing criminal justice system. Meaningful participation and equitable treatment are pre-conditions to holding a sincere respect for any system, particularly a system of justice. However, aboriginal peoples' views of conflict and its resolution have absolutely no voice in the current order. We use the phrase 'meaningful participation' as an alternative to the term 'access', as it is a term which more accurately represents our view of the situation. Aboriginal peoples have 'access' to the criminal justice system which is all too generous. Our representation in the offender populations has been outrageously high.[12] We have serious reservations regarding whether, in the context of our experience to date, the criminal justice system can even be termed a 'justice' system for aboriginal peoples.

The historical fact that the Canadian criminal justice system has absolutely failed to recognize and incorporate aboriginal cultures has important structural consequences. Aboriginal people do not need further access to the system which exists. What is needed is meaningful participation in the criminal justice system and less 'access'. By meaningful participation we suggest that aboriginal people must be encouraged to participate in the system by defining the meaning, institutions and standards of justice in their own communities. Also, all peoples must be partners in developing a criminal justice system outside aboriginal communities that can and does reflect aboriginal cultures. Thus far, aboriginal peoples have simply struggled to survive their experiences in an alien criminal justice system. To become meaningful participants would require an enormous shift in our experience and in conventional Canadian thinking about criminal justice.

A number of questions are obviously yet to be asked regarding our meaningful participation in the justice system. For example, how does an aboriginal person experience the current justice system?[13] The overall perspective of an aboriginal person toward Canadian legal institutions is one of being surrounded by injustice without knowing where justice lies, without knowing whether justice is possible. . . . The impact of racism—of another culture having power over yours—is not easily undone. Simply getting this reality acknowledged requires a 'healing,' in the aboriginal sense of that process. A shift must occur so that aboriginal leaders, academics, justice activists and 'offenders' will be given the authority necessary to shape answers for ourselves which are culturally appropriate.[14]

The search for justice within the criminal justice system has resulted only in systemic injustice for aboriginal peoples, either as victims of crime[15] or as accused persons.[16] How pervasive are these experiences? What courses of action represent ways out? We believe that the era of collecting data about the over-representation of aboriginal people in the criminal justice system must end. This gross over-representation is well documented and obvious. It is now time to begin to focus on meaningful change, to correct over-representation and to generate respect by implementing changes which allow aboriginal cultural practices to be recognized and supported. This is not to say that our hearts are not heavy with the burden of living with our family members and friends, our leaders and children, in Canadian prisons: they are heavily burdened. It is difficult to participate enthusiastically in reform efforts while our communities have been deprived of their members. . . .

The Supreme Court of Canada has made it clear that the key to equality rights analysis is an examination of the larger context of discrimination. We must assess whether differential treatment has had an adverse impact upon certain groups in a manner contrary to that envisioned for a society that is pluralistic, free and democratic.[17] The Court is interested in correcting and ameliorating historic disadvantage and recognizes that this does not mean that all groups should be treated alike.[18] In fact, different treatment is often more appropriate.[19] Arguably, there is a built-in notion of respect for difference in this conception of equality.[20] However, if one looks both at the context for discrimination and at historical disadvantage and its impacts with relation to aboriginal peoples, it becomes apparent that something very different from similar treatment is required.

From an aboriginal perspective, equality as a legal concept is often too narrowly cast in that it does not encompass a discussion of aboriginal and treaty rights or collective rights claims. . . . However, from the outset, it is important to ensure that the mandate of the Minister's Reference is viewed in this particular and novel legal and constitutional context.

It is not only the Ministry of Justice that recognizes and embraces the need for change of this nature. It is becoming more and more widely believed that aboriginal-Canadian relations can no longer be ignored. In discussing the aftermath of Kanasatake, Kanawake, Oka and the Mercier Bridge, the Canadian Human Rights Commission expressed deep concern over the current state of affairs:

> It is deeply regrettable that it has taken conflict and violence to bring about a realisation of the urgency of reform of aboriginal affairs. We believe that aboriginal and non-aboriginal Canadians alike see the present juncture as an opportunity to apply ourselves to the long-neglected national task of redesigning the aboriginal and non-aboriginal relationship in a spirit of collaboration and good faith. This process should get under way immediately and should tackle the fundamental questions in a thorough and innovative way.[21]

. . . In light of this, what do the terms 'equal access,' 'equitable treatment' and 'respect,' mean to an aboriginal person? 'Equal access' may, at first glance, be interpreted to require an analysis of equality in the access to the criminal justice system. However, because equality conjures up images of sameness or similar treatment (especially in the context of defining aboriginal rights), and is often tested merely by some form of data collection exercise, this interpretation is not completely helpful in this context. Equality is sometimes measured by how well aboriginal people can be integrated into the existing system.[22]

Reliance on policies of integration and assimilation within the criminal justice system has doomed to failure many past efforts aimed at amelioration of our conditions. Further, assimilationist policies are antithetical to our desire for cultural survival—integration is not desired, rather the aboriginal goal is autonomy and respect for difference. Equal access framed in assimilationist terms could conceivably mean inequity when the position of aboriginal peoples is placed in historical, cultural and linguistic perspective. For example, equal access for aboriginal and non-aboriginal people to a system of sentencing which is insensitive to the history and culture of aboriginal peoples does not take basic differences into consideration and contradicts the progressive notion of equitable treatment and respect. For this reason, a broader interpretation of the Reference, focusing on the dual nature of respect and sensitivity to the cultural, historical and linguistic position of aboriginal peoples must inform the Law Reform Commission's study of, or any reform-minded approach to, the Canadian criminal justice system.

What must be remembered as we begin to face this new challenge together is that the shape of the answer is not singular. There is no single answer that will speak to the diversity of experience, geography and culture of aboriginal people and our communities. To give but one example, the problems and solutions will be different for aboriginal peoples living on reserves or Inuit or Métis communities, as compared to those living in urban centres. Any reasoned response must be tailored to answer both the internal dimension of criminal justice problems (i.e. for aboriginal communities) and the external dimension (i.e. for aboriginal individuals living away from their communities).[23]

An additional but related factor required for reform is an appreciation and sensitivity towards aboriginal political objectives. . . .

We see it as pivotal not only to understanding the sources of our discontent with the existing system, but also to providing direction for the 'development of new approaches to, and new concepts of, the law in keeping with and responsive to the changing needs of Canadian society.'[24] Eventually, and ideally at an early stage, changes in the criminal justice system will have to be placed before aboriginal peoples for their input and consent. Arguably, this requirement to seek input and gain the consent of aboriginal peoples is established by international human rights covenants.[25]

B. Aboriginal Rights and Criminal Justice: Legal Premises

While we advocate a broad interpretation of the mandate placed before the Law Reform Commission, we also perceive political constraints on any study in this area dictated by what are, in our view, confused images of aboriginal peoples' experience and aspirations vis-a-vis criminal justice. The Minister of Justice has suggested on numerous occasions that 'separate' justice systems or 'alternative' justice systems are incompatible with the Rule of Law and are simply not open for discussion. . . . This position misconceives the aboriginal proposal as some kind of lawless zone which would be exempt from criminal sanctions. . . . Aboriginal rights are inherent and not contingent on Crown recognition. For example, the application of the *Criminal Code* may be seen, in the context of aboriginal rights recognized in s. 35 of Part II of the *Constitution Act*, 1982, as an infringement of long-standing justice practices by aboriginal peoples or of treaty guarantees. The basis of aboriginal rights has been accepted in numerous cases to be their inherency or the fact that certain rights or practices have been exercised for long periods of time. . . .

It is important to appreciate that aboriginal peoples are different keeping in mind all of the points we have outlined thus far. Aboriginal cultures are non-Anglo-European. We do not embrace a rigid separation of the religious or spiritual and the political. We have extended kinship networks. Our relations are premised on sets of responsibilities (instead of rights[26]) among individuals, the people collectively and toward land. Our cultures do not embrace discipline and punishment as organizing principles in the same fashion as Anglo-European peoples' do. Aboriginal peoples live with a basic connection to the natural order, which we see as the natural law.[27] This means that family connections, i.e. natural connections, are more important in controlling anti-social behaviour. The lessons offered by a family member, particularly if that person is an Elder, are more significant than any other type of correctional interaction. The personal, familial interaction is the consensual social fabric of aboriginal communities. It is this which makes aboriginal communities distinct culturally and politically from Canadian social institutions.

Aboriginal peoples are *different*. Also, aboriginal communities are *separate* geographically and socially from Canadian society. Our territories are frequently in remote areas and aboriginal people are more closely dependent upon the land for survival than Canadians who live, for the most part, on a narrow strip of territory hugging the United States border. Aboriginal peoples, given that we are both different and separate, simply cannot be considered as part of Canadian society for the purpose of designing a comprehensive criminal justice system. We are not necessarily culturally, linguistically or historically part of Canada or Canadian legal and political institutions. We are different and separate, set apart by our cultures, languages, distance and histories.

To suggest, then, that aboriginal peoples must be treated equitably and with respect by the criminal justice system means that we must be treated differently for the simple reason that we are different. This does not mean lesser treatment as we have so often been afforded. Especially insofar as criminal justice institutions reach *within* our communities, the criminal justice system can only work if premised on the notion that aboriginal peoples are different and separate. Therefore, aboriginal people must be allowed to design and control the criminal justice system inside their communities in accordance with the particular aboriginal history, language and social and cultural practices of that community. The justice system in aboriginal communities will, of necessity, be different than elsewhere (namely in non-aboriginal society) in Canada. It will not be a lesser system and it will not be Canadian law—it will be our system and our law. It will be the system required for the preservation of our peoples and the exigencies of our notion of justice based on principles of balance and harmony. . . .

C. Aboriginal Political Goals and Criminal Justice

The development of new approaches to criminal justice responsive to the changing needs of Canadian society necessitates an examination of the aboriginal political agenda to discern the direction in which aboriginal peoples are heading and the implications of aboriginal political goals for the area of justice. The aboriginal political agenda can be capsulized around one key aspiration or motivation: self-determination. There is much discussion about what self-determination means and the term is often interchanged with self-government. Two Mohawk women describe the personal experience of government relations in the following way:

> When an aboriginal person, who knows what s/he is talking about, speaks of 'self-government,' s/he means the particular system of government that was given to the people when they were placed in their territory on Turtle Island. This government needs no sanction through legislation or otherwise; rather, the 'others' need only honour the original agreements to co-exist, and through their actions, show respect for our ways. However, because so many of our people don't know our ways, they have become involved in processes whereby they have attempted to gain recognition of our 'right to self-government,' instead of working on finding ways to effectively assert and exercise our own governments.[28]

Aboriginal peoples, including Indian, Inuit and Métis, have unanimously articulated a desire for federal, provincial and territorial government recognition of their inherent right to 'self-government.' We use the term 'self-determination' instead because it is broader and emphasizes the rights of peoples and not states to choose their form of governance. . . . Aboriginal people see the need for self-determination as the central and essential element to meaningful progress. It means officially recognizing aboriginal peoples' interest in jurisdictional authority and providing the resources necessary to sustain our communities and cultures. It is seen as the first step in ameliorating the grave social conditions under which many of us live our lives. Self-determination is our primary political agenda item for the very reason that control over our own lives, lands and community is the only way out of the widespread oppression we face. . . .

Self-determination means aboriginal design, control and management of institutions and programs. It also means control over fiscal arrangements. It obviously encompasses, at least from a community-based perspective, control over civil and criminal justice matters including dispute resolution structures. Within many reserve communities, this means the internal development and control over powers of criminal law.[29] For off-reserve or external matters, there is a desire for an increased aboriginal presence in the administration of criminal justice and a greater awareness of racism and the differential impact of norms and processes on aboriginal individuals. The extent and form of initiatives taken in urban and rural non-reserve areas will depend on the access and connection, including distance, to the internal mechanisms and structures which need to be developed within aboriginal reserve communities. . . .

Centuries of mistrust have been built upon the centuries of ill-founded approaches to aboriginal-Canadian relations. If we are to turn the tide and enter into a progressive relationship, then the historical mistrust must be resolved through genuine initiatives. Many aboriginal political leaders would suggest that anything short of recognition of self-determination in criminal justice matters is inconsistent with the goals of equal access, equitable treatment and respect, as discussed above. If further mistrust and suspicion are to be avoided, the federal government must recognize that the aboriginal political agenda is genuine and legitimate. . . .

One important discussion which has not yet taken place in any significant way concerns the role of women in self-determined initiatives in our communities, and specifically in justice initiatives.[30] It has historically been the strength of women that has led aboriginal people away from the tragedies of oppression. At Alkali Lake, it was one woman who 'sobered-up' and then 'sobered-up' her family, which in turn triggered a great change in the entire community.[31] . . .Aboriginal people do not separate justice in any of our relations, be they relations of leadership, government, criminal justice or civil justice. We cannot stress enough the importance of the work that must be done in rediscovering this set of women's responsibilities and sharing them within our communities. We would be negligent if we failed to mention that the imposition of the *Indian Act*[32] and its patriarchal structure has been a causal factor of great importance in the suppression of aboriginal women's roles in our communities.[33]

The oppressiveness of attempts to force the assimilation of aboriginal peoples, such as the *Indian Act* regime, must not be understated. In an effort to better our peoples, the delicate balance and harmony in the relationship of aboriginal men and women was compromised. . . . The devastation of the family unit cannot be minimized because familial relationships are integral to the community's ability to be active in matters of criminal justice. Progress on criminal justice matters requires progress on other fronts, including the socio-economic situation, land rights and family and child welfare services. There is a further causal link between the destruction of cultural relationships between the sexes and a vulnerability to the sanctions of the criminal justice system:[34]

The conflict of some Native women with the law may be linked in a variety of ways to the aforementioned role strain experienced by Indian men. First, Native women may retaliate in kind against physically abusive Native men. Secondly, Native women may escape from a violent or otherwise abusive situation at home and migrate to an urban area where discrimination by the larger society, combined with a usually low level of skills and education, may relegate them to the ranks of the unemployed or the unemployable. That in turn increases the probability of resorting to alcohol or drug abuse, or to prostitution, all of which increase the probability of conflict with the law.[35]

The importance of addressing the relationship between aboriginal women and the pursuit of justice within our communities wherever they are located cannot and should not be understated.[36] . . .

Aboriginal self-government will require a refashioning and, in many instances, a re-imagination of Canadian concepts of crime, punishment and victimization, and of our current, collective reactions to anti-social behaviour. . . . This is, in our view, the inevitable direction not only of aboriginal demands for self-determination, but of recent social science inquiry as well. Mere tinkering with criminal statutes, in a unilateral way by government, is antithetical to the movement for self-determination and contrary to the legitimacy it has gained in many circles including those of government.[37]

Notes

1. R.S.C. 1985, c. C-46.
2. Although the authors have taken issue with this terminology in other contexts, in a desire not to confuse the issues, the expression adopted in Canadian constitutional documents, 'aboriginal peoples', has been used throughout this manuscript. Section 35(2) of Part II of the *Constitution Act, 1982*, specifies that the expression 'aboriginal peoples' includes the 'Indian, Inuit and Métis.' 'Aboriginal peoples' refers collectively to the descendants of the First Peoples of the territory now known as Canada.
3. Here, we would like to echo a concern similar to that expressed by the Correctional Law Review in their report, A Framework for the Correctional Law Review (Working Paper No. 2, Part I, 1986) at 19. In that document, concern is expressed regarding the lack of a determined and express philosophical grounding of correctional policy and legislation which is perceived as necessary for a principled, integrated and workable system of justice.
4. We wish to recognize that this paper will be most accessible to those who have an academic background and/or

legal training. The purpose of the paper is to educate the Law Reform Commission personnel, and it is therefore written in a language and style accessible to them. Consequently, and unfortunately, it will not be accessible to many aboriginal people; the very people who have inspired us to participate in this project. If we were writing for the aboriginal community our participation and expression would be very different.

5. The authors wish to emphasize that notions of discipline, punishment, and rehabilitation as they are understood within the Canadian criminal justice system are *not* necessarily the norms and values that have gained respect within traditional aboriginal justice practices.

6. One example of the total alienation of the criminal justice system, and in particular the structure of the court process was explained to the Marshall Commissioners by Bernie Francis, as cited in *The Mi'kmaq and Criminal Justice in Nova Scotia: A Research Study 1989, Volume 3 of the Report of the Royal Commission on the Donald Marshall Jr., Prosecution* (Halifax: Government of Nova Scotia, 1989) at 47:

   [M]any Micmacs translated the judge's question, 'how do you plead: guilty or not guilty?' as 'Are you being blamed?' Heard in this way, the natural response is to answer in the affirmative, which can then be interpreted by the court to mean 'guilty'.

   This comment does not capture the entire gravity of the situation. There is no word for 'guilt' in most aboriginal languages. An accused, when standing in court, hearing, 'are you being blamed'; only needs to look around at the formal and official surroundings, the court personnel, and the police officers, to determine that in fact s/he is!

7. This does not mean that it would be impossible to codify aboriginal systems of law. That is a choice that may be necessitated by the technical society in which we live today. This choice should be left with each individual aboriginal community that chooses to participate in any process of reclaiming traditional relations of justice.

8. The Correctional Services of Canada indicated, in their *Final Report of the Task Force on Aboriginal Peoples in Federal Corrections* (Ottawa: Solicitor General, 1988), that at the time of admission to a federal institution 67.2 per cent of all Aboriginal offenders were residing in communities with a population of greater than 10,000 people. Urbanization is commonly cited as a causal factor specific to so-called 'aboriginal criminality'. The background to this statement must be explored before any automatic conclusions may be drawn. Aboriginal peoples are often transitory, moving frequently between cities and their communities. Those who come to the cities looking for work experience discrimination and often are forced by their unemployment to return to their reserves. But it is not an either/or proposition. The transitoriness of aboriginal persons also stands as evidence of a cultural focus on connection and community above materialistic values which would be actualized more readily away from the reserves. This is a factor which is not paralleled and therefore not usually relevant in the assessment of the crime patterns of non-aboriginal persons. The conclusion is that aboriginal persons who offend should not be treated differently based on where they were when the offence was committed. Even when residing in urban centres, many aboriginal people remain connected to the communities of their birth in highly significant ways. Interfering with this connection or severing it through the imposition of mainstream criminal sanctions which are not culturally sensitive can have life-long adverse impacts which go deep into the life and identity of an aboriginal person. Failure to consider the connectedness of aboriginal populations to a community is one quality which has made past 'solutions' ineffective in redressing systemic discrimination within the criminal justice system.

9. For a discussion see P.A. Monture, 'A Vicious Circle: Child Welfare and First Nations' (1989) 3 C.J.W.L. 1 at 12.

10. For a discussion see Monture, *supra*, note 15 at 4–7.

11. Detailed assessments of any component of the Canadian criminal justice system are beyond the scope of this report. Although numerous reports have been undertaken over the last five years with a view to reforming the system, none have included systematic and rigorous analysis of its cultural implications. This work will only be necessary if agreement can be reached between government leaders, non-aboriginal and aboriginal, which supports the notion of a single justice system for all peoples. If we move in the direction of parallel or separate systems of justice, it will not be necessary to understand these complex cultural factors in their totality. Change can be based on the recognition that the old system was unjust without requiring such a detailed understanding of the content of that injustice.

12. For example the 'Daubney Report,' *Taking Responsibility: Report of the Standing Committee on Justice and the Solicitor General on its Review of Sentencing, Conditional Release and Related Aspects of Corrections* (Ottawa: House of Commons, 1988) at 211 indicates that while aboriginal people comprise two percent of the Canadian population we currently comprise 9.6 per cent of the federal inmate population. These figures are even greater in the west and the north, reaching 31 per cent in the prairie region.

    See also, M. Jackson, *Locking Up Natives in Canada: A Report of the Canadian Bar Association Committee on Imprisonment and Release* (Ottawa: Canadian Bar Association, 1988) at 2–4. Jackson reveals that the situation for aboriginal women is more extreme: 'A treaty Indian woman was 131 times more likely to be admitted' to a provincial correctional centre in Saskatchewan than a non-Native (at 3).

13. See F. Sugar and L. Fox, 'Nitsum Peyako Seht'wawin Iskwewewaak: Breaking Chains' (1989–90) 3 C.J.W.L. 465; and also, F. Sugar, 'Entrenched Social Catastrophe: Native Women in Prison' (1989) 10 *Canadian Woman Studies* 87; for a preliminary documentation of aboriginal women's

perspectives on their experience of the federal correctional system. In the summer of 1990, a video was produced by the Canadian Broadcasting Corporation at the Prison for Women in co-operation with the Correctional Service of Canada. In this video, 'To Heal the Spirit', a number of the aboriginal women speak to their life experiences including the experience of criminal justice. It is an excellent video and can be obtained from Media Tapes and Transcripts, 60 Queen Street, Suite 600, Ottawa, Ontario, K1P 5Y7. The telephone number is (613) 236-4695.

14. For example, this was the overwhelming message heard in the Law Reform Commission's consultation with aboriginal individuals in March 1991.

15. The most notorious case here is that of Helen Betty Osborne, one focus of the Aboriginal Justice Inquiry of Manitoba.

16. Donald Marshall, Jr's experience of discrimination as an aboriginal accused was a highly publicized and scrutinized example.

17. In *Andrews, supra*, note 7 at 171, Justice McIntyre notes:

    The promotion of equality entails the promotion of a society in which all are secure in the knowledge that they are recognized at law as human beings equally deserving of concern, respect and consideration.

18. See *Andrews, ibid.* at 175; and *R. v. Turpin* [1989] 1 S.C.R. 1296 at 1325.

19. In *R. v. Big M Drug Mart* (1985) 18 D.L.R. (4th) 321 (S.C.C.) at 362, Justice Dickson states:

    The equality necessary to support religious freedom does not require identical treatment of all religions. In fact, the interests of true equality may well require differentiation in treatment.

    And in *Andrews, supra* note 7 at 164, Mr. Justice McIntyre comments:

    It must be recognized . . . that every difference in treatment between individuals under the law will not necessarily result in inequality and, as well, that identical treatment may frequently produce serious inequality.

20. Madam Justice Wilson has cautioned that:

    [I]n these early days of interpreting s. 15, it would be unwise, if not foolhardy, to attempt to provide exhaustive definitions of phrases which by their nature are not susceptible of easy definition and which are intended to provide a framework for the 'unremitting protection' of equality rights in the years to come.
    Turpin, supra note 28 at 1326.

21. 'A New Commitment: Statement of the Canadian Human Rights Commission on Federal Aboriginal Policy' (21 November 1990) at 2.

22. This is the lesson that should have been learned during the 1969 'White Paper on Indian Policy' experience which is documented in H. Cardinal, *The Unjust Society: The Tragedy of Canada's Indians* (Edmonton: M.G. Hurtig, 1969).

23. Aboriginal communities have, in fact, grown in major Canadian cities with a population of aboriginal people.

The friendship centre movement has fostered the maintenance and development of these communities.

24. As provided in Minister's Reference letter of 8 June I 990, paragraph 2.

25. Particularly if a United Nations complaint currently before the United Nations Human Rights Committee against Canada is borne out. See *Mi'kmaq Tribal Society v. Canada*, CCPR/c/39/D/205/1986, released 21 August 1990.

26. P.A. Monture, 'Reflecting on Flint Woman' in R. Devlin, ed., *Canadian Perspectives on Legal Theory* (Toronto: Emond Montgomery, 1990) 351 at 352–5.

27. For a discussion of what this means from an aboriginal perspective see O. Lyons, 'Spirituality, Equality, and Natural Law' in L. Little Bear *et al.*, eds, *Pathways to Self-Determination: Canadian Indians and the Canadian State* (Toronto: University of Toronto Press, 1984) 5. Similar concepts are also discussed in T. Porter, 'Traditions of the Constitution of the Six Nations' in L. Little Bear *et al.*, eds, *ibid.*, 11; Chief John Snow, 'Identification and Definition of Our Treaty and Aboriginal Rights,' in M. Boldt *et al.*, eds., *The Quest for Justice* (Toronto: University of Toronto Press, 1985).

28. Ossennontion & Skonaganleh:ra, 'Our World' (1989) 10 *Canadian Woman Studies* 7.

29. This is too narrowly east because traditional forms of dispute resolution focus on restoring the balance in the community. This means responding to offenders, victims and the community as a whole. Traditional justice, therefore, spans what Canadian law thinks of as criminal and civil jurisdictions.

30. That this work is to be accomplished within our communities (and among the women) is of pressing importance. There is currently no aboriginal political organization which is meaningfully grappling with this issue.

31. The experience of the community of Alkali Lake has been documented in two Canadian Broadcasting Corporation productions prepared for the television program 'Man Alive.' They are: 'The Spirit That Moves' produced in 1987 and 'A Circle of Healing, Part II, When the Eagle Lands on the Moon' produced in 1989.

32. R.S.C. 1985, c. I-5.

33. In the report completed by the Ontario Advisory Council on Women's Issues, *Native Women and the Law* (Toronto: Advisory Council on Women's Issues, 1989) at 17, this causal connection between the *Indian Act* and the criminal justice system is described:

    Although it does not appear to be documented, the effect of Bill C-31 on the crime rate of Native women seems obvious. If bad socio-economic conditions are major causal factors in Native female crime, and given that Bill C-31 works against the betterment of women who have lost their status, Bill C-31 can then be said to contribute to the conditions which breed anger and desperation that result in crime, if not a direct cause of crime.

34. *Ibid.* at 20.

35. C.P. LaPrairie, 'Native Women and Crime in Canada: A Theoretical Model' in Adelberg & Currie, eds., *supra*, note 56 at 109.

36. A second reason for the importance of rebuilding the traditional relationships between men and women is the fact that aboriginal women are traditionally the transmitters of culture. It is primarily the mother's responsibility to ensure that the children are taught the proper way to be. This is not to belittle the role of father and this comment should not be understood from within an ethnocentric cultural perspective. If women cannot live in a healthy way with their total environment, their ability to fulfill their traditional responsibilities is compromised. This jeopardizes the health and well-being of the generations yet to come. Many would suggest that allowing this situation to continue is tantamount to cultural genocide.

37. Rt. Hon. B. Mulroney, *supra*, note 82.

Chapter 27

Sexual Violence as a Tool of Genocide

Andrea Smith

[Rape] is nothing more or less than a conscious process of intimidation by which all men keep all women in a state of fear. (Brownmiller, 1986)

Rape as 'nothing more or less' than a tool of patriarchal control undergirds the philosophy of the white-dominated women's antiviolence movement. This philosophy has been critiqued by many women of colour, including critical race theorist Kimberle Crenshaw, for its lack of attention to racism and other forms of oppression. Crenshaw analyzes how male-dominated conceptions of race and white-dominated conceptions of gender stand in the way of a clear understanding of violence against women of colour. It is inadequate, she argues, to investigate the oppression of women of colour by examining race and gender oppressions separately and then putting the two analyses together, because the overlap between racism and sexism transforms the dynamics. Instead, Crenshaw advocates replacing the 'additive' approach with an 'intersectional' approach. . . .

Despite her intersectional approach, Crenshaw falls short of describing how a politics of intersectionality might fundamentally shift how we analyze sexual/domestic violence. If sexual violence is not simply a tool of patriarchy but also a tool of colonialism and racism, then entire communities of colour are the victims of sexual violence. As Neferti Tadiar argues, *colonial relationships are themselves gendered and sexualized*. . . .

Within this context, according to Tadiar, 'the question to be asked . . . is, Who is getting off on this? Who is getting screwed and by whom?' (Tadiar, 1993). Thus, while both Native men and women have been subjected to a reign of sexualized terror, sexual violence does not affect Indian men and women in the same way. When a Native woman suffers abuse, this abuse is an attack on her identity as a woman and an attack on her identity as Native. The issues of colonial, race, and gender oppression cannot be separated. This fact explains why in my experience as a rape crisis counsellor, every Native survivor I ever counselled said to me at one point, 'I wish I was no longer Indian.' As I will discuss in this chapter, women of colour do not just face quantitatively more issues when they suffer violence (e.g., less media attention, language barriers, lack of support in the judicial system) but their experience is qualitatively different from that of white women.

Ann Stoler's analysis of racism sheds light on this relationship between sexual violence and colonialism. She argues that racism, far from being a reaction to crisis in which racial others are scapegoated for social ills, is a permanent part of the social fabric. 'Racism is not an effect but a tactic in the internal fission of society into binary opposition, a means of creating 'biologized' internal enemies, against whom society must defend itself' (Stoler, 1997). She notes that in the modern state, it is the constant purification and elimination of racialized enemies within the state that ensures the growth of the national body. 'Racism does not merely arise in moments of crisis, in sporadic cleansings. It is internal to the biopolitical state, woven into the web of the social body, threaded through its fabric' (Stoler, 1997).

Similarly, Kate Shanley notes that Native peoples are a permanent 'present absence' in the US colonial imagination, an 'absence' that reinforces at every turn the conviction that Native peoples are indeed vanishing and that the conquest of Native lands is justified. Ella Shohat and Robert Stam describe this absence as,

> an ambivalently repressive mechanism [which] dispels the anxiety in the face of the Indian, whose very presence is a reminder of the initially precarious grounding of the American nation-state itself . . . In a temporal paradox, living Indians were induced to 'play dead,' as it were, in order to

perform a narrative of manifest destiny in which their role, ultimately, was to disappear. (Shohat and Stam, 1994)

This 'absence' is effected through the metaphorical transformation of Native bodies into a pollution of which the colonial body must constantly purify itself. For instance, as white Californians described them in the 1860s, Native people were 'the dirtiest lot of human beings on earth' (Rawls, 1997). They wear 'filthy rags, with their persons unwashed, hair uncombed and swarming with vermin' (Rawls, 1997). . . . In the colonial imagination, Native bodies are also immanently polluted with sexual sin. Theorists Albert Cave, Robert Warrior, H.C. Porter, and others have demonstrated that Christian colonizers often likened Native peoples to the biblical Canaanites, both worthy of mass destruction (Cave, 1988; Porter, 1979; Warrior, 1991). What makes Canaanites supposedly worthy of destruction in the biblical narrative and Indian peoples supposedly worthy of destruction in the eyes of their colonizers is that they both personify sexual sin. . . .

Because Indian bodies are 'dirty', they are considered sexually violable and 'rapable', and the rape of bodies that are considered inherently impure or dirty simply does not count. For instance, prostitutes are almost never believed when they say they have been raped because the dominant society considers the bodies of sex workers undeserving of integrity and violable at all times. Similarly, the history of mutilation of Indian bodies, both living and dead, makes it clear that Indian people are not entitled to bodily integrity. . . .

> I saw the body of White Antelope with the privates cut off, and I heard a soldier say he was going to make a tobacco-pouch out of them. (Wrone and Nelson, 1982)

> Andrew Jackson . . . supervised the mutilation of 800 or so Creek Indian corpses—the bodies of men, women and children that he and his men massacred—cutting off their noses to count and preserve a record of the dead, slicing long strips of

flesh from their bodies to tan and turn into bridle reins. (Stannard, 1992) . . .

The project of colonial sexual violence establishes the ideology that Native bodies are inherently violable—and by extension, that Native lands are also inherently violable.

As a consequence of this colonization and abuse of their bodies, Indian people learn to internalize self-hatred, because body image is integrally related to self-esteem. When one's body is not respected, one begins to hate oneself (Bass and Davis, 1988). Anne, a Native boarding school student, reflects on this process:

> You better not touch yourself . . . If I looked at somebody . . . lust, sex, and I got scared of those sexual feelings. And I did not know how to handle them . . . What really confused me was if intercourse was sin, why are people born? . . . It took me a really long time to get over the fact that . . . I've sinned: I had a child. (Haig-Brown, 1988)

As her words indicate, when the bodies of Indian people are designated as inherently sinful and dirty, it becomes a sin just to be Indian. Native peoples internalize the genocidal project through self-destruction. As a rape crisis counsellor, it was not a surprise to me that Indians who have survived sexual abuse would often say that they no longer wish to be Indian. Native peoples' individual experiences of sexual violation echo 500 years of sexual colonization in which Native peoples' bodies have been deemed inherently impure. . . .

In a recent case among the Aboriginal peoples of Australia, a judge ruled that a 50-year-old Aboriginal man's rape of a 15-year-old girl was not a serious crime, but an example of traditional culture. He ruled that the girl 'knew what was expected of her' and 'didn't need protection' when raped by a man who had been previously convicted of murdering his former wife. An 'expert' anthropologist in the case testified that the rape was 'traditional' and 'morally correct' (Shah, 2002). According to Judy Atkinson, an Aboriginal professor, survivors have reported numerous incidents

of law enforcement officials dismissing reports of violence because they consider such violence to be 'cultural behaviour'. 'We are living in a war zone in Aboriginal communities,' states Atkinson. 'Different behaviors come out of that,' she says. 'Yet the courts of law validate that behavior' (Shah, 2002).

Taussig comments on the irony of this logic: 'Men are conquered not by invasion, but by themselves. It is a strange sentiment, is it not, when faced with so much brutal evidence of invasion' (Taussig, 1991). But as Fanon notes, this destructive behavior is not 'the consequence of the organization of his nervous system or of characterial originality, but the direct product of the colonial system' (Fanon, 1963).

Tadiar's description of colonial relationships as an enactment of the 'prevailing mode of heterosexual relations' is useful because it underscores the extent to which US colonizers view the subjugation of women of the Native nations as critical to the success of the economic, cultural, and political colonization (Tadiar, 1993). Stoler notes that the imperial discourses on sexuality 'cast white women as the bearers of more racist imperial order' (Stoler, 1997). By extension, Native women are bearers of a counter-imperial order and pose a supreme threat to the dominant culture. Symbolic and literal control over their bodies is important in the war against Native people, as these testimonies illustrate:

> When I was in the boat I captured a beautiful Carib woman. . . . I conceived desire to take pleasure. . . . I took a rope and thrashed her well, for which she raised such unheard screams that you would not have believed your ears. Finally we came to an agreement in such a manner that I can tell you that she seemed to have been brought up in a school of harlots. (Sale, 1990)

> Two of the best looking of the squaws were lying in such a position, and from the appearance of the genital organs and of their wounds, there can be no doubt that they were first ravished and then shot dead. Nearly all of the dead were mutilated. (Wrone and Nelson, 1982) . . .

The history of sexual violence and genocide among Native women illustrates how gender violence functions as a tool for racism and colonialism among women of colour in general. For example, African American women were also viewed as inherently rapable. Yet where colonizers used sexual violence to eliminate Native populations, slave owners used rape to reproduce an exploitable labour force. (The children of Black slave women inherited their slave status.) And because Black women were seen as the property of their slave owners, their rape at the hands of these men did not 'count'. As one southern politician declared in the early twentieth century, there was no such thing as a 'virtuous colored girl' over the age of 14 (Davis, 1981). . . .

Immigrant women as well have endured a long history of sexual exploitation in the US. For instance, racially discriminatory employment laws forced thousands of Chinese immigrant women into prostitution. To supplement their meager incomes, impoverished Chinese families often sold their daughters into prostitution. Other women were lured to the US with the promise of a stable marriage or job, only to find themselves trapped in the sex trade. By 1860, almost a quarter of the Chinese in San Francisco (all female) were employed in prostitution (Almaguer, 1994).

Karen Warren argues that patriarchal society is a dysfunctional system that mirrors the dysfunctional nuclear family. That is, severe abuse in the family continues because the family members learn to regard it as 'normal'. A victim of abuse may come to see that her abuse is not 'normal' when she has contact with less abusive families. Similarly, Warren argues, patriarchal society is a dysfunctional system based on domination and violence. 'Dysfunctional systems are often maintained through systematic denial, a failure or inability to see the reality of a situation. This denial need not be conscious, intentional, or malicious; it only needs to be pervasive to be effective' (Warren, 1993).

At the time of Columbus's exploits, European society was a dysfunctional system, racked by mass poverty, disease, religious oppression, war, and institutionalized violence. For example, in the Inquisition, hundreds of thousands of Jewish people were slaughtered and their confiscated property was used to fund Columbus's voyages. . . .

Furthermore, European societies were thoroughly misogynistic. The Christian patriarchy which structured European society was inherently violent, as has been thoroughly documented (Daly, 1978; Dworkin, 1974; Barstow, 1994; Ehrenreich and English, 1979; Ruether, 1974, 1975; Stannard, 1992). For example, because English women were not allowed to express political opinions, a woman who spoke out against taxation in 1664 was condemned to having her tongue nailed to a tree near a highway, with a paper fastened to her back detailing her offense (Gage, 1980). Hatred for women was most fully manifested in the witch hunts. In some English towns, as many as a third of the population were accused of witchcraft (Stannard, 1992). The women targeted for destruction were those most independent from patriarchal authority: single women, widows, and healers (Ehrenreich and English, 1979).

The more peaceful and egalitarian nature of Native societies did not escape the notice of the colonizers. In the 'colonial' period, it was a scandal in the colonies that a number of white people chose to live among Indian people while virtually no Indians voluntarily chose to live among the colonists. According to J. Hector St. John de Crevecoeur, the eighteenth-century author of *Letters from an American Farmer*, 'Thousands of Europeans are Indians, and we have no example of even one of these Aborigines having from choice become Europeans!' (Stannard, 1992). Colonists also noted that Native peoples rarely committed sexual violence against white prisoners, unlike the colonists. . . .

In contrast to the deeply patriarchal nature of European societies, prior to colonization, Indian societies for the most part were not male dominated. Women served as spiritual, political, and military leaders, and many societies were matrilineal. Although there existed a division of labour between women and men, women's labour and men's labour were accorded similar status (Jaimes and Halsey, 1992). As women and men lived in balance, Native societies were consequently much less authoritarian than their European counterparts. . . .

Of course, in discussing these trends, it is important not to overgeneralize or give the impression that Native communities were utopian prior to colonization. Certainly gender violence occurred prior to colonization. Nevertheless, both oral and written records often note its relative rarity as well as the severity of the punishment for perpetrators of violence. . . .

European women were often surprised to find that, even in war, they went unmolested by their Indian captors. . . . Between 1675 and 1763, almost 40 per cent of women who were taken captive by Native people in New England chose to remain with their captors (Namias, 1993).[1] In 1899, an editorial signed by Mrs Teall appeared in the *Syracuse Herald-Journal*, discussing the status of women in Iroquois society.

> They had one custom the white men are not ready, even yet, to accept. The women of the Iroquois had a public and influential position. They had a council of their own . . . which had the initiative in the discussion; subjects presented by them being settled in the councils of the chiefs and elders; in this latter council the women had an orator of their own (often of their own sex) to present and speak for them. There are sometimes female chiefs . . . The wife owned all the property . . . The family was hers; descent was counted through the mother. (Lopez, n.d.) . . .

Thus, the demonization of Native women can be seen as a strategy of white men to maintain control over white women. This demonization was exemplified by the captivity narratives which became a popular genre in the US.[2] These narratives were supposedly first-person narratives of white women who were abducted by 'savages' and forced to undergo untold savagery. Their tales, however, were usually written by white men who had their own agenda. For instance, in 1823 James

Seaver of New York interviewed Mary Jemison, who was taken as captive by the Seneca. Jemison chose to remain among them when she was offered her freedom, but Seaver is convinced that she is protecting the Indian people by not describing their full savagery. 'The vices of the Indians, she appeared disposed not to aggravate, and seemed to take pride in extolling their virtues. A kind of family pride induced her to withhold whatever would blot the character of her descendants, and perhaps induced her to keep back many things that would have been interesting' (Seaver, 1975). Consequently, he supplements her narrative with material 'from authentic sources' and Jemison's cousin, George (Seaver, 1975). Seaver, nevertheless, attributes these supplements to her voice in this supposed first-person narrative. . . .

Paula Gunn Allen argues that colonizers realized that in order to subjugate indigenous nations they would have to subjugate women within these nations. Native peoples needed to learn the value of hierarchy, the role of physical abuse in maintaining that hierarchy, and the importance of women remaining submissive to their men. They had to convince 'both men and women that a woman's proper place was under the authority of her husband and that a man's proper place was under the authority of the priests' (Allen, 1986a). She further argues:

> It was to the advantage of white men to mislead white women, and themselves, into believing that their treatment of women was superior to the treatment by the men of the group which they considered savage. Had white women discovered that all women were not mistreated, they might have been intolerant of their men's abusiveness. (Allen, 1986b)

Thus in order to colonize a people whose society was not hierarchical, colonizers must first naturalize hierarchy through instituting patriarchy. Patriarchal gender violence is the process by which colonizers inscribe hierarchy and domination on the bodies of the colonized. Ironically, while enslaving women's bodies, colonizers argued that they were actually somehow freeing Native women from the 'oppression' they supposedly faced in Native nations. Thomas Jefferson argued that Native women 'are submitted to unjust drudgery. This I believe is the case with every barbarous people. It is civilization alone which replaces women in the enjoyment of their equality' (Pearce, 1965). The *Mariposa Gazette* similarly noted that when Indian women were safely under the control of white men, they are 'neat, and tidy, and industrious, and soon learn to discharge domestic duties properly and creditably.' In 1862, a Native man in Conrow Valley was killed and scalped with his head twisted off, his killers saying, 'You will not kill any more women and children' (Rawls, 1997). Apparently, Native women can only be free while under the dominion of white men, and both Native and white women have to be protected from Indian men, rather than from white men.

A 1985 Virginia Slims ad reflected a similar notion that white patriarchy saves Native women from oppression. On the left side of the ad was a totem pole of cartoonish figures of Indian women. Their names: Princess Wash and Scrub, Little Running Water Fetcher, Keeper of the Teepee, Princess Breakfast, Lunch and Dinner Preparer, Woman Who Gathers Firewood, Princess Buffalo Robe Sewer, Little Woman Who Weaves All Day, and Woman Who Plucks Feathers for Chief's Headdress. The caption on top of the totem pole reads: 'Virginia Slims remembers one of many societies where the women stood head and shoulders above the men.' On the right side of the ad is a model adorned with makeup and dressed in a tight skirt, nylons, and high heels, with the familiar caption: 'You've come a long way, baby.' The message is that Native women, oppressed in their tribal societies, need to be liberated into a patriarchal standard of beauty, where their true freedom lies. The historical record suggests, as Paula Gunn Allen argues, that the real roots of feminism should be found in Native societies. But in this Virginia Slims ad, feminism is tied to colonial conquest—(white) women's liberation is founded upon the destruction of supposedly patriarchal Native societies.

Today we see this discourse utilized in the 'war on terror'. To justify the bombing of Afghanistan,

Laura Bush declared, 'The fight against terrorism is also a fight for the rights and dignity of women' (Flanders, 2004). These sentiments were shared by mainstream feminists. Eleanor Smeal, former president of the National Organization for Women (NOW) and founder and president of the Fund for a Feminist Majority said, 'Without 9/11, we could not get the Afghanistan tragedy in focus enough for the world powers to stop the Taliban's atrocities or to remove the Taliban. Tragically, it took a disaster for them to act definitively enough' (Smeal, 2001).

It seems the best way to liberate women is to bomb them. Meanwhile, the Revolutionary Association of Women of Afghanistan (RAWA), whose members were the very women who were to be liberated by this war, denounced it as an imperial venture. . . .

So why does a group like the Fund for a Feminist Majority ignore the voice of RAWA? Again, even within feminist circles, the colonial logic prevails that women of colour, indigenous women, and women from Global South countries are only victims of oppression rather than organizers in their own right. . . .

Historically, white colonizers who raped Indian women claimed that the real rapists were Indian men (Wrone and Nelson, 1982). Today, white men who rape and murder Indian women often make this same claim. . . .

Of course, Indian men do commit acts of sexual violence. After years of colonialism and boarding school experience, violence has been internalized within Indian communities. However, this view of the Indian man as the 'true' rapist serves to obscure who has the real power in this racist and patriarchal society. Thus, the colonization of Native women (as well as other women of colour) is part of the project of strengthening white male ownership of white women.

And while the era of Indian massacres in their more explicit form has ended in North America, the wholesale rape and mutilation of indigenous women's bodies continues. . . .

One wonders why the mass rapes in Guatemala, Chiapas, or elsewhere against indigenous people in Latin America does not spark the same outrage as the rapes in Bosnia in the 1990s. In fact, feminist legal scholar Catherine MacKinnon argues that in Bosnia, 'The world has *never* seen sex used this consciously, this cynically, this elaborately, this openly, this systematically . . . as a means of destroying a whole people [emphasis mine]' (MacKinnon, 1993). Here, MacKinnon seems to have forgotten that she lives on this land because millions of Native peoples were raped, sexually mutilated, and murdered. Is mass rape against European women genocide, while mass rape against indigenous women is business as usual?

The historical context of rape, racism, and colonialism continues to impact women in North America as well. This legacy is most evident in the rate of violence in American Indian communities—American Indian women are twice as likely to be victimized by violent crime as women or men of any other ethnic group. In addition, 60 per cent of the perpetrators of violence against American Indian women are white (Greenfield and Smith, 1999).[3]

In times of crisis, sexual violence against Native women escalates. When I served as a nonviolent witness for the Chippewa spearfishers who were being harassed by white racist mobs in the 1980s, one white harasser carried a sign that read, 'Save a fish; spear a pregnant squaw.' During the 1990 Mohawk crisis in Quebec, Canada, a white mob surrounded an ambulance carrying a Native woman who was attempting to leave the Mohawk reservation because she was hemorrhaging after giving birth. She was forced to 'spread her legs' to prove she had delivered a baby. The police at the scene refused to intervene. An Indian man was arrested for 'wearing a disguise' (he was wearing jeans), and was brutally beaten at the scene, with his testicles crushed. Two women from Chicago Women of All Red Nations (WARN) went to Oka to videotape the crisis. They were arrested and held in custody for 11 hours without being charged, and were told that they could not go to the bathroom unless the male police officers could watch. The place they were held was covered with pornographic magazines. . . .

Sexual Violence and Impunity

The ideology of Native women's bodies as rapable is evident in the hundreds of missing indigenous women in Mexico and Canada. Since 1993, over 500 women have been murdered in Juarez, Mexico. The majority have been sexually mutilated, raped, and tortured, including having had their nipples cut off. Poor and indigenous women have been particularly targeted. Not only have the local police made no effort to solve the cases, they appear to be complicit in the murders. Amnesty International and other human rights organizations and activists have noted their failure to seriously investigate the cases—the police have made several arrests and tortured those arrested to extract confessions, but the murders have continued unabated. Furthermore, the general response of the police to these murders is to blame the victims by arguing that they are sex workers or lesbians, and hence, inherently rapable (Hewitt, 2003; Nieves, 2002). For instance, one former state public prosecutor commented in 1999, 'It's hard to go out on the street when it's raining and not get wet' (Amnesty International, 2003).

Similarly, in Canada, over 500 First Nations women have gone missing or have been murdered in the past 15 years, with little police investigation. Again, it seems that their cases have been neglected because many of the women were homeless or sex workers. Ada Elaine Brown, the sister of Terri Brown, president of the Native Women's Association of Canada, was found dead in her bed in 2002. She was so badly beaten her family did not recognize her. According to Terri Brown: 'The autopsy report said it was a brain aneurysm. Yeah, because she was beaten to a pulp' (Diebel, 2002). . . .

[In the US,] because sexual assault is covered under the Major Crimes Act, many tribes have not developed codes to address the problem in those rape cases the federal government declines to prosecute. Those with codes are often hindered in their ability to investigate by a wait that may last more than a year before federal investigators formally turn over cases. In addition, the Indian Civil Rights

Act (ICRA) of 1968 limits the punishment tribal justice systems can enforce on perpetrators.[4] For instance, the maximum time someone may be sentenced to prison through tribal courts is one year.[5] Also, Native activist Sarah Deer (Muscogee) notes that the US can prohibit remedies that do not follow the same penalties of the dominant system. . . .

To further complicate matters, tribes covered under PL 280, which gives states criminal jurisdiction, must work with state and county law enforcement officials who may have hostile relationships with the tribe. And because tribes are often geographically isolated—reservations are sometimes over 100 miles from the closest law enforcement agency, with many homes having no phone—local officials are unable to respond to an emergency situation. Racism on the part of local police officers in surrounding border towns also contributes to a lack of responsiveness in addressing rape cases. And since the federal government does not compensate state governments for law enforcement on reservations, and tribes generally do not pay local or federal taxes, states have little vested interest in providing 'protection' for Indian tribes.

Finally, American Indian tribes do not have the right to prosecute non-Indians for crimes that occur on reservations. In *Oliphant v. Suquamish Indian Tribe* (1978), the Supreme Court held that Native American tribes do not have criminal jurisdiction over non-Native peoples on reservation lands. This precedent is particularly problematic for non-PL 280 tribes, because tribal police cannot arrest non-Indians who commit offenses. Furthermore, state law enforcement does not have jurisdiction on reservation lands. So, unless state law enforcement is cross-deputized with tribal law enforcement, *no one* can arrest non-Native perpetrators of crimes on Native land (Deer, n.d.).

In response to these deplorable conditions, many Native peoples are calling for increased funding for criminal justice enforcement in tribal communities. . . . It is undeniable that US policy has codified the 'rapability' of Native women. Indeed, the US and other colonizing countries are engaged in a 'permanent social war' against the bodies of women of colour and indigenous women, which threaten their legitimacy (Stoler, 1997). Colonizers evidently recognize the wisdom of the Cheyenne saying 'A nation is not conquered until the hearts of the women are on the ground.'

Notes

1. I am not arguing that the nonpatriarchal nature of Native societies is the only reason white women may have chosen to live with their captors, but that it is a possible explanation for why many chose to stay.

2. It is difficult to ascertain the true nature of Indian captivity of white people based on these narratives because of their anti-Indian bias. For instance, *A Narrative of the Horrid Massacre by the Indians of the Wife and Children of the Christian Hermit* sets out to prove that Indians are so biologically cruel that there is nothing else for whites to do than exterminate them. However, even the narrator admits that Indians killed his family because he 'destroyed their village'. He further states that Natives 'are kind and hospitable, but toward those who *intentionally* [italics mine] offend them, the western savage [sic] is implacable' (*A Narrative of the Horrid Massacre by the Indians of the Wife and Children of the Christian Hermit* [St. Louis: Leander W. Whiteney and Co., 1833]). June Namias suggests that captivity of white people became more brutal as the conquest drove Native people to the point of desperation. She also says that since captivity narratives by Jesuits seem to be the most graphic in nature, it is possible that they embellished their stories to enhance their status as martyrs and encourage greater funding for their missions (Namias, *White Captives*). Francis Jennings argues also that there were some practices of torture among the Iroquois, though not other northeastern tribes, and that it became more pronounced as the conquest against them became more brutal. He states, however, that Native people never molested women or girls (Francis Jennings, *Invasion of the Americas* [New York: Norton, 1975]). Richard Drinnon believes that most male captives were killed, except that some might have been adopted into the tribe to replace those that had been killed in battle. Women and children were not killed (Richard Drinnon, *Facing West* [New York: Schocken Books, 1980]). All of these discussions are based on Native practices after colonization and the infusion of violence into their societies.

3. Native youth are also 49 per cent more likely to be victimized by violent crime than the next highest ethnic group—African Americans (National Center for Victims of Crime, http://www.ncvc.org).

4. The Indian Civil Rights Act was passed ostensibly to protect the civil rights of Indian peoples, but the effect of this act was to limit tribal sovereignty over tribal members if tribal acts infringed on the 'civil rights' of its members, as

understood by the US government. Consequently, tribes are limited in the types of strategies and punishments they can use to address sexual violence to the types of strategies and punishments that are seen as acceptable by the US government.

5. For history of Indian policy, see Sharon O'Brien, *American Indian Tribal Governments* (Norman: University of Oklahoma, 1989); Luana Ross, *Inventing the Savage: The Social Construction of Native American Criminality* (Austin: University of Texas Press, 1998); Carole Goldberg, *Planting Tail Feathers* (Los Angeles: American Indian Studies Center, UCLA, 1997). For more resources on current criminal justice policy, see the website of the Tribal Law and Policy Institute, Los Angeles, CA, available at http://www.tribal-institute.org.

References

Allen, Paula Gunn. 1986a. *The Sacred Hoop*. Boston: Beacon Press.

Allen, Paula Gunn. 1986b. 'Violence and the American Indian Woman', in Maryviolet Burns, ed., *The Speaking Profits Us*. Seattle: Center for the Prevention of Sexual and Domestic Violence.

Almaguer, Thomas. 1994. *Racial Faultlines*. Berkeley: University of California.

Amnesty International (Mexico). 2003. 'Intolerable Killings: Ten years of abductions and murders in Ciudad Juarez and Chihuahua', 11 August.

Barstow, Anne. 1994. *Witchcraze*. New York: Dover.

Bass, Ellen, and Laura Davis. 1988. *Courage to Heal*. Harper & Row: New York.

Brownmiller, Susan. 1986. *Against Our Will*. Toronto: Bantam Books.

Cave, Albert. 1988. 'Canaanites in a Promised Land', *American Indian Quarterly* (Fall): 277–97.

Daly, Mary. 1978. *Gyn/Ecology*. Boston: Beacon Press.

Davis, Angela. 1981. *Women, Race and Class*. New York: Vintage.

Deer, Sarah. n.d. 'Expanding the Network of Safety: Tribal Protection Orders and Victims of Sexual Assault'. Unpublished paper.

Diebel, Linda. 2002. '500 Missing: Aboriginal Canadians Take Fight for Justice for Invisible Victims to UN', *Toronto Star*, 30 November.

Dworkin, Andrea. 1974. *Woman Hating*. New York: E.P. Dutton.

Ehrenreich, Barbara, and Deirdre English. 1979. *For Her Own Good*. Garden City: Anchor.

Ella, and Robert Stain. 1994. *Unthinking Eurocentrism*. London: Routledge.

Fanon, Frantz. 1963. *Wretched of the Earth*. New York: Grove Press.

Flanders, Laura. 2004. 'What Has George W. Ever Done for Women?', *The Guardian*, 26 March.

Gage, Greenfield, Lawrence, and Steven Smith. 1999. *American Indians and Crime*. Washington, DC: Bureau of Justice Statistics, US Department of Justice.

Haig-Brown, Celia. 1988. *Resistance and Renewal*. Vancouver: Tilacrum.

Hewitt, Bill. 2003. 'A Wave of Murders Terrorizes the Women of Ciudad Juarez', *People*, 25 August.

Jaimes, M. Annette, and Theresa Halsey. 1992. 'American Indian Women: At the Center of Indigenous Resistance in North America', in M. Annette, ed. *State of Native America*. Boston: South End Press.

Lopez, Andre. n.d. *Pagans in Our Midst*. Mohawk Nation: Awkesasne Notes.

MacKinnon, Catherine. 1993. 'Postmodern Genocide', *Ms.*, July/August.

Matilda Joslyn. 1980. *Women, Church and State*. Watertown, MA: Persephone Press.

Namias, June. 1993. *White Captives*. Chapel Hill, NC: University of North Carolina Press.

Nieves, Evelyn. 2002. 'To Work and Die in Juarez', *Mother Jones*, May/June.

Pearce, Roy Harvey. 1965. *Savagism and Civilization*. Baltimore: Johns Hopkins Press.

Porter, H.C. 1979. *The Inconstant Savage*. London: Gerald Duckworth & Co.

Rawls, James. 1997. *Indians of California: The Changing Image*. Norman: University of Oklahoma.

Ruether, Rosemary Radford, ed. 1974. *Religion and Sexism*. New York: Simon & Schuster.

Ruether, Rosemary Radford. 1975. *New Woman, New Earth*. Minneapolis: Seabury Press.

Sale, Kirpatrick. 1990. *The Conquest of Paradise*. New York: Plume.

Seaver, James. 1975. *Narrative of the Life of Mrs. Mary Jemison*. New York: Corinth Books.

Shah, Sonia. 2002. 'Judge Rules Rape of Aboriginal Girl "Traditional" ', *Women's E-News*, 29 November; available at http://www.feminist.com/news/news126.html.

Shohat, Smeal, Ellie. 2001. Fund For a Feminist Majority.

Stannard, David. 1992. *American Holocaust*. Oxford: Oxford University Press.

Stoler, Ann. 1997. *Race and the Education of Desire*. Chapel Hill: Duke University Press.

Tadiar, Neferti. 1993. 'Sexual Economies of the Asia-Pacific', in Arif Dirlik, ed. *What's in a Rim? Critical Perspectives on the Pacific Region Idea*. Boulder, CO: Westview Press.

Taussig, Michael. 1991. *Shamanism, Colonialism and the Wild Man*. Chicago: University of Chicago Press.

Warren, Karen. 1993. 'A Feminist Philosophical Perspective on Ecofeminist Spiritualities', in Carol Adams, ed., *Ecofeminism and the Sacred*. New York: Continuum.

Warrior, Robert. 1991. 'Canaanites, Cowboys, and Indians', in R.S. Sugirtharajah, ed., *Voices from the Margin*. Maryknoll: Orbis.

Wrone, David, and Russell Nelson, eds. 1982. *Who's the Savage?* Malabar: Robert Krieger Publishing.

Part Nine

Additional Readings

Amnesty International Report. *Stolen Sisters: A Human Rights Response to Discrimination and Violence Against Indigenous Women in Canada*. Ottawa: Amnesty International, 2004.

Chan, Wendy, and Kiran Mirchandani, eds. *Crimes of Colour; Racialization and the Criminal Justice System in Canada*. Peterborough, ON: Broadview Press, 2002.

Native Women's Association of Canada. *Aboriginal Women and the Legal Justice System in Canada*. 2007. Available online at http://www.nwac-hq.org/en/documents/nwac-legal.pdf.

Reber, Susanne. *Starlight Tour: The Last, Lonely Night of Neil Stonechild*. Toronto: Random House Canada, 2005.

Smith, Andrea. *Conquest: Sexual Violence and American Indian Genocide*. Cambridge, MA: South End Press, 2005.

Relevant Websites

Native Women's Association of Canada (Sisters In Spirit)
http://www.nwac-hq.org/sisters-spirit-research-report-2010
Sisters in Spirit is a research initiative conducted by the Native Women's Association of Canada. The 2010 report is a culmination of five years of research on murdered and missing Indigenous women in Canada and can be found at the following link.

Report of the Aboriginal Justice Inquiry of Manitoba
http://www.ajic.mb.ca/volume.html
The Manitoba Government created the Public Inquiry into the Administration of Justice and Aboriginal People, commonly known as the Aboriginal Justice Inquiry. The Inquiry was created in response to the trial in November 1987 of two men for the 1971 murder of Helen Betty Osborne in The Pas. The Report can be found online on this website.

Films

Circles. Dir. Shanti Thakur. National Film Board of Canada, 1997.

Finding Dawn. Dir. Christine Welsh. National Film Board of Canada, 2006.

Go Home, Baby Girl. Dir. Audrey Huntley. CBC, 2005.

Two Worlds Colliding. Dir. Tasha Hubbard. National Film Board of Canada, 2004.

Key Terms

Social cohesion
Starlight Tours
Systemic racism
Sexual violence

Genocide
Systemic injustice
Meaningful participation
Self-determination

Discussion Questions

1. Andrea Smith asserts that sexual violence and colonialism are intimately interconnected. What does she mean by this and what are the implications? What roles do white women and white men play in colonial sexual violence? How are Indigenous women and/or men of colour constructed in the colonial imaginary and how do these constructions impel colonial/white heteropatriarchy?

2. While white women are often understood in Western thought as the originators of feminism, Andrea Smith and other authors in this anthology trouble this notion and offer alternative understandings of the origins of feminism and/or women's equality. In this vein, discuss Andrea Smith's assertion that the demonization of Indigenous women was a strategy

of white men to maintain control over white women. What examples does she give, and other authors of this anthology have also given? What implications does this have for white feminism?

3. Green insists that decolonization is vital to both colonizer and colonized: map the different components of this argument. How is dehumanization an essential part of colonialism? Why does Green argue it is necessary for Canada to deal with racism and colonialism? What are the ramifications if it does not?

4. How has the Canadian criminal justice system in reality resulted in systemic injustice towards Indigenous peoples? What steps need to be taken for true justice to take place?

Activities

Read the Amnesty Internal Report about the Missing/Murdered Indigenous women and/or the Sisters in Spirit campaign (the latter can be found in the Native Women Association of Canada's website). How do colonialism, racism, sexism, and classism intersect in the events surrounding the lives and treatment of these Indigenous women? How did the police treat those cases? Are there any indications of systemic injustice?

Locate at least three cases of police's treatment of Indigenous peoples in your area. What were the main issues? How are these cases connected to the articles covered in this part of the anthology (e.g. was a relationship of trust, co-operation, respect existent or not; could an argument be made that systemic racism played a part in the treatment of Indigenous people)? What do you suggest could have and/or should be done in order for a better relationship between the parties to occur?

Invite a local anticolonial activist to discuss about issues of hatred and violence against Indigenous peoples in your area and to strategize about ways in which to organize to bring public awareness and social change.

Conclusion

On 27 September 2009, Prime Minister Stephen Harper announced to members of the G20 Summit—and the international community—that Canada is unique in being a country unmarked by histories of colonialism. 'We have no history of colonialism,' he told world leaders, 'so we have all of the things that many people admire about the great powers but none of the things that threaten or bother them.' Indigenous peoples and Canadians alike listened in shock and disbelief. In saying these words, the Prime Minister seemed to contradict his own apology made to residential school survivors in Parliament about colonialism in June 2008. Moreover, his suggestion was that Indigenous efforts to challenge and rupture colonialism and dispossession are merely a 'bother' and 'threat' to the great powers of the world.

It is not uncommon to hear sentiments like these in Canadian society. Regrettably, they are not only limited to this country's leaders. In the classes we teach, we hear from educated Canadians that colonialism is a thing of the past, entirely disconnected from the present. These attitudes reflect a common sense or taken for granted set of assumptions about the nature of colonial dominance, the nature of history, and the making of the nation. In some cases, these attitudes are shaped by hostility toward Indigenous peoples, anti-Indian organizing, and unwillingness to acknowledge histories of land dispossession, even institutionalized racism. On the other hand, these attitudes stem from misunderstanding, ignorance about contemporary colonialism, and a lack of clear vision informed by original nation-to-nation principles.

In writing this anthology, we have hoped to provide readers with a more thorough understanding of the racism that structures the colonial present. We have hoped to show that it is no longer possible to ignore Canada's origins as a colonial creation of both British and French settlers. The disparities outlined by Indigenous scholars in the realm of education, social class, and criminal justice are each living vestiges of Canada's colonial history, as alive and well in the twenty-first century as it was in the nineteenth. In summary, we also hope this book will spur readers to further contemplate and reflect on some of our major conclusions, including:

1. That neither racism nor Indigenous peoples are disappearing into the twenty-first century;
2. That the options available for repairing the mistrust and disavowal structuring modern colonial consciousness have already been set out in early historical and nation-to-nation-based agreements, such as Guswanteh or Two Row Wampum;
3. That poverty and economic marginalization continue as obstacles, requiring us to revisit colonial legacies, and—in the first historical instance—the dispossession of lands before fully understanding, repairing, and eradicating them;
4. That Indigenous peoples continue to face serious disparities in educational attainments despite ameliorative efforts, the nature of which require us to consider histories of difference-making, antiracist, and anticolonial pedagogies, along with—and sometimes even before—strategies aimed at cultural awareness and revitalization (see inside back cover illustration);
5. That institutionalized racism is not disappearing, especially as this has been directed toward Indigenous women, men, and nations through the Indian Act, Indian status distinctions, proposed amendments to the Indian Act under Bill C-3, and other interlocking systems of oppression based on sexism, colonialism and patriarchy;
6. That racialized violence (e.g., Stonechild, Stolen Sisters, Ipperwash, Caledonia, Burnt Church, and Gustafsen Lake) continues to take place in Canada embodying, in itself, the ongoing physical—and symbolic—removal of Indigenous peoples from their lands into the twenty-first century; and
7. That our resistance and resilience as peoples is not disappearing as is evidenced by the contributions we continue to make in reformulating academia (see Mihesuah, 1998), the arts, sports, and legal reform in Canada.

Dismantling colonial dominance requires breaking with cycles of oppression founded in the first instance upon histories of racism and sex discrimination. As we have shown, racism may seem altogether unrelated to other systems of oppression like sexism, social class exploitation, and even heteronormativity. But Indigenous scholars have nuanced how these systems work together simultaneously to structure distinct kinds of discrimination for Indigenous nations, women, and to a lesser extent in published literature, two-spirited individuals. Racialization, sexism, and heteronormativity have quite simply intersected historically to place Indigenous men and women at a disadvantage relative to the state, the justice system, and to each other. We therefore suggest that any meaningful discussions about racism and Indigeneity in Canada take these complex inter-relationships into account, as they profoundly shape and structure the experiences of Indigenous peoples.

Colonial injustice is racialized injustice. In the first instance, the Indian Act set into motion a way of thinking about identity, governance, and nationhood in racialized terms. It also made compulsory, a racialized order of Indian Act govern-ance on Crown lands reserved for Indians. As Indigenous scholars, we believe it is incumbent upon us to revisit these early historical precedents, especially since much of our lives are shaped by them. On the one hand, we agree with scholars who insist that we refuse at every turn the invitation to citizenship (Henderson, this anthology) and who reject the fashioning of sovereignty grievances under racial minority statuses (Porter, 1999). At the same time, we cannot help but be concerned by race and racialization, largely because it is so fundamentally tied to colonialism in the first instance. For better or worse, racism shapes the everyday experience of Indigenous peoples in Canada, but it does not prevent us from naming and then resisting its parameters.

Racism cannot fully be understood, nor reconciled, so long as Indigenous peoples are administered as Indians under federal legislation. The word 'Indian' is a race-based concept but, as John Raulston Saul (2009: 8) makes clear, it does not belong to Indigenous peoples, nor is it one that is desirable to us, or that rightfully defines our nation-to-nation-based relationships. 'If today's land claims [sic], treaty rights, and membership in particular seem to be dependent on definitions of race', writes Saul, 'that is entirely the outcome of a European-imposed approach, one that had nothing to do with the Aboriginal idea of expandable and inclusive cir-cles of people' (ibid.). Saul points to histories of dominance through which lands were deemed *terra nullius*—empty or unoccupied—and to nation-to-nation-based relationships and identities becoming racialized. He draws attention to the origins of Canada wherein racialized categories of difference became entrenched in law, economics, and politics.

Canada's earliest categories of racial difference are contained in the Indian Act (RSC, 1985). This piece of federal legislation remains with us today, and has come to define the relationship between Indigenous nations and Canada, in effect ren-dering all prior treaty and nation-to-nation agreements with our peoples null and void. We appreciate that current relationships may have become shaped by mon-etary wealth and its unequal distribution, but we also recognize the spirit of our initial agreements. Our original agreements were about responsibilities and how to best live amongst one another. We think these prior arrangements set an important historical precedent, and we regard the current system of colonial rela-tions between Indigenous peoples and Canada as completely unacceptable. Indigenous peoples must be self-determining and to share in the significant royal-ties that are derived from this land.

The Indian Act is currently being challenged on the basis of blatant sex dis-crimination (see *McIvor v. Canada, Registrar, Indian and Northern Affairs*, 2007; see also Silman, 1987). These are important legal matters; however, we also feel that someone should raise the matter of racialization, or racialized injustice as a con-stitutional challenge (see Cannon, 2008; see also forthcoming). As mentioned in the Introduction of this anthology: the very first act of colonial injustice in Canada is racialized injustice. It is none other than the process through which Indigenous peoples became Indians for state administrative purposes and for the sake of dispossessing us of the lands that are required for capitalist expansion and exploitation. We have meant to draw attention in this anthology to racialized injustice as the earliest form of colonial dominance in Canada, a matter that can no longer go unnoticed or unchallenged in the law (ibid.).

We have hoped to show that racialized thinking represents a double-edged sword for Indigenous peoples. While we might wish to avoid its usage, Indianness shapes the opportunities and outcomes made available to us by the colonizer. It is also tied to a genocidal project that legally requires our total disappearance as nations. In a material sense, the category Indian rests on a blood quantum logic that, as Kauanui (2008: 34–5) points out, enacts, substantiates, and then disguises the further appropriation of lands. In order to justify the appropriation of Indigenous territories, the colonizer has always to mark the bodies of Indigenous peoples as Indians through policy-making and other symbolic, highly gendered practices of difference making. Blood quantum logic effects the denigration of our genealogical connection to territory or place. It is premised on our dilution, reducing our nations in turn to racial minorities instead of sovereign nations.

However paradoxical it may seem, we cannot help but reconcile histories of racism and racialization in Canada without engaging in precisely the same racialized discourses that produced them. As Anishinabek scholar Dale Turner writes: 'It is no secret that for Aboriginal peoples to participate effectively in Canadian legal and political cultures they must engage the normative [liberalist] discourses of the state' (2006: 81). In a similar, albeit different manner, Lawrence (2004: 230) explains:

> It is one thing to recognize that Indian Act categories are artificial—or even that they have been internalized—as if these divisions can be overcome simply by denying their importance. Legal categories, however, shape peoples' lives. They set the terms that individuals must utilize, even in resisting these categories.

Our colleagues suggest to us that the socio-legal and political contexts that prevent Indigenous nationhood, as well as identification approaches to identity and citizenship, require our intense scrutiny and unwavering political will. Histories of racialization require us as nations to posit Indianness—and at once resist it—in a dual-gestured, combative force against colonial and racialized injustice.

Despite what is believed in some circles, Indigenous peoples are not at all disappearing. Between 1951 and 2001, the 'Aboriginal ancestry population' grew sevenfold, while the Canadian population as a whole only doubled (Statistics Canada, 2003: 5). Today, some of us are registered as status Indians, while others go federally unrecognized and without reserve lands. Still others blend effortlessly into decidedly urban, multicultural milieu, invisible to many Canadians as Indigenous peoples because of a politics of authenticity structuring the representation of our everyday lives. Indeed, Indigenous peoples are quite literally rendered invisible and unintelligible, not simply by our own choice or determination, but rather by a highly racialized and structured way of thinking about Indianness as if we were a static or unchanging essence, untouched by modern conveniences or even privileges based on social class, education, and skin colour.

In writing this anthology, we have hoped to show how racism pervades the everyday representation of Indigenous people, from criminal justice, to poverty, to the availability of clean and safe drinking water in reserve communities like Kashechewan Cree Nation (*Globe and Mail*, 28 October 2005). There has tended to be a jealously guarded gap in the knowledge that is presented and possessed about Indigenous peoples in Canada. Much of it stems from what John Steckley (2003: 58–63) and Métis scholar Emma LaRocque (1993: 212) have referred to as a 'social problems' or 'victim blaming' approach to Indigenous disparities. The reality is that Indigenous peoples tend to become visible when—and only when—they fit into the social problems category of analysis. These perceptions play themselves out in both the living rooms and classrooms of Canada. More often than not, 'statistical outliers', including a decidedly middle class of Indigenous peoples, receive limited public attention, or they are rendered invisible or inauthentic.

The tendency to represent Indigenous peoples in these ways concerns us greatly. As we have shown, it is true that status Indians and majority Canadians experience enormous disparities in education, income, health, and well-being. The statistics have been well documented and—in a somewhat peculiar way—are called rapidly to mind by many individuals in our classrooms. But when issues affecting all Canadians like poverty, racial profiling, the H1N1 pandemic, or the availability of clean and safe drinking water become a convenient means of showcasing social problems among Indians, it forces us as Ukwehuwe to contemplate the purpose being served. In the absence of critical reflection or tangible solutions, statistical information and media coverage of Indigenous disparities has become a modern-day form of violence and assault on Indigenous nations. We believe these practices of representation must be reconciled, especially as the construction of racialized subjects is—and has been—so fundamental to reproducing racism under contemporary colonialism.

As nations of individuals, Indigenous peoples are determined to maintain our presence and livelihood. Many of us work tirelessly in communities to address the social issues we are currently facing. Collectively, we have resisted, survived, dealt with, and indeed envisioned a way forward, often in the face of adversity. We continue to make steadfast contributions to the arts, sports, academia, and legal reform in Canada. Our communities offer programs that are culturally specific and appropriate, many of them seeking to reclaim and revitalize the language, traditions, and teachings of our people. These successes demonstrate our perseverance and our resistance to colonialism. They are indicative of a widespread resurgence taking place in our nations to maintain our Indigenous ways of knowing, our stories, and our ways of being. We believe this resurgence is key to securing reparations and to combating racism.

Guswentah, or Two Row Wampum, is exemplary of the kinds of continuity and resurgence we are meaning to highlight. We believe this ancient agreement holds an original set of instructions that are key to showing how Ukwehuwe and non-Indigenous peoples might secure redress for contemporary injustices like colonialism and racism. The principles embodied in the Two Row Wampum delineate an original partnership, the maintenance of separate jurisdictions, and a clear commitment to self-determination. Not only do these principles remind us of the unbroken assertion of sovereignty (Mitchell, 1989), they are furthermore useful for revisiting, and rethinking, matters of governance, land grievances, citizenship, criminal justice, education, economics, and the family. In each of these areas, we have witnessed the greatest intrusion of colonial dominance and racism. In each of these areas, colonialism has sought to undo the sovereignty of our nations.

Combating racism in Canada does not at all require a re-invention of the proverbial wheel. Instead, it requires a return to original principles and partnerships. In doing so, we start by acknowledging that Indigenous territories cannot be reduced to Indian reserves, governance to Indian Act band councils, or citizenship to Indian status. Reserves, Indian status, and band council governments embody the very kinds of infringement that were, in the very first instance, motivated by racialized thinking. Each of them was an affront to Indigenous jurisdiction and sovereignty. We have shown in this anthology that Indigenous scholars each share in this understanding, albeit differently, and that reconciliation requires the restoration of sovereignty and jurisdiction. Whether it is in calls for Indian control of Indian education, restorative justice and sentencing circles, or even the right to determine our own citizens, reparations start with revisiting principles of autonomy and governance contained in historic arrangements.

In our view, Guswentah provides a model for Indigenous peoples and Canadians to work together at rejuvenating and indeed developing partnerships of shared responsibility, mutual respect, reciprocity, and obligation. These are qualities that define Canada's original nation-to-nation and treaty arrangements. Without fully realizing them, it is impossible to exercise our responsibilities aimed at individual, economic, and collective well-being, internal governance, or the protection of lands. Nor can we engage in a project of restorative justice without being first able to make those who have committed crimes responsible to both their communities and to their victims. Through qualities of mutual responsibility and respect, it is possible to create cooperative alliances, and to envision environmentally sustainable futures (Grossman, 2005; Hill, 2008). At the same time, we are not naïve to the tremendous obstacles standing in the way of exercising our sovereign rights and responsibilities.

We do not assume that all Canadians will look favourably upon the sovereignty of Indigenous peoples, or without great skepticism, opposition, and resistance. Today, many fail to see these rights as being historical instead of race-based. We hope this anthology has shown that our original nation-to-nation agreements are not at all based on race, but rather partnerships established in the earliest origins of Canada, as well as a special relationship with the Crown. As Fleras (quoted in Wallis and Fleras, 2009: 78) writes:

> Aboriginal peoples . . . are political communities who are sovereign in their own right, while sharing the sovereignty of Canada through multiple and overlapping jurisdictions. By virtue of their original occupation and political rights, Aboriginal peoples possess a special (nation-to-nation) relationship with the Crown, together with a corresponding set of entitlements (rights) that flow from that relationship . . . the discourse of rights must supersede that of race in any debate over constitutional change . . . And only by trumping race by playing the rights card is there much likelihood of a post-colonial social contract between Aboriginal peoples and Canada based on principles of power sharing, partnership, and participation.

The idea of Indigenous rights as race-based, or even as constituting reverse racism, pervades modern colonial consciousness. As an ideology, it allows for the maintenance of racist beliefs while championing democratic values (Henry, Tator, Mattis, and Rees, 1998: 19). Even though the Supreme Court of Canada has denounced the idea of reverse racism in *R v. Kapp* (2008), the ideology continues to provide justificatory arguments enabling the coexistence of racism and democracy (Henry, Tator, Mattis, and Rees, 1998). We see this as a major challenge when it comes to fully understanding and reconciling histories of racialization and colonial injustice. But there are additional challenges as well.

How do we ensure, for example, a more integrated analysis and understanding of sex discrimination and racialized injustice? How have the gendered components of racism and the racialized components of sexism been disregarded in politics the media and Canadian courts of law around issues involving missing Indigenous women, Indigenous identity, citizenship, and the history of nation-building? These are questions that require a separate series of analyses, additional and ongoing from what we have been able to provide here. At this critical point in history, we also need to contemplate what is being asked of Canadians, especially with respect to colonial reparations and responsibility.

While we in no way wish to denigrate the apology offered to residential school survivors in June 2008, we ask questions that are similar to those of then President Beverley Jacobs of the Native Women's Association of Canada. 'Words must turn into action,' as Jacobs (2008: 224) put it, 'What is it that this government is going to do in the future to help our people?' We realize there are no easy answers to these questions, but the urgency and care that is required in approaching them cannot be underestimated. It is incumbent on Canada to look to the lessons learned in other countries that have already sought to reconcile the colonial past. An apology is only restorative, as Sara Ahmed (2005: 76) has written of the Australian context, 'when the shamed other can "show" that its failure to measure up to a social ideal is temporary'. In issuing its apology, or for that matter taking responsibility for its genocidal history, Canada and its citizens must be careful to avoid reissuing the injury of colonialism through either a disabling guilt, or the failure to take responsibility for historical injustice altogether.

Recent developments surrounding the dismantlement of the Aboriginal Healing Foundation (AHF) concern us greatly. We believe they are inconsistent with Canada's apology for residential schooling, and as Bev Jacobs notes, are entirely discordant with aims to take responsibility for the history of residential schools. We furthermore echo the concern of Murray Sinclair, the current Chair of Canada's Truth and Reconciliation Commission (TRC), who in speaking publicly on 22 March 2010 at the University of Western Ontario, called on Parliament to address the cutting of AHF in order for TRC to reach its mandate. The AHF provides a necessary and essential source of programming supports for residential schools resolutions that are holistic, culturally relevant, Indigenous centered, controlled, and administered. Priority must be placed on providing these and other resources for the TRC to effectively meet its mandate.

Funding and supports are not the only issues to consider. Indeed, Indian residential schools resolutions cannot take place in the absence of critical reflection and responsibility, nor can reparations for colonialism in general. Canadians cannot simply be asked to 'feel good about feeling bad', or as Roger Simon (2010) explains:

> [T]he act of acknowledging victimhood [cannot be] reduced to an affective transaction in which one both recognizes and 'feels for' the pain of others, a situation in which there is no need to ask difficult questions that might implicate one's psychic, social and economic investments in the conditions and institutions responsible for the genesis and prolongation of that pain.

In seeking to reconcile colonial pasts, specifically histories of racialization and residential schools, it is necessary for Canadians to relinquish structural advantages acquired through both colonialism and privilege. As Simon (ibid.) suggests, it will require 'asking non-Aboriginal Canadians to work out where we "fit in" to Aboriginal history, not just where Aboriginal history fits into the history of Canada'.

Canada's Truth and Reconciliation Commission will inevitably confront the enormity of issues we are describing. At some point over the next several years, and as part of its mandate surrounding public education, it will need to determine a suitable course of action surrounding the testimonies it will summon from our ancestors and familial relations who attended residential schools. It is our hope that these testimonies lead to truly transformative action and pedagogy, enabling histories of colonial injustice and racialization to be reconciled. Confusion must not exist for a moment in the minds of ordinary Canadians about what to do with these testimonies. As Simon (ibid.) suggests, something more than feelings of outrage are required. It will not be enough to 'sit outside of relations of injustice, to observe, judge, and condemn these relations . . . without considering and/or taking responsibility for one's implication in their reproduction' (ibid.).

Having said that, what does it mean to ask Canadians, especially new Canadians, to take responsibility for colonial injustice in the way that Simon is suggesting? Finding answers to that question needs to be taken seriously. Indeed, emerging scholarship has explored the kinds of scholarly and intellectual relationships that exist between Indigenous peoples and 'racialized diasporic communities' (Amadahy and Lawrence, 2009; Lawrence and Dua, 2005). The matter of new Canadians being asked to take responsibility for racialized injustice when they are often fleeing violent, racist situations themselves is also on the minds of those in charge of finding colonial reparations. Speaking publicly at a recent engagement at the University of Toronto School of Law in December 2009, Murray Sinclair, the current Chair of Canada's TRC, spoke of the challenges in calling on new Canadians to take responsibility for colonialism. He stated:

> We have been challenged to determine what . . . we are going to say to new Canadians who themselves are unable to accept responsibility for anything that they've done because they're not the ones who did this. . . . But what I say to them is this: if you are to properly enjoy the benefits of this society . . . you have to take responsibility for the fact that what you have now, what you are gaining now, is something . . . that was taken away improperly.

Sinclair raises what we believe is and will be one of the most difficult and pressing challenges facing Canadians and Indigenous peoples into the twenty-first century. It demands that we work across differences to think about what possibilities exist and how new relationships might be envisioned.

What sets of challenges and limitations surround the building of antiracism coalitions between racialized diasporic communities and Indigenous peoples in both theory and in practice? This question requires ongoing scholarly research and analysis (Amadahy, 2008). Our hope is that outcomes will lead to the founding of new partnerships. At best, the building of coalitions in particular stands to open new fields of scholarly research and decolonizing inquiry. We view the following as a set of gestures and activities aimed at critical coalitions building, a process which is sure to open fruitful, decolonizing avenues of research and exploration.

1. The No One Is Illegal movement (www.nooneisillegal.org) seeks, as an activist political organization, to challenge racialized inequality associated with Canada's Immigration Act—and to respect, learn more about, and acknowledge First Nations self-determination. We view these aspirations as important because they concentrate on people's relationship to the land, to Indigenous peoples, and with each other (see Haig Brown, 2009).

2. The Women's Legal Education and Action Fund (LEAF) released a press statement on 5 May 2010 detailing its support of the Sharon McIvor legal action that challenges racialized and gender inequality as it is directed toward Indigenous men and women under section 6(2) of Canada's Indian Act. We view LEAF's efforts as important because they are respectful of gender and race discrimination and they seek to build coalition across women's differences.

3. An activist writes:

   At the reclamation site, some settler activists came and wanted to fight the police. They yelled, threw things, and egged the other side on, getting out people all worked up. We have to live there. Remember, no white people were arrested that raid but 50 of our people have been charged. If they want to help, they have to listen, take direction, and stick around' (quoted in Amadahy, 2008: 27).

   We are interested in work that explores the kinds of ethnographic complexity contained in the activist's quote. The citation holds significant pedagogical currency, especially if one considers the formidable task of working across differences and what this might mean in everyday practice.

4. An 'Anonymous Racialized Activist' (quoted in ibid., 29) writes:

   Relationships between racialized and indigenous people are not great. Racialized immigrants are suffering, but sometimes they create a hierarchy of suffering and put themselves on the top, which is problematic. There's a lack of understanding of how fundamental the eradication of indigenous culture is to a settler society. All the '–isms' in settler society exist, but you can't forget its foundations . . . we benefit from the continuing violations of indigenous sovereignty and are, in many ways, complicit in this colonial project.

We think the building of coalitions between racialized and Indigenous communities holds enormous potential where shedding light on racism and the colonial experience is concerned. In fact, we believe that talking about our differences stands to transform the very way in which we view notions of privilege and disadvantage both theoretically and in practice.

5. A 'Refugee' (quoted in ibid., 27–8, emphasis added) writes:

> I didn't come here as a settler, I came here as a refugee. That makes a great difference and *we can only know about that if we talk about it*. You can't say many of the racialized people here are privileged but they still don't know anything about Aboriginal history or people. I see myself as having a role there.

We recognize the complexity of privilege and disadvantage as this is experienced in relation to other people. Having said that, we feel some of the most valuable kinds of insight and teaching stem from our relationships with each other. These kinds of complexity need to be addressed in Canada.

At worst, working across differences may result in 'postures of innocence' (Amadahy and Lawrence, 2009: 105; Fellows and Razack, 1998), making it difficult or even impossible to develop a new vision of mutual responsibility and coexistence. In reconciling histories of racism and colonial injustice, we feel it will be important to avoid thinking hierarchically about the oppressions between us. This point is made eloquently by Patricia Hill Collins (2003: 332) who writes:

> Once we realize that there are very few pure victims or oppressors, and that each one of us derives . . . penalty and privilege from the multiple systems of oppression that frame our lives, then we will be in a position to see the need for new ways of thought and action . . . [without which we remain] locked in a dangerous dance of competing for attention, resources, and theoretical supremacy.

In contemplating the future of self-determination and colonial reparations, one thing is for certain: racist beliefs and practices continue in Canada despite ameliorative efforts to curb their effects. In writing this anthology, we have hoped to show how this is so. However, we believe that much can be gained by working across differences, rejuvenating original partnerships and agreements, and endeavouring collectively with all Canadians to combat racism. In the words of the Lakota Chief Sitting Bull 'Let us put our minds together and see what kind of life we can make for our children.' These are words that require our tenacity and spirit. The time is now. We cannot afford not to.

Postscript

On 12 November 2010, after a prolonged three-year abstention, Canada became a signatory to the UN's *Declaration on the Rights of Indigenous Peoples* (United Nations, 2007). As a postscript to this edition, we believe it is important to acknowledge the significance of this development overall, and in relation to reconciling histories of racism, colonialism, and Indigeneity in Canada. We share the enthusiasm and sentiment of both the Native Women's Association of Canada (2010) and the Assembly of First Nations (2010) in seeing Canada's endorsement as a noteworthy step toward reconciliation, but only if it is aimed at restitution (ibid; Alfred, 2007). It must carry a commitment to ensure that we are able to exercise our responsibility as self-determining peoples (Monture, 1999: 36), including the rejuvenation and honouring of historic treaty and nation-to-nation agreements. It remains to be seen what will take place now that the UNDRIP has been signed, especially since Canada is not legally bound by its terms (Indian and Northern Affairs Canada, 2010). As Trask (2002; 2003: 36–37) has written, there is reason to be hopeful, above all because Part VI repudiates the doctrine of discovery and terra nullius upon which settler-colonial states are premised (Introduction and Chapter 8, this volume; Behrendt et al., 2010). Of course, the language of rights requires critical interrogation, especially if, as Taiaike Alfred (2009: 184) proposes, rights are themselves coterminous with liberal democracy, which is 'by design and culture, incapable of just and peaceful relations with Indigenous peoples'. With respect to the UNDRIP and the broader question of colonial reparations, we therefore concur with Corntassel (2008: 116) and others (ibid: 130) that 'sustainability must be a critical benchmark for indigenous self-determination processes.' Restitution takes place not only through a discourse of legal rights and recognition, but when we are able to define, as Tsalagi scholar Andrea Smith (2010: 60) points out, 'the terms of discourse itself' (also Coulthard, 2007).

References

Alfred, Taiaiake (Gerald). 2009. 'Restitution Is the Real Pathway to Justice for Indigenous Peoples', pp. 179–87 in Gregory Younging, Jonathan Dewar, and Mike DeGagné, eds., *Response, Responsibility, and Renewal Canada's Truth and Reconciliation Journey*. Ottawa: Aboriginal Healing Foundation.

———. 2005. *Wasáse: Indigenous Pathways of Action and Freedom*. Peterborough, ON: Broadview Press.

Assembly of First Nations. 2010 (19 November). 'A Communiqué from National Chief Shawn A-in-chut Atleo on Canada's Endorsement of UNDRIP', available at www.afn.ca/misc/NC-Bulletin-UNDRIP.pdf

Behrendt, Larissa, Tracey Lindberg, Robert J. Miller, and Jacinta Ruru. 2010. *Discovering Indigenous Lands: The Doctrine of Discovery in the English Colonies*. Oxford, UK: Oxford University Press.

Corntassel, Jeff. 2008. 'Toward Sustainable Self-Determination: Rethinking the Contemporary Indigenous Rights Discourse', *Alternatives: Global, Local, Political* 33: 105–32.

Coulthard, Glen S. 2007. 'Subjects of Empire: Indigenous Peoples and the "Politics of Recognition" in Canada', *Contemporary Political Theory* 6: 437–60.

Indian and Northern Affairs Canada. 2010 (12 November). 'Frequently Asked Questions Canada's Endorsement of the United Nations Declaration on the Rights of Indigenous Peoples', available at www.ainc-inac.gc.ca/ap/ia/dcl/faq-eng.asp

Monture, Patricia. 1999. *Journeying Forward: Dreaming First Nations Independence*. Halifax, NS: Fernwood Publishing.

Native Women's Association of Canada. 2010 (12 November). 'Statement of Support on the United Nations Declaration on the Rights of Indigenous Peoples', available at www.nwac.ca/media/release/17-11-10

Smith, Andrea. 2010. 'Queer Theory and Native Studies: The Heteronormativity of Settler Colonialism', *GLQ: A Journal of Lesbian and Gay Studies* 16 (1–2): 41–68.

Trask, Haunani-Kay. 2003. 'Restitution as a Precondition of Reconciliation: Native Hawaiians and Indigenous Human Rights', pp. 32–45 in Raymond A Winbush, ed., *Should America Pay? Slavery and the Raging Debate over Reparations*. New York: Amistad/Harper Collins Publishers, Inc.

———. 2002. 'Indigenizing Human Rights', pp. 213–24 in Majid Tehranian and David Chappell, eds., *Dialogue of Civilizations: A New Peace Agenda for A New Millennium*. London: I.B. Tauris Publishers.

United Nations. 2007. *United Nations Declaration on the Rights of Indigenous Peoples*, available at www.un.org/esa/socdev/unpfii/en/declaration.html

Glossary

Aboriginal community development A holistic community development model rooted in traditional Aboriginal values of sharing and community with the ultimate goal of restoring healing and decolonizing Aboriginal communities (Silver et. al, 2006: 133).

Aboriginalism '[T]he ideology and identity of assimilation, in which Onkewehonwe are manipulated by colonial myths into a submissive position and are told that by emulating white people they can gain acceptance and possibly even fulfillment within mainstream' (Alfred, 2005: 23).

Acculturation '[P]henomena which result when groups of individuals having different cultures come into continuous first-hand contact, with subsequent changes in the original patterns of either or both groups' (Linton, 1940: 463–4).

Antiracism A field of theoretical and historical study, as well as a set of ideas that inform activist practice. The 'anti' in antiracism signifies a commitment to undo and identify racist ideas that form the root of white supremacist and Eurocentric knowledge systems. Unlike 'non-racism', antiracism theory and practice encourages the undoing of racist ideas in our own minds and ways of understanding the world (van Dijk, 1993).

Assimilation Defined by Davis Jackson (2002: 74) as 'the loss, by an individual, of the markers that served to distinguish him or her as a member of one social group, and the acquisition of traits that allow that person to blend in with, and succeed in, a different social group'.

Authenticity A state of being authentic, real, and genuine. Colonial powers have used concepts of authenticity to quantify 'Indianness', through, for example, blood quantum. To be recognized as a 'real Indian' and therefore to hold Indian status, individuals must fit the qualifications created by the colonizer.

Banking concept A term used by Paulo Friere to refer to a pedagogical style, approach, and/or educational framework that 'views the students' minds as "containers" to be filled by teachers [knowledge] thus allowing [for] the imposition of one worldview over another, sometimes with a velvet glove' (Battiste, 1986: 37)

Binarism A way of thinking and/or knowledge that creates, justifies, and reinforces the idea that phenomena in the world exist in binary either/or opposites. Examples of binary thinking include the creation of Evil versus Good, White versus Black, Female versus Male, etc.

Cartesian dualism Renee Descartes, a seventeenth-century philosopher, understood the mind as non-physical. Cartesian dualism is often called the mind/body split, whereby the mind is understood as separate from the body. This dualism constructs a binary or sense of separateness between the mind and body.

Cognitive assimilation The tendency in education to devalue—either by force or implicit curricular measures—Indigenous traditions and replace them with Western educational modes and methods (see Battiste, 1986).

Colonial imaginary A set of ideas that makes up the colonial narrative. This narrative or imaginary establishes how the colonizer imagines the world and sees own self in it. The colonial imaginary has key racial tropes and root ideas that make sense of and justify the colonial project.

Colonization A process of conquest whereby one nation establishes a colony on another nation's territory with the intent of taking power, land, and resources. European colonialism dates from the fifteenth century onwards, and involved the brutal establishment of European sovereignty on stolen non-European territory. Colonialism is not only about material accumulation but requires the production of ideologies that justify the theft and violent practices at its root (Said, 1979; 1994).

Compulsory heterosexuality A term first developed by lesbian feminist poet Adrienne Rich (1993). The term defines the phenomenon of making heterosexuality compulsory—something that is required and enforced through threat of violence whether ontological, psychological, physical, or emotional and through everyday taken-for-granted relations and state practices.

Cultural revitalization A movement in education and/or policy that 'calls for the celebration, affirmation, and revitalization of Indian cultures and peoples' (St Denis, 2004: 35). St Denis outlines the way in which an 'adherence to cultural revitalization encourages the valorization of cultural authenticity and cultural purity among aboriginal people [helping] to produce the notion and the structure of a cultural hierarchy' (ibid., 37).

Decolonization A process of struggle whereby colonized nations and peoples reject colonial authority and (re)establish freedom, recognized self-determining governing systems, and self-determined existence on their territories.

Dehumanization A process through which a person or group of people is rendered as less than human. Dehumanization is often the first step in legitimizing and systemizing violence against particular bodies. Dehumanization can be a singular individual act, but in the case of Canadian colonialism there is a political, social, legal, and institutional system of dehumanization.

Democratic racism '[A]n ideology in which two conflicting set of values are made congruent with each other. Commitments to democratic principles such as justice, equality, and fairness conflict but coexist with attitudes and behaviours that include negative feelings about minority groups, differential treatment, and discrimination against them' (Henry and Tator, 2006: 22).

Dispossession '[T]he forcible and relentless . . . theft of [Indigenous] territories, and the implementation of legislation and policies designed to effect their total disappearance as peoples . . .' (Lawrence, 2002: 23–4).

Enculturation The process through which an individual learns and is taught cultural competency.

Eurocentric models A reference to Eurocentric bias, which is a view that takes the West/Europe as the normative or universal standard for measuring, understanding, and describing the world.

Eurocentrism A product of 'Europe's ascent to global dominance, the imperatives of commercial expansionism are advanced in language proclaiming that the outcome of history is inevitable, even as it frequently ascribes to very local and specific historical circumstances and unwarranted authority derive from false claims of universality' (Hall, 2003: 71).

Fourth World A term that is used to refer to some 350 million Indigenous peoples in the world, and also to the 'unifying nature of Indigenous action in the struggles against colonialism throughout the world' (Corntassel and Alfred, 2005: 610).

Fractured identity Refers to identity outcomes effected by transracial adoption and/or the expectations placed on Indigenous peoples to think of their identities and experience in dichotomous, either/or terms.

Gender discrimination This term refers broadly to the systematized inequitable treatment of a person or group of persons based on gender. Gender discrimination was systematized and institutionalized in the Indian Act through years of 'blatant sex discrimination toward Aboriginal women under section 12(1)(b)' (Cannon, 2007: 35).

Genocide Genocide refers to the physical or cultural erasure/elimination/extermination of a people by another group of people. Andrea Smith (2006: 68) writes that '[The logic of genocide] holds that indigenous people must disappear. In fact, they must always be disappearing in order to allow non-indigenous peoples rightful claim over this land.'

Heteronormativity A concept defined as 'the notion that heterosexuality is the only "natural" orientation' (Schick, 2004: 249).

Homelessness A reference to individuals that live on the street, stay in emergency shelters, or who have otherwise unsafe or unstable housing. Homelessness often affects 'those who have suffered from the effects of colonization and whose social, economic, and political conditions have placed them in a disadvantaged position' (Baskin, 2007: 32).

Imperialism The domination of another land and people through economic and political control established by violent or coercive force. Edward Said writes: '(n)either imperialism nor colonialism is a simple act of accumulation and acquisition. Both are supported and perhaps even impelled by impressive ideological formations that include notions that certain territories and people *require* and beseech domination' (Said, 1994: 9).

Indian Act Defined by Henry, Tator, Mattis, and Rees (1998: 130) as:

> the legislation that has intruded on the lives and cultures of status Indians more than any other law. Though amended repeatedly, the act's fundamental provisions have scarcely changed. They give the state powers that range from defining how one is born or naturalized into 'Indian' status to administering the estate of an Aboriginal person after death . . . the act [sic] gave Parliament control over Indian political structures, landholding patterns, and resource and economic development. It covered almost every important aspect of the daily lives of Aboriginal peoples on reserve. The overall effect was to subject Aboriginal people to the almost unfettered rule of federal bureaucrats. The act

[sic] imposed non-Aboriginal forms on traditional governance, landholding practices, and cultural practices.

Indian The label 'Indian' has been an external descriptor, meaningless to the Indigenous peoples of the Americas prior to colonization. As a common identity, it was imposed on Indigenous populations when settler governments in North America usurped the right to define Indigenous citizenship, reducing the members of hundreds of extremely different nations, ethnicities, and language to a common raced identity as 'Indian'. (Lawrence, 2002: 23).

Indigenous knowledge Indigenous knowledge includes systems of thought, ways of being, ways of knowing, and ways of thinking that are held and developed by Indigenous nations and peoples. There is not one Indigenous knowledge system, but often, Indigenous systems of knowledge hold key similarities rooted philosophical ideas and understandings about humanity and the world.

Institutional racism '[R]acial discrimination that derives from individuals carrying out the dictates of others who are prejudiced or of a prejudiced society' (Henry and Tator, 2006: 352).

Institutionalized patriarchy Refers to 'male dominance in personal, political, cultural, and social life, and to patriarchal families where the law of the father prevails' (Code, 2000: 378).

Intergenerational impacts Refers to the present-day trauma experienced by individuals whose parents, grandparents, or ancestors attended residential schools (Ing, 2006: 157).

Involuntary enfranchisement A process through which Indigenous peoples lose Indian Act status through involuntary activities. Involuntary enfranchisement continues today for the grandchildren of women who married non-Indians before 1985 because, unlike the grandchildren of men, they do not choose do become non-Indians under section 6(2) of the Indian Act (Cannon, 2007: 39).

Legal assimilation Legal assimilation is the word that is used to describe the act of losing legal status of Indian Act status in Canada (Cannon, 2007: 38).

Matrilocal/Matrilineal societies Refers to kinship organization and residence patterns organized through the female line of descent. Women in the vast majority of matrilineal and matrilocal societies hold economic and political power unknown in patriarchal societies.

Matrimonial real property Refers to 'the house or land that a couple occupies or benefits from while they are married or living in a common-law relationship' (Bastien, 2008: 90). Until only recently, 'provincial laws regarding matrimonial real property have generally been found not to be applicable on First Nation lands through a number of Supreme Court decisions' (Anishinabek Nation, 2007: 4).

Meaningful participation 'Meaningful participation and equitable treatment are pre-conditions to holding a sincere respect for any system, particularly a system of justice. . . . By meaningful participation we suggest that aboriginal people must be encouraged to participate in the system by defining the meaning, institutions and standards of justice in their own communities. Also, all peoples must be partners in developing a criminal justice system outside Aboriginal communities that can and does reflect Aboriginal cultures' (Monture-Okanee and Turpel, 1992: 249).

Nation-building The process of building and maintaining a nation. It can refer to Indigenous nation-building processes following from colonialism, or to the process of colonial nation-building. According to Lawrence (2002), nation-building is central to the maintenance of settler colonialism. As mythology, it refers to the way in which 'Canada maintains its posture of being "innocent" of racism and genocide' (ibid., 26).

Poverty An economic state in which an individual or group is impoverished. Baskin (2007: 39) writes: 'For Aboriginal peoples, poverty is a direct result of colonization which destroyed the original economic basis of our communities.'

Racial profiling Racial profiling 'occurs when law enforcement or security officials, consciously or unconsciously, subject individuals at any location to heightened scrutiny based solely or in part on race, ethnicity, Aboriginality, place of origin, ancestry, or religion or on stereotypes associated with any of these factors rather than objectively reasonable grounds to suspect that the individual is implicated in criminal activity' (Tanovich, 2006: 13)

Racialization The process by which people are formed into a racial category, and through which racism is justified by representations of these groups. 'Sociologists refer to this process, whereby a heterogeneous, linguistically diverse population is singled out for different (and often unequal) treatment in Canada, as racialization' (Li, 1990: 7).

Racism '[T]he assumptions, attitudes, beliefs, and behaviours of individuals as well as the institutional policies, process, and practices that flow from those understandings' (Henry and Tator, 2006: 5).

Representation The way in which a person, place, or thing is commonly represented by another.

Residential schooling A colonial system of schooling enforced on Indigenous nations aimed at effecting cultural genocide and assimilation on children, many of whom were forcibly removed and abducted from their families and communities. The residential school experience is characterized by forced removal form families; systemic and ritualized physical and sexual assault; spiritual, psychological, and emotional abuse; and malnutrition, inhumane living conditions, death, and murder.

Resurgence 'Regeneration of power gives us the strength to continue to fight; restoring connection to each other gives us the social support that is crucial to human fulfillment; reconnection to our own memory roots us in a culture; and reconnection to spirit gives us a strong and whole mind. These are the elements of resurgence' (Alfred, 2005: 256).

Romanticism The representation of noble, innocent and idealized 'Indians'. Often romantic colonial images have 'Indians' disappearing through their innocence.

Royal Commission on Aboriginal Peoples (RCAP) 'The Royal Commission on Aboriginal Peoples was the largest and most expensive public inquiry undertaken in Canadian history. . . . The commission interviewed Aboriginal from across the country . . . as with most inquiries, the RCAP Report . . . condensed hundreds upon hundreds of interviews and [was condensed] into five converted volumes . . . [wherein] the more radical Aboriginal views [e.g., assertions of sovereignty] were marginalized in favour of more moderate ones' (Denis and Andersen, 2003: 379)

Self-determination The right of all peoples to determine their own destiny. 'International and human rights norms contained in many instruments to which Canada is a signatory clearly provide for the protection of group rights and also underscore the right of all peoples to self-determination. Self-determination means that peoples must determine their own destiny' (Monture-Okanee and Turpel, 1992: 255).

Self-government Self-government is based on an *a priori* concept of governance as defined through Canadian federal policy and the Department of Indian and Northern Development. It is often understood to stand in lesser and inferior relation to self-determination, which refers in general to an inherent set of rights given to Indigenous peoples by the Creator.

Sequential literacy Refers to the ability to read, understand, and write a sequential phonetic script of written letters. European languages are written in this manner (see Battiste, 1986).

Settler violence A specific form of violence, often genocidal in nature, that occurs in ongoing colonial contexts. It refers to the systemized ideological, political, social, symbolic, spiritual, military, and state violence enacted with impunity by settlers on Indigenous nations and individuals.

Sexual violence Violence that is of a sexual or sexualized nature. It can include 'individual' acts of violence as well as systemic forms of violence enacted through political, state, and social institutions, practices, and policies. As Andrea Smith (2005: 8) writes, 'sexual violence is not simply a tool of patriarchy but also a tool of colonialism and racism.'

Silenced history Histories that are silenced in official records and in the dominant telling of history. Silenced histories are those histories that are marginalized and erased through various power systems that control the production and dissemination of knowledge. Bonita Lawrence insists that 'in order for Canada to have a viable national identity, the histories of Indigenous nations, in all their diversity and longevity, must be erased. Furthermore, in order to maintain Canadians' self-image as a fundamentally "decent" people innocent of any wrongdoing, the historical record of how land was acquired—the forcible and relentless dispossession of Indigenous peoples, the theft of their territories, and the implementation of legislation and policies designed to effect their total disappearance as peoples—must also be erased' (Lawrence, 2002: 23).

Squaw Drudge/Indian Princess binary A binary classification finding its roots in the patriarchal Victorian virgin/whore dichotomy. Colonial imperatives—fuelled by racist ideology—intensified the binary racializing the sexuality of Aboriginal women.

Starlight tours The 'practice of [police] taking Indigenous people out of town and leaving them, sometimes to freeze to death. This practice is also used against non-Native homeless people' (Green, 2007: 507).

Stereotype Representations created by a dominant group to typecast and classify the 'Other'. These stereotypical representations, whether 'positive' or 'negative', are used to justify objectification, control, and oppression by the dominant group (for example, 'Native people are lazy'). This hyper-disseminated stereotype works to justify the systematic impoverishment of Indigenous nations by blaming indigenous people for the economic conditions created by the colonizer.

Structural determinants Factors that arise from or are effected by social and political structures (e.g., colonization, Eurocentrism).

Structural racism '[I]nequalities rooted in the system-wide operation of a society that exclude[s] substantial numbers of members of particular groups from significant participation in major social institutions' (Henry and Tator, 2006: 352).

Symbolic literacy Refers to the ability to read, understand, and write a system of language that uses symbols rather than sequential phonetic scripts (see Battiste, 1986).

Systemic injustice A context whereby injustice is systematized and institutionalized for a group of people. In the case of Canada, a colonial white settler state, Turpel and Monture-Okanee indicate that 'the overall perspective of an Aboriginal person toward Canadian legal institutions is one of being surrounded by injustice without knowing where justice lies' (Monture-Okanee and Turpel, 1992: 250).

Systemic racism While racism is often equated with abhorrent individual prejudice or ignorance, systemic racism is a form of power that controls power relations between dominant and oppressed racial groups. In the case of Canadian colonialism, the manufacturing of the racial group 'Indian', occurred alongside the creation of racist political, social, and economic systems used to maintain white settler dominance and the control of lands.

The Other The theoretical term used to refer to the creation of an us/them binary, where normality is understood in the 'us' and the abnormality, sub-humanity, or inferiority is understood as belonging to 'them'—the Other.

Transracial Native adoption The adoption of Indigenous children into non-Indigenous families. Shandra Spears (2003: 81–2) writes: '[T]he removal of entire generations of Native children from our communities and families is a genocidal blow to our Nations, and we feel that violence in our bones.'

Treaty An agreement made between international actors, between sovereign and self-determining Indigenous Nations, that becomes a *sui generis* part of international law (Henderson, 2002).

Two-spirited A pan-Indigenous term that identifies Indigenous people who do not fit into Western binaries of sex, gender, and/or sexuality.

Urbanity/Indigeneity The tendency to view Indigenous peoples as either urban- or reserve-based and, in binary fashion, the imaging of both spheres as separate and distinct, with 'reservation Indians depicted as the "real" Natives and urban Indians depicted as hopelessly assimilated and alienated from their cultures' (Smith, 2008: 204; also see Ramirez, 2007).

White-settler society A white settler society is one that is established through processes of colonialism and genocide effected by Europeans on non-European soil (Razack, 2002: 2–3). 'Settler states in the Americas are founded on, and maintained through, policies of direct extermination, displacement, or assimilation' (Lawrence and Dua, 2005: 123).

Bibliography

Alfred, Taiaiake (Gerald). 2005. *Wasáse: Indigenous Pathways of Action and Freedom*. Peterborough: Broadview Press.

———. 1999. *Peace, Power, Righteousness: An Indigenous Manifesto*. Toronto: Oxford University Press.

———. 1995. *Heeding the Voices of Our Ancestors: Kahnawake Mohawk Politics and the Rise of Native Nationalism*. Toronto: Oxford University Press.

Alfred, Taiaiake, and Jeff Corntassel. 2005. 'Being Indigenous: Resurgences Against Contemporary Colonialism', *Government and Opposition* 40 (4): 597–614.

Ahmed, Sara. 2005. 'The Politics of Bad Feeling', *Australian Critical Race and Whiteness Studies Association Journal* 1: 72–85.

Amadahy, Zainab. 2008. 'Listen, Take Direction and Stick Around: A Roundtable on Relationship-Building in Indigenous Solidarity Work', *Briarpatch* June/July: 24–9.

Amadahy, Zainab, and Bonita Lawrence. 2009. 'Indigenous Peoples and Black People in Canada: Settlers or Allies?', pp. 105–36 in Arlo Kempf, ed., *Breaching the Colonial Contract: Anti-Colonialism in the US and Canada*. New York: Springer.

Andersen, Chris, and Claude Denis. 2003. 'Urban Native Communities and the Nation: Before and After the Royal Commission on Aboriginal Peoples', *Canadian Review of Sociology and Anthropology* 40 (4): 373–90.

Anderson, Kim. 2000. *A Recognition of Being: Reconstructing Native Womanhood*. Toronto: Second Story Press.

Anishinabek Nation. 2007. Matrimonial Real Property Regional Consultations. March.

Baskin, Cyndy. 2007. 'Aboriginal Youth Talk about Structural Determinants as the Cause of Their Homelessness', *First Peoples Child & Family Review* 3 (3): 31–42.

Bastien, Elizabeth. 2008. 'Matrimonial Real Property Solutions', *Canadian Woman Studies* 26 (3 & 4): 90–3.

Battiste, Marie. 1986. 'Micmac Literacy and Cognitive Assimilation', pp. 23–44 in Jean Barman, Yvonne Hébert, and Don McCaskill, eds., *Indian Education in Canada: Volume 1: The Legacy*. Vancouver, BC: UBC Press.

Borrows, John. 1997. 'Wampum at Niagara: The Royal Proclamation, Canadian Legal History, and Self-Government', pp. 155–72 in Michael Asch, ed., *Aboriginal and Treaty Rights in Canada: Essays on Law, Equality, and Respect for Difference*. Vancouver: UBC Press.

Cannon, Martin J. 2008. 'Revisiting Histories of Gender-Based Exclusion and the New Politics of Indian Identity', A Research Paper for the National Centre for First Nations Governance.

———. 1995. 'Demarginalizing the Intersection of "Race" and Gender in First Nations Politics'. Unpublished MA Thesis, Queen's University.

Code, Lorraine. 2000. *Encyclopedia of Feminist Theories*. New York: Routledge.

Collins, Patricia Hill. 2003. 'Toward A New Vision', pp. 331–48 in Michael S. Kimmell and Abby L. Ferber, eds., *Privilege: A Reader*. Boulder, CO: Westview Press.

Cornet, Wendy. 2003. 'Aboriginality: Legal Foundations, Past Trends, Future Prospects', pp. 121–47 in Joseph Eliot Magnet and Dwight A. Dorey, eds., *Aboriginal Rights Litigation*. LexisNexis Butterworths.

Davis Jackson, Deborah. 2002. *Our Elders Lived It: American Indian Identity in the City*. DeKalb, IL: Northern Illinois University Press.

Doxtator, Deborah. 1996. 'What Happened to the Iroquois Clans?: A Study of Clans in Three Nineteenth Century Rotinonhsyonni Communities'. Unpublished PhD Dissertation, University of Western Ontario.

Fellows, Mary Louise, and Sherene Razack. 1998. 'The Race to Innocence: Confronting Hierarchical Relations Among Women', *Journal of Gender, Race and Justice* 1 (2): 335–52.

Fleras, Augie. 2009. ' "Playing the Aboriginal Card": Race or Rights?', pp. 75–8 in Maria Wallis and Augie Fleras, eds., *The Politics of Race in Canada: Readings in Historical Perspectives, Contemporary Realities, and Future Possibilities*. Toronto: Oxford University Press.

Green, Joyce, ed. 2007. *Making Space for Indigenous Feminism*. Halifax, NS: Fernwood Publishing/Zed Books.

———. 2006. 'From Stonechild to Social Cohesion', *Canadian Journal of Political Science* 39 (1): 507–27.

Grossman, Zoltan. 2005. 'Unlikely Alliances: Treaty Conflicts and Environmental Cooperation Between Native American and Rural White Communities', *American Indian Culture and Research Journal* 29 (4): 21–43.

Haig-Brown, Celia. 2009. 'Decolonizing Diaspora: Whose Traditional Land Are We On?', *Cultural and Pedagogical Inquiry* 1 (1): 4–21.

Hall, Anthony J. 2003. *The American Empire and The Fourth World: The Bowl With One Spoon*. Montreal, QC: McGill-Queen's University Press.

Harris, Cheryl I. 1993. 'Whiteness as Property', *Harvard Law Review* 106 (8): 1707–91.

Haudenosaunee Confederacy. 1983. 'Statement of the Haudenosaunee Concerning the Constitutional Framework and International Position of the Haudenosaunee Confederacy', in *House of Commons Minutes of Proceedings and Evidence of the Special Committee on Indian Self-Government*, Issue # 31, Appendix 36. Ottawa: Queen's Printer.

Henderson, James (Sákéj) Youngblood. 2002. 'Sui Generis and Treaty Citizenship', *Citizenship Studies* 6 (4): 415–40.

Henry, Frances, and Carol Tator. 2006. *The Colour of Democracy; Racism in Canadian Society*, 3rd edn. Toronto: Thomson Nelson Canada.

Henry, Frances, Carol Tator, Winston Mattis, and Tim Rees. 1998. *The Colour of Democracy: Racism in Canadian Society*, 2nd edn. Toronto: Thomson Nelson Canada.

Hill, Susan M. 2008. ' "Travelling Down the River of Life Together in Peace and Friendship Forever": Haudenosaunee Land Ethics and Treaty Arrangements as the Basis For Restructuring the Relationship with the British Crown', pp. 23–45 in Leanne Simpson ed., *Lighting the Eighth Fire: The Liberation, Resurgence, and Protection of Indigenous Nations*. Winnipeg, MB: Arbeiter Ring Publishing.

Ing, Rosalyn. 2006. 'Canada's Indian Residential Schools and Their Impacts on Mothering', pp. 157–72 in D. Memee Lavell-Harvard and Jeanettee Corbiere Lavell, eds., *'Until Our Hearts Are On The Ground': Aboriginal Mothering, Oppression, Resistance and Rebirth*. Toronto: Demeter Press.

Jacobs, Beverley. 2008. 'Response to Canada's Apology to Residential School Survivors', *Canadian Woman Studies* 26 (3 & 4): 223–5.

Johnston, Darlene M. 1986. 'The Quest of the Six Nations Confederacy for Self-Determination', *University of Toronto Faculty Law Review* 44 (1): 1–32.

Kauanui, J. Kehaulani. 2008. *Hawaiian Blood: Colonialism and the Politics of Sovereignty and Indigeneity*. Durham, NC: Duke University Press.

LaRocque, Emma. 1993. 'Three Conventional Approaches to Native People in Society and in Literature', in Brett Balon and Peter Resch, eds., *Survival of the Imagination: The Mary Donaldson Memorial Lectures*. Regina, SK: Coteau Books.

Lawrence, Bonita. 2004. *'Real' Indians and Others: Mixed-Blood Urban Native Peoples and Indigenous Nationhood*. Vancouver, BC: UBC Press.

———. 2003. 'Gender, Race, and Regulation of Native Identity in Canada and the United States: An Overview', *Hypatia* 18 (2): 3–31.

———. 2002. 'Rewriting Histories of the Land: Colonization and Indigenous Resistance in Eastern Canada', in S. Razack, ed., *Race, Space, and the Law: Unmapping a White Settler Society*. Toronto: Between the Lines.

Lawrence, Bonita, and Ena Dua. 2005. 'Decolonizing Anti-Racism', *Social Justice* 32 (5): 120–43.

Li, Peter. 1990. *Race and Ethnic Relations in Canada*. Toronto: Oxford University Press.

Linton, Ralph. 1940. *Acculturation in Seven American Indian Tribes*. New York: Appleton-Century.

Lyons, Oren. 1989. 'Power of the Good Mind', pp. 199–208 in Joseph Bruchac, ed., *New Voices from the Longhouse: An Anthology of Contemporary Iroquois Writing*. New York: The Greenfield Review Press.

Magnet, Joseph Eliot. 2003. 'Who are the Aboriginal People of Canada?', pp. 23–92 in Joseph Eliot Magnet and Dwight A. Dorey, eds., *Aboriginal Rights Litigation*. LexisNexis Butterworths.

Martinot, Steve. 2003. *The Rule of Racialization: Class, Identity, Governance*. Philadelphia: Temple University Press.

Mihesuah, Devon A., ed. 1998. *Natives and Academics: Research and Writing About American Indians*. Lincoln, NE: University of Nebraska Press.

McIvor v. Canada (Registrar, Indian and Northern Affairs). 2007. BCSC 827.

Mitchell, Grand Chief Michael. 1989. 'Akwesasne: An Unbroken Assertion of Sovereignty', pp. 105–36 in Boyce Richardson, ed., *Drum Beat: Anger and Renewal in Indian Country*. Ottawa: Summerhill Press/The Assembly of First Nations.

Monture, Patricia. 2008. 'Women's Words: Power, Identity, and Indigenous Sovereignty', *Canadian Woman Studies* 26 (3 & 4): 154–9.

———. 1999. *Journeying Forward: Dreaming First Nations Independence*. Halifax, NS: Fernwood Publishing.

————. 1995. *Thunder In My Soul: A Mohawk Woman Speaks*. Halifax, NS: Fernwood Publishing.

Monture-Okanee, Patricia, and Mary Ellen Turpel. 1992. 'Aboriginal Peoples and Canadian Criminal Law: Rethinking Justice', *University of British Columbia Law Review* (Special Edition) 26: 239–77.

Porter, Robert B. 1999. 'The Demise of the Ongwehoweh and The Rise of the Native Americans: Redressing the Genocidal Act of Forcing American Citizenship Upon Indigenous Peoples', *Harvard Black Letter Law Journal* 15: 107–83.

R. v. Kapp. 2008. SCC 41.

Ramirez, Renya. 2007. *Native Hubs: Culture, Community, and Belonging in Silicon Valley and Beyond*. Durham, NC: Duke University Press.

Razack, Sherene H., ed. 2002. *Race, Space and the Law: Unmapping a White Settler Society*. Toronto: Between the Lines Press.

Rich, Adrienne. 2003. 'Compulsory Heterosexuality and Lesbian Existence', in Henry Abelove, Michele Aina Barale, and David Halperin, eds., *The Lesbian and Gay Studies Reader*. New York: Routledge.

Said, Edward W. 1994. *Culture and Imperialism*, 1st Vintage Books edn. New York: Vintage Books.

————. 1979. *Orientalism*. New York: Vintage Books.

Schick, Carol. 2004. 'Disrupting Binaries of Self and Other: Anti-Homophobic Pedagogies for Student Teachers', pp. 243–54 in James McNinch and Mary Cronin, eds., *I Could Not Speak My Heart: Education and Social Justice For Gay and Lesbian Youth*. Regina, SK: Canadian Plains Research Centre/University of Regina.

Saul, John Ralston. 2008. *A Fair Country: Telling Truths About Canada*. Toronto: Penguin Canada.

Sharma, Nandita, and Cynthia Wright. 2008–9. 'Decolonizing Resistance, Challenging Colonial States', *Social Justice* 35 (3): 120–38.

Silman, Janet. 1987. *Enough is Enough: Aboriginal Women Speak Out*. Toronto: Women's Press.

Simon, Roger. 2010. 'Towards a Hopeful Practice of Worrying: The Problematics of Listening and the Educative Responsibilities of the IRSTRC', in Pauline Wakeham and Jennifer Henderson, eds., *Reconciling Canada: Historical Injustices and the Contemporary Culture of Redress*. Toronto: University of Toronto Press.

Simpson, Audra. 1998. 'The Empire Laughs Back: Tradition, Power, and Play in the Work of Shelley Niro and Ryan Rice', pp. 48–54 in Doris I. Stambrau, Alexandra V. Roth, and Sylvia S. Kasprycki, eds., *IroquoisArt: Visual Expressions of Contemporary Native American Artists*. Altenstadt, DE: European Review of Native American Studies.

Sinclair, Murray. 2009. 'Truth and Reconciliation: They Came for the Children'. University of Toronto, Faculty of Law, 11 December.

Smith, Andrea. 2008. *Native Americans and the Christian Right: The Gendered Politics of Unlikely Alliances*. Durham, NC: Duke University Press.

————. 2006. 'Heteropatriarchy and the Three Pillars of White Supremacy', pp. 66–73 in *Color of Violence: The Incite! Anthology. Incite!: Women of Color Against Violence*. Cambridge, MA: South End Press.

————. 2005. *Conquest: Sexual Violence and American Indian Genocide*. Cambridge, MA: South End Press.

Sorenson, John. 2003. 'Indians Shouldn't Have any Special Rights', in Judith C. Blackwell, Murray E. G. Smith, and John Sorenson, eds., *Culture of Prejudice: Arguments in Critical Social Science*. Peterborough, ON: Broadview Press.

Spears, Shandra. 2003. 'Strong Spirit, Fractured Identity: An Ojibway Adoptee's Journey to Wholeness', pp. 81–94 in Kim Anderson and Bonita Lawrence, eds., *Strong Women Stories: Native Vision and Community Survival*. Toronto: Sumach Press.

Statistics Canada. 2003. 2001 Census Analysis Series: Aboriginal Peoples in Canada (A Demographic Profile). Ottawa, ON: Ministry of Industry.

St Denis, Verna. 2004. 'Real Indians: Cultural Revitalization and Fundamentalism in Aboriginal Education', pp. 35–47 in Carol Schick, JoAnn Jaffe, and Aisla M. Watkinson, eds., *Contesting Fundamentalisms*. Halifax, NS: Fernwood Publishing.

Steckley, John. 2003. *Aboriginal Voices and the Politics of Representation in Canadian Introductory Sociology Textbooks*. Toronto: Canadian Scholars Press.

Sunseri, Lina. 2005. 'Indigenous Voice Matters: Claiming Our Space through Decolonising Research', *Junctures* 9: 93–106.

————. 2000. 'Moving Beyond the Feminism versus the Nationalism Dichotomy: An Anti-Colonial Feminist Perspective on Aboriginal Liberation Struggles', *Canadian Woman Studies* 20 (2): 143–8.

Tanovich, David M. 2006. *The Colour of Justice: Policing Race in Canada*. Toronto: Irwin Law.

Thobani, Sunera. 2007. *Exhalted Subjects: Studies in the Making of Race and Nation in Canada*. Toronto: University of Toronto Press.

Tobias, John L. 1983. 'Protection, Civilization, Assimilation: An Outline History of Canada's Indian Policy', pp. 39–55 in Ian A.L. Getty and Antoine S. Lussier, eds., *As Long As The Sun Shines And Water Flows: A Reader In Canadian Native Studies*. Vancouver, BC: UBC Press.

Turner, Dale. 2006. *This Is Not A Peace Pipe: Towards a Critical Indigenous Philosophy*. Toronto: University of Toronto Press.

van Dijk, Teun A. 1993. *Elite Discourse and Racism*. New York: Sage Publications.

Venne, Sharon Helen. 1981. *Indian Acts and Amendments 1868–1975, An Indexed Collection*. Saskatoon, SK: University of Saskatchewan, Native Law Centre.

Wallis, Maria, and Augie Fleras, eds. 2009. *The Politics of Race in Canada: Readings in Historical Perspectives, Contemporary Realities, and Future Possibilities*. Toronto: Oxford University Press.

Weis, L., A. Proweller, and C. Centrie. 1997. 'Re-Examining "A Moment in History": Loss of Privilege Inside White Working-Class Masculinity in the 1990s', pp. 210–28 in M. Fine, L. Weis, L.C. Powell, and L.M. Wong, eds., *Off White: Readings on Race, Power, and Society*. New York: Routledge.

Wente, Margaret. 2008. 'What Dick Pound said was really dumb—and also true', *The Globe and Mail* 25 October: A21.

———. 2005. 'Crisis in Kashechewan', *The Globe and Mail* 28 October: A1.

Williams, Paul, and Curtis Nelson. 1995. *Kaswantha*. Ottawa: Royal Commission on Aboriginal Peoples [paper no. 88a].

Wotherspoon, Terry L., and Vic Satzewich. 1993. *First Nations: Race, Class and Gender Relations*. Toronto: Nelson.